For Reference

Not to be taken from this room

CONTEMPORARY ETHICAL ISSUES

Business Ethics

A Reference Handbook

CONTEMPORARY ETHICAL ISSUES

Business
Ethics
A Reference Handbook

John W. Dienhart and
Jordan Curnutt

ABC-CLIO
Santa Barbara, California
Denver, Colorado
Oxford, England

Library of Congress Cataloging-in-Publication Data

Dienhart, John William.
    Business ethics : a reference handbook / John W. Dienhart and Jordan Curnutt
       xiv, 445 p. 15×22 cm. -- (Contemporary ethical issues)
    Includes bibliographical references and index.
    ISBN 0-87436-863-4 (alk. paper)
    1. Business ethics--Dictionaries.   I. Curnutt, Jordan. II. Title. III. Series.
HF5387.D57   1998
174'.4'03--dc21   98-42277
                                         CIP

03 02 01 00 99   10 9 8 7 6 5 4 3 2

ABC-CLIO, Inc.
130 Cremona Drive, P.O. Box 1911
Santa Barbara, California 93116-1911

For Rosie

For RPC—*siempre*

CONTEMPORARY ETHICAL ISSUES

Contents

4 The Employee, 151

5 The Environment, 267

6 Codes of Ethical Conduct, 325

7 Biographical Sketches, 337

8 Business Organizations and Associations, 353

9 Reference Material, 363

Glossary, 401

Court Cases, Federal Statutes, and Agencies, 429

Index, 439

CONTEMPORARY ETHICAL ISSUES

Preface

Our original goals for this book were two: to write a comprehensive reference book for business ethics by providing brief discussions of major topics in the field and to provide a theoretical orientation to integrate these topics. As we were working on the book, we discovered that we could also produce a business ethics textbook if we arranged the topics (Chapters 2–5) thematically instead of alphabetically.

We devote a chapter to each of the following topics in business ethics: the consumer, the corporation, the employee, and the environment. Within each chapter we have integrated subtopics. In Chapter 2, The Consumer, for example, we begin with a discussion of the ethics, economics, and legal aspects of advertising. Advertising gives consumers information about products and their proper use, which leads to product safety. The section concludes with a discussion of finance, which concerns the ways in which we acquire the resources to buy products. Despite this thematic arrangement, the chapters and subtopics can also be read as independent units.

To provide a theoretical framework, Chapter 1 includes introductory discussions of ethics, economics, and law. We discuss economics and law because nearly every ethical issue in business has economic and legal aspects. We discuss the topics in business ethics using the concepts found in this introductory chapter. We provide references in the topics to the introduction when we use technical or specialized terms.

Finally, Chapters 1–5 can be used as an introductory business ethics text. This book has at least two features that can make it more attractive than other texts in business ethics. First, it is presented in a way that is accessible to students of many different levels. Second, it is brimming with research ideas. In our discussion of topics in business ethics, we mention the views of many authors and give explicit references to where more information can be found. If readers want still more direction, they can turn to Chapters 6, 7, 8, and 11, where we discuss ethical codes, professional organizations, print and nonprint resources, and law, respectively.

As a reference work, this book is uniquely helpful. Beyond a bibliography of print and nonprint resources (including websites), we have also included information about ethical codes, professional and business organizations devoted to business ethics, short biographies of the leading figures in business ethics, and a list of important court decisions, laws, and regulatory agencies.

This book can be used as a main text, a supplementary text, or a recommended text for a course in business ethics. It will be especially helpful for inexperienced students working on projects or papers in business ethics.

CONTEMPORARY ETHICAL ISSUES

Acknowledgments

This book has been significantly improved through the kind and careful assistance of Rosemarie Puerta Curnutt, Roger Curnutt, Peter Spuit, and Clark Wolf. We are deeply grateful for their efforts. We would also like to thank all those people who are doing and thinking about business.

CONTEMPORARY ETHICAL ISSUES

Chapter 1:
Introduction

In the late 1970s when the systematic study of business ethics was just beginning, people started speeches, books, and articles by asking the question, "Is business ethics an oxymoron?" An *oxymoron* is a contradiction in terms. Other oxymorons are "legal bribe," "deafening silence," and, perhaps, "airplane food." In the past ten years, however, this question has been asked only rarely. Understanding why it was once popular, and why business ethicists do not address it anymore, can help us understand the nature of business ethics.

What Is Business Ethics?

The view that business ethics is an oxymoron rests on two assumptions:

1. Business is concerned with promoting *self-interest*
2. Ethics is concerned with promoting the *interests of others*.

These two assumptions, which were taken from the history of ethics and theology, as well as popular culture, guided the early discussions of business ethics. Hence, it was natural to worry about the oxymoronic nature of business ethics.

As the field of business ethics matured, it became clear that each of these two assumptions are only partly true. Business ethicists learned this in two ways: first, by paying attention to how business people really act, and second, by examining how self-interest fits with other ethical concerns.

By listening to and working with business people, business ethicists discovered that not all business behavior is purely self-interested. Business people want to make money and be promoted, to be sure, but most of them also want to be good to their families and friends, to be loyal to their country, and to be fair. Given these considerations, we can modify the first assumption as follows:

1. Business people are motivated by four concerns: self-interest, personal relationships (family and friends), national interests, and fairness.

By reflecting on the history of ethics, business ethicists have seen that one of the primary tasks of ethics is to understand how these four motivations fit together. Hence, we can reformulate the second assumption as follows:

2. Ethics examines how self-interest, personal relationships (family and friends), national interests, and fairness fit together.

The Roots of Business Ethics

The roots of business ethics are in philosophy, theology, and in the business community itself. In this book we focus on Western philosophy and business practices. We recognize the importance of other traditions, but we do not cover them here. One of the foundations of the Western value system is the belief that each individual human has **intrinsic value**. This is a special value of elevated worth that goes beyond whatever it is that makes something valuable as a tool. To be intrinsically valuable is to be valuable as an end, independently and above usefulness, an idea often characterized in terms of rights to respect, self-determination, and freedom, and various duties correlative with these. We will have occasion to investigate this foundational value in more detail in Chapter 5, The Environment.

In the fourteenth, fifteenth, and sixteenth centuries, business began to grow rapidly in Europe. One of the main instruments of this growth was regional and international trade. The development of business during this period led to four changes that are still with us today. First, regional and international trade required more resources (**capital**) and was more risky than domestic business. The **common stock** company evolved as a way to acquire capital and reduce risk. The common stock company acquired capital by selling shares of the company to many owners. This spread risk among many people, reducing the risk each individual bore. Second, in order to reduce risk further, a new kind of service arose: insurance. Third, financial and banking companies arose to deal with the new concentration of capital and to trade shares of stock. Fourth, the nation-state became an active partner with business, providing a stable environment that supplied a monetary system, guaranteed property rights, and provided a court system to resolve contractual disputes.

When Europe traded with the Middle East and Asia, they exchanged ideas as well as goods. These ideas included the rediscovered works of the ancient Greeks, especially Aristotle, whose work had been preserved by Muslim scholars. The rediscovery of Aristotle and awareness of other cultures led to a view that we call **humanism**. Humanism holds that human beings are free to think and choose as they will, the center or apex of moral value. Humanism does not reject God but instead pushes God and religion generally into the background. According to humanism, God created human beings so that each person could pursue his or her own path. Human beings did not necessarily need the church to tell them what to do with every step of their lives. Instead, the church was thought of as providing general spiritual guidance. Thomas Jefferson must be counted among the most notable humanists in American history.

Humanism and the growth of business fit well together, but they both conflicted with established religion. A major conflict arose over **usury**, which originally referred to the practice of charging any interest on loans. Usury was a crime and a sin in medieval Europe. (Today, usury is illegal only when the interest rate is excessive). For business to grow, however, people had to borrow money. Unfortunately, no one will lend money if they are not compensated for **opportunity cost**, or cost of the opportunities they will miss while the loan is still unpaid. By the seventeenth century, the needs of business won out and charging interest for loans was a common practice.

Business surged again in the eighteenth and nineteenth centuries during the Industrial Revolution, and especially during the decades following the American Civil War. The number of common stock companies increased dramatically as new machinery, methods of production, and distribution in large markets required huge amounts of capital. In the United States, a Republican-controlled Congress, always sympathetic and supportive of business enterprises, placed very few obstacles in the path of commerce. But the growing cities were ill equipped to handle the hundreds of thousands of people who came from the Old World and rural America to work in the new factories. It was in this environment that business ethics, as we know it today, began.

One of the earliest groups to deal with problems created by the new business setting was the Young Men's Christian Association (YMCA), founded in London in 1844 (Heald 1988). The YMCA was created to aid the many young men who were far away from family and friends. In the aggressive and accelerated atmosphere of the teeming cities, many fell away from their Christian beliefs, and turned to alcohol and other illicit activities. The YMCA was dedicated to helping them retain their religion. Arriving in America just after the Civil War and coincident with the rise of big business, the YMCA spread rapidly, especially in the railroad industry, where many men were away from home for long periods of time. Many business people in the United States believed that the YMCA was responding to problems that were created by business, and they gave large donations to support it.

The funding of the YMCA is one of the first examples in the United States of the business community accepting responsibility for problems it helped create. Subsequently, there were many other examples of business people accepting responsibility for the harms and troubles business created. For example, Joseph Wharton, a Quaker and a Philadelphia business person, gave a large sum of money to begin the first collegiate school of business, The Wharton School of Finance and Economy, which is still part of the University of Pennsylvania. Wharton's goal was nothing less than the reform of business people themselves, whom he said were too ready to take wealth from others rather than providing needed goods and services to the community (Heald 1988). The Wharton School continues to promote this goal today, with one of the most active centers for business ethics in the country.

Despite Wharton's attempt to look at the ethics of business activity itself, business ethics still focused on ills, such as overcrowded cities and pollution, created by the growing industrial state. Because of this, from the late nineteenth century until the 1960s most talk of business ethics focused on business philanthropy: contributing to the well-being of the communities by giving to education, parks, youth programs, and other similar projects.

The Maturing of Business Ethics

In the 1960s business ethics started to take a serious look at the ethics of business itself: its people, practices, policies, and organizations. One of the classic studies was done in 1967 by Raymond Baumhart, S.J., who surveyed the ethical attitudes of business people by asking them to define the term *ethical*. Some had no idea what it meant. Most offered a definition, however: Fifty percent said that ethics was whatever their feelings told them was right; 25 percent said ethics was what their religion told them; and 18 percent said that ethics was the Golden Rule (Valesquez 1992). The fact that fully half of the respondents defined ethics by what they *feel* is shocking, because acting on what we "feel" can lead to immorality as well as to ethical conduct. Baumhart's study lit a fire in many quarters of academia, and colleges rapidly began to add courses in business ethics to the standard business curriculum and in philosophy departments.

In 1979 two textbooks were published that played a major role in defining and guiding the development of business ethics: *Ethical Issues in Business: A Philosophical Approach*, edited by Thomas Donaldson and Patricia Werhane; and *Ethical Theory and Business*, edited by Tom L. Beauchamp and Norman E. Bowie. These two books, currently in their fifth editions, introduced readers to traditional ethical theories, such as those described in the next section. These theories were then used to analyze readings and cases on advertising and marketing, management–employee relationships, government regulations, and other business issues.

The general development of business ethics can be tracked by noting changes in subsequent editions of these books. Three major changes are observable. The first of these was the inclusion of more case studies depicting managerial and policy dilemmas, including cases from law. The second change, connected to the first, was more emphasis on ethical reasoning to illustrate actual business decision making. The third change was the inclusion of material on international business, reflecting the growing expansion of world trade. The shift in these textbooks to more case studies and to concrete ethical reasoning resulted from several factors. Understanding these factors will help us understand the present state of business ethics.

One factor leading to these three changes was instructors' classroom experience of teaching business ethics: It was not always clear how to apply abstract ethical theories to business problems. Second, as business ethicists began to consult for and work in the business community, they found that business people wanted concrete advice about how to think through problems like whistleblowing and affirmative action; they were not interested in abstract theory. Third, in the late 1980s and early 1990s business ethicists began to meet and talk with business school faculty who dealt with social issues in management (SIM). SIM dealt with many of the same issues as business ethics, but from the perspective of social science.

Social science uses a descriptive approach. SIM researchers used the tools of social science to *describe* how business people and organizations understand social and ethical expectations, and how they influence action. Further, researchers studied whether acting or failing to act from these expectations affects the financial performance of corporations. In contrast, business ethics uses a prescriptive approach: Business ethics researchers use the tools of philosophical ethics and theology to prescribe or recommend what business people and organizations *should* do.

Integrating the prescriptive and descriptive approaches can enhance our understanding of business better than either approach alone. There are two reasons why the integration of these two fields is beneficial. First, business ethicists must understand how business works in order to give effective advice to business people. Second, for social scientists to describe the ethical aspects of business, they must understand what features of the work environment are morally problematic and why.

It is impossible to predict the future of business ethics, but we can extrapolate from some current trends. We have seen how business ethics is moving away from the focus on abstract ethical theory and toward more concrete questions of how ethics fits into everyday business practices. This trend is likely to expand in several directions. Especially clear and prominent evidence of the course of such expansion is the hundreds of companies that now have ethics programs, and the many that have full-time ethics officers devoted to examining how ethics fits into their companies and industries. The allocation of corporate resources to ethics has been spurred by at least two significant factors. First, research is beginning to suggest that companies that treat employees, vendors, suppliers, and other **stakeholders** well tend to do better than those companies that do not. That is, financial performance seems to improve for companies that act from traditional ethical virtues, such as honesty and loyalty. Second, the *U.S. Sentencing Guidelines for Corporate Crime* provides incentives for companies to develop ethics programs (see Chapter 3, The Corporation—The Nature and Structure of the Corporation, Law: *Sentencing Reform Act of 1984*). For example, if an employee bribes a government official and is caught, the fine to the corporation can be reduced up to 95 percent if the company has an active and meaningful ethics program (United States Sentencing Commission Manual 1991).

The move away from abstract ethical theory to more concrete ethical questions is exhibited by philosophers paying more attention to economic and legal questions, as well as to issues about how people learn moral values. For their part, business academics as well as those in economics and law are paying more attention to ethical questions about what constitutes ethically good law and economic policy. These overlapping interests have led to a collaboration between these groups that has not occurred before. For example, the Society for Business Ethics (SBE), founded in 1979, is the largest and most prestigious professional group devoted to business ethics. It was founded by philosophers and in its early years its membership was dominated by philosophers. The SBE now includes so many people from business, economics, and law that philosophers are a minority. This change in membership of the SBE signals a deep and healthy change in the field of business ethics that is likely to continue.

The Tools of Business Ethics

We will use principles of ethics, economics, and law as tools to analyze and evaluate issues in business ethics. We have organized these issues according to their impact on the four main "players" in the business world: the consumer, the corporation, the employee, and the environment.

Consumers are the target of advertising, and the safety of the products marketed by business is of primary concern to them. Of course money is required in order to be a consumer, so we follow our discussion of advertising and product safety with a look at consumer finance. In the next chapter, we explain the nature and structure of the corporation, putting us in a favorable position to address questions regarding corporate relations with society and with other corporations; these matters revolve around the social responsibilities of business, the propriety of the business combination or trust, and the merging and acquiring of corporations. Employer duties to the employee are the focus of our fourth chapter, which surveys a host of vexing problems in a complex moral and legal arena: foremost among these are affirmative action and discrimination, employee health and safety, privacy, sexual harassment, the terms and conditions of employment, and whistleblowing and loyalty. Finally, corporations depend on the environment for the raw materials and resources that are ultimately entered into commerce and fuel the economy;

here, our primary interest shifts from specific principles guiding decision and action, to the underlying moral and legal status presupposed by those principles. We will investigate the standing before the law and the enlightened conscience of those features of the natural world on which business and all people depend, and the duties corporations might have to them: animals, plants, forests, and ecosystems.

We believe a fruitful method of investigating these matters proceeds by bringing to bear upon them the conceptual devices provided by ethics and economics, followed by an overview of what the law says. In the remainder of this introduction, we explain what those concepts are and how the legal issues will be presented.

Ethics

We do not consciously think about most of our decisions and actions. Consider what you have done today: You woke up, got dressed, ate breakfast, drove to work or school, and the list goes on. Sometimes, when you are late, you make a conscious decision to skip one of these things, or, if you are ahead of schedule, you may add something—but most mornings you have a routine, or **script**, that you follow without thinking about it. Examining this seemingly trivial fact can reveal a great deal about how we make ethical decisions.

Why do we have scripts? One reason is **bounded rationality**: We have limited rational capacities and a finite amount of time to exercise them (Simon 1976). If we had to think through and make conscious decisions about every action, like when to get up, which toothbrush to use, which bowl to use for cereal, etc., we would not have time to go to school, pursue a career, raise children, and seek the many other things that enrich our lives. The solution to this problem is a script. When acting from a script we act almost automatically, devoting our mental time and resources to more important things. For example, if you have an important presentation, you can think about it and plan it as you get dressed, eat breakfast, and drive to work. The fact that you have scripted your morning allows you to think about your presentation and other things that are important to you.

Scripts would not work unless other people cooperated by acting in expected ways. To illustrate, consider that when you live in a family or with roommates, you can't script your morning behavior if they take your toothpaste, use your towels, and eat your food. Living with others requires that the people involved develop scripts that fit together. Even if you live alone, you depend heavily on the scripts of others to make your life possible. The water you drink, the food you eat, and the energy you use for heating, cooling, transportation, and a thousand other things are possible only because millions of people are acting from coordinated scripts in your community, region, nation, and globe.

These coordinated scripts do not happen by accident, nor could they. Scripts arise within and are guided by **social institutions** (North 1990).

According to Norman Uphoff, "[Social] [i]nstitutions are...complexes of norms and behaviors that persist over time by serving collectively valued purposes" (Uphoff 1993). Institutions can be *practices* like marriage and making promises, *documents* like the Bible or the United Sates Constitution, *roles* like police officer and church leader, and *organizations* like the United States Senate or General Motors. What all of these institutions have in common is their ability to organize and stabilize patterns of behavior that allow individuals to script their conduct while achieving important social goals. These scripted routines, in turn, allow us to use our limited rational powers to think about our lives with others and plan for our future.

What does this have to do with ethics? Everything. Look at some of the institutions mentioned in the above paragraph: promising, the Bible, the police, the church, the U.S. Senate. Each of these institutions consists of principles and rules that define some behavior as ethical and other behavior as unethical. As long as people live their lives according to institutional rules, we can script our behavior. The more people depart from institutional rules, the less we can script our behavior. The less we can script our behavior, the more attention we have to pay to everyday acts. The more attention we must pay to everyday acts, the less time we have for family, friends, and career.

As we can see, institutions are valuable because they allow us to script behavior necessary for social life. *This ability to script behavior is also what makes institutions so dangerous.* If we live in a society with slavery, as existed in the United States before the Civil War, or with a program of genocide, as existed in Nazi Germany, we are not likely to think very much about it, because these institutions are part of our everyday lives. Trying to change them requires a lot of effort and a lot of discomfort. At least two good reasons determine why this is so. First, peoples' jobs and social status are dependent on their institutional framework; changing the institutions will change peoples lives. Second, institutions are highly interrelated; changing or getting rid of one institution can result in changes throughout the society. Slavery in the United States, for example, was deeply integrated with a system of agriculture, private property, and government. So to attack slavery was to attack these other institutions as well. The same can be said of the Jewish genocide in Nazi Germany: To attack the death camps was to attack the entire German political system. The importance of these institutions to those in power can be measured by the effort it took to change them. In the United States, it took five horrific years of civil war to end slavery. In Europe, it took six even more horrible years of world war to end the Nazi regime. These wars were among the bloodiest in human history.

Assuming that institutions guide our behavior in scripted, unthinking ways, ethical decisions arise when we are stopped from acting in these institutional, scripted ways. This can happen for two reasons: We are faced with a situation that is not covered by one of our scripts, or we are faced with a situation covered by two or more scripts that prescribe different actions. One way to find some guidance is to search for a social rule that will tell us what to do.

Look for ethical rules to guide our decision making.

Standard scripts do not effectively guide
our decision making.

For example, suppose you are a manager negotiating a salary with a new employee for a job. The prospective employee has a background in software development that would be highly beneficial to the company. In the industry, these jobs pay between $45,000 and $60,000, but you are willing to pay up $80,000. Should you tell the truth, that you will pay her a $20,000 premium if she will join your company? Or should you say that you are willing to pay her, say, $55,000, to see if you can hire her for less?

The relevant ethical rule here would seem to be: "Tell the truth." If that were the only consideration, then you should tell the prospective employee that you are willing to pay $80,000. But the ethical rule about telling the truth is *not* the only consideration. First, you are in a bargaining situation, and the standard rule of truth telling may not apply in the same way as it does in other situations. Further, as a manager, you also have a moral duty to represent the interests of the owners of the company. As a manager, then, one of the ethical rules relevant to this example is "Don't waste the owners money."

Look for ethical principles to reconcile conflicts
between ethical rules.

Ethical rules conflict with each other, and so do not
effectively guide our decision making.

Our standard scripts do not effectively guide
our decision making.

The duty not to waste the owners' money suggests that you should not reveal your willingness to pay $80,000, at least not early in the bargaining process. Another managerial responsibility is to maintain an efficient workforce. What will happen if other software programmers find out that a new employee is making $20,000 to $35,000 more than they are? When ethical rules conflict, as in this example, we can look to ethical principles to help us resolve the conflict.

Moral rules are very specific. For example, the *rule* to tell the truth leaves little doubt about precisely what behavior is mandated. Moral principles are much more general that rules. Principles like "Promote the good of all" and "Act fairly," on the other hand, are far more open-ended and allow greater space for moral maneuvering. We can identify these four broad categories of ethical principles:

1. Promote self-interest or self-development
2. Promote nurturing family relationships and friendships
3. Promote the well-being of nonfamilial groups like organizations, religions, and nations
4. Respect the intrinsic value of human beings by respecting their rights, being fair, and/or acting justly.

Many of the moral problems that arise in the business setting, as illustrated by our hiring case, are generated by conflicts between rules. Appealing to these more general principles can help sort out matters and steer us toward a solution. This is our strategy in the coming pages as we examine the core issues of business ethics. Right now, let's take a closer look at each of these broad categories of principles, explaining how they work. We will not try to decide whether some are better than others, but we will indicate how each can provide a resolution to morally problematic business situations.

Principles that Promote Self-Interest: Egoism   Ethical principles that focus on self-interest or self-development must first specify what human interests are. For instance, if we think happiness is our most important interest, the ethical principle will be "Do whatever promotes my happiness." If we think that knowledge is our most important interest, the ethical principle will be "Do whatever promotes my knowledge." If we think that the health of our spirit is our most important interest, the ethical principle will be "Do whatever promotes the health of my spirit." As these examples show, being self-interested does not mean that we will be narrowly selfish or that we will foolishly act on impulse. Ethical theorists use the term *enlightened self-interest* to indicate rational and nonimpulsive forms of self-interest. We will examine two kinds of enlightened self-interest, aggressive self-interest and contemplative self-interest.

Aggressive Self-Interest   The twentieth-century novelist and philosopher, Ayn Rand, argued that our interests were defined in terms of rationality and self-awareness. To promote our interests we need to study and be truthful to ourselves. Rand argued that we should aggressively pursue our self-interest without regard to the interests of others. If we all did this, we would—paradoxically—make a better society, because the well-being of society is nothing more than the sum of the well-being of the individuals in the society. Rand praised capitalism and successful capitalists who knew what they wanted and were not afraid to fight for it.

Contemplative Self-Interest   The Greek philosopher Epicurus (341–270 B.C.E.) argued that enlightened self-interest prompts us to be honest, loyal, and kind, because acting in these ways encourages others to treat us well, which should increase our own pleasure and happiness. If we are selfish and crude, people will not want to work with us or help us in times of need.

Epicurus argued that a peaceful, pain-free existence was the best possible life. The most common cause of unhappiness is not having our desires fulfilled, and so the best strategy for promoting our interest is to reduce our desires to essential needs: food, clothing, shelter, friends, and education. A large and growing number of people, sometimes referred to as *downshifters*, have adopted some of Epicurus's beliefs. Downshifters are people who have left high-powered, well-paid jobs for part-time jobs or lower-key full-time jobs so they can spend more time with their family, friends, and their own interests and hobbies (Goldberg 1995).

Both Epicurus and Rand argue that promoting our self-interest is hard, but rewarding, work.

Principles that Nurture Personal Relationships: Care   The care ethic uses personal relationships between friends and family members as the model for all human relationships. Good relationships nurture their members into full, compassionate human beings. Caring for others can be interpreted in at least two ways. First, we could interpret care as helping others pursue any projects they may have: This would be a *passive care ethic*. Second, we could interpret care as helping others pursue their projects, but also, when appropriate, to help them critically evaluate their projects: This would be an *active care ethic*.

Passive care has two problems. First, it makes the caring person a virtual slave of the *cared-for*. Second, it does not acknowledge that people can have hateful and harmful projects, such as those advocated by neo-Nazi groups. To be an active carer, we need to understand the point of view of the cared-for. The point of caring is to encourage strong, nurturing relationships between the carer and the cared-for, as well as with other individuals. This means that there are limits to helping others. For example, if we are asked to help someone harm another, we should not help. If the harm is great enough, we may be required to stop the person intending it. There also are limits to *how* we should help others. If a friend is becoming too dependent on us, the best way to help the person become independent may be to sever the relationship, at least temporarily. This is sometimes called *tough love* because it is tough for all involved.

Principles that Promote the Good of the Group: Utilitarianism Ethical principles that focus on nonfamilial groups must first specify two things: (1) the identity of the group and (2) the nature of group well-being. The answer to question (1) could be a limited group of human beings. Some examples are a company, a religion, a nation, a region, a gender, a race, even a group like a criminal gang. The group could also be universal, like that comprised of all human beings. The answer to question (2) could be put in terms of financial well-being, happiness, pleasure, law and order, or religious codes, to name only a few.

Utilitarianism is an ethical principle that focuses on the well being of a designated group. The eighteenth- and nineteenth-century British philosophers Jeremy Bentham, David Hume, John Stuart Mill, and, in our own time, the Australian philosopher, J. J. C. Smart, have all espoused different forms of utilitarianism. The two dominant forms of utilitarianism are **act utilitarian-**

ism and **rule utilitarianism**. According to act utilitarianism, morally right actions are those that best promote the well-being of everyone affected by the act. Although this seems like a good principle, it has many problems. One major problem stems from the fact that we do not have enough information or reasoning power to figure out how our actions are going to affect all those that they will affect. Consider, for example, whether you should pay back a loan to a friend. How do you know doing so is the best of all alternative acts open to you? What if a good charity asks you for money, and you don't have enough money to give to the charity and to pay back your friend? If you believe that giving the money to the charity will improve group well-being more than paying back your friend, act utilitarianism would prescribe that you give to the charity.

Many of the problems with act utilitarianism do not appear with rule utilitarianism. According to rule utilitarianism, we should follow the rule that expresses a general pattern or practice of behavior that promotes the good of everyone. The problem now is selecting the rule that does this. We will discuss two methods for making this determination.

Strict Rule Utilitarianism The first method for choosing the best rule, proposed by the Scottish philosopher and historian David Hume (1748), is called *strict rule utilitarianism*. It is quite simple: Follow the rule that your society endorses. This is the best rule because it is the rule most likely to preserve stability, law, and order. According to Hume, the crucial factor in promoting social well-being is being able to correctly anticipate what others will do. Social rules are the means by which we do this. Consider the example about paying back the loan to your friend, above. We loan money to others in the first place because we have a solid expectation that loans will be repaid. Hence, we should as a general rule or practice pay back loans, even when the particular act of paying back the loan may not promote the good of all.

In cases in which there is no rule to follow, one should be created that is simple, clear, and easy to follow. This simplicity means that it will prescribe actions that are sometimes contrary to the group good, as in the loan case above. But we must live with these particular bad consequences. After all, the social order that results from these simple, easy-to-follow rules helps us far more than we are hurt by the bad consequences of particular acts of following the rules.

Flexible Rule Utilitarianism The second method for choosing the best rule, *flexible rule utilitarianism*, acknowledges that rules are very important for social stability and that social stability is necessary for social well-being. However, there are times when following the rule would be disastrous for all concerned, and in these cases we should break the rule. This was the position of the nineteenth-century British philosopher John Stuart Mill. He argues that while promoting group well-being is the first and most important principle of morality, societies also have "secondary rules" that tend to promote group well-being (Mill 1859). Examples of secondary rules are: "Tell the truth," "Be helpful to your friends," "Be a good student," and many others. Telling the truth promotes happiness in this way: When members of a group tell the truth, they have good information and fewer wasted activities, both of which promote happiness. We can give the same kind of justification for secondary rules regarding loyalty and promises.

In case there is no secondary rule to follow, one should be created that is easy to follow, but if we know in advance that it will prescribe some acts that harm the group, we should construct the rule to avoid these problems. Unfortunately, almost any rule can prescribe actions that are harmful, no matter how carefully it is formulated. Consider the murderous regimes of Hitler and Stalin. Following the rule of loyalty in cases like these harms groups. In the case of paying back a loan to a friend, above, if you know that your friend is going to use the money to buy a gun and kill someone, then you should not pay back the loan. The focus on group well-being can require us to break secondary rules, but *only* in extreme cases. In less extreme cases, we should trust in the secondary rules, even if we think that everyone would be better off if we lied, cheated, or broke some other secondary rule.

Principles that Promote Respect for Dignity and Rights: Intrinsic Value Ethical principles that focus on human intrinsic value must specify what makes humans intrinsically valuable and how intrinsic value should be respected. Two approaches are often directed at these two issues. The first approach is to identify the intrinsic value of human beings in terms of their rational capacities. Respecting intrinsic value means treating others as free, choosing beings, not as things to be manipulated by us. The second approach is to interpret human intrinsic value in terms of rights: Respecting intrinsic values means nothing more than not violating the rights of others.

Human Dignity The German philosopher Immanuel Kant (1724–1804) and the American philosopher John Rawls, professor emeritus at Harvard University, take the first approach. They argue that we should act only on those motives to which everyone could rationally agree. Consider the case in which you falsely promise to pay back a loan, knowing that you will not repay, but also knowing that you will not get the money unless you say that you will. Such false promising violates the dignity of the lender because you are treating that person as an object, as a kind of machine, to increase your wealth. In doing so, you act in a way that the lender would never agree to, because if he knew you were making a lying promise, he would not lend the money.

This sounds like the Golden Rule, but it is much stronger than the Golden Rule. The Golden Rule tells us to act only in those ways that we would want others to act toward us. But what if we are suicidal? In this case, the Golden Rule would allow us to murder others, because we would be willing to be murdered. Kant argues that *the value of human life rests on our ability to freely choose*, not on our emotional beliefs or attitudes.

The Right to Property The British philosopher John Locke (1632–1704) and the American philosopher Robert Nozick (currently at Harvard University) take a rights approach to intrinsic value. Locke's views are enshrined in the U.S. Declaration of Independence. When Thomas Jefferson wrote that "all Men…are…endowed by their Creator with certain unalienable Rights, that among these are Life, Liberty, and the Pursuit of

Happiness," he was borrowing heavily from Locke (although Locke said "property" not "happiness"). Arguing that individuals create government to protect their right to property and personal security, Locke asserted that there were only two limits on how we could use our property. The first limit is that we should never use our property to infringe on the rights of others. The second limit is that we must not acquire so much property that others are robbed of their opportunities to appropriate property they need to live fulfilling lives. Locke further contended that if the government oversteps its duties and violates our rights to life, liberty, and property in extreme and systematic ways, citizens have the right to replace that government. The political leaders of our country located in this position a powerful moral foundation for the American Revolutionary War.

We have been examining ethical principles in the hope that they would give us the guidance that rules failed to supply. But of course moral principles can come into conflict too. What happens then? Let's look again at our hiring example: Suppose that during the job interview you remember that you promised your daughter that you would go to her basketball game that evening. You ask the candidate if she can meet again tomorrow, but she is flying out to interview with Cisco Systems early the following morning. Cisco Systems is one of the most prestigious computer companies in the United States. If you withhold your bottom-line offer, you will negotiate a long time, missing your daughter's basketball game. However, if you tell the prospective employee that you are willing to pay $80,000, and no more, you can end the negotiations quickly—and make the beginning of the basketball game. In this case, the principle of being a caring parent seems to conflict with the principle of respecting the rights of the owners. Should you be a good business person or good parent in this case? When ethical principles conflict, we can turn to ethical theory.

Develop an ethical theory to reconcile conflicts
between ethical principles.

↑

Ethical principles conflict with each other, and so do not
effectively guide our decision making.

↑

Ethical rules conflict with each other, and so do not
effectively guide our decision making.

↑

Our standard scripts do not effectively guide
our decision making.

Developing an ethical theory may sound too intellectual or too difficult for most of us, but this is not the case. We adopt an ethical theory whenever we choose one moral principle over others. Many of the individuals we mentioned in the discussion of ethical principles argued for the view that one ethical principle was more important than any others.

1. Epicurus argued that self-interest is the supreme principle of morality, and that the other three principles could be explained in term of self-interest. He argued that we should care for others, promote the good of the group, and obey the law because it is in our interest to act in these ways.
2. Nel Noddings argued that care is the supreme principle of morality, and that if we act from care we end up promoting our interest and helping our group.
3. John Stuart Mill argued that promoting the welfare of our group is the supreme principle of morality, and that doing so will help ourselves, our friends and family, and be just.
4. Robert Nozick argued that the supreme principle of morality is to respect the rights of others, and that this will promote individual interests. Nozick thought that caring for others was a private affair, and he simply denied that we have a duty to promote the good of the group.

Another way to deal with conflicts between ethical principles is to develop an ethical theory called *pluralism*. A pluralistic theory accepts two or more principles as equally good; conflicts between principles are resolved on a case by case basis. This is the approach taken by Manuel Velasquez in his book, *Business Ethics: Concepts and Cases* (1992). Velasquez takes the principles of group well-being, rights, and justice to be equally compelling. In an article coauthored with Gerald Cavanagh, SJ, and Denis Moberg, he argues that we need to add the care perspective to this list (Cavanagh 1995). Dienhart (1995) argues for a pluralistic view that includes self-interest, care, utilitarianism, and intrinsic value.

Consider once more the hiring example, above, in which acting as a good business person seemed to conflict with telling the truth and with being a good parent. A pluralistic theory would urge us to examine which principle was most at risk. For example, if the business is flourishing, and you believe that you will end up paying $80,000 in any case, and the relationship with your child is poor, pluralism may well prescribe going to the basketball game. Or, if your family life is strong, and the business weak, pluralism could prescribe continuing the negotiation and missing the game.

In the next section we will see that many of these ethical principles and theories are used in economics.

Economics

Economics is the study of how people and society *choose* to employ scarce resources that could have alternative uses in order *to produce* various commodities and *to distribute* them for consumption, now or in the future, among various groups [and individuals] in society (Samuelson and Nordhaus 1995; emphasis added).

Economists examine the connections between choice, production, and distribution at the *macro* and the *micro* levels. *Macroeconomics* examines the economy as a whole—studying, among other things, the relationship between output, productivity, and prices at a national level. One of the most important topics of macroeconomics is how societies establish the basic rules of the economic game. It is these basic rules that determine the relationships between consumers and producers. In our view, society acts as an arbiter between the interests of consumers and producers. How we think society should arbitrate this relationship depends on our ethical views, as described above. *Microeconomics* deals with specific issues in business organizations or in particular markets. We will focus on the basic economic rules and laws that form the background of business behavior.

What are Markets? *Markets exist wherever trade exists.* This covers everything from bartering between primitive hunter-gatherers to the New York Stock Exchange. Markets are defined by the following four conditions (Gwartney and Stroup 1982). It is these conditions that determine the basic rules of the economic game.

Competition Competition exists whenever we have more demand than supply. Because all human societies have demands that exceed supply, the question is not whether we will have competition, but how we will organize it. Communist states reduce competition at the level of production, but because they produce well below demand, they create a great deal of competition between consumers. Communist governments have discovered that this situation causes a great deal of dissatisfaction and unrest among the citizenry. Free-market countries, on the other hand, have competition between producers for consumer dollars. This can provide a wide variety of goods, which reduces competition between consumers.

There are three ways to structure competition: perfect competition, monopolistic competition, and oligopolistic competition. *Perfect competition* occurs when there are many producers of goods that are virtually identical in quality. Markets for agricultural commodities sold by farmers, such as wheat and corn, are close to being perfect. The advantage of perfect or near-perfect markets is that no one producer can dictate the price or supply. This allows demand for the product to set the price of the product.

Monopolistic competition exists when we have items featuring certain qualities that others cannot copy, but these qualities are not essential to the usefulness of the product. This is especially true for brand names. No one but Eddie Bauer can sell down coats with the Eddie Bauer name, giving this catalog company a monopoly on articles of clothing that are so labeled. However, because the coats from Lands' End will be very similar, a buyer who is dissatisfied with Eddie Bauer can buy a Lands' End coat, providing competition. Because there is competition for buyers between these and other catalog companies, along with the many fixed stores that sell similar products, no one producer can dictate the price or supply. Once again, this allows demand for the product to set the price of products.

Oligopolistic competition prevails when a product is so expensive to create that only a few producers can survive in a market. Automobile, cruise ship, and airplane manufacturing all operate in oligopolistic markets. At this writing there are only two manufacturers of commercial aircraft: Boeing in the United States, which started in the 1920s, and Airbus in Europe, which began in 1970. The initial costs of producing aircraft are extremely high—so high that the governments of Germany and France had to put up millions of dollars to get Airbus started and to sustain it for the first years of its existence. Its first plane was certified in 1974, and the company was on the verge of going out of business until it began selling to U.S. air carriers in 1979 (Airbus 1998).

The problem with an oligopoly is that, because there are a small number of producers, companies can conspire to control supply and therefore get higher prices than they would get in a competitive market. If Boeing and Airbus cooperated with one another and agreed to divide up the market and to charge prices higher than the market would otherwise generate, they can do so. This means that money that might have gone to education, hospitals, and other such essential institutions, goes to aircraft manufacturers instead. This is bad for the taxpayers and for society. As we will see in Chapter 3, The Corporation, business is subject to a variety of antitrust laws that are designed to prevent them from using their market power to raise prices.

Monopolistic markets exist when there is just one supplier of a product to a given set of consumers, and therefore no competition between producers. For most products, monopolies are bad for consumers and society because the controlling business limits supply, driving up prices. However, some monopolies are "natural."

Natural monopolies obtain when it is cheaper for the consumer to have only one provider. Until recently, telephone, gas, and electric utilities were considered natural monopolies, and so they were allowed to do business without any competition. These monopolies are natural because of the tremendous cost of setting up the *infrastructure* required to deliver these products. If more than one company tried to operate in the same area, it would have to completely duplicate the infrastructure, despite having fewer customers over which to spread these costs. In other words, if a new utility were to try to compete with an existing one, it would have to charge higher prices! Of course, consumers would not pay higher charges, so no company would try to compete for these customers.

The computer technology that came of age in the 1980s was the beginning of the end of natural monopolies. Now that we have sophisticated ways of keeping track of how much electricity and gas flows through wires and pipes, many companies can use the same infrastructure to deliver these products. Hence, the problem of duplicating infrastructures has disappeared. This has allowed the U.S. government to use legislation and the courts to bring competition to public utilities. We first saw this phenomenon in 1982 when the

United States sued AT&T to allow Sprint and MCI to use AT&T's long-distance phone lines. Fearing a court-imposed settlement, AT&T agreed to split up into seven regional companies, and a long-distance company, with only the long distance company keeping the name of AT&T. This agreement, formalized in a consent decree (*U.S. v. American Tel. & Tel. Co.*, 552 F. Supp. 131), went into effect in 1984. We now have several different long-distance phone companies competing for our business. Phone competition is beginning to occur at the regional and local levels, and even gas and electric utilities are starting to compete for residential customers (Salpukis 1996).

Property The most fundamental way societies organize competition is by establishing the rules of property. At the most general level, the property rules of a nation establish whether private or state property will dominate. In the United States and in most of the world, private property is the dominant form of ownership. In China, Vietnam, North Korea, and Cuba, the state owns the capital and the means of production, while individuals own personal property: clothes, food, sometimes a car or a home.

Property rules were at the heart of the AT&T breakup mentioned above. The United States sued AT&T because it was using its property rights to infrastructure to inhibit competition. AT&T retained its long-distance service, but it had to lease long-distance lines to competitors at **fair market prices**. In effect, the consent decree changed the competitive environment of telephone service by altering AT&T's property rights.

Risk-Reward Relationships Business involves risk. At the level of production, businesses ordinarily must take risks to develop and sell products. One of the biggest risks of doing business is the possibility that the basic rules of the economic game might change. Government sets these basic rules, and government can change them, as happened with AT&T. For consumers, there is a risk that the product will not work as advertised. To reduce consumer risk, businesses give guarantees or warranties, especially on complex and expensive items like televisions and cars. Guarantees are backed by government rules and laws. The reduction in risk encourages people to buy more products. This increases production and at the same time gives manufacturers an incentive to produce quality products. Monopolies bear almost no risk, since they have no competitors. This is why AT&T fought so hard against Sprint and MCI. AT&T lost because the U.S. Supreme Court decided that competition was more important than preserving the property rights AT&T had to its infrastructure.

Information We must have good information about products and businesses if we are to make rational decisions about what to purchase. For businesses to succeed, they must have good information about the basic rules governing property, risk-reward, and competition. In general, better information promotes more efficient markets.

Descriptive Economics and Normative Economics Descriptive economics is the study of how economic systems and economic organizations *do* work. Normative economics is the study of how economic systems and economic organizations *should* work. The basic assumption behind most descriptive economics is that we act to promote our personal, financial well-being. Normative economics investigates how we should structure the basic rules of the economic game so that self-interested people will promote desirable social outcomes.

Normative economics relies on descriptive economics in several ways. Suppose we agree that people do act to promote their own economic self-interest (descriptive economics), but we think that self-interest sometimes has bad effects on organizations and society (normative economics). For example, private property is supposed to promote group well-being because people will take better care of what they own than of what they do not own. If people take good care of their property, and most property is privately held, this will promote the well-being of the group. However, there are instances in which private property and self-interest have undesirable outcomes. In the AT&T case, for example, self-interest and the rules of property gave AT&T the right to refuse to lease its line to Sprint and MCI. The U.S. Supreme Court decided this was bad for consumers, and so they altered AT&T's property rights.

Externalities are another way in which private property and self-interest can create bad outcomes. Externalities can be negative or positive, but even positive externalities can be harmful. Let's begin with negative externalities.

Negative externalities occur when business activities harm those who are not *voluntary* parties to the business activities. It does not matter whether this harm is intentional or not. It does not even matter if those within the transaction attempt to avoid harming those external to the transaction. The essence of a negative externality is *the lack of consent* of those who are harmed. Pollution is a clear case of an externality. A large chemical plant, for example, can cause air and water pollution that harms the health and property of many people (see Chapter 5, The Environment—Environmental Economics: Society).

Positive externalities occur when business activities *benefit* those who are not voluntary parties to the business activities. For example, suppose a company opens a plant in a high-crime area. To protect their investment, management hires security guards. The presence of the security guards may reduce crime in the area surrounding the plant. The residents would receive the benefits of lower crime without paying for it. In another case, the building of Disneyland in California increased land values of those who owned land near the new theme park, generating significant positive externalities.

Before we leave these introductory remarks about economics, we need to discuss the concept of **comparative advantage**. The theory of comparative advantage was first advanced in 1776 by the British economist and philosopher, Adam Smith (1776). Smith is widely recognized as the grandparent of modern economics. He argued that one of the primary ways that a nation becomes wealthy is to produce goods that it makes efficiently, and to trade for those goods it cannot make efficiently. This is known as comparative advantage, because a country should make its decisions about what to produce by *comparing* its productive resources with those of other countries. Smith thought this would happen naturally if government did not interfere with the business decisions of individual entrepreneurs. When a country has a productive *advantage*

Table 1
Law Reinforces Ethical and Economic Values

	Self-Interest	Personal Relationships	Group Interest	Intrinsic Value: Rights, Fairness
Competition	Laws	Laws	Laws	Laws
Property	"	"	"	"
Laws	"	"	"	"
Information	"	"	"	"

with respect to a product, it should produce that product. When a country has a productive disadvantage with a product, it should let other countries produce it. If all countries produced what they made best, and traded for the rest of their needs, we would all be better off, getting the best products for the least cost and with the least waste.

In our discussions of the economic implications of the issues in business ethics, we will examine how society, through its institutions of government, uses these economic categories and concepts to establish and regulate the relationships between consumers and producers.

Law

Societies use law to *reinforce* ethical rules, and to monitor and enforce rules governing competition, property, production-reward relationships, and information. This is called the **reinforcement view of law**. According to this reinforcement view, law is a product of how societies weave together the four economic conditions just outlined, and the four ethical values discussed in Ethics, above.

Table 1 will be different for different countries, and different for the same country at different times. Further, reasonable people can disagree about how to fill it in order to represent a particular state of affairs. Still, we can use it as a tool to understand the ethical and economic values that ground a country's legal system. Table 1a represents how we could use this table in the United States. To keep things simple, we will use standard interpretations of economic and ethical categories. We will also give only one example per cell to illustrate how law can *support* or *conflict* with institutional values, practices, and relationships.

Law emerges out of the need to guarantee ethical and economic relationships that are central to our well-being. For example, at the intersection of Risk-Reward and Personal Relationships we find the Family and Medical Leave Act. This act was signed by President Clinton to strengthen family relationships while still allowing efficient workplaces. At the intersection of Property and Intrinsic Value, to take another illustration, we find laws that prohibit government from taking personal property without a fair and open

Table 1a
Legal Intersection of Ethics and Economics for the United States

	Self-Interest	Personal Relationships	Group Interest	Intrinsic Value: Rights, Fairness
Competition	Open markets allow individuals to choose good products for good prices	Child labor restrictions promote family stability, protect children	Anti-trust laws increase product quality	State regulation of natural monopolies ensures fair(er) prices
Property	Private property laws allow us to pursue our interests as we see fit	Inheritance laws promote family continuity	Laws protecting the environment promote group well-being	Due process laws preventing the arbitrary seizure of property are fair
Risk-Reward	Taxes interfere with the pursuit of wealth and security for oneself	Family and Medical Leave Act promotes caring family relationships	Laws shielding managers from lawsuits promote the economic wealth of the group	Reducing voting age from 21 to 18 during the Vietnam War gave those drafted the right to vote
Information	Privacy laws prevent disclosure of our medical information to others	Food labeling laws promote family well-being	Freedom of information necessary for economic growth	Laws requiring managers to inform workers about workplaces dangers respect employee rights

21

hearing about the legitimacy of the taking. We leave the interpretation of the other cells to the reader.

What Are the Laws? We will have numerous occasions to note how the laws most important for business embody this reinforcement view and demonstrate the intersection of ethics and economics. But we must recognize that law is not static and fixed; it is fluid and dynamic. Any discussion of business and the law can only represent a snapshot of the current, and often temporary, state of things, along with views of what has gone before. This caveat should be kept firmly in mind while reading about the legal dimensions of ethical issues in business. Given the energetic nature of business practices, the flexibility of law, and the complex ways in which each adapts to the other, it is likely that some of the statutes and cases presented here will have been superseded, or at least modified, by the time a particular reader has the opportunity to examine this material. That is the nature of the beast. To stay current with the most recent developments, we recommend perusal of the *Congressional Quarterly Weekly* and the *Federal Register* (see both below), as well as the standard print, video, and radio resources of the news media.

Each chapter's section on law begins with an introduction to that area. These introductions vary in length, depending on the grasp of the legal history and terminology that the reader needs in order to appreciate the issues at stake. A subsection called Selected Cases, Statutes, and Regulations follows, in which we examine specific items of the law affecting business practice. These items are usually arranged chronologically according to how a particular legal arena has developed over time; sometimes they form discrete units unrelated to those around them. We recommend that the Law section be read in sequence, from the introductory material through the particular laws; however, individual cases and statutes can be profitably read independently of any others.

Our selection of items of law is not close to comprehensive. There are tens of thousands of court cases and many hundreds of laws relevant to business practices. Instead, we have tried to focus on the especially foundational, seminal, enduring ones, or those representing key legal principles. We have emphasized the two primary sources of laws applicable to business: (1) acts of Congress that establish both federal laws and the administrative agencies that issue federal regulations and enforce various laws; and (2) judges' decisions in courts at the federal level, comprising case law. We discuss both of these in more detail below.

We concentrate on federal standards for two reasons. First, Article VI, Section 2 of the U.S. Constitution declares that federal laws are the supreme law of the land, and state or local laws conflicting with them are unconstitutional; this is known as the **Supremacy Clause**. Article I, Section 8 of the Constitution gives Congress the power "to regulate commerce... among the several states," an authority that has been interpreted to include not only business activity between states, but also business activity that simply affects interstate commerce. This **Commerce Clause** coupled with the Supremacy Clause ensures that the federal government will be the preeminent force setting legal standards for business.

The second reason we will focus on federal standards is that state laws are not only profuse, they are also highly variable. Even a bare outline of the legal issues surrounding business ethics at *both* the federal and state level would require several volumes. The best we can do here is sketch the main contours of the legal terrain in which business must find its way.

Acts of Congress: Statutory and Regulatory Law   An act of Congress exemplifies the legislative branch of government as a source of law. Rules promulgated from this source are called federal statutes. Such laws begin as *bills* introduced by one or more members of Congress. The bill is assigned to the appropriate committee or subcommittee that studies the subject matter addressed by the bill. After hearings and testimony concerning the proposal, and various drafts have been composed, the committee votes on the bill. If the committee vote is affirmative, the bill is then referred to all the members of the House and Senate for a full vote. The *Congressional Quarterly Weekly* tracks this process, including the different versions of the bill under consideration.

If both houses of Congress pass the bill, it is then forwarded to the president. When the president signs off on a bill, it becomes a law or statute. It is then "codified" or recorded in its final form in the *United States Code* (U.S.C.). The U.S.C. is arranged according to fifty different categories or "Titles". Within each title, specific statutes are listed by section number (they are also arranged by chapter and subchapter but these are almost never included in standard citations). For example, the citation for the *Occupational Safety and Health Act of 1970* is 29 U.S.C. §§651–678. This indicates that this statute is found under Title 29 ("Labor") of the *United States Code*, beginning at section (§) 651 and ending at §678.

Acts of Congress sometimes also create federal administrative agencies (state legislatures may create state administrative agencies as well). For example, the *Occupational Safety and Health Act* created the *Occupational Safety and Health Administration*, more commonly known as OSHA. Under the authority provided by the enabling legislation (the act of Congress), OSHA and the other agencies of the legislative branch of government promulgate federal regulations; these rules function as laws along with the specific statutes enacted by Congress. They are codified in the *Code of Federal Regulations* (C.F.R.), which is organized and cited in the same manner as the U.S.C. The majority of federal administrative agencies are part of the executive branch and the president's cabinet. The Department of Labor, the Commerce Department, the Department of Housing and Urban Development, among others, also issue federal regulations.

The point of these agencies and departments is to form a group of professionals who are experts in a particular field; the application of their expertise is intended to effectively regulate a specific industry or area of commerce by writing rules. Proposed regulations and those that have been officially implemented are published each day in the *Federal Register*; established regulations are compiled annually in the C.F.R. Additionally, the federal agencies and the executive branch departments each have their own websites, easily located by using any one of the major search engines and entering the name of the agency.

Nearly every university and public library owns the U.S.C., and many also have the C.F.R. Much of the material in both of these law books is also accessible on the Internet. The Cornell University Law School offers a website with the complete text of many statutes from the U.S.C.; its address is http://www.law.cornell.edu/uscode/. The C.F.R. is available at the U.S. Government Printing Office website: http://www.access.gpo.gov/nara/cfr-table-search.html.

The statutes and regulations most important to business are predominantly **civil laws**, although some are classified as **criminal law**. The distinction between the two types basically turns on the penalties for breaking the law. Criminal law provides for imprisonment and probation, possibly fines as well (payable into the government treasury), and perhaps even capital punishment. Because of the severity of the sanctions, conviction under the criminal law requires a unanimous decision by members of a jury who are convinced "beyond a reasonable doubt." In contrast, civil law violations are punishable only by fines, called *monetary damages*, which are payable to the prevailing party in the law suit, and *injunctions*, which are court orders either to do something required by law or to stop doing something prohibited by law. A judgment against the accused in a civil case requires a finding only that the "preponderance of the evidence" indicates a violation. Typically, only a majority vote, and not a unanimous decision by the jury, is sufficient. Some cases are tried before a judge alone.

Judges' Decisions: Case Law   The decisions of judges in state and federal courts are a third source of law. Their judgments are based on a case-by-case interpretation of constitutions (state or federal), and the relevant statutes and regulations. Judges look to these documents to guide and validate their decisions, and these decisions become law. Sometimes, however, judges must make decisions in cases in which the Constitution does not provide any explicit direction, the issue has not been addressed before by a court, and lawmakers have not supplied an applicable statute or regulation. In such "cases of first impression," judges must create the law by issuing a ruling that establishes a precedent.

The decisions judges make in the absence of constitutional guidance, and when neither statutes supplied by lawmakers nor regulations promulgated by regulatory agencies are available, constitute the common law. The rules of the common law are based on judges' understanding of prevailing social customs or practices, or what seems appropriate or reasonable in the particular circumstances of the case at hand or are based on what judges decided in earlier, similar cases. State and federal legislatures sometimes react to this "judge-made law" by writing the decision into subsequent legislation, or by passing laws that counteract a judge's decision with which they disagree.

As mentioned above, criminal and civil laws affecting business are compiled in books of statutes and regulations, such as the *United States Code* and the *Code of Federal Regulations*. These books provide ready access to inventories listing what exactly the laws are. It would be helpful to have similar books of common law, but the problem is that these laws do not emanate from a rule-making body in any systematic fashion. Instead, they arise here and there, now and then, from judges working in different jurisdictions, hearing often widely disparate sorts of cases.

Fortunately, members of the American Legal Institute have poured over thousands of cases and distilled the principles of common law from them. Staffed by numerous legal practitioners, jurists, and scholars, the institute was formed in 1923 with a mission to promote the clarification and simplification of the law. This mission has produced two sets of volumes entitled *Restatements of the Law*. Included in the two sets, which are designated as *First* and *Second Restatements*, respectively, are volumes covering the main areas of common law: agency, contracts, torts, property, and international relations. These volumes have become the standard legal reference source for lawyers, legislators, and judges alike.

It is important to emphasize that the *Restatements* do not have the force of law; unlike state and federal constitutions and books of statutes and regulations, they are best thought of as advisory materials. When lawmakers, administrators, and judges use the *Restatements* to inform their deliberations, it is the statutes, regulations, and opinions they then write that are law. We will have occasion to refer to the *Restatements* in the chapters that follow when discussing certain aspects of the common law that apply to business.

The opinions of judges in particular cases, whether forming the common law or interpreting codified criminal or civil law, are published in various court reporters. The U.S. court system is arranged hierarchically with the Supreme Court at the top. The decisions of the Supreme Court are published in the *United States Reports*, a publication of the federal government, and in the *Supreme Court Reporter*, issued by West Publishers of St. Paul, Minnesota. These opinions are cited by naming the parties to the dispute, followed by the volume and first page where the opinion can be found in the publication, and the year the decision was rendered. For example: *McDonnell Douglas Corp. v. Green*, 411 U.S. 792 (1973). The first name refers to the **plaintiff** in the case, the party filing the complaint; the second name refers to the **defendant**, the individual responding to the suit. The citation indicates that this case can be found in volume 411 of *United States Reports* (abbreviated "U.S.") on page 792, and that it was decided in 1973. Our citations of Supreme Court cases almost always refer to *United States Reports*. In the most recent cases, however, we have cited the *Supreme Court Reporter*—abbreviated as S. Ct.—simply because the independent, private publisher gets the opinions in print much faster than the federal government. Supreme Court opinions can also be accessed on the Internet at the *Findlaw* website; the address is **http://www.findlaw.com/ casecode/supreme.html**.

Although the Constitution does not explicitly say so, since the historic *Marbury v. Madison* case (5 U.S. 137 [1803]), the Supreme Court has been regarded as having the *power of judicial review*. This is the right to decide the constitutionality of every law, whether state or federal. Because the Supreme Court is the final arbiter of the law in the United States—there is no appeal of its judgments—it has ultimate power to restrict legislative and executive branch activity. For these reasons, Supreme Court decisions are the most important authorities in case law, and so they tend to dominate our discussion.

Next in judicial importance below the Supreme Court, and so also occupying a prominent place in our discussion of business law, is a system of United States Courts of Appeals. These federal courts are divided into 13 *circuits* according to 12 geographical regions and the federal circuit. Opinions of the various circuit courts are found in the *Federal Reporter*, also provided by West Publishing. For example: *Spaulding v. University of Washington*, 740 F.2d 686 (9th Cir. 1984). Spaulding is the plaintiff, the University of Washington the defendant, and the opinion is found in volume 740 of the *Federal Reporter, Second Series* (abbreviated "F.2d"), beginning on page 686. The case was decided by the Ninth Circuit Court of Appeals in 1984. Notice that in this citation, and in *McDonnell Douglas* above, a corporation or an institution can be either a plaintiff or a defendant.

Below the circuit court level are 96 federal district courts. These are grouped geographically, and each state typically has one or two federal districts, depending on population. These opinions are cited in the same manner as those of the other federal courts, with a volume and page number sandwiched around an abbreviation for the relevant publication, and the year of the decision tagged on at the end. District court opinions are found in the *Federal Supplement*, also published by West, and cited as "F. Supp." We do not identify the specific district court rendering an opinion.

There are also many courts in each state judicial system, including a supreme court, appellate courts, and superior and municipal courts. Many of these decisions are collected in West's National Reporter System, which divides the country into seven geographical regions, with these abbreviations: Atlantic (A.), North Eastern (N.E.), North Western (N.W.), Pacific (P.), South Eastern (S.E.), Southern (S.), and South Western (S.W.). We do discuss or mention a few especially important cases decided on the state level, and here the citation proceeds in the familiar pattern, inserting the appropriate regional reporter abbreviation between the volume number and the page on which the decision begins.

Finally, we should point out that various administrative agencies also have their own publications describing their rulings on particular issues. We will be concerned to some extent with the *Federal Trade Commission Reports (FTC)*, which records hearings and rulings of the Federal Trade Commission, and the *Securities & Exchange Commission Reports (SEC)*, which presents similar material from the Securities and Exchange Commission. If they are not challenged, FTC and SEC rulings stand as law; however, they are frequently appealed, and in that case the matter enters the federal court system.

Almost any big city public library or major university library will have one or both of *United States Reports* and the *Supreme Court Reporter*. However, the federal and regional reporters tend to be harder to find outside of law school libraries. Municipal and county courthouses often have their own libraries and usually include these resources. Most of them are open to the public. A library collection often contains only the reporters for the region in which the library is located. Fortunately, many of these federal decisions can be retrieved on the Internet. Circuit court decisions can be found on the Cornell University Law School website at this address: http://supct.law.cornell.edu/Harvest/brokers/circuit-x/fancy.query.html. *Findlaw* also offers some federal district court opinions at http://www.findlaw.com/casecode/district.html. Another reference source is multivolume sets of books that group together cases from different jurisdictions involving a particular subject or similar range of legal problems. Of special importance to the study of business ethics and the law are these sets published by the Bureau of National Affairs in Washington, D.C.: *Individual Employment Rights* (IER), *Fair Employment Practices* (FEP), and *Occupational Health and Safety Cases*. These materials collect federal district and appellate court cases involving employee-related issues, and they are widely available in the libraries of postsecondary education.

Also, many libraries carry a number of "cases and materials" texts. These compilations feature a wealth of court opinions focused on a specific range of legal problems, along with explanatory material. They are offered by a variety of different publishers. The student of business ethics and law should find these items especially helpful: Brenda Barrett, *Cases & Materials on Occupational Health & Safety Law* (Holmes Beach: Gaunt Inc., 1995); Daniel J. Gifford, *Federal Antitrust Law: Cases & Materials* (Cincinnati: Anderson Publishing, 1997); David G. Owen, *Products Liability & Safety: Cases & Materials* (Westbury, CN: Foundation Press, 1997); David L. Ratner, *Securities Regulation: Cases & Materials* (St. Paul, MN: West Publishing, 5th ed., 1997); Philip Weinberg, *Environment Law: Cases & Materials* (Bethesda, MD: Austin & Winfield Publishers, 2nd ed., 1998); Michael J. Zimmer, *Cases & Materials on Employment Discrimination* (New York: Panel Publishers, 4th ed., 1997).

Business ethics involves the investigation of the intersection of ethics, economics, and law. Although ethical concepts are the main focus in this book, we examine them as they arise in economic and legal contexts. This concludes our discussion of the general features of business ethics. In the coming chapters, we discuss specific issues. We use the tools of ethics, economics, and law to present and analyze these issues, according to how they arise for, respectively, the consumer, the corporation, the employee, and the environment.

References: Airbus. 1998. Website: http://www.airbus.com/about_mini.html.

Cavenaugh, G. F., D. J. Moberg and M. Velasquez. 1995. "Making Business Ethics Practical." *Business Ethics Quarterly* 6: 363–374.

Dienhart, John W. 1999 (forthcoming). *Institutions, Business, and Ethics*. New York: Oxford University Press.

Goldberg, Carey. 1995. "The Simple Life Lures Refugees from Stress." *The New York Times*, National Edition (21 September): B1, C1.

Gwartney, James D. and Richard Stroup. 1982. *Economics: Private and Public Choice*. 3d ed. New York: Academic Press.

Heald, Morrell. 1988. *The Social Responsibility of Business*. New Brunswick: Transaction Press.

North, Douglass. 1990. *Institutions, Institutional Change and Economic Performance*. Cambridge: Cambridge University Press.

Salpukis A. 1996. "Electric Utilities to Provide Access for Competitors." *New York Times* National Edition (25 April): A1.

Samuelson, Paul A. and William D. Nordhaus. 1985. *Economics*. 3d ed. New York: McGraw-Hill.

Simon, Herbert. 1976. *Administrative Behavior*. 3d ed. New York: The Free Press.

Smith, Adam. 1976, 1776. *The Wealth of Nations*. Edited by Edwin Cannan. Chicago: University of Chicago Press.

United States Sentencing Commission Manual. 1991. Sj8A1.3 1 November.

Uphoff, Norman. 1993. "Grassroots Organizations and NGO's in Rural Development: Opportunities with Diminishing States and Expanding Markets." *World Development* 21 (4): 607–622.

Velasquez, Manuel. G. 1992. *Business Ethics: Concepts and Cases*. 3d ed. Upper Saddle River, NJ: Prentice Hall.

CONTEMPORARY ETHICAL ISSUES

Chapter 2:
The Consumer

We live in a consumer-oriented society. Everywhere we go we see the products, advertisements, and logos of Nike, AT&T, General Motors, and many others. Most of our lives are devoted to taking care of what we already own or to earning money to buy more things. Critics argue that we lead dreary lives that are consumed by consuming (Jones 1997).

This dreary view of consumerism misses a fundamental point. We seek consumer goods to promote the well-being of ourselves, friends, and families. We want nice cars, homes, clothes, educations, and even toasters, because they make the lives we live with others more pleasant. Producers know that consumers want these things, so they spend money and time creating them. Producers also know *why* we want them, so they spend money and time marketing them.

Introduction

In this chapter we will discuss advertising, product safety, and finance from the consumer's point of view. The central ethical issue for all three topics is *honesty*: Are consumers given correct and sufficient information about the nature of the products and services they use? If not, should government pass laws to ensure that consumers get good information and safe products? This last question addresses an issue that is often foremost in the minds of business persons: the justification of the regulation of business by government.

Protecting Consumers

Two general views pertain to the matter of government regulation designed to protect consumers. The first one is called the **free market approach** (FMA), which holds that government intervention with transactions on the free market is not necessary because all the information consumers need to make informed purchases will be supplied there. The second approach is called the **imperfect market approach** (IMA), which holds that we need government regulation because free markets fail in ways that can be very harmful to individuals and society (Samuelson and Nordhaus 1985).

Free Market According to the FMA, consumers seek information about products that will satisfy their needs. It is the consumers themselves that decide what is best for them. Most product information comes from the producers. If the product is affordable and meets consumer needs, they purchase the product. If the product works as advertised, both producers and consumers are better off than they were before the transaction: The producer recoups money spent on production (including profit margins) and consumers have a product that helps them live better than they could before.

However, if the product does not work for the consumer, The producer will lose repeat business as consumers turn to other producers. If enough consumers turn to other producers, the producer in question will go out of business and competing companies will prosper. Because producers know they have to give good information to survive, they do not mislead consumers. For these reasons, the FMA holds that the free market itself provides a sufficient incentive for producers to make safe products, and supply thorough, accurate information about them. Because the market supplies all the information consumers need, it is wasteful to spend taxpayer money on government laws and agencies to ensure good consumer information.

Imperfect Market According to the IMA, free markets contain many features that provide businesses with powerful incentives to give consumers misleading and false information. First, consider that there are many products that we buy very few times. In this case, repeat business is not very important. This is especially true in large markets. For example, many people buy exercise equipment from **infomercials**. Suppose that a company plans to sell say, 250,000 thigh-busters and then move on to another project. In a nation the size of the United States, with 280 million people, a producer can sell all of the units before there is time for customer dissatisfaction to affect sales. These products are often sold as if the inventor is the one marketing the product. In reality, it is likely that the inventor has signed a contract with a company that markets the product. The name of the company providing the support is usually not mentioned, so consumers with bad experiences with exercise products cannot avoid the company in the future. In these kinds of cases, IMA suggests that government should intervene to ensure that marketing campaigns are truthful.

Second, consumers often have difficulty evaluating products they buy because of **asymmetric information**: The producers know much more about their products than consumers (Pearce 1992). This means producers can make products that look good but that do not perform well. Let's take exercise equipment again. Many people buy exercise equipment they do not use, and it is likely that many blame themselves for this. In reality, it may be that the equipment is badly designed, hard to use—or even dangerous—and that not using it is the correct, rational response. Because most people cannot differentiate well-designed from badly designed exercise equipment, they will not know the problem lies in faulty equipment. In another kind of case, the product may be too complicated for consumers to evaluate, and if they have problems they will not know whether to attribute the problems to themselves or the product. This is the case with most people when they buy their first computer. They try to install a new program or printer, and the computer crashes: The screen goes blank, and using the mouse and keyboard has no effect. It is very hard to determine what went wrong.

Third, some businesses sell products and services, like food, air travel, automobiles, and medicine, the failure of which can cause illness and death. If we wait to let the free market sort out good from bad with these products, many consumers will be injured or killed. The IMA holds that government should intervene in these cases to make sure that such products are safe and work as intended.

Fourth, there are two kinds of consumers, **primary consumers** and **secondary consumers**. Primary consumers buy products and services that they themselves will use. Secondary consumers use products and services bought by others. Most adults are primary *and* secondary consumers: They buy things for themselves, but while they are at work, walk down the street, or turn on to an interstate highway, they use and rely on things bought by others. Some people, like infants and the very ill, are secondary consumers only.

The FMA works better with primary consumers, because they have intimate knowledge of their own needs. When people buy things for others, however, the buyers lack this intimate knowledge. Further, buyers may not care very much about the needs of secondary consumers, focusing instead on saving their own money and time. Lack of knowledge and lack of concern put secondary consumers at more risk than primary consumers. For example, airplane passengers are secondary consumers of the plane, the services the plane received, and the food served. Because these products can put passengers at significant risk, IMA holds that government should intervene to assure safety and quality.

The FMA can respond to some of these problems. For example, distrust of company information has led to the growth of magazines, like *Consumer Reports*, that evaluate products for quality, ease of use, and safety. Underwriters

Laboratory came into existence to assure consumers of product safety. Supporters of the FMA argue that if government did not protect us in so many ways, private producers would supply information about airplanes, cars, medicine, and other dangerous products and services, and that the cost of acquiring and distributing this information would be less than what the government spends.

Which approach is the right one? Most commentators argue for a **mixed economy** in which the free market is allowed to function unless it produces serious harms (Samuelson and Nordhaus 1985; Gwartney and Stroup 1982). This is the approach in the United States, as we will see in our discussions of ethics, economics, and law.

Advertising

Companies use advertising and marketing to inform consumers about their products, and to motivate consumers to buy them. *Advertising* refers to the presentation of product information in media like billboards, newspapers, radio, television, and now, the Internet. *Marketing* is a broader term, because it can be used to refer to an entire scheme or strategy for promoting a product. A marketing plan typically includes decisions about pricing, when and where to release products, advertising campaigns, coupon strategies, rebates, and a host of other things designed to encourage the public to buy the product.

Ethics

Advertising has two principal functions, which are sometimes at odds with each other: To give consumers information about products and to persuade consumers to buy products (Santilli 1983).

When we view advertising and marketing as ways of communicating information, they are subject to ethical rules that govern communication in general, such as "Tell the truth" and "Do not deceive others." When we view advertising in its persuasive functions, it takes on characteristics similar to a promise because it asserts that the product really has the qualities being described. As such, advertising is subject to ethical rules such as "Keep your promises" and "Only make promises you can keep." Truth telling and promising can be justified by the four ethical principles discussed in Chapter 1, Introduction.

Truthful and accurate advertising became a problem as the United States developed a national market. Before the Civil War, most consumer markets were local. This meant that consumers and producers were often known to each other. If there was trouble with a product, the consumer could go to the producer. If the producer failed to live up to reasonable standards, others would find out quickly, and the producer could go out of business.

By the end of the Civil War, transportation and communications systems were in place that allowed for national markets. For example, businesses in

Chicago and New York could place advertisements in papers across the country, and use the U.S. mail or other forms of transportation to ship products to consumers. Although national markets have many advantages (see Economics, below), one distinct problem is that producers and consumers no longer know each other, making it much easier for producers to mislead and defraud consumers. Consider a newspaper advertisement, placed in 1897, that promised a sure-fire method for getting moths out of carpets, clothes, and other fabrics upon which moths like to feed. Those consumers who sent in the requested 50 cents got back a set of instructions telling them to soak the fabric in kerosene and burn it (further described in Law, below). This kind of fraud would very likely not occur in a small town where the seller and buyer both reside, and if it did, the fraud could only be perpetrated a few times, perhaps just once, before others would find out.

A survey of 330 advertising executives revealed that they had two fundamental concerns (Hunt and Chonko 1987). First, they worried about persuading consumers to buy useless products. For example, every Christmas, products such as pet rocks come out (complete with care and feeding instructions) that people buy as gifts. These gifts end up in the attic or the garbage in a very short time. The economist John Kenneth Galbraith goes on to argue that persuading people to buy useless products encourages people to produce useless products (Galbraith 1984). In a world in which so many people do not have decent food, housing, or education, it seems that we should be working to end those problems, and not designing, producing, and marketing pet rocks.

These advertising executives also worried about persuading consumers to buy unhealthy products. Consider the case of Leo Burnett, a major advertising firm in Chicago, that handles the marketing for Marlboro cigarettes and McDonalds. Should they continue advertising these products when it is well known that cigarettes and high-fat, high-sodium foods are dangerous to our health? What would consumers say?

Promoting Self-Interest: Egoism In theory, aggressively self-interested consumers do not spend money on products unless they are reasonably sure that they will benefit from them. These consumers do enough research to make sure that the products they are buying actually perform as the producers say they will, and that the products are sufficiently reliable given their price. It seems that this point of view would be in favor of the free market approach, because aggressively self-interested consumers would not want to waste tax money on activities that they do for themselves.

An argument for the free market based on the perspective of the aggressively self-interested consumer only works if we assume that individuals have the time and skill to evaluate the many products they buy. This assumption is false. Think about the many products you buy in a week: food, medicine, gasoline, toothpaste, gum—the list goes on. When a new product comes out that claims to be superior in some way, you give it a try. You do not have the time to research every one of those products to see how truthful and accurate its advertising is. Nor do you have the knowledge or skill to evaluate all the different information relevant to such diverse products as toothpaste and television sets, computers and calligraphy courses.

Despite these problems with evaluating products, aggressively self-interested consumers do not have to turn to government regulation. Instead, they can argue that the need for this kind of information will be supplied by other business people who publish and sell magazines and newsletters, such as *Consumer Reports*, that evaluate products for consumers. Although this may solve the expertise problem, it does not solve the problem of time. Do we have time to research all the products we buy?

Aggressively self-interested consumers would not be too worried about being sold products they do not want or need. They would side with philosophers like Robert Arrington (1982), who argue that we can choose to resist even the most persuasive advertising. It is simply a matter of knowing who we are and what we want. According to aggressively self-interested consumers, those who seem to succumb to advertising for cigarettes and fast food are really *choosing* to do so.

Contemplatively self-interested consumers believe that we should reduce our desires. The strategy of trying to meet all the desires we happen to have is a recipe for pain and conflict. We are born with a few desires—the desire for food, warmth, friendship, clothes, and education. Although we cannot eliminate these desires, we can choose how to fulfill them. The contemplative self-interested person, like Thoreau (1970), would try to fulfill them in the simplest and least costly way. By spending very little on consumer goods, there is less need to work, and the less we work the more time we have for friends, family, and self-development. From this point of view, the first question consumers should ask is not whether the advertising is truthful, but whether the product advertised is something they really need. Contemplative, self-interested consumers would not worry too much about Leo Burnett's advertising of cigarettes and McDonalds, because they avoid the consumerist approach to life all together, and so they would not smoke cigarettes or eat fast food.

Still, contemplatively self-interested consumers do consume. Can they evaluate well all the products they buy, or do they need some other source providing evaluations, like independent consumer magazines or government agencies? If there were no consumer magazines or government agencies, then it is unlikely that contemplatively self-interested consumers would want to create or lobby for them, because that would be a lot of trouble that would interfere with their contemplative lives. However, where such magazines and government agencies already exist, as they do in the United States, these consumers would take advantage of them, as long as they were easily available and had accurate information about products they might buy.

Nurturing Personal Relationships: Care   Caring consumers focus on supporting the projects of those for whom they care, those we above called **secondary consumers**. We will restrict our discussion to how caring consumers would decide to make purchases for a small group of secondary consumers, usually friends and family, whom we sometimes call the "**cared-for.**"

Passive caring consumers would try to get products that would help their friends and family pursue their projects. These passive carers would not consider how the cared-for chose their projects or how they decided that a particular product would help them. When these consumers buy clothes, food, and other standard items for others, passive caring seems reasonable. But when the cared-for want cigarettes, drugs, or money for gambling, passive caring seems inappropriate.

Passive carers view government regulation of advertising in more than one way. On the one hand, they might want government regulations that prevent cigarette advertising, because they would prefer that their loved ones do not smoke. This would be especially true if they believe that advertising can make us want things that we would not otherwise want (Crisp 1987). However, they might be so devoted to supplying the needs of their family and friends that they would not want the government to interfere in any way.

Active caring consumers would also try to get products that would help their family and friends pursue their projects. Active carers would try their best to let the cared-for make their own decisions about their personal projects and how best to fulfill those projects. However, active carers will be ready to challenge their friends and family if the carers believe that their projects are dangerous to themselves or others. To decide whether to intervene, active carers will pay close attention to the cared-for's history and personality, their relationship with that person, as well as other important relationships the person has.

To illustrate, suppose that Gina and Mary are good friends, and that Mary is trying to give up smoking. On several occasions, Mary told Gina not to let her smoke. As an active carer, Gina knows that she cannot really prevent Mary from smoking: That is up to Mary. Gina cannot follow Mary around all the time, and even if she did, what could she do if Mary insisted on smoking? Further, Mary's request is inappropriate, since it seems to place the responsibility for Mary's smoking on Gina.

As an active carer, however, there are several things Gina might do. She might suggest going with Mary to classes that help people stop smoking. She might volunteer to be Mary's "phone buddy," that is, be ready to talk to Mary at any time to help her avoid cigarettes. Mary would also try to make sure that she and Gina do not go to places that display cigarette advertising or have lots of people smoking. Depending on their relationship, Gina might also talk about the legitimacy of Mary's initial request that Gina not let her smoke.

Whether active carers would be in favor of government regulation of advertising would depend, in part, on how effective they believe advertising is. If they take the Arrington view (1982) that we can simply ignore advertising if we want to, these consumers would not have much of a reason to encourage government to regulate advertising. However, if they believe, with Roger Crisp (1987), that advertising can manufacture desires in us for things that we really do not want or need, then this is a good reason to have government regulation of advertising, at least for products that are clearly harmful.

Promoting the Good of the Group: Utilitarianism Utilitarian consumers want to make sure that advertising and marketing benefit the group. Marketing and advertising benefit the group if they give consumers enough information to make good decisions about what products they want to buy. If consumers believed that the free market (see above, Market Approaches to Regulation) provided enough incentives for producers to supply true, accurate information, there would be no need for government intervention. However, utilitarian consumers would be in favor of government regulation if they believed that consumers could be hurt or killed by using products that had been inaccurately advertised.

Strict utilitarian consumers would argue for regulations that hold producers liable for harm caused by false information no matter what the intent of the producer. This doctrine of **strict liability** (see Law, below) can be defended in at least two ways. First, many products are dangerous, and the best way to compel producers to be especially careful is to make them liable for all harm their products cause, even if there was no negligence on their part. This may sound unfair, but from the utilitarian perspective, fairness is only valuable if it promotes the group good, and in this case it does not. Second, if we exempt producers from some kinds of liability, consumers will not know when to pursue a claim on the basis of misleading advertising. This will raise their risk, and therefore the cost of consumption. Flexible rules for deciding liability when products cause injuries would result in lawsuits that have no merit, because consumers would then pursue litigation simply in hopes of getting some money. Flexible rules would also result in legitimate claims not being pursued, because consumers are not likely to understand the flexible rules.

A strict rule utilitarian view about persuasive advertising would hinge on whether we adopt the Arrington (1982) view that we can easily resist advertising, or the Crisp (1987) and Galbraith (1984) view that we can easily be persuaded by advertising. It would also depend on whether the products advertised are dangerous or harmful. For example, if we couple the Arrington view with benign products, like rubber bands and Post-It notes, it is hard to see why a society should spend its time and money regulating that kind of advertising. However, if we couple the Crisp/Galbraith view with dangerous and harmful products, like cigarettes and alcohol, we get a compelling reason for government regulation.

Flexible utilitarian consumers who believed that government regulation is needed might argue that strict rules regarding accurate information are too costly, because they do not acknowledge that advertisements for dish soap cannot harm the group the way that cigarettes can. The government should spend its money where it can prevent the most harm. When little or no harm is likely, little or no regulation is needed.

Another problem with strict rules regarding information is that not all information about products is essential for consumers to make good decisions. For example, the way a car absorbs the energy of a front-end collision is important for safety. Whether the car looks good after four years of driving over salted, wintery roads is important to resale value. Whether the seats have good lumbar supports is virtually meaningless to safety or resale. Because the risks consumers take on the basis of these different claims are different, the penalties for misleading advertising, if any, should also be assessed differently.

Still, the flexible rule utilitarian view of persuasive advertising is similar in some ways to the strict rule utilitarian view. Both views base their regulatory decisions on whether we can resist advertising and whether the product is dangerous. Flexible rule utilitarian consumers would insist, however, that the laws be written so that they can be applied in a reasonable way, that is, allowing for exceptions.

Respecting Dignity and Rights: Intrinsic Value   Consumers who subscribe to intrinsic value theory demand that advertising be truthful because that is the way to respect people as (1) dignified, choosing beings (Crisp 1987) and (2) as bearers of fundamental rights (Jackson 1990). When consumers are deceived, their choices are coerced. For example, if they choose to buy a vehicle advertised as safe, and it turns out that it is not safe, their freedom of choice was infringed by the bad information. Relying on this bad information can result in injury and death (see, for example, Selected Cases: *Leichtamer v. American Motors Corp.*, below).

Consumers who subscribe to intrinsic value also focus on rights. It is generally assumed that all people, consumers included, have the right to accurate information, especially in matters that affect their life and health. As we noted, advertisements are like promises to consumers. Given this, it is not surprising that consumers expect them to be kept.

Both interpretations of human intrinsic value could justify government intervention. Given the limited time and resources of most consumers, government regulation protects their ability to choose on the basis of accurate information, and therefore freely. Similarly, rights theory could focus on the need for producers not to break their promises. This does not mean that intrinsic value theorists would be in favor of all government regulations. Government regulation must not violate the rights of business owners and managers to choose how they will act and live.

Under the intrinsic value approach, regulating persuasive advertising would be dependent on the extent to which the audience can make a free, informed choice. As we saw, Crisp and Galbraith think we are all vulnerable in this way. But even if we adopt Arrington's view that we can resist or ignore advertising, we can still agree that some groups are especially vulnerable.

Taylor R. Durham (1984) argues that we cannot evaluate advertising in the abstract. In the real world, advertising aims at particular groups and tries to identify the best way to persuade that group. This can be a problem when groups have characteristics that make them more vulnerable than the average adult, such as children. Many believe that children's advertising should be regulated more carefully because children are more easily persuaded. The very ill can be vulnerable to false claims concerning new or untested medicine, and the elderly who live alone are vulnerable to telephone and door-to-door sales when they are lonely.

Economics

Efficient markets require clear and enforced property rights, clear relationships between risks and rewards, good information, and competition at the producer and consumer levels. Advertising and marketing deal with the third condition, information. Consumers use information to decide how to spend their money (which is a form of property). This information lets them assess the risk they are willing to take in order to enjoy the benefits (rewards) from a product. They know, however, that in the competitive environment, producers have an incentive to make their products look as good as possible.

Society   Accurate information about products promotes efficiency. If consumers know what they are buying, they are likely to meet their needs with that one purchase. However, if people are misled about the nature of products, they will purchase goods that do not meet their needs. When consumers buy faulty products, they may take them back, seek different products, or live with the loss. All three options are inefficient. Bad information can also cause consumers to lose trust in the free market, giving them an incentive to turn to government. Government action is costly, but if consumers demand it, there is no way to avoid it.

The cost of government regulation is very difficult to calculate, partly because it has so many aspects. We will consider two ways to measure the cost of government regulation: total cost and **marginal cost**. The *total cost* of government covers everything needed to create and maintain government, including the buildings, salaries, gas and electricity, and other overhead expenditures necessary to run it. It includes all branches of government: legislative, executive, judicial. It also includes all levels of government: federal, state, city, and township. The *marginal cost* of government is what it costs to add one more regulation. Even when we add in the cost of lobbying, this cost is a minute fraction of the total cost. Because the marginal cost of law is low, it is easy to pass new laws.

Society should integrate the consumer's need for good information and the producer's need to survive and flourish in a competitive environment. We now turn to a discussion of the economic needs and interests of these two groups.

Consumers   Consumers spend time and money when they investigate products to see if advertisements are accurate. We can characterize these costs as a kind of insurance. Consumers are insuring the accuracy of advertising and marketing.

If consumer research on products is a form of insurance, consumers will try to get as much insurance as they can for the least cost. Two ways enable consumers to insure the accuracy of advertising and marketing: They can do the research themselves or they can pay others to do the research. Consumers who do their own research must buy or somehow acquire the product in question. The consumer must also have the time, talent, and equipment to evaluate the product. The costs of doing one's own research are almost always more than paying someone else to do the research.

If we are going to pay for the research, we need to find a source for this information. For example, we may buy a copy of *Stereo Magazine* to read reviews of a particular CD player. Magazines spread the cost of research among thousands of readers. With products like medicine, airplanes, and food, the risks are great enough that we want to ensure that there will be as few problems as possible, and so consumers turn to government. When government pays the cost of insuring information, it spreads the cost over millions of taxpayers. Individual consumers cannot calculate the marginal cost of a particular government regulation to themselves and, even if they could, the cost would be very small because it is distributed among so many people.

The less consumers pay for insurance, the more time and money they have for their primary concerns, such as having fun, promoting their career development, strengthening family relationships, increasing the well-being of their country, and/or working to make social institutions more fair and just.

Producers Advertising and marketing are essential to the economic well-being of a company because these devices are the ways in which companies inform and try to convince consumers to buy their products. As we saw above in Market Approaches to Regulation, producers have more knowledge about their products than consumers. This **asymmetric information** often creates a situation in which companies have an incentive to mislead consumers, or, at the very least, an incentive not to spend much time making sure their marketing is not misleading. It is for these reasons that citizens pressure government to get involved.

It would seem that business would oppose all government regulation of marketing and advertising. However, this is not always true. For example, as we also saw above, many advertising executives are worried about misleading the public, especially when the products are harmful or useless (Hunt and Chonko 1987). Businesses with these concerns would welcome reasonable government regulation that requires accurate advertising because it would give help to convince them to create accurate advertising. Further, in this situation being honest would not put a company at a competitive disadvantage because all companies would have to be truthful.

We must admit, however, that even with regulations, companies try to be as persuasive as possible within the rules. If they find a legal means to advertise inaccurately in a way that may boost sales, they have an incentive to do so (see Bowie and Murphy 1995, for a case study that exemplifies this issue). This does not mean that we should have no rules, because the rules still prevent many cases of inaccurate advertising. Further, these rules can increase consumer trust, thus making all advertising more effective.

International Issues

The same ethical and economic issues arise for advertising and marketing in international business as arise in domestic business. However, international advertising and marketing issues have different dynamics for two reasons. The first reason is that there is no established international law to set standards for fair advertising and marketing. The absence of effective international law allows well-funded companies to manipulate consumers in countries with weak governments in ways they could not in more-developed nations. This problem is slowly being addressed, mainly through international trade agreements like the *North American Free Trade Agreement* (NAFTA), and the *General Agreement on Tariffs and Trade* (GATT), as administered by the *World Trade Organization* (WTO), along with the **European Union** (EU). Agencies of the United Nations have also been effective in helping to set standards for international advertising and marketing.

The second reason international advertising and marketing issues have different dynamics is that cultures have different expectations about what constitutes good information. What is acceptable in one country may be forbidden in another. Consider **puffery**, which is the glorification of products in vague and general terms such as "We have the best ribs in town," and "Ivory Soap is the most pleasant soap you can use." Puffery is allowed in the United States, but forbidden in Germany. German laws require that all claims regarding the effectiveness of products be substantiated by data. In Germany, Ivory would have to define what is meant by "pleasant"—smells better, cleans better, is gentle to hands, etc.—and have data to support that claim.

One of the most widely discussed problems of international marketing concerned Nestle's marketing of infant formula in third-world countries. In the 1960s the birth rate of first-world countries was stabilizing (Wood 1994). To increase sales, producers of infant formula needed to find new markets. Nestle, a Swiss company, engaged in a controversial marketing plan designed to convince women in third-world countries to give up breast feeding and switch to Nestle's infant formula. The most controversial part of the marketing plan involved hiring "milk nurses," saleswomen dressed as nurses, to give away free samples to poor women and to convince them that bottle feeding was the modern, safe, and most effective way to feed infants. Once women used the free samples, their own breast milk would diminish, forcing them to continue bottle feeding.

Bottle feeding in conditions of poverty in third-world countries has at least two problems. The first is the poverty itself. Formula is expensive, and to make it last longer, women would often dilute it, resulting in malnutrition. Water is another problem. For many of the poor in third-world countries, water sources are contaminated, and since many of the women had no education, they were unaware of the importance of boiling water to make it safer. Hence, many babies became sick and died because polluted water was used to prepare their formula.

In 1977 a worldwide boycott was launched against Nestle for their marketing strategies of infant formula. Other producers of infant formula also became targets of activist groups. This led the industry to develop an international code of marketing in 1981 that prevented giving free samples as well as several other practices to market infant formula. This code was developed under the auspices of the World Health Organization and the United Nations agency UNICEF. Nestle at first rejected the code, but agreed to it in 1983. By 1988 it appeared that Nestle was again using many of the tactics forbidden by the WHO/UNICEF code, and a new boycott was started. By 1991 Nestle once more agreed to stop offering free samples of formula, except to those impoverished women who truly needed it (Wood 1994).

Law

As early as 1872 Congress attempted to crack down on the numerous mail-order schemes of the time by passing stringent postal fraud laws. Unfortunately, these measures did little to check the flood of con men who ran rampant during the late 1800s and early 1900s. In 1911 alone the Post Office estimated that these charlatans, through the U.S. mail, cheated Americans out of $77 million. In those turn-of-the-century days, advertising was confined almost exclusively to the newspapers; the con man could set up his scheme simply by purchasing a cheap ad encouraging the locals to mail in money in return for all manner of inventions, real estate, alleged cure-alls, and baubles reputed to be of high value. One classic example of such fraud is a newspaper ad from 1897 promising to deliver, for 50¢, a foolproof method for eliminating moths from rugs, clothes, and other articles. Those who mailed in their money received instructions on how to soak the item with kerosene and ignite it. Another ad from 1882 offered to send, for $1, an engraving approved by Congress and the president's family of the recently assassinated President Garfield, and engraved, the ad proclaimed, by expert federal artisans. Each person mailing in their money received a 5¢ postage stamp featuring a likeness of the late president.

It was not until 1914 that Congress instituted comprehensive legislation designed to protect the public from a wide range of potentially injurious business practices, and created a regulatory agency authorized to promulgate and enforce protective laws. A survey of the Federal Trade Commission Act and the Federal Trade Commission are the appropriate starting points for a discussion of advertising and the law. Nevertheless, it was not until a 1938 amendment to the act that fraudulent advertising was vigorously attacked by federal law. In the cases, statutes, and regulations that follow, we trace the evolution of federal laws prohibiting false and deceptive advertising, and the process of specifying precisely when such advertising occurs. Additionally, we look at the important relationship between advertising and the claims of liability that arise when products injure consumers.

Selected Cases, Statutes, and Regulations

Federal Trade Commission Act of 1914, 15 U.S.C. §§41–51   The original congressional intention behind the act was to preserve fair competition between businesses by preventing restraints on trade (see Chapter 3, The Corporation—Antitrust Issues, Law). The restraint on trade of primary concern here was the business monopoly. Monopolies tend to drive up prices, which is contrary to the public interest, so the consumer protection initially provided by the act was indirect. However, over time, the regulatory power of the Federal Trade Commission (FTC) evolved to form an agency the most significant impact of which is on the methods and content of advertising and marketing.

The signal event in this development was the adoption of the Wheeler-Lea amendments of 1938 that added this phrase to section 5 of the Federal Trade Commission Act: "[U]nfair or deceptive acts or practices in or affecting commerce are declared unlawful." The five presidentially appointed FTC commissioners are thus empowered to order companies to refrain from engaging in unjust activities and from using deception. This is primarily accomplished by protecting the public from false and deceptive advertising, especially for food, drugs, and cosmetics, although all consumer products are included. The FTC has the authority to require companies who have employed such deception to disclose additional information or correct false information presented in ads. Much of the case law involving advertising concerns a determination of just when a particular ad is "deceptive." We will examine a representative sampling of such cases below.

Before proceeding, an important difference between two regulatory agencies should be noted. While the FTC deals with the false and deceptive *advertising* of all consumer products, the **Food and Drug Administration** (FDA) as authorized by the *Food, Drug, and Cosmetic Act of 1938* (and various amendments), regulates the accuracy of *labeling* on these particular products. Nonetheless, the regulatory tasks of these two agencies were blended with the Cigarette Labeling and Advertising Act of 1966 (15 U.S.C. §§1331–1341). This Act, along with a 1970 amendment, produced a requirement to label every package of cigarettes and every print media ad with a warning concerning the health hazards of smoking, and a ban of all radio and television advertisements for cigarettes. Despite this regulation, neither the FDA nor the Consumer Product Safety Commission has ever asserted their authority over tobacco products as a product safety issue (for more on the FDA, the Food, Drug, and Cosmetic Act, tobacco, and the Consumer Product Safety Commission, see Product Safety, Law, in this chapter).

Advertising can itself raise troubling problems for product safety and liability. When a manufacturer, through its advertising, states or implies that a product is safe or will perform for its intended use, a type of promise is made that imposes a duty on the manufacturer. If the product is not safe or does not perform as advertised, the promise has been broken and liability may be imposed. These promises come in the form of warranties. Any act, representation, affirmation of fact, or promise made by the manufacturer creates an **express warranty** that the product will perform as represented. An **implied warranty** refers to an assurance that arises simply by placing a product on the market that it will function correctly (types of liability in product safety matters are further discussed in that section of this chapter). We will consider some important cases for advertising and product liability below.

Manufacturers or retailers can employ false or deceptive advertising, and incur liability for resulting damages in several different ways: *Deceit* occurs when advertising is intended to mislead; *fraudulent concealment* refers to the withholding of information that must be disclosed; *negligent misrepresentations* are false or inaccurate statements that the manufacturer should have known were false. **Strict liability** may also be imposed. This holds the manufacturer liable for harm resulting from the misrepresentation of the product even though there was no negligence or fraud involved.

The FTC exercises its authority over advertising in two basic ways. First, the FTC issues various sorts of trade regulations. These rules may apply to all commercial advertising or they may be specific to certain industries, but in either case they have the force of law. As an example of a regulation applying to any business, in 1972 the FTC banned all use of the advertising practice commonly called bait-and-switch (16 C.F.R. Part 424). This technique begins when a product is advertised at a certain price. When the consumer arrives to purchase the product, either it is not on hand, or it has not been marked at the advertised price, thus redirecting the consumer's attention to some other, typically more expensive product. Similarly pervasive rules concern ads employing personal testimonials or endorsements. These must honestly portray the beliefs and experiences of the endorser, they must be representative of what an ordinary consumer would experience when using the product or, if "expert" testimony is utilized, the authority must have the qualifications to be recognized as an expert in that area.

Additionally, the FTC issues "Industry Guides" describing the rules and regulations for advertising in numerous specific industries as diverse as those manufacturing mirrors, watches, waist belts, ladders, and sleeping bags. To take a few examples, jewelry advertisers are prohibited from using the word "gold" unless the product is entirely composed of 24-karat gold, a clear and conspicuous statement of the country of origin must accompany every ad for any wool product, and advertisements for household furniture must disclose the use of veneers or simulated materials.

The FTC also regulates business by filing complaints against companies they believe are engaging in unfair or deceptive trade practices. These complaints may originate with members of the general public, consumer groups, Congress, other regulatory agencies, or business organizations. The company charged with the violation may simply agree to an FTC **consent order**. If the company does not agree, and wishes to challenge the allegation, a hearing is convened before an **administrative law judge** (ALJ) (see also Chapter 4, The Employee—Health And Safety, Selected Cases Occupational Safety and Health Act).

The ALJ listens to testimony from both sides, examines the applicable federal law, and eventually renders a decision. The entire process, whether culminating in an agreement to a consent order or in a decision by the ALJ, can be tracked through the federal government publication *Federal Trade Commission Reports* (also abbreviated FTC; some of our cases below cite this reference). The judgment of the ALJ may be appealed through the federal circuit courts of appeals, and those proceedings will be recorded in the *Federal Reporter*. Once the order of the ALJ becomes final, either by the company accepting it or an appellate court affirming it, failure to comply can result in a fine of $10,000 for each day of continued violation.

Lanham Act of 1946, 15 U.S.C. §1125   The target of this congressional action is the use of comparative advertising. The act allows a company to sue another when agents for the firm believe that damage either has been caused or is likely to be caused to their business interests as the result of the other's false advertising. Individual consumers are also entitled to sue companies that employ false statements or representations in an advertised comparison of products. Notice that the act does not require proof of actual injury, only a showing that injury is likely. For many years after the act was passed, companies could recover for injury only when they lost sales (or were likely to) as a result of false claims made by a second company about its own products (such as in the *L'Aiglon* case below). But eventually Congress recognized that damage could be caused when one company makes false statements concerning another's products. The Trademark Law Revision Act of 1988 (15 U.S.C. §§1051 *et seq*.) included an important amendment to the Lanham Act prohibiting any advertising that disparages a competitor's product. *Disparagement* is a false statement that tends to diminish respect for, or confidence in, a product by impugning its quality.

Also, during the several years immediately following its passage, the courts' interpretations of the act were quite lenient toward corporations and their advertising agencies. At least 30 complaints had to be filed against an advertiser before a case would even be heard. This indulgence changed abruptly in 1954 with *L'Aiglon Apparel, Inc. v. Lana Lobel, Inc.* 214 F.2d 649 (3d Cir. 1954). L'Aiglon had manufactured a distinctively styled woman's dress with a suggested retail price of $17.95, and widely marketed it through a series of ads showing a photograph of the dress. A retailer called Lana Lobel sold a different dress through mail order for $6.95 (remember, this was 1954!). However, Lobel's ads showed a picture of the L'Aiglon dress, not their own, thus falsely representing it as available for $6.95. L'Aiglon filed suit under the Lanham Act, and even though this was the first complaint against Lobel, the case was litigated. The plaintiff successfully argued that the misrepresentation had been damaging because some sales were lost to Lana Lobel and others were lost due to the false belief that L'Aiglon was selling a dress worth $6.95 for $17.95.

Under the Lanham Act, there are three different remedies available to injured parties: **injunctions**, corrective advertising, or monetary damages. Injunctions are the most common remedy and result in a halt in the publication of the offending advertisements, but are granted only if the plaintiff can show that irreparable damage will ensue if the ads are not stopped. A court may also order a company that created a deceptive ad to use its own money to correct the false statements.

Monetary damages for false comparative advertising were unheard of until 1984 and *U-Haul International, Inc. v. Jartran, Inc.*, 601 F. Supp 1140 (D. 1984). Jartran's ads claimed that their self-move rental prices "to almost any city" were cheaper than U-Haul's. Unfortunately, the Jartran prices advertised were not their regular prices but promotional rates undisclosed as such, while U-Haul prices were the regular ones plus a distribution fee, also not disclosed. In the litigation process, a series of consumer surveys (evidence often used in Lanham Act cases for this purpose) showed that the false and deceptive ad campaign did influence decisions on which self-move company to choose. The court awarded U-Haul $20 million in actual damages (for lost sales), $20 million in punitive damages (as punishment for wrongdoing), court costs, and attorneys' fees. Jartran is no more.

Rogers v. Toni Home Permanent Company, **147 N.E.2d 612 (Ohio 1958)** This historic case decided by the Ohio Supreme Court marked the first time that liability for a breach of warranty for a defective product was assigned to a manufacturer that did not sell the product directly to the injured consumer. Previously, only the immediate *seller* of a product could be sued for a breach of warranty—and not the distant manufacturer that actually made the product—because it was thought that no contract of any kind existed between the consumer and the manufacturer. Lured by the manufacturer's advertising claims and by statements on the package, Ms. Rogers bought a Toni Home Permanent set labeled "Very Gentle." Apparently, she followed the instructions carefully but the results were disastrous. Her hair would not dry, and when she removed the curlers supplied with the kit, most of her hair came out with them, leaving only about half an inch of stubble.

The court's precedent-setting ruling found that the manufacturing company was liable for these damages, not the retailer who sold it to Ms. Rogers. After all, the sellers of most merchandise are simply conduits for products that are shipped in sealed containers. The buying public typically relies exclusively on advertisements presented by the manufacturer when choosing products. The court concluded that the producer of these goods should be accountable for damages when consumers make purchases on the basis of their advertising. Although the company was not being sued for the advertising claim, the advertising served as proof of what Rogers reasonably expected from the product; this creates an express warranty that was violated when the product failed to perform as expected.

FTC v. Colgate-Palmolive **380, U.S. 374 (1964)** Here we have the seminal case concerning a very important method of television advertising. Given the technological limitations of TV for viewing real objects and events (not special effects), and given the time constraints involved in airing commercials, which typically are one minute in duration or less, claims that are in fact true cannot be accurately represented in the ads. Is this sort of deception an illegal representation?

The particular type of TV advertising of concern here is the *mock-up*, a model built to depict an actual situation. In 1959 Colgate-Palmolive promoted its product Rapid Shave by using one of these models. In the commercials, the shaving cream was applied to what appeared to be sandpaper, and then a razor was shown shaving the substance clean. This "sandpaper test" was supposed to demonstrate the "supermoisturizing power" of Rapid

Shave and its capacity to handle the toughest beard. In fact, the substance was a piece of plexiglass covered with sand, not sandpaper. The problems the advertising agency had confronted were that, although Rapid Shave could indeed shave sandpaper, it required eighty minutes of soaking time to do it, and on TV a sheet of sandpaper appeared to be nothing more than colored paper—hence, the need for the mock-up.

The FTC issued a cease-and-desist order on the grounds that the moisturizing effects of the product had been misrepresented and that viewers were misled into adopting the false belief that they had seen an actual demonstration of sandpaper being shaved. The FTC ordered further that all future use of undisclosed simulations of this type be halted. The First Circuit Court of Appeals rejected the order and the case went to the Supreme Court.

Chief Justice Earl Warren's majority opinion sided with the FTC. He found that the use of the mock-up to falsely represent what was in fact true was no different in principle from an advertiser falsely stating that a respected source had testified to a product's quality, or falsely stating that certain product claims had been verified by a testing agency. Even if the claims were true, in each case an attempt is made to persuade a potential buyer with something false: There was no testimony or testing, and the consumer is perceiving a simulation, not reality.

Warren also approved the FTC ban on undisclosed mock-ups. In finding for Colgate-Palmolive, the appellate court had compared shaving sand-covered plexiglass with using mashed potatoes in an ice cream commercial; real ice cream melts under hot studio lights just as real sandpaper requires a prolonged soaking time and looks like colored paper. Warren rejected the analogy. The crucial difference is that the mashed potato prop was not used as proof of a product claim, while the "sandpaper test" mock-up clearly was. The key here is that an undisclosed simulation is deceptive when the information it presents relates to claims about the quality of the product, and thus is likely to affect a consumer's decision about whether or not to buy it. Such material information must be truthful (see *In re Cliffdale Associates, Inc.* below for more on "materiality").

The last gasp for undisclosed mock-ups came several years later with an instance nearly as famous as the Rapid Shave case. *In re Campbell Soup Co.*, 77 FTC 664 (1970), concerned TV ads showing a bowl of soup chock full of vegetables. However, this representation had been achieved by inserting clear, glass marbles in the bottom of the bowl, causing the solids in the soup to stay near the surface. Like Colgate-Palmolive, Campbell Soup Company argued that the limitations of the medium required using the mock-up to portray the actual viscosity of the product. The FTC disagreed and declared that using the marbles was intended to create false beliefs in consumers that interfere with their ability to make rational choices. Because the matter had already been settled by the Supreme Court in *Colgate-Palmolive*, Campbell Soup gave up and accepted a consent order.

Warner-Lambert Co. v. FTC, 562 F.2d 749 (D.C. Cir. 1977) This famous case decided by the District of Columbia Circuit Court of Appeals illustrates two key issues in the regulation of advertising: (1) the amount of evidence required to affirm a cease and desist order from the FTC, and (2) the scope of FTC power to correct false advertising. The roots of the case go back as far as 1921 when Warner-Lambert first began marketing Listerine as a product that provides certain benefits for those wishing to avoid colds. After many years of such claims, in 1975 the FTC ordered Warner-Lambert to stop representing, either directly or by implication, that Listerine would prevent or cure colds or have any effect on the severity of colds. Additionally, the FTC directed Warner-Lambert to disclose in future ads that "Contrary to prior advertising, Listerine will not help prevent colds or sore throats or lessen their severity." The company denied that their ads stated or implied that Listerine alone would cure or prevent colds, rather that when combined with a healthy diet and sufficient rest, Listerine produced fewer, less severe colds. They backed up these claims with data from two different studies. Further, Warner-Lambert argued that the FTC had overstepped its regulatory authority by ordering the corrective disclosure.

Judge J. Skelly Wright was unpersuaded by Warner-Lambert's defense. He agreed with the FTC's findings that, among other things: (1) Gargling does not allow the active ingredients of Listerine to reach the body's cells where the cold virus lodges, and (2) even if they could reach those areas, they could not penetrate the tissue cells, (3) Listerine has no significant beneficial effect on a sore throat, and (4) the results of Warner-Lambert's studies were unreliable— there was no legitimate placebo, and the subjects, many of whom were Warner-Lambert employees, knew they were being treated for colds.

On the matter of the FTC's authority to order corrective advertising, Wright again sided with the commission. Citing previous judicial decisions and the FTC's own policy, he introduced two conditions for justifying corrective advertising: First, the original ads gave rise to a false belief about the product; second, the belief persists after the false advertising ends. Wright found that both conditions obtained, especially the second, given the extensive time period in which the false claims concerning Listerine's curative powers had been made. However, Judge Wright would not allow the Commission's order to include the phrase "Contrary to prior advertising" as this smacked of a malicious desire to humiliate the advertiser.

***Leichtamer v. American Motors Corp.*, 424 N.E.2d 568 (Ohio 1981)**
Deceptive advertising can also play a critical role in the awarding of punitive damages in product liability cases (as in comparative advertising; see above, the *Lanham Act* and *U-Haul International, Inc. v. Jartran, Inc.*). Punitive damages are essentially cash payments to the injured party from the guilty party as punishment for wrongdoing. This case demonstrates not only how advertising fuels such damage awards, but also how such awards can be made even when the consumer is negligent in his use of the product (recovery for damages even with consumer negligence was first established by the Michigan Supreme Court in *Bahlman v. Hudson Motor Car Co.*, 288 N.W. 309 (Mich. 1939).

In April 1976 Paul and Cynthia Vance and their friends Carl and Jeanne Leichtamer went for a ride in the Vance's Jeep CJ-7. While descending the slope of an abandoned strip-mine, the Jeep's rear end pitched over and the vehicle completed one and one-half revolutions, coming to a rest upside down. The Vances were killed and the Leichtamers were severely injured, Jeanne winding up a paraplegic.

Testimony at the trial left little doubt that Paul Vance's decision to drive down the slope was an exceedingly careless one. Nonetheless, the court found that the Leichtamer's injuries were significantly aggravated by the collapse of the factory-installed rollbar. Yet the Jeep had been specifically promoted as a vehicle that could safely negotiate steep and rugged terrain, and the rollbar in particular was touted as providing "added protection" and a "must" for off-road enthusiasts—as the Vance's were. Punitive damages were appropriate because advertisements depicted the likely use of the Jeep for ascending and descending precipitous hills while ignoring the substantial dangers inherent in such an activity. Furthermore, American Motors had failed to test the roll-bar to determine if it really did provide added protection. A total of $2.2 million in damages was awarded, over half of which were punitive.

***In re Cliffdale Associates, Inc.* 103 F.T.C. 110 (1984)** This Federal Trade Commission ruling signaled a major modification in the criteria employed by the FTC for identifying deception, and thus has great historical and contemporary significance. Throughout the 1970s Cliffdale Associates marketed a device called the "Ball-Matic Gas Saver Valve," claiming that it produced significant increases in gas mileage. When installed on a car engine, the valve admits additional air into the carburetor, increasing the ratio of air to fuel. Ads touted personal testimonials and scientific research that asserted dramatic improvements of from 8 percent to 40 percent. In fact, no credible scientific tests were ever performed, and the testimonials were all from people connected with the company. In finding against Cliffdale Associates, the FTC enumerated the three necessary conditions for a sales practice to be found deceptive, all of which were satisfied in the Ball-Matic ads: (1) There is a representation or omission of fact that is (2) "likely to mislead consumers acting reasonably under the circumstances," and (3) the representation or omission is material.

The first condition presents nothing new, but numbers (2) and (3) do. Consider number (2) first: In the decades following the passage of the Federal Trade Commission Act of 1914 (see above), the primary component of an illegal advertisement was its tendency or capacity to deceive. Especially germinal in establishing this criterion was the Supreme Court case of *FTC v. Raladam Co.*, 316 U.S. 149 (1942). Raladam marketed a product called "Marmola," claiming that it was effective for producing weight reduction. In fact Marmola had little or no tendency to cause an individual consuming it to lose weight. The FTC ordered the company to pull the ads. Attorneys for Raladam argued that whether or not the advertising was deceptive, there was no evidence that any injury had occurred as a result of the ads, or that anyone actually was deceived by them. Justice Hugo Black rejected this argument and ruled that no actual injury or deception needed to be proved in order to sustain the FTC's cease and desist order, only a showing of a "tendency or capacity to deceive." The difference between a "tendency to deceive," as in the *Raladam* case, and what is "likely to mislead," here in *Cliffdale*, is the difference between a mere possibility and a definite probability. In either case, there is no need to show that any deception actually occurred, but the new definition requires a higher degree of proof and thus, in effect, affords less protection for the consumer. And, of course, decreased consumer protection means increased protection for business. This was a clearly identifiable trend during the 1980s while the Reagan administration held sway, and an obvious swinging of the pendulum from the heyday of the FTC in the 1970s, especially as evidenced by *Warner-Lambert Co. v. FTC* (see above). Indeed, for one day in 1980, the FTC ceased to exist as a regulatory agency when Congress withheld all funding. The lawmakers demanded that President Carter give them veto power over FTC rulings, and no money would be released until he did. He did.

The reasonably acting consumer mentioned in (2) above is the commerce version of the **reasonable person standard**. This standard was first formulated in an 1837 English case (*Vaughan v. Menlowe*) and has been used countless times since then by courts in England and this country. It refers to the ordinary person of average prudence and common sense, who exercises commonplace levels of care and skill (see also Chapter 4, The Employee—Sexual Harassment, Law: *Ellison v. Brady* and the **reasonable woman standard**).

Although *Cliffdale Associates* appeals to this standard of reasonableness, the FTC and the courts have not always looked for this standard when identifying deception. For many years following the Wheeler-Lea amendments (see above Federal Trade Commission Act) and especially after the seminal Supreme Court decision in *FTC v. Standard Education Society*, 302 U.S. 112 (1937), what can only be called an "ignorant man" standard was employed. The prevailing opinion was that a finding that only one person was deceived, and even if that person was incompetent or a fool, was sufficient to establish a claim of deceptive advertising, no matter how unintended the deception, or how unreasonable it was to be deceived. *Gelb v. FTC*, 144 F.2d 580 (2d Cir. 1947) clearly demonstrates the ignorant person standard then operative. A product sold under the brand name "Clairol" was advertised as being capable of "permanently" coloring hair; that is, it permanently colors hair to which the solution is applied. The FTC argued that the ad was misleading because the solution did not color hair that had not yet grown in. No matter that only a fool would believe that it did—the court agreed with the FTC.

The restoration of the reasonable person standard began in 1973 with *In re Coca-Cola Co.* 83 F.T.C. 746. The complaint against the Coca-Cola Company was that the marketing of their "Hi-C" beverage implied that it was made from fresh orange juice and had a similar nutritional value, when neither was the case. The FTC disagreed with the complaint on the grounds that the advertising representations were "not reasonably likely" to lead anyone to believe anything contrary to fact. By the time of the *Cliffdale* decision, the reasonable person standard was deeply embedded into the FTC's reasoning process. This too represents a weakening in safeguards for the consumer, as it seems to make the uninformed and credulous—or those who are simply careless or unsophisticated—legally acceptable prey for deceptive advertising.

The third criterion of deceptive advertising mentioned in *Cliffdale* is that the representation or omission is "material." This case also indicates a shift in FTC policy concerning this criterion. *Cliffdale* announced that a claim is *material* if it is likely to affect the consumer's choice of a product. A material representation is deceptive when the consumer would have made some other choice had there been no deception: To compromise one's choice in this way constitutes an injury. In previous FTC and court rulings, any fact that was important to consumers had been considered material, regardless of whether those facts affected their choices and irrespective of any harm or injury. This new understanding of a deceptive material statement places a greater burden of proof on plaintiffs to show that consumers actually or probably did rely on the misrepresentation when making the decision to buy. This is much more difficult to do than merely showing that the statement was important to consumers. Once more, we see an inclination to make things easier for business.

***Haelan Laboratories, Inc. v. Topps Chewing Gum, Inc.*, 202 F.2d 866 (2d Cir. 1953)** Advertisements commonly use professional actors to sell various products, but real people often serve just as well, or better. But if an ad appropriates a person's image without his or her consent, isn't that a way of deceiving the consumer? And isn't the person portrayed also harmed? It has been a settled matter in case and statutory law for many years that an ordinary citizen's **right to privacy** prohibits advertisers from using his or her image without consent. The precedent was the 1905 Georgia Supreme Court case, *Pavesich v. New England Life Insurance Co.*, 50 S.E. 68 (Ga. 1905). A photo of Paolo Pavesich had appeared in an advertisement published in the *Atlanta Constitution*, falsely identifying him as a New England Mutual Life Insurance policy holder. Moreover, Pavesich had not agreed to the use of the photo. He was awarded $25,000 in damages for injured feelings (see also Chapter 4, The Employee—Privacy, Law).

Different standards of privacy and consent were applied to public figures for many years. These were established in *O'Brien v. Pabst Sales Co.*, 124 F.2d 167 (5th Cir. 1941). David O'Brien was an All-American football player for Texas Christian University in 1938, and perhaps the most widely publicized athlete of that year. In 1939 Pabst Brewing Company published a calendar that included a picture of O'Brien in his TCU uniform. O'Brien argued that he had not given his permission to use the photo and because he was personally opposed to alcohol consumption, the publication of his image in connection with beer sales was very embarrassing. The court was not sympathetic; O'Brien's status as a public figure who had regularly sought national exposure entailed that he had waived his right to privacy. Therefore, companies need not obtain the permission of public figures before using their images.

In response to this ruling, several states passed privacy laws that protected celebrities as well as ordinary citizens, but in most states images of famous people were fair game for advertisers. *Haelan Laboratories, Inc. v. Topps Chewing Gum, Inc.* changed all that. It presents the controlling case for the use of photographs or film of celebrities in advertising. A conflict arose in the early 1950s between two chewing gum companies, quarreling over the right to use a baseball player's photo. Haelan Labs was in the chewing gum business, and had secured a baseball player (not named in the opinion) to promote its product. The player had signed a contract giving the corporation the exclusive right to use his photograph in connection with selling gum. Topps, a competitor in the chewing gum market, convinced the player to sign a second contract with them, granting permission to use his photograph to sell Topps gum. Haelan sued Topps, charging that the rival company had invaded Haelan's exclusive right to use the photos of the player.

Topps claimed that Haelan's contract with the player simply released Haelan from liability for the use of his photographs, which, without the contract, would have violated his right to privacy as provided by a New York statute. This right to privacy, Topps argued, is personal and not assignable to a corporation or anybody; in that case, the player's contract with Haelan did not give the company any sort of exclusive property right or other legal interest in the use of his image. Judge Frank did not buy this argument. In ruling for Haelan, Frank asserted a **right to publicity**, which he defined as "the right to grant the exclusive privilege of publishing [a] picture." This right protects a public person's commercial interest in the use of his or her identity, and in effect entitles a celebrity to authorize a business to publish a picture of that identity to the exclusion of other corporations. This is precisely what the player had done with Haelan. After this case, advertisers have routinely secured celebrity permissions before utilizing their images in any way.

Onassis v. Christian Dior, New York, Inc., 472 N.Y.S.2d 254 (N.Y. App. Div. 1984)   This landmark case represents a further refinement of the **right to publicity** announced in *Haelan Laboratories v. Topps Chewing Gum, Inc.* (see above). It ordained that this right also requires consent when advertisers use people who merely *look like* public figures. A series of Dior ads featured a trio of individuals depicted in a variety of situations, one of which was a wedding. A number of well-known people appeared in the wedding ad along with one completely unknown person, a secretary named Barbara Reynolds. The trouble for Dior was that Ms. Reynolds bore a striking resemblance to Jackie Onassis, and Dior knew it—indeed that is why they hired her for the spot.

Although Dior claimed that the use of the look-alike was merely for humor, the court was not amused. There was no question that Dior intended viewers to believe, and it was quite likely that they would believe, that Onassis herself was appearing in the ad. The humor was intended to promote Dior products, and because Onassis had always deliberately avoided any connection with commercial products, the right to publicity asserted in *Haelan Laboratories* applied here as well. Her embarrassment and annoyance were recompensable injuries.

In a similar case just one year later, a video rental service called National Video attempted to avoid the legal problems of using look-alikes by publishing a disclaimer at the bottom of one of their ads. Printed in national magazines, the ads featured a person who looked at lot like Woody Allen. The small disclaimer read: "Celebrity double provided by Ron Smith's Celebrity Look-Alikes" (incidentally, National Video was the same company that provided Dior with Barbara Reynolds). Even this was not sufficient to avoid liability. Allen won his suit in *Allen v. National Video, Inc.*, 610 F. Supp 612 (1985). After this and the *Onassis* case, any advertiser wishing to employ celebrity look-alikes hastened to secure the permission of the real person, or supply a very prominent disclaimer.

Not only is it illegal to use real people who look like celebrities (without their consent or conspicuous disclaimers), it is also illegal to use devices that simulate the appearance of celebrities. In the late 1980s Samsung Electronics ran a television commercial set in the twenty-first century and featuring a robot outfitted to resemble the game show hostess Vanna White. Ms. White did not consent to the ad and was not paid, so she sued for misappropriation of her right to publicity. She won and was awarded $403,000 (*White v. Samsung Electronics America, Inc.*, 971 F.2d 1395 (9th Cir. 1992).

The right to publicity does not stop with one's appearance. It is also illegal to use impersonators who *sound* like celebrities. Frito-Lay hired a professional musician to promote a new variety of corn chips by singing a song inspired by a Tom Waits tune. That in itself was not a problem, but the person hired to do the commercial sang in a manner distinctly reminiscent of Waits's raspy, gravely voice. As Waits had, at that time, steadfastly refused to do any commercials, he, like White, claimed misappropriation of the right to publicity. Waits too won his suit, receiving $375,000 in compensatory damages and $2 million in punitive damages (*Waits v. Frito-Lay, Inc.*, 978 F.2d 1093 (9th Cir. 1992).

Product Safety and Liability

Whenever we use a product, there is some risk. If someone is harmed, responsibility is determined by the nature and quality of the product, the kinds of consumers for whom the product is intended, and the way the product was used.

Consider an ordinary, wooden-handled hammer, designed and sold to pound in average-sized nails. If, due to a defect, the handle is not secured to the steel head and the head flies off and severely injures someone, the manufacturer can be held liable for the harm. If the hammer is promoted as one that is easy for children to use, because of its size and weight, and it injures a child because it is actually not easy for a child to use, the company can be held liable even though there are no defects in the hammer itself. Finally, if the hammer flies out of a person's hand and injures someone because the handle is greasy, the producers of the hammer would not be held liable, because it was not used in normal conditions.

Theories of Responsibility for Harm

There are three ways to determine who is responsible when a product causes harm: the **due care theory**, the contract theory, and the social cost theory (Velasquez 1992).

The due care theory states that if the producer is negligent, that is, does not use due care to ensure that a product is safe, the producer can be held liable for damages caused by the product's defects. Due care is evaluated by the **reasonable man standard**: How would a reasonable person design, manufacture, and promote a product? The answer to this question depends, in part, on the state of technology. For example, a car produced now is much safer than one produced 20 years ago because of technological advances in seat belts and air bags; there is also a better understanding of how cars absorb the energy of impacts.

Due care also depends on the audience for whom the product is intended and how it is labeled. For example, a device for measuring blood pressure that is sold to the general public needs to be presented and labeled differently than those sold to hospitals. Finally, due care also requires that any known risks be clearly communicated to the consumer (Boatright, 1997).

The main problem with the due care theory is that it does not focus on the product, but on how the product was produced and labeled. As such, a consumer who is harmed by a product has to show that the manufacturer acted negligently. This can be very difficult to prove, even when the charge is correct (Boatright 1997).

The **contract theory** of producer liability holds that producers are liable only if they have a contract with the person who uses the product. This was the basis of product liability law in the United States until the beginning of the twentieth-century (McCall 1997). There are several problems with this theory. One problem with this theory is that consumers almost never agree to contracts when they buy products. One way to overcome this problem is to argue that there is an implied contract between seller and buyer because a reasonable person would expect or presuppose such an agreement. The mere fact of selling implies a guarantee that the product is safe for its intended use. The Uniform Commercial Code (see Law: Introduction, below), specifies what kinds of warranties can be implied.

The **social cost theory** holds companies responsible for harms that result from defective products even if the companies exercised due care and warned consumers of all reasonable risks. The social cost theory recommends that producers be held to the standard of **strict liability** (see below, Law: Modern Legal Remedies), which holds producers responsible for all defective products, regardless of the intentions of the producers or any actual or implied contracts. This is much easier to apply, and so less costly to apply, than the due care theory, where you have to prove negligence, or the contract theory where you have to establish the existence of an actual or implied contract. Social cost theory is based on the fact that harm is always costly. If individuals cannot cover the costs of their injuries and maladies from defective products, society pays the cost with taxes to provide medical treatment and other services. Social cost theory holds that the most efficient way to allocate these costs is to make the producers pay.

Producers can defend themselves against the due care and contract theories by arguing that their product was not properly used. For example, drunk drivers cannot successfully sue a car company for an accident that was caused by their drunken driving. Producers can defend themselves against the social cost theory by arguing that the product was substantially altered when it caused harm. For example, in the case of the injury caused by a hammer in which the handle was covered with grease, the company would not be held liable because the product was substantially altered at the time of the accident (see also Law: Defending Against Liability, below).

In what follows, we will examine ethical and economic aspects of product liability from the consumer's point of view. We will then see how these ethical and economic considerations are reinforced by law.

Ethics

Promoting Self-Interest: Egoism   Aggressively self-interested consumers evaluate products by their risk-reward ratio. As long as the reward is greater than the risk, these consumers will *consider* buying the product. However, aggressively self-interested consumers will want to buy the product that has the *best* risk-reward ratio. This means that they are willing to accept a lot of risk if the rewards are sufficiently great. For example, some consumers buy recreational products to get the thrill of excitement: The more dangerous the activity, the greater the thrill. Consider hang-gliders: Hang-gliding is very thrilling to some, but if the glider crashes, the rider can be killed or seriously injured. Suppose that the rider does crash, and is seriously hurt. If the consumer is aggressively self-interested, the crash may open new opportunities to sue the company and seek government benefits.

Aggressively self-interested consumers would be in favor of the social cost theory of product liability, since it is easier to sue on this theory than on the due care or contractual theory. (Aggressively self-interested business people take the opposite point of view.) They would also be in favor of a legal system in which lawyers work for contingent fees, that is, lawyers collect money only if they win their cases.

Lawyers in the United States often work for contingent fees. Many think that this system encourages frivolous suits, because plaintiffs do not have to put any money at risk. However, there are at least two factors that prevent frivolous suits. One is the force of Rule 11 (Fed.R.Civ.P.11). Rule 11 allows defendants to charge plaintiffs and their lawyers with bringing frivolous lawsuits; if the defendants prevail, this can result in significant fines. In addition, lawyers have an incentive to take only those plaintiffs who have a good chance of winning, because if the plaintiffs lose, the lawyer gets no money. Given that lawyers can easily spend hundreds of thousands of dollars in developing a case, even on simple suits, they are not likely to accept frivolous cases.

Aggressively self-interested consumers could disagree about whether the free-market approach or the imperfect market approach is better. The free market approach would tend to produce more products, giving these self-interested consumers more ways to pursue their interests. However, as we noted in our discussion of advertising and marketing, consumers do not have the time to evaluate products, and must rely on third parties. If government can monitor product safety less expensively than an individual consumer, an aggressively self-interested consumer would prefer government regulation. This does not mean that these consumers would approve of all product safety regulations, only those that kept products safe, while limiting, as little as possible, the supply and innovation of products.

Contemplatively self-interested consumers also pay attention to the risk-reward ratio of product safety, but instead of trying to get the greatest rewards, these consumers try to minimize risk. Instead of hang-gliding, these contemplative consumers might join a health club and work out. They would be careful to exercise within their limits, because the goal is to have a good time to become healthy, not to lift more or run faster than anyone else. If a product is unsafe and they are injured, they may sue or try to find other ways to promote their contemplative interests. However, the process of suing others is to willingly engage in conflict, so the stakes would have to be high for contemplatively self-interested consumers to pursue this course of action.

Contemplatively self-interested consumers would endorse social cost theory, because, if they need to sue a manufacturer to avoid a great loss, social cost theory will minimize the level of conflict. They would also endorse government regulation if it made their lives easier. They would be less worried than aggressively self-interested consumers about not getting as much product innovation, because their goal is to live simply and peacefully.

Nurturing Personal Relationships: Care   Passive caring consumers try to make sure that their friends and family use safe products. To do this, these consumers want information about the quality and safety of products. Because they are passive, these consumers might have trouble influencing the **cared-for** to choose safe products or to urge them to use products safely if these others did not want to do so. For this reason, passive caring consumers would be in favor of government regulation that promoted safety, because this unpleasant, but important task, is left to others. Like self-interested consumers, they would be in favor of social cost theory, but for the reason that it makes suing producers easier for their friends and family.

Active carers are willing to question the purchase of dangerous products by others. Active carers would do this carefully, trying not to impose their own idiosyncratic values on others. To make sure they are not improperly imposing their values, active carers would pay close attention to the history and personality of the cared-for. For instance, suppose a teenager wants to buy a motorcycle, and the parents object because it is too dangerous. Active caring parents would consider their relationship with the child. Will forbidding the purchase severely damage the parent-child relationship? Is the child going to get a job in order to make the monthly payments for the motorcycle, and will the job be good for the child because it promotes responsibility, or will working interfere with the child's education? What about alternatives, such as a car? Even a subcompact is safer than a motorcycle. If parents and child eventually agree on a motorcycle, the next task would be to find the safest one at a price that would be affordable, and to make sure that the child has the proper lessons. To do this, parents and child need good information to evaluate motorcycle safety.

Active carers would be in favor of government regulation if the regulations helped to ensure the safety of complex and potentially dangerous products like motorcycles. The more harm a product can cause, the more regulation would be justified. Active carers would also argue that consumers are responsible to choose and use products correctly, and to accept responsibility for their own mistakes.

The theory of product liability endorsed by active carers would be different, depending on how other aspects of society are handled. For example, due care would be fine as long as there were other ways to deal with unforeseen harms. Suppose a manufacturer acts with due care in the production of asbestos. Asbestos was once thought to be a wonderful product for insulation because it had a high R-value and did not burn. It was later discovered that asbestos filaments in the air, when inhaled, lodge in people's lungs, slowly reducing their ability to breath (Beauchamp 1998). This condition, asbestosis, affects tens of thousands of people. Having asbestosis makes most people unable to work, so they forfeit all wages from the time they become ill. These sick individuals need medical care that is very expensive. If the sick individuals are the major wage earners in a family, the family will suffer, perhaps go on welfare or food stamp programs.

According to the due care theory, this company would not be responsible for the illness, deaths, and other costs that result from asbestos. If the society had a good social welfare system that could support these ill individuals and cover medical costs, active caring consumers could endorse the due care theory. However, given the conditions in the United States today, where the social welfare system has never been very good and what there has been is being dismantled, active carers would probably endorse the social cost theory and its requirement of strict liability.

Promoting the Good of the Group: Utilitarianism Utilitarian consumers are primarily concerned with how product safety affects the entire group. They would want government rules to promote product safety only if the group was better off with these rules than without them. These consumers would be willing to live with the death and injury of innocent victims as long as the cost of preventing these deaths was greater than the cost of allowing them. (Compare this analysis with the other three ethical views.) Consider the Tylenol case. Eight people died from taking Tylenol, a pain-reliever manufactured by Johnson & Johnson, that had been poisoned by persons unknown. As a consequence of those eight deaths, the packaging of all over-the-counter medicine and food has changed radically. Although there is no estimate about the cost of these changes, it surely has run into the billions of dollars by now.

A utilitarian would have a hard time justifying this great cost to prevent such a small number of deaths, unless the new packaging had other benefits. Some of these benefits include improved consumer confidence in the products they buy. If even a few people continued to die from tainted over-the-counter medicine, sales would go down drastically, affecting jobs and tax revenues. When we add in these other benefits, a utilitarian consumer could endorse government regulations requiring secure packaging. If government rules are justified, they can be flexible or strict.

Strict rule utilitarian consumers would endorse the social cost theory and its insistence on strict liability (Velasquez 1992). Think again about the asbestos case, discussed above. In order to understand utilitarian reasoning, we must recognize that *someone* will have to pay for these losses. The sick individual can almost never pay. That leaves the company and the society at large to take on the costs. According to strict utilitarian theory, the most socially efficient way to pay for these costs is to make the business that produced the product responsible, in other words, to impose **strict liability**. There are two related reasons why this would be efficient. First, when companies know they are strictly liable, they will be more careful than if the liability rules rest on due care or contract theory. Second, holding businesses responsible in this way allows them to build these harms into the cost of the product, which then gets spread out over all the consumers who buy the product.

Flexible rule utilitarian consumers would argue that the strict liability makes business *too* careful. Because business would be afraid of being sued and having virtually no defense, they would not produce goods that would harm people, like medicine, automobiles, and even toasters. Flexible rule utilitarian consumers would argue that the due care and contract theories of product liability are better, because they allow companies more defenses. With more defenses, companies would be more willing to produce products.

Respecting Dignity and Rights: Intrinsic Value Intrinsic value consumers believe that people have a special dignity based on the fact that we are (1) free, choosing beings and/or (2) bearers of fundamental rights. In either case, it is wrong for producers to offer products that are not safe.

Consumers who adopt the first kind of intrinsic value would argue that consumers have a responsibility to choose and use products safely, since they have a duty to treat themselves with dignity. By making a choice, consumers assume reasonable and foreseeable risks in using the product. Because the consumer makes a choice, other ethical rules come into play, such as, "We are responsible for our own actions" and "Do not blame others for the undesirable consequences of your own actions." For example, it is not the manufacturer's fault if a carpenter who buys a hammer hits and breaks his thumb while pounding in a nail, because hitting one's thumb is a reasonable and foreseeable risk of using a hammer.

However, the manufacturer would be responsible if the head of the hammer flies off and puts out the carpenter's eye, assuming the hammer is relatively new and has not been damaged. The manufacturer has the duty to make sure that its products are safe. Selling unsafe products, knowingly or through negligence, violates consumers' right to choose because the product is misrepresented. When consumers buy misrepresented products they do not get what they choose.

Consumers acting from intrinsic value would be in favor of government regulation as long as it did not take away our responsibility for our freely chosen actions. Within these limits, regulation of potentially dangerous products can be justified when consumer evaluation is too difficult or time consuming. Grocery shoppers do not have the time or the expertise to test all the food they buy for harmful bacteria. Requiring secure packaging of over-the-counter medicine is also justified because we do not have the time or skills to evaluate each pill or capsule. However, in cases in which consumers are at fault, the law should be careful not to let them blame the manufacturer. Bearing the responsibility of one's choice is inseparable from the choice itself.

The focus on responsibility would make human dignity consumers favor the due care and the contract theories, since both tie responsibility to choice. It would be difficult for them to endorse social cost theory and its advocacy of strict liability, since the very notion of strict liability are liable regardless of their intentions. There is one set of circumstances, however, in which these consumers would endorse the social cost/strict liability theory. One component of this set of circumstances would be a substantial and clear warning to companies that, in the future, they will be held strictly liable for the harm caused by products. The beginning of enforcement could be several years down the road, allowing companies to choose to produce new products, if they want to. Under these circumstances, owners and managers would retain the right to choose in the face of strict liability, since they would have knowledge of the risks.

Consumers who take a property rights view would agree that manufacturers are responsible for defects resulting from design and manufacturing. If consumers are harmed by products, they can turn to the courts, which will determine responsibility. Consumers with this point of view would be opposed to social cost/strict liability theory, because companies would be punished—by losing their property in fines and awards to plaintiffs—without having done anything wrong.

If we focus on the property rights of consumers, however, we can endorse strict liability. Consumers paid good money for a product they believed was safe, and not only was the product not safe, but it injured them in ways that required them to spend money (a kind of property) to repair damage to themselves and to their property. So, when products injure people, and no one did anything wrong, the property rights view must choose between respecting the property rights of the company or the harmed consumer.

George Brenkert (1997) argues that consumers who ground ethics in property rights should hold the company responsible through the policy of strict liability. Companies profit not only because they sell products, but because they operate in an entire *social-economic system*. Because companies profit from this system, they should also pay their part for maintaining the system. Part of this cost is paying for the harms their products cause, even when no one is at fault.

Economics

Efficient markets require clear and enforced property rights, clear relationships between risks and rewards, good information, and competition at the producer and consumer levels. Product safety concerns the distribution of risks and rewards between society, consumers, and producers.

Society Society wants and needs businesses to produce certain products, including goods that are also potentially dangerous: automobiles, airplanes, trains, firearms, electrical appliances, and so on. If used correctly, these products help promote a productive and happy society because we use them to pursue our personal, familial, and career interests and goals. The more business supplies these products and services in an efficient way, the more people will be satisfied with their lives, all other things being equal.

This qualifying phrase, "all other things being equal," means that, given two lives, equal in all respects except that one person is always getting products that don't work and the other one gets products that typically do work, the second person will be happier than the first. Specifically, the notion that better products and services will make us happier with our lives does not mean products and services will make us happy. It is certainly true that money can't buy love. However, if you have a love and are happy, having products that work is better than having products that don't work.

Under the typical economic assumption that we act from self-interest, we can expect that consumers will try to make producers bear all the risks, while producers would want consumers to bear all the risk. Society, in the form of government action, seeks to mediate this conflict.

Consumers Consumers are not likely to buy potentially dangerous products if producers are not responsible for harms due to faulty design or manufacture. The more a producer assumes liability for the harms of a product (at a given price), the more likely consumers will buy the product. Consumer advocates, like Ralph Nader, claim that consumers have a right to safe products. In purchasing a car, for example, a consumer has a right to expect that the car is as safe as technology and costs allow. This does not mean that consumers have a right to the safest car possible. A rational consumer should expect, for example, that a $35,000 Volvo will be safer than a $15,000 Ford Contour. Still, the consumer has a right to expect that each of the cars will be as safe as their prices and current technology allow them to be.

The Ford Pinto, for example, a car first built and marketed in the 1970s, had a design flaw that made it more likely to explode in rear end collisions than similar cars on the market. A protective plate, costing between $5 and $25 per vehicle, could have prevented these explosions. Yet Ford resisted putting in this plate because it was too expensive. This was not an issue of making the Pinto the safest car on the road, but of making it safer for minimal cost. The Pinto sold well because the producers had more information than the consumers. Once these problems became public, through civil and criminal suits, Ford stopped producing the Pinto.

Producers Producers are not likely to produce potentially dangerous products if they bear all the liability for the harm caused by their products. The less responsibility they have for the harm their products cause, the more likely they are to produce those products.

There is a conflict between the desire of producers to minimize their responsibility for the harm their products cause and the desire of consumers to have producers assume all responsibility for those harms. Ideally, society attempts to resolve this conflict through law in a way that keeps production and consumption at levels that promote the good of all and that respects the rights of individual consumers. Although it is probably not possible to reach this ideal, it serves as a standard by which we can evaluate how law divides risk between producers and consumers.

International Issues

The Nestle's infant formula case described above in the section on Advertising is also a case of product safety. In that case, Nestle's was selling a product that is safe and can even be beneficial for consumers who have enough money to pay for it and who have access to clean water. Because many families in third-world countries did not have these advantages, the infant formula became an unsafe product for that demographic group. At least three reasons prevented the governments of those countries from forbidding Nestle to offer its products. First, third-world governments do not have the money, time, or legal infrastructure to monitor the millions of products that they import. Second, international business provides money and jobs that many third-world countries do not want to lose. Third, international businesses can use their power to influence the government to leave them alone.

A new development is the growing regionalization and internationalization of product safety standards (Galluccio 1996). International trade has grown phenomenally since the end of World War II. A large part of this growth is the result of the *General Agreement on Tariffs and Trade* (GATT), which has more than 100 countries as members. Founded in 1948, the major goal of GATT was to reduce barriers to trade (Dienhart 1999). Initially these barriers were in the form of tariffs, which are essentially taxes charged a company on imported goods. By the 1980s tariffs came down or were eliminated in many areas. When this happened, GATT turned to nontariff barriers, such as product safety standards. If a country had peculiar or very strict safety standards that make it difficult for imports to pass, then this is an effective trade barrier.

To address this problem, countries are beginning to join together to standardize product safety standards. For example, the **European Union** has set standards for product safety that apply to all member countries. Canada has agreed to accept safety certification from independent organizations in the United States and the United States has reciprocated. The Pacific Rim trade bloc, ASEAN, is also moving to standardize product safety standards (Wagner 1996). Market forces, including distributors and trade associations, are driving the acceptance of international standards together with regulators and regional trade groups such as the EU, the Asia Pacific Economic Co-Operation forum (APEC), and NAFTA.

Law

Many of the manufactured goods we buy are simple and harmless. Coffee mugs, dish towels, and bookends, to name a few, are easily mass-produced items that don't go wrong and hurt people. On the other hand, numerous products are very complicated and can be extremely dangerous. Automobiles, firearms, and table saws, to name a few of these, when defective or misused, are sources of misery and tragedy. And it is also true that seemingly innocuous items—a salad from the local fast-food joint—can lead to severe illness and even death. When consumer products cause harm, the incident very often winds up being discussed in great detail in the courts of our country. Legal responsibility for the harm must be fixed, and compensation, even punishment, for the wrongdoing must be determined. Our topic now is how the law attributes this responsibility when people are injured by consumer products, and how this liability might be evaded.

Privity and Liability   The notion that manufacturers might be legally responsible for the harm caused by their products was virtually unheard-of until this century. Those very few cases prior to this time in which injured consumers received some compensation were all based on a written contract that was in some way violated when the damages occurred. The necessity of a contract in order to recover for harm caused is known in law as the **requirement of privity**. It is a harsh doctrine that not only left most consumers without any available legal remedy, it also prevented the family or friends of the injured party, or innocent bystanders, from recovering anything. Contributing significantly to the anticonsumer, industry-centered atmosphere of the nineteenth and early twentieth centuries was a predominating attitude of *caveat emptor*, or *buyer beware*. Manufactured goods were relatively simple in those days, and customers were routinely invited to try something out before buying it. Given the opportunity for a trial run and the straightforward nature of the item, it was thought appropriate to hold that, once the purchase was made, the consumer was stuck with the product and any resulting injury.

The requirement of privity and the strength of *caveat emptor* were both severely weakened by the landmark case of *MacPherson v. Buick Motor Co.*, 217 N.Y. 382 (N.Y. App. Div. 1916). The case concerned a defect in a wooden wheel supplied by a manufacturer to Buick for their automobiles. Donald MacPherson had been seriously injured when the wheel collapsed and he was thrown from the vehicle. Because the defect should have been noticed during the assembly of the car, the court ruled that Buick was negligent, and therefore owed MacPherson damages, even though there was no contract to that effect. The ruling principle here was that simply by the act of placing a product on the market, a manufacturer assumes a duty of "care and vigilance" to the consumer, and to all others who might be injured due to a defect.

Another major blow to privity came in *Baxter v. Ford Motor Company*, 35 P.2d 1090 (Wash. 1934). Baxter lost an eye when a rock struck the windshield of the car he was driving and the glass shattered. The Washington Supreme Court ruled that Baxter was owed compensation because Ford had advertised that the windshields of their cars were shatterproof: "so made that [they] will not fly or shatter under the hardest impact." Wording like this creates a **warranty** (see below), despite the absence of a contractual relation. This case also illustrates how a product liability claim can arise from false or deceptive advertising; the plaintiff in such a suit must prove that an advertisement misled him or her into believing the product was safe, and the purchase was made on that basis. Some of these sorts of advertising-driven liability cases are discussed above in the section Advertising, Law. The requirement of privity was finally defeated in 1960 with the historic *Henningsen v. Bloomfield Motors* case (see below).

Modern Legal Remedies Today, explicit contract or not, injured consumers may avail themselves of legal remedies provided in three different areas:

1. **Common law of torts** A "tort" is an action that injures someone in some way, but it is not criminal behavior and does not involve breach of contract. For example, consider a person driving down a road who fails to allow enough room for a bicycle rider, and so hits and injures him. The driver has clearly done something wrong, but, legally speaking, she has not deliberately *assaulted* the bicyclist, which would be criminal behavior, nor has she violated the terms of any contract with him. Tort laws are thus created by judges when they render opinions for injury cases such as this. Torts are classified according to how fault or *liability* for the injury is assessed. When a consumer product harms someone, a tort may be committed, and fault is assigned as either due to **negligence** or as a matter of **strict liability**.

    (a) **negligence** A negligent activity is one that creates an unreasonable risk of harm with a resulting injury; this high risk of injury may be caused by negligence in the design, manufacture, or inspection of the product, or by a failure to warn of the danger.

    (b) **strict liability** This is the attribution of legal responsibility for injury regardless of the intentions or reasonableness of the liable party. Generally, any damages resulting from a product with a defect (strict liability does not apply to services) that presents an unreasonable danger to a consumer are those for which strict liability may apply, whether or not the defect was known about or should have been known about. This means that any and all parties in the chain or distribution—manufacturers, distributors, retailers—can be found liable for damages caused by a defect even though all possible care was exercised in the preparation and sale of the product (see below, *Greenman v. Yuba Power Products, Inc.*, for the landmark case).

2. **Uniform Commercial Code (UCC)**   The UCC is a set of rules authored by legal scholars of the American Law Institute and the National Conference of Commissioners on Uniform State Laws (for more on the UCC, see Finance, Law: Credit, below). These rules apply to almost every sort of transaction necessary for exchanging complex consumer goods: buying and selling merchandise. Before the UCC was written, commercial law varied widely from state to state, and this proved to be quite an obstacle to business as the American economy blossomed nationwide during this century. Hundreds of lawyers, law professors, and judges began drafting the UCC in 1942 and the first edition was published 10 years later; there have been numerous revisions and amendments since then, the latest in 1990. It has been adopted in its entirety by 49 states (Louisiana has adopted only a part of it), the District of Columbia, and the U.S. territories. It is the only national law not enacted by Congress.

Article 2 of the UCC provides for three sorts of warranties, assuring consumers that a product will perform in a certain way:

(a) **express warranty**   An affirmation of fact, explicitly stated verbally or in writing, or created by a description or a sample of the product, that the item meets certain standards of quality, performance, or condition. The terms "warranty" or "guarantee" need not be used to create an express warranty, nor are sellers required to offer such warranties.

(b) **implied warranty of merchantability**   A promise arising out of the mere fact that a sale has been made. Simply by selling a labeled and packaged product to someone, a merchant promises that the item is fit to be used for the purposes for which it was produced.

(c) **implied warranty of fitness for a particular purpose** This warranty arises when a seller knows the specific purpose for which a product has been purchased, makes a statement that the product will serve this purpose, and the buyer depends on the seller to select the necessary item for that purpose. The UCC incorporates within this type of warranty an implied warranty of "fitness for human consumption" that applies to food. Restaurants, including fast-food outlets, grocery stores, and vending machine operators, are all subject to this warranty.

3. **Federal and state statutes**   Various federal and state statutes contain provisions making the sellers of defective products, and those who deceive consumers, liable for resulting injuries. These statutes often overlap or duplicate UCC rules and the principles of tort law.

Defending Against Liability   Consumers' claims of liability may be defeated by sellers in several different ways:

1. **Consumer misuse**   Manufacturers and sellers can demonstrate that the consumer's conduct with regard to the product was in some way inappropriate. The personal injury resulted from the consumer's own negligence, hypersensitivity, or misuse; in other words, the consumer brought the harm on himself or herself. Some courts have rejected defenses that appeal to the consumer's own conduct on the grounds that the misuse was *invited* or *foreseeable* by the manufacturer. For example, in *LeBouef v. Goodyear Tire and Rubber Co.*, 623 F.2d 985 (5th Cir. 1980), an injury occurred as a result of tread separation in the right rear tire of a Mercury Cougar. Even though the owner's manual warned that the Goodyear tires were not safe for prolonged driving over 90 miles per hour, and the tread had separated at a speed of over 100 miles per hour, the court still found Ford liable for damages. Because Ford had marketed the Cougar as a high-performance vehicle for younger people, it was to be expected that occasionally speeds exceeding the safe operating level of the tires would be achieved; the misuse was foreseeable. Ford should have done a better job of warning Cougar owners of the problem or used better tires.

2. **Consumer acknowledgment of danger**   Sellers cannot be found strictly liable for failing to warn of widely recognized dangers, such as the fact that guns shoot bullets or that power saws cut materials. Nor will liability be imposed if it can be proved that the consumer knew and appreciated the risks associated with the product, and voluntarily accepted those risks.

3. **Intervening event**   A seller can only be held strictly liable for damages caused by a product if the item reaches the consumer without substantial change in its condition. If the merchandise is materially altered or modified in a way that causes an injury—say, a safety guard is removed by a distributor—the original seller is not at fault for the harm.

4. **State-of-the-art defense**   In this defense, the claim is that the designing and marketing of a product employed the most advanced knowledge and technology available, and any injuries

were unavoidable or unforeseeable given the most current information and procedures. This appeal seems to work best when the extent of the injury is not especially wide. The more pervasive the harm to the public generally, the less effective the defense. For example, in *Bashada v. Johns-Manville Products Corp.*, 90 N.J. 191 (1982), the New Jersey Supreme Court rejected the contention of Johns-Manville that it had exercised due care with regard to asbestos as defined by the scientific knowledge and technology at the time. The company should have advanced the current state-of-the-art for due care or not used the product.

Selected Cases, Statutes, and Regulations

The Food and Drug Administration   Perhaps the most important consumer items produced by businesses are food and drugs. Not only is food essential for human survival and well-being, and for many people this goes for a variety of drugs too; these substances can have disastrous effects on health when contaminated or in some way corrupted. The first recorded law in the United States prohibiting the adulteration of food was a Massachusetts statute of 1785. Over the next century, a number of other states passed food and drug laws. However, many states had no such laws and enforcement was often lax in those that did. The need for federal regulation became obvious. Finally, in 1906 Congress passed the Federal Food and Drug Law (34 Stat. 768), or the Wiley Act, as it was more commonly known.

Harvey Wiley had been appointed chief of the Bureau of Chemistry in 1883 and had immediately become a tireless campaigner for federal food and drug laws. Due to his role in this process, and the scientific nature of food and drug investigation, the administration of the new law was assigned to the Bureau of Chemistry. In 1927 enforcement of the federal laws was handed over to the newly formed Food, Drug, and Insecticide Administration, which was subsequently renamed the Food and Drug Administration (FDA) in 1931. Like the Bureau of Chemistry, the FDA was originally a division of the Department of Agriculture, but it was transferred in 1940 to the Federal Security Agency, which was in turn renamed, in 1953, the Department of Health, Education, and Welfare (HEW). In 1979, HEW was split into several new administrative agencies, and the FDA was placed in the Department of Health and Human Services.

The Wiley Act defined "adulterated" and "misbranded" foods and drugs, and prohibited their shipment across state lines. However, its inherent weaknesses were soon exposed. For one thing, the promoter of a totally ineffective patent medicine could escape liability simply by showing that he personally believed that the false therapeutic claims were true. Also, food adulteration persisted because the Wiley Act did not provide judges with the authority to enforce the standards promulgated by the FDA. In response to these unsatisfactory circumstances, and influenced by the reformist climate of the new Roosevelt administration, Congress went to work and drafted a new law, one that (with amendments) regulates the production and distribution of food and drugs to this day: The Food, Drug, and Cosmetic Act.

Food, Drug, and Cosmetic Act of 1938, 21 U.S.C. §§301 *et seq.* This law (FDCA; and various amendments) is the cornerstone of the regulatory authority of the Food and Drug Administration (FDA; see above). Over the years it has become quite complicated, but its basic rule prohibits the distribution or importation of adulterated or misbranded products. These two terms are defined in great detail in the FDCA, and they have been further refined in subsequent amendments. The main ideas are these: "adulterated" refers to products that are defective, unsafe, dirty, or produced in unsanitary conditions; "misbranded" includes statements, designs, or pictures that are false or misleading, and the failure to provide required information in labeling. The Federal Trade Commission is charged with ensuring that *advertising* for consumer products is accurate and truthful (see Advertising, Selected Cases: Federal Trade Commission Act, in this chapter).

Although the FDCA, as administered by the FDA, prohibits the selling of adulterated or misbranded food, the Department of Agriculture is responsible for inspecting all meat and poultry that is intended for human consumption. This is a holdover from the days when the FDA was housed in the Department of Agriculture (see the Food and Drug Administration, above). Adulterated and misbranded cosmetics are illegal, and FDA regulations require cosmetics to be labeled, their ingredients identified, and warnings displayed if the product is in any way dangerous to human health. "Cosmetics" is defined as substances and preparations for cleansing (except for soap), altering personal appearance, or promoting attractiveness. Producers wishing to apply color additives to food, as well as to cosmetics or drugs, must secure FDA approval before they can be used (Color Additives Amendment of 1960, 21 U.S.C. §376 [a]).

Owners or operators of drug manufacturing plants must be registered with the FDA, and manufacturers must submit a vast amount of scientific data proving safety and effectiveness before the agency will approve any drug for marketing. The process can take many years, and the FDA can withdraw approval of any previously licensed drug. These and other regulations were written in the Drug Amendments of 1962 (21 U.S.C. §321). The FDA publishes its "New Drug Regulations" annually (along with other standards) in Title 21, *Code of Federal Regulations.* One of its best-known, drug regulations followed the deaths of seven people in 1982 after they ingested cyanide-laced Tylenol; the now familiar tamper-resistant packaging required for many over-the-counter drugs dates from this tragic incident.

The Medical Device Amendments of 1976 (321 U.S.C. §§360 *et seq.*) for the first time established a comprehensive framework for regulating equipment used in medicine. The main idea here is just that, like drugs, manufacturers of medical devices need to show that their products are safe and effective before they can go on the market. Further amendments in 1990 required those who use medical devices to report to the FDA whenever deaths or serious injuries were related to medical devices. This applies to hospitals, nursing homes, ambulance services, and medical clinics, among others. In such cases, the FDA has the authority to order manufacturers to halt the distribution of the defective equipment, and health care professionals to stop using it; the equipment might also be recalled.

Companies that package food in airtight containers, mainly cans and glass, must also satisfy registration requirements. Food processors are required to file processing information, such as cooking times and temperatures, for each type of food packed in this way. Various amendments have strengthened the food regulations initially presented in the FDCA, and have taken the form of further congressional actions. For example, the Infant Formula Act of 1980 (21 U.S.C. §350a) established, among other things, nutrient standards for all infant formulas. This act was itself amended in 1986, requiring the FDA to determine standards for quality control testing, record keeping, and recall procedures for infant formulas.

Most recently, the Nutrition Labeling Health and Education Act of 1990 (NLHEA; 21 U.S.C. §343) requires that the labels of all processed foods (about 20,000 different varieties) contain a "Nutrition Facts" panel indicating the calories, fat, saturated fat, cholesterol, sodium, carbohydrates, sugars, fiber, and protein in the product for a specified serving size. The NLHEA builds on the Fair Packaging and Labeling Act of 1966 (15 U.S.C. §§1451–1461), which requires that food products list the ingredients in order of quantity. All consumer goods must bear a label identifying the product, the name and location of the manufacturer, packer, or distributor, and the net quantity in the package. Meat, poultry, restaurant food, and prepared food sold in grocery stores or delicatessens are exempted from this law.

Magnusson-Moss Warranty Act of 1975, 15 U.S.C. §§2301 *et seq.* Just one year before this federal act was passed, a congressional subcommittee reviewed 200 warranties and determined that only one of them was without ambiguities, exemptions, and disclaimers. Clearly, the protections afforded by the Uniform Commercial Code warranties (see Law: Modern Legal Remedies, above) were not enough. This legislation was intended to compel sellers to supply their customers with the information needed to pursue a claim that the warranty has been breached. It does not require merchants to offer a warranty, nor does it affect implied warranties of merchantability and fitness (see also Law: Modern Legal Remedies, above). However, when a written warranty is made, and the cost of the item exceeds $15, the "warrantor" (person making the warranty) must disclose, among other things: the names and addresses of the warrantor(s), the product or parts covered, a statement of what the warrantor will do if the warranty is violated, and the length of time the warranty is effective. This act also formally establishes a consumer's right to sue for damages as well as for attorneys' fees and court costs.

Henningsen v. Bloomfield Motors, Inc., **161 A.2d 69 (N.J. 1960)** Claus Henningsen bought a new 1955 Plymouth Plaza "6" Club Sedan for his wife Helen to use. Just ten days after picking up the car at a Chrysler dealer in Bloomfield, New Jersey, Helen was driving home from a trip to Asbury Park. She suddenly heard a loud noise under the hood and felt something crack.

The steering wheel spun in her hands, turning the car sharply to the right, and the car crashed into a brick wall. Helen was injured and the Henningsen's insurance company determined that the car was a total loss. It had 468 miles on the odometer.

Claus had agreed to a sales contract with the dealer stipulating only that defective parts would be replaced within 90 days of the purchase or 4,000 miles, whichever came first. Liability for injuries caused by a defective part was excluded from this contract. The question faced by the court was whether or not this contractual exclusion prevented recovery for Helen's injuries.

Judge John Francis decided that it would be patently unjust to disallow recovery simply because the contract did not specify liability for personal injury. He based this conclusion on two main considerations. First, the relative bargaining positions of consumers and manufacturers are vastly different, especially when it comes to buying cars. At this time, nearly every American car was sold using a standardized contract issued by the Automobile Manufacturers Association. Dealers were not allowed to alter the terms, so there was no competition whatever concerning warranties. Buyers had no choice but to purchase cars on the manufacturer's terms—or do without a car. However, that is not a realistic alternative in a society where an automobile is a necessity. Second, car buyers are not in a position to examine the product and determine whether or not it works properly. They must rely almost entirely on the expertise of the manufacturer and the dealer. This trust places a heavy burden on companies to provide what consumers expect: safe products. Compensating consumers for injuries caused by a manufacturer's products is thus a cost of doing business, contract or not.

Greenman v. Yuba Power Products, Inc., 377 P.2d 897 (Cal. 1963) Probably the most important **strict liability** case for product safety, this one concerns a machine called the "Shopsmith," manufactured by Yuba Power Products. A power tool combining a drill, saw, and lathe, the Shopsmith was a Christmas 1955 gift to Mr. Greenman from his wife. Two years later, while Greenman was using the machine as a lathe, a piece of wood suddenly flew out and struck him in the head, causing severe injuries.

Testimony at the trial revealed that the set screws used to hold sections of the machine together were not adequate. Vibration of the machine while in use caused the screws to loosen, allowing the part holding the wood in place to move away, thereby ejecting the wood from the lathe at a high velocity. Judge Traynor of the California Supreme Court ruled that Yuba Power Products was **strictly liable** for Greenman's injuries. Although the company had been negligent in the construction of the tool, and in effect an express warranty was created by claims made in the product brochure, these factors were irrelevant to the decision. In other words, even if there had not been any negligence whatever, and even if there had been no warranty of any kind, the company would still be liable. The mere fact that a product has been placed on the market entitles the consumer to assume it is safe for the purposes for which it was built. The Shopsmith was not safe; it was used in the intended way, causing injury due to defect. Manufacturers are strictly liable for such injuries.

Traynor's seminal formulation of strict liability as a controlling legal principle in defective products cases was not one he had invented for *Greenman*. He had first expressed the doctrine, famously, in *Escola v. Coca-Cola Bottling Company*,150 P.2d 436 (Cal. 1944), though here it was not the basis of the decision. In this case, a restaurant waitress had been severely cut when a Coke bottle exploded in her hand. The California Supreme Court ruled that the company was liable due to negligence, but Judge Traynor's concurring opinion stated that Coke would have been at fault even if no negligence had been found at all: that is strict liability.

Consumer Product Safety Act of 1972, 15 U.S.C. §2051　This act of Congress created an independent regulatory body, the Consumer Product Safety Commission (CPSC), that has the power to issue standards, require warnings, and ban dangerous merchandise entirely. Every consumer product is subject to regulation by the commission, with the exception of cars, food, liquor, and firearms. Tobacco too is not regulated by the CPSC, but this is not to say that the safety of tobacco is regulated by some other government agency. The unfettered nature of an industry that manufactures and distributes a dangerous product has long been very troubling for those concerned with product safety. However, recent developments such as the Supreme Court decision in *Cipollone v. Liggett Group* (see below) and suits aimed at tobacco companies by state attorneys general have changed matters dramatically.

The mission of the CPSC has three facets. First, the commission is to gather data concerning injuries caused by consumer products. This information is compiled primarily through a network of hospital emergency rooms that report to CPSC headquarters in Washington, D.C., every day. CPSC also conducts their own investigations of accidents involving consumer goods. Second, the commission actively studies consumer products for safety-related problems. If, as a result of their investigations, the CPSC finds that some product does present a hazard of illness or injury, the agency may develop safety standards that must be satisfied by the manufacturer. These studies are announced in the *Federal Register* and consumers or consumer organizations themselves are given the opportunity to participate in developing safety standards. This is the commission's third responsibility: to promulgate federal regulations consistent with its interpretation of the act.

Occasionally, CPSC finds that some product presents too great a risk to consumer safety to be allowed on the market and that no standard will provide protection. The product may then be banned entirely. In the past, CPSC has outlawed the sale and manufacture of such products as lawn darts, furniture with lead paint, all-terrain vehicles, and merchandise containing asbestos.

***Dow Chemical Company v. Alfaro*, 786 S.W.2d 674 (Tex. 1990)**　This is a crucial case in which it was established by the Texas Supreme Court that U.S. companies can be liable for harm caused by their products in foreign countries. In the process, the *forum non conveniens* **doctrine** as a defense to liability for such harm was resoundingly defeated. Generally, an appeal to *forum non conveniens* is aimed at rejecting the jurisdiction of a particular court (the *forum*) on the grounds that litigating the case there would involve difficulties (*non conveniens* or "inconveniences") that do not obtain in some other court. If the appeal is successful, the case is dismissed in one jurisdiction and moved to another.

The factors that determine a legitimate instance of such inconvenience were originally set out by the Supreme Court in *Gulf Oil Corporation v. Gilbert*, 330 U.S. 501 (U.S. 1947). These factors are, first, the cost to and ease with which the litigants can access documents and witnesses, and, second, various public interests such as the burden on the courts, and appropriate deference to foreign courts. Although the *Gilbert* case involved questions of jurisdiction between American states, *forum non conveniens* was subsequently employed many times by multinational corporations wishing to elude a variety of troublesome legal issues arising overseas. However, cases dismissed from American jurisdictions on this basis rarely ever went to trial in foreign courts. The decision here in *Alfaro* put multinationals on notice that the appeal to *forum non conveniens* is unlikely to work for product safety issues. As of this writing, there has been no definitive ruling on the issue from the federal court system.

Domingo Castro Alfaro, and a number of other people, worked on a banana plantation in Costa Rica. The farm was owned by the Dole Fresh Fruit Company. During the late 1970s Alfaro and his coworkers were often required to handle a pesticide manufactured by Shell Oil and Dow Chemical. The Environmental Protection Agency (EPA) had already banned the use of dibromochloropropane (DBCP) in the United States—a fact known to the Costa Rican government, but the agency's authority does not extend beyond this nation's borders. Alfaro and the others suffered serious mental and physical injuries, including impotence, as a result of exposure to DBCP. They filed suit in a Texas district court, but the case was dismissed when Dow and Shell pleaded *forum non conveniens*. An appellate court reversed this ruling and the state supreme court upheld the reversal.

Judge Doggett's concurring opinion noted that none of the factors described in the *Gilbert* case obtained here. On the contrary, he argued that allowing *forum non conveniens* violated a number of public policy concerns, rather than advanced them. After instancing some of the atrocities perpetrated by American multinationals in foreign countries, Doggett urged the complete abolition of *forum non conveniens*. This is the best way to provide a check on the conduct of multinational corporations, whose reliance on an obsolete and parochial doctrine has provided them with a way to evade legal responsibility for their own misdeeds.

Forum non conveniens has not been abolished, and its application varies. Indeed, some courts have widened the scope of the cases in which it is applicable. For example, a recent decision by the Florida Supreme Court (*Kinney System, Inc. v. Continental Insurance Co.*, 21 F.L.W. S43 [1996]) overturned a previous ruling that allowed using the doctrine only when all the litigants were not residents of Florida. This means that American jurisdictions may be rejected even when some of those involved are U.S. citizens. Although the

Alfaro case effectively spelled the demise of *forum non conveniens* in product liability, it remains viable in other areas effecting business.

Cipollone v. Liggett Group, Inc., 505 U.S. 504 (U.S 1992) Rose Cipollone was 17 years old when she began smoking cigarettes in 1942. For the next 40 years, she smoked one or two packages every day. She started with Chesterfields and then switched to L&M in 1955, both manufactured by Liggett. In 1968, she switched to Virginia Slims, and later to Parliament, both brands manufactured by Philip Morris, Inc. In 1974, she started smoking a low-tar brand called True, made by Lorillard, Inc. Mrs. Cipollone was diagnosed with lung cancer in 1981, but continued to smoke regularly until she had a lung removed one year later. She still smoked occasionally, and secretly, until she was finally declared terminally ill in 1983. She died in 1984.

Just over one year before she died, Mrs. Cipollone and her husband had filed suit against these various manufacturers, charging that she had been personally injured by their product. She stated in her deposition that over the years, a variety of cigarette advertisements had led her to believe that smoking was safe, glamorous, and a practice of beautiful people and liberated women she wished to emulate. The Cipollones asserted liability on the part of the tobacco companies grounded in, among other reasons, a failure to warn of the dangers of smoking, breach of an express warranty that smoking did not present any significant health hazard, fraudulent misrepresentation of medical and scientific data indicating these health hazards, and conspiracy among the companies to conceal or misrepresent these data.

The tobacco companies argued that warnings on the cigarette packages, as required by the Cigarette Labeling and Advertising Act of 1969 (see this chapter, Advertising, Law: Federal Trade Commission Act) preempted the Cipollones' lawsuit for the period in which the warnings were required. A federal district court agreed with this defense, and the Third Circuit Court of Appeals affirmed. The Supreme Court reversed part of this decision and affirmed part of it.

Justice John Paul Stevens's majority opinion upheld the lower courts' finding concerning the failure to warn. The Labeling Act did defeat the claim of liability because the point of the labeling was to provide some measure of warning. The precise wording of the act precluded an argument that there should have been additional or clearer warnings. However, Stevens observed that the language of the act should be read "narrowly," attending closely to the exact meaning of the sentences.

Under this narrow interpretation, the labeling acts did not bar lawsuits against cigarette companies based on breach of express warranty, misrepresentation, or conspiracy. Rather, the act barred only those lawsuits concerning warnings. Despite that favorable judgment, the Cipollone family withdrew the lawsuit in late 1992.

Although this decision did not directly benefit the Cipollone family, it did open a floodgate of lawsuits from private citizens, and from numerous state attorneys general, who hoped to recoup many millions of dollars in state money used to fund public health care for tobacco-related illnesses.

Finance

Money is not important in itself; it is only a means to secure or promote other goods we want. We use money to buy a house, car, pay for higher education, save for vacation, raise a family, and the many other things that become part of our lives. Most of us, however, do not have cash on hand to pay for these things. Instead, we use **financial instruments**: loans, credit, savings and checking accounts, stocks and bonds, and mortgages. Because financial instruments are so important to our well-being, access to them is a central ethical issue.

As we discussed in the Chapter 1, Introduction—Roots of Business Ethics, financial institutions like banks and insurance companies developed to meet the changing needs of business as it has developed in the past 1000 years. By 1400, the nation-state was well on its way to replacing the feudal social system. Part of the reason the nation-state emerged was the demand from business people for stable monetary systems and systems of credit. England, for example, made such rapid economic progress from 1700 to 1900 because the national government established a monetary system and a court system that business people could trust.

The financial system we have in the United States, which establishes our currency, guarantees our banking deposits, regulates the stock market, and many other things, is simply a more complicated version of the financial systems that started long ago. Despite this complexity, trust and honesty are still the central and necessary virtues of economic systems. If we could not be reasonably certain that (most) people will repay loans, we would not lend money. If banks cannot be reasonably sure that (most) people will pay the minimum required on their credit card balances, there would be no credit cards. In what follows, we will see how ethical and economic principles shape the relationships between consumers and lenders, and how law codifies and reinforces those relationships.

The taking of excessive risks by, and unjustified trust of, financial institutions was at the heart of the economic crash of 1929, which brought the Great Depression to the United States. As banks sought higher profits, they engaged in risky investments, many of which involved stocks and bonds. When the stock market crashed, people went to the banks to get their money. Much of the money individuals deposited in banks was in the stock market or loaned out to individuals and businesses who could not repay. The banks did not have the money to give their depositors. Millions of people lost their life savings; their plans for themselves and their families disappeared overnight.

In the presidential race of 1932, Franklin Delano Roosevelt promised to end the depression by reforming the nation's financial sector. He was elected by a substantial majority. His victory was paired with a large Democratic majority in the House and Senate. The 1932 election was the beginning of a new approach to government and its relation to business. One of the first things Roosevelt did was to restrict banks from engaging in risky investments and loans. While the U.S. banking industry is presently being deregulated by the federal government, our banks are still among the most regulated, and the safest, in the world.

In our discussion of consumer finance, we will focus on loans and the stock market. Recent figures show that individuals are investing in the stock market more than ever. For the first time in 50 years, stock investments make up the major portion of household wealth, accounting for 28 percent. In 1987, stock investments made up only 13 percent of total household wealth. When financial wealth is separated out from household wealth, stock ownership forms 48 percent of that; in 1990, stock represented less than 24 percent of financial assets (Wyatt 1998). We will use the following scenario to explain ethical and economic aspects of consumers buying stock.

Many people buy stock on "margin," which means that they pay only 10 percent of the stock price and borrow the rest, usually from a stockbroker. In a volatile market that is generally going up, an investor might buy quite a bit of stock in this way. For example, suppose John calls Jordan, his stockbroker. John asks Jordan to buy 1000 shares of Kripke, Inc., at $10 a share. Jordan knows that John doesn't have $10,000 cash on hand, and wonders if this is a prudent purchase. John pays only a 10-percent margin, so he only has to give Jordan $1,000 for $10,000 of stock. The $9,000 loan, say, is due in 30 days. There is interest of $100 and a commission of $75. If Kripke stock goes up 10 percent, John can tell Jordan to sell his stock for $11,000, pay off the loan, its interest, and the new commission to Jordan for another $75, and walk away with around $750. Not bad for making a couple of phone calls. The more the stock goes up, the more money John makes.

The price of stock can also go down. If it does, John still owes $9,000. Let's suppose that the stock goes down to $50, and John must now repay the loan. He sells his shares for $5,000, and now he must come up with $4,000 plus the interest and commission to Jordan, or $4,250. His original investment of $1,000 lost half its value, so all told, John lost $4,750. Not so good for making a couple of phone calls.

This case raises several question about ordinary consumers who buy stocks; we will discuss three of them. First, where did John get the information about Kripke, Inc., that made him think that its stock was going to go up in value? Did he get it from the newspaper, did Jordan recommend it, did he hear something from a friend who works at Kripke, Inc.? Second, what kind of business is Kripke, Inc. Do they make bicycles, software, weapons, or what? Third, what is the responsibility of Jordan to advise clients like John who take on a lot of risk. Should Jordan just do what John says, and nothing more?

Ethics

Promoting Self-Interest: Egoism   Aggressively self-interested consumers will borrow money to invest in the stock market in order to increase their wealth. They are willing to accept a lot of risk if the rewards are big enough. How can consumers calculate risk?

When it comes to the stock market, most of the information that a typical investor has comes from the companies themselves. Because selling stock is a way for companies to generate capital, it would seem that these companies would have an incentive to make themselves look good to investors (see *Escott v. BarChris Construction Company*, below). This was a contributing factor in the stock market crash of 1929. Many companies were claiming to be financially healthy when they were not. Given this experience and others like it, aggressively self-interested consumers would not trust the information companies give.

Given the need for reliable information, aggressively self-interested financial consumers would want enough government regulation to ensure the availability of good information. This became clear in 1929 and laws requiring accurate financial reporting by companies such as the Securities Act of 1933 were soon passed (see Selected Cases, below).

Contemplative self-interested consumers will borrow money to invest in the stock market in order to secure a peaceful, conflict-free life. They would not buy stock on margin, as John did, above, unless they could afford to lose the $10,000 without disrupting their lives. These investors would prefer to borrow money on items like houses, that are more likely to keep or increase in value. In the event that they lose their jobs, or some other financial catastrophe occurs, they can sell the houses and be debt free. Contemplative self-interested consumers would tend to be in favor of government regulation of financial markets, especially if they believe that aggressively self-interested companies and consumers could damage the system.

These contemplative consumers would also be in favor of government regulation because of **asymmetric information**: Lenders know so much more than consumers about loans and how to package them. The cost of a home loan, for example, is a combination of interest rates, points, appraisal fees, mandatory insurance, property taxes, and other items. If there were no law that mandated that loan costs be standardized, like the Truth in Lending Act (the Consumer Protection Act of 1969, see Selected Cases, below), lenders would package their loans in many different ways to make them look less expensive than they really are. If loan costs are described differently at different financial institutions, consumers will have a difficult, if not impossible, time deciding which is the best deal. Of course, government regulation is only as good as the government that makes and enforces it. These contemplative consumers would have to trust government more than the market to be in favor of government regulation.

Nurturing Personal Relationships: Care   According to the care ethic, our primary responsibility is to promote nurturing, caring relationships with family and friends. Carers would borrow money to invest in stocks if it promoted the well-being of their personal relationships.

Passive carers measure the health of their relationships by how well they serve the need of friends and family (those **cared-for**). These carers would invest and save in ways that those who are cared-for would want them to act. This strategy can work if friends and family have good judgment and are trustworthy; if they are not, this strategy could lead to a great deal of trouble. A passive carer could go deeply in debt to please or serve others, only to have the cared-for not help repay the money.

Passive carers could be in favor of government regulation of lending if it would protect them from taking unwise loans. In an intriguing approach, Robert Fredrick and W. Michael Hoffman (1990) argue that the ordinary investor is playing a game that they do not, and probably cannot, understand. However, it is a game that can ruin their lives and the lives of loved ones. Because of these high stakes, the authors suggest that there be some regulation governing who can buy stocks. For example, investors could be given tests to make sure that they understand how markets work and the risk they are taking. Fredrick and Hoffman compare this to driving tests, to make sure that drivers know the rules of the road. On the other hand, passive carers might be opposed to government regulation if it restricts their ability to help friends and family. They would at least want enough government oversight to keep the financial system stable, so they could make use of it when needed.

Active carers would promote the well-being of relationships by trying to get as much information about those things intimate others want. Borrowing and investment itself takes time and demands repayment, which can affect caring relationships. Whether active carers should spend this time and commit themselves to future payments depends on what the cared-for are going to do with the loan.

For example, suppose the loan is acquired in order to buy a large-screen television with a premium sound system. Because watching television focuses family members on the TV and not on each other, an active carer would tend to reject borrowing money for this purpose. There are circumstances, however, where a carer would encourage such a loan. For example, suppose the family as a whole made videos of family activities as well as video art projects. In this case, the large-screen TV could bring family together. Saying that active carers will examine their own and others, reasons for borrowing does not mean that they will impose their personal values on friends and family. Instead, a discussion about the propriety of borrowing can be a way for the relationship to become richer and deeper.

Promoting the Good of the Group: Utilitarianism   From a utilitarian point of view, financial instruments should be designed to promote group well-being by creating and managing the capital that creates jobs, national economic growth, and a sound tax base.

Financial instruments are sold and delivered in many different ways by thousands of people across the nation. The government has many rules and regulations that standardize financial transactions to create a level playing field and ensure honesty. This is necessary if people are going to make efficient use of these financial instruments. Should these rules be strict or flexible?

Strict rule utilitarians would argue that because of the **asymmetric information** that obtains between sellers and consumers of financial instruments, we need strict rules to ensure that consumers are not defrauded. Consider the problem of **insider trading**. Insider trading occurs when someone inside the company supplies private information to people outside the company, giving these outsiders special advantages (for the legal issues, see below, Selected Cases: Securities Exchange Act of 1934). For example, suppose that Kripke,

Inc., was just about to sign a contract that would increase its revenues by 200 percent. When the deal becomes public, Kripke's stock will greatly increase in value. A senior manager of Kripke tells John about the deal. John calls Jordan with the order to buy 1,000 shares of Kripke.

There are several problems with insider trading of this kind. First, there are likely to be many people who own Kripke stock who are selling it just as John is buying. They are at a substantial disadvantage to John. If John is caught, and goes to jail, the news of this will discourage other investors, who will be afraid of losing money because they do not have inside information. Not only will consumers distrust the stock market, they may come to distrust many other kinds of business relationships that involve experts—like accountants and lawyers— who are supposed to act on behalf of their clients. This is consistent with Jennifer Mills Moore's argument that insider trading violates the **fiduciary relationship** that is at the heart of a free-market system, in which experts are paid to provide services for others (Moore 1990). General distrust of fiduciary relationships will reduce investment, making less capital available to business. This will harm all of us as tax revenues go down, jobs are lost, and quality products are harder to find. Because of these problems, there should be strict rules forbidding all insider trading.

Flexible rule utilitarians would argue that the strict utilitarian view is unrealistic. First, *making* a strict rule and *enforcing* it strictly are two different things. When strict rules are applied to many different situations, they end up harming people in situations in which the rule does not work. To illustrate, suppose a married couple in a restaurant overheard John and the manager from Kripke talking about the impending rise in Kripke's stock. They use this information to make hundreds of thousands of dollars, which they use to send their children to college and set up a retirement fund. Although the couple made money from insider information, it would be ridiculous to prosecute them, because using inside information in this way does not harm the market or promote people's distrust of the market. Most would view the couple as lucky, not dishonest. Further, their luck did not merely include hearing the information, but the fact that the information was accurate! They took a risk, a big one to get such a large return.

Take another example: Suppose we make it a rule that stockbrokers must tell clients all relevant information when they make stock purchases. We will need to decide what is relevant information. Suppose we make a strict rule that stock brokers must send a prospectus (see Selected Cases: Securities Act of 1933, below) of the company in question, and offer explanations of the prospectus as needed. To make sure that explanations have been offered, we need another strict rule requiring brokers to record all of their meeting and telephone conversations with clients.

Flexible rule utilitarians would argue that forcing stockbrokers to record all of their meeting and telephone conversations is ridiculous. First, they waste the time of experienced investors who know what they want to do. Second, brokers will have to spend much more time with each client, thus reducing the number of clients they can serve. This will drive the cost of commissions higher, because brokers will not want to take a pay cut. The list of objections goes on. A better rule is one that required brokers to exercise **due care** when dealing with clients, making sure that they know the risks of investment. This rule means that brokers need to spend more time working with inexperienced investors and less time with experienced investors.

Flexible rule utilitarians can admit that more individuals will lose their money because of bad information under flexible rules than under strict rules, but that these individual losses will be more than overcome by the increase in jobs, tax revenue, and quality products that will result from the money that goes into the stock market.

Respecting Dignity and Rights: Intrinsic Value   One way to respect human dignity is to respect people as free to make their own decisions and to live by the consequences of those decisions. Let's go back to John buying the stock of Kripke, Inc., and look into what it is that Kripke does. Let's suppose it is the mid-1980s, a time when South Africa is still an oppressive, immoral regime. Kripke makes computer software that helps the South African regime keep track of blacks as they move from their "homelands" to work in white-only areas.

Consumers who respect human dignity may very well avoid buying stock in Kripke because, as William Irvine (1987) argues, it helps people do evil, immoral things to other people. On a more personal level, it would be like giving a sadist money to buy instruments of torture. These consumers might also want the economic system to forbid sale of Kripke stock because the company promotes such horrible activities.

The idea that we should have a rule or law not to let immoral companies sell stock would be very hard to formulate, and if formulated, very hard to enforce. Yet, preventing immoral companies from selling stock is something we already do, at least indirectly. Widely endorsed laws that prevent selling drugs and child pornography, for example, prevent the incorporation of companies for those immoral purposes. Because there are no formal companies of these kinds, they cannot sell stock.

Consumers who respect the dignity of others may, under certain conditions, buy stock in companies engaged in what they regard as immoral activities, if they think they can be a voice of change. As owners, they have a right to speak at company shareholder meetings, and air their concerns in other ways. For example, Christian fundamentalists could buy stock in the Disney Corporation, hoping to stop the broadcast of *Ellen*, a television show on ABC, which is owned by Disney. *Ellen* presents lesbianism as an acceptable life style, a view that many conservative Christians reject (Rich 1997).

Consumers who take a property rights view might take a completely different approach, by insisting that consumers have the right to invest in any company they want, as long as the company does not commit illegal acts. Insofar as the past South African regime was not illegal, they should be able to invest in any company that does business with it. These consumers would have violently disagreed with the Comprehensive Anti-Apartheid Act of 1986, which was passed by Congress despite a presidential veto by Ronald Reagan.

This act banned new investments and loans, ended direct United States–South African air travel, and restricted the import of many South African goods (Encyclopaedia Brittanica 1997).

Rights consumers can act in many of the same ways as those who rely on dignity if a company engages in conduct they believe is immoral. They could sell the stock, because they do want their property to be used in those ways. Or, they could buy stock, hoping to use their property rights to change company policy.

Economics

Society We have looked at four different ethical points of view. No matter which one(s) is the best, they are all represented in our society. In a free, democratic society, each person is free to build his or her own ethical personality. Our ethical personality consists of how we interpret and rank the four ethical points of view: self-interest, care, group well-being, and intrinsic value. The social task, then, is to create a society that allows each person to pursue these values to the greatest extent compatible with others having the same opportunities. When we apply this to the stock market, we need to look at the social functions fulfilled by companies that sell stock, the brokers who mediate its sale, and the individual buyers of stock.

From the social point of view, stock markets serve two related functions. First, they supply the money (capital) for companies to produce products, grow and distribute food, build houses and apartment buildings, and all the other things we need to live our lives. This productive activity provides jobs and tax revenues that builds roads, schools, and other parts of the social and physical infrastructure (Samuelson and Nordhaus 1985; Gwartney and Stroup 1982).

Second, stock markets provide an important investment opportunity for consumers who have money they do not need for day-to-day living. The long-range rates of returns for the stock market are much greater than savings accounts, government bonds, or commercial debt. For those planning for retirement or any other project requiring long-term investments, the stock market is a likely choice.

Stock markets, then, form an intersection between companies and individual investors. Society needs to shape that intersection in a way that is good for investors and companies. If the rules give companies too much power, investors will pull out, and the market will crash. If the rules give investors too much power, then companies will not offer stock, and stock markets will diminish or disappear. We will now look more closely at the economic needs of consumers and producers.

Consumers Consumers need an economic base to create and direct their lives. As we saw, stock ownership is the major way that people use to promote their economic security. But as we also saw in Chapter 1, Introduction—The Tools of Business Ethics, consumers want economic security for several reasons, most of which have nothing to do with money (Rivoli 1995). Most people want to live peacefully with their friends, family, and fellow citizens; to participate in the religion of their choice; and to pursue opportunities for self-development and enjoyment, such as education and travel. Many also want other things they think will make them happy, such as cars, fancy houses, large-screen TVs, and other luxury items.

The stock market is the way that many people think they will acquire the funds to reach these goals. That they invest as heavily as they do in the stock market indicates that they have a high level of trust in the stock market. One reason they trust the market is their belief that the law will protect them from fraudulent corporations and stockbrokers. These laws came into effect to fix the problems that led to the 1929 stock market crash; the reader should notice that none of the federal cases or statues mentioned in Law, below, are dated earlier than 1933.

Despite these laws, there is no way to prevent some market crashes. Most economists believe that there are natural **business cycles**, and the government can, at best, soften the downturns. This means that the high returns of the stock market come with higher risk. For example, suppose you invest in the market when it is high, but when you need the money, the market is low. Although markets can bounce back quickly, that does not matter if you have to take your money out now. Also, the market can stay low for long periods of time. The market did not recover from the 1929 crash until the early 1950s. The decade of the 1970s also saw stagnant stock markets.

If the stock market fails, individuals will have to use savings and other assets, like homes, cars, and even pension funds, in case of emergency. However, we cannot count on savings, because U.S. citizens save so little. We also cannot count on pension funds, because they are heavily invested in the stock market. This leaves homes and cars to cover our emergency needs. If the stock market crashes and stays low for a year or more, there will be a national emergency. People will reduce the amount of consumer goods they buy, which will put people out of work, and reduce the tax base we will need to help them. Those who lose their jobs will soon lose their homes, unless the government intervenes with a law that forbids **foreclosures** of primary residences (see below, Law: Credit).

The consequences to consumers of a national financial collapse are horrible, to say the least. This means consumers have a deep and broad interest in a stable system, which, given the experiences of 1929, can only be ameliorated by sound government regulation.

Producers   Financial institutions fill two important social roles that can, at times, conflict:

1. The business role. Financial institutions are designed to make money for their owners (stockholders). This means that they seek out all possible legal ways to make money.
2. The social role. Financial institutions are the backbone of our economic system. They serve as the intermediary between companies and individual investors. Without a stable financial system, business activity would be severely reduced, harming all members of

society. According to the first role, financial organizations want to increase their profits as much as possible. They make profits from the commissions they charge individual investors. If the commissions are too high, investors will be driven away, and that will mean less money for the company. If they are too low, then not enough people will participate in the securities industry where stocks, bonds, and other financial instruments are bought and sold (for more details, see Law: Credit, below).

The market is the perfect answer to the problem of setting commissions. Let commissions rise until individual investors start investing less money to avoid the high commissions. When this happens, commissions will stabilize, or perhaps go down a little. An equilibrium will be reached between the commission investors are willing to pay and commissions stockbrokers are willing to work for. Unfortunately, this equilibrium will be achieved only if all the players have good information. Because brokers have more information than individual investors, the government passes laws to give brokers incentives to inform individual investors of risks.

Because government regulations are costly to business and taxpayers, it would be much cheaper for all concerned if business could regulate itself. There are several reasons why this is not likely to happen. Perhaps the most compelling reason is that companies would try to **free ride** on the good behavior of others (Gwartney and Stroup 1982). Free riding occurs when an individual or company gets the benefits of something without paying the cost.

To see how free riding works, consider the following thought experiment: Suppose that financial houses, in an effort to avoid government regulation, get together and adopt a set of consumer protection rules. As this becomes known, consumers should increase their trust, and therefore their investments. Suppose further that one firm decides to violate the rules only when they can make a lot of money and only when the chances of getting caught are slim. They will make more money than competing firms, which have no way to verify that all companies follow the rules.

All companies know the problem of free riding, and know that some will cheat in just the way we described. Inevitably, the companies will be found out, and the public will lose trust in the financial sector, lowering investments and profits. Government will step in and take over, and it will be some time before consumer confidence is restored. The cost of going through a failed attempt at self-regulation, plus the cost of the government regulation that follows is higher than the cost of initially accepting government regulation. So, it does not make economic sense for business to try to regulate itself.

International Issues

As we have just noted, American financial institutions are more regulated than banks in other countries. This allows foreign banks to take on riskier ventures, and so to make more money. United States banks argue that they have trouble competing in the world market. They have a point. But, as we saw with the Great Depression, there is a trade-off between risk and gain. If foreign banks begin to fail, American banks may feel awfully lucky to have been forced to invest and loan safely. This does not mean that U.S. banks are immune from problems. Current regulation may become ineffective with new technology and social changes. Further, U.S. banks are tightly connected with foreign banks and projects. Should these foreign banks fail, the ripple effect could easily be felt in this country.

Perhaps one of the most important differences between domestic and international finance is that there is no world government to control international financial issues as there is for domestic finance. Despite this, there are ways that international financial issues can be influenced. The **World Bank** and the **International Monetary Fund** (IMF) were set up for this very purpose.

The IMF was created after World War II to help relieve imbalances in international trade. These imbalances result from one of two factors: either a country exports (sells) more than it imports (buys), running a trade surplus; or a country imports (buys) more than it exports (sells), running a trade deficit. The IMF acts as a reserve bank that uses funds from surplus countries to loan money to deficit countries to cover their financial debts to richer countries. With the power of lending comes the power of influence. IMF loans are often made on condition that the borrowing country change its financial system so that it is more likely to increase exports and pay back the debt. The World Bank was created at the same time to make loans to countries for development projects, such as dams, roads, and airports, that were too risky for private lenders.

The Collapse of Thailand's Currency In 1996, the World Bank reported that Thailand's economy was the fastest growing economy in the world (Butler 1997). This news made the already substantial foreign investments in Thailand grow to new heights. However, in the summer of 1997, the Thai *baht*, the major unit of Thai currency, dropped 20 percent. This drop led major investors to pull out of Thailand as fast as they could.

What happened in Thailand? The story is very similar to what happened in the U.S. during the savings and loan crisis. In the 1980s, Congress reduced the regulation governing savings and loans. This allowed savings and loans to make very risky investments and also made it easier for corporations to defraud their own organizations for personal gain. As a result, many savings and loans failed. Since savings and loans are so important to the financial well-being of the country, and because the money lost was insured by the federal government, taxpayers paid the bill to clean up the mess.

The financial institutions in Thailand were never regulated very well, but when the country was poor, this was not a great problem. In the mid-1980s, Thailand's economy grew very fast. The officer's of Thailand's financial institutions acted like those who controlled U.S. savings and loans. For example, Thai financial institutions made risky loans to fund commercial real estate ventures like luxury hotels and apartment buildings. In the summer of 1997, 300,000 apartments were empty, as were many rooms in the new hotels. This made it difficult for developers to pay back their loans, causing banks to become insolvent.

There was another economic factor compounding the problem. In 1984, Thailand tied the value of the *baht* to the U.S. dollar. By tying their currency to the dollar, the Thai government promised that the *baht* will always be worth the same amount of U.S. dollars. They did this to reassure investors the the *baht* was secure. During much of the 1980s the dollar was relatively cheap, keeping exports from Thailand cheap. However, as the dollar strengthened in the 1990s, the *baht* also became more expensive. As the *baht* increased in value, Thailand's exports became more expensive, resulting in fewer exports. Fewer exports, in turn, decreased funds coming into Thailand. Bad financial real estate loans and lower exports caused the Thai economic system to collapse, forcing the devaluation of the *baht*.

The Thai government issued many statements blaming Thailand's problems on greedy financiers who prey on developing countries. The financiers and developed countries responded by saying that the same financial system that brought down Thailand is the very system that helped Thailand become so wealthy. They further argued that Thailand's weak internal financial controls were the heart of the problem.

In the fall of 1997 the IMF stepped in to help Thailand with a $17.2 billion loan, which at that time was the second biggest loan in IMF history. Most believe that the Thai economy is still fundamentally sound, and expect it to revive. Yet the cost of this help is high. In exchange for the loan, the Thai government has agreed to create a new agency, the Asset Management Company, to oversee financial institutions, a new deposit insurance agency, and they have allocated to themselves broad powers that allow the government to replace officers of troubled financial institutions.

Law

The essential role that consumers play in commerce depends entirely on their ability to produce money in exchange for goods and services, or to infuse with capital enterprises that supply goods and services. When cash is on hand for a simple exchange—you give a ten-dollar bill and receive a tank of gasoline—the trading is straightforward. But when the cash is promised to be delivered in the future, or when money is used to make money, things become much more complicated. Consequently, a vast array of legal rules have developed intended to order and regulate these financial matters. In this section, we first introduce the main ideas that inform the laws governing consumer credit and investments; we then examine some of the most important examples of those laws.

Credit   Few of us could acquire very many of the consumer goods that we believe make our lives worthwhile without credit. Sellers hand over things like homes, cars, computers, refrigerators, clothes, and food even though we return little or no cash at all in the immediate exchange. What we do give them is some form of a promise that the balance of the cost of the item will be paid at some future time. This agreement turns sellers into our creditors. In the meantime, we get the goods—and a debt. In a very literal sense, our country is a nation of debtors. Consumer debt now stands at over $1 trillion.

Most of the legal rules governing the use of credit are found in the Uniform Commercial Code. The UCC was written by legal scholars of the American Law Institute and the National Conference of Commissioners on Uniform State Laws, and applies to almost every sort of transaction that involves buying and selling merchandise. Before the UCC was developed, commercial law varied widely from state to state. This was a serious impediment to business as the American economy blossomed nationwide during this century. Hundreds of lawyers, law professors, and judges began drafting the UCC in 1942 and the first edition was published ten years later. There have been numerous revisions and amendments since then, the latest in 1990. The UCC has been adopted in its entirety by 49 states (Louisiana has adopted only a part of it), the District of Columbia, and the U.S. territories. It is, in effect, the only national law not enacted by Congress.

There are two general types of credit: *unsecured* and *secured*. Unsecured credit is so called because it is given without any *security* (collateral) that would promote payment of the debt. Here, the lender or creditor relies entirely on a written or verbal promise to repay the *principal* (the amount owed), typically with some interest. The most common example of unsecured credit is a credit card issued by a bank. Unsecured credit is considered a greater risk for a lender, so the interest rate is higher; if the debtor *defaults* (fails to repay the debt), the creditor has lost on the deal. Unsecured credit makes a lender feel insecure.

The security that is lacking in unsecured credit is something that will make the creditor feel secure in making the loan. It is something that will alleviate his or her worries about repayment because the lender will get something as compensation in the event of default. This is the point of offering security or collateral for credit. Here's a simple case: say Jordan asks John to loan him $100. Jordan promises to repay. John is wary of his ability to repay, not necessarily because John thinks he's not as good as his word, though John might think this, but because, well, things happen, and sometimes people just can't come up with the money they owe. So John agrees to the loan if Jordan provides him with security—that is, in order to get the money from John, Jordan needs to come up with something that will make John feel secure, confident that he will not come out a loser. Jordan offers his CD player. John is satisfied: if Jordan doesn't repay him, at least he gets the CD player.

The *security interest* that John, as Jordan's creditor, has in the CD player is a security interest in personal property. This sort of security obtains when Jordan uses such goods or equipment, as well as any stocks or bonds or intangible property like any patents he might have, as collateral for credit. However, what if Jordan uses his CD player as security for a $100 loan from John *and* for another $100 loan from somebody else? If Jordan can't pay either John or the other person, who gets the CD player? What John wants to do is *perfect* his security interest by filing a financial statement; this device gives him an exclusive right to the collateral against any other creditors Jordan might have.

A security interest may also be held in **real property**. This is an interest in land ("real estate"), but also includes any buildings on a tract of land as well as the trees, crops or plants generally, soil, and minerals found there. Such a security interest is called a **mortgage**, and it is most often held by a bank that has lent money to a person so that he or she can purchase a piece of real property. Homes are typically bought by using the property itself as collateral (security) for the large amount of money needed to make the purchase. The holder of a mortgage is entitled to sell the property if the money is not repaid by the borrower who used the land to secure the loan. This is known as a **foreclosure sale**.

It costs money to borrow money. Creditors in the banking business often speak of "selling loans." The price of a loan—the cost of credit—is its interest rate, which is a (possibly variable) percentage of the loan amount or a monthly balance on the loan, calculated over a specified amount of time. Creditors are not free to charge whatever interest rate they wish. **Usury laws** set the upper limits on interest rates; these vary from state to state and are not included in the UCC. Usury laws were enacted principally to protect unsophisticated or desperate borrowers from falling prey to "loan sharks" or other unscrupulous individuals who would otherwise charge exorbitant rates of interest.

When a debt is past due, a creditor may bring legal action against the debtor. If a court passes judgment against the debtor, there are several methods by which the creditor is entitled to recover. *Attachment* is basically a seizing of the debtor's property by the creditor. *Execution* occurs when a sheriff is ordered by the court to seize the debtor's property, which is then sold at auction; the proceeds go to the creditor, although the debtor is entitled to any amount exceeding that which is owed. Most states exempt a certain amount of the value of the debtor's real property, and some personal property from attachment or execution. A **homestead exemption** allows a debtor to retain some portion of the value of his or her residence, while furniture, clothing, pets, vehicles, and tools of one's trade usually cannot be seized.

The third alternative for creditors is **garnishment**. This is a right to a debtor's property that is in the possession of some third party. The property most often subject to garnishment is the debtor's wages, held by his or her employer. Funds belonging to the debtor in the possession of banks may also be garnished. Title III of the Consumer Credit Protection Act protects debtors from overzealous garnishment by creditors: Debtors have a right to retain either 75 percent of their weekly earnings (after taxes, of course) or 30 hours of work paid at the current minimum wage, whichever sum is greater.

Unless there is a state law expressly forbidding the seizure, the UCC allows creditors to employ self-help in order to take possession of ("attach") the goods pledged as collateral. Many creditors hire repossession companies to seize cars, equipment, and other sorts of secured property, but the repossession cannot be done by using force, threats of force, fraud, or violence.

Investments   When a person puts money into a business, or into real estate, he or she does so intending eventually to receive in return more money than was originally put in. The point of investing money is to make a profit. Money can be invested in a number of different ways. One of the most popular methods is to buy some amount of **stock** in a company. Someone who buys stock is buying a slice of a corporation; this is the usual way that companies raise money to finance their operations. Stocks thus represent ownership rights in a company: a stockholder is a part-owner, entitled to some portion or *share* of the company's profits. Stocks are classified as *preferred* or *common*. Holders of preferred stocks have priority over common stockholders, so they receive their interest payments or dividends (a portion of the profits) first. Whatever is left over, if any, is then distributed to common stockholders.

Bonds, debentures, and *notes* are also standard devices for investing money. Unlike stocks, these financial instruments do not give investors any ownership rights. Instead, they establish a creditor-debtor relationship in which the corporation has borrowed money from the investor. The corporation agrees to pay interest on the amount borrowed and promises to repay the principal at some time in the future: This is the *date of maturity.* The interest on the "loan" is the profit the investor intends to realize.

A bond typically matures after 30 years or more, and represents a corporate debt that is secured by some form of collateral (usually real estate or personal property). In the event the bond matures and the corporation is unable to pay the principal, a bondholder may foreclose on the collateral (take possession of it or sell it). A debenture is essentially an unsecured bond that is based on the corporation's general credit standing. If the corporation encounters financial problems, the debenture holder becomes just another creditor who must wait until the claims of secured creditors are satisfied. Notes may be either secured or unsecured, and they mature in five years or less.

Other methods of investing include investment contracts, certificates of interest, and profit-sharing agreements. With these devices—as with stocks, bonds, debentures, and notes—an individual invests money in some common enterprise with the expectation that profits will result from the efforts of other parties. Collectively, all these financial instruments are known as **securities**. Consumer investing is centrally concerned with the buying and selling of securities.

A security has no value in itself: Like a dollar bill, it is a virtually worthless piece of paper. The value of a security resides in the entitlement it gives its holder to the profitability of the corporation (or some other entity) issuing the security. As profits rise, or their rising becomes increasingly likely, a security also rises in value. When profits fall, or the prospects of profit look dim, the value of a security diminishes. Thus, a security is a kind of fluid currency that is not consumed or used by purchasers, nor is it, strictly speaking, produced by a corporation or other issuer. It can simply be created in unlimited quantities and at very little cost.

The buying and selling of securities is heavily regulated by both the federal government and the various state governments. We will see how this is done shortly, but first it is important to understand *why* securities need to be regulated. Imagine that a corporation has an excellent opportunity to expand into a burgeoning market, but needs capital to do so. The company basically has two means of generating the necessary capital: Borrow money, or sell portions of the company (or both). Money can be borrowed from a bank through a commercial loan, or it can be borrowed from the public by issuing bonds to people like you and us. The company can also sell common or preferred stock to new owners, who are, again, people like you and us. In either case, the source of the funds—the bank or members of the general public like us—wants to have accurate information about the past and present earnings of the company, and its future earning potential with the intended expansion. A bank will not lend money to finance a marginal firm with a project that is unlikely to succeed, and we will not invest in one either.

Now a bank, as a professional financial institution, has a staff of experts whose job it is to evaluate corporations in terms of these factors. We do not have a staff of experts at our disposal. Where do we get our information? The most obvious source is the company itself, but of course the company has a profound interest in obtaining our money. The temptation here to sacrifice objectivity and accuracy is just too strong to allow a corporation to police itself. Hence, external regulation aimed at the public interest appears to be in order.

Similarly, suppose now that Jordan is on the board of directors of a large corporation, and the board has just decided to substantially increase its dividends to stockholders. Such an increase will likely produce a higher demand for the stock, which will raise its price. Knowing this, and before the announcement of the raise in the dividend, Jordan buys 1000 shares of stock in his own company from John, who is selling them at the current market price, say, $10 a share. The next day, the dividend is announced, there is a run on the stock, and its value jumps to $12 a share. Jordan now has $12,000 of stock for which he only paid $10,000. John has been cheated here, and Jordan has exploited his position "inside" the company to do so. Again, government regulation is needed to deter this kind of internal fraud.

With the rise of big business after the Civil War (for details, see Chapter 3: The Corporation—Antitrust Issues, Law), the volume of trading in securities soared. These transactions were wholly unregulated, and the sort of deception and fraud exemplified above was common. Misconduct of this nature in large part precipitated the great stock market collapse in 1929, after which Congress recognized that it was time to do something: Pass laws designed to control securities exchanges.

Selected Cases, Statutes, and Regulations

Consumer Credit Protection Act of 1969 15 U.S.C. §§1601 *et seq*. This federal law is essentially a consumer protection act, aimed at shielding debtors from the various abusive, deceptive, and unfair practices creditors had employed in the past. It is more commonly known as the Truth-in-Lending Act (TILA). The Federal Reserve Board has the authority to promulgate regulations while interpreting and enforcing the act. TILA requires that certain information be disclosed by creditors for consumer transactions of less than $25,000 and for real estate loans of any amount. Among the items of which debtors must be informed are: the cash price of the product or service; the down payment; the finance charge with annual percentage rate; the number, amounts, and due dates of payments; and penalties for late payments.

TILA was amended in 1988 with the Fair Credit and Charge Card Disclosure Act (15 U.S.C. §1643), requiring disclosure of terms for credit cards, including the annual percentage rate, any membership fee, any minimum finance charge, and any transaction charge. Credit card holders are liable to pay for purchases even if they exceed the established limit on the card. Charges on lost or stolen cards must be paid by the cardholder but only up to $50; there is no liability if the issuer of the card is notified that it is missing before any charges are made.

Fair Credit Reporting Act of 1970, 15 U.S.C. §§ 1681 *et seq.* (FCRA) This is Title VII of the Consumer Credit Protection Act (see above), and it has two basic purposes: first, to set guidelines for credit bureaus that compile and sell credit reports; and, second, to entitle consumers to access to these reports so that they may be checked for accuracy. The guidelines established by FCRA specify that credit bureaus can provide credit reports only for certain reasons, such as to make decisions concerning extending credit, for underwriting insurance, as ordered to do so by a court of law, or to evaluate job applicants or current employees (see also Chapter 4: The Employee—Privacy, Law: The Right to Privacy). Consumers, at any time, have the right to know all of the information contained in their individual credit reports, where this information came from, and the names of all those who have received a copy of the credit report within the last six months, or the last ten months for all current and prospective employers.

Consumers also have the right to challenge any of the information contained in a report. Information that is proved to be incorrect or cannot be verified must be deleted from the consumer's credit file. If a consumer insists that some item is inaccurate, but the error cannot be substantiated, he or she may compose a 100-word document stating what is believed to be the correct account. This statement becomes part of the consumer's permanent record and must be included in any subsequent distribution of the credit report.

Consumer reporting agencies are not only required to keep accurate records, they must also delete obsolete information. Bankruptcies occurring more than 14 years prior to the date of the report cannot be included. After seven years, such items as lawsuits, tax liens, accounts placed for collection or written off as bad debts, arrests, indictments, or convictions cannot be reported. Violations of this or any other of the provisions of FCRA may be punished with damages, including punitive damages, court costs, and attorneys' fees.

In a landmark Supreme Court case involving FCRA, a credit bureau was found liable for compensatory and punitive damages when it inaccurately reported a bankruptcy filing. Greenmoss Builders, Inc., a Vermont construction company, was denied a bank loan because Dun & Bradstreet, Inc. (D&B), a credit-reporting agency, notified the bank that Greenmoss had filed a bankruptcy petition. This notation resulted when a 17-year-old high school student employed part-time at D&B mistakenly attributed to the company a personal bankruptcy petition that had been filed by an *employee* of Greenmoss. The Court ruled that D&B had defamed Greenmoss even though their misstatement had no malicious intention and was circulated to a very small audience. Nonetheless, it was false and it was published to others. Greenmoss was awarded $358,000 (*Dun & Bradstreet, Inc. v. Greenmoss Builders, Inc.*, 472 U.S. 749 [1985]).

Equal Credit Opportunity Act of 1975, 15 U.S.C. §1691 (ECOA) This federal law was originally written to prevent discrimination against women in credit transactions. Prior to this time, women— especially unmarried ones—often had difficulty obtaining credit due to their lower financial status relative to men. ECOA prohibits denying credit to a person based on sex or marital status. A 1976 amendment extended this protection to include race, color, national origin, religion, age, or receipt of income from public assistance. A creditor cannot ask any questions regarding these features, and the marital status of an applicant can only be considered if the spouse's income is used to establish credit. In addition, creditors are forbidden from asking questions about plans for childbirth or contraceptive practices. A creditor who rejects an applicant must provide a statement containing the specific reasons for the rejection. ECOA applies to banks, finance companies, retail stores, credit card issuers, and any other creditor who arranges credit in the ordinary course of doing business.

Fair Debt Collection Practices Act of 1977, 15 U.S.C. §1692 (FDCPA) Just as the Consumer Credit Protection Act (see above) provides safeguards against the abusive and unfair practices of creditors, the FDCPA protects debtors from the same sort of misconduct perpetrated by the collection agencies that creditors employ. This statute applies only to *debt collectors*, defined as those who collect debts for other people, so creditors who pursue debtors themselves are not subject to FDCPA. Debt collectors are forbidden from using obscene or abusive language, or harassing debtors, or threatening them with violence or imprisonment. Additionally, debt collectors are not allowed to contact debtors at various times and places, including any time that is inconvenient (generally between 9:00 p.m. and 8:00 a.m.), public places, or the debtor's place of employment. Nor can a debtor be contacted if he or she has legal representation, or if the debtor states in writing that he or she refuses to pay the debt and does not want to be contacted again by the collector.

Securities Act of 1933, 15 U.S.C. §§ 4 *et seq.* This federal law is aimed at regulating the distribution of securities by the issuer to ensure "truth in securities." This is primarily accomplished by requiring the issuer to file a **registration statement** with the Securities and Exchange Commission (SEC), a federal agency created by the Securities Exchange Act of 1934 (see below). Unless the kind of security offered or the nature of the transaction qualifies for an exemption from the requirement (see below), Section 5 stipulates that all securities offered to the public in interstate commerce must be registered. *Interstate commerce* has been interpreted very broadly to signify the business activities of any issuer who makes out-of-state telephone calls or who uses the U.S. mail to send or receive items crossing state lines.

The registration statement is usually prepared by a lawyer, with the assistance of an underwriter, and must contain several different items: descriptions of the securities to be sold, how the proceeds from the sale will be used, the nature of the business, and the structure of management in the business; any pending litigation must also be detailed, along with the degree of competition in the industry and any other special risk factors. A prospectus must also be included even though the information it contains substantially duplicates that found in the registration statement. The prospectus is intended to supply a complete financial picture of the would-be issuer of securities to the potential investor, so it is written in far less technical language than the registration statement, and emphasizes the best features of the corporation. It is essentially an advertisement.

The issuer is forbidden from selling or offering to sell securities before the registration statement has been filed. Nor can the issuer "condition the market" in anticipation of the sales by publishing articles or advertisements testifying to the bright prospects of the company. Such public relations work can commence once the statement is filed. If the SEC approves, the registration ordinarily goes into effect 20 days after filing. The securities are then usually purchased by an underwriter, whose market expertise has aided the issuer in preparing the registration statement. The underwriter is a kind of wholesaler of securities who then resells them to a dealer; the public makes their purchases from the dealer.

Not all types of securities have to be registered with the SEC; for example, those issued by banks, governments, charitable organizations, common carriers, and those that mature in nine months or less are exempt. Additionally, some types of security transactions do not need to be registered; these exempt transactions are nonetheless regulated by federal securities laws prohibiting fraud and deception, so even here investors must be provided with financial statements and other evidence. Exempt transactions include those in which ordinary investors resell securities they have purchased, and in which companies whose business is substantially confined to one state try to raise capital from local investors for use in that state.

Probably the most important exempt transaction for many corporate issuers is *private-placement*. This exemption allows issuers to forego registration when attempting to raise capital from accredited investors. These sorts of investors are typically other corporations. Because corporations have the appropriate staffing with the expertise necessary to obtain and assess the relevant information from the issuer, government oversight is not required. Individuals may also qualify as accredited investors, so long as they have a net worth of at least $1 million, or personal income for each of the previous two years of at least $200,000, and at least the same amount can be reasonably expected for the current year.

Section 24 provides that anyone who violates the Securities Act may be *criminally* liable. This means the possibility of imprisonment for a maximum of five years. Criminal actions are prosecuted by the Justice Department. Sections 11 and 12 impose civil liability for violations. Section 12 liability concerns selling securities without registering them when a registration statement is required; injured purchasers can cancel the sale or sue for damages. Section 11 liability concerns inaccurate statements of fact or omissions of relevant facts in the registration statement. The landmark case of *Escott v. BarChris Construction Company* (see below) established that all signatories to a false or misleading registration statement can be held individually liable.

Securities Exchange Act of 1934, 15 U.S.C. §§77a–77aa The Securities and Exchange Commission (SEC) was created by this act. An independent regulatory agency, the mission of the SEC is to ensure adequate financial disclosures by securities issuers so that investment decisions made by the general public are based on accurate information. The five commissioners are appointed by the president and approved by the Senate for staggered five-year terms, so every 5 June a new commissioner is selected. As a bipartisan agency, no more than three SEC commissioners can be members of the same political party.

The SEC does not make judgments or promulgate regulations concerning the price of the offerings or the risk involved; indeed, it is illegal to state or imply in a prospectus that the commission has the authority to disallow a securities offering based on its merits. Instead, the SEC is charged with investigating complaints of violations and conducting enforcement proceedings when violations occur. These proceedings may be one of three types: (1) a request for an injunction or a court order from a federal district court to require the company to surrender (*disgorge*) illegal profits, (2) a referral of the case to the Justice Department for criminal prosecution (an individual may be fined up to $1 million and imprisoned for ten years, and a corporation may be fined up to $2.5 million), or (3) a hearing to be held before an administrative law judge (ALJ). (See also this chapter, Advertising, Law.) The ALJ reads briefs and hears oral argument from both sides, and then renders a decision that may result in a number of different sanctions against securities issuers and traders. This decision may be appealed to the U.S. circuit court of appeals.

Although the Securities Act of 1933 (see above) regulates the original issuance of securities, the focus of the Securities Exchange Act of 1934 is on subsequent trading. It requires reporting companies to periodically file financial reports with the SEC. These reporting companies are securities issuers of three sorts: (1) those with assets of more than $5 million and at least 500 shareholders, (2) those whose stocks are traded on a national securities exchange, or (3) those that have filed a registration statement pursuant to the Securities Act of 1933. Reporting must be done annually and quarterly; monthly reports are required if a significant business event, such as a merger, occurs.

Probably the most important law in the act is **Rule 10b–5** (section 10[b]). This rule makes it illegal "to employ any device, scheme, or artifice to defraud" or "to engage in any act, practice, or course of business which operates or would operate as a fraud or deceit upon any person in connection with the purchase or sale of a security." Rule 105-b applies to reporting companies and all transfers of securities. Although the expression is not used in Rule 10b–5, it has been interpreted to prohibit **insider trading**. This prohibition was explicitly stated and strengthened by two statutes enacted in the 1980s. The Insider Trading Sanctions Act of 1984 (15 U.S.C. §§78a–78c) authorized the SEC to place civil liability on anyone who has purchased or sold securities using information not available to the public, or who has provided this information to others who then exploit it for securities transactions. The Insider Trading and Securities Fraud Enforcement Act of 1988 (15 U.S.C. § 78u) provides stiffer civil and criminal penalties, establishing the liability of those who employ inside traders and fail to adequately supervise them. It also gives a cause of action to contemporaneous traders, that is, people who trade securities in the same market at the same time as the insider.

What is insider trading? Interestingly, the federal statutes do not define the concept. The theory is that a definition would be too restrictive and that clever insiders would find a way around it. The general idea, though. is that insider trading occurs when a company employee or advisor uses crucial information unavailable to the general public in order to make a profit or avoid a loss in securities trading. This activity is illegal because the insider has an unfair advantage over the public. An individual who uses this information for his or her own benefit is generally called a *true insider*. Someone who passes this information along to another person is known as a *tipper*; the receiver of the lucrative facts is the *tippee*. The tippee is legally liable for acting on the information if he or she knew or should have known that it was not public (see below, *Dirks v. SEC*). The tipper is liable for the profits realized or the loss avoided by the tippee.

Section 16 requires that all statutory insiders file reports with the SEC disclosing their ownership and trading in their company's securities. A statutory insider is any executive officer, director, or 10-percent shareholder. These insiders must relinquish to the company any *short-swing* profits; this is money made on securities transactions within six months of each other. For example, if an officer bought 100 shares of his or her employer's stock at $10 per share and then sold them at $12 per share less than six months later, the officer would have to hand over the $200 profit to the corporation.

International Securities Enforcement Cooperation Act of 1990, 15 U.S.C. §§78a–80b Securities are traded on common markets around the world, and other countries too have laws against insider trading and securities fraud. Although the U.S. laws are probably the most stringent in the world, the European Community has directed all its member countries to adopt laws against insider trading. England and France have led the way in this effort. On the other hand, although Japan is a major player in the world economy, its insider trading law has seen very spotty enforcement. The purpose of this Act of Congress is to authorize the SEC to cooperate with foreign securities officials, provide financial records to them, and to penalize securities traders in this country who violate foreign securities laws.

The SEC has signed a memorandum of understanding (MOU) with several foreign countries, including Brazil, Canada, Great Britain, France, and Japan. This is essentially an agreement between the SEC and its foreign counterparts to cooperate in the enforcement of each other's securities laws. The MOU allows the SEC to obtain information concerning the location of bank accounts in foreign countries where illegal profits might be ensconced or evidence of foreign business fronts from which insider trading in this country may be carried out.

Escott v. BarChris Construction Corp., 283 F. Supp. 643 (D. 1968). This historic case set the standard for civil liability under Section 11 of the Securities Act of 1933 (see above). The main issue here is the legal culpability of individual corporate officers for misinformation disseminated to investors. BarChris Construction Corporation worked mainly in the erection and sale of bowling alleys in New York. Early in 1961 various officers of the company decided to seek financing from public investors by selling debentures. Consequently, a registration statement and prospectus were prepared, as required by the Securities Act, both of which were eventually approved by the SEC. Tens of thousands of dollars worth of debentures were sold.

Unbeknownst to the investors, the registration statement and prospectus contained numerous errors. Among others, the assets of BarChris were inflated while the liabilities were reduced, both by 15 percent; the sales for the most recent quarter were overstated by 32 percent and the profits overstated by 92 percent; hundreds of thousands of dollars of loans were not disclosed and the backlog of orders was grossly inflated. Within one year, BarChris was failing financially, so the company filed for Chapter 11 reorganization under federal bankruptcy laws. Shortly thereafter, BarChris defaulted on interest payments due to those who bought the debentures. Barry Escott and other investors sued the executive officers of the company and the accountants who worked with them, charging them with violating Section 11 by submitting misrepresentations and omissions of material facts.

The defendants appealed, raising the *due diligence* defense for a Section 11 allegation: This is the claim that they had reasonable grounds to believe and did in fact believe that at the time the registration statement became effective, its assertions were true and that there were no significant omissions. One by one, Judge McLean addressed the liability of each of the defendants and found in favor of Escott. The chief executive officer, being thoroughly conversant with all aspects of the business, could not have believed that there were no untrue statements or material omissions. The president and vice-president were also liable, even if they had neither read nor understood the documents, simply because they signed them. The controller must have been aware of at least some of the inaccuracies or omissions; after all, his position required being apprised of the company's finances. Finally, the senior accountant of the consulting firm was also liable, despite his inexperience (he was not a CPA at the time and had never worked in the bowling alley industry); he committed numerous errors and oversights. The bottom line established in this case is that each person who signs a registration statement must make a reasonable effort to determine whether or not the facts contained therein are accurate. Otherwise, individual liability may be imposed.

SEC v. Texas Gulf Sulphur Co., 401 F.2d 833 (2d Cir. 1968) This is a key case in the development of the law concerning insider trading and illegal tipping. It started in November 1963 in Ontario, Canada. There, at an exploratory drill hole, Texas Gulf Sulphur Company (TGS) struck it rich. Or so it seemed. Assay reports from the core of the drilling indicated a mineral deposit loaded with copper, zinc, and silver. Workers quickly concealed the drill site and began conspicuous drilling elsewhere. The problem was that TGS did not own any mineral rights around the exploratory site, although the process of acquiring the land there was initiated. Within a few months, rumors were flying that TGS had made a rich mineral strike. These rumors were denied at first—indeed, TGS issued a press release claiming it was too soon to reach any firm conclusions about the deposit—but then a press conference announcement admitted that the rumors were true. By May 1964 TGS stock had more than tripled in value.

The SEC charged two TGS executives, David Crawford and Francis Coates, with using information not available to the public for their own benefit. Both had traded heavily in company stock, realizing a significant profit. The district court found that Crawford had engaged in illegal insider trading but Coates had not. The court of appeals agreed on Crawford and found Coates liable as well. Crawford had indisputably contacted his broker with instructions to buy TGS stock before the press conference was held. However, Coates had waited until after the press conference before placing his order. The district court relied on this fact in vindicating Coates, and on the principle established by *In re Cady, Roberts & Co.*, a 1961 SEC ruling (40 SEC 907).

Cady was one of the first true insider trading cases (it never went to court) and is historically very important for setting the legal boundaries for securities transactions. In *Cady*, a corporate director tipped a brokerage firm about an impending reduction in the corporation's dividends; the broker dumped much of the affected stock before the news was made public. The SEC decreed that the director had acted illegally, and that corporate officers have a duty to either (1) abstain from trading until the relevant information has been made public, or (2) disclose information that is accurate, complete, and truthful. In *Texas Gulf Sulphur*, the district court ruled that Coates had satisfied duty 1: He did delay his order until the announcement had been made. But the appeals court held that this was not good enough. The press conference ended at approximately 10:10 a.m. Coates was talking to his broker by 10:20 a.m. The duty set out in *Cady* requires an insider to allow a reasonable amount of time for the dissemination of the news through the standard media before acting on that information. Coates had not done this.

Dirks v. Securities and Exchange Commission, 463 U.S. 646 (1983) Raymond Dirks was an officer of a New York brokerage firm specializing in the investment analysis of insurance companies. In March 1973, Dirks was given some disturbing information by Ronald Secrist. According to Secrist, the assets of an insurance company called Equity Funding had been enormously, and fraudulently, exaggerated. As a former officer of Equity Funding, Secrist claimed first-hand knowledge of this, and also indicated to Dirks that other employees had contacted regulatory agencies about the fraud—but to no avail. Secrist wanted Dirks to investigate the matter and publicly reveal the wrongdoing.

Dirks visited Equity Funding's headquarters in Los Angeles, and there received conflicting information: Senior management denied that any fraud had occurred while other employees verified what Secrist had told him. He spent two weeks on this investigation, and during this time Dirks discussed the allegations with a number of clients and investors, some of whom quickly unloaded their Equity Funding securities. The company's stock fell from $26 per share to $15, trading on the New York Exchange was suspended, and California insurance authorities, after impounding Equity Funding's records, confirmed the fraud.

The SEC then launched its own investigation into Dirk's role in exposing the fraud. The SEC found that Dirks was liable as a tippee—Secrist was the tipper—who had aided and abetted violations of Rule 10(b)–5 of the Securities Exchange Act (see above) by informing holders of Equity Funding securities that the financial records of the company had likely been fraudulently altered. He should have made a public disclosure before passing on this information. The District of Columbia Circuit Court of Appeals agreed with the SEC.

The Supreme Court rejected this judgment. To justify the reversal, Justice Powell turned to the Court's precedent-setting decision in *Chiarella v. United States* (445 U.S. 222 [1980]). Vincent Chiarella worked in the composing room of Pandick Press in New York. In his capacity as a "mark-up man," he handled five secret announcements of corporate takeovers. Although the names of the companies involved were not to be revealed until the night of the final printing, Chiarella correctly guessed who the targeted companies were. He bought stock in these firms and then sold the shares immediately after the takeovers were made public, realizing a healthy profit. The court found that Chiarella did not have a duty to disclose the information he had deduced because he was not an agent or a fiduciary of the corporation, and he had not received confidential information from the target companies. Chiarella was entitled to use the nonpublic information to his benefit.

The SEC ruling in *Dirks* conflicts with *Chiarella* by suggesting that *all* traders must have equal information before trading. Powell and the majority firmly stifled the SEC ruling, and in the process clarified the nature of tippee liability. The test for tippee liability begins with the tipper: if the tipper violated a duty of trust and confidence to the corporation, then there may be a *derivative* violation by the tippee. If there is no breach of duty by the tipper, then there can be none by the tippee. So did Secrist, as the tipper, violate his fiduciary duty? That is determined by the reason why he disclosed the information to Dirks in the first place; if the disclosure was motivated by personal gain, then a breach of duty has occurred. However, this was *not* the case with

Secrist: He received no monetary benefit from the revelation and wished only to expose the fraud. Moreover, Dirks had no fiduciary duty to Equity Funding or its shareholders, he did not obtain the information illegally, and was not expected to keep it confidential.

References: Arrington, Robert L. 1982. "Advertising and Behavior Control." *Journal of Business Ethics.* 1: 3–12.

Beauchamp, Tom L. and Norman E. Bowie. 1997. *Ethical Theory and Business.* 5th ed. Upper Saddle River, NJ: Prentice Hall.

———. 1998. "Reserve Mining's Silver Bay Facility." In Tom L. Beauchamp, *Case Studies in Business, Ethics, and Society.* 4th ed. Upper Saddle River, NJ: Prentice Hall.

Boatright, John R. 1997. *Ethics and the Conduct of Business.* 2d ed. Upper Saddle River, NJ: Prentice Hall.

Bowie, Norman E. and Partick E. Murphy. 1995. "Natural Cereals." In John R. Boatright, *Cases Studies in Ethics and the Conduct of Business.* Upper Saddle River, NJ: Prentice Hall.

Brenkert, George G. 1997. "Strict Products Liability and Compensatory Justice." In *Ethical Theory and Business.* Edited by Tom L. Beauchamp and Norman E. Bowie. 5th ed. Upper Saddle River, NJ: Prentice Hall.

Butler, Steven. 1997. "It was too easy to make money." *U.S. News and World Report* 123 (4): 41.

Crisp, Roger. 1987. "Persuasive Advertising, Autonomy, and the Creation of Desire." *Journal of Business Ethics* 6: 413–418.

DesJardin, Joseph and John J. McCall. 1996. *Contemporary Issues in Business Ethics.* 3d ed. Belmont, CA: Wadsworth.

Durham, Taylor R. 1984. "Information, Persuasion, and Control in Moral Appraisal of Advertising Strategy." *Journal of Business Ethics* 3: 173–180.

Fredrick, Robert E. and W. Michael Hoffman. 1990. "The Individual Investor in Securities Markets: An Ethical Analysis." *Journal of Business Ethics* 9: 579–589.

Galbraith, John Kenneth. 1984. *The Affluent Society.* 4th ed. Boston: Houghton Mifflin.

Galluccio, Gregory S. 1996. "International Certification." *Appliance Manufacturer* 44 (2): 96.

Gwartney, James D. and Richard Stroup. 1982. *Economics: Private and Public Choice.* 3d ed. New York: Academic Press.

Hunt, Shelby and Lawrence Chonko. 1987. "Ethical Problems of Advertising Agency Executives." *Journal of Advertising* 16: 16–25.

Irvine, William B. 1987. "The Ethics of Investing." *Journal of Business Ethics* 6: 233–242.

Jackson, Jennifer. 1990. "Honesty in Marketing." *Journal of Applied Philosophy* 7(1):51–60.

Jones, Judy. 1997. "Can't Shop, Won't Shop." *New Statesman* 126 (4360): 39.

Moore, Jennifer Mills. 1990. "What is Really Unethical about Insider Trading?" *Journal of Business Ethics* 9: 171–182.

New York Times. 1997. "Thai Economy Gets Some Relief," *New York Times* (NL), Oct. 18: B14.

North, Douglass. 1990. *Institutions, Institutional Change, and Economic Performance.* Cambridge: Cambridge University Press.

Pearce, David W., ed. 1992. *The MIT Dictionary of Modern Economics.* 4th ed. Cambridge, MA: MIT Press.

Rich, Frank. 1997. "The Ellen 'Striptease.'"*The New York Times on the Web.* April 10.

Rivoli, Pietra. 1995. "Ethical Aspects of Investor Behavior." *Journal of Business Ethics* 14: 265–277.

Samuelson, Paul A. and William D. Nordhaus. 1985. *Economics.* 3d ed. New York: McGraw-Hill.

Santilli, Paul C. 1983. "The Informative and Persuasive Functions of Advertising: A Moral Appraisal." *Journal of Business Ethics.*

"Southern Africa: The Unraveling of Apartheid." 1997. *The Encyclopaedia Britannica CD.* Chicago: Encyclopaedia Britannica, Inc.

Thoreau, Henry David. 1970. *The Annotated Walden: Walden; or, Life in the Woods.* Edited by Philip Van Doren Stern. New York: C. N. Potter.

Velasquez, Manuel G. 1992. *Business Ethics: Concepts and Cases.* 3d ed. Upper Saddle River, NJ: Prentice Hall.

Wagner, Christopher. 1996. "Safe Products and Global Trade." *OECD Observer* Oct–Nov, n202: 13–15.

Werhane, Patricia H. and R. Edward Freeman. 1997. *The Blackwell Encyclopedic Dictionary of Business Ethics*. Malden, MA: Blackwell Publishers.

Wood, Donna. 1994. *Business and Society*. 2d ed. New York: Harper Collins.

Wyatt, Edward. 1998. "Share of Household Wealth in Stocks Is at 50-Year High." *New York Times*, Cyber Edition, February 11.

CONTEMPORARY ETHICAL ISSUES

Chapter 3:
The Corporation

Corporations are organizations designed to achieve or promote a goal (Simon 1976). Business corporations have a compound, or two-part, goal: (1) the *production of a product or service* (2) *for profit*. Managers use corporate goals to direct and evaluate corporate behavior. For example, managers of Microsoft make decisions based on the fact that the corporate goal is the production of software for profit; the managers of Ben and Jerry's make decisions based on the fact that the corporate goal is the production of ice cream for profit. *The goal of a business corporation is never profit alone.* Profit for a business corporation is like breathing for a human being: While it provides the resources necessary for its continued existence, it does not give purpose or specific direction to behavior.

The Nature and Structure of the Corporation

What is a corporation? What sort of entity is it? What does the way a corporation is arranged have to do with morality? Do corporations have legal obligations and rights? Can a corporation commit a crime and be punished for wrongdoing?

A corporation as an organization devoted to commerce is uniquely defined by these features:

1. **Perpetual existence.** This feature most readily distinguishes the corporation from other forms of business enterprise, such as a partnership, a proprietorship, or a franchise. Unless the owners agree to dissolve the corporation, or it goes bankrupt, corporate existence continues in perpetuity through a succession of owners and managers. A partnership ends when one of the partners dies, as does a proprietorship when the owner dies, while a franchise is always at the mercy of the franchiser.

2. **Share ownership.** A corporation is owned by individuals who possess shares of **stock**. A stock is a certificate validating the shareholder's ownership of some portion (a *share*) of the corporation. This certificate gives the owner a legal claim to a percentage of the corporation's profits (see also Chapter 2: The Consumer—Finance, Law: Investments). Stocks can be sold at any time, and their sale may or may not have a significant effect on the business. Small corporations are usually managed by stockholders, so that a sale could radically alter the corporation.

3. **Limited liability of owners.** The liability of shareholders for a corporation's debt is limited by the amount of capital they invested when they purchased shares. For example, a shareholder who owns stock worth $1000 typically cannot be legally required to surrender more than that amount if the company should be held liable to creditors or for damages. However, some situations warrant *piercing the corporate veil*: This is to disregard the corporation and hold the owners personally liable for the corporation's debts and obligations.

4. **Centralized management.** The owners of the corporation elect a board of directors to make policy decisions concerning the operation of the corporation. The directors then appoint various corporate officers to run the company on a day-to-day business. The directors and officers, along with the lower-level managers hired by the officers, form the corporate management.

A corporation is a form of property that can itself own property. Shareholders own the corporation and the corporation owns the buildings, equipment, and other assets and instruments of the business. Because the corporation, and not the shareholders, owns the business property, the corporation receives all of the benefits, costs, and risks of doing business. This arrangement allows shareholders to *take the benefits* out of the corporation, *leaving costs and risks* behind (Berle and Means 1968). This is the primary feature that limits their liability.

Stockholders do bear some risk, of course, but their limited liability confines their risk to the price they paid for their stock. If a corporation incurs billions of dollars of debt that it cannot repay, the stockholders are not responsible for any of it. Their possible rewards, on the other hand, are limitless, as the early buyers of Microsoft and IBM have discovered. Not only can the price of their shares increase, they can also receive healthy dividends.

Corporate managers also have limited risk. If they run a business into the ground, they are not liable for those bad decisions unless they acted illegally or were negligent in the pursuit of their duties. On the other hand, their rewards are without limit. Bill Gates, the person behind Microsoft, is worth about $80 billion at the time of this writing.

Corporations have functional areas designed to help them reach their goals. Most corporations have accounting, finance, marketing, and human resources (what used to be called personnel) departments, and one or more individuals to coordinate these functional areas. In a small business, like a local dry cleaner, one person may handle several or even all of these functions. In a large multinational corporation, these functional areas can be staffed by hundreds, even thousands, of individuals with their own intricate layers of management (Chandler 1977).

As Figure 1 indicates, the board of directors is the link between the owners and management. The board of directors not only hires the chief executive officer (CEO), it is supposed to monitor the CEO and important corporate financial indicators, such as profit margins, revenues, market share, and debt-to-asset ratios. The board does not monitor day-to-day operations; that is the job of management.

Ethics

Although the structure of corporations may seem to be independent of ethics, nothing could be further from the truth. The entire corporate structure is built on ethical relationships that tie organizational members together. The purpose of the board of directors has an ethical core: to protect the interests of the owners. If board members do not do this, they are violating their ethical duties as defined by their job. Similarly, the CEO has a duty of honesty and fidelity to the board. *These ethical duties define and are part of managerial relationships*, they are not separate from, or external to, managerial relationships (Dienhart 1999).

Most human beings have a variety of motives: self-interest, care for others, loyalty to their groups, and a desire for justice and fairness, although not all of these motivations are equally strong in all people (Dienhart 1999). When we take on the role of investor, manager, or employee, this role can strengthen some of our motivations and weaken others. To assume a role, then, can profoundly affect what we think is important and how we should go about achieving it. We will discuss the four ethical points of view as they would be expressed by people in the roles of investor, manager, and employee roles.

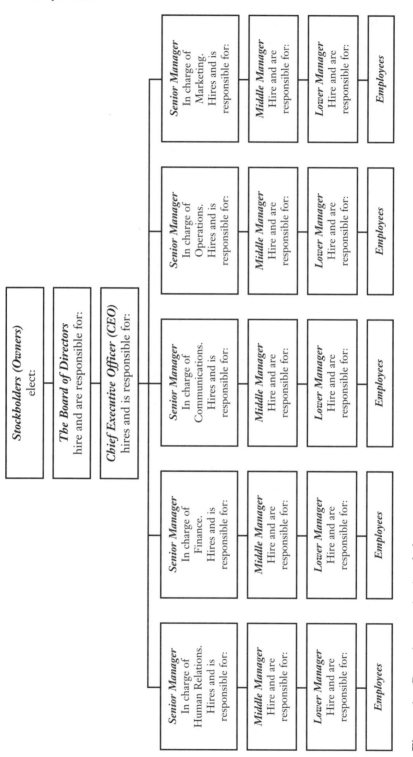

Figure 1 Generic organizational chart.

Promoting Self-Interest: Egoism   When investors buy stock in a corporation, they expect to benefit financially from their investments. These benefits include peace of mind as well as the purchase of goods and services they believe will make them better off. Individuals will not invest in a corporation unless they can be reasonably sure that managers will use corporate resources to promote the financial interests of investors. A self-interested investor, then, would favor a corporate structure that monitors senior management, as described in Figure 1. Corporate structures that include monitoring can be understood as a *response to investor demand* (Williamson 1985).

A rational, self-interested manager understands that people will not invest in corporations unless they can be reasonably sure that their money will be used to benefit investors. On this view, rational, self-interested managers will agree to a corporate structure that monitors their behavior. Unless there is such monitoring, there will be no corporation in which they can pursue their interests. This does not mean that managers will not try to promote their interests at the expense of the owners, only that they accept the fact that the investors want them to be monitored. One managerial strategy to avoid monitoring is to pack the board with people who are sympathetic to managerial interests. Packing boards allows managers to have the appearance of being monitored while avoiding most of the problems of being monitored.

Managers who try to pack the boards are starting to face a great deal of resistance. Pension funds have been especially vocal. The California Public Employees Retirement System (Calpers), with $126 billion in assets, has exerted pressure on such companies as General Motors, Eastman Kodak, and IBM to change their directors because their revenues and market shares were declining. Calpers asked for changes, and got them, because they are major investors. Calpers is now thinking about seeking directorships in companies in which they have investments (Lublin 1997). TIAA-CREF, the major pension fund for college teachers, has also been active. At the beginning of 1998 TIAA-CREF tried to pressure Walt Disney Co. into replacing several directors who are closely allied with Michael Eisner, the CEO, and other top Disney managers. The proposal failed, but the pressure is on (Orwall 1998).

If we focus on the self-interest of the owners and the managers, we get a conflict that is known as the **agency problem** (North 1990). The agency problem can be described in the following way: Managers are supposed to act as agents for the owners, but the self-interest of managers gives them an incentive to promote their own welfare. Regulations, laws, and boards of directors are ways in which society tries to solve the agency problem.

Rational, self-interested employees understand that managers will not hire them unless managers can be reasonably sure that the employees will do the jobs they are hired to do. Self-interested employees will agree to a corporate structure that monitors their behavior. Of course this does not mean that some employees will not try to get more pay for less work, only that they accept the fact that managers will try to stop them.

Nurturing Personal Relationships: Care   Caring stockholders will focus on how the corporation affects the relationships of those connected to the corporation. Caring owners will want to ensure that those who work for the corporation have time for family and friendships. Caring owners will also want the work environment to promote and encourage friendly relationships between *all* organizational members.

It may seem odd to think of caring stockholders, but there are several cases in which they have made a difference. Many religious groups bought stock in companies doing business in the former Republic of South Africa. They were protesting the apartheid system of racial segregation and exploitation. Polaroid was the object of stockholder pressure because the South African government was using Polaroid technology to make the pass cards that blacks had to carry when they were in public (Beauchamp 1998).

Caring managers will want to respond to the needs of the owners, because owners have entrusted managers with important assets. They also need to care for employees. Caring managers must integrate their care for owners and employees, because the care ethic holds that we should not harm one group of people to care for another group. Polaroid's managers formed a committee composed of management and labor to investigate how their products were being used. After spending time in South Africa, the committee made several recommendations that the company followed. One of the recommendations was to stop doing business with the South African government, but to keep manufacturing facilities there (Beauchamp 1998).

Caring employees will focus on doing their job well in order to produce safe products of high quality. Employees with families will want to ensure that their job is compatible with developing and maintaining loving, nurturing family relationships. Caring employees will also be concerned with respecting the relationships of other corporate members, whether they are employees or managers. Again, Polaroid shows how caring employees can exert their force, since it was a group of employees who brought pressure on management (Beauchamp 1998).

Promoting the Good of the Group: Utilitarianism   Utilitarian investors will buy stock in companies they believe will benefit the group. The group in question could be a particular religion, a political party, a gender, a nation-state, as well as a number of other choices. Consider religion. Members of a particular religion might buy stock in companies that have religious foundations or that acknowledge the importance of religion. They might not buy stock in companies that produce products that conflict with their religious principles. This is what happened when fundamentalist Christian groups urged members to sell Disney stock, because it aired *Ellen*, a television show that presented homosexuality in a positive light (Rich 1997). These same people, however, might buy Disney stock, so that, as owners, they voice their protests about *Ellen* directly to management.

Utilitarian managers have a ready-made group whose interests they can promote: the owners. In fact, managers must, by law, promote the financial interest of the owners. However, like the owners, they have many other groups they could choose to promote. Let's consider managers who are dedicated to promoting the interests of the corporation *and* the nation. There are many ways to promote the good of both groups; we will look at corporate philanthropy.

Corporate philanthropy has a long history in the United States, going back to the railroads, our first major industry, that helped fund the YMCA (Heald 1988). During World Wars I and II, businesses helped organize campaigns to get materials, like rubber, to recycle for the war effort. In the 1930s, during the height of the Depression, many managers saw the importance of giving to charitable causes. Unfortunately, there were obstacles to corporate philanthropy. One of the main obstacles was that it was illegal for managers to use corporate money in a way that was not likely to have direct benefits for the company. In 1935, largely due to business pressure, Congress passed the Revenue Act, which allowed corporations to deduct 5 percent of their taxable income from their taxes (Heald 1988).

Utilitarian employees also have a ready-made group whose good they can promote: the employees. However, like the owners and managers, employees could promote the interests of many other groups. Often, employees who promote the good of the corporation also promote the good of the employees. However, employee and corporate interests can conflict when employees are asked to advance corporate welfare by relying on cheap, risky production methods that can harm employees but add to corporate profits.

Respecting Dignity and Rights: Intrinsic Value   Owners who focus on dignity and rights will want managers to form a corporate structure that respects human rights and dignity. Hence, a major concern about the corporate structure is whether it has good information flow that allows decision makers to make informed, free decisions.

Another important feature will be how the corporation handles problems and mistakes. As we saw in the Polaroid case, above, the dignity of South African black employees was systematically violated. South African laws did not allow black employees to be promoted. These employees could not eat or congregate with white workers. Many Polaroid owners voiced objections, arguing that it was mistake for Polaroid to have set up production there. Polaroid established a committee to examine the issue, and, in the end, pulled out of South Africa completely.

Managers who respect human rights and dignity will never use employees or other stakeholders merely as means to promote the good of the corporation. Each employee has the right to direct his or her own life, even at work. However, this does not mean that employees can do anything they want in the workplace. When they freely agree to the company's terms and conditions of employment (see Chapter 4: The Employee), they are morally and legally obligated to keep their agreement. Managerial respect for human dignity and rights can conflict with their responsibility to pursue the corporate goal of production for profit. Imagine that managers discover how they can get a product to market faster, and so increase profits; unfortunately, this requires employees to work overtime, in violation of a long-standing informal agreement that employees are free to turn down requests for overtime.

Employees who respect human rights and dignity will focus on doing the job they promised to do at a reasonable pace. They will also realize that the changing business environment can require them to work with management to alter the terms and conditions of employment. This does not mean that employees have to agree with all management requests. In the overtime case mentioned in the preceding paragraph, the employees could recognize a need to alter the way overtime is handled without simply accepting management's order to work more now.

It is in this kind of case that the right kind of organizational structure is crucial. If the organization has structural mechanisms that allow affected parties to participate in resolving problems and pursuing opportunities as they arise, management will not be as likely to choose a position that violates the dignity of the employees.

Economics

Society   Corporations are at the heart of contemporary social life. Incorporated businesses produce almost everything we use, from essentials like medicine, housing, clothing, and transportation, to luxury goods and other items that enrich our lives. Corporations are also becoming more involved in education at all levels.

Corporations yield great social benefits because of the way they reassociate risks and rewards for owners and managers. As we saw above, owners and managers can reap great rewards at minimal risk. This lower risk attracts the money and talent needed for large-scale production. The contemporary corporation is quite different from what it was 200 years ago. In the following, we will look at corporate history in the United States, to reveal the nature, power, and limits of corporations (Berle and Means 1968).

Until the late eighteenth and early nineteenth centuries, most businesses were treated as ordinary private property. If someone walking down the street was harmed by a flying metal shard that came off a horseshoe as a blacksmith was pounding it into a horse's hoof, the blacksmith's personal property and his livelihood would be in jeopardy. As the United States expanded west and as the eastern markets matured, needs developed for goods, like canals and railroads, that could not be produced using the business practices current and the resources available at the time.

The major problem in creating a business for national markets was that it takes many investors to provide the enormous amount of money required for these projects. Potential investors would not invest unless there were controls on how managers allocated business resources. Another problem was controlling risk. Potential investors would not invest unless their personal property was protected from those who made claims against the business. The corporation was the answer to both of these problems.

The first U.S. corporations were few in number and were created to provide infrastructure goods, likes canals and railroads. These early corporations could be formed only with the explicit assent of a state legislature. Corporate charters restricted corporate spending to activities specifically designed to promote the corporate goal, which was narrowly defined in the charter. For example, if a corporation was formed to build a canal and at a later point the managers or owners wanted to go into the barge-building business, they had to get the permission of every single owner. This gave each owner veto power. Larger changes, such as a substantial reorganization of the **capital structure**, would require legislative approval. These restrictions protected owners by ensuring that their money would not be spent against their wishes (Berle and Means 1968).

As we saw, incorporation shields the owners' property from claims against the corporation. Although shielding the private property of shareholders was good for the owners, it put the general public at risk.

One way to think about this is that risk does not disappear with a wave of the legal wand. All law can do is *redistribute* risk. We can illustrate this with two examples. First, consider a corporation that goes bankrupt, leaving many of its suppliers unpaid. They can remain unpaid even if the owners (stockholders) have enough money in private accounts to pay them. These vendors bore the risks, not the owners. Second, consider a small company with few resources that produces mercury. By a terrible, unforeseeable accident, it causes billions of dollars of environmental damage. The company cannot begin to pay for the cleanup costs. Further, whatever private property the owners and managers have is protected from confiscation. The general public bears the risk, not the owners or managers.

These redistributed risks that define the corporation are the main reason why corporations were so tightly regulated when they first appeared. However, as markets grew and technology became more complex, the demand for incorporation grew beyond what state legislatures could handle. There was also pressure from the business community to make incorporation easier. By the early twentieth century, most state legislatures passed laws that set standards for incorporation. These laws of incorporation were administered by states' attorneys general. As the twentieth century progressed, the standards for incorporation became easier and easier to meet (Berle and Means 1968). At present, in most states, a person can form a corporation by filing fairly simple incorporation papers and paying a small fee.

As incorporation became easier, the state's role of protector got moved from overseeing the incorporation of business to monitoring the activities of business. Hence, we have the growth of regulation, first with respect to the economic infrastructure—for example, promoting a competitive environment—and later with respect to labor, community, and environmental issues.

Consumers Corporations succeeded because they produced goods and services that met consumer demand better than noncorporate businesses. Initially, large-scale production requires a great deal of money and time, but, after the initial investment, products can be made very inexpensively. This was a boon to consumers, who could buy things, like automobiles, that formerly only the very rich could afford. Henry Ford was one of the first to understand this, and many other entrepreneurs followed in his footsteps.

One problem consumers face is the very feature that makes corporations so useful: the risk consumers take in buying and using a product is borne by them and the corporation, not by the managers or the owners. Because managers and owners bear less risk for their decisions, they have an incentive to make decisions that put consumers at risk. Of course, to remain a viable company, good managers will not knowingly manufacture products that will fail for all those who use them. But there are cases, like that of the Ford Pinto, in which the failures are few but disastrous. Ford was willing to take this risk because the financial cost of preventing it was more expensive than settling law suits for those who needlessly lost their lives (Gioia 1992). Cases like these provide good reason to regulate business practices to *prevent* such states of affairs from arising, rather than relying on the executive and judicial branches to correct harms that have already occurred.

Producers Owners and managers have the possibility of great rewards with relatively low risk. They get this attractive risk-reward relationship because government gives them limited liability. On the other hand, producers do not like government interfering in their business practices.

Although it is true that government regulation can harm business, it must be remembered that corporations exist only because there are governmental laws that define them and authorize their existence. If it turns out that governmentally sanctioned corporations allow or encourage harm to the public and the environment, then the government is responsible for these harms to some extent, and would be remiss if it did not try to repair the harm and prevent future ones.

There are some cases in which the government has decided that it is useful to pierce the corporate property veil and make managers personally responsible for their actions (see also below, Law: Corporate Crime). One of the more well-known laws that does this is the Foreign Corrupt Practices Act (FCPA), passed in 1977 and amended in 1988. This law was passed in the wake of the Lockheed scandal, in which the CEO of Lockheed bribed officials of the Japanese government to buy Lockheed's commercial airliners. The FCPA makes managers personally responsible for bribing government officials of foreign countries, imposing both jail and fines for such behavior. If fines are imposed, the company cannot pay them; the fines must be paid by the offending manager.

International Issues

Corporations across the globe are structured in a manner that provides for a board of directors that monitors senior management. Boards of directors in many countries, including the United States are under increased scrutiny and pressure. One vehicle that businesses use to educate themselves about these pressures and to learn from each other is the Conference Board. Established in 1916, the board has two goals: to improve the enterprise system and to enhance the contributions that business makes to society. It is a nonprofit, nonadvocacy group.

The Conference Board sponsors the European Council on Board Effectiveness. The European Council has 16 corporate members, including Allied Irish Banks, BP Oil International, and Heineken N.V. The council's mission "reflects the growing importance of enhancing corporate perform-ance and the need to respond to an increasingly complex corporate gover-nance environment" (The Conference Board 1988a).

Rather than viewing the board of directors as simply reacting to manage-ment proposals, the council reflects the United States emphasis on helping direct a company's strategic plans regarding product emphasis, **market pene-tration**, and dealing with different cultures and foreign governments. A board of directors that has members from different cultures, for example, may be more sensitive to how management proposals will be accepted in **host** nations.

Another international organization, the Caux Round Table, is made up of senior business executives from Japan, Europe, and the United States. The mission of this organization is "to promote principled business leadership and responsible corporate practice in support of successful and sustainable busi-ness activity and the common good of the world-wide communities served" (Caux Round Table 1998).

This mission has substantial effects on corporate structure, because it implies that the good of a company will be defined not merely in terms of maximizing the financial return to stock owners, but also in terms of how well it promotes the "common good of the world-wide communities served." To promote this common good, the interests of these worldwide communities need to be represented in the company so that management decision making can consider it. In other words, new information channels need to be added to corporate structure. One way to do this, as we just saw, is to use the board of directors to supply information about community needs.

Law

A corporation is a special sort of legal entity, often referred to as a *legal fiction*. This means that the law regards a corporation as if it were a real, natural per-son, when in fact it is not. For the purposes of a legal system, the most perti-nent features of a person are his or her legal rights, a person's culpability in violating the rights of others, and his or her susceptibility to punishment meted out by the judiciary. We find that all these features have been dupli-cated in defining the legal status of a corporation.

The Rights of Corporations During the late 1700s and early 1800s the key features of a corporation—especially ownership by stockholders, their limited liability, and the continual existence of the firm (see above)—were generally regarded by policy makers as privileges. Individuals wishing to form a corporation had to convince state legislatures that their proposed enterprise would serve some public good. If lawmakers were convinced, they granted a *corporate charter*: This was a permission and an agreement to incorporate for a certain purpose and to conduct business in a certain way. At least through the 1820s, much of state legislative activity was the consideration of incorporation proposals and the awarding of charters. By the 1850s legislatures had grown tired of this process, and the states adopted general incorporation statutes that specified the requirements anyone needed to meet in order to form a corporation.

The legal standing of a corporation was first articulated in a famous 1819 case involving a charter bestowed by the state of Rhode Island on Dartmouth College. The Supreme Court held that a corporate charter granted to the school was a contract between the corporation and the state, and, like any contract, it could not be unilaterally changed at the discretion of one of the contractors (*Dartmouth College v. Woodward*, 4 Wheaton 518 (1819). Henry Wheaton was the third of the young Court's reporters, serving at a time before the task was accomplished by anonymous government clerks. Wheaton compiled 12 volumes of arguments and opinions from 1816 to 1827). *Dartmouth* suggests that a corporation is a fictional person under the law that (who?) can contract with real persons, the state, or other corporations. Corporate property is entitled to protection by the law just as human property is. This means that a corporation, like a person, is a *legal entity*—one that has legal rights. In his majority decision, Chief Justice John Marshall observed that "A corporation is an artificial being, invisible, intangible, and existing only in the contemplation of law. Being the mere creature of the law, it possesses only those properties that the charter of its creation confers upon it…. Among the most important are immortality, and, if the expression may be allowed, individuality."

This finding was solidified in 1886 and 1889 with two more landmark Supreme Court decisions. In the first case, *Santa Clara County v. Southern Pacific Railroad Company*, 118 U.S. 394 (1886), Chief Justice Morrison Waite infamously preempted any debate concerning a controversial position by simply announcing that the **Equal Protection Clause** of the Fourteenth Amendment to the Constitution applies to corporations as well as natural persons. This phrase prohibits government from "deny[ing] to any person within its jurisdiction equal protection of the laws," and suggests that it is not the case that corporations are by their very nature unworthy of legal rights. Moreover, in *Minneapolis & St. Louis Railroad Company v. Beckwith*, 129 U.S. 26 (1889), the court held that a corporation is a person under the meaning of the **Due Process Clause** of the Fourteenth Amendment to the Constitution. This phrase prohibits government from "depriv[ing] any person of life, liberty or property without due process of law." It implies that a corporation cannot be arbitrarily or capriciously divested of its property or its freedom to engage in commerce. In a historic case discussed below, the Supreme Court has gone so far as to affirm that First Amendment rights of free expression are also held by companies (*First National Bank of Boston v. Bellotti*).

Nonetheless, the Supreme Court has stopped short of proclaiming that all constitutional rights belong to business. Most notably, the justices have determined that the Fifth Amendment protection against self-incrimination does not apply to a corporation (*Bellis v. United States*, 417 U.S. 85 [1974]). Therefore, business records are not protected from disclosure even though they may incriminate people who work at the business.

Punishing Corporations   The Supreme Court decisions in *Dartmouth College*, *Santa Clara County*, *Beckwith* (see above), and others, established that a corporation has the status of an artificial person with legal rights. Yet real persons not only have legal rights, they can also unlawfully violate the rights of other people, and break other laws as well. Real persons are then held legally responsible or *liable* for these transgressions, and thus merit punishment for them. So if a corporation has rights, similar to a real person, should not a corporation also be held responsible for its wrongdoing, and be punished accordingly? For many years, judges and legislatures answered "no" to this question simply because they held that a corporation could not be guilty of committing a crime.

In order for a person to be found guilty of most crimes, two conditions must be satisfied: (1) The individual must have performed the forbidden act (or failed to perform a required act, such as filing an income tax return); and (2) the person must have intentionally, purposefully, and with knowledge of its criminal nature, committed the prohibited act. This latter requirement is known as *mens rea*, or the "guilty mind." (Some statutes impose **strict liability** for lawbreaking: Finding that the commission of the act is sufficient to establish guilt, and a determination of *mens rea* is unnecessary. See also Chapter 2: The Consumer—Product Safety, Law: Modern Legal Remedies.) The common law held that a corporation was incapable of satisfying condition (2): It could not have a guilty mind. It followed from this that it would be inappropriate to punish a corporation, because, after all, it was not guilty of any wrongdoing.

Gradually, during the first quarter of this century, courts began to abandon this view, and today corporations are often subject to civil sanctions. A corporation can be held liable for the misconduct of its employees. (Company managers and subordinates can be held liable for their own civil and criminal wrongdoing. Managers can be liable for the wrongdoing of their subordinates, even if they were unaware of the misconduct, and subordinates are not necessarily absolved of responsibility simply because they were carrying out the unlawful orders of their managers.) So how is a corporation to be punished? In the famous words of an English jurist, a company has no pants to kick and no soul to damn, and of course it cannot be arrested and thrown in jail.

Yet a company can be fined, have its license revoked, or its property confiscated. As we will see below, the Sentencing Reform Act of 1984 specifies various formulae for determining just how much money a corporation must surrender in cash or property, depending on the seriousness of the offense and the degree of culpability.

Corporate Crime   Corporations can run afoul of the law in any one of the areas that occupy our study in this book. A manufacturer who sells a defective product can be found liable for injuries resulting from the defect, and punished accordingly. Although a corporation cannot be imprisoned, it can be fined and forced to surrender very large amounts of money. Similarly, a company that engages in discriminatory employment practices can also be found guilty of wrongdoing and compelled to compensate the person so wronged, either by reinstatement or issuing back pay, or both. And, again, a corporate polluter may be severely fined for dumping hazardous or toxic waste. These legal wrongs are perpetrated against consumers, employees, and ordinary citizens, all of whom can bring lawsuits against the offending firm. But corporations can also engage in illegal conduct against other corporations. One of the most common occurrences of business-on-business crime is the attempt to appropriate a trade secret. Literally billions of dollars are at stake here, not only in measures taken to protect such secrets, but in the profits to be realized by their misappropriation.

A trade secret is basically information of some sort that gives a company a competitive advantage over others because the information is not known (for more on trade secrets, see Chapter 4: The Employee—Whistleblowing and Loyalty, Law: Employee Loyalty). This competitive advantage can be eliminated if the secret is uncovered, hence corporations have a powerful incentive to obtain these lucrative facts, and the owners of trade secrets have just as much motivation to keep them concealed. For many years, it was a settled matter of law that it is illegal to obtain a trade secret by trespassing on a corporation's property, or by breaking and entering, or by violating a duty of confidentiality. But what if the information was secured without any illegal conduct at all? As we will see below, this question confronted the courts in the seminal case of *E.I. DuPont DeNemours & Company v. Christopher*, a case that set new standards for *industrial espionage* and, along with other litigation, eventually produced federal laws against stealing trade secrets.

Selected Cases, Statutes, and Regulations

***First National Bank of Boston v. Bellotti*, 435 U.S. 765 (1978)**   The First Amendment to the Constitution announces, in part, that "Congress shall make no law...abridging the freedom of speech."

This right of free speech has at once been among the most cherished and the most controversial features of our Constitution. The freedom to speak our minds is one of the defining qualities of Americans and the American way of life, but the last century has seen much debate centered on the scope of this right: Does it allow a person to say *anything*? If not, what principles limit the right? In recent years, a new facet of the controversy has emerged in the business world. Does a corporation have the right to freely express itself? Commercial speech extolling the virtues of a company's product must be truthful and accurate (see Chapter 2: The Consumer—Advertising, Selected Cases; Federal Trade Commission Act), so corporations are not free to express themselves with false or inaccurate advertising. But what about corporate speech concerning matters of public interest? Should a corporation be allowed to exert influence on the electorate?

In the fall of 1976 a proposition was to appear on a general election ballot in Massachusetts. The proposition asked voters if they would approve an amendment to the state constitution permitting the legislature to impose a graduated tax on the income of individuals. The First National Bank of Boston, along with another banking association and three corporations, strenuously opposed the ballot question, believing that it would have profoundly detrimental effects on the state economy. They wanted to make their view available to the general public by purchasing space and time in numerous media outlets around the state. Unfortunately, a state law specifically prohibited a corporation or business association from spending any money for the purpose of influencing voters, unless the ballot question directly affected the business; furthermore, the statute explicitly stated that issues concerning income tax do not directly affect business. The plaintiffs sought a legal opinion on publicizing their position on the proposition, and State Attorney General Bellotti informed them that doing so would be a violation of the law.

The Massachusetts Supreme Court agreed with Bellotti that the state was permitted to limit corporate speech in this way. Massachusetts, Bellotti argued, has a compelling interest in maintaining voter autonomy, free from corporate persuasion, and in protecting stockholders who disagree with management opinions. The United States Supreme Court rejected this argument. Writing for a five to four majority, Justice Lewis Powell pointed out that there was no evidence whatever that corporations were interfering with voters' independence, and, moreover, the limitation on corporate expression obtained even if stockholders unanimously agreed with the corporation's opinion. He went on to say that the First Amendment provided no support for the view that "speech that otherwise would be within the protection of the 1st Amendment loses that protection simply because its source is a corporation." It is unconstitutional, Powell concluded, for a legislature to determine what subjects may be discussed or who may discuss them, whether a person or a corporation.

Sentencing Reform Act of 1984, 18 USC §§3551 *et seq.* This statute established the United States Sentencing Reform Commission. The commission was charged with developing sentencing guidelines for federal judges to follow in the sentencing of criminals. Although called guidelines, the standards set forth by the commission are not mere recommendations but are considered binding rules. In 1991 the commissioners issued their standards for sentencing organizational defendants, focusing on corporations, but also including partnerships, labor unions, unincorporated organizations and associations, and other sorts of business enterprises. The keystone in the guidelines is a series of formulas that are utilized to calculate the fines imposed on guilty corporations. The leading idea behind the formulas is that the amount of the fine should be a function of the severity of the offense and the firm's degree of culpability.

The level of offense is determined by the seriousness of the crime, the amount of loss suffered by the victim, and the amount of planning that went into the violation. The various numerically ordered offense levels are correlated with base fines of various amounts: For example, crimes at level six and lower involve a base fine of $5000, while those at or above level 38 carry a fine of $72.5 million.

Once the offense level is set, the *culpability score* is calculated. This variable is essentially a multiplier applied to the base fine coordinate with the offense level; the fine will be increased if the culpability is high, decreased if it is low. The maximum multiplier is four, so that a corporation (1) employing more than 5,000 people with (2) a prior history of similar criminal conduct, where (3) corporate officers were involved in or tolerated the criminal activity, and (4) court orders were violated or investigations obstructed, would have the base fine for the particular offense multiplied four times. A culpability score of less than zero will reduce the base fine; for example, a $10 million base fine times 0.2 results in an actual fine of $2 million. Subzero scores can be achieved if the company had an effective program to prevent and detect violations before the offense occurred, and if the misconduct was reported by the company itself, followed by cooperation with authorities and acceptance of responsibility.

***E.I. DuPont DeNemours & Company v. Christopher*, 431 F.2d 1012 (5th Cir. 1970)**   This is the leading case in what is known as *industrial espionage*: corporations stealing trade secrets from one another. It marked the first time that the issue reached the federal appellate court level, and the case was considered for review by the Supreme Court, although the request was ultimately denied. The primary importance of *DuPont* is that it established exactly how acquiring a trade secret could be illegal even when the usual circumstances formerly held to make the acquisition unlawful are absent. Until this time, a plaintiff needed to show that the accused had obtained the trade secret by breaching a confidential relationship, by trespass, by robbery, or through some other illegal conduct. In this case, none of these illegal behaviors were employed by the defendants. Just as significant, this case was one of the major factors that eventually produced the Uniform Trade Secrets Act and the Economic Espionage Act (see both below).

In March 1969 the DuPont Company was well along in constructing a new plant in Beaumont, Texas. The purpose of the facility was to produce methanol, and DuPont had invested a great deal of time and expense into developing an original process. The company regarded this process as a trade secret, and so it made a further investment to protect this valuable information. A tall fence topped with barbed wire was erected around the entire site, all doors and gates into the site were equipped with locks and attended by a security guard, and no admittance was allowed without proper identification. On this March morning, employees noticed a single-engine plane circling above the plant; it made a number of passes and then flew away. By that same afternoon, an investigation by DuPont personnel revealed that the plane was occupied by two brothers, Rolfe and Gary Christopher, and they had taken a number of aerial photographs of the construction site.

In its complaint, DuPont noted that since the construction of the plant was not complete, parts of the new methanol production process were exposed to view from directly above the construction site; photographs taken from this vantage point would allow a person well versed in methanol production to determine what the new process was. DuPont sued the Christophers, claiming that they had illegally obtained the company's trade secret. The company demanded that the photos be handed over and the name of the firm that had hired the brothers be disclosed. Further, DuPont asked both for damages to cover losses sustained as a result of the circulation of the photos, and an injunction to prevent any further circulation.

The Christophers defended themselves by pointing out that they had not committed any legal wrong with their aerial photography. Their activities occurred in public airspace, they did not violate any federal aviation regulation, they had no duty of confidentiality to DuPont, and they did not engage in any other fraudulent or illegal conduct.

Judge Goldberg of the Fifth Circuit Court of Appeals agreed with the Christophers that none of the standard grounds for identifying theft of trade secrets applied in this case. Nonetheless, he rejected the notion that only these traditional factors signify illegal acquisition of a trade secret. The crucial issue is whether or not the secret was obtained properly or improperly. According to Goldberg, *proper* or lawful methods include *reverse engineering*— that is, acquiring a product from a competitor and taking it apart to see how it works—or discovering the covert process through independent investigation and research. *Improper* or illegal methods of acquisition avoid expending the energy, time, and money required for such engineering and discovery, and simply take the secret from the corporation without permission and when precautions to maintain the secrecy have been employed. This sort of avoidance and taking was precisely what the Christophers did. DuPont won their lawsuit.

Uniform Trade Secrets Act of 1985, National Conference of Commissioners on Uniform State Laws   This is a piece of model legislation, drafted by experts in the law. Like other sorts of *uniform laws*, such as the Uniform Commercial Code (see Chapter 2: The Consumer—Product Safety, Law: Modern Legal Remedies), the UTSA is purely advisory. It is a model of what the law should be, and does not have legal force until it is incorporated into state or federal statutes by legislators. As of this writing, 40 states have enacted various statutes that closely follow the UTSA, so its provisions are fairly representative of state law in this area. The Economic Espionage Act of 1996 (see below), the first federal law criminalizing the theft of trade secrets, may or may not supersede the UTSA, depending on the wishes of state legislatures. Together, the two acts provide a comprehensive picture of trade secrets law.

UTSA prohibits the misappropriation of a trade secret by any person. A **trade secret** is defined as information, a formula, program, device, pattern, method, technique, or process that (1) derives economic value from not being generally known, and (2) is the subject of reasonable efforts to maintain its secrecy. *Person* here refers to any natural person, and any commercial or legal entity, such as a corporation or a government agency. The crucial element of *misappropriation* is defined in two different ways: (1) the acquisition of a trade secret by a person who knows the trade secret was acquired by improper means; (2) disclosure or use of a trade secret without consent by a person who (a) used improper means to acquire the trade secret, or (b) received the trade secret from someone else who used improper means to acquire it. *Improper means* includes theft, bribery, misrepresentation, breach of a duty to maintain secrecy, or espionage through electronic or other methods (see above, *E.I. DuPont DeNemours & Company v. Christopher*).

The courts may issue injunctions ordering that the misappropriation, especially the use of a trade secret, be halted, and actions designed to protect trade secrets may also be ordered. Damages awarded to injured parties can include both the actual loss and the unjust enrichment caused by the misappropriation, and this amount can be doubled in cases of willful and malicious misappropriation. Attorney's fees may also be awarded.

Economic Espionage Act of 1996, 18 U.S.C. §§1831–1839   Unlike the *Uniform Trade Secrets Act* (UTSA; see above), which has been adopted by most of the states, this federal law (EEA) makes the theft of trade secrets a criminal offense. This act gives the U.S. attorney general and staff of the Justice Department the authority to prosecute the theft of trade secrets in the United States or internationally, whether obtained electronically (such as from the Internet) or by stealing a piece of paper. The EEA forbids any person from using a trade secret for his or her own benefit, or for the benefit of others, with the intention that or knowing that such use will injure the owner of the trade secret. Moreover, attempts or conspiracies to acquire or use trade secrets are also proscribed.

Like the UTSA, *person* means not only individual human beings, but all manner of business enterprises and organizations, as well as government entities. Illegal acquisition of a trade secret includes nearly every conceivable means, including theft, concealment, deception, drawings, sketches, downloads, transmissions, copying, photocopying, or in some other way duplicating without consent. It is also illegal to receive, buy, or possess a trade secret knowing that it has been misappropriated by another person.

The definition of a trade secret is essentially the same for the EEA as that offered by the UTSA, although expanded slightly to account for developments in the technology of creating and storing information. As with the UTSA, trade secrets are so designated because they have economic value and because reasonable attempts have been made to conceal the information. The big difference between the EEA and the UTSA comes from the sanctions applied for offenses. Under the UTSA, violations were subject only to civil penalties: These are misdemeanors in which fines are determined by the money made and lost. With the EEA, the penalties are much stiffer: Individual violators can be imprisoned for as many as ten years, 15 if the information benefits foreign entities, and fined $500,000. Corporations may be fined up to $5 million, or $10 million if the offense "benefits a foreign government, instrumentality, or agent." It should be noted that the attorney general is not required to seek criminal indictments first: Injunctions to stop the misappropriation and protect the owner of the trade secret may be issued at any time in the legal proceedings.

Further, the EEA allows the U.S. government to seize any property obtained from the proceeds of violations, or any property used or intended to be used in committing a violation. Finally, the EEA applies to offenses committed outside the United States, if an individual is a U.S. citizen or resident alien, or if a corporation was incorporated or organized in this country.

Corporate Social Responsibility

In our discussion of corporate structure, we said that the goal of a business corporation is to supply a product or service for a profit. The issue of corporate social responsibility raises the issue of whether this compound goal is sufficient. Should corporations also actively promote the good of others by contributing to social and charitable causes?

The Nobel Laureate, Milton Friedman, argues that corporations should focus on business, not society. In "The Social Responsibility of Business is to Increase Its Profits" (1970), first printed in *The New York Times Magazine*, Friedman argues that the free market system in which business operates is set up to benefit all *as long as managers pursue profits*. These social benefits can be measured by jobs and products. The pursuit of profit also protects the property rights of stockholders, who own the company. The owners invested their money on the condition that managers increase profits, not social well-being (see the discussion of corporate structure, above). Social well-being, argues Friedman, is the duty of the government.

R. Edward Freeman (1984, 1997) and others insist that corporate responsibility extends much further than the production of products for profits. Freeman argues for a **stakeholder view** of corporate responsibility, which he contrasts with Friedman's more narrow stockholder view. According to the stakeholder view, all those with legitimate stakes in the corporation need to be considered by managers. These include stockholders, but are not limited to them. Typically, stakeholders also include customers, employees, communities in which the company operates, suppliers, and creditors: all those who are significantly affected in various ways by corporate conduct. The newest addition to the stakeholder theory is the natural world. Some have argued that domesticated and wild animals, plants, even entire species and ecosystems should be included among those with a stake in the consequences of business activity (for more details, see Chapter 5: The Environment—Environmental Ethics).

The disagreement between Friedman and Freeman hinges on an issue known as the **agency problem**. An agent is someone who acts for another, called the **principal**. The traditional view of their relationship is that the principal hires the agent to do things the principal cannot or does not want to do. For example, we go to a physician when we are sick because the physician has knowledge and expertise that we do not. The physician acts as our agent. Because the physician has much more knowledge than we do, we must *trust* him to act in ways that are good for us. For example, when a physician says that we should have an expensive operation, he should recommend this because it is in our interest, not because he wants to buy a new Mercedes.

Almost all business as we know it today depends on managers acting as agents for others. The traditional stockholder view, espoused by Friedman, argues that managers should act to promote the economic welfare of owners, subject only to restraints provided by the law. This is a narrow view of what is required of management. Freeman, advocating his stakeholder view, claims that managers should act as agents for *all* those affected by the corporation, and thus adopts a wider view of those to whom managers owe obligations; these duties go well beyond making money for the company's owners.

We will take the managerial point of view when examining the different ethical theories. In this context, agency is a decidedly ethical issue, because it concerns the moral obligations of managers to a host of beneficiaries who are affected by corporate behavior. However, we cannot fully understand the moral issues unless we examine the economic relationships of business. Since the issue of corporate social responsibility concerns business obligations that go beyond legal rules, in this section we omit a discussion of law.

Ethics

Promoting Self-interest: Egoism   Aggressively self-interested managers could favor either the traditional stockholder view or the stakeholder view, depending on which view is more likely to be in their interest. It might seem that these self-interested managers would prefer the traditional view, because they will have fewer constituencies to serve. However, the stakeholder view could also be very appealing to aggressively self-interested managers. With so many constituencies, it will be harder to monitor managerial decisions, giving managers more opportunities to pursue their own interests.

There are two reasons why the stakeholder view will give aggressively self-interested managers more opportunities to pursue their interests. First, the corporate structure has been designed to protect shareholders, not stakeholders. This means that managers can represent self-serving behavior as promoting stakeholder interests. Imagine that the husband of a CEO sets up a charity for unwed mothers. The husband, however, uses most of the donations to pay his own salary, leaving very little for the unwed mothers. His wife, as CEO, can contribute a great deal of money to this charity on the grounds that these unwed mothers are stakeholders: They live in the communities in which her husband's company does business. The end result, however, is that the CEO and her husband get rich while appearing to serve the poor and underprivileged.

Contemplative, self-interested managers could also prefer either the stockholder or the stakeholder theory, depending on which one is likely to give them more peace of mind. The stakeholder theory would be appealing because managers are more likely to know about conflicts in advance, allowing them to prepare for them. However, the stockholder view could also be appealing because the rules and laws governing managerial behavior have been developed to fit with the stockholder view. These rules and laws create expectations of how managers should act. Violating these expectations can cause considerable conflict. Granted, this could cause other stakeholders to cause conflict, but senior managers are insulated against this conflict unless it escalates into a regional or national problem.

Nurturing Personal Relationships: Care   Passive carers, it would seem, would favor the stockholder theory over the stakeholder theory because there are fewer stakeholders to serve. If a passive caring manager were to use a stakeholder theory, his or her job could easily be unworkable. It is very unlikely that there is a solution that could satisfy groups as diverse as laborers, suppliers, owners, and the community, to mention only a few.

Active caring managers who hold the stockholder view would also have a difficult time. Their major problem is that the stockholder theory is founded on the belief that managers should promote the good of owners even if that is very disruptive to other stakeholders. If closing a plant will benefit the owners more than any other act, these managers would have to believe that doing so will promote caring relationships. However, when they see the damage to families and the poverty that follows plant closings, they would have a hard time believing that this is the best way to encourage caring relationships.

Active caring managers who adopt the stakeholder view would also have quite a task. From this point of view, stakeholders are tied together in a complex web of relationships (Wicks, *et. al.* 1994). Because it is a central tenet of the care ethic that caring for one person does not justify treating others badly, these managers would have to obtain huge amounts of information before acting.

Unlike the passive caring managers, these active carers would not be bound by the current interests of the different stakeholders. Instead, they would look for solutions that help stakeholders develop better relationships with each other and with the company. By actively trying to reinterpret the interests of stakeholders, these managers have a better chance than passive caring managers to bring stakeholders together.

Promoting the Good of the Group: Utilitarianism   Strict utilitarian managers would tend toward the stockholder view for two reasons. First, they would argue that management's social role is to pursue profits within legal constraints. Pursuing profits creates jobs, satisfies consumer demand, and promotes efficiency. Efficiency is important because it reduces prices and saves valuable resources for future use. It is the social role of government to pursue social goods like justice, fairness, and equality. If corporations try to provide consumer goods and promote social goals, they will do both jobs badly.

Second, strict utilitarian managers would prefer the stockholder view because it gives self-interested managers the least chance to enrich themselves at the expense of society. This is because the restraints on managers have been developed according to the stockholder model.

Finally, strict utilitarian managers would point out that corporations generate and have access to a tremendous amount of money. As such, corporations provide a tempting target for stakeholder groups. Any policy that gives self-interested people outside the corporation power over what goes on inside the corporation would be detrimental to corporations, and therefore to society itself. Consider the case of Maytag. Maytag decided to close a plant that made vending machines, and the workers sued Maytag for breach of contract. The employees stated that they had asked managers several times if their jobs were secure, and the managers answered that the jobs were secure. When Maytag closed the plant, lawyers for the employees argued that these statements made by management created an implicit contract to keep the plant open. The case ended in the summer of 1995 with the employees being awarded $11.5 million (Kilbourn 1995).

The Maytag case is just the kind of thing strict utilitarian managers fear: uncertainty about who has rights to corporate resources and who can make decisions about corporate property. If management constantly fears lawsuits by stakeholder groups who think they have been wronged, managers cannot make the best economic decisions about production and marketing. This will have a chilling effect on productivity and the economic welfare of the nation.

Flexible utilitarian managers would tend to support the stakeholder view. These managers would agree that they should promote the interests of owners, but they would point out that products and the processes by which they are produced are much more dangerous than they were when corporations first appeared in the nineteenth century. Environmental pollution from chemical and nuclear waste are new problems and managers need to have the flexibility to deal with them. The production and trade in weapons also poses many more dangers than it did in the early days of corporate formation.

Consider the case of the "cop-killer" bullet. These bullets get their name from their capacity to pierce body armor (bulletproof garments), which are worn mainly by police. The bullets were outlawed by a federal statute, but the statute defined them as made of metal. The new cop-killer bullet was made of plastic. The company at first defended its product as allowed by the law. Public reaction was so negative, however, that the company withdrew the bullet until the law could be clarified (*New York Times* 1995a). A flexible rule utilitarian stakeholder manager would have considered the social impact of the bullet at the development stage, and could have stopped production until the law governing these kinds of bullets was clarified.

Finally, flexible rule utilitarian managers would point out that stakeholders have interests that they pursue by appealing to the legislative and judicial branches of government. Think for a moment about these stakeholders and their interests. Consumers have an interest in safe products. Individuals living in communities in which business operates have an interest in having a clean environment. Labor has an interest in getting fair and adequate compensation, and the list goes on. Unless corporations account for the interests of these stakeholders, especially when they are adversely affected by management decisions, those stakeholders will appeal to legislatures and the courts for regulation and restitution. These appeals can be more costly to management than considering stakeholders' interests in the first place.

Flexible rule utilitarian managers would have a completely different view of the Maytag plant closing case discussed above. Instead of viewing it as a problem with flexible rules, they would view it as one event in the continuing evolution of contract law. Managers who are not aware of this evolution, which has been going on for centuries, are bound to be harmed by it. Managers who understand the evolution of law, and are not captured by the myth of strict rules, can use this flexibility to promote the well-being of their corporations and of society as a whole.

The evolution of law is hard to see in areas like contract law because it moves so slowly. But in other areas, like law governing the Internet, the evolution is noticeable, as business people, academics, private persons, nonprofit organizations, and others fight for rules that will promote their own views of what the Internet will look like (Harmon 1998).

Respecting Dignity and Rights: Intrinsic Value A manager committed to respecting human dignity would tend toward the stakeholder model. This is the position that Freeman (1997) takes. Respecting human dignity means that those affected by a corporate decision have the opportunity to voice their concerns. A key word here is *opportunity*. Managers should not coerce stakeholders into giving their views about managerial decisions. The focus on opportunity, however, means that stakeholders must be given enough information to make an informed decision about whether to express their voice.

The human dignity approach to the Maytag case would be a very different one than either of the utilitarian views discussed above. The focus on dignity would require these managers to respect employees as free, choosing beings, who need good information. The Maytag managers' statements were promises, which the employees took seriously. On the basis of these promises, employees bought houses, cars, and planned for vacations. Note that it is not important to this analysis whether the managers lied or were mistaken. What is important is that they obligated the company in particular ways.

A manager committed to respecting property rights would tend to support the stockholder view, since stockholders are the only ones who have clearly defined property rights to the corporation. Such a manager would have several objections to the stakeholder view.

First, managers have explicit contracts, which are legally enforced promises, to promote shareholder wealth. Managers should not, of course, harm innocent stakeholders in their pursuit of profit. But this does not mean that they have an obligation to *help* innocent stakeholders live better lives. To do this with company money and time is to cheat the stockholders out of their dividends and capital gains. In the Maytag case, however, these property rights managers could agree with the human dignity managers. If the Maytag managers did make explicit promises that the plant would stay open, and if employees did not pursue other job opportunities on the basis of these promises, managers contracted away their right to close the plant when they did.

Managers committed to respecting human dignity have at least two responses to the property rights view. First, they would argue that it is not always easy to tell what is in the best interest of stockholders. Suppose that managers have three plans from which to choose, and each of them seems to promote shareholder financial interests equally well. Suppose further that two of these alternatives would have terrible consequences for nonowning stakeholders, and that the third alternative benefits nonowning stakeholders. In this case, managers should promote the interests of *nonowning* stakeholders

Second, a corporation can have goals that include more than promoting the financial interests of the owners. Companies can be committed to all sorts of causes, like cleaning up the environment, or fostering cultural diversity. Levi Stauss, for example, won the 1997 Ron Brown Award for Corporate Leadership, which honors companies for enhancing the well-being of their employees and the communities in which they live. Levi Strauss won this award for its continuing commitment to the promotion of racial diversity and harmony; this commitment goes back at least 40 years, when the company integrated its workforce before there were laws requiring it (The Conference Board 1998b). A corporation adopting goals that are not ultimately financial ones does not violate its fiduciary duty to the owners as long as they are made aware of this; potential owners should also be given prior notice that such goals are being pursued.

Economics

Society   Whether society is better off with managers acting from the stockholder or stakeholder view is a descriptive *and* a normative issue. The stockholder view promotes social well-being as long as the law and the rest of the economic infrastructure are designed so that the pursuit of corporate interest is (usually) going to promote social interest. The discussion of the consumer in Chapter 2, above, and of antitrust issues, below, provide a great deal of evidence that the legal and economic infrastructure historically has not provided this safe background, and the economic incentives to do so are still meager.

Another problem with the stockholder view is found in a feature that we would normally think of as virtue: the insistence that managers be free to pursue profits in all legal ways. This will effectively curb socially destructive management behavior only if those who make the laws are independent of the business community. However, business groups are constantly trying to affect government policy in ways that are good for business, but not necessarily good for the society as a whole (Wood 1994). Lobbyists from many industries converge on Washington, D.C., and state legislatures, and try to influence lawmakers to write statutes and regulations that promote their special interests, which can conflict with wider group interests. The reader should note that this argument does not mean that ethical managers should break the law—that would be absurd. The argument only tries to establish that following the law may well not be enough to ensure that managers promote social good as well as corporate good. One way to do this is to pay attention to many stakeholders.

Even though the social weaknesses of the stockholder view may push us to the stakeholder view, it is not at all clear that managers using their consciences to promote a good society are going to create a better society than managers promoting the interests of owners. One problem with the stakeholder model is that managers would have a difficult time coordinating information about social projects, which would be necessary for such projects to be successful. Two other problems are those mentioned by Milton Friedman (1970): Managers are not trained to promote social goods, nor do they have a political mandate to change society.

Although these problems with the stakeholder theory are real, they merely show that stakeholder interests must be pursued with caution, especially in unclear cases. Many cases are clear, however. Managers would not be accused of imposing their values on others if their explicit policy was that all corporate members should treat each other with courtesy and respect. As we saw in our discussion of human dignity and rights, above, Levi Strauss received an award for doing this very thing. Nor would managers be accused of imposing their own social agenda if they told their sales staff, as they do at Whetherill Associates, that their first obligation is to make sure that customers get the right product, even if that means referring them to a competitor (Paine 1994).

Just as there can be widespread agreement about the benefits of acting in particular ways, there is also widespread agreement about the harms of acting in particular ways. Similarly, a manager can refuse to dump dangerous chemicals in a river that supplies drinking water, even if it is legal, and even if it increases profits. Here the harm is so clear, judging it wrong does not rely on an idiosyncratic view about social good.

Consumers Consumers are likely to reject the stockholder view, since consumer interests can easily be disregarded in a way that promotes the interests of owners. Granted, the market provides substantial checks on this, because a company can succeed only if consumers are satisfied with its products. However, as we noted in Chapter 2: The Consumer, there are many cases in which the market fails to punish companies who reward owners at the expense of consumers.

Although consumers should prefer the stakeholder view, they are not the only stakeholder that management needs to consider. Managers could defer to employees or suppliers in a particular case that would put consumers at risk. Because of this, consumers are likely to prefer a dignity- or rights-based stakeholder approach, since that approach will always consider their interests as important in themselves. This does not guarantee that consumers would always get what they want, only that they are fairly considered.

Producers It would seem that producers should be in favor of the stockholder view, because law and popular opinion emphasizes this **fiduciary** relationship. However, there are many good reasons to prefer the stakeholder view. One reason is that producers are likely to get better information using the stakeholder view, enabling them to make decisions that are more likely to work. Sometimes, these decisions may not favor owners, at least in the short term. For example, when the Tylenol scare occurred in the 1980s, Johnson & Johnson (J&J) immediately recalled all the Tylenol in the United States (see Chapter 2: The Consumer). Senior managers did this against the advice of their legal staff, who worried that a recall would be viewed as an admission of guilt if J&J were sued. Marketing people at J&J also worried that the recall would hurt the Tylenol brand more than the poisonings themselves.

The legal and marketing staff at J&J turned out to be wrong. The recall established J&J as a trustworthy producer that was willing to accept responsibility. Indeed, not long after the crisis, the Tylenol brand once again became a market leader. J&J's recall promoted owner interests in the long run, yet it was the corporation's focus on consumer well-being that motivated the recall. Focusing on the consumer, not surprisingly, benefitted the owners of this consumer-driven company.

International Issues

International issues in corporate social responsibility are very similar to domestic issues. One difference is that there is no single government that can coordinate or sanction these special efforts. A second difference is the variety of cultures involved; what might count as social responsibility in one country may be an insult, or even illegal, in another country.

Still, there are some clear cases of corporations going beyond their legal duties. One of the most famous is Merck's approach to the disease of river blindness, a disease that affects millions of poor people in third-world countries. Merck developed a drug to treat river blindness. They hoped that they could find a nonprofit organization, like the UN or the World Health Organization, to distribute and administer the drug. No organization was willing to do it (The Business Enterprise Trust 1991). At that point, Merck decided that the cure was too important to waste, and they decided to bear the full financial burden of making, distributing, and administering the drug. Did this hurt Merck financially? Judging by its current price, the answer is "no." Merck has one of the best-performing stocks in the past two years.

Why did Merck spend all this money on a project that was guaranteed to lose money? The surface answer is that the company's mission statement asserts that the company focus is on relieving human sickness and promoting health. The deeper answer, perhaps, is that this commitment cannot be fulfilled by only pursuing projects that are likely to be profitable. If Merck discovers a drug that can cure millions of people of a terrible disease, but the afflicted cannot pay, what should the company do? If they do not develop the drug, that would send a message to scientists that they should not pursue unprofitable projects, which can hinder their science as well as their spirit. By pursuing the drug to cure river blindness, Merck was telling its scientists, "You do the research, we'll take care of the company." This is a message that research scientists love to hear. It makes them more productive, and so benefits Merck and its owners.

Antitrust Issues

Antitrust laws and regulations are designed to promote competitive markets. They first arose in the United States at the end of the nineteenth century as a response to the behavior of companies like Standard Oil, which captured most of the oil market, and the E.C. Knight Company, which captured 98 percent of the sugar market (for more details, see below, Law).

As we saw above, in the section on the nature and structure of the corporation, reduced risk to owners and managers, along with growing markets, make it possible for corporations to amass great wealth. At the turn of the century, this wealth allowed commodities like oil, sugar, and tobacco, to be dominated by one company even though there was no economic reason for this high level of dominance (see Chapter 1: Introduction—The Tools of Business Ethics, Economics). These companies used their size and increased bargaining power to drive out competitors, not to supply superior products and reasonable prices (Gwartney and Stroup 1982).

When a company obtains a monopoly, or joins with others to form a **trust** (see also below, Law), it is almost impossible to compete with it. For example, if an entrepreneur were to start up an oil company to compete with Standard Oil, Standard Oil could undercut its new competitor's prices. Because of its size, Standard Oil could sell its products at a loss until the competitor went out of business, and then raise its prices once more. This strategy not only drove competitors out of the market in the 1870s and 1880s, but it kept competitors from coming in.

A political movement, called **Populism**, began to grow during that time, and exerted pressure on the government to stop these monopolies (Lambe and Spekman 1997). Populists believed that the new concentration of wealth associated with the growth of large corporations was inconsistent with the political and economic origins of the United States. What were those origins? Before the Civil War, businesses were small, and the economy was agrarian. With businesses being roughly equal in size, and dealing mostly with local markets, no business could dominate another one except by producing a better product at a lower price, which is the goal of competition.

Populists had motives and a rationale for their dislike of monopolies and trusts. It is helpful to distinguish motives from rationales because having bad or questionable motives does not mean that one's rationale is bad. A *motive* is a personal reason for acting; a *rationale* is a justification for action. For example, your motive for going to the grocery store could be that you are out of your favorite cereal; your rationale is that your family is out food. Often, motives and rationales are the same. In the case of going to the grocery store, your motive and rationale could be the same: your family needs food.

Populists had motives that were many and varied. One motive was anger at losing a way of life that would never return, and many were jealous of the growing number of wealthy business people. We are not concerned with motives here, but with rationales. The major rationale was that free markets are the best way to ensure individual freedom. At the surface level, this freedom is expressed in the ability of producers to enter and exit markets at will. It was this freedom that monopolies and trusts violated.

At a deeper level, market freedom is about the hopes and aspirations that are expressed in the U.S. Declaration of Independence. If a few companies and families own most of the wealth, and can successfully exploit the mechanisms of law to keep others from becoming wealthy, we will end up with a class system in which people are not treated equally, and are not guaranteed the right to life, liberty, and the pursuit of happiness, or property.

Ethics

Promoting Self-interest: Egoism Whether aggressively self-interested managers would be in favor of antitrust laws would depend on whether the specific laws in question benefitted them. For example, Bill Gates, founder and CEO of Microsoft, is aggressively fighting a lawsuit brought by the Justice Department that alleges Microsoft is violating antitrust laws (*New York Times* 1997b). Microsoft Windows dominates the market for operating systems used in personal computers. However, its dominance in this market is not the problem, because there is general agreement that Windows became popular because it fit better with existing technology and served the needs of business and consumers at lower costs than competitor operating systems. The Justice Department suit concerns how Microsoft is using its legitimate dominance with Windows to gain an unfair advantage in the market for Internet browsers. Specifically, the suit charges that Microsoft is designing new versions of Windows so that it runs much better with Microsoft Internet Explorer than with its major competitor, Netscape Navigator. This violates Section 3 of the *Clayton Act* (see Selected Cases, below) which prohibits **tying arrangements**. Tying arrangements occur when a company makes the purchase of one product conditional on the sale of another. Say that Black & Decker would sell its cordless drills to Target only if Target would also buy its battery chargers; this would be an illegal tying arrangement (see also *Eastman Kodak Company v. Image Technical Services, Inc.*, in Law, below).

This battle has found its way into the U.S. Senate. In November 1997 Orin Hatch said: "Microsoft now has the ability to virtually annihilate any competitive product it wants by bringing it into the next version of Windows;" he added that "there's evidence that they [Microsoft] are *aggressively* seeking to extend that monopoly to the Internet, and policy makers have to be concerned about it" (Wilke 1997, emphasis added). Texas is also suing Microsoft for interfering with the state's efforts to investigate Microsoft for violation of Texas antitrust law. Texas claims that Microsoft has required producers who use its operating system to inform them before they give any information to state or federal authorities about Microsoft (*New York Times* 1997c).

Aggressively self-interested managers who are not managing monopolies should be in favor of antitrust laws because these laws would increase their opportunities to become wealthy. For example, the CEO of Netscape has said that he is in favor of the Justice Department's suit against Microsoft, and blames the loss of Netscape's market share on Microsoft's monopolistic practices.

Contemplative self-interested individuals, who think that it is in their interest to work less and live a more retiring life, are unlikely to become managers, and so this issue would not arise. However, there are a growing number of managers, sometimes referred to as *downshifters*, who have become disenchanted with the hectic pace of business (Noble 1994). They have quit their high-paying, high-stress jobs in order to take up less demanding pursuits. Those tempted by downshifting who work for monopolies might welcome antitrust laws precisely because it gives them another reason to quit.

Nurturing Personal Relationships: Care   Passive caring managers would pursue monopolies if doing so would please the important people in their lives. These managers are in a difficult position if the people they are trying to please have different views. For example, if one family member believes that managers should optimize financial returns, while another believes managers should provide a nurturing environment for mothers with small children, passive carers would be faced with a dilemma. A passive carer would have to decide which relationship was most important, and act to please the person in that relationship.

Active caring managers want to make sure that the people affected by their decisions are able to pursue projects of their own choosing. While antitrust law would prohibit some projects, such as price fixing, it would present far more and better opportunities for the cared-for than it prevents, because these people would be free to participate in the market of their choice, assuming they have the talent and the capital.

Still, it must be remembered that active caring managers are partial to personal, intimate relationships. By opening up more business opportunities, these caring managers are creating conditions in which people will spend time doing business instead of being with their families. Active carers need to pay attention to their own families. Further, being an active carer is a difficult, demanding approach to management. The more time these managers spend trying to create a system that benefits the personal relationships of others, the less time they will have for their own personal relationships.

Promoting the Good of the Group: Utilitarianism   Strict rule utilitarian managers would focus on the internal and external rules governing their jobs. If managers are expected to maximize shareholder wealth, and if trying to obtain a monopoly is a legal and effective way to do this, utilitarian managers would try to establish them.

In the United States, not all monopolies are illegal. **Natural monopolies**, like electric and gas utilities, are allowed, because adding other producers raises consumer prices (Samuelson and Nordhaus 1985; also see Chapter 1: Introduction—The Tools Of Business Ethics: Economics). As we will discuss in Economics, below, the thesis that there really are natural monopolies is becoming difficult to sustain. A company can also acquire a legal monopoly if the market dominance results from having a better product.

Flexible rule utilitarian managers would also try to pursue legal monopolies, and, under the right conditions, illegal monopolies. For example, managers might believe that the laws preventing monopolies are misguided. They would use their monopolistic behavior to challenge and, they hope, to change the law. Some analysts think that this is what Microsoft is doing in its fight with the Justice Department. Reports from Microsoft indicate that this battle is really about whether private companies or the federal government should control production and innovation in the software industry (Lohr and Markoff 1998).

Some economists, like Brian W. Arthur (1994), agree that the battle goes much deeper than the market for Internet browsers. However, Arthur construes the deeper battle somewhat differently than does Microsoft. Relying on a concept known as "path dependency," he argues that software is much different from oil and tobacco, the industries that were the target of the first federal antitrust laws. Software, especially operating systems, has economic properties that can make it a natural monopoly.

If a product has path-dependent characteristics, it becomes less expensive to use as more people use it. A computer operating system has path-dependent characteristics for several reasons; we mention two. First, once the operating system is developed, it is almost cost-free to reproduce it. In fact, the more people buy the operating system, the less it costs! Compare this to commodities like oil and lumber; the more we use lumber, the less of it there is, which tends to increase prices. Also, lumber requires a costly production and distribution system that must be constantly maintained. All of this increases the price of lumber over time.

The second reason that an operating system is different from other commodities is because word processing and spreadsheet programs have to be tailored to a particular operating system. Since people want to share data with each other, they must not only use the same word processing and spreadsheet programs, but they must also use the same operating system. So, it makes sense for consumers to choose the operating system used most by other people. While these reasons show how Windows may legitimately dominate the market, they do not hold equally well for Internet browsers. This second reason, for example, does not hold for browsers.

Respecting Dignity and Rights: Intrinsic Value   Managers relying on human dignity and fairness would focus on the process by which antitrust laws are enacted. If the process is fair, then the laws that come out of this process are fair.

If the laws that prohibit monopolistic behavior have been passed in a fair process, then these managers should obey the law. Saying this does not mean the managers think that the laws are good laws for promoting business or society, *only* that they are fair. If these managers thought that the country would be better off with different laws, they could very well encourage a change by hiring **lobbyists** or employing other means to change the law. This is what Sprint and MCI did in the early 1980s when they challenged the laws that let AT&T have a natural monopoly.

If monopolistic behavior is not legally prohibited, managers should pursue monopolies if that is the best way to maximize the financial well-being of the company. However, managers are also citizens. If they believe that allowing monopolies harms innocent people, they would pursue ways to make the laws more stringent. If promoting stricter antitrust laws is not in the best interest of their companies, these managers would have a conflict between their duty as citizens and their duty as corporate officers. Which duty they should fulfill would depend on how much damage the two courses of action would create.

Managers relying on a natural rights view would focus on the property rights of owners and their contractual obligation to promote the financial well-being of the owners. Natural rights managers could reject or support antitrust laws, depending on how they are written. They would reject antitrust laws as unnecessary impediments to business if they believed that such laws interfered with the property rights of owners. Like flexible rule utilitarians, they would be willing to pursue monopolistic behavior in order to challenge antitrust laws. Natural rights managers could also support antitrust laws if they thought that they allowed more people to exchange property rights (see the discussion of Nozick and Locke's Proviso in Chapter 1: Introduction—The Tool of Business Ethics).

International Issues

Monopolies at the global level can be at least as destructive as domestic monopolies. However, because we are dealing with business across borders, the opportunities for monopolies and the ways they can be restricted are different. One difference is that a nation can protect an industry from outside competition. If this industry has a monopoly or an **oligopoly** that is operating as a monopoly, the consumers of this nation will pay higher prices than they would in a competitive environment.

Japan has been accused of protecting its industries in the way just described. The Japanese government has made it difficult or impossible for foreign companies to compete in the retail industry, the computer industry, and the financial industry, to name only a few. However, international pressure is starting to change this. In December 1997 more than 100 countries, including the United States and Japan, signed an accord to open up domestic financial markets to foreign competition (Andrews 1997). Pressure from the world community prompted Japan to make this concession; representatives of many nations argued that since Japan has become rich selling their goods in other countries, Japan needs to open up its markets to foreign competition. In a separate agreement with the United States, signed earlier, Japan agreed to open its securities markets to U.S. firms. Once again, the issue of fairness and reciprocity arises. The United States is Japan's largest single customer. If Japan wants to sell its products here, it must let us sell our products there. This should benefit both countries, as the notion of **comparative advantage** suggests (see Chapter 1: Introduction—The Tools Of Business Ethics, Economics).

Lest we leave the impression that the United States and its companies are always on the right side of the monopoly debate, we should mention that Microsoft is also being investigated for antitrust activities in the **European Union** (Wolff 1997) and in Japan (Dow Jones Newswires 1997). The Europeans and the Japanese are interested in the same issues that have prompted the U.S. Department of Justice investigation: Is Microsoft tying its Internet browser to its software in a way that puts other browsers at a serious disadvantage?

Economics

Society   From the social-economic perspective, monopolies tend to reduce supply, lower quality, and raise prices, all of which are bad for society. Monopolies are good only in the case of *natural monopolies*.

Historically, natural monopolies occurred in industries that had infrastructural costs that were so high that it did not make sense to duplicate them, such as those that provide gas and electricity. In the gas industry, for example, hundreds of thousands of miles of pipelines had to be laid and maintained. If another company wanted to compete in providing gas in the same area, they too would have to lay and maintain pipelines. This would result in both companies charging higher prices, because each would have to cover the costs of their pipelines with fewer customers. Of course, companies do not enter markets when they know that they will have to charger higher prices than the current providers. It was market incentives that kept competitors out of the market, not the federal government, and this is why these monopolies were called natural. Most economists agree that natural monopolies require some sort of public oversight, because competition does not exist to keep prices down and quality high. Every state in the union has a public utilities commission to regulate these natural monopolies.

Natural monopolies are rapidly becoming a thing of the past, as new technology allows different providers to use the same infrastructure. The first example of this occurred with the court-ordered breakup of AT&T in the early 1980s. MCI and Sprint successfully argued that computer tracking and new switching systems allowed multiple companies to use the same phone lines and keep their billing separate. In the 1990s we find the same thing occurring for gas and electric utilities (Salpukis 1996).

Transforming natural monopolies into **oligopolies** does not eliminate the need for public oversight, but it does change the nature of that oversight, because oligopolies can easily collude to restrict supply, withhold technological advances, and keep prices high.

Consumers   Consumers want the best product price/quality ratio possible. Ideally, this ratio should occur at several price levels, as it does for automobiles, to enable people with different economic resources to purchase products.

Consumers are normally indifferent about the market structure that delivers their products as long as they get the quality and service they want at a fair price. One exception to this is the growing public belief in the value of free markets. Since the late 1970s, when President Carter began deregulating the airline industry, the American public has fairly consistently elected candidates who advocated more open markets and less government intervention. Unfortunately, oligopolistic market structures lend themselves to collusion, so forbearing to regulate corporations in oligopolies will likely result in unfree markets.

Producers   In an unregulated environment, producers would work to achieve monopolies, and failing that, oligopolies. The reason is simple: The fewer players there are in a market, the more power a producer has to manipulate product supply and quality in a way that benefits the producer. The more producers there are, the more power the consumers have, because consumer choice will drive producer behavior.

However, as we have discussed, some products can only be produced in oligopolies, thus limiting consumer choice. In this case, consumers turn to government to protect them from oligopolistic collusion, which restricts supply and innovation and results in price increases.

We should point out that the consumer demand for regulation conflicts with the consumer demand, noted above, for free, unregulated markets. We can understand this conflict if we focus on the consumer's desire to obtain the best product price/quality ratio. Consumers tend to believe that competition is the most efficient way to satisfy this desire. Yet they also find that producers in oligopolies (although consumers generally do not know enough economics to describe these producers in this way) are not very responsive to consumer demand, and in these cases consumers make their demands felt in the voting booth. What drives consumers in both cases is the desire for products with the best price/quality ratios, but they do not often see that the means they demand for this—regulated and unregulated markets—conflict.

Law

Antitrust law contains some of the most complicated and controversial legal rules found in American legislation and jurisprudence. Although the basic principle guiding the law in this area seems simple—businesses should treat each another and consumers fairly and honestly—putting that principle into practice is terribly difficult. There have been thousands of court cases and there are hundreds of state and federal statutes addressing antitrust law. All we can do here is summarize the most important congressional actions and provide an overview of some key or representative judicial findings. We begin with a brief outline of the historical factors that produced this complex legal morass.

The quarter century immediately following the Civil War saw the meteoric rise of big business in America. The economy of the country changed from one based on agriculture and a rural way of life to one based on industry and centered on large urban enclaves. Numerous factors have been cited for this development. Certainly among the most significant of these was a

Congress controlled by Republicans—a party traditionally dominated by business interests. Perhaps more important was a flood of European immigrants, and a steady flow of Americans into the cities, having abandoned a rural way of life. This created an enormous pool of cheap labor (see also Chapter 4: The Employee—Health and Safety, Law; Introduction). A dramatic increase in capital available to private investors paid for their work, and for a rapid succession of technological advances in production equipment, communication, and transportation. Large-scale manufacturing, which reduced cost per unit, along with centralized management, and diversified, national markets followed.

The primary outcome of these events was the formation of various **trusts**. In this context, a *trust* refers to a combination of several firms, initially competitors in the same market, that have banded together. With such unification, competition shifts to those who are not allied with the trust. Because the trust has enormous financial and material resources at its disposal, these unallied firms are at a severe disadvantage. Unable to compete, smaller businesses are either forced to cooperate with the trust or cease operations altogether. The industry is thus **monopolized**: One seller controls a market for a particular good or service. The problem with this state of affairs for consumers is that the absence of competition allows the monopoly to restrict the supply of the commodity in order to drive up prices and increase its profits. With the large labor pool, trusts also can exercise great control over the terms and conditions of employment (see Chapter 4: The Employee—Health and Safety, Terms and Conditions, Law).

By the late 1880s monopolies had been established in the oil, steel, coal, sugar, tobacco, and textile industries, and in the railroads, among others. Trusts had completely overthrown what had been the norm—balanced competition between businesses of approximately equal strength—and replaced it with corporate oligarchies enjoying near-total control. This practice became extremely unpopular with the American people. It was perceived by ordinary citizens and by Congress as terribly threatening to basic principles of fair and open competition, and distinctly contrary to the public interest.

Congress's first concerted attempt to rectify this situation was directed against the railroad industry, which had formed the first great business combination. The Interstate Commerce Act of 1887, 49 U.S.C. §§501–507, instituted federal regulation of the transportation of merchandise by rail, particularly grain. State regulation of the railroads had been repeatedly struck down by the courts as an unauthorized interference with interstate commerce. This act also created the first federal administrative agency, the Interstate Commerce Commission. Universal rather than industry-specific antitrust laws began three years later with the Sherman Antitrust Act of 1890 (see below, and also Chapter 4: The Employee—Terms and Conditions, Law: Labor Unions). The purpose of the Sherman Act, like all antitrust laws, was to promote good faith competition within industries and honest dealing with customers. Over the intervening 100 years and more, the concept of antitrust has been elaborated and refined in great detail.

Originally, under the Sherman Act, the penalty for violating an antitrust law was a fine of just $5,000 and no more than one year in jail. As recently as 1975 the maximum fine was still only $50,000—mere pocket change for a large company. Finally, in 1976 as part of the Antitrust Procedural Improvements Act (15 U.S.C. §1311), the sanctions were significantly increased to as much as $1 million for corporations for each violation, while individuals may be fined up to $250,000 and spend three years in prison. Today, following the Antitrust Amendments Act of 1990, the fines stand at $10 million for corporations and $350,000 for individuals. Court-ordered injunctions to cease the anticompetitive practices may be issued instead of, or in addition to, these penalties.

Responsibility for the enforcement of antitrust laws is relegated to these four entities:

1. **Justice Department.** The antitrust division of this executive branch agency is headed by the assistant attorney general and staffed by several hundred lawyers and economists. The Justice Department files charges of violations in the appropriate federal district court.

2. **Federal Trade Commission.** The FTC hears complaints of antitrust violations and makes decisions in these cases, and also issues trade regulations. The agency's decisions may be appealed through the federal circuit courts of appeal (for more on the FTC, see below, Selected Cases: Federal Trade Commission Act of 1914, and also Chapter 2: The Consumer—Advertising, Law).

3. **State regulations.** Many states have their own antitrust laws. Additionally, state attorneys general are authorized to file lawsuits in federal district courts on behalf of citizens of that state (this is called a *parens patriae* claim).

4. **Private citizens.** Any individual or corporation can seek damages or an injunction if they believe they have been injured by anticompetitive business practices. This feature is unique to antitrust law: corporations may be sued by the federal government, injured competitors, *and* private litigants. Because of this potential for attack on numerous fronts, many large corporations employ copious legal staffs that do nothing but antitrust work.

Not every type of business is subject to antitrust laws. Express exemptions have been established by various statutes, and the courts have identified other implied exemptions. These industries are either regulated by their own particular agencies or they are regarded as needing special protection. Some examples of exempted businesses include:

- **Regulated industries.** The banking, securities, communications, and transportation industries are governed by agencies devoted to their particular commodities.

- **Labor unions.** Congress has rejected the view that a person's labor is a commodity or article of commerce. Workers are permitted to band together without fear of illegally restraining trade (see Chapter 4: The Employee—Terms and Conditions of Employment, Selected Cases: Clayton Act).

- **Professional baseball.** In 1922 the Supreme Court held that because baseball was not engaged in interstate commerce, antitrust laws did not apply to it (*Federal Baseball Club of Baltimore, Inc. v. National League of Professional Baseball Clubs*, 259 U.S. 200 [1922]). This result was reaffirmed 50 years later (*Flood v. Kuhn*, 407 U.S. 258 [1972]), and attempts in Congress in 1995 to statutorily remove baseball's antitrust exemption failed.

Selected Cases, Statutes, and Regulations

Sherman Antitrust Act of 1890, 15 U.S.C. §§1–7   Named for Senator John Sherman of Ohio, the key sections of this act are the first and second ones. Section 1 declares that any contracts or combinations that restrain interstate commerce are illegal. Section 2 prohibits monopolization and attempts or conspiracies to monopolize. Unfortunately, the act did not specify precisely what business practices result in a "restraint of trade," nor did it define exactly what it means to "monopolize" a market. The broad language seems to have been intentional, evidencing a willingness to leave the process of clarifying and interpreting the act to the federal judiciary and the Supreme Court. First, we consider Section 1 violations.

In a long series of decisions dating as far back as 1899, four basic categories of market behaviors were determined by the courts to be **per se violations of Section 1** of the Sherman Act. *Per se violations* are those that are illegal "in themselves," meaning they cannot be justified by any other considerations. To prevail in court, a plaintiff need only prove that any one of these behaviors occurred:

1. **Price fixing.** This is an agreement by competitors in the same market to set or "fix" prices at a certain amount. (The rule of per se illegality was first announced explicitly by the Supreme Court in a price-fixing case, *United States v. Trenton Potteries*, 273 U.S. 392 [1927].) Firms accused of this practice sometimes defend themselves by claiming that agreeing on prices adds beneficial stability to the market or in some other way serves the public interest (see below *National Society of Professional Engineers v. United States*). The courts are rarely persuaded by this defense.

2. **Dividing markets.** This means splitting a market into geographical regions or simply allocating territories, with the competitors agreeing not to interfere in one another's regions.

3. **Group boycotts.** This occurs when firms stipulate certain conditions of business to outside firms or refuse to deal with them altogether (see below, *United States v. Parke, Davis & Company*). This was a common practice of the nineteenth-century trusts.

4. **Resale price maintenance.** A vertical price restraint or fixing that occurs when a producer tries to impose either maximum or minimum prices on a wholesaler or retailer whom the producer supplies. This sort of price fixing can be combined with a business boycott ([3] above) in which a supplier refuses to deal with a retailer unless the goods are resold at the stipulated price (see also *United States v. Parke, Davis & Company*, below).

Numbers 1 through 3 are examples of *horizontal restraints* of trade: agreements between competitors. In contrast, *vertical restraints* of trade are agreements between different levels of the distribution chain, for example, between a manufacturer and a retailer. Number 4, above, is a vertical restraint.

It took more than two decades for the Sherman Act to have any significant impact on big business in America. Early antitrust suits were not taken seriously. Indeed, in the first such case, a huge sugar refining company controlling 98 percent of the market was held not to have violated the act (*United States v. E.C. Knight Company*, 156 U.S. 1 [1895]). Finally, in 1911 two of the country's most powerful trusts were broken. *Standard Oil Company v. United States*, 221 U.S. 1 (1911), and *United States v. American Tobacco Company*, 221 U.S. 106 (1911), marked the first time that the act was successfully brought to bear against giant corporations.

These two cases are important not only as benchmarks in the development of per se illegality, but more significantly they display the initial specification of the second test for lawfulness under Section 1: **the rule of reason** standard (see also *National Society of Professional Engineers v. United States*, below). Standard Oil and American Tobacco controlled 95 percent of their respective markets, and the Supreme Court ruled that this percentage was contrary to law. However, the Court also noted that some restraints of trade were "reasonable," while others were not, thus allowing large companies to operate legally so long as their business practices were not unreasonable. Unfortunately, no clear specification of what was reasonable and what was not, or precisely how to make determinations of reasonableness, appeared in these decisions.

In another Supreme Court decision several years later, Justice Louis Brandeis offered what is usually credited as the seminal formulation of the rule of reason. In *Chicago Board of Trade v. United States*, 246 U.S. 231 (1918), Brandeis noted that the question of whether an agreement between companies, or a government regulation, is legal cannot be settled simply by appeal to the "restraint of trade" criterion found in Section 1 of the Sherman Act. Any agreement or regulation at all restrains trade. The key issue, he wrote, is "whether the restraint imposed is such as merely regulates and perhaps thereby promotes competition or whether it is such as may suppress or even destroy competition."

Antitrust law under Section 1 can then be understood as including two standards of illegality: (1) per se violations (such as those behaviors listed above), and (2) a balancing test for the reasonableness of the restraint of trade: If it is unreasonable, then it is illegal.

Section 2 of the Sherman Act prohibits monopolizing or attempting to monopolize any part of trade or commerce. Notice that what is forbidden here is the *act* of monopolizing, or trying to monopolize, not the *condition* of there being a monopoly. This is because there are certain situations in which market domination is unavoidable and even desirable. If such circumstances obtain, a business can successfully defend itself against charges. Courts have recognized two such situations of defensible monopoly: (1) natural monopoly, as when demand for a product may be limited to what one company can produce, or when a small town may not be able to support more than one grocery store or newspaper; and (2) superior business acumen, through which a monopoly is acquired by superior skill, foresight, or industry (see below, *Berkey Photo, Inc. v. Eastman Kodak Company*).

A Section 2 case addresses three main features:

1. **Relevant market.** The market that is being illegally dominated is defined both in terms of the *product* involved and the *geographical area* served. The product market is determined by the *cross-elasticity of demand* test established by the Supreme Court in *United States v. E.I. DuPont DeNemours & Company*, 351 U.S. 377 (1956). If customers stay with a product even as the price continues to rise, then that item probably constitutes the market. However, if consumers switch to a substitute soon after the prices start rising, the substitutes must be included in the market. The geographical market is defined as the area in which the various competitors sell the product at issue.

2. **Monopoly power**. This is the extent of the ability to control prices and exclude competition. Although no rigid test or mathematical formula is employed, the general guidelines are that a market share exceeding 70 percent is monopoly power, while less than 20 percent is not.

3. **Monopolizing.** This feature makes plain that the target of the Sherman Act is any attempt, successful or not, to exclude competitors from the market, and not the mere existence of a dominating force in a market. For example, any intentional action in violation of Section 1 (or any other antitrust law) is an act of monopolizing that violates Section 2.

Clayton Act of 1914, 15 U.S.C. §§12–21   Congress was not satisfied by a number of Supreme Court decisions during the first decade or so of this century. The Sherman Act contained loopholes that produced rulings in cases such as *Standard Oil Company v. United States* and *United States v. American Tobacco Company* (see both above), which, though "trust-busting," were too vague and still allowed big business too much latitude in their efforts to squelch competition. This dissatisfaction led to the passage of the *Clayton Act*. One of the major purposes of this act was to state more clearly what business practices qualify as monopolistic.

Section 2 proscribed **discriminatory pricing**, that is, the practice of charging different consumers different prices for the same commodity (this item needed further refinement; see below, the Robinson-Patman Act). Section 3 made **tying agreements** per se illegal. This kind of agreement occurs when a company makes the sale of one product, A, conditional on the purchase of a second product, B. The buyer wants A, but cannot get it unless B is also purchased (see below, *Eastman Kodak v. Image Technical Services*). Section 4 of the Clayton Act allows for treble (triple) damages for any person injured by violation of antitrust laws. Section 7 prohibits any merger or acquisition that results in a substantial decrease in competition and tends to create a monopoly by, for example, acquiring the stock of a competing company. Finally, Section 8 prohibits a single individual from simultaneously serving on the boards of directors of two or more companies in competition with each other.

It is important to distinguish the burden of proof required to show violations of the Clayton Act from that required by the Sherman Act. Violations of the Sherman Act require proof of an *actual* adverse impact on business competition; this is shown by establishing that either a per se illegal activity occurred, or that the practice was an unreasonable restraint of trade (the "rule of reason" approach; see above, the Sherman Act). This is a backward-looking investigation into past behavior. On the other hand, a violation of the Clayton Act requires only a *probability* or a tendency to restrain trade. Thus, enforcement of this act involves a prediction of the consequences of certain business practices; this is a forward-looking perspective.

Federal Trade Commission Act of 1914, 15 U.S.C. §40 *et seq.* This act is closely linked with the Clayton Act, and, along with the Sherman Act, was conceived as a third line of defense against anticompetitive business practices. Section 5 covers conduct that violates either the letter or the spirit of the Sherman Act or the Clayton Act, and is detrimental to public policy by being unethical, oppressive, or causing substantial injury to consumers or competitors. The Federal Trade Commission Act created the Federal Trade Commission (FTC), and gave this agency the authority to prevent persons or firms from engaging in unfair methods of competition and unfair or deceptive practices effecting interstate commerce. The FTC exercises this authority by issuing interpretative rules, policy statements, trade regulations, and guidelines defining unfair or deceptive practices. The original congressional intention behind the act was to protect consumers indirectly by regulating the monopolistic practices that tend to increase the prices of products while reducing their quality. However, by the 1970s the FTC was almost entirely concerned with the regulation of business practices that most directly affect consumers: advertising, selling, lending, warranties, and packaging (see

Chapter 2: The Consumer—Advertising, Selected Cases; Federal Trade Commission Act).

Robinson-Patman Act of 1936, 15 U.S.C. §13   Technically an amendment to Section 2 of the Clayton Act (see above), the bill sponsored by Senator Joe Robinson and Representative Wright Patman is commonly known by the names of it's two authors. The Clayton Act did prohibit the sort of price discrimination in which a business charges two different customers different prices for the same item, but at the same time the act allowed such variations in pricing when the *quantity* of goods sold varied. This meant that a large retailer with substantial buying power (lots of money) could purchase large quantities of a commodity for a cheaper price than could a smaller business that could not afford the capital expenditure required to make a purchase of similar size. Therefore, the large retailer could set lower prices for the item than the small retailer could, and then dominate the market. During the 1930s large grocery chains exploited this loophole by undercutting the retail prices set by the small, neighborhood "Mom and Pop" stores. Unable to compete, many went out of business.

Alarmed, Congress closed this loophole in 1936. The Robinson-Patman Act stipulates that illegal price discrimination must involve sales to at least two different buyers at approximately the same time. The sale must involve a commodity, that is, a tangible thing or object of some kind, and not an intangible like advertising or title insurance. Only sales involving items of like grade and quality can be tested for discriminatory pricing; two goods that are physically or chemically indistinguishable are alike in this way, no matter how they are labeled or trademarked (this was established by the Supreme Court in *FTC v. Borden Company*, 383 U.S. 637 [1966]). To recover damages, an individual or firm must show an actual injury caused by the price discrimination. The injured party may be either the retailer who did not receive the lower price, called *primary line injury*, or the customers of the retailer who did not receive the lower price, called *secondary line injury*.

United States v. Parke, Davis & Company, 362 U.S. 29 (1960)   In a historic case, *United States v. Colgate & Company*, 250 U.S. 300 (1919), the Supreme Court held that a producer may declare a price of resale to retailers, and then notify those retailers that the company will refuse to deal with them unless that price is maintained. This is called the *Colgate* doctrine. Although the doctrine sounds like a straightforward violation of Section 1 of the Sherman Act, allowing per se illegal resale price maintenance coerced by boycotting, subsequent lower court decisions indicated that the ruling would be interpreted very narrowly. In this case the Supreme Court established the limits of allowable refusals to deal.

Parke Davis manufactured about 600 pharmaceutical products, marketed nationally through drug wholesalers and retailers. In 1956 Parke Davis announced a resale price maintenance policy in its wholesalers' and retailers' catalogues, stipulating that the company would sell its products only to wholesalers that observed the company's pricing schedules. Shortly thereafter, however, a number of units of Peoples' Drug Stores in the Washington, D.C.

and Richmond, Virginia, areas began selling several of Parke Davis's vitamin products at substantially less than the suggested minimum retail price, thus violating the price-maintenance policy. In response, representatives of Parke Davis visited the five wholesalers who supplied the maverick drug stores and informed them that the company would not sell them any further merchandise if the wholesaler continued to sell to any retailer that did not observe the minimum price. Further, the wholesalers were told that their competitors had been apprised of Parke Davis's intentions in this matter. All five wholesalers agreed to go along with the scheme.

The U.S. government sought a court-ordered injunction against Parke Davis to terminate the policy of threatening wholesalers with a boycott, citing Section 1 of the Sherman Act. The district court dismissed the complaint, citing the *Colgate* doctrine in defense of Parke Davis. The Supreme Court disagreed, ruling that the Parke Davis policy was a clear violation of the Sherman Act. The problem was that Parke Davis did not merely announce the price policy and then refuse to deal with those who did not adhere to it. The company went much further by enlisting the wholesalers in a cooperative enterprise to shut out noncomplying retailers. Justice William Brennan wrote in the majority decision that by "involving the wholesalers to stop the flow of Parke Davis products to the retailers, thereby inducing retailers adherence to the suggested retail price, Parke Davis created a combination with...the wholesalers to maintain retail{...} prices and violated the Sherman Act."

National Society of Professional Engineers v. United States, **435 U.S. 679 (1978)** One way for corporations to **fix prices**, and so run afoul of Section 1 of the Sherman Act, is to make agreements regulating competitive methods, agreements tending to stifle any real competition altogether. This is precisely what happened in the engineering profession. Members of the National Society of Professional Engineers (NSPE) agreed, and their canon of ethics explicitly required, that any competitive bidding for engineering jobs be scrupulously avoided. The rule and practice was for an engineer to refuse to negotiate or to even discuss the matter of his or her fees until after the prospective client had selected the engineer for a particular project. Indeed, the NSPE rule obligated an engineer to withdraw from consideration for a job if the client required fee information.

The rationale behind all this was that the disclosure of fee information would make price comparisons available to a prospective client, who would then naturally seek out less expensive services. Because offering lower prices would tend to increase the demand for a particular engineer's consultation, there would be a strong temptation for engineers to cut corners in order to offer cheaper rates, thereby endangering public safety. After all, engineers are intimately engaged in the study, design, and construction of bridges, office buildings, airports, factories, and other structures used by large numbers of people.

The U.S. government sought to nullify the NSPE rule prohibiting competitive bidding. The district court and the circuit court of appeals agreed that the rule violated Section 1. The Supreme Court consented to hear the case.

Citing a previous precedent in which a bar association's rule prescribing minimum fees was found illegal, Justice John Paul Stevens's majority decision observed that the engineer's rule was just as clearly in violation. However, he continued, certain business practices of members of a professional association might survive judicial scrutiny by passing the **rule of reason** test (also see the Sherman Act, above).

The NSPE argued that their practices did indeed pass the test because the prohibition on price competition prevents inferior work and promotes ethical behavior, resulting in public benefits. Stevens pointed out that this was a misunderstanding of the rule of reason: A reasonable restraint on trade is one that encourages competition, while an unreasonable one deters or destroys competition. He wrote: "[The NSPE] ban on competitive bidding prevents all customers from making price comparisons in the initial selection of an engineer, and imposes the Society's views of the costs and benefits of competition on the entire marketplace." *This* is what is unreasonable, not that allowing competitive bidding poses some threat to public safety. In composing the Sherman Act, the legislature held the view that competition not only produces lower prices, but better goods and services as well.

***Berkey Photo, Inc. v. Eastman Kodak Company*, 603 F.2d 263 (2d Cir. 1979)** Identifying violations of Section 2 of the Sherman Act has been a troublesome matter for the courts. The main problem is that Section 2 forbids *attempting* to establish a monopoly, and that requires some determination of the intentions of a corporation. How do you tell when a business intends to monopolize a market?

For many years, Kodak has been the preeminent force in the "amateur conventional still camera" market. Beginning in the 1920s with the *Brownie* box camera, Kodak has always been the leader in selling small, simple, and relatively inexpensive cameras designed for the mass market. For example, in 1964 Kodak cameras accounted for 90 percent of all market revenues. In 1972 Kodak introduced the 110 system, called the *Pocket Instamatic*, and a new type of cartridge-loading film, *Kodacolor III*. The new system was enormously successful. Berkey was a much smaller camera manufacturer in competition with Kodak that also attempted to enter the new 110 market, but did very poorly. Berkey charged Kodak with attempting to monopolize the 110 market with the introduction of the new format, a violation of Section 2 of the Sherman Act.

Berkey argued that because other companies could not compete without offering similar products, Kodak was in a position to set industry standards both for camera manufacturing and film manufacturing. Indeed, Kodak's dominance in film production as well as in cameras prevented other companies from introducing any new formats other than those already controlled by Kodak. A camera without film is worthless. Most importantly, Kodak provided no advanced notice of the new 110 system, which would have at least allowed rivals to enter the new market at the same time. All this indicated an attempt to monopolize.

The district court found for Berkey to the tune of over $15 million, but Chief Judge Kaufman of the Second Circuit Court of Appeals overturned that decision. Section 2, he declared, allows a corporation to succeed through capitalizing on its resources for invention and innovation: This is essentially the defense of superior business acumen. Kodak was not under any duty to predisclose its innovations because a policy of such disclosure would be so unclear that innovations would tend to be stifled. The first company to design a new product has a right to the lead time that follows from the success. Furthermore, Kodak could not be deprived fairly of the benefits of this success just because the company manufactures film for the new format.

Berkey is often contrasted with another famous Section 2 case decided by the Second Circuit Court of Appeals, *United States v. Aluminum Company of America*, 148 F.2d 416 (1945). Alcoa's standing in the aluminum market was rather similar to Kodak's in the camera and film market: Alcoa enjoyed a 90 percent share in the new aluminum ingot market, and had completely dominated the industry for years. Although the company claimed that it never excluded any competitors, that its dominance was the result of expertise and efficiency, Judge Learned Hand was unpersuaded. He pointed out that Alcoa continually expanded its production capacity, and then promoted demand for the product just to the extent that it could meet that demand while effectively anticipating and deterring all competition. Hand concluded that "Alcoa meant to keep, and did keep, that complete and exclusive hold upon the ingot market with which it started. That was to monopolize that market." Clearly, Hand's and Kaufmann's respective views of what indicates a corporation's intention to monopolize are very different.

Eastman Kodak Company v. Image Technical Services, Inc., **504 U.S. 451 (1992)** Section 3 of the Clayton Act (see above) prohibits **tying arrangements**. These occur when a company makes the purchase of some good or service conditional on the purchase of some other good or service. The case we consider now is one of the few Section 3 disputes heard by the Supreme Court, and presents an interesting attempt to evade the statute.

Kodak manufactures and sells photocopiers and micrographics machines (microfilmers, microfilm viewers, scanners). This equipment and its parts are not compatible with any other manufacturer's equipment and parts. For some years, Kodak was the exclusive supplier of parts and service to buyers of their machines, but in the early 1980s independent service organizations (ISOs) entered the market. ISOs provided service and parts for Kodak equipment at significantly lower prices than Kodak; some customers even purchased Kodak parts and employed ISOs to install them.

In 1985 and 1986, Kodak implemented two new policies designed to make it much more difficult for ISOs to undercut their service operations. First, Kodak severely limited the availability of parts to ISOs. Second, the company began selling replacement parts only to owners of Kodak equipment who used Kodak to service and repair their machines. These two policies were very successful: Many ISOs went out of business and numerous others suffered substantial loses in business revenue, while Kodak service sales returned to previous levels. Reacting to a dire situation, various ISOs began suing Kodak in 1987, charging it with establishing an illegal tying arrangement:

what customers wanted was Kodak parts (to be installed by ISOs), but in order to get them, buyers had to purchase Kodak service as well.

Kodak responded with the observation that an illegal tying arrangement can only exist when there are two products to tie together. However, parts and service constituted just one item involved in commerce: repair. Therefore, no such arrangement could have obtained because there was only one product at issue. The district court bought this argument, but the Ninth Circuit Court of Appeals and the Supreme Court did not. The sale of replacement parts and the provision of services to install these parts and repair Kodak machines are two separate and distinct markets. Kodak did have sufficient power in the market for parts to substantially restrain competition in the market for service, especially considering its machines were not compatible with those of any other manufacturer. And that is illegal.

Mergers and Acquisitions

When one company *merges* with another, both companies cease to exist and a new company comes into being. When one company *acquires* another company, the acquiring company continues to exist and the acquired company ceases to exist.

Companies *merge* with other companies because they believe there is a business advantage to do so. For example, Company X, a luggage manufacturer, might merge with Company Y, another luggage manufacturer, because they each have something the other wants. Company X may have a patent on a new rolling system for suitcases while Y has an established brand name and a developed distribution system. When they merge, the new company will save a great deal on management costs, because it will need only one CEO, one president, and one vice-president for each of the other functional areas.

The advantages to the new corporation are often disadvantages to other groups and individuals. For example, many senior managers lose their jobs. Also, mergers and acquisitions often result in closing or moving plants to new locations, harming employees, the community, and suppliers. Mergers can also create monopolistic markets in which goods are scarce and prices are high (see Antitrust Issues, above).

A company acquires another company to get an increased market share, a developed and productive research and development program, or some other business advantage. There are several reasons why a company would seek to acquire, rather than merge with, another company. For one thing, a merger is all but impossible if the target company does not want to merge. For another, cash flow and other financial aspects can be more favorable for an acquisition than a merger in a particular case.

A special kind of acquisition, known as a **management buyout** (MBO), occurs when managers of a **common stock company** buy all of the stock from the stockholders. The company then becomes privately owned by the managers. Another way to describe this is that the managers, who once worked for the owners, are now the managers and owners. In 1979 the monetary value of MBOs was $636 million (News Release 1984). By 1986 this number grew to an estimated $40.9 billion (Profile 1986). Even adjusting for inflation, this is a phenomenal increase.

One way to explain the increase in MBOs is by appeal to managerial learning. After managers looked at the results of the 1979 MBOs, they learned that it was a very good way to maximize shareholder wealth, which is their primary ethical duty. Share prices go up because there is huge demand for the stock when the managers try to buy it.

There is another, more skeptical way to interpret the growth of MBOs. This interpretation starts with the fact that managers are buying the corporation they are selling. As sellers of the corporation, they are supposed to act in the best interest of the owners, which means getting the highest possible price for the corporation. However, as buyers, which they also are, they are trying to acquire the company for the lowest price. The suspicion is that managers may favor their own interests when faced with this kind of conflict (Bruner and Paine 1988). The board of directors is supposed to monitor management, but they will not always be successful (see The Nature and Structure of the Corporation). As knowledgeable as the board may be, it must be remembered that the board members get most of their information about the company from the managers themselves. If the managers know that a new discovery or some other event is going to increase the value of the company, they could conceal it from the board. Management could then buy the company for its current value, and when the new event occurred, the managers, now the new owners, would reap all the benefits.

Ethics

Promoting Self-Interest: Egoism Aggressively self-interested managers would seek to merge, acquire, or buyout if it promoted their chosen goals, such as advancing a career or accumulating wealth. The discussion above suggests that MBOs would be especially attractive to aggressively self-interested managers. However, every case is different, and it could be that merging with or acquiring another company might promote the interests of an aggressively self-interested manager better than an MBO.

Interestingly enough, aggressively self-interested managers could approve of a merger, acquisition, or buyout that would eliminate their jobs. There are many specific scenarios in which this could occur, but we will consider only one. These managers would approve of a change in company ownership if they thought that their job loss was occurring at a time when the probability was very high that they would get an equally good job, and they would get a good compensation package for being forced out. Their reasoning would go something like this: The mere attempt at a merger, acquisition, or buyout indicates that it makes economic sense to change corporate ownership. So, even if this plan fails, other attempts are likely to follow. If the job loss occurs now, managers' chances of maintaining their current level of employment are good. The chances are unknown for the future.

As we have mentioned, contemplatively self-interested people are not likely to become managers. However, managers might become contemplatively self-interested if they get tired of the hectic corporate pace. These managers might welcome being forced out of their jobs. On the other hand, they might also dread being forced out if, for example, they were near retirement, and losing their jobs wiped out most of their retirement benefits.

Nurturing Personal Relationships: Care   Using care to evaluate mergers and acquisitions is difficult because care applies first and foremost to close personal relationships, like those we have with friends and family.

Passive caring managers would pursue or interfere with a merger or acquisition depending on what those in their most important relationships wanted. The goal of the passive carer is to preserve the relationship by doing what others want. This is a notoriously risky way to sustain relationships, as it excludes a person whose interests are central to a good relationship: the carer. By focusing on others, passive carers do not pay enough attention to themselves.

Passive caring managers would tend to be very biased against owners in MBOs, because these managers are going to look out for their family and friends more than the owners. This lack of concern for shareholders can be exacerbated if the managers initiating the buyout are friends.

Active carers want to help others pursue their personal projects. They also argue that we should not harm some to care for others. These managers would look at how the change in corporate ownership affects the personal relationships of all those affected. For example, it is not unusual for plant closings to be accompanied by an increase in suicide and divorce.

These drastic consequences, however, must be evaluated in terms of the alternatives. If it turns out the plant will close, no matter what, an actively caring manager could approve of the merger. Caring managers would be adamant, however, about warning employees of the merger as soon as possible, helping them get new jobs, and offering counseling services to help them through difficult periods.

Finally, actively caring managers would have to pay attention to their own friends and family. If the merger or acquisition was good for those relationships, that is a good reason for the manager to pursue it. If the merger was not good for their relationships, actively caring managers would try to opt out of the company.

Promoting the Good of the Group: Utilitarianism   Using strict rule utilitarianism, managers would pursue a change in corporate ownership if that is the best way to fulfill their duties as specified by social rules. They would want to follow these social rules because that is the best way to maintain law and order, which is necessary for economic planning and growth. One set of these rules, both formal and informal, gives managers a fiduciary duty to owners. As citizens, however, they are subject to rules that require us to not harm others.

When social rules conflict, managers should follow the rules that are most important to social well-being. There is no way to tell in advance whether in a particular case managerial rules that require maximizing shareholder return will override general social rules that prohibit harm. We can say, however, that when the harm is slight and the benefit to shareholders is great, the manager should promote the interests of shareholders. Only in the most harmful and/or illegal cases should the manager forgo promoting the well-being of shareholders. Violating the expectation that managers act in the interests of owners would reduce or eliminate investment in corporations, destroying the very institution that makes contemporary life possible.

Using flexible rule utilitarianism, managers would agree that stability and rule following are important for a successful society. They would also accept that we must live with the unfortunate consequences of otherwise valuable rules. However, flexible rule utilitarian managers have more opportunities to pay attention to other stakeholders and the society as a whole. These managers could pursue a merger/acquisition in the face of significant community harm if it generated enough good consequences to outweigh the bad. However, the good created must be certain and must be so much greater than the harm that a reasonable, disinterested observer would approve of the merger/acquisition.

Respecting Dignity and Rights: Intrinsic Value   Managers relying on human dignity and fairness would acknowledge the privileged rights of owners. But that would be only the beginning of their analysis. They would also look at the many implicit agreements and legitimate expectations of other stakeholders. If a merger or acquisition violated these agreements and expectations in ways that harmed stakeholders greatly, this could lead managers to reject the transition. Would these managers then be violating their freely chosen fiduciary duty to the owners? The answer to this question would depend on the way managers had acted in the past. Consider a company like Levi-Strauss, which has a long tradition of paying attention to the interests of all stakeholders. Levi-Strauss is proud of its commitment, and is not shy about distributing press releases about it. If senior management decided not to acquire a company because that would harm many innocent stakeholders, this should come as no surprise to the owners. However, if a company had no history of social action, and decided not to acquire a company because that would harm many innocent stakeholders, the managers of this corporation would be violating their fiduciary duty.

Managers relying on property rights would merge if it benefitted shareholders more than any other course of action. Although managers could regret the loss to nonowning stakeholders, their first duty would be to protect and promote the property rights of the owners. There is one exception, however: Locke's proviso. Robert Nozick interprets Locke's proviso to require that "enough and good enough" be left for the use of others when dealing with resources necessary for human life (see Chapter 1: Introduction—Ethics: Principles that Promote Respect for Dignity and Rights). For example, if a merger would create a monopoly that would prevent people from obtaining food or water, then it should not be done, no matter how much the owners are benefitted.

International Issues

Although culture may be relative, economics may not be. We have seen throughout this chapter that international issues regarding corporate structure, social responsibility, and antitrust resemble the domestic issues very closely. We find the same resemblance with mergers, acquisitions, and buyouts. The **European Commission** antitrust unit is investigating two mergers of four of the most prominent accounting firms in the world. If these mergers go through, the Big Six, referring to the six largest accounting firms in the world, will become the Big Four. Price Waterhouse is planning a merger with Coopers & Lybrand in a deal valued at $13 billion. In another merger, KPMG Peat Marwick plans to merge with Ernst & Young in a deal worth $15 billion. The worry is that these mergers will reduce competition and create conflicts of interest. With fewer accounting firms, competing companies, for example, General Motors, Mercedes, and Volvo, are more likely to be represented by the same accounting firm. The problem is that the accounting firm may not be able to keep the information from competing firms separate.

The **European Union** may be sensitive about mergers and acquisitions because they are preparing for 1999, when 11 of 15 member countries will use a single currency, the *Euro*. With one currency, analysts believe there will be a frenzy of mergers and acquisitions, with larger companies taking over smaller ones. At present, there are 1200 small and medium-sized businesses traded on the stock exchanges in Europe. That number could be reduced to 350. There are presently 270 banks in the European Union; that number could go as low as five or six (Lewis 1997).

Economics

Society By definition, the social point of view concerns all stakeholders, not merely owners, and so the evaluation of mergers must include all those affected by a merger. The standard view of free markets suggests that allowing mergers would be the social policy that would maximize wealth, except when mergers lead to monopolistic, anticompetitive behavior.

This free market view seems to have been the policy of the United States recently. Last year, mergers of U.S. companies totaled $100 trillion. This was 50 percent more than the previous year, which itself set merger records (Wayne 1998). Mergers have been most noticeable in the financial and telecommunications industries. In an irony not lost on most commentators, the seven "Baby Bells," which were created in 1984 when the U.S. Supreme Court broke up AT&T, are beginning to merge (Schiesel 1997). The government has been letting these mergers occur because they believe they are both good for consumers, giving them lower prices, and good for companies, giving them higher revenues.

Consumers Consumers are better off if mergers improve the quality of products and reduce their costs. Consumers are worse off if mergers result in monopolies that reduce the supply of products, pushing prices up and quality down. The interests of consumers in this case are nearly identical with the interests of society, because we are all consumers.

But why do mergers between the Baby Bells reduce prices? With fewer companies, shouldn't competition decrease and prices go up? The answer, in this case, is "no." This is because mergers between the Baby Bells are horizontal mergers (for more details, see below, Law). Horizontal mergers occur when companies do the same kind of things, in this case, providing local and regional phone service in a given area: the Pacific Coast, the Midwest, the South, to name three. When these regional companies merge, the level of competition does not change, because they already had monopolies in their given areas. Merging does reduce many of their costs, however, and these savings can be passed on to consumers.

Producers   This new wave of mergers is happening for a very old reason: economies of scale. As we discussed above, merged companies can cut their administrative overhead in half. The cost of other operations, such as mailing bills and marketing products, will also go down. Further, the pay and benefits for senior managers can be much larger in these more wealthy, merged companies. The question arises then, why would these new telecommunication companies pass savings in their costs on to customers? These businesses have an incentive to keep prices where they are, and even raise them, and use the money to give themselves pay raises, to increase dividends, or to hike research and development budgets.

There are two forces that can keep these new companies honest. One is the state public utilities commissions (PUCs) that regulate phone rates. They will demand that phone companies justify rate increases, and if a company saves money from a merger, the PUC can demand rate reductions. The second force keeping them honest is the federal government. The Department of Justice can intervene to stop mergers if they see that consumers are suffering. They can also sue merged companies in order to break them up again.

It is hard to say how effective these government agencies are in protecting consumers. However, even if rates do go down, telecommunication companies will benefit more, and sooner than the average customers will.

Law

The trusts of the late nineteenth century that came to be so vilified by the American people were often formed through the merger of two or more companies or through the purchase of one or more companies by another. Unfortunately, Congress's move to dissolve and prevent trusts in 1890 with the enactment of the Sherman Act was not very effective in deterring the mergers and acquisitions that often resulted in monopolization. Attempting to rectify this situation in 1914, Section 7 of the Clayton Act (also see above, Antitrust Issues, Selected Cases) was written explicitly to prohibit mergers and acquisitions that tend to lessen competition or create a monopoly. The problem was that Section 7 only prohibited mergers resulting from stock sales and not those achieved through the acquisition of assets. Business exploited this loophole for many years until the section was amended by the Celler-Kefauver Act of 1950, 15 U.S.C. §18, to include this sort of acquisition and all other varieties of combination.

The Clayton Act was amended again in 1976 with the Antitrust Procedural Improvement Act, 15 U.S.C. §1311, requiring businesses to notify the Justice Department and the Federal Trade Commission (see above, Antitrust Issues, Law: Federal Trade Commission Act) of all large mergers. This gives those agencies 30 days to investigate for anticompetitive consequences. A *large merger* is defined as one in which the acquiring company has at least $100 million in assets or annual sales and the acquired company has at least $10 million in assets or annual sales.

As in a Section 2 case under the Sherman Act, a Section 7 case under the Clayton Act (as amended) must identify the relevant market in order to determine whether a particular merger or acquisition has a monopolizing effect. Here too, the key aspects are the product being offered in commerce and the geographical area where it is available. The *elasticity of demand test* (see above, the Sherman Act) indicates both the functional interchangeability of products and where the competition lies. The geographical area may be local, statewide, regional, or national. Once the relevant market is fixed, the court must decide if the merger or acquisition is likely to substantially lessen competition or create a monopoly.

Section 7 of the Clayton Act is not violated if it can be proved that one of the merging companies is failing. The standard of proof required here was set out by the Supreme Court in *Citizen Publishing Company v. United States*, 394 U.S. 131 (1969). A failing business is one in which: (1) Bankruptcy is imminent, and must be pursued in order to save the company; and (2) the company has made an honest effort to find other buyers and there are none.

There are three basic types of mergers that may be scrutinized for Section 7 violations:

1. **Horizontal mergers.** This is a merger between two or more companies that compete in the same business and geographical market. These are the most closely examined mergers, as they obviously result in a more concentrated market, although the degree of concentration varies with the number of firms in competition. A four-firm market in which two of the firms merge is clearly far more concentrated than a 40-firm market in which two of them merge. The Supreme Court has determined just how concentrated a market can be before monopolization occurs. In *United States v. Philadelphia National Bank*, 374 U.S. 321 (1963), the court offered two necessary conditions for an illegal horizontal merger: (a) The corporation formed after the merger would have 30 percent or more of the market share, and (b) the merger would result in an increased market concentration of 33 percent or more.

2. **Vertical mergers.** This type of merger results when the operations of a supplier and a customer are integrated. These are less problematic than horizontal mergers because the merging firms serve different markets; nonetheless, anticompetitive effects can ensue. Thus, a proposed merger between Ford Motor Company and Autolite, a spark plug manufacturer, was disallowed by the Supreme Court because it would not only eliminate any potential for Ford itself to enter the spark plug industry (and stimulate competition in doing so), but the merger would also remove Ford as a major buyer of spark plugs (*Ford Motor Company v. United States*, 405 U.S. 562 [1972]).

3. **Conglomerate mergers.** These are mergers that do not fit into any other category because they typically involve corporations either doing business in unrelated fields or selling different products in a broad market area. For example, a merger between a popcorn maker and a coal company would be of this type. Conglomerate mergers may be anticompetitive, and hence illegal, if the combination gives a firm an unfair advantage over its competitors. A particularly important case of this nature was *Federal Trade Commission v. Procter & Gamble Company*, 386 U.S. 568 (1967). The Supreme Court would not allow P&G, the leading seller of household cleansers, to merge with Clorox, the leading seller of liquid bleach. The merger was prohibited because the Court believed that smaller firms would be much more reluctant to enter the liquid bleach market when faced with the giant P&G than they would be against the smaller Clorox Company.

Selected Case

Brown Shoe Company, Inc. v. United States, **370 U.S. 294 (1962)** This classic merger case is one of the most famous antitrust decisions rendered by the Supreme Court. It concerns a proposed merger, with both horizontal and vertical aspects, between G.R. Kinney Company, Inc. and Brown Shoe Company, Inc. In the 1950s Kinney was not only a major manufacturer of shoes, it was also the largest independent chain of family-owned shoe stores in the nation. Kinney's assets exceeded $18 million and it sold more than 8 million pairs of shoes each year through its 350 retail outlets. Brown Shoe was the fourth largest shoe manufacturer in the United States with assets of about $72 million, and sold more than 25 million pairs annually. Kinney and Brown Shoe announced in 1955 that they would combine, thus producing both a vertical merger (Brown's manufacturing plants would find retail outlets in Kinney's stores and vice versa), and a horizontal merger, because both companies had been competing in retailing and manufacturing shoes.

The federal government sought an injunction denying the merger on the grounds that it violated Section 7 of the Clayton Act. The district court ruled against Brown Shoe, holding that the proposed merger was an illegal combination in restraint of trade, and prohibiting the company from having or acquiring any interest in Kinney stock or assets. The Supreme Court affirmed that judgment.

Chief Justice Earl Warren's majority opinion found first that the shoe industry in general was undergoing an increasing number of vertical mergers, which had as a result a distinct tendency to reduce competition. The merger at issue was another example of this growing trend. After defining the relevant product market as men's, women's, and children's shoes in the medium- and low-price range, and the geographical market as the entire nation, Warren went on to examine the vertical and horizontal aspects of the proposed merger. Vertically speaking, the merger being contemplated was that between the fourth largest shoe manufacturer in the country, Brown Shoe, and the operator of the largest chain of retail shoe stores, Kinney. It was clear that such a merger would shut out the largest share of the current market that could possibly be otherwise open to competitors.

In regards to the horizontal aspect of the merger, Warren noted that the resulting market share would still only be about 5 percent for retail shoe sales. But the market was severely fragmented and that percentage represented a commanding position in the industry. If it were allowed, competitors of the merged company might well be entitled to their own mergers seeking a similar share. "The oligopoly Congress sought to avoid would then be furthered," Warren observed. "We hold that...this merger...may tend to lessen competition substantially in the retail sale of men's, women's, and children's shoes in the overwhelming majority of those cities in which both Brown and Kinney sell [shoes]."

References: Andrews, Edmund L. 1997. "Agreement to Open Up World Financial Markets Is Reached." *New York Times* CyberTimes (Dec. 13).
———. 1998. "A European Inquiry on Accounting Mergers." *New York Times* CyberTimes (21 January).
Arthur, Brian W. 1994. *Increasing Returns and Path Dependency in the Economy.* Ann Arbor: University of Michigan Press.
Beauchamp, Tom L. 1998. "Polaroid In and Out of South Africa." In *Case Studies in Business, Ethics, and Society,* Tom L. Beauchamp, ed. 4th ed. Upper Saddle River, NJ: Prentice Hall.
Beauchamp, Tom L. and Norman E. Bowie, eds. 1997. *Ethical Theory and Business.* 5th ed. Upper Saddle River, NJ: Prentice Hall.
Berle, Adolf and Gardiner Means. 1968. *The Modern Corporation and Private Property.* Revised ed. New York: Harcourt Brace and World.
Blackstone, William T. 1984. "Ethics and Ecology." In *Business Ethics: Readings and Cases in Corporate Morality.* New York: McGraw-Hill.
Bruner, Robert F. and Lynn Sharp Paine. 1988. "Management Buyouts and Managerial Ethics." In *Ethical Theory and Business,* Tom L. Beauchamp and Norman E. Bowie, eds. 1997. 5th ed. Upper Saddle River, NJ: Prentice Hall.
Business Enterprise Trust, The. 1991. Merck & Co., Inc.
Caux Round Table. 1998. Website: http://www.cauxroundtable.org/mission.htm
Chandler, Alfred. 1977. *The Visible Hand.* Cambridge, MA: The Belknap Press of Harvard University Press.
Conference Board, The. 1998a. Website: http://www.conferenceboard.org/expertise/frames.cfm?main=gov.cfm.
Conference Board, The. 1998b. Website: http://www.ron-brown-award.org/ronbrown/winners.html

Dienhart, John W. 1999 (forthcoming). *Institutions, Business, and Ethics*. New York: Oxford University Press.

Dow Jones Newswires. 1997. "Japanese Agency Says It Will Investigate Microsoft." *The Wall Street Journal Interactive Edition* (22 October).

Freeman, R. Edward. 1984. *Strategic Management: A Stakeholder Approach*. Boston: Pitman Publishers.

————. 1997. "A Stakeholder Theory of the Modern Corporation." In *Ethical Theory and Business*, Tom L. Beauchamp and Norman E. Bowie, eds. 5th ed. Upper Saddle River, NJ: Prentice Hall.

Friedman, Milton. 1970. "The Social Responsibility of Business is to Increase Its Profits." *The New York Times Magazine* (13 September).

Gerston, Larry H., Cynthia Fraleigh, and Robert Schwab. 1988. *The Deregulated Society*. Pacific Grove, CA: Brooks/Cole Publishing.

Gioia, Dennis. 1992. "Pinto Fires and Personal Ethics: A Script Analysis of Missed Opportunities." *Journal of Business Ethics* 11: 379–380.

Gwartney, James D. and Richard Stroup. 1982. *Economics: Private and Public Choice*. 3d ed. New York: Academic Press.

Harmon, Amy 1998. "In Cyberspace, Is There Law Where There Is No Land?" *New York Times* Cybertimes (16 March).

Heald, Morrell. 1988. *The Social Responsibility of Business*. New Brunswick: Transaction Books.

Kilbourn, P. 1995. "Appliance Maker Agrees to Pay for Moving Away." *New York Times* (16 August): A8.

Lambe, C. Jay and Robert E. Spekman. 1997. "Anti-Competitive Practices in Marketing." In *The Blackwell Encyclopedic Dictionary of Business Ethics*, Patricia H. Werhane and R. Edward Freeman, eds. Malden, MA: Blackwell Publishers Inc.

Lewis, Paul. 1997. "Much of Europe Seems Unready for Single Currency." *New York Times* CyberTimes (27 December).

Lohr, Steve and John Markoff. 1998. "Why Microsoft Takes Hard Line With Government." *New York Times* Cyber Edition (12 January).

Lublin, Joann S. 1997. "Calpers Clears Plan That May End Policy of Not Seeking Board Seats," *The Wall Street Journal* Intereactive Edition (26 December).

News Release. 1984. Doremus and Company. Chicago. Jan. 12. Quoted in Robert F. Bruner and Lynn Sharp Paine. "Management Buyouts and Mangerial Ethics." In *Ethical Theory and Business*, Tom L. Beauchamp and Norman E. Bowie, eds. 1997. 5th ed. Upper Saddle River, NJ: Prentice Hall.

New York Times 1995a. "Designer of New Ammunition Is On Defensive After Criticism." (1 January): Sec. 1, p. 7.

New York Times. 1997b. "Microsoft Says Antitrust Case Aims to Stall Improvements in Windows." *Interactive Journal*. News Roundup (11 November).

New York Times. 1997c. "Texas Charges That Microsoft Interfered With Antitrust Probe." *Interactive Journal* News Roundup (7 November).

Noble, Barbara. 1994. "Making Family Leave a Reality; Benefits Exceeded Burdens in Law's First Year, the Labor Department Says." *The New York Times* National edition (31 July): F19.

North, Douglass. 1990. *Institutions, Institutional Change, and Economic Performance*. Cambridge: Cambridge University Press.

Orwall, Bruce. 1998. "Disney Rebuffs CREF Bid For 'More Independent' Board." *Wall Street Journal* Interactive Edition (24 February).

Paine, Lynn Sharp. 1994. "Managing for Organizational Integrity." *Harvard Business Review* (March–April).

Profile. 1986. Mergers & Acquisitions. May/June 71. Quoted in Robert F. Bruner and Lynn Sharp Paine. "Management Buyouts and Managerial Ethics." In *Ethical Theory and Business*, Tom L. Beauchamp and Norman E. Bowie, eds. 1997. 5th ed. Upper Saddle River, NJ: Prentice Hall.

Rich, Frank. 1997. "The Ellen 'Striptease,'" *The New York Times* on the Web. (10 April).

Salpukis A. 1996. "Electric Utilities to Provide Access for Competitors." *New York Times*, National edition (25 April): A1.

Samuelson, Paul A. and William D. Nordhaus. 1985. *Economics*. 3d ed. New York: McGraw-Hill.

Schiesel, Seth. 1997. "Mergers May Be Good for Competition." *New York Times* (12 November).

Simon, Herbert. 1976. *Administrative Behavior*. New York: The Free Press.

Wayne, Leslie. 1998. "Wave of Mergers Recasts the Face of Business." *New York Times* Cybertimes (19 January).

Wicks, Andrew C., Daniel R. Gilbert and Edward R. Freeman. 1994. "A Feminist Reinterpretation of the Stakeholder Concept." *Business Ethics Quarterly*. 4: 475–497.

Wilke, John R. 1997. "Hatch Attacks Microsoft on Eve of Senate Hearings." *The Wall Street Journal* Interactive Edition (3 November).

Williamson, Oliver E. 1985. *The Economic Institutions of Capitalism*. New York: The Free Press.

Wolf, Julie. 1997. "EU Launches Probe of Microsoft and European Service Providers." *The Wall Street Journal* (22 October).

Wood, Donna. 1994. *Business and Society*. 2d ed. New York: Harper Collins.

CONTEMPORARY ETHICAL ISSUES

Chapter 4:
The Employee

For many of us, the work that we do is one of the primary facets of our self-identity, of who we are. Think of how you would describe yourself to another person. Your job would certainly be one of the foremost features about yourself that you would immediately instance, if not the preeminent one. And even for those for whom a job does not hold such pride of place, certainly their dreams of an ideal, or just a much better line of work are persistent—and that sort of dreaming also significantly defines us. And of course, the salary we receive allows us to enjoy much of that which we believe enhances the quality of our lives.

We begin then with the foundations of this working arrangement that means so much to us: the terms and conditions of employment. We survey the moral and legal principles that inform and shape the agreements we make with our employers, and the working environment in which we labor. For employees, two critical issues are confronted every day in their occupational relationship with their employers: the health and safety of the workplace and the extent to which the employer may intrude upon personal privacy on, and off, the job. Equally incisive, but perhaps more controversial, is the matter of discrimination on the job and the remedial intention of affirmative action. This concern broadens the focus to include the process of being hired for a job, and presents one of the most influential and sweeping items of legislation affecting employees: Title VII of the Civil Rights Act. This federal law leads us to sexual harassment, officially identified by the judiciary as an instance of illegal discrimination based on sex. Finally, we shift from an examination of the rights of employees and the benefits due to them, to the obligations employees owe to their employers, and how that requirement might be compromised when employers engage in misconduct.

Terms and Conditions of Employment

Few things are more important to us than our jobs. We use our jobs to make a life for ourselves and our families. Our self-worth, for good or ill, is often dependent on our jobs. During the nineteenth and the early twentieth centuries, employees were subject to the **employment at will** (EAW) doctrine, which allows managers to fire employees "for good cause, for no cause, or even for a cause morally wrong" (see also Law: Employment at Will, below). Employees could also quit for any of these "causes." The EAW doctrine applied to all employee–employment relationships that were not governed by contracts. The basis of the doctrine is equality and **autonomy**: employer and employee are equally free to end their relationship "at will."

Employment at will puts management and labor on an equal plane only if the demand for jobs is roughly equal to the demand for labor. If the demand for labor is greater than the number of workers, workers have the upper hand. In conditions of labor scarcity, EAW gives employees the freedom to quit if management does not meet their requests for more pay and benefits. Since managers know that employees can quit and find other jobs, and that it will be difficult to fill these jobs, they will give in to employee demands for more pay and benefits. Those looking for work find that companies will compete for their labor by offering more money and benefits than what they believe other companies are offering.

If there are more workers than jobs, managers have the upper hand. In a condition of job scarcity, managers can use EAW to fire workers in order to hire cheaper ones. For most of the twentieth century in the United States, there have been more workers than jobs. In an effort to obtain job security and decent wages, employees began to form unions. We tell the story of this struggle in Law, below. For now, we can say that business resisted unions and that, until 1935 the legislative and judicial branches of government helped business fight unions. In 1935, six years into the Great Depression, the federal government passed the National Labor Relations Act (NLRA), which helped workers form unions in several different industries.

Union employees work under contracts that their union has negotiated with management. This contract specifies the terms and conditions of employment, not anything as open-ended as EAW. The doctrine still applies to all workers who are not members of unions, and who do not have some other contract stipulating the terms and conditions of employment. Some observers view the NLRA as the first step in eroding the EAW doctrine (Radin and Werhane 1996; Flynn 1996), because in its wake the number of workers subject to the doctrine was significantly reduced.

Beginning in the 1960s several more laws have been passed that limit management's use of EAW: the Civil Rights Acts of 1964 and 1991, which prohibit hiring and firing on the basis of race, color, religion, and national origin (see below, Discrimination and Affirmative Action); the Worker Adjustment and Retraining Notification Act of 1988, which requires management to warn employees of layoffs in several kinds of conditions (see below, Law); The Family and Medical Leave Act, which allows employees to take up to 12 weeks unpaid leave without penalty; and the Americans with Disabilities Act, forbidding hiring and firing on the basis of handicaps that are not relevant to the job (see also below, Discrimination and Affirmative Action). Each time laws like these are passed—and there are more than just those mentioned here—fewer people are subject to EAW.

Employment at will has also had some direct attacks. For example, the doctrine was directly challenged as the states and the federal government passed minimum wage laws, laws stipulating a 40-hour work week, and health and safety laws. These laws prohibited some kinds of employment conditions and requirements, and so forbade employers from firing employees if they refused to work in conditions contrary to these laws (see below, Selected Cases: *West Coast Hotel v. Parrish*).

Ethics

Promoting Self-interest: Egoism   Whether EAW is in the aggressive self-interest of employees depends on the state of the labor market. If there are more jobs than qualified workers, then employees can aggressively pursue their self-interest by demanding more pay. Either employers meet the demand or lose employees. Labor costs should continue to escalate until the number of jobs and the number or applicants are roughly equal. In this case, employees would have no need for unions, as that would be an extra cost without any added benefits. In fact, under these conditions, unions would impede self-interest. Unions negotiate long-term contracts that cannot be easily adjusted to the changing labor markets.

However, if the number of qualified workers is greater than jobs, employers can aggressively pursue their self-interest by pushing down wages and keeping more money for themselves. EAW allows employers to fire employees who refuse to accept pay cuts. Other qualified workers readily take their place. This reduction in labor costs continues until the number of qualified workers and jobs are roughly equal. Under these conditions, aggressively self-interested workers would fight against EAW in whatever way they could, such as by forming unions. Hence, they would be in favor of the NLRA and other laws, statute or common, that impeded management's ability to secure the lowest labor costs.

When labor markets fluctuate between job shortages and job surpluses, aggressively self-interested employees need to play the odds. If they believe that job shortages are the rule, they should opt for unions; otherwise, they should not. One thing they need to keep in mind, however, is that once unions are started, it is hard to get rid of them.

Whether EAW is in the contemplative self-interest of employees is somewhat independent of the state of the labor market. Contemplatively self-interested employees who have the upper hand with employers would bargain for long-term contracts, more training, or more medical benefits. These employees would opt for unions and other safeguards, since they are more interested in security than getting the highest possible pay in a particular labor market.

Nurturing Personal Relationships: Care   Caring employees and employers will respond to the supply and demand for labor. Passive caring employees would be willing to take advantage of job surpluses if the **cared-for** think this is the right thing to do or need resources that the employee can get in these conditions. However, passive caring employees would not take advantage of these conditions if their family and friends thought that doing so was wrong. Passive carers could even join a union in these conditions if they were pressured to do so by family and friends.

Active carers have a different approach, because they consider all the relationships they are in as having value. In a condition of job surpluses, these employees will be careful not to take advantage of employers. In general, active carers will damage less important relationships to improve more important ones only as a last resort. Hence these employees would be wary of laws that force employers to act in certain ways, as that would interfere with active carers forming their own, unique relationships with employers.

Despite the need to pay attention to the contextual details of their relationships with employers, active carers would accept government regulation if it were necessary to prevent exploitation of workers. For example, active caring employees may want to make sure that they can help family members in ways that require more money, more time off, or more medical benefits. In this case they would be in favor of the NLRA, since it makes forming unions easier, and acts like the Family and Medical Leave Act, which requires employers to give employees up to 12 weeks of unpaid leave to take care of home and medical needs.

Promoting the Good of the Group: Utilitarianism   Utilitarianism is an **impartial principle**. Utilitarian employees would approve of EAW as long as it promoted the overall social good. This evaluation would have to consider all participants in the employer-employee relationship. This includes consumers and the communities in which the participants live. So, unlike self-interested and caring employees, utilitarian employees would not give special consideration to themselves, family, or friends when evaluating employment relationships.

Employment at will is the default, or natural, state of affairs because it would obtain in the absence of contracts or social rules that require employers to treat employees in specific ways. The utilitarian question, then, would seem to be whether to limit the doctrine, not whether to have it. Unfortunately, this is not *the* utilitarian question.

The utilitarian question must always be put in the context of *the state of affairs at the time the decision is being made*. So, if EAW has already been limited, as is the case today, the utilitarian question concerns what it would cost to limit it more, or limit it less. Because there is an abundance of statutory and common law that limits EAW, and because these laws overlap each other, it is very difficult to calculate the cost of changes. In what follows, we take into account this contextual requirement. Our question will be, "Given the present state of affairs in which EAW is limited by statute and common law, how would employees who adopt strict and flexible utilitarian evaluate these restrictions?" For our purposes, we will stipulate first that the relevant group is all those who are affected by the decision, and second that their good is to be measured in financial terms.

A strict rule utilitarian employee focuses on stability and order. The thesis is that managers and employees need to know, at least in general terms, what the future will be like in order to negotiate their relationship. If the current state of affairs is going to change, this brings uncertainty, putting both parties at risk. On this reasoning, we cannot just compare costs and benefits between the present situation and the situation that we hope to make, we must also include *all the costs of moving from the present system to the one we hope to create*. We will also need to include the risks of other people interfering so that we do not get where we want to go, as well as the risks of having the desired state of affairs fail to achieve the benefits we expect.

As an example of this, consider the NLRA, discussed above. This law was supposed to even the playing field between business and labor, but instead it seemed to favor labor over business. This led to the Taft-Hartley Act, which attempted to restore balance between business and labor (for more, see Selected Cases, below). This is just the kind of problem strict rule utilitarians would warn against. EAW was working fine. There was no evidence that it created the Great Depression, yet the NLRA became law because of political pressure. This led to other laws designed to remedy mistakes contained in the NLRA. The statute also opened the door to many other laws that interfere with employer-employee relationships in unpredictable ways.

Strict rule utilitarian employees would have to include all the **transaction costs** of changing the current laws and rules, and this could be very expensive. These costs could easily exceed the benefits of the change. If any change is to occur, however, the rules that define the new state of affairs must be strictly enforced, so that employees can make accurate judgments about how to construct their employment relationships.

Flexible rule utilitarian employees would argue that strict rule utilitarianism will not work because the world is too complex and changes too fast.

Rather, we need to have rules that make the economy predictable enough and rewarding enough for business and employees to invest their money and effort, but not so strict that rules, like EAW, will be followed even when they clearly hurt the group. The need to have the NLRA limited by the Taft-Hartley Act does not mean the NLRA should never have been passed. This kind of tinkering with public policy is just what we should expect, since we have limited information and **bounded rationality**. As for other laws that affect EAW, like the Civil Rights Act and the Family and Medical Leave Act, flexible rule utilitarian employees would approve of them if they tend to make the group better off. Although these laws impose costs on business, they also have many social benefits, such as ensuring that all people can have an equal chance at a good job and the parents can stay home to take care of sick children. It is these benefits that prompted the laws in the first place.

Respecting Dignity and Rights: Intrinsic Value We will discuss two views of intrinsic value: the first emphasizes our capacity to make free decisions, and the second view holds that our intrinsic value is based on natural rights, which give rise to duties on the part of others to respect these rights.

Werhane (1983) argues that the reciprocity of the employment relationships gives each side rights and duties. Based on this reciprocal relationship, employees should be treated with dignity, which includes, at least, notification of termination. This reciprocity can be understood as a relationship between two parties, one of whom has intrinsic value, the employee, and one of which does not, the corporation. Of course, a human being who has intrinsic value negotiates for the company, but the employment relationship holds between the employee and the corporation. Since human beings have intrinsic value, it prevents their being used merely as a means to promote the financial well-being of a corporation. This does not imply that employees' jobs are guaranteed; it does mean that they should only be fired, refused promotion, or reprimanded for doing something wrong, or terminated only when a fundamental shift in technology or a demand that makes their job superfluous has occurred. Because the EAW allows workers to be fired simply because managers feel like it, the doctrine is immoral on its face.

Note that the immorality of EAW is not dependent on the nature of the job market, nor is it dependent on anyone actually using it in capricious and cruel ways. It is immoral because it endorses action that is itself immoral. Consider a parallel case. Suppose that parents were allowed to abandon their babies in trash cans if they cried for more than 36 continuous hours. This would be an immoral law even if no parents took "advantage" of it.

DesJardins (1985), and DesJardins and McCall (1985), argue that the principle of fairness gives employees **due process** rights. This means that employers cannot fire employees without going through a process to determine if they are being fired for the right reasons. DesJardins and McCall's argument is intriguing, since business used this very rationale to argue against limiting EAW (see Law: Employment at Will, below). Business's argument was simple: Jobs are the property of a business, and for government to use *statutes* to interfere with a business's right to hire, fire, and promote was to deprive them of their property without due process. We emphasize the term *statute* because court action to limit EAW would, by its very nature, be due process.

In a contrary view, Maitland (1989) relies on the natural rights view of Robert Nozick, and argues that the property rights of owners to control their jobs outweighs any need a particular employee may have for a particular job. In the spirit of Nozick (1974) we can argue that if people want to acquire property rights to a job, they need only begin their own business. Nickel (1978–1979) agrees that no employee has the right to any particular job, but that people have a general right to employment. Lee (1989) argues that while employees may not have a right to their jobs, they are owed something like it, in the form of job protection.

International Issues

Employment is a necessary condition for human survival for most of the world's population, so it is no surprise that issues raised by EAW in the United States have corollaries in other countries. The nature of the employment relationship in a country tends to mirror the dominant cultural relationships found there. For example, EAW fits well with the U.S. ideology of rugged individualism. Even England, from which our court system and common law derived, does not have EAW. The doctrine arose in America because it suited the needs of a developing country that was partial to business interests (Ballam 1995).

U.S. employment practices are quite different from those in Japan, where most managers—but less than half of all employees—have lifetime employment. Although lifetime employment fits well with the group-oriented Japanese culture, the corporation's promise to the employee of a guaranteed job for life is not given without the expectation of something in return. Employees are expected to devote their lives to the company. This means, among other things, work days that routinely last 10 to 12 hours, six days a week, and an implicit promise never to leave the company (Sethi, *et. al.* 1984).

In England, the Tory governments of Margaret Thatcher and John Major admired the business practices of the United States, including EAW. Although they could not institute anything like the doctrine, they did make moves to reduce, by 10 million, the number of employees who could challenge dismissals they believed were unfair (Dyer 1996). This new policy was almost certainly a response to a British court decision a year earlier that increased the number of employees who could challenge dismissals they believed were unfair (Moorman 1995).

Employment in China presents yet another way to structure employer-employee relationships. Like Japan, the Chinese are definitively a group-oriented culture: Devotion to the group and to its leaders are essential parts of Chinese life. Since the communist revolution in 1949, industry in China has been owned by the state, and workers expect that their devotion will be rewarded with state-supplied care from the cradle to the grave. As the Chinese economy begins to be more market driven, however, the government is challenging these workers' expectations. In a dramatic move in March 1998, the newly elected prime minister of China, Zhu Rongji, said that state industries will be sold to private investors and that all housing will be commercialized (Eckholm 1998). These policies will have dramatic effects on hundreds of millions of Chinese, who will have to do more to look after themselves.

Economics

Society   From the social point of view, business provides products, services, jobs, training, technology, and taxes. As described in Chapter 3: The Corporation, government passes laws of incorporation, which make corporations possible. Proponents of EAW argue that the doctrine is necessary if we are to have free, efficient markets. Free markets are usually justified by the claim that they provide for the greatest sum total of happiness in a society: they "maximize utility." By their very definition, free markets require that individuals be free to compete for any job for which they are qualified. It seems that limiting EAW would limit the competition for jobs. Is this true? The answer is "yes" and "no." Let's look at the "no" answer first.

The answer is "no" because some limitations on EAW do not interfere with domestic competition in the labor market so long as they set standards that apply to everyone, such as the minimum wage and the 40-hour week. Because these apply to all participants, no applicant is given greater or lesser opportunity to get a job, and no company has a greater or lesser chance of attracting employees. Yet the answer is also "yes," because limitations on EAW do alter the competitive environment of the labor market. Fortunately, this is sometimes exactly what we want. Consider the case of child labor. If we look back in human history, we see that child labor was the norm in hunter-gatherer tribes and in small, traditional agricultural societies. It worked well in those environments because children learned skills they would need as adults.

In large, technology-based societies, child labor is a disaster for the child and the group. Child workers do not get much schooling, and without an education, they will be unable to participate and contribute to the larger society. The lack of education is especially harmful because there appear to be *developmental windows* of education. That is, if children do not learn elementary math by a certain age, they will never be able progress to algebra, trigonometry, and calculus. This is also true of reading skills. If children do not learn to read at an early age, they may never acquire the kind of reading skills that are required in order to excel in college and in the business world.

Although restrictions on EAW do restrict free labor markets, this is often demanded by society. These restrictions are implemented to achieve other social goals, such as allowing individuals to find and keep employment, without which they would not be able to support themselves or their families. If people cannot afford to support themselves, others will pay the price for this in the form of taxes, and an additional cost in social discontent. To avoid these unwelcome consequences, society has chosen to limit EAW.

Consumers Consumers typically do not know if the products they buy and the services they use are produced by employees who are treated well. The only way they might know this is if disgruntled workers or their advocates bring this information to the consumer. In the mid-1990s this is just what happened. Advocates of labor in third-world countries revealed that Kathie Lee Gifford's line of clothing, sold in Wal-Mart discount stores, was made by children in third-world factories (Polter 1997). These children were paid pennies per hour, forced to work 12 to 15 hours per day, and were yelled at and hit by their bosses if they did not work fast enough. At first Ms. Gifford denied it, but when she discovered that it was true, she vowed to change the conditions under which her clothing was made.

A similar event occurred in the 1970s when the people who pick California grapes tried to form a union. Because the pro-union laws passed in the 1930s that had helped factory workers did not apply to agricultural workers (see Law, below), the owners simply fired union officials and the workers who wanted to join the union. In order to press their cause, union leaders and sympathizers led a nationwide boycott on grapes. Although this did not stop the sale of grapes, it did hurt the grape industry, forcing the producers to talk to the unions. As of this date, however, little progress has been made.

These two cases reveal a close connection between ethics and economics. The public demands that companies not use their power to force unfair arrangements on employees. This is clear, as Mrs. Gifford, Disney, Nike, and others are working to clean up labor practices in their overseas production.

Producers The employment at will doctrine gives managers the right to hire and fire at will, allowing them to terminate bad employees and secure good ones, so it is no surprise that they support it. If managers think it makes good economic sense to develop a more long-term relationship with a worker or workers, they can negotiate an employment contract tailored to the specific situation. As we have seen in our discussion of EAW, this kind of managerial discretion died long ago, and it is not likely to return.

The most business can hope to accomplish is a weakening of the laws that limit their control over hiring and firing. One of the most important ways that business influences legislation is by contributing to the campaigns of politicians who promise to reduce government regulation. President Reagan, who garnered many dollars from a wide variety of business interests, was a vocal critic of government regulation, and did all he could to reduce it. George Bush followed in Reagan's footsteps. The 1991 Civil Rights Act was supported by Bush because it got rid of quotas in hiring **protected classes**, which seemed to be allowed by the 1964 Civil Rights Act. Whether the 1991 Act has this effect is not clear, but it is clear that the number of employee suits charging business with discrimination has gone up dramatically since 1991 (Chlopecki 1997).

Despite these moves to weaken regulation, there is a public demand to treat people well, and not merely as resources or factors of production. This demand is expressed directly when consumers avoid products made by employees who are treated badly, and expressed indirectly, through the medium of government regulation.

Law

During the last century and well into this one, it was almost always the employer who set the terms and conditions of employment: who was hired, the rate of pay, the nature of the work, the causes of dismissal, and so on. This was especially so during the latter half of the nineteenth century, when the Industrial Revolution caught hold of America, and a small percentage of the population accumulated enormous amounts of capital, constructed empires, and established a buyer's market for human labor. As the factories grew larger and employed more people, and waves of immigrants arrived at U.S. ports, the individual worker found himself or herself in an extremely weak position to bargain with a capitalist about a job. In this context, it is little wonder that by the turn of the century, workers throughout urban America rigorously pursued a strategy begun in New York City during the 1820s: They organized themselves into groups in order to increase their bargaining power and to promote terms and conditions of employment more favorable to workers. Usually, this bargaining power was wielded in the form of a work stoppage or *strike*.

Labor Unions   The judicial and legislative branches of government were generally not receptive to this exercise of employee power. Much of the nineteenth century saw the courts siding with business when strikes occurred, viewing them as the infliction of economic harm. The Sherman Antitrust Act see also Chapter 3: The Corporation—Antitrust Issues, Law) was passed in 1890 as an antidote to the huge monopolies or **trusts** that had developed over the previous 30 or 40 years, particularly in the oil and beef industries, and in the railways. Although the point of the Sherman Act was to stimulate business competition and outlaw the practice of eliminating competitors, the first section of the statute became a tool to prevent workers from organizing into unions. Section 1 declares illegal any business practice "in restraint of trade or commerce." Many courts around the turn of the century, culminating in the Supreme Court decision *Loewe v. Lawlor*, 208 U.S. 274 (1908), ruled that union strikes and boycotts violated Section 1 of the Sherman Act. **Injunctions** to end the union action were typically accompanied by law enforcement officers intent on compelling compliance.

Nonetheless, by this time public sentiment seemed clearly on the side of organized labor, and in 1914 Congress passed the Clayton Act (see also Chapter 3: The Corporation—Antitrust; Law Issues). Section 6 stated that a worker's labor is not to be considered a good available in commerce, and that a labor union was not an illegal combination acting in restraint of trade. Obviously, the congressional intent was for organized labor to evade the provisions of the Sherman Act, but courts again tended to side with big business by finding many exceptions to the Clayton Act. Striking workers, they said, were exempted from the Clayton Act's protection because they were no longer employees, union organizers were exempted because they were not employees, as were those who signed *yellow-dog contracts*. The appropriate cease and desist injunction followed.

A **yellow-dog contract** was actually a clause in a contract stipulating that employment was conditional on the refusal to join a union. Despite being consistently upheld by the courts, including the Supreme Court (see *Coppage v. Kansas*, below), this sort of employment condition was banned in 1926 with the passage of the Railway Labor Act, 45 U.S.C. §§151–188. This act also created the National Mediation Board; the board's mission is to promote voluntary conciliation between management and the union, and to propose binding arbitration if no settlement is reached.

In 1932 Congress finally solved the recurring problem of antiunion sentiment in the judicial system by enacting the Federal Anti-Injunction Act, more commonly known as the Norris-LaGuardia Act, 29 U.S.C. §§101–115). This move was transparently motivated to take the matter out of the hands of the courts altogether: Labor disputes were no longer under their jurisdiction; the injunction could no longer be used to hammer down union protests. This act also marks the beginning of direct congressional activity in support of organized labor. Just a few years later, the National Labor Relations Act (see Selected Cases, below) was passed, probably the single most important piece of legislation favoring workers who organize on their own behalf.

Today, about 25 percent of America's labor force are union members. For them, the terms and conditions of employment are negotiated on their behalf by a labor union. In addition, virtually all workers in federal, state, and local governments are covered by applicable civil service laws that define the employer–employee relationship in the public sector. This constitutes about 20 percent of all workers. So approximately half of all employees must deal with employers individually. What is the nature of this relationship?

Employment at Will   It is a settled matter of common law that when an employer and an employee willingly enter into an agreement to exchange goods (money) for services (labor), the relationship continues only so long as both parties will that it do so. This arrangement is known as **employment at will** (EAW). As we have seen above in Ethics, the main idea of EAW is that employer and employee alike are entitled to strike any sort of deal that they find mutually acceptable, without being hindered by external forces. Unless they specifically agree otherwise, each may end the relationship at any time. The first clear statement of EAW in common law is usually attributed to H. G. Wood and his 1877 book *A Treatise on the Law of Master and Servant*. Wood canvassed nineteenth-century court cases involving the *master–servant*, or employer–employee, relationship and concluded that any general or indefinite hiring is done "at will." The doctrine was first given legal ratification in a case challenging a termination of employment. In *Paine v. Western & A.R.R.*, 81 Tenn. 507 (1884), the Tennessee Supreme Court declared: "All may dismiss their employee(s) at will, be they many or few, for good cause, for no cause, or even for a cause morally wrong."

During the 1870s businesses began to argue that their claim to independence from government regulation was validated by the **Due Process Clause** of the Fourteenth Amendment to the Constitution (see also Chapter 3: The Corporation—Law; The Rights of Corporations). This clause prohibits government from "depriv[ing] any person of life, liberty or property without due process of law." Businesses focused on the liberty and property rights affirmed in the clause, reasoning that the machinery and raw materials they utilized to manufacture products were their property, and they were free to use their property as they wished. Federal laws regulating their businesses violated this right. Initially, this argument was not well received by the courts: in 1877 the Supreme Court upheld an Illinois law regulating the prices charged by grain elevator operators (*Munn v. Illinois*, 94 U.S. 113 [1877]). But the resistance of the judiciary was gradually worn down, especially when the due process argument was applied to the terms and conditions of employment.

After all, a person's labor is his property, and, according to the interpretation favored by business, a person is just as free to sell his or her labor as a commodity to an employer as an employer is free to use his or her money to buy labor. The Due Process Clause protects both parties from the government interfering with their agreements concerning the exchange of their property. Thus, the doctrine of at-will employment was given a powerful constitutional justification. At the end of the nineteenth century, and well into the twentieth, the judiciary found this appeal to be quite convincing.

Two historic Supreme Court cases elevated the doctrine to a constitutional right. In *Lochner v. New York*, 198 U.S. 45 (1905), the high Court rejected a New York statute limiting the number of hours a baker could work to 60 per week precisely because the law violated the Due Process Clause of the Fourteenth Amendment; the clause entitles employers and employees to contract on mutually acceptable terms. And in *Coppage v. Kansas*, 236 U.S. 1 (1914), the Supreme Court struck down another state statute, this one making it illegal to require prospective employees to sign yellow-dog contracts, that is, agreements not to join a labor union. The statute was unconstitutional because—again—it violated a right to contract freely for employment. (As noted above, Congress eventually outlawed yellow-dog contracts with the Railway Labor Act of 1926.)

Because the highest court in the land was not imposing any restrictions, and indeed shielding the doctrine with the Constitution, appeal to EAW sanctioned a variety of abuses of workers. Perhaps the best example of this, representing the apogee of the doctrine, is found in *Comerford v. International Harvester Corporation*, 235 Ala. 376 (1938). Here, the Alabama Supreme Court rejected the claim of a man who was fired because his wife refused to have sex with his job foreman. The court observed that since Mr. Comerford was an at-will employee, he could be fired for any reason or for no reason at all. However, at nearly the same time Alabama was depriving a man of his job because his wife would not prostitute herself, the Supreme Court was dealing a major blow to the due process foundation of at-will employment. *West Coast Hotel v. Parrish* signaled the beginning of the end for EAW as an unrestricted employment practice (see below).

Selected Cases, Statutes, and Regulations

National Labor Relations Act of 1935, 29 U.S.C. §§142 *et seq.* The National Labor Relations Act (NLRA), also known as the **Wagner Act**, after its sponsor, Senator Robert Wagner, set up an infrastructure to provide for the continued vital existence of labor unions. The NLRA contains five major features:

- **Employee rights.** Section 7 declares that workers have the right to organize into unions, to join and assist unions, and to bargain collectively with their chosen representatives. Union management is entitled to recommend a strike if an agreement cannot be reached; a majority of the union membership must vote for a strike. Strikes causing property damage or personal injury, or those in which employees occupy the employer's premises, are illegal. The right to picket is *implied* by NLRA, not stated. Picketing is lawful unless it is accompanied by violence, obstructs customers or nonstriking employees of the struck business, or prevents pickups and deliveries. The NLRA does not cover all workers; among others, government employees, agricultural workers, airline and railroad employees, and managers and supervisors are excluded.

- **National Labor Relations Board (NLRB).** The NLRB administers and enforces the Wagner Act. The five-person board is appointed by the president and subject to Senate approval. It has two primary functions: (1) to oversee the selection of the union representative in collective bargaining; and (2) to investigate complaints of unfair labor practices and prosecute those they find.

- **Employer unfair labor practices.** Section 8(a) lists these as interfering with employees who form or join unions, discrimination against employees for union activity (see also Whistleblowing and Loyalty, this chapter), domination of union administration by company officials, and refusing to engage in collective bargaining with the designated representative of the employees.

- **Good faith bargaining.** Section 8 also requires employers and employee representatives to "meet at reasonable times and confer in *good faith* with respect to wages, hours, and other terms and conditions of employment." (Emphasis added.) Good faith bargaining is perhaps best understood in terms of what it is not. Bargaining in *bad* faith is an unfair labor practice, and includes such things as insisting on illegal terms of contract, refusing to execute a written contract, unions refusing to agree on a reasonable contract period, and employers unilaterally changing wages, hours, or working conditions. The courts have found that refusing to bargain at all, that is, entering negotiations with a take-it-or-leave-it attitude, is not bargaining in good faith (*NLRB v. General Electric Company*, 418 F.2d 736 (2d Cir. 1959); see also *NLRB v. Truitt Manufacturing Company*, below, for another key feature of good-faith bargaining). Employers are not required to make concessions, but nor should they arrive at the bargaining table intending to give nothing at all.

- **Bargaining unit.** Section 9 details the procedures for creating or designating a union to represent employees in various *bargaining units*. The process begins when either an employer, an employee, or an already established union files a petition with the regional NLRB office indicating substantial employee support. The bargaining unit may be formed as a wholly new union, in cooperation with an existing union, or, what is most often the case, as part of an existing union. An election is then conducted by the NLRB office, and the winner is designated the exclusive bargaining representative. *Exclusive* means that employers must bargain with this representative and no other, and employees are prohibited from making individual contracts with employers, even if they voted against unionization entirely.

The Wagner Act legitimized and empowered the unions in an unprecedented fashion, which is to say that there was a corresponding diminution of power for many of the nation's employers. So it did not take long for business to challenge the constitutionality of the NLRA. Employers typically argued that the Tenth Amendment to the Constitution reserves the regulation of labor for the individual states, not the federal government. The Supreme Court was unpersuaded; *NLRB v. Jones & Laughlin Steel Corporation*, 301 U.S. 1 (1937) affirmed that the Wagner Act was constitutional.

Taft-Hartley Act of 1947, 29 U.S.C. §§141 *et seq.* The decade following the enactment of the National Labor Relations Act (NLRA; see above) was one in which unions experienced enormous growth and exercised unparalleled power. Congress had intended the NLRA to level the labor playing field by raising up the workers, but the field kept tipping and before very long the balance of power shifted in favor of the unions. Between 1945 and 1947 industrywide strikes occurred in the railroads, coal mining, lumber, automobile manufacturers, and others, and public sympathy for unions began to wane.

The Taft-Hartley Act, formally known as the Labor-Management Relations Act, was designed to counteract this new imbalance by adding Section 8(b) to the NLRA, defining unfair labor practices on the part of unions. These included coercing an employee to join a union, establishing a *closed shop* (causing an employer to discriminate against nonunion employees), and causing an employer to pay for work that was not done. Taft-Hartley also requires unions (not just management) to bargain in good faith, gives federal courts the authority to enforce collective bargaining agreements, and prohibits federal employees from striking. Finally, the president was given the authority to seek an injunction for up to 80 days for strikes that would create national emergencies, and the Federal Mediation and Conciliation Service was created to handle such strikes.

Section 14(b) also allowed the states to reject unions entirely: "Nothing in this Act shall be construed as authorizing the execution or application of agreements requiring membership in a labor organization as a condition of employment in any State or Territory in which such execution or application is prohibited by State or Territorial Law." In other words, states can pass **right-to-work laws**. Strictly speaking, right-to-work laws do not make unions illegal, rather they prohibit the formation of either a **union shop** or an **agency shop**. In a union shop, an employee must join a union (typically within one month of being hired), and an employer must discharge an employee who does not join. In an agency shop, employees are not required to join the union, but they must pay an *agency fee* that is equivalent to union dues. By outlawing these shops, the practical effect is to ban unions, because a state thereby removes all incentives to form a union in the first place. Right-to-work laws are often enacted to attract businesses to a nonunion and therefore lower-wage labor environment. Today, 21 states have these laws; about three-quarters of them are found in the South and Southwest.

Landrum-Griffin Act of 1959, 29 U.S.C. §§153 *et seq.* Congressional hearings during the 1950s revealed that many unions were rife with corruption and various abuses of power. To rectify the situation, Congress again amended the National Labor Relations Act (NLRA; see above) with the Labor-Management Reporting and Disclosure Act, more commonly known as the Landrum-Griffin Act, named after its two sponsoring senators. The main thrust of the act is to exert greater internal control over union activities, particularly by requiring unions and employers to file financial disclosure forms, and by providing penalties for misconduct on the part of union officials. The act also forbids ex-convicts and communists from holding union offices.

Landrum-Griffin added several more unfair labor practices to Section 8 of the NLRA. For example, unions and employers are prohibited from making **secondary agreements**; this occurs when an employer with whom the union does *not* have a dispute agrees not to make purchases from another employer with whom the union *does* have a dispute. **Hot-cargo contracts** are also prohibited: These are agreements by an employer with a union to refrain from dealing with nonunion employers. Interestingly, the Supreme Court had ruled that such contracts were constitutional (*United Brotherhood of Carpenters and Joiners, Local 1976 v. NLRB*, 357 U.S. 93 (1958), but Congress rejected the idea just one year later.

***West Coast Hotel v. Parrish*, 300 U.S. 379 (1937)** Here we have one of the earliest cases in which limits were placed on the doctrine of employment at will (see above), and the first time the Supreme Court upheld them. This case concerned a woman named Elsie Parrish and a statute enacted in the state of Washington that authorized the fixing of minimum wages for women and minors. Mrs. Parrish worked as a maid at the West Coast Hotel in Olympia. Although the statute required employers to pay at least 32¢ per hour, she received less. Relying on an earlier Supreme Court decision (*Adkins v. Children's Hospital*, 261 U.S. 525 (1923), the hotel argued that the minimum wage requirement violated a right to freedom of contract, a right that the hotel discerned to follow from the **Due Process Clause** of the Fifth Amendment, and that competent adults were free to enter into contracts on terms mutually acceptable to the affected parties.

Chief Justice Charles Evans Hughes was unpersuaded. His majority opinion observed first that liberty rights are not absolute; in a host of cases the Supreme Court has restricted the freedom of contract between employers and employees. (Hughes did not mention *Coppage v. Kansas* or *Lochner v. New York*; see both above, Employment At Will). In these cases, the restrictions were justified in order to promote health, safety, "wholesome conditions of work, and freedom from oppression" in the workplace. These same considerations applied to the Washington statute, particularly in the case of women whose "physical structure and performance of maternal functions place [them] at a disadvantage in the struggle for subsistence." Ironically, the sexist flavor of Justice Hughes's remarks here produced a benefit for women because there was no minimum wage law for men at this time.

Hughes went on to assert that even though the parties to a contract are competent adults, the state is entitled to interfere when the parties do not stand on an equal footing. This is certainly the case when an employer has a pool of many prospective employees to choose from, while an individual worker cannot simply go out and select a job. Finally, Hughes pointed out that not only is at-will employment detrimental to workers, but taxpayers generally are adversely effected when they must make up the difference between the wages offered and those that are required to achieve a decent standard of living. Washington's minimum wage law was thus ruled constitutional and the *Adkins* decision was overturned.

Fair Labor Standards Act of 1938, 29 U.S.C. §§201–215 Inspired by *West Coast Hotel v. Parrish* (see above) and other minimum wage cases, as well as by the terrible conditions and oppressive hours inflicted on workers during the job-thin Depression years, Congress passed the Fair Labor Standards Act (FLSA) in 1938. The main features of FLSA were (1) a definition of overtime (any hours exceeding 40 in one week must be compensated at one-and-one-half times the normal rate of pay); (2) a setting of the minimum wage (25¢ in 1938; 60 years later it stands at $5.15 per hour); and (3) provisions for child labor. The act withstood a constitutional challenge in *United States v. F.W. Darby Lumber Company*, 312 U.S. 100 (1941). The FLSA has been amended many times. Some of the highlights include: the Equal Pay Act (see this chapter, Discrimination and Affirmative Action, Law) requiring that women and men receive the same rate of pay for jobs of equal skill, effort, and responsibility; coverage for employees of hospitals and educational institutions; and strict guidelines for determining and accruing compensatory time (time off work instead of cash payments).

The FLSA applies to employers whose annual sales are at least $500,000, or that are involved in interstate commerce. Because receiving or sending mail or making phone calls across state lines qualifies as interstate commerce, nearly every workplace is included. Some of the major exemptions from the FLSA are executive, administrative, and professional employees, farm workers, amusement park employees, newspeople on small, local newspapers, personal companions, and babysitters.

Individuals under 18 years old are not allowed to work any job designated by the secretary of labor as hazardous (e.g., mining, logging, roofing), and children under 14 cannot work any job except newspaper delivery. Children between the ages of 14 and 16 are allowed a maximum of 3 hours work on a school day and 8 hours on a nonschool day; they are never permitted to start work before 7 A.M. and, except in summer when they may work until 10 p.m., they must quit work by 7 P.M. Minors of any age may work in the entertainment industry, but here too their hours are strictly limited. State child labor laws are typically more stringent (except for age restrictions) than these minimum standards set by the FLSA, especially in California and New York where many children are employed in entertainment and various other forms of commercial media. Children working in agriculture are exempt from these laws.

NLRB v. Babcock and Wilcox Company, **351 U.S. 105 (1956);** *LRB v. Truitt Manufacturing Company*, **351 U.S. 149 (1956)** These two Supreme Court cases, decided just one week apart, set precedents for two vital issues concerning the actions of employers toward unions. The first issue pertains to whether employers must allow union organizers, who are not themselves employees, to solicit workers at their nonunionized place of employment. Is a union organizer entitled to recruit on the workplace premises? The second problem deals with contract negotiations: typically, the main topic of such negotiations is the rate of pay, and employers almost invariably claim that they cannot afford what the union wants. Is the employer required to prove that this claim is true?

Consider first the question of union involvement on nonunion premises. Babcock & Wilcox manufactured boilers and accessories on a 100-acre tract, employing 500 nonunionized employees. When union organizers attempted to distribute union literature in the company parking lot and talk to employees about organizing, they were deterred by a Babcock & Wilcox policy that prohibited the distribution of any sort of pamphlet on company property. Unfortunately, the nearest public access to the plant was too close to the highway to safely distribute the material, and attempting to do so there presented a traffic hazard. After investigating the union complaint, the National Labor Relations Board (NLRB) charged the company with an unfair labor practice in violation of the National Labor Relations Act (NLRA; see above); in particular, interfering with employees' attempts to form or join unions.

When the case reached the Supreme Court, Justice Reed's majority opinion was that the company was not guilty of any violation, but he also specified when such a violation might occur. He allowed that employers are entitled to prohibit the distribution of union leaflets on their private property so long as union organizers are able to reach workers through other available means of communication, such as telephone calls and mailings. However, he added that employers may not exclusively target unions for this ban, while permitting other organizations to distribute their materials. Reed noted in conclusion that, while the NLRA does not permit employers to interfere with, coerce, or discriminate against employees exercising their rights to organize, it also does not require them to allow their place of business to be used for organization efforts when other means are readily available. The decision implies that if unions do not have other readily accessible alternatives to communicate their message to workers, employers must allow them the use of company property to do so.

The second key question concerning employer practices is the substantiation of claims of an inability to pay wage increases. A union representing some of Truitt Manufacturing's employees requested a wage increase of 10¢ per hour. Truitt responded that the company could not possibly pay more than 2.5¢ without going out of business. When the union asked for financial records that would support Truitt's position, the company refused to supply anything, contending that such information was not relevant and that the union had no legal right to it. The NLRB found that by refusing to provide any evidence of its financial situation, Truitt had not bargained in good faith, a violation of Section 8 of the NLRA. Truitt was ordered to produce the evidence.

The Fourth Circuit Court of Appeals declined to enforce the order. Yet, in another case, the Second Circuit Court of Appeals had agreed with an NLRB judgment of bad-faith bargaining when another company had refused to make financial disclosures (*NLRB v. Jackson Manufacturing Company*, 196 F.2d 680 (1953). This clash of circuit court decisions led the Supreme Court to offer a definitive answer. The answer sided with the NLRB. Justice Hugo Black articulated what has come to be known as the **honest claims doctrine**. Black wrote that "[g]ood-faith bargaining necessarily requires that claims made by either bargainer should be honest claims. This is true about an asserted inability to pay an increase in wages. If such an argument is important enough to be present in the give and take of bargaining, it is important enough to require some proof of its accuracy."

Petermann v. International Brotherhood of Teamsters, **344 P.2d 25 (Cal. 1959)** This landmark decision of the California Supreme Court is famous for placing a severe restriction on the doctrine of **employment at will** while serving as the controlling case for the important issue of dismissal for refusing to break the law. It is also interesting because it involves an at-will employee working for a labor union, who was at the same time a member of that union.

Peter Petermann was a member of Local 396 of the International Brotherhood of Teamsters; he was also the unit's business agent. An investigative committee of the California legislature issued a subpoena to Petermann, ordering him to testify before the committee about the financial status of Local 396. According to Petermann, upon learning of his subpoena, the secretary-treasurer of his unit instructed him to make false statements during his testimony. Petermann did not comply with the demand to commit perjury, and answered truthfully all questions put to him by the committee. The next day, the secretary-treasurer informed Petermann that he was no longer the business agent for Local 396, and shortly after that Petermann was handed a card stating that his membership in the union had been terminated. He sued for back pay lost after the discharge and for reinstatement in the union.

The court noted that, since Petermann had not been promised employment for any specified length of time, he was an at-will employee, signifying a relationship that could be discharged at any time. However, the at-will rule was not absolute and could be limited by more weighty considerations. In this case, the court found that public policy concerns outweighed the prevailing standards of this particular employment relationship (for more on public policy and dismissals, see this chapter, Whistleblowing and Loyalty, *Palmateer v. International Harvester Company*). The concern at issue here is the simple administration of justice: If employers were allowed to terminate their employees for refusing to commit perjury, the public welfare would be seriously threatened. To make job security contingent upon criminal conduct is to encourage wrongdoing by both the employer and employee, and thus jeopardize the very point of legal rules, which is simply to promote honesty and fair dealing. Petermann won his suit.

Cases of this nature were rare during the 1960s but by the 1970s litigation involving employees claiming they were fired for not engaging in illegal activity began to increase, and nearly every decision favoring the plaintiff appealed to the public policy concern first articulated in *Petermann*. One such case that presaged a wave of similar litigation was decided by the Michigan Supreme Court in 1978. Frank Trombetta successfully argued that he was unjustly fired because he would not agree to alter sampling results in pollution control reports required by the state; falsification of such documents was prohibited by state law (*Trombetta v. Detroit, Toledo & Ironton Railroad Company*, 265 N.W.2d 385 [Mich. 1978]). And in 1980 the California Supreme Court had occasion to reaffirm its decision in *Petermann* by applying public policy concerns in finding for another discharged at-will employee who had refused to commit an illegal act. Gordon Tameny was fired for refusing to participate in a price-fixing scheme in violation of state antitrust laws, but the court would not allow the discharge (*Tameny v. Atlantic Richfield Company*, 610 P.2d 1330 [Cal. 1980]).

One of the first dismissals invalidated by appeal to public policy, however, did not involve an employee refusing to commit an illegal act. Olga Monge received a promotion at Beebe Rubber Company on the understanding that she date her job foreman; when she then refused to do so, she was demoted and finally fired. In ruling for Monge in its 1974 decision, the New Hampshire Supreme Court held that the public good is served by employment practices that promote a stable economy and by balancing workers' job interests and employers' interests in running a business; a dismissal such as this, motivated by malice and bad faith, is contrary to the public good (*Monge v. Beebe Rubber Company*, 114 N.H. 130 [1974]).

Perry v. Sindermann, 408 U.S. 593 (1972) From 1959 to 1969, Robert Sindermann worked as a teacher in the Texas state college system. The last four years he was professor of government and social science at Odessa Junior College, working a series of one-year contracts. During the 1968–1969 academic year, Sindermann was elected president of the Texas Junior College Teachers Association; he then began to vocally advocate the conversion of the college to a four-year institution, a move adamantly opposed by the board of regents. A newspaper ad appeared, bearing Sindermann's name, that was very critical of the regents' position. In May 1969 Sindermann's contract expired and the regents voted not to offer him another one for the next year. They produced a statement charging him with insubordination, but no specific reasons were given for not renewing his contract. Sindermann was denied an opportunity to challenge the regents' decision.

Sindermann sued the regents in federal district court on two grounds: The decision not to rehire him because of his public remarks violated his right to free speech, and the refusal to allow him a hearing violated his right to due process as guaranteed by the Fourteenth Amendment. The district court ruled against Sindermann, but the circuit court of appeals reversed that judgment. The Supreme Court then agreed to consider the issue.

What is interesting and germinal about this case is the appeal to the **Due Process Clause** of the Fourteenth Amendment. That clause prohibits the state from taking a person's life, liberty, or property without due process of law. For many years in the late nineteenth century and well into the twentieth, businesses had argued that their property included the machinery, materials, and money needed to manufacture a product, while a worker's labor was his property. Government intervention in agreements made by employers and employees concerning the disposition of their respective property in a working relationship was a violation of due process (for details, see above, Law: Employment At Will). Now, Robert Sindermann is claiming that the *job* itself qualifies as his property, and taking it away from him without a hearing is a failure of due process.

The Supreme Court agreed. In the landmark majority decision, Justice Potter Stewart first noted that the issue of the free speech violation could not be settled, but did not need to be in order to find in Sindermann's favor. Stewart determined that Sindermann did indeed have a legitimate property interest in his job: Odessa College and the state university system fostered a binding understanding that so long as a teacher performs satisfactorily and cooperates with colleagues and staff, continued employment would be assured. Given this understanding, and the lack of evidence that his performance was not satisfactory, Sindermann held an entitlement to his job that demanded the opportunity for a fair hearing before it could be taken away from him. Thus, a job is a form of property under the Fourteenth

Amendment; employees cannot be deprived of their jobs without due process.

Reid v. Sears, Roebuck & Company, 790 F.2d 453 (6th Cir. 1986)
Some judicial history is needed to best appreciate this important case. We start with Charles Toussaint and Walter Ebling, two people working different jobs in Michigan. Both men were given verbal assurances by their respective employers that they would not be fired without just cause. However, Toussaint was asked to resign, and Ebling was fired after he exercised a very lucrative stock option in the company. In deciding the two cases together, the Michigan Supreme Court ruled in favor of Toussaint and Ebling. Although both were at-will employees, they had each been given an implied contract as a result of being told that their jobs were secure, and because of certain statements made in their employee manuals (*Toussaint v. Blue Cross & Blue Shield of Michigan* and *Ebling v. Masco Corporation*, 292 N.W.2d 880 [Mich. 1980]). The idea that an at-will employee might have such an implied contract providing protection against unjust discharge originates with this case.

This seminal finding of a state high court was put to the test at the federal level in a case several years later involving three individuals who were dismissed without just cause from their jobs at different Michigan Sears stores. All three claimed that, despite the fact that they were at-will employees, Sears needed to show just cause. They cited *Toussaint* and *Ebling* as the controlling precedent.

The circumstances of the various discharges were not unequivocal. Mary Ann Reid wanted to help her mother file an insurance claim for a stolen car battery, so she asked a coworker to produce receipts for two batteries, one for the battery that had been stolen and the second for a replacement. Both batteries had been purchased at Sears, but the receipt for the stolen one had been lost and the original receipt for the replacement was not in the name of the policy holder. Reid was fired when the scheme was exposed, though she claimed the discharge was part of an ongoing Sears practice of replacing higher paid full-time employees with lower paid part-timers. John Serra was fired for selling regularly priced merchandise at discount prices; he claimed that the purchases were made on rainchecks and that the dismissal was really in retaliation for disagreements concerning sales policies. Mary Batchelor was fired for failing to pay for a bottle of nail polish she had removed from the cosmetics department and taken to the store locker room; she said she intended to pay for the item and was fired to pad the store manager's record of apprehended shoplifters.

Chief Judge Lively found a significant difference between this case and *Toussaint* and *Ebling*. Reid, Serra, and Batchelor had all signed an employment application explicitly stating that they would be employed at the will or pleasure of the Sears, Roebuck Company. This crucial factor is precisely what Blue Cross & Blue Shield and Masco had not supplied in their employment applications, thus giving rise to the successful claims of an implied contract. This observation in effect validates the state supreme court decision at the federal level. Lively further noted that the clear statement in the Sears application was all that was required to create an express contract for employment at will. Consequently, there could not be an implied contract requiring just cause of dismissal.

NLRB v. Retail Store Employees Union, Local 1001, **477 U.S. 607 (1980)** Is it legal for a union to publicize the fact that a business with whom it has no dispute is handling the products of another business with whom it does have a dispute? The National Labor Relations Act (NLRA; see above) suggests that the answer is "no." Section 8 prohibits union efforts to coerce or restrain individuals who are not involved in a labor dispute from "using, selling, handling, transporting or otherwise dealing in the products of any other producer...or to cease doing business with any other person." However, in the landmark case *NLRB v. Fruit and Vegetable Packers* (377 U.S. 58 (1964), *Tree Fruits* for short), the Supreme Court found that some types of publicity are legally permissible.

In *Tree Fruits*, a union striking certain Washington fruit packers (the primary employer) set up picket lines at several area supermarkets (the secondary employer) in an attempt to persuade shoppers not to buy the produce of the struck packers. The Court held that there is a distinction between picketing that is intended to close down all commerce with a secondary employer unless it cooperates with the union, and picketing that merely attempts to influence consumers to avoid the products of the primary employer. The former type of picketing does violate NLRA, while the latter does not. Thus the *Tree Fruits* **Principle** holds that (peaceful) picketing of a secondary employer is permissible so long as the object of the protest is a particular product and not the business as a whole. Picketing the supermarkets was vindicated.

Retail Store Employees Union, Local 1001 presents a further development of this principle. This case also involved a business interest in Washington, this time the Safeco Title Insurance Company, located in Seattle. Certain Safeco employees were members of Local 1001 when union negotiations with the company broke down and a strike was called. Picketing commenced at Safeco's Seattle office, and at the offices of five local title companies with whom Safeco had a close business relationship, even though Local 1001 was not the collective bargaining representative for any of the employees at those other title firms. This demonstration at a secondary employer implicates the *Tree Fruits* principle.

The National Labor Relations Board (NLRB; see above, National Labor Relations Act) charged Local 1001 with an unfair labor practice in violation of Section 8 of NLRA. The union defended the picketing of a secondary employer by appeal to the *Tree Fruits* case. However, Justice Lewis Powell's majority decision discerned a crucial difference between this case and that one. Although the picketing of the other title companies did target a particular product and not the business itself, the nature of the title company business is such that a secondary protest does strike at the entire enterprise. Unlike the *Tree Fruits* case, in which a successful protest would induce the retailer to simply discontinue the product due to poor sales, effective union influence on the clients of the title companies would either cause clients to cease patronizing them altogether, or cause the companies to sever their relationship with Safeco. Powell found that both outcomes were in violation of NLRA.

More recently, the Supreme Court had occasion to offer yet another modification of the *Tree Fruits* principle. This time the publicizing of union dissatisfaction was not picketing, rather, it was the distribution of handbills at the entrances of a shopping mall in Tampa, Florida. The owner of the mall, Edward DeBartolo, had contracted with a local construction company to build a department store at the shopping center. The union, claiming that the company paid substandard wages, urged customers to boycott *all* the mall's stores until DeBartolo employed a construction firm that offered a fair rate of pay. DeBartolo demanded that the NLRB order the union to stop the distribution of the handbills.

Like *Tree Fruits* and *Retail Store Employees Union, DeBartolo Corporation v. Florida Gulf Coast Trades Council* (485 U.S. 568 (1988), concerns union protests directed at secondary employers. However, it is not like *Tree Fruits* because the protest was not about a particular product, it was instead directed at all retail businesses in the mall and therefore *all* their products. This resembles *Retail Store Employees Union* and suggests a favorable outcome for DeBartolo, except there is a dissimilarity from that case too. Remember, *Retail Store Employees Union* involved *picketing*, while here we have the distribution of handbills; the trade union did not form picket lines or in any way patrol the mall. The unanimous opinion of the Supreme Court, authored by Justice Byron White, found this to be the decisive factor. Because there was no picketing, violence, patrolling, or intimidating conduct, there was no attempt on the part of the union to coerce or compel consumers to take their business elsewhere. Moreover, the Court could not locate any evidence that Congress, in drawing up Section 8 of NLRA, intended to ban the peaceful dispersal of handbills as a form of union publicity.

Worker Adjustment and Retraining Notification Act of 1988, 29 U.S.C. §2101 More commonly known as the Plant Closing Act or the WARN Act, this federal statute requires employers with 100 or more employees to give their workers at least 60 days advance notice before proceeding with plant closings or layoffs. If the employees are represented by a union, the company must notify the union; if there is no union representation, each employee must be notified individually.

Not all layoffs and plant closings are covered by the act, and there are certain circumstances in which an employer does not have to give notice. Notification must be given for large or mass layoffs: these are defined as either work reductions of 33 percent or more of the labor force, or when at least 50 employees are to be laid off during a 30-day period. Notification must be given for plant closings when the shutdown results in the loss of 50 or more employees over a 30-day period, whether the closing is permanent or temporary. An employer does *not* have to give notice of a shutdown or layoffs in either one of two circumstances: (1) the decision resulted from business circumstances that were not reasonably foreseeable at the time the notice should have been given; or (2) the company was vigorously pursuing sales or a capital investment that would have avoided (or at least postponed) the shutdown or layoff, *and* the employer had a good faith belief that giving notice would have prevented the necessary sales or investment from occurring.

Health and Safety

In a normal year, 10,000 workers are killed on the job and nearly 3 million are injured. The yearly cost for these deaths and injuries is estimated to be $8 billion (Grcic 1997). Job hazards can arise in a number of different ways. The clearest instance is when the job itself is dangerous, for example, fire fighting. Job hazards can occur even when the job is not itself dangerous, but the speed at which the employee must complete the job is dangerous, such as running a punch press faster than safety allows; and when the job is not dangerous, but the environment in which the job is performed is dangerous, as in a battery factory when assembly line and office workers are exposed to airborne pollutants (together with their fetuses! See below, Discrimination and Affirmative Action, Selected Cases: *International Union v. Johnson Controls, Inc.*).

Traditionally, health and safety issues have been viewed as creating conflicts between employees who want a safe workplace and managers who do not want to spend the money to make workplaces safe. This simplistic view is changing for many reasons. One reason is that the contemporary global market is making good labor very important. The raw materials, information, and technology on which business relies can be transported anywhere and acquired by anyone; skilled and reliable employees are not so easy to come by. Rather than focusing on how to keep costs low, companies are beginning to focus on how to make products better, and that requires, among other things, employees who are motivated and efficient. To create such a workforce further requires, *at a minimum*, a workplace that is as safe and as healthy as the product and the technology allow (Birkner and Birkner 1997).

The U.S. government has laws, regulatory agencies, and regulations that mandate safe workplaces. The most important law for employee health and safety is the Occupational Safety and Health Act. This law created the Occupational Safety and Health Administration (OSHA), which promulgates regulations for all types of workplaces (see Law, below). This government action is a result of citizen pressure following grisly workplace accidents and the realization that accidents on the job are costly to society.

Ethics

Promoting Self-Interest: Egoism Aggressively self-interested employees would accept workplace risks up to the point at which the risks exceed or equal the benefits. For example, construction workers would volunteer for dangerous assignments, such as fitting steel girders at the top of skyscrapers, if the pay was great enough. These employees would be wary of OSHA regulations if these rules prevented them from taking risks they believed were justified.

One problem with the aggressive approach is that the nature and amount of risk often is not clear. The actual risks depend on, among other things, the safety training and precautions the company has mandated, the quality and experience of the workers and management at the site, the quality of the materials used, and the speed at which the job is supposed to be done. Some of these safety factors are beyond OSHA control, making it difficult for employees to assess risks even in highly regulated workplaces.

Contemplatively self-interested employees, wanting to avoid pain and conflict, would be in favor of OSHA, because this regulatory agency would have a great deal of information that workers do not have, and it has the authority and power to make management improve workplace safety. However, as we just discussed, OSHA cannot control everything, which makes it difficult for employees to make reliable risk-benefit calculations. Given this difficulty, the safest course of action is to make sure that risks are always very low, so that given the inevitability of mistakes, there is never very much at stake. Complying with OSHA regulations and creating safe working conditions also causes conflicts between employees and management, so these employees would be constantly weighing how much discord is necessary in order to make a workplace safe, against how high is the level of danger they are trying to reduce.

As always, we must remember that acting in a self-interested way varies with one's interests. We can't know how a self-interested person will act unless we know precisely what interests he or she has and how that person believes these interests can be promoted.

Nurturing Personal Relationships: Care   Passive caring employees would be in favor of a safe workplace so long as their friends and family thought it was important. If they come from families that prize risk taking, they may not be very concerned with workplace safety unless they are clearly in imminent danger. Or, if they come from families that distrust government, they might reject OSHA simply because it is a government agency. On the other hand, if passive caring employees come from families that trust government, they could easily support OSHA and its rules.

Active caring employees would want a safe workplace because they need to be healthy (and alive!) to maintain and nurture their relationships. Sickness and injury put a great deal of strain on relationships, because extra time and money must be spent attending to the sick or injured person. Although these are situations in which the selfless virtue of care is exhibited, caring individuals should do what they can to avoid being the ones in need.

These employees would be in favor of OSHA as long as it is effective and does not damage personal relationships in the workplace. This presents a problem for active caring managers, because OSHA can order managers to make changes that the managers think are costly and useless. To remedy this, active caring employees would try to work with management to create a safe workplace that meets OSHA standards. For example, Richardson (1997) argues that employee-management teams can efficiently promote and monitor workplace safety. This approach fits nicely with Birkner and Birkner's insight, above, that competitive advantage results from employee expertise. Employee-management teams are a vehicle for transferring information and fostering cooperation between employees and management that can result in better products at lower costs.

Of course, all is not sweetness and light. How should active caring employees act if managers do not care about a safe workplace? If the danger is sufficiently great, and managers cannot be convinced to reduce it, caring employees may report management to OSHA. If that takes too long, they may refuse to do the job and walk out, as two workers did at Whirlpool (see below, Selected Cases: *Whirlpool Corporation v. Marshall*). Finally, even managers and employees who care about each other may care more about their families. These differences in caring can lead to conflicts when employees need to be with their families, say, at parent-teacher conferences, and at work, needing to complete a project that must be finished by tomorrow.

Promoting Group Good: Utilitarianism Utilitarian employees would be in favor of workplace safety up to the point at which costs exceed benefits. For example, if it cost $2 billion per year to make U.S. chemical plants safer, that amount would be justified if it prevented $2 billion or more in diseases, injuries, and deaths. However, if the savings were under $2 billion, utilitarian employees would recommend against spending that amount of money. For example, in *Industrial Union Department, AFL-CIO v. American Petroleum Institute*, the U.S. Supreme Court seemed to argue that companies do not have to devise protective measures for workers if the costs of doing so greatly exceed the danger (the Court argued later in *American Textile Manufacturers Institute Inc. v. Donovan* that this was not their reasoning; see both of these cases in Selected Cases, below).

Strict rule utilitarian employees would argue that strict rules are necessary so that all parties to the employment relationship know what to expect. If rules of safety are flexible, employees will not know what the work conditions will be from one time to another. If they constantly have to adjust their behavior, costs are increased to all concerned. If these employees do not trust managers, they would want strict rules because such rules make it harder for managers to cheat on safety in order to save money.

Flexible rule utilitarian employees would argue that strict rules are too costly to enforce. The stricter the rules, the more managers are likely to resist them, and the more managers resist rules, the more monitoring government will have to do. Government monitoring is expensive, soaking up tax dollars that could be spent on education, health, and other programs that could help the group more. Moreover, government monitoring is intrusive, invading the private domain of business. This is an attack on the free market that we need to avoid.

Further, the *cost of monitoring* must be added to the cost of making workplaces safer. For example, if it takes $1 billion in enforcement costs to make managers spend $2 billion to make chemical plants safer, then the total cost of making these plants safer is $3 billion. Given the cost-benefit reasoning described above, there must be an added $1 billion in benefits to justify this greater cost.

Flexible rules that employees and managers adapt to their workplaces would be much better and less costly. For example, instead of having rules that set strict limits for how much benzene can be in the air inside a factory, employee-management teams, of the kind suggested by Richardson, above, could work together to find ways to limit exposure to benzene, perhaps by rotating workers in and out of dangerous areas more frequently. Managers could also create incentive programs to reward employees for ways to make the workplace safer (Laabs 1997). Government, in turn, could reward companies with effective employee-management teams that reduce workplace hazards and accidents.

Respecting Dignity and Rights: Intrinsic Value   Employees who evaluate problems in terms of human dignity would argue that they are owed a safe workplace because no amount of savings can justify harming a human being. This view is consistent with the U.S. Supreme Court's ruling in *American Textile Manufacturers Institute Inc. v. Donovan*. In this case, the Court specifically rejected the cost-benefit ratio suggested in *AFL-CIO v. American Petroleum Institute* (see Selected Cases, below).

Although human dignity does view human life as beyond price, it bases this value on the human ability to make *free choices*. If we focus on free choice, then the level of workplace safety would be dependent on the amount of risk employees are willing to accept. This view would seem to work against a regulatory agency like OSHA, because it imposes standards on companies without consulting the employees. One way around the problem of imposing standards would be to adopt the employee-management team approach to worker safety discussed in Promoting the Good of the Group, above. This approach would give employees a voice in the amount of risk they are willing to take.

Human intrinsic value can also be expressed in terms of rights. The English philosopher John Locke (1632–1704) argued that every person has an inalienable right to life, liberty, and property. Robert Nozick, currently at Harvard University, agrees. These rights, sometimes called *natural* or *human* rights, are based on the more fundamental right to be free from interference in the pursuit of legitimate projects central to our individual well-being. Because experiencing physical harm is one way that our pursuit of life and liberty can be impeded, we have a right to be free from it. These rights are reflected in laws that make murder and assault criminal offenses, and, of course, these laws apply within and outside of the workplace.

However, like the view of human dignity, the property rights view argues that employees can accept whatever risks they want, as long as taking those risks does not violate the rights of others. Employees are responsible for their injuries and deaths if they freely accept those risks. Genuine consent with regard to the risks must be based on good information: Unless workers have information about facts that are pertinent to safety, they cannot freely accept the risks for the simple reason that they do not know what the risks are. Further, the workers must not be coerced into accepting the risks. For example, if taking a dangerous job is the only way they can support their families or themselves, the decision to accept the risks may not be truly voluntary. OSHA was created, in large part, because workers can easily find themselves in this position. Unfortunately, OSHA applies to all workplaces and all employees, so that workers who do want to accept risks for extra pay are prevented from doing so.

The circumstances at Johnson Controls illustrates many of these issues. Women at the division of Johnson Controls that makes car batteries were forbidden to work in areas of the plant with high lead levels in the air (Lawrence 1995). This exclusion was based not on the possibility of harm to the women, but to the children they might bear. There was good evidence that exposure to lead could result in genetic damage to ova, which, in turn, could lead to birth defects. One woman "voluntarily" had herself sterilized so she could work in these dangerous areas. Employees wanted to work in these areas because doing so was the only way to get promoted. After the women and their union sued Johnson Controls for sex discrimination, the case eventually went up to the U.S. Supreme Court, and the justices ruled in favor of the women (see also below, Discrimination and Affirmative Action, Selected Cases: *International Union v. Johnson Controls, Inc.*).

International Issues

The United States and Europe have some of the strictest worker safety and health laws in the world. To avoid these standards, and the costs of implementing them, many companies move manufacturing to countries that have standards that are not as strict, or no standards at all. This tactic works only with goods that are relatively easy to manufacture, as is the case in the footwear, apparel, and toy industries. Companies like Gap, Nike, and Mattel have their corporate offices in the United States, but they assemble or make their goods in places like Thailand, Vietnam, and Mexico. Generally, American companies do not own these manufacturing and assembly plants. Instead, they contract for the work. The same plant, for example, could make toys and toy components for Mattel, Hasbro, and several other companies.

In December 1996 "Dateline NBC" aired an exposé of Mattel's production plants in Thailand. According to the report, Mattel was paying 13-year-old girls $2 a day to make doll clothes for Barbie. As a result of public pressure, Mattel announced that it would institute a set of worldwide production standards to protect workers. In an unusual move, Mattel agreed to allow independent auditors access to all the manufacturing and assembly plants they own and with whom they contract (*New York Times* 1997a). And just one year later, in November 1997, Nike was found to have subjected workers at a plant in Vietnam to dangerous fumes and excessive overtime, a potentially lethal combination. This report was leaked by their auditing firm, Ernst & Young.

In response, Nike said it was already correcting the problems with their Vietnam operations (*Wall Street Journal* 1997).

In a new development, U.S. labor unions are beginning to develop alliances with unions in other countries. These alliances are strengthening third-world unions, allowing them to make demands for safe and healthy workplaces. A Mexican government official said these alliances were an unnecessary intrusion by U.S. labor, which, he claimed, had no legitimate interests in these internal, Mexican affairs (Dillon 1997). U.S. labor would reject the view that they have no legitimate interests in Mexican labor practices. First, the North American Free Trade Agreement (NAFTA) made it much easier for American companies to manufacture goods in Mexico. The result of this movement was a loss of union jobs in the United States. Second, NAFTA is not just about the transfer of jobs to Mexico, but technology and production methods as well. It would be naive for Mexican officials to expect that American companies would set up operations in their country and not carry with them the seeds of U.S. labor unions. Third, all of the ethical views we discussed above are universal, which means that if they apply at all, they apply equally well in all countries. If unsafe workplaces violate the rights of U.S. workers, these conditions violate the rights of Mexican workers, too.

Economics

Society   From the social point of view, we want the best products at the least cost; if this means putting some workers at great risk, it may be worthwhile to subject workers to such dangers. There are two ways to respond to this economic utilitarian argument. First, we could counter with the claim that because human beings have infinite value (as we discussed in the preceding section) they can never be put in the same equation with things or money.

Second, we could challenge the view that putting workers at significant risk saves money. To make this point we need to distinguish product cost from **social cost**. Product cost refers to all the factors of production—materials, buildings, electricity—that the manufacturer has to pay for to produce the product. Social cost refers to the total cost of producing a product; this includes all production costs, as well as costs for negative **externalities** (see Chapter 1: Introduction—Economics) like air pollution, disposal of the product when it is no longer used, and harms to workers not covered by the employer. If there are no negative externalities, product cost equals social cost. However, there are almost always negative externalities.

As an example of how externalities work in occupational health and safety, consider the fact, mentioned above, that approximately $8 billion are spent annually on death and injuries in the workplace. If that entire $8 billion was paid by the businesses in which the injuries occurred, then there would be no externalities regarding medical and funeral costs. Yet we know that many of the workers injured are underinsured or not insured at all (LaBar 1997). These costs are then borne by the family, and, if they cannot pay, consumers and taxpayers pay.

There are two things wrong with externalizing production costs. First, it is simply unfair: People who do not use the product are forced to pay for some of its production. Second, significant production externalities for a product keep prices low and these low prices create a demand for the product that is greater than it would be if all the externalities were included in the cost. Producers respond to this excess demand by increasing production, which increases the number of deaths and injuries.

Consumers The consumer generally has very little information about the conditions under which products are made and delivered. However, if we assume that consumers are motivated to promote their own economic welfare by buying the most inexpensive product, that should encourage them to buy items made in cheap, unsafe conditions, because, as we discussed, this will reduce the price of the product.

However, recent events have shown that consumers do care about the conditions under which their products are made. U.S. consumers are very concerned about child labor, and companies that market primarily or significantly to children are especially vulnerable to this criticism. As we discussed in International Issues in this section, toy and apparel companies, like Mattel and Nike, have had consumers pressure them to improve working conditions for their employees.

More and more, we see consumers making a demand for ethical workplaces and we see business responding to this demand. An optimistic interpretation of this demand is that consumers believe that human life is intrinsically valuable; they are not willing to trade lower prices for increased human misery.

Producers Because managers work for the owners (stockholders) of the company, they have an ethical obligation to produce products as efficiently as they can. The more efficient managers are, the more money they can return to the owners. No matter how efficient managers are, however, they will make no money unless there is a demand for their product.

For the first 150 years of the Industrial Revolution, products were evaluated in themselves, that is, they were evaluated by how well the product satisfied consumer needs at a particular price. However, as we have just seen, consumers are beginning to demand safe and respectful workplaces. This means that consumers demand not only products at competitive prices, but products with ethically acceptable production histories.

There are other reasons beyond consumer demand for producers to prefer safer, more expensive workplaces to cheaper, more dangerous workplaces. One reason is the cost of employee turnover. As jobs become more technical, it takes longer for employees to master them, and until employees master their tasks they have lower output. Dangerous workplaces tend to have more turnover than safe ones, so working there requires that more time be spent training employees. Another reason to prefer safer work places is to increase worker commitment and loyalty. Herbert Simon (1995) argues that worker loyalty is necessary because most tasks cannot be specifically defined, and so employees are the ultimate decision makers about how well they complete their tasks. Employees can do their tasks well and quickly or they can do them adequately and slowly. If employees believe that their workplace is unnecessarily dangerous, they will not feel the kind of commitment to make them go the extra mile to ensure that things are done right.

Finally, we need to remember that the managers and owners of companies are also citizens and consumers. Hence, some of the demand for safe workplaces comes from them. Levi Strauss, for example, has a policy for evaluating its overseas sources of material and assembly of jeans, Dockers, Slates, and the many other clothes they make. They take this stand because they believe it is the right thing to do. In the early 1990s they carefully examined plants in China that were producing quality goods at a good price. Nevertheless, they decided that the labor force in China was so badly treated that they could no longer do business there. At great cost to themselves, they pulled out of China and turned to other sources (Paine 1994b).

If there are so many financial and ethical advantages of safe workplaces, why don't managers implement them? One reason is that managers make mistakes just like we all do. They may not have the right information or the right frame of mind to evaluate the information that is presented to them. Another reason may lie in the perception of risk: This can be altered according to whether or not we choose the task. Consider something simple, like telling an employee to drive across town to deliver a package. The employee will almost invariably view that trip as more risky than if she chose to drive that identical route, say, to visit a friend.

If this connection between choice and the perception of risk seems odd to you, just consider how you feel when you are a passenger in your own car. Even if the person driving drives as well as, or even better than, you, typically you feel more at risk than when you are driving. On this analysis, managers may honestly think that a workplace is safe because they chose it, while the workers are just as sure it is not safe, because they did not choose it. Once again, we see the importance of employee-management teams as suggested by Birkner and Birkner (1997), above.

Another reason managers and employees may perceive workplace safety differently is because they have different sources of information. If the managers have not worked at the dangerous tasks they are supervising, they may simply not know the risks of the job or the best way to minimize these risks. Another problem may be the managerial job itself. Managers focus on the daily, monthly, and quarterly accomplishment of objectives, and these are often in terms of sales or number of units produced, not measurements of risks reduced or avoided. This managerial focus on numbers does not lend itself to thinking about workplace safety. Failing to meet numerical goals can prompt management to push for more productivity until there is an accident, at which point the manager might see that unreasonable demands led to the accident. Yet, there are at least two factors that may cause managers to fail to see how they contributed to the accident. First, if managers admit that they have made unreasonable demands, they would have to accept personal responsibility for the harm, and that is very painful. Second, employees might use this information to sue the company. Managers could be fired for accepting liability.

Given the stakes involved, the complexity of setting standards, and the different information that managers and employees have, it is not surprising that conflicts over health and safety issues have ended up in the courts. Nor is it surprising that legislation and regulatory agencies have been created to ensure workplace safety. It is these issues to which we now turn.

Law

The rise of big business and the explosion of industry that followed the Civil War was made possible by a huge influx of foreign immigrants and a mass population movement from the country to the city where the factories were located. With the employment market saturated, human labor was cheap and plentiful. Much of the labor required was unskilled, so there was little economic motivation to invest in training or safety; it was always cheaper and easier just to replace killed or injured workers rather than protect them from workplace hazards, or give them the expertise needed to avoid high risk situations. Workers themselves tended to be complacent and accepting of dangers—the risks were just part of the job and could not be eliminated. This may have been another manifestation of a general attitude that life was full of toil and struggle that must simply be endured, and in any case, that was the way it had always been. There was little sense that things could be made better. In such a buyer's market, business could set the terms and conditions of employment (see also this chapter, Terms and Conditions of Employment, Law; and Chapter 3: The Corporation—Antitrust Issues; Law).

Tragic accounts of the terrible circumstances under which many in America's workforce labored, especially in mining and large-scale construction projects, are a staple of the century that preceded federal intervention on behalf of America's workers. One of the most notorious examples from the time was the building of the transcontinental railroad, linking Sacramento, California with Omaha, Nebraska. Still ranking as one of the largest construction projects in the nation's history, 20,000 men, virtually all of them Chinese and Irish, toiled in unspeakable conditions for three years. We will never know the exact numbers, but certainly the "Iron Road" spanning the country was bought at the cost of thousands of deaths and injuries.

In those days, occupational health and safety legislation was unheard of. Neither did the courts and the common law offer much help for America's workers. Lawsuits against employers were rare and awards for damages were even more uncommon. Employees who sued their employers, charging liability for a workplace injury, were almost certain to lose their jobs, and fellow workers who might testify on behalf of the injured victims ran a very substantial risk of the same fate.

Beginning in the 1920s, the risks to many workers increased as technology became more sophisticated, especially with the rapid development of the chemical and related industries. The first effort to provide protections against occupational injuries were various workers' compensation laws passed by many states. These laws required employers either to buy insurance covering damages or pay employees' medical bills. Unfortunately, due to a lack of resources, the state agencies responsible for administering workers' compensation were not very effective, and the vast majority of employees were not covered by them anyway. Moreover, standard-setting was still controlled by the leaders of business and industry, individuals whose motivations were more often their own economic interests rather than the welfare of their employees. Finally, in 1970 primary responsibility for the regulation of working conditions was passed to the federal government.

Selected Cases, Statutes, and Regulations

Occupational Safety and Health Act of 1970, 29 U.S.C. §§651–678

The Occupational Safety and Health Act imposes a broad obligation on nearly all private employers to maintain a workplace that is as safe and healthy for employees as is reasonably possible. Federal, state, and local governments, independent contractors, and family farms are exempted, as are industries regulated by other federal safety legislation (e.g., coal mining).

The employer's obligation is fulfilled in two ways. First, the act's "general duty clause" requires an employer to provide a job and a work environment free from "recognized hazards" that cause or are likely to cause illness, injury, or death. In addition to this catch-all requirement, employers also have a specific duty to comply with the particular standards set by OSHA that are tailored to certain kinds of jobs. There are literally thousands of these specific standards, and they cover such items as fire prevention procedures, the type of personal protection clothing needed, training methods to ensure safety on the job, and the proper construction and maintenance of a vast variety of equipment.

This congressional Act also created the Occupational Safety and Health Administration (OSHA), the administrative agency charged with issuing and enforcing national regulations on workplace safety. OSHA is provided with technical support by the National Institute for Occupational Safety and Health (NIOSH), whose mission is to research ways to make jobs safer. OSHA and NIOSH are divisions of the Department of Labor, overseen by the secretary of labor.

When OSHA, backed by the scientific expertise of NIOSH, proposes a rule, public hearings are held to discuss the proposal. Oral and written evidence from public interest groups, concerned citizens, professional associations, and representatives of industries and unions are considered. After this input has been accounted for, the final form of the rule is published in the *Code of Federal Regulations* (CFR).

Possible violations of the rules are investigated by OSHA compliance officers, either by administratively initiated inspections or as a result of complaints filed by employees. If a violation is confirmed, then the regional OSHA office issues a citation detailing any fines due for the infraction, what conditions must be changed, and how long the employer has to make the required changes. The solution to the safety problem and the timetable for fixing it are known as the *abatement plan*. If the problem is especially severe, posing an imminent danger to workers, or if the employer has a record of violations, OSHA may seek an injunction—this is a court order demanding the elimination of the workplace hazard. OSHA also gives employees the right to walk off the job without fear of reprisals in extreme situations presenting an immediate and substantial threat to personal safety.

Employees are entitled to contest OSHA's abatement plan; almost invariably this is on the grounds that it is inadequate to address the hazard. The case is then referred to the Occupational Safety and Health Review Commission (OSHRC), an agency independent of OSHA. In the event that the findings of OSHRC are unacceptable to one of the parties involved, the case is submitted to an **administrative law judge** (ALJ), whose specialty is to adjudicate disputes concerning the rules of administrative agencies. After hearing evidence from the disputants, the ALJ renders a decision. This decision may be appealed to the federal court system, perhaps all the way to the Supreme Court.

OSHA is focused on prevention. Restitution for damages suffered on the job is a matter for worker's compensation. Ensuring worker's compensation is the major role left to the individual states, and all 50 states do have laws requiring businesses that meet certain criteria to provide their employees with this compensation. Thus it is strictly speaking not a benefit, but a legally mandated *right*. About half of the states have their own occupational safety and health laws that are usually similar to federal laws. About two-thirds of the states have laws prohibiting employers from firing workers who file OSHA complaints. This, in effect, duplicates an OSHA statute making it illegal for an employer to discharge or otherwise discriminate against workers who instigate or participate in an OSHA investigation (see also this chapter, Whistle Blowing and Loyalty, Law: Introduction).

Marshall v. Barlow's Inc., **436 U.S. 307 (1978)** An essential ingredient in the regulatory power of OSHA is the inspection of workplaces by compliance officers in search of violations. Section 8(a) of the Occupational Safety and Health Act authorizes inspectors to search any employment facility for this purpose, but there is no mention whatever of first obtaining a search warrant. The Fourth Amendment to the Constitution protects citizens from unreasonable searches and seizures, explicitly stating that a "Warrant" is required, issued only on "probable cause." This has been understood to mean that before a search or seizure can be carried out, law enforcement officials must present their reasons for wanting to do so to a judge, swearing that the facts they allege are true: this is to show **probable cause**. The judge then decides if the search is justified or *warranted* (see also this chapter, Privacy, Law: Introduction). Does the Fourth Amendment protect places of business from unjustified intrusions by officers of administrative agencies?

On a morning in September 1975 an OSHA inspector arrived at Barlow's Inc. of Pocatello, Idaho, a business specializing in the installation of electrical and plumbing apparatus. The inspector identified himself and asked Ferrol Barlow, the president and general manager of the company, for permission to examine the premises. Barlow inquired if there had been any complaints about his business, and if the inspector had obtained a warrant. Upon receiving a negative reply to both questions, Barlow refused to allow the inspection to proceed.

Secretary of Labor F. Ray Marshall argued that warrantless searches to enforce OSHA regulations were "reasonable" within the meaning of the Fourth Amendment, because requiring warrants would not only unduly burden the courts, but actually prevent inspections and make those accomplished less effective. A district court and ultimately the Supreme Court were not convinced.

In his majority opinion, Justice Byron White analyzed the origins of the Fourth Amendment in the American colonial experience. In those days, agents of the British king plagued merchants with arbitrary inspections in search of smuggled and untaxed goods. Moreover, White continued, the significant privacy interests protected by the Fourth Amendment apply to employers regulated by federal statutes as well as to private citizens governed by criminal laws. To allay fears that requiring warrants of OSHA would be too restrictive, because "probable cause" in criminal law typically requires solid evidence of violation, White introduced the notion of *reasonable standards of inspection*. This is a weaker standard under which a showing of how a particular search advances the general administrative plan for enforcing OSHA regulations is sufficient for issuance of a warrant.

Justice White concluded that there are indeed exceptions to the warrant requirement for inspecting businesses. These exceptions involve industries that have been strictly regulated and closely scrutinized by the federal government for many years, for example, liquor and firearms. Electrical and plumbing installation was not one of these tightly monitored industries. Barlow should have been presented with a warrant.

In an important Supreme Court decision in 1981, the list of exceptions to the warrant requirement was expanded to include another industry whose health and safety standards are regulated by the Department of Labor. *Donovan v. Dewey* (452 U.S. 594 [1981]) involved a warrantless inspection of the Waukesha Lime and Stone Company of Wisconsin. A federal mine inspector had been ordered out of the quarries by the company president, Douglas Dewey, while the inspector was attempting to determine whether health and safety violations detected in a previous examination had been corrected. Dewey demanded a warrant.

The Supreme Court upheld the constitutionality of the Federal Mine Health and Safety Act of 1977, 30 U.S.C. §§801–804, which allowed inspections without advance notice. Justice Thurgood Marshall ruled that warrantless searches are permissible when they are necessary to further a regulatory scheme of a federal agency, and when the owner of the business is aware of their likelihood. Given the substantial federal interest in improving the health and safety of miners, and given that the mining industry is among the most hazardous, with one of the worst health and safety records, warrantless inspections are indispensable "if the law is to be properly enforced and inspection made effective."

Industrial Union Department, AFL-CIO v. American Petroleum Institute, 448 U.S. 607 (1980)   This is the first case in which a challenge to the regulatory power of the Occupational Safety and Health Administration (OSHA) advanced to the highest judicial level. More importantly, it raised serious problems for determining just how safe the workplace should be. The central element in this case is a colorless, aromatic gas called benzene. Virtually all the benzene produced is used in the petrochemical and petroleum refining industries, mainly in the processing and manufacturing of tires, paint, pesticides, and gasoline. Scientists at the National Institute for Occupational Safety and Health (NIOSH), the research arm of OSHA, had long suspected that benzene was linked with cancer, especially leukemia. A connection between the gas and leukemia had been theorized as far back as the 1920s, and various studies in the 1960s and 1970s seemed to support a connection. In 1977 NIOSH submitted a report that detailed a leukemia death rate for workers at two rubber plants in Ohio at five times the national average. The report asserted a correlation between the deaths and exposure to benzene in the plants: Exposure levels measured in excess of 10 parts benzene per million parts of air (ppm), then the current OSHA limit. Shortly thereafter, OSHA issued an emergency standard ordering that workers' exposure to benzene be reduced to 1 ppm.

The oil industry objected to the new standard on the grounds that there was insufficient evidence that benzene was a serious health hazard for their employees; moreover, the costs of compliance with the 1 ppm limit were very high, running into thousands, even tens of thousands of dollars for each employee. After the Fifth Circuit Court of Appeals ruled in favor of the American Petroleum Institute, the AFL-CIO, on behalf of its members in the oil industry, sought review of the case by the Supreme Court.

Justice John Paul Stevens and a close majority affirmed the Fifth Circuit. They concluded that OSHA had overstepped its rule-making authority by advancing an unduly strict standard that would benefit relatively few employees at an excessive cost. Employers cannot be expected to provide risk-free environments regardless of the cost; they are required to maintain a workplace where there is no substantial risk to health. Stevens pointed out that OSHA had demonstrated that there was some threat to worker's health at exposures above 10 ppm, but they had not demonstrated that any significant benefit would be provided by dropping the allowable limit below 10 ppm. That is what they needed to prove. OSHA was compelled to return the standard to 10 ppm.

Over the next several years, research at NIOSH on benzene exposure led to a new OSHA standard, which became effective in 1988. The new limit was set at 1 ppm over an eight-hour shift. This did not, however, reignite the controversy, since advances in filtering and monitoring technology required by the Environmental Protection Agency (see Chapter 5: The Environment) had reduced the level of benzene exposure to just over 1 ppm. The cost of compliance was then far less than it was in 1977.

American Textile Manufacturers Institute Inc. v. Donovan, 452 U.S. 490 (1981)   The Supreme Court's ruling in *Industrial Union Department, AFL-CIO v. American Petroleum Institute* (*API*, see above) might give the impression that the Court was endorsing a **cost-benefit analysis** approach to regulating employee health and safety. This is a decision-making procedure whereby the price tag of a certain policy is compared with its advantages. If the price exceeds its returns (measured numerically), the policy is to be rejected. *API* seemed to reject the 1 ppm limit because the price was too high, while very few were being served by it; this suggests that acceptable levels of risk for workers are to be determined by balancing costs and benefits. Does the Supreme Court hold that certain risks for some workers are acceptable if the costs of eliminating or reducing them outweigh the benefits of doing so? In *American Textile Manufacturers Institute Inc.*, decided only one year after *API*, we find the Court turning away from calculating costs and benefits.

Like *API*, this case concerns an OSHA regulation for a hazardous substance encountered in the workplace, and, again like *API*, the crucial issue revolves around the operative principles that ground the rules. In 1978 OSHA issued the "Cotton Dust Standards," stating the permissible exposure limits (PELs) for contact with the airborne particles produced during the manufacture of cotton products. The PELs applied to eight-hour work days and varied with the type of processing, ranging from 200 micrograms per cubic meter of air ($\mu g/m^3$) for yarn manufacturing, to 750 $\mu g/m^3$ for slashing and weaving operations. Unlike *API*, in which the carcinogenic effects of exposure to various amounts of benzene were not entirely clear, there was here conclusive evidence that inhaling cotton dust was the primary cause of a variety of respiratory ailments collectively known as *byssinosis* or *brown lung*.

The American Textile Manufacturers, in the interest of the cotton industry, objected to the new OSHA standards. They asserted that the new regulation was very expensive—OSHA's own estimate was $656 million for compliance—and would still produce an incidence of low grade byssinosis of 13 percent. On the other hand, American Textile's proposed standards (500 $\mu g/m^3$ for yarn production, for example) were far cheaper to implement, with a low-grade byssinosis incidence of 25 percent. They demanded that OSHA demonstrate that the disparity between the costs and benefits of the agency's PELs did not obtain, and that the two were reasonably close to one another.

Raymond Donovan, in his capacity as secretary of labor, responded that the Occupational Safety and Health Act (see above) did not require OSHA to engage in a cost-benefit analysis in order to determine the propriety of its regulations, and the District of Columbia Circuit Court of Appeals agreed. The Supreme Court seconded the D.C. Circuit. In the majority opinion, Justice William Brennan looked closely at the language of the Occupational Safety and Health Act. In section 6(b)(5), the statute authorizes the secretary of labor to set standards for hazardous materials "to the extent feasible" for ensuring that no employee will be impaired due to exposure to the hazard. After consulting several dictionaries, Brennan reported that *feasible* means "capable of being done." He concluded that the act limits standards of health and safety to those that can be accomplished, not those whose benefits exceed their costs. In promulgating regulations for dealing with hazardous substances in the workplace, OSHA is not required to take the cost of compliance to employers into account, but only the technological feasibility of eliminating the hazards. Thus **feasibility analysis** replaces cost-benefit analysis.

Whirlpool Corporation v. Marshall, **445 U.S. 1 (1980)** The Whirlpool plant in Marion, Ohio, is devoted to assembling household appliances. Appliance parts are moved through the plant by a system of conveyors installed above the plant floor. Occasionally, these parts fall from the conveyors, so a huge wire net is suspended to protect the workers below. Maintenance workers are responsible for removing the parts caught by the net, and this sometimes requires stepping onto the screen. In 1973 and 1974 several of these workers fell part way through the screen and two fell to the floor; the second one who hit the floor was killed. Soon after this incident, Virgil Deemer and Thomas Cornwell were ordered by their supervisor to perform routine maintenance on a section of the screen. They refused on the grounds that the work was unsafe. The foreman told them to punch out, which cost them the remaining six hours of pay on their shift, and he wrote up reprimands on both employees, which were deposited in their respective personnel files.

Section 11(c)(1) of the Occupational Safety and Health Act (OSH Act) prohibits an employer from discriminating against or discharging any employee who exercises any of the rights provided by OSHA regulations. In 1979 OSHA issued a regulation that entitles an employee to refuse any assigned task if he or she has a reasonable apprehension of death or serious injury and a reasonable belief that no less drastic alternative is available. Secretary of Labor Marshall, on behalf of Deemer and Cornwell, filed suit in district court, claiming that the loss of pay and the reprimands for refusing to work constituted discriminatory treatment in violation of Section 11(c)(1). Marshall sought restitution of the lost wages and the removal of the reprimands from Deemer's and Cornwell's files.

The district court rejected the claim. Although the 1979 regulation fully justified the two men in refusing the task, the court ruled that the regulation was invalid; thus Whirlpool's disciplinary action was not discriminatory since it did not violate any right held by Deemer and Cornwell. The Sixth Circuit Court of Appeals and the Supreme Court reversed this decision. Justice Potter Stewart and a unanimous court agreed that the regulation conforms to the OSH Act's fundamental objective of preventing deaths and serious injuries on the job. Moreover, the regulation is consistent with the **general duty clause** of the OSH Act, requiring employers to provide their workers with a job and a workplace free from life-threatening hazards. The Court thus upheld the constitutionality of a right to refuse work. This right obtains when: (1) an employee, acting on good faith, reasonably believes that the working conditions pose an imminent risk of death or serious injury, and (2) the employee has reason to believe that the risk cannot be avoided by any less disruptive course of action.

Privacy

Employee privacy covers a variety of issues, but at the heart of them all is the right of individuals to use information about themselves as they see fit. In the United States, this right is tied to the value we place on the individual. Although the right to privacy is never mentioned explicitly in the Constitution or its amendments, the Supreme Court has argued that it is implied by the Fourth Amendment, which protects against unreasonable searches and seizures of one's person, home, papers, and effects; the Fifth Amendment, which protects against self-incrimination; and the Fourteenth Amendment, which protects against the loss of one's life, liberty, or property without due process of law (for more, see below, Law: The Right to Privacy). All of these amendments were passed to protect individual citizens from *government*. At the times these amendments were ratified, there were no corporations as we know them today. Most businesses were small, and no one of them could have much influence over the everyday lives of many citizens.

Because these privacy protections were passed to prevent government from interfering with the private lives of individuals, it is not always clear how they apply to individuals at work. For example, while the police are forbidden to walk into your home and search your desk without a warrant, it is not clear that this protection prevents an employer from searching an employee's desk at work. If the employer does have the right to search an employee's desk, does that extend to personal property found in the desk, such as letters, purses, or wallets? (See *O'Connor v. Ortega* in Selected Cases, below.) Employers can monitor phone calls and e-mail that are work-related, but this does not give them the right to listen in or record *personal* calls (see Selected Cases: Omnibus Crime Control and Safe Streets Act, below). Drug testing is one of the more hotly debated issues when it comes to employee privacy. Under what circumstances can companies require their employees to undergo drug tests?

Drug use in the United States is widely acknowledged to be one of the most important problems of our time. It is estimated that 20 percent of those between the ages of 18 and 25 use drugs, and that 12 percent of those between the ages of 26 and 34 use drugs (Wood 1994). Drug use in the workplace costs $60 billion each year, accumulated through accidents and lost productivity (Lipman 1995). Drug use has also been involved in highly publicized accidents, like the one that killed Princess Diana (Henely, 1997).

Unfortunately, testing for drugs usually can be done only with invasive techniques that require individuals to give parts of their bodies, such as hair, fingernails, or bodily fluids, to researchers. This is distasteful to many, and, further, it allows the company to discover a great deal of information about their employees that goes well beyond drug use. The bodily material collected for these tests can reveal genetic abnormalities, diseases, and medical conditions that a person does not want to disclose and to which the company has no moral or legal right.

The American Management Association found that 80 percent of the firms they surveyed in the United States test their employees for illegal drug use. In 1987, that figure was 22 percent (Greenberg 1996). Although some companies fire employees who test positive for illegal drugs, the majority recommend treatment. There is evidence that treatment programs, if designed correctly, can be very effective. For example, Oregon Hills Steel began a drug identification and treatment program in 1980. By 1993, the accident rate fell 60 percent. There were other benefits as well: Employee productivity increased by *140* percent and the average number of days that employees missed in one year dropped from 14 days to 1.5 days (Wood 1994). In our discussion of the ethics and economics of privacy, we will focus on drug testing. Due to the broad range of constitutional issues activated by this topic, as well as its inherently controversial nature, employee drug testing will also be our emphasis in the section on law, though other privacy matters will also be surveyed there.

Ethics

Promoting Self-interest: Egoism   Aggressively self-interested employees who are *drug free* should favor mandatory drug testing, because drug use by fellow employees likely endangers them. However, they would want assurance that the results of these tests are confidential and that no other medical information is gathered from these tests without their permission.

Aggressively self-interested *drugs users*, it would seem, would be against mandatory drug testing. However, aggressive self-interest does not require us to pursue whatever desires we have. As we defined *aggressive self-interest* in Chapter 1: Introduction—The Tools of Business Ethics, it requires rigorous self-discipline and study to *discover* what our true interests are. Since it is widely recognized that illegal drug use harms us and our relationships, aggressively self-interested employees who are drug users should welcome drug testing as an incentive to get their lives under control.

Contemplatively self-interested employees should favor mandatory drug testing, because, in the long run at least, it seems very likely to reduce conflict. Drug-using employees are not only dangerous, but they tend to miss work more than others, as we saw in our discussion of Oregon Steel Mills, above. When employees miss work, this puts extra stress on the employees who are there. Drug testing will either prompt drug users to seek treatment, or it will get them out of the workplace.

Promoting Personal Relationships: Care   Caring employees would base their judgment of mandatory drug testing on how those tests affected their relationships.

Passive caring employees would take whatever view their family and friends would want them to take. For example, if the passive caring employee has a drug problem, and the employee's family wanted the employee to keep working, they would urge the employee to fight against drug testing. Or, if the family had recently lost a child to a drug-related accident, in the workplace or elsewhere, they may be very much in favor of drug testing. The passive caring employee would then adopt this pro-drug testing view, even if it meant he or she would test positive and would have to quit drugs or quit his or her job.

Active carers would also consider how drug testing would affect their relationships, but they would not let others be the sole determinant of what counts as a good relationship. Rather, they would evaluate whether what their family and friends wanted was likely to lead to strong, nurturing relationships. Because drugs tend to pull us inward, focusing us on ourselves and our own immediate pleasure, they do not bring people closer together. If mandatory drug testing helped to reduce this destructive behavior, that would be a reason for active carers to support it. Active carers would also be very wary of drug testing that would give employers other information that they could use to harm employees or their relationships.

Finally, active carers would also try to look at the root cause of drug use and the best ways to prevent it. The National Bureau of Economic Research (1997), for example, found that having a job is an important part of recovering from drug use. This means that drug testing is only the first step in a program of rehabilitation, and the focus should be finding ways to keep drug users employed as they go through treatment.

Promoting the Good of the Group: Utilitarianism   According to strict rule utilitarianism, mandatory drug testing would be justified if it promoted group well-being better than any other rule. Drug testing is likely to have beneficial effects only in jobs where many people's safety is at risk, such as piloting airplanes and driving buses. If it turned out that drug testing revealed information about employees, and this information did not promote group welfare, this would have to be subtracted from the overall group good promoted by the testing. It must be stressed, however, that as long as the total amount of good promoted by the policy exceeded all other policies, utilitarian employees should accept it even if they suffer in ways that are unfair. For a utilitarian, fairness should be pursued only if it promotes group well-being; if an unfair policy promotes the good of the group better than any other policy, they would implement the unfair one.

Strict rule utilitarian employees, like active caring employees, would also look at the root causes of drug use. Kenkel and Wang (The National Bureau of Economic Research 1997) found that, compared to nonalcoholic men, alcoholic men tended to have lower fringe benefits. A possible utilitarian response to this would be to pass laws that increase fringe benefits. The same study and another independent study found that there were more drug users in smaller firms than in larger ones (Rose 1997), and that smaller firms did not test for drugs as often as larger ones. One explanation of this is that drug users are purposefully seeking employment with companies that do not test for drugs. If so, strict utilitarians might be in favor of laws mandating drug testing, since voluntary testing seems to push the problem to smaller companies that cannot afford to handle it.

Whether these tests should be used to obtain other information about employees, such as their genetic disposition to contract certain diseases, or whether they are infected with HIV, would depend on whether this promoted the good of all. Fairness would not be an issue in itself. What would be important, however, would be employee reactions to policies they *perceive* to be unfair. If a perception of unfairness caused employees to work less diligently and to miss more days, this could be a good reason not to implement policies perceived to be unfair.

Flexible rule utilitarian employees would be more willing to mandate drug testing only for employees, such as pilots, bus drivers, and policeman, whose incompetence and bad judgment can harm many others. For example, St. Louis requires random drug testing of airport police officers, those with commercial drivers licenses, and of public safety personnel (Looney 1996). The reasoning here is clear: Test those who put the public at most risk.

In another case, the National Transportation Safety Board (NTSB) mandates drug testing for harbor pilots, but does not specify how those tests should be administered. Harbor pilots guide ships into harbors, because ship captains cannot be expected to know the best and safest way to enter and leave the many harbors they visit. The NTSB is now investigating the administration of drug tests after a harbor pilot in Portland, Maine, steered a Liberian tanker into a bridge, dumping 180,000 gallons of oil into the harbor and closing the bridge for a week. The pilot admitted that he successfully avoided positive results from testing because he was able to schedule his own dates for testing (Baldwin 1997). For jobs like these, nationally mandated drug testing is likely to be cost effective. But to require it of all employees is very likely a waste of money. Each company should make its own judgment about whether to implement drug testing. If the data shows, as suggested above, that drug problems are greater at companies that have difficulty affording testing, flexible utilitarian employees would be in favor of using public funds to help them, as long as the benefits outweigh the costs.

Respecting Dignity and Rights: Intrinsic Value   Employees who use human dignity to evaluate mandatory drug testing would assert that such testing is an invasion of an individual's privacy. Privacy is not an absolute value, however, to be respected at all costs. If there is good reason to believe that a particular person is going to endanger others because of drug use, mandatory drug testing can be justified.

It should be noted that this justification applies to a *particular person*, not a group of people who have characteristics that are associated with drug use (see Davidson 1988, for a similar argument). For example, the National Bureau of Economic Research (1997) reported that drug use is higher for blue collar workers. This would not justify random testing of blue collar workers, because many nondrug users would have their privacy invaded when there is no reason to suspect them of drug use. Another study found that fewer white collar workers are tested for drugs than blue collar workers (Quintanilla 1997). The mere fact that blue collar workers are tested more does not by itself imply that their dignity is being violated, rather it may be that blue collar jobs are more likely to put people at risk than white collar jobs.

Another feature of respecting human dignity is making sure individuals know the "rules of the game" when they take a job. For example, if a job applicant is told in advance that random drug tests were mandatory, that person could decide to take the job or not. If the person took the job, that would imply his or her consent to random drug testing (see *Barlow* 1977, for a similar case).

Employees who evaluate drug testing policies on the basis of property rights would have to consider two kinds of property: the proprietary information employees have about themselves, and the property of others they may damage or illicitly disseminate because of drug use. Mandatory testing is justified if the rights protected are more important than the rights that are violated. For those who take privacy rights to be more important than property, mandatory testing is justified only to protect substantial items of property or to protect human well-being. For those who think that property rights are inseparable from personal well-being, as do Nozick (1974) and Maitland (1989), then random drug testing can be justified when the potential losses to property are much lower. This kind of reasoning could even justify random testing of groups, like blue collar workers, if it could be shown that this group had a significant percentage of drug use.

International Issues

Investigating the international aspects of employee privacy poses several challenges. (In our discussion we will rely on a report by Americo Rodriguez, 1995, that focuses on North, Central, and South America.) First, there are very few explicit legal or cultural rules that apply to privacy in general, much less to employee privacy. This means that the definition and scope of employee privacy must be inferred from other rules and standards. This is what has happened in the United States, and the same is happening in many other countries. The lack of traditional, explicit rules regarding employee privacy is just what we should expect, because the modern corporation is only 75 to 100 years old, and the right to privacy itself is a relatively new moral and legal concern.

A second problem is that employee privacy is connected to many other issues. In one country employee privacy may be entwined with political freedom, in another country gender discrimination, and in another, medical records. Although privacy is an essential part of understanding these issues, it is not identical to any one of them.

A third problem with investigating international aspects of employee privacy is that understandings of privacy are often a function of culture. For example, the United States and Uruguay both assert that there is firm distinction between private life and public life, while Canada claims that no firm line can be drawn between these two spheres. These differences in the view of what is private and public lead to differences in the laws and rules of employee privacy.

There are some common threads to the laws protecting employee privacy in different countries. One such thread is that many countries restrict employers from requiring information that is not relevant to the job. Unfortunately, countries tend to have different views about what is relevant. For example, Argentina allows employers to ask virtually anything about a job applicant's health; in the United States questions about health have to be directly related to the job.

Another privacy issue concerns employee records. Canada requires companies to destroy information gathered on prospective employees who are not hired. Most other countries in the Americas say nothing about these kinds of records.

Although there are different views on the exact definition of privacy, the ones discussed here all have group well-being and human dignity as their foundation. There is a general agreement on at least three principles: (1) Employees are paid to do certain duties, and it is legitimate and appropriate to ask them questions that directly bear on the job, (2) employees have dignity and rights that they do not lose at their place of employment, and (3) society should integrate and balance the privacy of the employee with the need of business to compile information about employees.

Economics

Society From the social point of view, privacy has advantages and disadvantages. John Stuart Mill argued that privacy is necessary for the marketplace of ideas, a mechanism for choosing the best ways to create an efficient, responsive economic system (Mill 1859). Privacy gives us the room to choose and live by our own ideas. When individuals live by their own choices, they become sources of information for others about how people *can* live. This information is added to the marketplace of ideas that other people and later generations can choose, alter, or reject.

However, privacy can also limit the marketplace of ideas, because, by its very nature, it allows individuals to keep their beliefs to themselves. This is a problem especially with information that can greatly harm society, such as the use of drugs by individuals in the workplace. As we saw in the introduction to this topic, drug use is ubiquitous and it causes billions of dollars of workplace injuries and deaths. These accidents not only harm the drug users, but their coworkers and the general public as well.

The notion of private property adds another dimension to privacy in the workplace. Employees often work in places owned by their employers. If an employer owns the desk, telephone, and computer, the doctrine of private property should allow the employer-owner access to them at any time. Yet this is not the case. Employees do not give up their rights to privacy when they go to work. As we discuss in the law section, below, legislation and court cases forbid employers from monitoring private phone calls and restrict the use of polygraphs, psychological tests, and drug tests to cases in which there is reasonable suspicion that a problem exists, such as when a person is disoriented or there is a likelihood of significant harm, as is the case with pilots.

The social-economic point of view, then, tries to balance the need for privacy with the need for information.

Consumers   Unlike the other employee issues we have discussed, privacy in the workplace has direct and indirect effects on consumers. Direct effects occur when consumers use services provided by business, such as riding in airplanes, buses, or trains, or when being treated by physicians or nurses. In these cases consumer lives and well-being depend on those in control being alert and ready to act. Also at risk are nonpassengers who could be killed or injured by out-of-control airplanes, busses, and trains. Hence it is not surprising that consumers are willing to pay for the extra cost of drug testing and psychological testing if these are going to make transportation safer.

Indirectly, consumers care about workplace privacy for many of the same reasons they care about safety and fairness in the workplace. Unfortunately, these two considerations can conflict, as we saw above. The more we protect privacy, the less likely we are to find out about drug use and psychological infirmities of employees. The more we find out about the drug use and psychological infirmities of employees, the less we protect privacy.

Producers   One way that producers think about employees is as resources for production, like steel and electricity. On this model, producers want as much control over these resources as possible. For employees this means drug testing, polygraphs, and psychological testing. However, these tests have financial and organizational costs; most obviously they cost money to administer. Tests can be more or less reliable, and more reliable tests usually cost more. Organizationally, there are also opportunity costs to the company: When employees are tested they are not producing products. There may be another substantial organizational cost as well: a lack of trust. Employees who are tested may feel that they are not trusted by management. Even if these tests are accurate and reveal who the drug users are, the 80 percent or more who do not use drugs may feel offended and will not be as willing to go the extra mile that businesses often need from employees for the company to excel.

Another problem with testing is inaccurate results. Drug tests may indicate drug use when there is none, psychological tests may indicate personality defects that do not exist or are not severe enough to interfere with an employee's performance, and polygraphs can indicate a subject is lying when he or she is not. In the case of drug tests, retesting is possible, perhaps with a more accurate and typically more expensive test. With psychological tests and polygraphs, retesting does not settle the issue, because the new tests are not necessarily more reliable. Producers might worry about eliminating good employees only if there is a tight labor market. If labor is plentiful, however, the company may not care if they reject a good candidate as long as they get another good employee from the labor pool in a reasonable amount of time.

If producers treat employees like human beings who are capable of making their own decisions, and not as factors of production, other strategies are available for treating privacy in the workplace. Consider again the situation at Oregon Steel Mills, mentioned above. First, the Employee Assistance Program (EAP) is run by a committee that is made up mostly of employees. Management had veto power, but agreed not to institute any plan that was not passed by the EAP. This kind of self-governance is the essence of treating employees as rational, valuable human beings.

Oregon Mills adopted the view that drug addiction is an illness, and that the company's efforts should focus on prevention, detection, and rehabilitation. To promote prevention, all employees were given drug training. This in itself might motivate some drug users to come forward, and for those employees not familiar with drugs it would help them deal with employees who do have drug problems. For detection, the EAP decided that all new employees would be tested, and that current employees would be tested if they showed erratic behavior or if they were on probation. Employees who test positive are urged to enter a drug treatment program that is paid for by the company. If they deny they are drug users, they may request another test. If the retest indisputably shows drug use, and the employee still refuses treatment, the individual is fired.

As noted in the introduction, the Oregon Steel Mills policy reduced accidents and absenteeism while increasing productivity. One of the reasons it works is not the mere mechanics of the program, but the fact the program was adopted *by* the workers *for* the workers, and so they had a lot invested in making it work.

Employee privacy is an issue that affects the individual rights of employees and consumers, public well-being, and the property rights of business owners. As such, it is not a matter to be decided by owners alone or by consumer demand. What is needed is a way to include the interests of consumers, owners, and employees. Integrating these interests is one of the central functions of government. As the reader will see in the discussion of law, below, statutes and court cases try to balance the need for personal privacy in the workplace and the need for society to protect itself. This is just what we expect if the reinforcement view of law is correct.

Law

Historically, employers have been very interested in the personal lives of their employees. Henry Ford is famous for dictating the sorts of interests and activities that were appropriate for his workers, and policing them to make sure that they measured up. Ford Motor Company's "Sociological Department" routinely dispatched inspectors to employees' residences to see that the houses were clean and tidy, while checking on employees' drinking habits, their frugality with money, and the frequency of their church going. Those who did not meet Ford's expectations did not last long with the company. Although today such measures seem extreme, if not unimaginable, many corporations are still much concerned with what those in their employ do and what they think, and not just when they are on the job. Drug tests, lie detectors, and personality tests administered to employees are all designed to get beneath and behind what is immediately manifest, while data bases collect information, and video and audio equipment monitors employee activities at work. Employers who rely on such devices would not appear to have much respect for their worker's right to privacy.

The Right to Privacy Yet is there really such a legal right to be respected? The phrase *right to privacy* does not occur in the Constitution, either in reference to the home or while on the job. Nonetheless, in 1965 the Supreme Court announced that privacy was a constitutionally protected right. *Griswold v. Connecticut*, 381 U.S. 479 (1965), concerned a state law making it a crime for any person to use any drug, article, or instrument to prevent conception. After Planned Parenthood of Connecticut opened a birth control clinic, the executive director and medical director of the facility were convicted of violating the statute by giving information, instruction, and medical advice to married persons regarding means of preventing contraception. The state supreme court affirmed their conviction, but a seven-to-two Supreme Court majority held that a statute criminalizing contraception violated the right to privacy. Where did the justices find this right?

In his famous majority opinion, Justice William O. Douglas claimed that the right was located in the "penumbras" and "emanations" of rights that are specifically stated in the Constitution; in other words, the right to privacy is *implied* by various other rights that are explicitly enumerated there. Douglas pointed to the Third Amendment, which requires the consent of the owner before a soldier can be quartered in a private residence, the Fourth Amendment, to be discussed below, as well as the Ninth, which guarantees rights retained by the people even though they are not mentioned in the Constitution, noting that all these create "zones of privacy" that are protected from government intrusion. The *Griswold* decision thus saw the right to privacy as essentially a right to be left alone.

What does this have to do with business? Drug testing is perhaps the best context in which to appreciate the impact on the workplace of this judicially discovered right, and it is perhaps also the most controversial employee privacy issue. The legality of this testing, as well as discussion of the constitutional grounds of a general employee right to privacy (and one for citizens too), typically centers on the Fourth Amendment, just as in the *Griswold* case. To understand why, we first need to look at what the Fourth says:

> The right of the people to be secure in their persons, houses, papers, and effects, against unreasonable searches and seizures, shall not be violated, and no Warrants shall issue, but upon probable cause, supported by Oath or affirmation, and particularly describing the place to be searched, and the persons or things to be seized.

Many hundreds of court cases have labored over the meaning of this amendment. These analyses have yielded the following facets of the Fourth Amendment:

- **Probable cause.** When a warrant is required, it is issued only on **probable cause**. This has been understood to mean that before a search or seizure can be carried out, law enforcement officials must present their reasons for wanting to do so to a judge, swearing ("by Oath") that the facts they allege are true: This is to show probable cause. The judge then decides if the search is justified or *warranted*.

- **Warrantless searches.** Not all searches require warrants. The courts have not interpreted the Fourth Amendment to mean that any reasonable search must have a warrant. The prohibition is really against searches that are "unreasonable."

- **Reasonableness.** Warrantless searches are permissible so long as they are *reasonable*. Just what makes a search reasonable has been hotly debated. In general, concern for the safety of law enforcement officers or for private citizens, where there is no significant cost to privacy interests, has been seen as a key feature in identifying a reasonable, but warrantless search.

- **Scope of protection.** Fourth Amendment protection extends to premises other than the home, including places of business. However, the scope of what is considered a reasonable, warrantless search expands as the expectation of privacy diminishes. In the home, there is a very high expectation of privacy, while in a busy restaurant there is very little. A reasonable search in a restaurant would likely be completely unreasonable at home. Similarly, the scope of reasonableness expands according to the degree to which a business is regulated. Highly regulated businesses (such as alcohol producers) are more vulnerable to warrantless searches than lightly regulated businesses (such as textbook publishers).

Prior to the landmark Supreme Court cases *Skinner v. Railway Labor Executives' Association* and *National Treasury Employees Union v. Von Raab* (see both below), scores of lower courts had considered the issue of workplace drug testing. Although there was still disagreement on some crucial points, a few consistent standards had emerged from these decisions. First, courts agreed that a urinalysis is a search, and therefore its legality is governed by the Fourth Amendment. Second, since the level of the drug in a person's system declines over time, the test must be given promptly, obviating the need for a search warrant. This means that a drug test is essentially a warrantless search. Third, since a urinalysis is a search, it must be reasonable to conduct one.

Unfortunately, there was little consensus in these early drug testing decisions about exactly when a test, as a warrantless search, is reasonable. Nearly every court held that testing was legal when there was an "individualized" and "reasonable suspicion" of drug taking; that is, the well-founded belief that some particular individual was under the influence of drugs. Various cases marked the boundaries of what counts as a reasonable suspicion. Many of these courts also held that individualized suspicion was *required* in order to justify the testing. Other courts, however, were willing to allow suspicionless or random drug testing. Random testing was ruled reasonable only under certain conditions, such as when: (1) significant interests in public safety are at stake, (2) the testing is done confidentially with minimal intrusion on personal privacy, and (3) employees have lower expectations of privacy on their jobs. Some courts found that random testing was reasonable for individuals working in heavily regulated businesses, such as horse racing and law enforcement.

As we will see, some of these matters were sorted out by the Supreme Court in the *Skinner* and *National Treasury* cases. In preparation for that discussion, we need first to recognize that a right to privacy, understood as a right to be left alone, can be subsumed under a broader sense of privacy not immediately countenanced by the *Griswold* decision. This wider sense includes the right to retain exclusive possession of certain information about oneself; stated negatively, this is the idea that people are entitled not to have personal details about their lives disclosed to the public without their consent. More directly than a right to be left alone, this sort of privacy right strikes at the use of polygraphs, character assessments, computer files, cameras, and microphones to gain access to facts about employees that they would not willingly reveal, and includes revelations of their drug use. Although this wider sense of privacy has never been ratified in a Supreme Court decision, and many legal scholars believe it cannot be prized out of the Constitution, it has nonetheless been written into many state and federal statutes, most notably the Employee Polygraph Protection Act and the Privacy Act.

Selected Cases, Statutes, and Regulations

Privacy Act of 1974, 5 U.S.C. §§552 *et seq.* This act evidences congressional recognition of three fundamental facts: (1) Information technology has placed a vast amount of data concerning the personal lives of American citizens at the disposal of the federal government; (2) this personal information could seriously harm individuals if disseminated to current or prospective employers, creditors, and insurance carriers; and (3) the right to privacy is a basic right guaranteed by the U.S. Constitution. In light of these facts, the Privacy Act allows federal employees to find out what information has been collected about them by federal agencies, and requires their written consent before any of this personal information can be disclosed to employers. There are exceptions to this disclosure rule. Written consent is not needed to divulge this information to: (1) employees of the agency collecting the information (if their employment position requires the data), (2) law enforcement agencies, (3) courts, (4) the Census Bureau, and (5) the National Archives. The act also limits the kind of information about federal employees that federal employers may compile, confining it to data relevant and necessary for accomplishing some agency purpose as mandated by Congress or the president.

There is little regulation of employee information in the private sector. A few states limit the kind of information employers can collect for personnel files, but most state regulations are confined to employee access to their files, and correcting erroneous information contained there. Many states have no employee privacy statutes whatsoever.

Omnibus Crime Control and Safe Streets Act of 1968, 42 U.S.C. §§3711 *et seq.* Title III of this statute prohibits employers from listening to the personal telephone conversations of their employees or making the substance of these conversations public. Listening in to private calls is permitted only with the consent of the employee. It is legal for employers to monitor business-related phone calls to and from the workplace, but if business calls are interrupted by personal conversations, the monitoring must be halted immediately. The act does allow employers to ban personal calls entirely while on the job, and employee conversations may be monitored for violations. However, once a personal call is detected, an employer is not permitted to listen to the entire conversation. Monitoring personal calls without employee consent may bring a fine of up to $10,000.

In 1986 Congress amended this act to include a prohibition on employers monitoring their employees' electronic communications, especially e-mail and video-teleconferences. So far, there have been no reported cases challenging employers monitoring video display terminals.

Fair Credit Reporting Act of 1970, 15 U.S.C. §§1681 *et seq.* Employers are entitled to access credit information on current and prospective employees from consumer reporting agencies (see also Chapter 2: The Consumer—Finance, Law; Credit). Credit histories of individuals are generally seen by employers as relevant evidence for decisions concerning hiring, retention, promotion, or reassignment. Because the information provided includes not only an individual's alacrity in paying bills, but also a list of the other companies requesting credit information, an employer can determine whether that person is looking for another job. There is no requirement to notify the individual about whom the information is sought unless what is asked for goes beyond the credit history to include—for example—material about other interviews. A more detailed background check requires the notification but *not* the consent of the employee or applicant, so long as this is justified by business necessity. Just what constitutes a **business necessity** can be controversial, and a person may sue a company for invasion of privacy if he or she believes the boundaries of this standard have been overstepped.

Employee Polygraph Protection Act of 1988, 29 U.S.C §§2001–2009 This congressional act, also known as EPPA, concerns the role of **lie detectors** in places of employment. The term "lie detector" refers here to any device used "for the purpose of rendering a diagnostic opinion regarding the honesty or dishonesty of an individual." EPPA prohibits the random or pre-employment use of these devices by private sector employers and requires them to post a conspicuous notice informing employees of the act's provisions.

The prohibition does not apply to federal, state, and local government employees, but nearly all honesty testing has been done in the private sector anyway. Additionally, some private sector businesses may use polygraphs in certain situations. Security firms that hire personnel to protect public health and safety (guards at power plants, for example) are exempt from EPPA, as are companies that manufacture and distribute pharmaceuticals. Certain businesses that contract with the Department of Defense may use polygraphs fairly liberally. Finally, any employer with a reasonable suspicion that a particular employee has been involved in theft or embezzlement from the company (or a similar illegal activity) may ask that person to submit to a polygraph examination.

Nonetheless, EPPA does give employees in these exempt areas some rights: The person to be tested must be given advance notice, and he or she has the right to stop the test at any time, the right not to be asked questions about race, religion, politics, or sexual behavior, and the right to a written list of the questions to be asked before the test takes place. Only licensed examiners can be used.

The secretary of labor is in charge of implementing and enforcing EPPA. Alleged violations of EPPA are actionable by the secretary in federal district court, and can be punished by court orders to stop the unlawful use of the lie detector tests, by reinstatement with back pay of the wronged employee, and by fines of up to $10,000.

Soroka v. Dayton Hudson Corporation, **1 Cal. Rptr. 2d 77 (Cal. Ct. App. 1991)** Few cases concerning psychological testing of current or prospective employees have made their way very high in the judicial system; no such case has ever been heard by the Supreme Court. The legal issues are unsettled on the federal level and quite various at the state level. Nonetheless, about 25 percent of all employers use some form of personality inventory in screening applicants for job openings. To date, this case, and the one following, seem to have been the most influential for establishing some standards for business.

Sibi Soroka applied for a job as a security guard at the Walnut Creek, California, Target store in 1989 (Dayton Hudson owns Target). As part of the interviewing process, Soroka was required to take a *Psychscreen* test: This consisted of 704 first-person statements to which he was to respond with "true" or "false." Soroka was quite disturbed by many of these statements. For example, some were about his religious beliefs: "I feel sure that there is only one true religion," and "My soul sometimes leaves my body." Others concerned his sexual inclinations: "My sex life is satisfactory," and "I am very strongly attracted to members of my own sex." Although Soroka completed the test and was hired, within a few months he had quit and was suing Target for, among a number of things, violation of the California Constitution's right to privacy.

Target's lawyers argued that the test was intended to ensure the emotional stability of the store's security force, not discover their religious beliefs or sexual orientation; this particular interest justified the invasion of privacy resulting from taking the test. The use of the test for screening applicants, they claimed, was "reasonable," because those looking for a job do not deserve as much protection as those already employed. Soroka responded that the right to privacy in the state constitution was intended to protect all persons, whether employed or not, and that Target needed to demonstrate a much stronger compelling interest in the private lives of its workforce to justify intrusion, not just that it is "reasonable."

The California court of appeals agreed with Soroka on all counts. Justice Reardon asserted that the protections of the state constitution make no distinction between applicants and employees, and that a violation of the right to privacy must be justified by a compelling interest arising from a distinctly job-related purpose. Target had failed to demonstrate any compelling interest or job-related purpose in the Psychscreen's statements about religious and sexual matters. He ordered that the use of the test be suspended and the case be remanded to the trial court. Target appealed, and in 1992 the California Supreme Court agreed to take the case. However, in 1993, Target reached a cash settlement with Soroka; the company also agreed to pay $1.3 million to those people who had taken the Psychscreen.

Cleghorn v. Hess, 853 P.2d 1260 (Nev. 1993)   Do employees qualify as the patients of the professionals who administer psychological tests to them? If so, then they are entitled to the results of those tests. Michael Cleghorn worked as an inspector for a company under contract to the Department of Energy (DOE) to provide security for nuclear weapons facilities in Nevada. As part of the collective bargaining agreement with Cleghorn's union, he was required to meet a certain DOE personality standard as measured by psychological testing. The tests were administered by a Dr. Hess. After taking a pre-employment test in 1982 and a second test in 1990, Cleghorn requested copies of his psychological records and test results. Hess refused.

Cleghorn sued, claiming that a Nevada statute required Hess to supply the health records to him upon demand; Hess countered that the statute does not apply because he is not in this instance a health care provider and Cleghorn was not, strictly speaking, his patient, primarily on the grounds that he did not give him any treatment. Chief Justice Rose of the Nevada Supreme Court agreed with Cleghorn. Rose found that (1) Hess was a health care provider, (2) Cleghorn was his patient because he sought medical services for examination *or* treatment, and (3) the records requested were medical records. This finding has significant implications for the psychological testing of employees. Although no case on this issue has been scrutinized yet by the Supreme Court, *Cleghorn* means that the well-established standards for the doctor-patient relationship hold here. Most important is the applicability of the standards of confidentiality and access to the information gathered by the health care professional.

Drug-Free Workplace Act of 1988, 41 U.S.C. §701–707   This act applies to companies that contract with the federal government for at least $25,000 worth of goods or services, and to any employer that receives federal grants. The basic idea is to compel employers to make a sincere effort to produce a job environment where the presence of drugs is eliminated. The act requires these businesses to send a notice to each of their employees, and to post in a conspicuous location the announcement that using alcohol and certain illegal drugs is prohibited. Additionally, the employer must educate workers on the dangers of drug use, the availability of counseling and treatment for drug problems, and the consequences for not seeking help. An employee convicted of drug use must notify his or her supervisor within five days, and notification of the conviction must be passed on to the contracting or funding federal agency within ten days.

Skinner v. Railway Labor Executives' Association, **482 U.S. 602 (1989);** *National Treasury Employees Union v. Von Raab*, **482 U.S. 656 (1989)** These two landmark cases were decided by the Supreme Court on the same day, marking the first time the high Court had considered the constitutionality of drug testing in the workplace. Although both cases involve random or suspicionless testing, there is an important difference between the two regarding the accompanying belief that drug use had occurred. *Skinner* concerns drug testing without an individualized suspicion; that is, testing a person for the presence of drugs without having any reason to believe that that person has actually taken drugs. There is here a generalized suspicion of drug taking, one that is not necessarily focused on any particular individual. On the other hand, in *National Treasury Employees* we have a fairly pure case of suspicionless testing. There is neither a suspicion diffused among the group, nor is any particular person suspected of taking drugs. Are these varieties of drug testing legal? Consider *Skinner* first.

In 1985 the Federal Railroad Administration (FRA) adopted two new regulations, both intended to address what was perceived to be a problem of drug and alcohol abuse by railroad employees. One regulation required blood and urine tests of train crew members following certain major accidents or incidents; the other, for the most part, authorized breath or urine tests (or both) of crew members when less significant accidents or incidents occurred, or when certain safety rules were violated. The Railway Labor Executives Association, a union of railroad workers, sued Samuel Skinner, the secretary of transportation and administrator of FRA, on the grounds that the regulations were unconstitutional.

The Ninth Circuit Court of Appeals found that the drug testing qualified as a search, and thus implicated the Fourth Amendment. The Ninth Circuit also found that concern for public safety overrode the privacy interests of railroad workers, and, because of these serious concerns, such a search did not require a showing of probable cause, only meeting the standard of reasonableness. Despite these findings favorable to the FRA, the regulations were ruled invalid. The problem was that the drug testing was conducted without an individualized suspicion: All crew members involved in the incident were tested whether or not any one of them was suspected of using drugs. For the Ninth Circuit, this made the testing—that is, the search—unreasonable.

The Supreme Court validated the Ninth Circuit's judgment that the drug testing required and authorized by the FRA regulations did constitute a search, and was thus subject to Fourth Amendment protection. Justice Anthony Kennedy, writing for the majority, also agreed that issuing a warrant justified by probable cause was not necessary to elude that protection. However, Kennedy rejected the notion that the reasonableness standard could not be satisfied without a showing of individualized suspicion: "[T]he government interest in testing without a showing of individualized suspicion is compelling. A substance-impaired railroad employee in a safety-sensitive job can cause great human loss before any signs of impairment become noticeable, and the regulations supply an effective means of deterring such employees from using drugs or alcohol."

Treasury Employees v. von Raab concerns a policy implemented in 1986 by the U.S. Customs Service, a division of the Treasury Department. The drug-screening program required all those in the service who applied for transfer or promotion to certain positions to undergo a urinalysis. Individuals wanting to work directly with drug interdiction, or in jobs requiring carrying firearms or handling classified material were required to be tested for the presence of certain illegal drugs. Here there was no suspicion of any kind: The program was not motivated by the belief that any of the applicants were taking drugs.

The union for employees of the Treasury Department sued Commissioner von Raab, head of the Customs Service, for violating their Fourth Amendment rights with the drug testing program. The district court agreed with the union and issued an injunction to halt the program, but the Fifth Circuit Court of Appeals vacated the injunction. Justice Anthony Kennedy and a majority of the Supreme Court agreed with Fifth Circuit.

As in *Skinner*, Kennedy first observed that the drug testing program was indeed a search and therefore must meet Fourth Amendment requirements. However, he argued that demonstrating probable cause and obtaining a warrant were not necessary because this would produce a wasteful expenditure of valuable resources without providing much protection of personal privacy. Despite the lack of probable cause or any suspicion at all, Kennedy held that the search was reasonable: Compelling government interests in both the integrity and heartiness of their frontline interdiction forces, and in the public safety, outweigh the privacy interests of those seeking promotions. He added that, "Although it is not motivated by any perceived drug problem among Service employees, the program is nevertheless justified by the extraordinary safety and national security hazards that would attend the promotion of drug users to sensitive positions."

Vernonia School District 47J v. Wayne Acton, 115 S. Ct. 2386 (1995)
Although this decision concerns athletes at a public high school, its legal implications are wide ranging. It not only expands the criteria for legally permissible, random or suspicionless drug testing first articulated in *Skinner v. Railway Labor Executives' Association* and *National Treasury Employees Union v. Von Raab* (see both above), it should also be taken as stating the conditions for overriding the privacy interests of employees faced with drug testing in the workplace as well.

The citizens of Vernonia, Oregon, perceived a marked increase in drug use among students in their secondary education schools during the late 1980s. A contemporaneous rise in disciplinary problems was believed to be linked to the drug surge and the emergence of student athletes as leaders of a drug subculture. After other measures failed to abate the problem, school district officials and participating parents adopted a "Student Athlete Drug Policy" in

1989, the substance of which consisted in weekly random testing by urinalysis of students engaged in interscholastic sports programs. Students were required to sign a form consenting to the testing and to obtain the written consent of their parents. In the fall of 1991 seventh-grader James Acton, desiring to play football, refused to sign the consent form. His parents also refused to sign. They sued the school district, claiming that the drug policy violated the Fourth and Fourteenth Amendments of the Constitution. The district court rejected the claim, but the Ninth Circuit Court of Appeals reversed, agreeing with the Actons.

The Supreme Court vacated the Ninth Circuit's decision. Justice Antonin Scalia presented a majority opinion focused on the reasonableness of the drug policy. He first noted that the high Court's earlier decision in *Skinner* established that a drug test qualified as a search under the meaning of the Fourth Amendment. Scalia went on to observe that the constitutionality of such a search turns on either "probable cause," which justifies the issuance of a warrant, or whether the search is a reasonable one. He considered three factors in making this determination concerning the Vernonia School District's policy: (1) the decreased expectation of privacy; (2) the unobtrusiveness of the search; and (3) the severity of the need for such searches.

For each factor, Scalia found for the school district: (1) The locker room atmosphere that pervades athletics undermines any expectations of privacy; (2) the searches were conducted in a manner little different from ordinary use of a public lavatory; and (3) the discipline and health problems associated with "children" using drugs produced an urgent need for the testing. Scalia warned "against the assumption that suspicionless drug testing will readily pass constitutional muster in other contexts." For the working world, "the relevant question is whether that intrusion upon privacy is one that a reasonable employer might engage in." Numbers 1 through 3 above suggest the sorts of criteria employers need to consider to effect "reasonable" random drug testing.

O'Connor v. Ortega, **408 U.S. 709 (1987)** One of the very few workplace privacy cases to be considered by the Supreme Court, this decision has profound ramifications for employee privacy. It concerns the extent to which the Fourth Amendment to the Constitution protects people from their employers while on the job. This amendment prohibits unreasonable searches and seizures (see above). Does the Fourth Amendment place similar constraints on employers and provide a similar refuge for their workers?

The long road to an answer to this question began in 1981 when Dr. Magno Ortega was dismissed from his position as chief of professional education at Napa State Hospital in California. Just two months before his discharge, Dr. Dennis O'Connor, the executive director of the hospital, had placed Ortega on administrative leave. O'Connor wanted to investigate charges that Ortega had improperly obtained a computer for the psychiatric residency program he directed, had sexually harassed two women, and had inappropriately disciplined a resident. At various times while he was on leave, members of O'Connor's "investigative team" entered Ortega's office and seized a number of items, both personal and work-related, from his desk and file cabinets. Some of this confiscated material was used as the basis for Ortega's discharge. He eventually sued for violation of his Fourth Amendment rights.

The district court ruled that the search was proper because there was a need to secure state property located in Ortega's office. The Ninth Circuit Court of Appeals disagreed, holding that Ortega had a reasonable expectation of privacy in his office and that the search violated the Fourth Amendment. The Supreme Court affirmed part of this judgment and reversed another.

The majority opinion, authored by Justice Sandra Day O'Connor, first observed that people have a legitimate expectation of privacy on the job: The Fourth Amendment does apply to searches and seizures by public employers of the private property of their employees. However, in some work situations, the expectation of privacy might not be a reasonable one; O'Connor recognized that conditions vary greatly, and it might not make sense to expect privacy if one's office is regularly accessed by coworkers and other visitors. Whether it is reasonable to anticipate that one's materials will remain secluded from others must be determined on a case-by-case basis. In this case, O'Connor agreed that Ortega was correct to suppose that his office would remain private. On the other hand, whether his Fourth Amendment rights were violated depended on whether his employer conducted a reasonable search. Determining that "requires balancing the employee's legitimate expectation of privacy against the government's need for supervision, control, and the efficient operation of the workplace." O'Connor opined that requiring a warrant or probable cause of an employer would be unduly disruptive and burdensome, that the appropriate standard was "reasonableness." The majority concluded that the evidence was insufficient to sustain the judgment that the search was unreasonable.

Discrimination and Affirmative Action

In the United States, affirmative action policies or plans (AAPs) attempt to increase the proportion of women and minorities (the legally **protected classes**) in jobs traditionally held by white males (members of an unprotected class). These policies are usually justified by invoking past injustices that prevented members of protected classes from competing on a "level playing field" with members of unprotected classes (Boatright 1997a). Sometimes AAPs are seen as additionally advancing the social goal of a more egalitarian society. AAPs add race and/or gender to the standard qualifications for hiring and promotion, but only as tie-breakers: If a protected class candidate and a nonprotected class candidate are *equally qualified*, the protected class candidate is chosen for the job (Phillips 1991).

Advocates of AAPs argue that affirmative action is necessary to overcome the competitive disadvantages faced by women and minorities due to current and past discrimination, and to make our employment more inclusive and representative of these disadvantaged groups. Opponents argue that these programs result in unfair **reverse discrimination** either because the injustices of the past were not so pervasive as to taint the present, or because those penalized by not getting a job for which they are qualified were not the ones who committed those past wrongs (Boxhill 1978). Further, these policies are bad for society as a whole because they will discourage qualified individuals from unprotected classes from entering the labor market.

Comparable worth concerns the specific issues of pay and **compensation** (Devine 1987). In general, women's wages are about two-thirds of men's wages, and many jobs traditionally held by women pay less than those traditionally held by men, even when women's jobs require more skill and training (see, for example, Selected Cases: *AFSCME v. State of Washington*, below). Comparable worth requires companies to pay equally for jobs of equal value to the company, even though the occupations are not identical, regardless of the gender of the workers.

One of the main problems with comparable worth is how to decide whether two jobs are comparable, and so should be paid the same rate (Waluchow 1988). Opponents argue that such policies are unworkable, undermine the market, ignore facts about women's work experience and seniority, and would backfire against women (Devine 1987; Paul 1989). Proponents argue that wage disparities are the result of discrimination, not the workings of the free market. Further, many contend that even if comparable worth is inefficient, fairness and justice, which are more important than efficiency, demand that we implement such programs (Hill 1987; Shrage 1987).

John Stuart Mill, the nineteenth-century economist and philosopher (see Chapter 1: Introduction—The Tools Of Business Ethics: Ethics), argued that an efficient economy must make jobs open to all talented members of society. If comparable worth programs created these opportunities, they could make the market more efficient, not less. Comparable worth policies can be found at the state and municipal level, but have largely been rejected at the federal level (Boatright 1997b).

In our discussion of ethics and economics, we will focus on AAPs.

Ethics

Promoting Self-interest: Egoism Aggressively self-interested members of protected classes would be in favor of AAPs as long as AAPs promoted their goals as employees. However, AAPs may help only selected members of protected classes. Boxhill (1978), for example, examines arguments that AAPs help only the most educated members of protected classes. Even if this true, however, AAPs would provide an incentive for members of protected classes to get an education. Aggressively self-interested members of protected classes might reject AAPs if they thought these policies would create animosity among their coworkers.

Aggressively self-interested members of *un*protected classes would tend to reject AAPs because these programs limit their opportunities to get jobs and promotions. However, unprotected class workers who are secure in their jobs could welcome AAPs if they believe these policies will add more qualified workers, making the workplace more efficient. AAPs could make the workplace more efficient because they encourage members of unprotected classes to get educations, bringing in talent that was lost before (see Promoting the Good of the Group, below).

Contemplatively self-interested members of protected classes would be wary of AAPs because of animosity by, and therefore conflict with, fellow employees. However, if AAPs were the only way they could get a decent job and support themselves, these employees would be willing to live with this conflict in order to avoid the greater problem of being homeless or of being unable to provide for their families. If contemplatively self-interested individuals were dependent on the income of members of protected classes, they would be in favor of AAPs, in the hope that these types of programs would increase the earning power of their providers. For example, a man could easily favor AAPs if he doesn't want to work and is dependent on the income of his female partner.

As we can see, whether self-interested individuals will approve or reject AAPs depends on their particular circumstances and how they define their interests.

Promoting Personal Relationships: Care Passive caring employees want to preserve and strengthen their relationships by avoiding conflict. To avoid conflict, they would approve of AAPs if the **cared-for** approve of AAPs. If the cared-for are against them, these employees would reject AAPs.

Under some circumstances, passive caring employees might not simply mirror the beliefs of others. For example, suppose a passive carer believes an AAP would help a cared-for, but the cared-for is opposed to AAPs. Passive carers could support the AAP if they could conceal their support from the cared-for. This would be consistent with the passive carer's desire to maintain the relationship, because the cared-for would not know of the support, and consistent with their desire to help the cared-for. Passive carers who take this approach might be developing an active caring ethic, because they are starting to think for themselves.

Active caring employees, who focus on helping others pursue their own projects, would point out that employment is the primary way that people support themselves and their families. Supporting ourselves and our families is a fundamental project, because, if we can't do that, we cannot pursue other projects, such as a career or a profession. So long as AAPs help members of protected classes get jobs and promotions, active caring employees should be in favor of them.

Active caring employees would have conflicts if they themselves were denied jobs or promotions by an AAP. Members of unprotected classes would be especially vulnerable to this problem; their concern would not be over their own losses, but how their losses would affect their families and friends. Another problem that active caring employees would have is that unprotected class employees would be harmed by AAPs, an effect sometimes known as **reverse discrimination**. Because a central principle of care is that we may not harm one person to help another, active caring employees are caught in a difficult position.

Promoting the Good of the Group: Utilitarianism John Stuart Mill, writing in England during the 1860s, argued that the strength of an economy is based on the talent of its workers. The more talent an economy has, the more productive and innovative it will be. Now, suppose there is a large group of individuals (Mill focused on women) who are not allowed to participate in the business world. Mill argued that excluding groups in this way harms everyone because of all the talent that is lost (Robson and Robson 1994). The same arguments can be made for race, religion, and all the other attributes that have been used to arbitrarily keep others out of the workforce.

Another utilitarian argument against using arbitrary standards, such as race or gender, in hiring and promotion rests on the importance of social stability. If large groups of people are not allowed to pursue good jobs, careers, and professions, they will seek to equalize this through crime or other behavior that is disruptive and costly to the society.

If utilitarian employees accepted the arguments just given, it does *not* follow that they would be in favor of government action to correct the problems, since government action can be more costly, in terms of money and repression, than the problems AAPs try to resolve. Sassen (1976) argues that programs like AAPs will have these unfortunate consequences, because government will have to impose some particular notion of what equality is, monitor companies closely to make sure they adhere to the rules, and punish those who do not. In *The Road to Serfdom*, F. A. Hayek argued that policies like these would lead to repressive, totalitarian governments that turn most citizens into paupers (Hayek 1944).

Strict utilitarians would probably agree with Sassen. David Hume, a strict rule utilitarian writing in the eighteenth century, made a very similar point when discussing the best way to distribute property. If we try to distribute property equally, he says, we will soon find that some people have lost it, others have destroyed have it, while others have used it for productive purposes, creating more property for themselves (Hume 1748). When faced with this new inequality, the government will have to redistribute jobs, which will also lead to inequalities. This process of distributing and redistributing jobs will go on forever. To illustrate Hume's point, suppose a government, trying to rectify inequality in jobs, gave each person a job for which he or she was qualified. Some would work hard and be promoted; others would do just enough to avoid getting fired and would never be promoted; while still others would get fired because they did not do their job well. Soon after the initial distribution, jobs would be unequal, and the government would have to redistribute them again. It is not hard to see the uselessness and intrusiveness of this program.

Another problem strict utilitarians would have with AAPs is that it is difficult to develop workable rules about preferential hiring that result in an efficient and smoothly functioning economic system. No strict rule could be formed because there is too much variation in the jobs that must be filled and in the characteristics of the people who do them. Managers need to have the flexibility to decide which candidate will best fill a position.

To see the problem managers have when hiring under AAPs, we must say something about the process of affirmative action hiring. The first step is to write a job description. This description serves as the standard for evaluating job candidates. Among all the people qualifying, the manager should choose the most qualified. If a protected class candidate and an unprotected class candidate are equally qualified, the manager should choose the protected class candidate. However, what if it turns out that the unprotected class candidate has a skill, not mentioned in the job description, that is very valuable to the company? The manager cannot hire the unprotected class candidate even though that person would be better for the job.

A flexible rule utilitarian would argue that these problems can be overcome by flexible rules. One strategy for making flexible rules work, which many organizations have already adopted, is to designate or hire an affirmative action officer to help managers apply AAPs correctly. In the case just mentioned, in which the job candidate who is not a member of a protected class has a skill not included in the job description, the affirmative action officer could suggest alternatives. For example, if there is another job in the company that the unprotected class candidate could fill, the company can hire both of them.

An affirmative action officer would need what Werhane (1994) and Johnson (1993) call *moral imagination*. Moral imagination consists of many things, but for our purposes, we can describe it as the ability to develop novel ways to understand and resolve problems. For instance, the problem of the unprotected class job candidate with a skill not listed in the job description was originally thought of as conflict between two people for one job, but by looking for other positions in the same company, new ways to resolve the problem are created. Even if there is no other job at the same company, other creative solutions are possible. The affirmative action officer may contact other companies in the same industry to see if they have a position for either of these candidates. In doing so, this officer could develop reciprocal relationships with other companies, allowing the industry to broaden its placement opportunities and labor market. These kinds of relationships are beginning to form through the auspices of the Ethics Officers Association, which is affiliated with the Bentley College Center for Business Ethics.

Whether utilitarian employees support strict or flexible rules, and whether they endorse or reject AAPs, they share a dedication to making society better in the future. Although it may seem hard to argue against such a lofty goal, it can be done. In the next section we will look at ethical views that focus on human dignity and rights. Both of these views give ethical weight to what happened in the past.

Respecting Dignity and Rights: Intrinsic Value   Employees can use the principle of fairness and human dignity to justify AAPs, because prejudices toward minorities and women unfairly keep qualified applicants out of the workforce (Ezorsky 1991). People get education and training to become qualified in a particular area, and if they are rejected because of their race or gender, this is unfair. AAPs can help prevent this unfairness.

Opponents of AAPs also rely on the principle of fairness and human dignity, and argue in the following manner: AAPs are immoral because they give members of protected classes an unfair advantage in two ways. First, the members of the protected classes did nothing in the past to earn the privilege of being chosen ahead of those in nonprotected classes. Contrast this with the case of veterans. Many government agencies give veterans preference when they apply for jobs, so veterans will get the job when they compete against equally qualified nonveterans. Few think this is unfair, partly because the veterans have earned their preference by enduring great personal risks; giving them job preferences is one way the country can pay them back, and even honor them for their contribution. The second reason that AAPs are unfair is that they punish people who did not create the problems that AAPs are supposed to combat. Members of nonprotected classes played by the rules of the game, got their education and training, and now the rules have changed on them, and to their detriment. AAPs, then, result in reverse discrimination (Pojman 1992).

Consider, for example, Laura Purdy's argument (1984) that managers should hire women whom they perceive to be less qualified than unprotected class candidates because women are often perceived as less qualified than they really are. To rectify this misperception, managers need to overcompensate. Even employees in favor of AAPs could reject this plan because it unfairly discriminates against nonprotected candidates. Though intriguing, Purdy's plan is not typical of AAPs. In fact, we know of no organization that actually tries to hire protected classes candidates it believes are unqualified. However, her argument does highlight the fact that AAPs can be designed in a number of ways. If we use fairness and human dignity as our moral base, we should make sure they are designed to protect *all* candidates as much as possible.

If employees take a property rights view, government-mandated AAPs are much harder to justify. If they focus on the owners of the corporation, these government plans infringe on their property rights to hire whom they wish. This right is sometimes expressed in the employment at will doctrine (see Terms and Conditions of Employment, above). The heart of this doctrine is that employers have the right to hire, fire, and promote whom they wish, for whatever reason they wish. Government-imposed AAPs, then, can only be justified if the rights they protect are more important than the property rights of owners.

Property rights are often limited to protect the rights of others. Firing a gun, for example, is prohibited in most cities in order to protect ordinary citizens from stray bullets. There are exceptions, of course. Police officers can fire guns in the line of duty and citizens can use legally acquired guns for self-defense. These restrictions and rules are not an infringement on the gun owners' property rights, but only on how they *use* their property.

The same kind of argument can be made in terms of the rights of corporate owners. If AAPs protect rights that are more important than the right of owners to give jobs to whomever they wish, then AAPs can be justified. J. Ralph Lindgren (1981) takes this approach when he argues that AAPs are not really programs designed to benefit protected classes, but instead they are programs intended to prevent *harming* protected classes. Being denied a job or promotion is a serious harm because jobs are how we earn a living for ourselves and our families. Leo Groarke (1990) argues that AAPs are justified because they are ways of making restitution to people who have lost a great deal due to past discrimination. Property rights theorists can view both of these considerations as more important than owner rights to choose employees.

We have seen that there are good reasons for AAPs and good reasons against AAPs. Which side has the strongest argument? We do not have to be in favor of AAPs in every circumstance, or opposed to them, if we believe that such programs are justified in some cases and not in others. Unfortunately, if we adopt a case-by-case approach, we have two new problems: First, we must determine what standards we should use to differentiate between justified and unjustified AAPs, and, second, we must settle on the procedures we use to implement these standards.

As we will see in Law, below, the case-by-case approach is very close to how the U.S. judiciary actually solves this problem. AAPs are allowed or mandated by executive order and federal statute; these orders and statutes set the initial standards for AAPs. Individuals can then appeal to the courts to enforce or to stop an AAP in a particular case. The courts' decisions set precedents that are used to evaluate similar cases in the future.

Passing statutes and evaluating them in the court system is time-consuming and expensive, but we do it because the stakes are very high, as they are with hiring, promotions, and firing. The case-by-case approach does not eliminate conflicts, but it ensures that the conflicts occur within a specific factual context to which we can apply ethical principles. Relevant questions of fact include: Did the company discriminate in the past? Are there qualified candidates from protected classes available? Are nonprotected class members being discouraged from seeking employment? These and other relevant questions can be asked, and answers are more likely to be found by examining cases on an individual basis.

International Issues

Affirmative action is practiced in many countries. The **European Union's** (EU) high court, which has as its jurisdiction all 15 member nations, upheld a German law that allowed government agencies to prefer women in a pool with equally qualified men. The court argued that discrimination against women in the past put them at an unfair disadvantage, and that AAPs were a legitimate way to make up for those disadvantages (Andrews 1997). Groups from all over Europe praised the ruling.

The EU court did not by this decision uphold all possible AAPs, because, first, the case spoke only to the issue of hiring women, and, second, it applied only to government agencies and organizations, not the private sector. Nonetheless, women's groups stated that they believed this ruling would affect the private sector as well. A third factor constraining AAPs is that the EU court also rejected the view that they could be designed as mechanical, rigid rules that do not allow for unforeseen events and characteristics (see the discussion of flexible rule utilitarianism, above, in Promoting the Good of the Group). In their support of the German AAP, the EU court specifically cited its flexibility, which allows managers to evaluate candidates on a case-by-case basis (Andrews 1997).

Thomas Sowell, in study of AAPs in several different countries, maintains that these policies do not promote the goal of job equality; in most cases, he argues, they do just the opposite (Sowell 1990). He cites studies of how AAPs affected the New Zealand Maoris, the Israeli Sephardim, the Malaysian Bumiputeras, Soviet Central Asians (in the former USSR), and South African whites (in the former Republic of South Africa). The AAP programs utilized in the first four examples failed for a number of reasons. One reason was that they benefitted only those minorities who were already doing well. Only those who had the requisite education and connections could make the AAPs work for them, while poorer members of the minorities were left behind. Another reason for failure was the backlash from those who believed they were victims of reverse discrimination. The only AAP program that clearly achieved its goal was the South African policy to hire and promote whites; and look at the repressive and violent government policies it took to make that work.

Economics

Society From the social point of view, AAPs can be justified if they promote or do not infringe on free markets. Free markets are usually justified in terms of utility. By definition, free markets require that individuals be free to compete for any jobs for which they are qualified. Such competition promotes the good of all, since the most qualified tend to get selected for jobs. The better that people do their jobs, the more efficiently companies manufacture products. This keeps prices low, quality high, and waste to a minimum.

Proponents argue that AAPs will increase the number of qualified candidates seeking employment because AAPs will encourage protected class members to get an education and the requisite training, thus expanding the talent pool for the business. Opponents of AAPs argue that companies will select lesser-qualified protected-class candidates to avoid government intervention and to avoid lawsuits from members of protected classes, causing business to be less efficient. Opponents further argue that choosing on the basis of race or gender will subject businesses to lawsuits claiming reverse discrimination (such as in *United Steelworkers of America v. Weber*; see Selected Cases, below).

When businesses spend time and money on litigation, they are less efficient at supplying products and services.

Consumers   Consumers typically do not know if the products they buy and the services they use are produced by protected classes or nonprotected classes. In some instances, minority-owned businesses may advertise that their products or services are produced and/or delivered by a protected class group, such as African-Americans or women, as a way to increase sales. But this is unusual, and when it happens it usually occurs in small neighborhood businesses or in specialty, niche markets, such as catalogue sales of unique clothes and crafts.

Producers   From the organizational point of view, corporations want the best employees for the lowest cost, because that will help them outperform the competition. One worry that businesses have about AAPs is that these programs will differentiate between *qualified* and *effective* employees. Qualified employees meet the standards listed in the job description, while effective employees are capable of doing the job well. The problem is that these might not be the same individuals.

Job candidates can be equally qualified but not equally effective for at least two reasons. First, there is the question of how broad or narrow the qualifications for the job are. If the standards are defined broadly, then two candidates could meet the standards, but one could be clearly better than another. For example, suppose an employer requires job candidates to know a particular computer language. Two candidates know the language. Candidate A, who is not from a protected class, has been working with the language for two years and has designed programs on the basis of it. The other candidate, B, who is from a protected class, has just learned the computer language. An AAP would recommend that the company hire the protected class candidate B, even though that person would be less effective than candidate A. These kinds of cases have forced employers to be more careful in their job descriptions, but this does not eliminate the problem, because not all relevant differences between candidates can be foreseen. Another problem is that narrow job descriptions exclude candidates that the company might hire because they have other traits that make them valuable.

Another reason why one employee may be more effective than another is because of his or her social skills. People who can work in teams, who are able to both lead and follow, depending on the situation, are essential to the success of most business organizations. Suppose that candidate B, above, has good references, a solid work history, and performs well in the interview situation, all these suggesting mature social skills. Candidate A, however, has references that indicate difficulties in working with others, such as rudeness and a failure to follow reasonable instructions in a timely fashion. In this case, the employer may be relieved that an AAP requires offering the job to B.

Producers need to be very careful when evaluating candidates on the basis of how well they get along with others. After all, effectiveness can never be legally evaluated as the ability of a protected class individual to work with prejudiced coworkers. For example, when women began joining police departments and fire departments, men objected that they would be uncomfortable, or worse, they refused to work with women. To give into these prejudices would simply perpetuate the discriminatory practices that AAPs were designed to eliminate.

Law

Introduction   When the Civil War ended, the country began the difficult process of reconstructing the Union. Of especially vital importance was the repatriation of southerners who had seceded, and the legal enfranchisement of blacks who had been enslaved. Two amendments to the Constitution addressed both these concerns. In 1865, Congress ratified the Thirteenth Amendment, prohibiting slavery or "involuntary servitude" anywhere in the United States. Three years later, the Fourteenth Amendment declared that all persons born in the United States were citizens of the United States, and further guaranteed that no state could deprive a citizen of the equal protection of the law, or of life, liberty, or property without due process of law. These phrases are known as the **Equal Protection Clause** and **Due Process Clause**.

To provide enforcement measures for the Thirteenth Amendment, Congress passed the first federal law protecting civil rights, the *Civil Rights Act of 1866*. Sections 1 and 2 of this act were then transferred into the *Civil Rights Act of 1871* and codified as Sections 1981 and 1982 (42 U.S.C.). Section 1981 states that "All persons within the jurisdiction of the United States shall have the same right in every State and Territory to make and enforce contracts...as is enjoyed by white persons." Since the employment relation is a contractual one, Section 1981 in effect prohibits discrimination in employment. However, in 1883 the Supreme Court ruled that such a prohibition in private sector employment was unconstitutional (the *Civil Rights Cases*, 109 U.S. 3 [1883]). Narrowly interpreting the Fourteenth Amendment, the Court held that *government* was precluded from infringing the rights of citizens protected by the Fourteenth Amendment, but private citizens were free to practice racial discrimination.

With the apparent blessing of the Supreme Court, there followed 80 years of discriminatory and segregationist literacy tests, poll taxes, and other measures collectively known as Jim Crow laws or the **Black Codes**. Title VII of the Civil Rights Act of 1964 (see below) put an end to all that, but it took four more years to affirm the original Civil Rights Act. In *Jones v. Alfred H. Mayer Company* (392 U.S. 409 [1968]), the Supreme Court ruled that the 1871 act was not unconstitutional after all, and that a refusal to sell property to blacks was a violation of Section 1982. Today, a discrimination suit can still be filed under the Civil Rights Act of 1871, though this is rare. There are advantages to doing so: Unlike Title VII, there is no minimum number of employees required and no administrative procedures to follow; instead, direct access to the courts is provided.

Title VII is the statute of choice for those filing discrimination suits, and the agency charged with administering Title VII, the Equal Employment

Opportunity Commission (EEOC; see Selected Cases: Title VII, below), also claims enforcement powers against other sorts of discrimination. After outlining Title VII and the mission of the EEOC, we consider in turn key cases and statutes concerning race, gender, age, pregnancy, and disability discrimination, followed by the related issues of equal pay and comparable worth.

Selected Cases, Statutes, and Regulations

Title VII of the Civil Rights Act of 1964, 45 U.S.C. §§2000e et seq. Officially called the Fair Employment Practices Act, but almost universally known as Title VII, this statute prohibits discrimination in employment. This means that there is a federal law forbidding employers in either the public or private sector from making certain decisions using race, color, religion, sex, or national origin as a relevant factor. These features define *legally* **protected classes** of people. Decisions concerning whom to hire, how much an individual will be paid (see also Equal Pay and Comparable Worth, below), what he or she will do, the grounds for discharge, and any other "term, condition, or privilege" of employment must not be based on ethnicity, nationality, religious beliefs, or gender. Additionally, these features must not be used in a way that presents obstacles to employment opportunities for either applicants or current employees. Title VII does not prohibit employment discrimination on the basis of sexual preference.

The act applies to every business organization with at least 15 employees, including labor unions (compare this with the Civil Rights Act of 1871, above, Introduction). Indian tribes and tax-exempt private clubs are excluded from coverage. Title VII can be violated either by **disparate** or adverse **impact** (see *Griggs v. Duke Power Company*, below) or by **disparate** or discriminatory **treatment** (see *McDonnell Douglas Corporation v. Green*, below). Violations may be penalized by **injunctions**, or awards of back pay, legal fees, or compensatory and punitive damages. The amount of damages varies according to the size of the company.

The act also created the Equal Employment Opportunity Commission (EEOC). The five commissioners are appointed by the president and are charged with the responsibilities of interpreting Title VII, investigating alleged violations of it, and enforcing their decisions concerning these allegations through the federal courts. The EEOC also administers the Equal Pay Act and the Age Discrimination in Employment Act, both to be discussed below.

An employer can defend against an allegation of disparate treatment of a member of a protected class on four different grounds:

- **Merit.** Employers are permitted to select, promote, and pay individuals based on their work or educational experience, and on professionally developed ability tests. The particular requirement that one person satisfies better than another must be job related.

- **Bona fide seniority system (BFSS).** Most employers use seniority systems to reward long-term employees, providing them with incentives to remain with the company. Allocation of wages, benefits, choice of working schedule, and other terms are lawful so long as they are not based on intentional discrimination. (See *Firefighters Local Union No. 1784 v. Stotts*, below.)

- **Bona fide occupational qualification (BFOQ).** Discrimination is permitted if it is based on a legitimate job requirement. For example, refusing to hire women as men's locker room attendants is justified because being male is a BFOQ in this instance. (See *International Union v. Johnson Controls, Inc.*, below.)

- **Business necessity.** This defense is not contained in the statute but was articulated and allowed by the Supreme Court in *Griggs v. Duke Power Company* (see below; the Court held there that this defense did not apply). A business necessity is established by showing that a discriminatory practice is required in order to achieve a legitimate business purpose in a safe and efficient manner. (See also *International Union v. Johnson Controls, Inc.*, below.)

Executive Order 11246 (1965)   This presidential directive of President Lyndon Johnson created **affirmative action**. The statute requires federal contractors and subcontractors to take positive steps to ensure that employees and prospective employees are treated fairly, without regard to their race, color, religion, or nationality. President Johnson's 1967 amendment to EO 11246 added sex, and President Richard Nixon's 1969 amendment added age and disability as features to be ignored in recruitment, hiring, and promotions (see also Age Discrimination in Employment Act and Americans with Disabilities Act, both below). In effect, EO 11246 is little more than an emphatic restatement of Title VII of the Civil Rights Act (see above), but in 1971 the Labor Department gave it some real impact.

The Office of Federal Contract Compliance Programs (OFCCP), a division of the Department of Labor (DOL), is charged with administering EO 11246. By this authority, DOL issued Order Number 4, requiring all companies with federal contracts exceeding $50,000 and with at least 50 employees to scrutinize their major job categories. They were to look for instances in which the percentage of women and minorities in these jobs was less than the percentage found in the local labor force. In these cases, the order called for the company to set DOL-approved goals for hiring and promotion, as well as timetables for meeting these goals. Since most large corporations and almost every *Fortune 500* company have federal contracts of the appropriate size, EO 11246, together with Order Number 4, imposed pervasive affirmative action requirements.

Race and Gender Discrimination

Griggs v. Duke Power Company, **401 U.S. 424 (1971)** This is a landmark case in which the Supreme Court had its first opportunity to interpret Title VII. It is best known for more clearly defining precisely what constitutes illegal discrimination. This definition derives from the insight that unfairness and injustice can occur in two rather different ways, one obvious and one not so obvious. First, when a company policy is formulated with the intent to discriminate on the basis of race or gender, this leads to treating individuals unequally, that is, **disparate treatment**. Second, unfairness can also occur even when there is no intent to discriminate, but a company policy results in different consequences for different individuals according to their race or gender; this is known as **disparate impact**.

Duke Power Company, located in North Carolina, had clearly discriminatory policies for many years: Blacks were employed only in the Labor Department, where the highest paying job was still less than the lowest paying job in the company's four other divisions. After the passage of Title VII, Duke Power instituted new policies designed to eliminate racial distinctions in its hiring and promotion decisions. Two requirements were now demanded of all applicants: (1) a high school diploma, and (2) a passing grade on both an intelligence test and a test of mechanical aptitude. A current employee desiring promotion had to satisfy either (1) or (2).

Thirteen black employees in the Labor Department sued Duke Power, in effect charging the company with discrimination of the disparate impact sort. One of those suing was Willie Griggs, a black male denied the position of coal handler. Griggs and his coworkers claimed that the two new requirements were discriminatory for two basic reasons: (1) At that time, white males were graduated from high school in North Carolina at three times the rate of black males; and (2) the passing scores on the two tests were set at the national median for high school graduates, this resulting in a failing grade for 94 percent of blacks. Chief Justice Warren Burger, writing the unanimous opinion, agreed with Griggs and his coworkers on both counts. Even though Duke Power did not intend to discriminate—there was no disparate treatment—nonetheless the new policy did maintain the outcomes of a racially biased schooling system and thus perpetuate a race-based disproportion in jobs—disparate impact. The major outcome of this decision is that an intention to discriminate is irrelevant for finding illegal discrimination.

McDonnell Douglas Corporation v. Green, **411 U.S. 792 (1973)** This precedent-setting case established the legal requirements and procedures for proving claims of **disparate treatment** in violation of Title VII when there is no direct evidence of discrimination. Factual or direct evidence of discrimination, such as witness testimony or documents expressing prejudicial motives, makes for a fairly straightforward case in favor of the plaintiff. Much more difficult is showing discrimination as a valid and compelling inference from various actions: indirect evidence.

Percy Green, a black male, worked as a mechanic for McDonnell Douglas in St. Louis for a number of years. In 1964, he and many other workers were laid off when the company instituted cost-cutting measures. A long-time civil rights activist and a member of the Congress on Racial Equality, Green vehemently objected to both his own discharge and the hiring practices of McDonnell Douglas generally, claiming they were motivated by racial bias. To express his convictions on these matters, Green participated in two sorts of illegal activities: first, a "stall-in," in which cars were parked on access roads to prevent employees from entering the plant; and, second, a "lock-in," in which a plant exit was padlocked to prevent employees from leaving. Shortly after the "lock-in," McDonnell Douglas advertised for mechanics. Green applied for his former position, but was not rehired. In response, he filed a complaint with the EEOC, charging that the company did not rehire him because of his race and because of his protest activities.

In rendering its decision, the Supreme Court, through Justice Lewis Powell's majority opinion, set the precedent for disparate treatment cases based on indirect evidence. Such cases proceed in three phases. In the first phase, four conditions must be satisfied to establish a presumption of racially discriminatory treatment: (1) The plaintiff (Green in this case) must belong to a racial minority, (2) the plaintiff must have applied for and been qualified for the job at issue, (3) the plaintiff must have been rejected, and (4) the job must have remained open and applicants continued to be sought. All four conditions were satisfied in Green's case. In the second phase, the defendant (McDonnell Douglas) is given the opportunity to rebut the presumption established in phase one: Some legitimate, nondiscriminatory reason for rejecting the employee must be given. Here, McDonnell Douglas offered as such a reason Green's involvement in illegal protest activities. This reason was accepted by the Court, and the decision was remanded (returned) to the Eighth Circuit Court of Appeals to consider the third phase. At this stage, the plaintiff must show that the reason offered in phase two is not the real reason, that it is merely a pretext for racially discriminatory motives. The Eighth Circuit found no evidence of pretext, and Green lost his case.

***United Steelworkers of America v. Weber*, 443 U.S. 193** (1979) In 1974 Kaiser Aluminum Company of Grammercy, Louisiana, and the local union, the United Steelworkers of America, instituted an affirmative action program (AAP) for its skilled craft labor force. This move was prompted by the large disparity between the racial composition of the local labor pool (39 percent black) and that of their craft workers (2 percent black). The program called for the seniority-based selection of equal numbers of blacks and whites as trainees for skilled craft work. However, since two different seniority scales were applied—one for blacks and another for whites—several whites were not selected for training, even though they had more time at the company than the blacks who were selected.

One of these rejected whites was Brian Weber. A lab analyst with ten years experience at Kaiser Aluminum, Weber had worked for the company longer than any of the black trainees. He sued the company and his own union, claiming that he was a victim of **reverse discrimination**, marking the first occurrence of this phrase in the legal lexicon. The AAP, Weber charged, was in violation of Title VII: an employment training program that unfairly discriminates against whites. A district court and the Fifth Circuit Court of Appeals agreed with Weber, ordering that race-based trainee selection be halted. However, hearing a challenge to affirmative action for the first time, the Supreme Court reversed these lower court decisions and Weber lost his lawsuit.

Justice William Brennan's majority opinion listed several key factors that defeated Weber's claim: (1) The prohibition on racial discrimination articulated in Title VII could not be interpreted as a condemnation of all race-conscious AAPs since that would defeat the purpose of the statute; (2) AAPs must be designed to eliminate racial inequalities in jobs that have traditionally been segregated; (3) AAPs must not result in whites being discharged; (4) serve as an insurmountable obstacle to further advancement; or (5) AAPs are to be temporary and flexible, so that hiring goals can be dropped when an appropriate representation is achieved. The majority found that the Kaiser Aluminum AAP did satisfy these criteria.

Several subsequent cases invoked these criteria in order to answer whites who claimed to have been unfairly passed over for jobs and promotions in favor of less well qualified or less senior minorities or women. For example, in *Johnson v. Transportation Agency, Santa Clara County*, 480 U.S. 616 (1987), a white male was denied a promotion despite scoring higher on an interview evaluation than the woman who was awarded the job. The factors cited in *Weber* were held to apply in this instance as well, and Paul Johnson too lost his lawsuit. *Johnson* was the first and, so far, the only reverse discrimination case involving gender to reach the Supreme Court.

Public Works in Employment Act of 1977, 42 U.S.C. §§6701–6710
This congressional action established a $4 billion fund to be distributed in the form of federal grants to state and local governments, primarily for public construction projects. The motivation behind the act was largely to dispense a financial shot in the arm to a national economy in the doldrums of a recession. But the act was also motivated by a certain conception of social justice: It created *set-asides* for minority-owned businesses. At least 10 percent of every government contract awarded out of the fund must be designated specifically for **minority business enterprises** or MBEs. An MBE was defined as a company whose ownership was at least 50 percent black, Hispanic, Asian, or American Indian.

The constitutionality of the act in its provision of set-asides for minority contractors was challenged almost immediately. In *Fullilove v. Klutznick*, 448 U.S. 448 (1980), several associations of New York construction contractors and subcontractors, and a heating and air conditioning firm, sued the secretary of commerce, Philip Klutznick, in his capacity as administrator of the act. Fullilove and associates alleged that the enforcement of the MBE requirement had caused them to lose contracts, and that it violated the **Equal Protection Clause** of the Fourteenth Amendment and the **Due Process Clause** of the Fifth Amendment. Chief Justice Warren Burger, writing for the majority, rejected Fullilove's suit. Burger argued that equal protection is maintained by the 10 percent minority set-aside provision, and that racial classifications are importantly related to the achievement of the congressionally mandated goal of remedying the present effects of past racial discrimination.

***Firefighter's Local Union No. 1784 v. Stotts*, 467 U.S. 561 (1984)** This was the first case in which an affirmative action program (AAP) was rejected by the Supreme Court. It began in 1977 when Carl Stotts, a black man and a captain in the Memphis, Tennessee, Fire Department, filed a class-action complaint. He charged the department and certain city officials with making hiring and promotion decisions that favored whites and discriminated against blacks, a violation of Title VII of the Civil Rights Act. After almost three years of negotiations, a *consent decree* (court-order settlement) was accepted in 1980. This decree, similar to one ordered in 1974, established an AAP with two goals, one for hiring and one for promotions. The hiring goal was to fill 50 percent of the job vacancies in the department with qualified black applicants. The promotions goal was to ensure that 20 percent of the promotions in each job classification be given to blacks. Unfortunately, the settlement contained no provisions for layoffs or any allowance for seniority.

In 1981 budget cuts in Memphis forced seniority-based layoffs of city firefighters according to the rule of "last hired, first fired." But under the new AAP, as well as the 1974 settlement, most of the newest hires were black. After first ordering that no blacks be laid off at all, a district court then modified its ruling so that the percentage of blacks in certain job categories would not be altered by the discharges. This resulted in some blacks retaining their jobs while some whites with more seniority lost theirs.

The Supreme Court overturned this lower court ruling. The majority opinion, authored by Justice Byron White, found that the Memphis Fire Department utilized a **bona fide seniority system** (BFSS) in decisions concerning layoffs. Section 703(h) of Title VII allows the application of different terms of employment, provided that such differences are not the result of an intent to discriminate because of race. A seniority system establishes different terms of employment for different employees, based on their tenure in the company. When these terms are not in any way motivated by an intent to discriminate, the system is *bona fide*, that is, a legitimate one made in good faith. The Court found no plan or design in the department's seniority system to disadvantage black workers, and, moreover, judged it unfair that the benefits of seniority be denied to white employees who had done nothing wrong.

***City of Richmond v. J.A. Croson Company*, 488 U.S. 469 (1989)** This case saw the Supreme Court continue to customize affirmative action programs by modifying the opinion on set-asides for MBEs (minority business enterprises) it had originally expressed in *Fullilove v. Klutznick* (see Public Works in Employment Act, above). At issue here was the Minority Business Utilization Plan adopted by the city of Richmond, Virginia, in 1983. According to this plan, the award of city construction contracts was contingent upon the company securing an MBE subcontractor at the rate of 30 percent of the total value of the contract. The MBE could come from anywhere in the United States.

That same year, Richmond invited bids on a construction project to purchase and install new urinals and toilets in the city jail. Croson Company, a regional plumbing and heating contractor, sought the city contract but was unsuccessful in securing an MBE. When it turned out that Croson was the only bidder on the project, a waiver of the 30 percent MBE requirement was requested. The waiver was denied and the city decided to rebid the contract. Croson sued Richmond on the grounds that the Minority Business Utilization Plan was unconstitutional by denying him equal protection under the law.

The Supreme Court agreed with Croson. Justice Sandra Day O'Connor reached this conclusion through the application of the standard of **strict scrutiny** to the Richmond plan, a standard the Court first applied in a contemporaneous reverse discrimination case, *Wygant v. Jackson Board of Education*, 476 U.S. 267 (1989). Strict scrutiny is a penetrating judicial examination activated when a fundamental right, such as the right of every person to equal protection under the law, is threatened by a statute. In the face of such a threat, defenders of the statute must show that it both (1) furthers a compelling interest, and (2) offers solutions that are narrowly tailored to that interest. Justice O'Connor argued that Richmond's 30 percent set-aside plan failed on both counts. It did not promote a compelling interest because there was no evidence that the city had previously discriminated against blacks in the awarding of construction contracts. And it was not narrowly tailored to remedy specific discrimination problems because it entitled any black, Hispanic, or Asian entrepreneur from anywhere in the country to an absolute preference over other citizens based solely on race.

***Adarand Constructors, Inc. v. Pena*, 115 S.Ct. 2097 (1995)**   In 1989, the Department of Transportation (DOT) awarded a contract to Mountain Gravel & Construction Company for highway construction in Colorado. The terms of the contract included a provision that Mountain Gravel would receive financial incentives if it subcontracted with firms controlled by "socially and economically disadvantaged individuals." This phrase was adopted from the Small Business Act and it was understood to refer to blacks, Hispanics, Asians, and Native Americans. As such, it is analogous to the MBEs (minority business enterprises) defined in the Public Works in Employment Act (see above). After seeking bids for the guardrail portion of the contract, Mountain Gravel received responses from Adarand Constructors, Inc., a white-owned company, and Gonzales Construction Company, a Hispanic-owned company. Despite the fact that Adarand submitted the lower bid for the work, Mountain Gravel awarded the subcontract to Gonzales. The chief estimator for the company explained that the decision was based on Gonzales's qualification as a firm controlled by socially and economically disadvantaged individuals, and the attendant additional payment that would be forthcoming from the federal government.

Adarand sued DOT and its secretary, Federico Pena. Adarand argued that giving contractors a financial incentive to hire subcontractors controlled by socially and economically disadvantaged individuals in particular, as well as the use of race-based presumptions in identifying such individuals in general, violates equal protection under the law as guaranteed by the Fifth Amendment's **Due Process Clause**. Both a district court and the circuit court of appeals ruled against Adarand, using a more lenient standard, *moderate* scrutiny, for examining federal programs involving racial classifications than the strict scrutiny standard utilized in *Croson* and *Wygant* (see both above) and applied to a local program.

This more lenient form of judicial review for federal programs was emphatically rejected by a plurality of the Supreme Court. Justice Sandra Day O'Connor asserted that all race-based classifications that produce unequal treatment must be subjected to the strictest judicial scrutiny, whether at the federal, state, or local level. This means, as in *Croson*, very specific plans that further compelling state interests. Because the lower courts had neither determined that such an interest was at stake, nor considered whether the provision for minority businesses was narrowly tailored to address that interest, their judgments were vacated and the case was returned to them for further consideration.

Age Discrimination

Age Discrimination in Employment Act of 1967, 29 U.S.C. §§621–634

Although Congress had debated age discrimination issues in the 1950s and age was considered as a component of Title VII, a specific federal statute was not passed until 1967. The Age Discrimination in Employment Act (ADEA) is very much like Title VII, except that there is just one protected class and it is defined exclusively by age. ADEA prohibits employers from making decisions concerning hiring, compensation, promotion, discharge, and other terms of employment on the basis of a person's age. Originally, all those up to age 65 were protected, but an amendment in 1978 moved the ceiling up to age 70, and another amendment in 1987 eliminated a ceiling age altogether, so that now the act applies to anyone over age 40. This means that an employer could maintain a policy of not hiring anyone under age 40, but could not establish a mandatory retirement age.

ADEA includes all private sector employers with at least 20 employees, labor unions with at least 25 members, and all state and local government employees. There are, however, groups of individuals who are excluded from the protected class due to their age, and there are exceptions to the prohibition where age-based decisions are permitted. Excluded individuals are tenured faculty in higher education at age 70, fire fighters and law enforcement officers who exceed state or local age requirements, corporate or institutional executives at age 65, and those holding public offices. Age-based decisions are permitted when they involve (1) **bona fide seniority systems** (BFSS), (2) **bona fide occupational qualifications** (BFOQs) (see below, *Western Air Lines v. Criswell*), or (3) **bona fide benefit plans**. Reasonable factors other than age, such as discharge for good cause, are also permitted as legitimate criteria for employment decisions. Violations may be penalized by awarding back pay, job reinstatement, legal fees, and by court orders (injunctions) requiring or proscribing certain actions. The ADEA is enforced by the Equal Employment Opportunity Commission.

Western Air Lines v. Criswell, 472 U.S. 400 (1985) This case is important because it established at the highest judicial level the essential ingredient for showing age as a **bona fide occupational qualification** (BFOQ): public safety. Until this time, the Supreme Court had not had the opportunity to clearly define the BFOQ exemption to the ADEA.

Captain Criswell was a pilot for Western Air Lines until age 60. He then retired, as directed by the mandatory age rule found in *United Air Lines v. McMann*, 432 U.S. 192 (1977), to be consistent with the ADEA. Criswell and another former pilot then requested reassignment as flight engineers (the "third seat") on Western aircraft requiring them. Their request was denied on the grounds that the mandatory retirement age applied to all three positions on the flight crew. Criswell and his colleague charged Western with age discrimination in violation of the ADEA. The airline defended the age rule by claiming a BFOQ exemption to the ADEA holds for flight engineers as well as pilots and first officers: The safe operation of the aircraft required limiting all those on the flight crew to individuals under age 60.

The Supreme Court disagreed with Western. Justice John Paul Stevens's majority opinion pointed out that the principle consideration for establishing a BFOQ defense to an age-based job qualification is whether an age limit is reasonably necessary for an overriding interest in public safety. This necessity can be proved by an employer showing either that (1) there is good reason to believe that all or virtually all persons over the age qualification would be unable to safely perform the duties of the job, or (2) it is highly impractical to individually test all the older employees for the abilities requisite to ensure public safety. In the opinion of the Court, Western did not demonstrate that either (1) or (2) obtained with respect to flight engineers.

An almost simultaneous Supreme Court case with very similar circumstances and the same result was *TWA v. Thurston*, 469 U.S. 111 (1985). In both of these judgments the Court was effectively authorizing principles relating mandatory retirement ages and public safety already reached in several lower court decisions, notably *Weeks v. Southern Bell*, 408 F.2d 228 (1969) and *Usery v. Tamiami Trail Tours*, 531 F.2d 224 (1976), both from the Fifth Circuit Court of Appeals.

Public Employees Retirement System of Ohio v. Betts, 492 U.S. 158 (1989) This case led to a crucial change in federal statutes concerning age discrimination. June Betts worked as a speech pathologist for the Hamilton County Board of Mental Retardation and Developmental Disabilities. Plagued with health problems, by 1985 Betts was 61 years old and, in the opinion of the Board, unable to continue working in any capacity for the county. She agreed to retire. The problem came about because as a participant in the Public Employees Retirement System (PERS), Betts was no longer eligible for disability retirement benefits, which end at age 60. This benefit would have given her considerably more money than the age-and-service rate she received. Betts filed an age discrimination charge against PERS with the EEOC, and filed suit in federal district court, claiming that the refusal of PERS to allow her disability benefits violated the Age Discrimination in Employment Act (ADEA; see above).

The lower court and the circuit court of appeals sided with Betts, relying heavily on an EEOC regulation adopted in 1979 which focused on the incidence of "subterfuge." The regulation, Section 1625.10, states that benefits for older workers may be reduced only in order to bring costs in line with those for younger workers. This circumstance did not obtain in the Betts case because younger workers already received the higher benefit.

The Supreme Court rejected this reasoning, holding that the language of Section 1625.10 was inconsistent with the ADEA, and thus the EEOC regulation was invalid. Justice Anthony Kennedy turned to a previous ruling, *United Air Lines v. McMann*, 432 U.S. 192 (1977), and was unable to find any evidence of subterfuge on the part of PERS. However, there is a significant difference between the two cases. In *McMann*, the retirement age was set by United Air Lines *prior* to the ADEA, so a scheme to evade a rule could not have occurred; on the other hand, in *Betts* the higher rate of disability retirement compared to age-and-service retirement came about as a revision to PERS in 1976, *after* the ADEA became law (1967). Does this difference affect the outcome? "No," Kennedy answered: In either instance, the burden is on the plaintiff (Betts, in this case) to provide factual evidence of subterfuge in order to justify the charge of discrimination.

The *Betts* ruling was a source of great dissatisfaction to many in Congress. This was expressed by the rapidity with which a new federal statute was drafted and signed into law. The Older Workers Benefit Protection Act of 1990, 29 U.S.C. §§621–623, is an amendment to the ADEA with three main revisions: First, it explicitly includes benefit plans (that is, retirement plans) as part of the specification of the employment practices covered, which was not clear in the original version of ADEA. Second, it eliminated the word *subterfuge* and allows age-based distinctions in wages, provided there is no intent to evade the ADEA. Third, the EEOC regulation (Section 1625.10) that was at the heart of the *Betts* decision was officially written into the statute: Henceforth, benefit costs for older workers are not allowed to be less than those costs for younger workers.

Pregnancy and Disability Discrimination

General Electric Company v. Gilbert, 429 U.S. 125 (1976)   Martha Gilbert and several other women were employees of a General Electric plant in Salem, Virginia. Each woman became pregnant at some time during 1971 and 1972, and each filed a claim requesting disability payments under GE's employees' benefit plan. All the claims were denied on the grounds that the plan did not cover disability due to pregnancy. The women then filed charges with the Equal Employment Opportunity Commission (EEOC) alleging that the refusal to pay disability benefits for time lost due to pregnancy and childbirth discriminated against them because of sex, a violation of Title VII. Damages were sought as well as an injunction directing GE to include pregnancy disabilities within the benefit plan on the same terms and conditions as other disabilities.

The district court and the circuit court of appeals held that GE's exclusion of pregnancy benefits was indeed an instance of sex discrimination in violation of Title VII. However, the Supreme Court reversed these decisions. Writing for the majority, Justice William Rehnquist noted the many similarities between this case and another high Court decision rendered just two years previously. In *Gelduldig v. Aiello*, 417 U.S. 484 (1974), a state insurance policy disallowing pregnancy benefits was challenged, not as a Title VII infringement, but as violative of the **Equal Protection Clause** of the Fourteenth Amendment. Rehnquist observed that the ruling principle in *Gelduldig* applied in this case as well: Legislatures are not required to include pregnancy in insurance coverage *unless* excluding the condition is simply a pretense intended to discriminate unfairly against women. There is no evidence, he continued, that GE's benefit plan is such a pretense. It does not use sex to bar anyone from benefit eligibility; instead, it removes one physical condition—pregnancy—from the list of compensable disabilities.

Pregnancy Discrimination Act of 1978, 42 U.S.C. §2000e(K) Also known as the PDA, this amendment to Title VII came about in large part as a reaction to the decision in *General Electric Company v. Gilbert* (see above). Congress rejected the notion that pregnancy can be legally ignored in benefit packages without discriminating against women: Title VII specifies that discrimination "because of sex" is illegal and that includes discrimination "on the basis of pregnancy, childbirth or related medical conditions." Employee benefits for women experiencing these physical conditions were not to be arranged any differently than benefits for those whose ability to work was impeded for other reasons. In other words, pregnancy is to be treated the same as any other illness. Or, perhaps more accurately, pregnancy is to be treated *at least* the same as any other illness. Subsequent to the passage of the PDA, the Supreme Court has allowed state laws in which pregnant women are provided with *superior* benefits than those available to men, notably in *California Federal Savings & Loan Association v. Guerra*, 479 U.S. 272 (1987).

International Union v. Johnson Controls, Inc., 499 U.S. 187 (1991) This fascinating and complicated case might just as well have been discussed in the health and safety section of this chapter, even though it was ultimately decided on Title VII grounds. But then again, the case concerns more than the health and safety of employees; the well-being of fetuses was also at stake. Let us explain.

Johnson Controls, Inc., a Milwaukee, Wisconsin, company, is the largest manufacturer of car batteries in the United States. These batteries typically contain significant quantities of lead. In 1977 the company informed its female employees of the various health hazards of lead and requested a signed statement from them indicating that they had been told of the risks of having a child while exposed to lead. Over the next several years, eight women became pregnant even though they had lead levels in their blood systems that the Occupational Health and Safety Administration had determined to be hazardous for fetuses. Alarmed, Johnson Controls issued a new policy prohibiting all pregnant women and all women "capable of bearing children" from working any job involving lead exposure. This new fetal protection policy had the immediate effect of forcing a number of women into lower paying clerical jobs. One woman chose sterilization in order to keep her job.

In 1984 several female employees (and one man) filed a class action suit charging that the new policy discriminated on the basis of sex in violation of Title VII. Fertile women were singled out, they argued, while fertile men were not, this despite evidence indicating that lead exposure detrimentally effects male reproductive capacities as well. Johnson Controls defended itself by replying that excluding women from these jobs was not only a **business necessity**, but also maleness was a **bona fide occupational qualification** (BFOQ) to perform them.

The Seventh Circuit Court of Appeals agreed with the company. The court accepted the business necessity defense because there was a substantial risk to fetuses, a risk that only obtains through women, and there was no nondiscriminatory alternative (the Seventh Circuit followed closely the reasoning of the Fourth Circuit Court of Appeals in *Hayes v. Shelby Memorial Hospital*, 726 F.2d 1543 (1984), one of the first fetal protection policy cases, in which a pregnant X-ray technician had been fired). The BFOQ defense was also accepted because employing men in these positions was "reasonably necessary" in order to spare others harm, namely, fetuses.

The Supreme Court unanimously rejected the Seventh Circuit's ruling. Using the Pregnancy Discrimination Act (see above) as his basis, Justice Harry Blackman's opinion ruled that all fetal protection policies were discriminatory. Therefore, only the BFOQ is appropriate for defending such a policy; the Seventh Circuit erred in considering business necessity. Johnson Controls' policy is indeed discriminatory because it excludes women solely on the basis of their child-bearing capability and ignores the risk to men. So was being a man a valid BFOQ? "No," Blackman declared: Fertile and pregnant women are no less adept at manufacturing batteries than are men, and the BFOQ defense is only relevant to the ability of the employee to perform the job safely. No fetus is being endangered by the manner in which a woman is making batteries.

Americans with Disabilities Act of 1990, 42 U.S.C. §§1201 *et seq*. The Americans with Disabilities Act (ADA) is organized into several titles, and for business the most important of these is Title I. Employment discrimination against qualified individuals with disabilities is prohibited by Title I in regard to job application procedures, hiring, compensation, training, promotion, and termination. All business enterprises with at least 15 employees are subject to the ADA, with the exception of corporations that are wholly owned by the United States. The basic requirement is that employers must make reasonable accommodations to assist disabled persons in the performance of job duties for which they are qualified, provided no undue burden is caused to the employer. These accommodations may include making existing facilities accessible to disabled persons, providing part-time or modified work schedules, acquiring special equipment or devices, and providing readers or interpreters. An undue burden would be one causing a significant decrease in work efficiency or requiring a substantial expense.

An **individual with a disability** is defined as a person with (1) a physical or mental impairment that substantially limits one or more of his or her life activities, or (2) a record of such impairment, or (3) is regarded as having such an impairment. The impairments that define disability include, among many others, cosmetic disfigurement, depression, cerebral palsy, mental retardation, multiple sclerosis, diabetes, and infection with HIV. Individuals with infectious diseases like AIDS or tuberculosis may be legally excluded from certain jobs if the illness presents "a significant risk to the health and safety of others that cannot be eliminated by reasonable accommodation." Recovering alcoholics and former drug users are protected by the ADA, but current users and alcoholics who continue to drink are not. Sexual preferences, sexual disorders, and gambling addictions are not considered disabilities. A qualified disabled person is one who, with or without reasonable accommodation, can perform the functions essential to a particular job.

Although Title I forbids an employer from asking a job applicant about the existence, nature, or severity of a disability, it allows questions about the applicant's ability to perform job-related tasks. Medical examinations cannot be requested before a job offer; once an offer has been made, the ADA permits employers to demand a medical exam. Employers may then also make the offer conditional on the results of the exam, so long as all new hires must also take the exam.

Equal Pay

Equal Pay Act of 1963, 29 U.S.C. §206(d)   During the Second World War, much of America's male work force was drafted into the armed services, producing a severe labor shortage. Women responded quickly, filling positions formerly dominated or wholly occupied by men. Soon, there was a need to address the issue of how much the women would be paid in these new roles. The National War Labor Board, established in 1942, declared that women should be paid the same wages as the men whose jobs they had taken; and so they were, for the most part, although no federal statute requiring equal pay was instituted. As the war years progressed, women consistently demonstrated their ability to perform their job duties at the same level of men, as testified by both factual data and government propaganda (such as Rosie the Riveter). After the war, the servicemen returned home and reclaimed their jobs; the women went back to the home and reclaimed housework.

By 1960 women constituted nearly 40 percent of the work force, and it had become obvious in Congress that an equal wage law was needed. In 1963 the Equal Pay Act (EPA) became federal law. The EPA prohibits sex discrimination in wages: Jobs that require equal skill, effort, and responsibility, and are performed under the same working conditions, must receive equal remuneration, regardless of the employee's gender. All private sector employees and all state and local government employees are covered; federal workers are excluded.

Under the EPA, differences in pay for the same job are justified only by virtue of (1) a seniority system, (2) a merit system, (3) a system in which wages are a function of the quality or quantity of the goods produced, or (4) factors other than sex (FOS)—for example, the profitability of a department in a clothing store. Violations of the EPA may be penalized in the form of monetary awards covering back pay and legal fees. Originally, the Department of Labor was the administrating office, so lawsuits and claims based on the EPA involved the secretary of labor. However, all administrative control of the EPA was transferred to the Equal Employment Opportunity Commission in 1978.

Corning Glass Works v. Brennan, **417 U.S. 188 (1974)**　Prior to 1925 all of Corning's inspectors in their New York and Pennsylvania plants were women, and all worked day shifts. Corning then established a night shift, but state laws of the time prohibited women from working it. As males began filling the nighttime inspector jobs, they soon requested and received significantly higher wages than the women working during the day. The plants unionized in 1944 and the wage differential was written into the collective bargaining agreement. Eventually the laws prohibiting women from night work were abolished and, after the passage of the Equal Pay Act (EPA; see above), the union agreed to open up all inspector shifts, regardless of time, to all employees, regardless of sex. In 1969 the wage difference between night and day work was eliminated, although current male inspectors retained their higher rate of pay.

Secretary of Labor Brennan sued Corning, seeking back pay for female inspectors on the grounds that the company had violated the EPA. Corning's first line of defense was that the jobs were not equal because the night work presented different working conditions. The Court disagreed and established a key precedent on the issue of working conditions. Justice Thurgood Marshall, in the majority opinion, pointed out that there were no significant differences in the "surroundings" and "hazards" for inspectors on any of the shifts. Corning then argued that night work qualifies as an FOS, a "factor other than sex," and, according to the EPA, a legitimate FOS justifies pay differentials. Marshall rejected this argument too; Corning had not shown that the higher pay for night inspectors was intended as compensation for the late time, rather than as additional payment for male workers. Finally, Marshall noted that the union solution of making all inspection shifts available to all employees did not solve the problem because the preexisting lower wages were not raised.

Comparable Worth

The phrase *comparable worth* has gained currency in discussions of business and society over the past 15 years, and introduces a concept different from that expressed in the phrase *equal pay for equal work*. Comparable worth is the idea that the value of two *different* jobs can be meaningfully compared in order to determine whether the wages offered for them are fair and equitable. If the jobs are comparable (rather than identical), but the wages are not, there would appear to be an inequity. The comparison is done by assigning numbers to various aspects of each job, for example, how much education is required, how much supervision, and what risks characterize the working conditions. The numbers are summed and the totals, and the wages, are compared.

Comparable worth, unlike equal pay, is not codified into federal law, but it may be implied there. Interestingly, early versions of the House and Senate bill of 1962 that became the Equal Pay Act (see above) contained language referring to "comparable" (rather than "equal") jobs. Perhaps it is ironic that Congresswoman St. George objected to this language and offered an amendment, later adopted in the final draft, calling for "equal work." This means that the issue of *comparable* worth cannot be addressed by a federal statute concerning *equal* pay. However, the issue might be addressed by a federal statute concerning civil rights: Section 703(h) in Title VII, also known as the Bennett Amendment, prohibits differentiating on the basis of sex in determining wages. Can Title VII be employed to remedy sex discrimination in wages based on a showing of comparable worth?

At this writing, the issue of comparable worth has not been definitively settled by the U.S. federal court system. It is worth noting, however, that Canada has moved forward on the issue. In 1990 the province of Ontario instituted a Comparable Worth Law. The details are complicated but the main point is that employers must evaluate a job according to skill, effort, responsibility, and working conditions if 60 percent of the people performing that job are women. Positions are evaluated by assigning points to these various features and then summing them; jobs that are within three points of each other are considered comparable and thus require equal compensation.

It remains to be seen whether the legislative or judicial branches of our government will follow the Canadian lead. Despite the silence so far, several significant court cases do have distinct implications for comparable worth.

County of Washington v. Gunther, 452 U.S. 161 (1981) This early Supreme Court case seemed to open the door for Title VII, and not just EPA remedies to wage discrimination. Alberta Gunther and three other women worked in the Washington County jail in Oregon, guarding female prisoners and performing various clerical tasks. In 1974 the county closed the women's section of the jail and transferred the female inmates to another county. Gunther and her coworkers were discharged. In response, they sued the county for back pay, claiming that (1) they were paid unequal wages for work that was substantially the same as that performed by male guards, and (2) part of the pay differential was attributable to intentional sex discrimination in violation of Title VII.

Both the district court and the Ninth Circuit Court of Appeals found that the women's work as guards was *not* substantially the same as that of the male guards: Among other reasons, each man was responsible for ten times as many inmates. Gunther's first claim was rejected. However, the district court and the Ninth Circuit disagreed on the second claim. The district court would not allow the appeal to Title VII on the grounds that the equal pay/equal work concept applies in the same way for both federal statutes. In other words, only a showing of very close similarity between jobs will do, not some notion of comparable worth. The Ninth Circuit overturned this decision and the Supreme Court affirmed the court of appeals.

Although unwilling to concede the implications for comparable worth, in his majority opinion Justice William Brennan pointed out the main problem: If Title VII wage cases were confined to an equal jobs context, then employers could base wages on gender, and women holding unequal jobs would not have the opportunity to prove discrimination. This ruling seems to remove the critical obstacle to claims of comparable worth: Plaintiffs must show that jobs are substantially *equal* in order to ground a case that differentials in pay evidence sex discrimination.

AFSCME v. Washington, 770 F.2d 1401 (9th Cir. 1985)   In 1976 a private job evaluation firm called Willis was commissioned by Washington State to rate a number of key jobs used as standards for setting pay for state employees. Willis's evaluation involved analyzing each job in terms of four categories: knowledge and skill, mental demands, accountability, and working conditions. Points were assigned to each category according to the extent to which that aspect was utilized or encountered by the worker. The results of this analysis were startling: Certain jobs received higher point totals than other jobs that paid considerably more, and the disparities seemed to fall along gender lines. For example, a registered nurse (a job dominated by women) received the highest rating at 573, while a computer analyst (a job dominated by men) was scored at 426. Yet, computer analysts were paid about 50 percent more than registered nurses.

Armed with these statistics, in 1981 the American Federation of State, County, and Municipal Employees (AFSCME) attempted to walk through the door opened in *County of Washington v. Gunther* (see above). AFSCME sued the state, claiming that the failure to pay women equitable wages, as indicated by Willis's comparable worth study, constituted sex discrimination in violation of Title VII. The union charged Washington with both adverse impact and disparate treatment (see *Griggs v. Duke Power*, above): Not only did the wage differences have adverse consequences for women, the state also intentionally discriminated against women. The district court ruled in favor of AFSCME, but the decision was subsequently overturned on appeal.

The Ninth Circuit Court of Appeals effectively closed the door on Title VII comparable worth suits that it had itself appeared to open four years earlier in *Gunther*. The court made two key points in overruling the lower court, arguments that it had already employed in a previous ruling (*Spaulding v. University of Washington*, 740 F.2d 686 [9th Cir. 1984]), and that were echoed in a subsequent Sixth Circuit case (*International Union v. Michigan*, 886 F.2d 766 [6th Cir. 1989]). First, neither the mere existence of comparable worth statistics indicating wage disparities, nor the bare knowledge of such disparities are sufficient proof of an intent to discriminate. Second, neutral market forces that give rise to wage disparities according to sex do not constitute specific employment practices, so companies cannot be held legally liable for them.

Despite the favorable judgment on appeal, Washington agreed to pay AFSCME $106 million.

Sexual Harassment

Since no one is in favor of sexual harassment, the central issue is how to define and enforce standards aimed at preventing and penalizing its occurrences. John Hasnas (1997) defines *sexual harassment* as "[t]he abuse of one's position of authority over an employee in order to extract sexual favors from the employee or to cause discomfort or humiliate the employee because of his or her sex."

Although sexual harassment has occurred throughout human history, it is only recently that societies are recognizing it as a serious problem. According to Feary (1997), a 1970s *Redbook* article (a magazine marketed for women) conducted one of the first surveys investigating sexual harassment, and found that 90 percent of women responding to the survey said they had "encountered" it. In 1992 *Working Mother* found that 60 percent of those they polled said they were victims of sexual harassment.

There have been several high profile cases of sexual harassment in the 1990s. In 1991 Anita Hill accused Clarence Thomas, then a nominee for the U.S. Supreme Court, of sexually harassing her (Williams 1997). Thomas was eventually confirmed by the Senate after Senator Orin Hatch, and others, undermined Hill's testimony by challenging her character. In 1996 the federal government filed a lawsuit against Mitsubishi Motors charging the corporation with sexual harassment, claiming that management verbally and physically abused women employees (Cohen 1997). This is the largest suit ever filed by the federal government, and it received national and international attention. Finally, Paula Jones is suing President Clinton for sexual harassment. Although her suit was dismissed, she is appealing that ruling.

In at least some instances companies do it right. For example, DuPont, the large chemical company based in Delaware, set up an innovative program to stop sexual harassment before the issue was taken seriously by the business community (Flynn 1997). Levi Strauss is another company that has a longstanding commitment to respecting its employees. (*The Conference Board* 1998). We will evaluate sexual harassment and policies that deter and punish harassment from the employee's point of view.

Ethics

Promoting Self-interest: Egoism Aggressively self-interested employees would want to develop reputations as good business people, so it is unlikely that they would sexually harass subordinates. One problem with sexual harassment is that it takes away time and energy that could be spent on doing one's job. Another problem is that sexual harassment is a mean and vicious act. Employees who sexually harass others are not trusted, even by those who are not direct recipients of harassment, and unless one is trusted, it is very hard to advance in a business career.

Aggressively self-interested employees could support or reject sexual harassment policies that deter and punish harassment, depending on the situation. In most cases, they would support sexual harassment policies, because sexual harassment is one way of not doing one's job. When coworkers do not do their jobs, it creates more work for their colleagues. If this happens in a team project, the project may be delayed or even fail, no matter how hard nonharassing employees work. However, if an employee's boss was a sexual harasser, an aggressively self-interested employee might join in to get promoted.

Contemplatively self-interested managers, who try to avoid pain and conflict, would not sexually harass subordinates. Sexual harassment creates conflict with others, and conflicts interfere with the pursuit of a pain-free life. These employees would favor sexual harassment policies that deter and punish sexual harassment as long as the policies did not cause more trouble and conflict than they prevented. This contrasts with aggressively self-interested employees who would approve of policies that caused conflict as long as they help these employees pursue their personal career interests.

Nurturing Personal Relationships: Care Passive caring employees would want to please those with whom they have close relationships. If these employees came from families organized according to the principle that men should always be in charge, they would be against policies preventing men from sexually harassing women. These same employees might be in favor of policies that prevent women from harassing men. However, because it is unlikely that a policy would only apply to women, these passive carers would have to reject it.

Active caring employees would not harass others and would be in favor of policies that prevented sexual harassment. Insofar as these policies required the threat of punishment, active carers would be in favor of this punitive incentive. Even so, as caring employees, they would want policies to prevent harassing in ways that could preserve and improve relationships. This would suggest that punishment should be used as a last resort for mild cases of sexual harassment, and a first step only in serious cases. These employees realize, nevertheless, how difficult it is to change the attitudes and behavior of sexual harassers, so they would agree with harsh punishments like demotion and firing for repeat offenders.

Promoting the Good of the Group: Utilitarianism Utilitarian employees would not universally condemn sexual harassment (or any act or policy, for that matter). From a utilitarian point of view, sexual harassment is wrong only if it harms the group. If sexual harassment in a particular instance helps the group, then it would be justified. The same holds for policies that punish or deter sexual harassment. If rejecting these policies helps the group more than policies that prevent and punish sexual harassers, it is morally required that they be rejected.

Utilitarian employees in the United States should recognize that sexual harassment harms the group. People have come to expect to be treated well in the workplace. Sexual harassment is a reprehensible act, and it can ruin company morale. Even employees who are against affirmative action (see above) can support policies to prevent sexual harassment, simply because this misconduct *harms* people in many different ways. First, there is the psychological damage that victims of harassment suffer; if the harassment continues for a long time, the victims can be permanently damaged (Boler 1998). Second, sexual harassment discourages others from entering the workplace, depriving the group of talent and using resources created or earned by others. Third, the failure to stop sexual harassment sends a specific message that it is appropriate and acceptable behavior, and, more generally, that degrading others in public is unproblematic.

Further evidence that the American public condemns sexual harassment is that federal and state laws proscribe this misconduct. A growing body of regulatory and case law provides money and other remedies to compensate victims of sexual harassment. If the general public were not in agreement with these legal trends, we would expect citizens and interest groups to appeal to government to change these policies. No such appeals have been made. Since there is widespread agreement on the evils of sexual harassment, people should be happy with rules that punish and deter it.

Strict rule utilitarian employees would want to pass rules that would be followed without exception: They would be in favor of **strict liability** standards as described in Law, below. Strict liability means that employers are responsible for their sexually harassing employees even if the employers have done everything they can to prevent it. The rationale for strict liability is twofold. First, it provides a powerful incentive to companies to be very, very careful—they know in advance that they will be responsible for sexual harassment no matter how careful they are. Although this may seem unfair because it could penalize corporations that are quite good along with those that are quite bad, this is a cost utilitarians are willing to pay to promote the general welfare. A second justification for strict liability here is that if sexual harassment does occur, and employees appeal to the courts, society does not have to spend court time and money to determine responsibility. By saving this money, the group as a whole is benefitted.

Although this strict policy might result in the punishment of innocent people and companies, as long as the rule promoted group well-being better than any other rule, utilitarian employees can accept these unfair results.

Flexible rule utilitarian employees would argue that strict liability would be bad for the group for two connected reasons. First, punishing people and companies unfairly erodes respect for the law by employees, managers, and citizens. Flexible rule utilitarians would prefer that the courts rely on the doctrine of *respondeat superior*, which holds the company responsible for its employees who are sexual harassers only if the company knew or should have known about the harassment. Although this is still a broad standard, it would not penalize companies that did their best to train and monitor employees to prevent sexual harassment. These employees realize that it is not merely the company that is harmed by fines: If the fines and other sanctions cause lay-offs, all the employees and the communities where they live are affected as well (Ralfalko 1994).

Flexible rule utilitarian employees could cite the Federal Sentencing Guidelines for Corporations as a good example of flexible rules (see also Chapter 3: The Corporation—The Nature and Structure of the Corporation, Selected Cases; Sentencing Reform Act). These guidelines apply criminal, not civil penalties, but they are pertinent here because of the flexible, incentive-based approach to fines and penalties. Imagine that ACME Company has defrauded consumers of $13.7 million, and it is ordered to refund that money to the cheated customers. Under the sentencing guidelines, if ACME had an effective ethics program, turned themselves in, cooperated with the investigation, and accepted responsibility for the fraudulent behavior, the company could be fined as little as $685,000. On the other hand, if ACME did not pursue any of these measures that mitigate its culpability, the fine could be as high as $54.8 million (Paine 1994a). Flexible rule utilitarian employees would argue that if civil cases concerning sexual harassment used a sliding scale similar to the sentencing guidelines, we could have effective enforcement and deterrence at the lowest possible cost.

Respecting Dignity and Rights: Intrinsic Value   Employees who rely on intrinsic value have an easier time evaluating sexual harassment than do utilitarians and egoists. Intrinsic value is easier to apply because it does not require us to calculate the consequences of our actions for ourselves, our groups, or our relationships. We only need to see if the intrinsic value of the victim is respected in the act of harassment. Since it is precisely this value that is being violated, sexual harassment is immoral. Employees who base their views on human dignity would strenuously oppose sexual harassment and would support policies and rules to prevent it.

In evaluating these rules and policies, only one thing is important: respecting the intrinsic value of all concerned, which includes those accused of harassment as well as the victims of harassment. Whether or not this policy makes the group happier, nurtures relationships, or promotes individual interests is irrelevant. This does not mean that all policies that stop sexual harassment are justified. If, for example, a sexual harassment policy required that anyone accused of sexual harassment be fired immediately, this could easily result in innocent people being fired. Due process rights are essential for those accused of harassment.

Employees who believe in respecting human dignity hold that human beings can never be used as a means to an end unless they voluntarily agree to be so used. By its very nature, sexual harassment violates this condition. Consider an instance of the *quid pro quo* type of harassment, in which a supervisor will promote an employee only if she has sex with him (see Law: Introduction; and Selected Cases: *Williams v. Saxbe*, below). The supervisor is using the employee as an object, not as a human being with infinite value. The other type of harassment, maintaining a sexually harassing environment, is degrading in another way. Jean Boler (1998), a class-action employee attorney, tells how women miners at Eveleth mines were constantly exposed to lewd and obscene pictures of naked women and sayings written on the walls. These pictures and writings were not there merely for male entertainment, but were intended to send the women miners a message: They do not belong in the mines nor are they qualified to be miners. This type of sexually harassing work environment was definitively rejected by a federal district court in the landmark case *Robinson v. Jacksonville Shipyards, Inc.* (see below, Selected Cases).

Employees who believe in natural rights would also be against sexual harassment. According to most rights theories, we have a right to conduct our lives without interference as long as we do not interfere with others. For example, we have the right to drive a car, but not when drunk, because drunk driving puts innocent people at risk. In a case of *quid pro quo* harassment, a person is coerced to do something he or she does not want to do. However, employees who focus on property rights might object to the **reasonable woman** standard, which says that harassment has to be seen from the perspective of the victim (see below, Selected Cases: *Ellison v. Brady*; also Bravo and Cassedy 1992). The problem with the reasonable woman standard is that it can portray women as less capable of making accurate judgments than men, and this can be a subtle way of degrading women.

International Issues

What counts as sexual harassment, and whether it is treated as a serious problem, quite often depends on the culture in which the behavior occurs. One study of managers in Japan found that they were much more likely to punish employees for embezzlement and giving away trade secrets than for sexual harassment. Managers were asked what they would do if (a) an employee embezzled $10,000, (b) an employee divulged company secrets, or (c) a male employee sent obscene e-mail messages to a female employee. Eighty-eight percent of Japanese managers said they would fire the embezzler, 66 percent would fire the divulger, and 11 percent would fire the harasser (*Industry Week* 1997).

This fits with the traditional attitude in Japan toward women. Until recently, for example, children's stories were written by men, who excluded female characters from the narrative (Sueyoshi 1997). The *New York Times* reports that many Japanese men seek sex with prostitutes who dress as school girls, read pornography in public, and are known to grope school girls on crowded commuter trains (*New York Times* 1997b). Special night clubs are starting to spring up in Japan that cater to women. The attraction? The clubs hire men to be polite and civil to women customers. Although there is evidence that attitudes are changing (*The Economist* 1997), it is, at the very least, not surprising that Japanese managers do not believe sexual harassment is a serious issue.

In April 1996 a Mitsubishi Motors plant in Illinois was sued by the U.S. government for verbally and physically harassing women in the workplace. As we mentioned in the introduction, this is the biggest suit of its kind ever filed by the federal government. In order to save its reputation and express the determination that the company would do better, Mitsubishi hired Lynn Martin, secretary of labor under George Bush, to investigate the allegations and propose a plan for improving the treatment of women. In February 1997 Martin released her plan, which included management training and sexual harassment workshops (Cohen 1997). It should be noted that hiring Martin and implementing her plan will *not* reduce Mitsubishi's liability in the harassment law suit.

Japanese culture has several elements that can help Mitsubishi and the Japanese companies avoid sexual harassment in the future. First, the Japanese have a history, at least since the end of World War II, of being **entrepreneurial**. Soon after the Mitsubishi law suit was announced, Japanese businesses began offering training programs in Japan for companies doing business in the United States. Another valuable trait of Japanese companies is that human resource managers tend to be more open with information than their counterparts in America. This would allow information about how to stop sexual harassment to move from company to company.

Economics

Society   From the social point of view, sexual harassment impedes business efficiency for several reasons. First, while they are harassing, managers are not doing their jobs, and they are interfering with the jobs of the harassed. Sexual harassment, then, raises the costs of products without any increase in the quality of those products. Second, those who are harassed will seek compensation for themselves and punishment for the harassers, consuming court time and company resources. Third, sexual harassment keeps qualified people out of the workforce. Their absence from the workforce is a double loss: We lose their talents *and* we need to support them because they are not employed.

Laws that discourage and punish discrimination can be formulated in many different ways. Efficiency dictates that we use the laws with the lowest costs to stop sexual harassment. One way to save money is to allow as much business control over harassment as is compatible with an effective program. The reason for this is simple: Developing plans for avoiding sexual harassment and monitoring companies to make sure they comply is very expensive. The more companies can develop and enforce their own plans, the more efficient the system will be.

Consumers   Like most employee issues, consumers have little knowledge of the way employees are treated. Yet, as with many other employee issues, sexual harassment can be very visible at times. Mitsubishi Motors is a case in point. In a demonstration of protest against the corporation's actions, picket lines went up across the country for a month or more. How much business Mitsubishi lost is not known, but they surely lost some sales in the highly competitive automobile retail market. These setbacks will be paid for at some point by consumers, managers, or owners.

Consumers also lose in other ways. If sexual harassment keeps qualified people out of the workforce, then the talents of these excluded workers, and their innovative ideas, are lost as well. This results in more costly, less innovative products (see Robson and Robson 1994 for a similar argument). Consumer prices can also go up because of the demands made on business by harassed workers, as we discuss in the next section.

Producers   One way that producers think about employees is little different from the way they think about other factors of production, like steel and electricity. On this model, it seems, producers would want to avoid sexual harassment for the reasons we have already discussed. It keeps qualified people out of the workplace, harassing and harassed individuals cannot do their jobs properly, plus there is the danger of expensive lawsuits brought by harassed employees.

Given the costs of sexual harassment, it seems that every company would formulate plans to eradicate it. Yet, companies do not formulate such plans. One reason for the inaction is that sexual harassment, if it is occurring, is very expensive to stop: Training, monitoring, and enforcement are all required. Therefore, managers often do not address this issue unless they must, and this is why employees go to the courts. The courts have the power to make management prevent sexual harassment if the employees can prove their cases. Once a company ends up in court, the costs can mount very rapidly. At this point, it can be less expensive to settle the case and institute programs to prevent sexual harassment in the future.

Law

Introduction   Section 703(a) of Title VII of the Civil Rights Act of 1964 (see this chapter, Discrimination, Law, above) prohibits employers from using an individual's gender as a term or condition of employment, but does not mention "sexual harassment." Early federal court decisions did not look favorably upon the notion that sexual harassment was actionable under Title VII (see below, Selected Cases: *Barnes v. Train, Corne v. Bausch & Lomb, Inc.*, and *Miller v. Bank of America*). Responding to these and other more favorable rulings, in 1980 the Equal Employment Opportunity Commission (EEOC; see also this chapter, Discrimination and Affirmative Action, Selected Cases, above) adopted Guidelines on Discrimination Because of Sex (with various amendments in 1988 and 1990). This document, among other things, declared that sexual harassment was a form of sex discrimination in violation of Title VII. It was then left to the federal courts to test the legality of this pronouncement.

The guidelines offer a definition; behavior of a sexual nature is sexually harassing when any of the following occur:

1. Submission to such conduct is made either explicitly or implicitly a term or condition of an individual's employment

2. Submission to or rejection of such conduct by an individual is used as the basis of employment decisions affecting such individual
3. Such conduct has the purpose or effect of unreasonably interfering with an individual's work performance or creating an intimidating, hostile, or offensive working environment

Numbers 1 and 2 describe what has come to be known as *quid pro quo* sexual harassment. The Latin phrase means "this for that," and refers to such circumstances as when a position or promotion is offered in return for sexual favors. The legal confines of these sorts of cases have been clearly marked in a series of federal district court rulings (e.g., *Barnes v. Costle* and *Williams v. Saxbe*). The Supreme Court has never heard a quid pro quo case and, after all, a circumstance in which one person says to another "I'll give you a raise (or other job benefit) if you give me sex" is fairly easy to identify. Rather more difficult to characterize are the sorts of cases expressed by number 3 in the guidelines. This is **hostile working environment** harassment, by far the most frequently heard complaint and the most discussed aspect of sexual harassment. Much judicial inquiry has gone into defining the features of such an environment and how it is determined when they obtain.

The guidelines also address the crucial issue of who is responsible for sexual harassment. When the harasser is shown to be a supervisor or agent of the company, **strict liability** is enforced. This means that the employer is legally responsible for the wrongdoing whether or not the employer knew of the activity or should have known. On the other hand, when the misconduct concerns fellow employees with no supervisory relationship, the employer's liability is confined to those cases in which the misconduct was known or should have been known. The company might also be responsible for sexual harassment perpetrated by nonemployees. The guidelines' view of legal responsibility has not been accepted in its entirety by the courts (see Selected Cases: *Meritor Savings Bank v. Vinson*, below).

A victim of proven sexual harassment may recover several different sorts of legal relief. If a discharge resulted or a promotion was withheld, the employee may be rehired or promoted; any lost salary or benefits can be awarded, as well as monetary damages for physical or emotional injury, and legal fees paid. A court may also order a company to revise its policies or conduct sexual harassment training.

Selected Cases, Statutes, and Regulations

Corne v. Bausch & Lomb, Inc., **390 F. Supp 161 (1975);** *Miller v. Bank of America*, **418 F. Supp 233 (1976)**   These are two of the first three cases of what came to be known as *sexual harassment* (the term was not used in either decision), and signaled an inauspicious start for the issue in the courts. By the standards developed later, *Corne* involved a **hostile working environment** and *Miller* was a *quid pro quo* case.

Jane Corne and Geneva DeVane worked as secretaries at Bausch & Lomb in Phoenix, Arizona, during the early 1970s. Their supervisor was Leon Price, a man who, they alleged, subjected them to "repeated verbal and physical sexual advances." Unable to endure the torment any longer, Corne and DeVane finally resigned in 1973 and promptly filed a complaint with the EEOC. They argued that Price's conduct was also directed toward other female employees, and so it was plausibly seen as a condition of employment: sex discrimination in violation of Title VII.

Judge William Frey ruled that Corne and DeVane had failed to state a claim under Title VII for three reasons: (1) Because Price's actions exhibited a personal inclination rather than a company policy, his conduct could not be construed as a discriminatory employment practice; (2) there is nothing in Title VII forbidding such sexual overtures when they have nothing to do with the job itself; and (3) if Title VII did proscribe such conduct, then liability could be avoided simply by accosting men in the same sexually charged way—a farcical idea.

The circumstances for Margaret Miller were rather different, but the judgment was the same. She was an NCR operator at the San Francisco branch of Bank of America. Miller claimed that her supervisor, Mr. Taufer, told her that she would get a better job if she agreed to have sex with him. When she refused, she was fired. Like Jane Corne, Miller charged her employer with sex discrimination in violation of Title VII.

And like the judge in *Corne*, Judge Spencer Williams was not convinced. In his judgment, he opined that Title VII was not intended to attribute liability to an employer for an isolated incident of misconduct between employees. Williams agreed with Judge Frey that the supervisor's proposition was personally motivated and had nothing to do with company policy, and, like Frey, he worried that allowing Title VII foundations to such claims would have ridiculous results. He suggested that merely flirting would be a violation of federal law.

***Williams v. Saxbe*, 413 F. Supp 654 (1976)** This piece of litigation was little noticed at the time but it is historically important as the first judgment for a plaintiff charging quid pro quo sex discrimination under Title VII. Diane Williams worked at the Community Relations Service of the Department of Justice in 1972 (William Saxbe was attorney general, head of the Department of Justice, at the time). During her tenure there, her supervisor, Harvey Brinson, made sexual advances toward her. She refused and was discharged.

Lawyers for the Justice Department argued along two different lines. First, the defense alleged that Diane Williams was fired because she turned Brinson down, not because she was a woman (for similar reasoning, see *Barnes v. Costle [Train]*, below). Second, Brinson's sexual proposition was not a department policy but an isolated incident with purely personal motivations (for similar reasoning, see *Corne v. Bausch & Lomb, Inc.* and *Miller v. Bank of America*, above). Judge Charles Richey rejected both these arguments. Anticipating Judge Robinson's argument in *Barnes v. Costle* (see below), Richey observed that Brinson's behavior was directed at Williams precisely because she was a woman. Had she not been a woman, she would not have been singled out in this way. Therefore, she was presented with an obstacle not confronted by male employees. Moreover, the fact that Brinson's conduct was a personal policy made it, in his capacity as supervisor, a department policy.

Although this case represents a historic victory for the civil rights of women, it was little more than a cry in the wilderness at the time. Nearly simultaneous with this decision, another district court was rejecting Adrienne Tompkins's Title VII claim against her supervisor, who had physically detained, assaulted, and then fired her for refusing to have sex with him (*Tompkins v. Public Service Electric & Gas Company*, 422 F. Supp 553 [1976]).

Barnes v. Costle, 561 F.2d 983 (D.C. Cir. 1977); Bundy v. Jackson, 641 F.2d 934 (D.C. Cir. 1981) Paulette Barnes began work at the Equal Employment Opportunity division of the Environmental Protection Agency in 1971 (Douglas Costle was the administrator of the EPA at the time). She was hired by Mr. Train, the director of the EEO division, as his administrative assistant. Shortly thereafter Train began to pursue Barnes sexually; his principle entreaty was that he would arrange a promotion for her if she would consent to a sexual relationship with him. Barnes steadfastly refused many such propositions. Eventually her job was eliminated and she was discharged.

Her federal district court case (*Barnes v. Train*) was the first instance in which the demand for sexual favors by an employee's supervisor was challenged as sex discrimination on Title VII grounds. However, Judge John Smith found that Barnes was discriminated against because she refused Train's sexual advances, not because she was a woman.

On appeal, Judge Robinson of the D.C. Circuit Court of Appeals found such reasoning to be specious. After pointing out that the sexual solicitation occurred precisely because Paulette Barnes was a woman, Robinson noted that this was a condition of employment not levied against any male employee. Since Barnes lost her job due to her failure to comply, her gender thus became a necessary factor for retaining her job: a clear instance of sex discrimination.

In this case we see the shaping of the legal contours of *quid pro quo* sexual harassment (though, again, that term was not used here). Judge Robinson's decision suggests two criteria for identifying such cases: (1) the **disparate treatment** of women as compared to men; and (2) a concrete employment consequence for noncompliance. On the issue of liability for the wrongdoing, Judge MacKinnon's concurring opinion proposed the legal doctrine of *respondeat superior*: The Latin phrase means "the boss has to answer for what the workers do," and implies that the employer is responsible for the illegal behavior of employees if he or she knew or should have known about it.

The D.C. Circuit further clarified the burdens for proving quid pro quo sexual harassment in the landmark case *Bundy v. Jackson*. Sandra Bundy had repeatedly spurned sexual advances from several men at the District of Columbia Department of Corrections, including those of Delbert Jackson, the director of the department. She argued that her persistent refusals caused significant delays and denials in promotions to which she was entitled.

In establishing discriminatory treatment based on sex, Chief Judge Wright applied and modified the criteria for discriminatory treatment based on race originally articulated in *McDonnell Douglas v. Green* (see this chapter, Discrimination and Affirmative Action, Law). The simplified first phase here turns on just two steps, written in the context of job promotions: (1) proof of a regular practice of chronic sexual harassment (this marked the first occurrence of the expression in a federal court decision), and (2) denial of a promotion for which the plaintiff was qualified and had a reasonable expectation of receiving. Confirming (1) and (2) gives rise to a presumption of illegal discrimination (phase two), but, as in *McDonnell*, the presumption can be defeated if the employer can supply a legitimate, nondiscriminatory reason for rejecting the applicant (phase three). The plaintiff then has the opportunity to show that the purported reason is not the real reason (phase four).

Despite these germinal conclusions on quid pro quo, *Bundy* is best known as the first judicial recognition of the **hostile working environment** form of sexual harassment. Over a period of more than two years, Sandra Bundy was also subjected to a steady stream of sexually stereotyped insults and demeaning propositions that she rebuffed at every turn. However, unlike *Barnes* and *Williams v. Saxbe* (see above), in which the women were fired for their refusals, there was no tangible employment consequence to Bundy. Was this nonetheless sex discrimination in the terms or conditions of employment? Judge Wright answered affirmatively. He relied heavily in this regard on *Rogers v. EEOC*, 454 F.2d 518 (5th Cir. 1971). In that case, the Fifth Circuit Court of Appeals found that discriminatory treatment of Hispanic *clients* created an offensive atmosphere for Hispanic *employees*, even though they were not treated unfairly, that is, they suffered no employment consequences. Wright accepted Bundy's claim that the conditions of employment include the psychological and emotional environment pervading one's work, and this aspect of her job had been "illegally poisoned."

Finally, on the issue of responsibility, the court cited and agreed with the EEOC's recently promulgated Guidelines on Discrimination Because of Sex (see above) and stated that, on remand to the District Court, the D.C. Department of Corrections should be held **strictly liable** for the wrongdoing of its employees. Notice that this is a stiffening of the court's view of legal responsibility when compared to the *Barnes* case.

Henson v. City of Dundee, 682 F.2d 897 (11th Cir. 1982)   Like *Bundy v. Jackson* (see above), this case contained both **quid pro quo** and **hostile working environment issues**, and like *Bundy*, its importance lies in the latter problem. Barbara Henson worked as a dispatcher for the police department of Dundee, Florida. Over the two-year period 1975–1977, she claimed that the chief of police, John Sellgren, subjected her and a female coworker to repeated sexual inquiries and vulgarities, as well as numerous requests to have sex with him, all of which she declined. Ultimately, she resigned and shortly thereafter filed a complaint with the EEOC, charging sexual harassment.

The district court had ruled for the city (as Sellgren's employer) on the grounds that Henson had not experienced any material job detriment as a result of Sellgren's conduct, and that she did not resign as a result of that conduct. Judge Vance of the Eleventh Circuit Court of Appeals reversed that ruling. Citing both *Rogers v. EEOC* and the *Bundy* case (see above), he asserted that Title VII does not require a plaintiff to show some tangible adverse consequence in order to establish a violation, and that sexually offensive working conditions undermine sexual equality.

More importantly, Vance formalized a five-step procedure for proving a hostile working environment:

1. The employee is a member of the protected class (all humans)
2. The employee experiences unwelcome sexual overtures, namely, those that is neither solicited nor incited, and are undesired or offensive
3. The harassment is based on sex, that is, but for her or his sex, the individual would not have been tormented (Vance cited *Bundy* here, but the precedent for this crucial factor is the neglected *Williams v. Saxbe* case; see above)
4. The harassment is so chronic that it disrupts the working conditions and creates an abusive environment, and
5. *Respondeat superior*: the employer is liable for the offense when the employer knew or should have known about it.

The court ruled that Henson had shown that each of numbers 1 through 5 was satisfied in her case.

We have then a firm judicial concept of what constitutes a hostile working environment, developed out of *Bundy* and especially here in *Henson*. But we have a conflict about legal responsibility in such cases: The D.C. Circuit says strict liability, while the Eleventh Circuit favors the weaker ***respondeat superior***. It was left to the Supreme Court to address this issue, and to finally enter the legal fray concerning sexual harassment.

***Meritor Savings Bank v. Vinson*, 477 U.S. 57 (1986)**   Michelle Vinson began work as a teller at New Jersey's Meritor Savings Bank in 1974. Over the next four years, she was promoted to head teller and then to assistant branch manager. Her supervisor throughout this period was Sidney Taylor, vice-president of the bank. According to Vinson, those four years were marked by constant sexual harassment from Taylor. She testified that initially she refused his advances but eventually acquiesced for fear of losing her job. During 1974–1977 she had sex with him 40 to 50 times, he forcibly raped her on several occasions, fondled her in the presence of coworkers, and once followed her into the women's restroom and exposed himself. Taylor denied all these charges. Vinson was fired in 1978 after she had taken two months of sick leave, deemed excessive by the bank. In response, she charged Meritor Savings with violating Title VII and sued for injunctive relief, compensatory and punitive damages against Taylor and the bank, and attorneys' fees.

The district court rejected her claim of sexual harassment on the grounds that the relationship with Taylor had been voluntary and there was no detrimental work condition imposed (indeed, she received several merit-based promotions). The District of Columbia Circuit Court of Appeals reversed that decision. Since the advances were unwelcome, they ruled, voluntariness was irrelevant; and it was unnecessary to show a tangible employment consequence to establish harassment. The D.C. Circuit also imposed strict liability on the bank, despite the fact that neither Vinson nor any other employee had ever lodged a complaint against Taylor.

The real significance of this case is that key features of the developing legal view of sexual harassment were confirmed by the Supreme Court for the first time. Writing for a unanimous court, Justice William Rehnquist set out these features as follows: (1) Sexual harassment is a form of sex discrimination in violation of Title VII; (2) hostile work environment is a genuine form of this harassment, and is illegal even when there is no loss of job benefits; and (3) the defining aspect of this form of harassment is that it is unwelcome, voluntariness does not matter.

In reaching this affirmation of the appeals court decision (and the reader will notice the influence), Rehnquist relied heavily on *Rogers, Bundy, Henson*, and the EEOC's Guidelines on Discrimination Because of Sex. However, the one sticking point was the question of employer liability. Rehnquist rejected the D.C. Circuit's judgment of strict liability in *Vinson v. Taylor*, but stopped short of validating respondeat superior in all hostile working environment cases. At this time, the federal courts seem to have adopted the policy of imposing strict liability only in quid pro quo cases, reserving respondeat superior for hostile working environment cases.

***Ellison v. Brady*, 924 F.2d 872 (9th Cir. 1991)** This was one of the first major sexual harassment cases after *Meritor Savings v. Vinson* (see above), and it continued the difficult process of legally characterizing the controversial notion of a **hostile working environment**. The main issue here is factor number 4 identified by Judge Vance in *Henson v. City of Dundee* (see above): A hostile working environment is one in which the harassment is so chronic that it disrupts the working conditions and creates an abusive situation. The problem is determining precisely when these circumstances obtain.

It began in 1986 at the Internal Revenue Service in San Mateo, California. Kerry Ellison worked there as revenue agent in the same office with Sterling Gray. Although the two barely knew one another, Gray became infatuated with Ellison, pestering her with frequent requests for dates and sending her several emotional letters and cards. Ellison complained to her supervisor and, as a result, Gray was admonished and transferred to the San Francisco office. When she learned that Gray would be returning to San Mateo, Ellison filed a formal complaint of sexual harassment with the IRS. After investigation, the Treasury Department (Nicholas Brady was secretary of the treasury at the time) determined that, according to EEOC regulations, Gray's conduct did not constitute a pattern or practice of sexual harassment. Ellison's complaint was rejected. The EEOC seconded the rejection but on the grounds that the IRS's measures to prevent Gray's conduct had been adequate.

The district court agreed with the judgment of the Treasury Department that Gray's behavior was not sexually harassing, calling it "isolated and trivial." Judge Robert Beezer and the Ninth Circuit reversed this judgment. Citing *Meritor*, the EEOC's Guidelines (see above, Introduction), and the court's own recent decision in *Jordan v. Clark*, 847 F.2d 1368 (1988), Beezer noted that the key to Ellison's case was showing that Gray's conduct was "sufficiently severe and pervasive to alter the conditions of Ellison's employment and create an abusive working environment." The question then becomes: Who is to say when this state of affairs occurs?

Beezer answered that the usual appeal to the *reasonable person* (the model and standard of all legal behavior) will not do here because it tends to be male-biased and ignore the experience of women. Instead, Beezer offered a **reasonable woman** or *reasonable victim* standard requiring that the alleged harassment be judged from the recipient's perspective. There are several implications of this view: (1) Employers do not have to take account of the idiosyncrasies of hyper-sensitive employees; (2) conduct may be harassing even when harassers do not realize their conduct creates a hostile working environment; and (3) the new standard is flexible and can change over time as views of the reasonable woman change.

***Robinson v. Jacksonville Shipyards, Inc.*, 760 F. Supp 1486 (1991)**
This is one of the most famous district court decisions impacting business, and a landmark case for the hostile working environment form of sexual harassment. Its major contribution to this type of litigation is found in its distinctiveness. The sort of work environment at issue here is unlike the more usual situation exemplified by *Vinson* and *Ellison* (both above) or *Harris v. Forklift Systems* (see below), although some elements of this variety were present. In these other cases, the predominant feature is a melange of unwelcome sexual advances and/or commentary. In *Robinson*, we find that this overt behavior is not the primary feature of the problem. This is the first case in which a judgment of a hostile working environment was predicated for the most part on the display of sexually explicit pictures, and so further elaborates on the nature of this type of harassment.

Lora Robinson worked as welder for more than ten years at Jacksonville Shipyards, Inc., in Jacksonville, Florida. During this time, she endured almost daily exposure to sexually graphic posters, calendars, and drawings depicting nude and partially clothed women in a variety of sexually suggestive postures. These displays were liberally distributed throughout the workplace and included many bared breasts and exposed pubic areas. Although graffiti containing sexual obscenities was conspicuous and a number of remarks of an explicitly prurient nature were directed at Robinson or uttered in her presence, the overwhelming atmosphere of the shipyards in which she worked was one sexually charged by the ubiquitous pictorials. After several years of silence, Robinson began to complain in 1985, lodging requests with her immediate supervisors that certain items be taken down. When little was done, she took her complaints to the shipyard superintendent, informing him that the pictures were degrading, humiliating, nauseating, and she wanted them removed. When the superintendent told her flatly that he would not remove the pictures, she then went to the vice-president of the yard, who also refused to do anything. After first entering a complaint with the local EEOC office, Robinson filed a lawsuit against her employer in 1986.

In coming to his decision, Judge Howell Melton relied on the five-step procedure inaugurated by Judge Vance in *Henson v. City of Dundee* (see above), each of which must be satisfied to find that a hostile working environment had prevailed: First, Robinson, as female, did belong to a protected class. Second, since no evidence was presented that she in any way solicited or incited the conduct, and she strenuously denied that she did, Robinson was subjected to unwelcome sexual harassment, primarily in the form of pictures of nude and partially nude women. Third, the harassing actions were based upon her sex; this is so because the actions were directed at her as a woman, and graphic pictorials of this sort have a disproportionately demeaning impact on women.

The fourth condition is often the most controversial, but Judge Melton found that, from both a subjective and an objective point of view, the harassment affected the conditions of employment. Subjectively speaking, Robinson was certainly deeply disturbed by the displays, and thus her ability to perform on the job was substantially altered. Jacksonville Shipyards did not dispute this, instead arguing that *objectively* speaking, she should not have been so affected that her job performance suffered. The court rejected this argument; the objective standard applicable here is that of the **reasonable woman** (see also *Ellison v. Brady*, above and *Harris v. Forklift Systems*, below), and, according to Melton, a reasonable woman would have found the working environment abusive. Finally, as the fifth necessary factor, the employer knew of the misconduct and not only did nothing to correct it, but actually endorsed it. Thus, liability was imposed on Jacksonville Shipyards, specifically on the vice-president of operations and the personnel manager.

Jacksonville Shipyards was ordered to immediately implement a comprehensive strategy for lodging sexual harassment complaints, and for investigating and resolving them. Additionally, the company was required to instruct all managers and supervisors on the proper methods of handling such complaints, while women employees were to receive training on resisting and preventing sexual harassment.

Harris v. Forklift Systems, Inc., **114 S. Ct. 367 (1993)** This case is the most recent consideration of sexual harassment by the Justices of the high Court, and represents their definitive finding to date on the nature of a **hostile working environment**. Like *Ellison v. Brady* (see above), the issue concerns the standards by which abusive or hostile working conditions are identified (see number 4 in *Henson v. City of Dundee*, above).

Teresa Harris worked as a manager at Forklift Systems, an equipment rental company, from 1985 to 1987. During this time, her supervisor was the president of the company, Charles Hardy. Harris reported that Hardy often insulted her for being a woman (he suggested on several occasions that since she was a woman, she was not very intelligent) and made numerous sexual innuendoes (he once suggested that he and Harris repair to the local Holiday Inn to discuss her raise). Harris complained to Hardy about his conduct; he was surprised, but apologized and promised to stop. However, after a brief respite the innuendoes began again, and Harris soon resigned. She then sued the company, claiming that Hardy's conduct had created an abusive work environment for her because of her gender.

The district court acknowledged that it was a close call, but decided that Harris had not proved her case. The court found that Hardy's conduct did not create an abusive situation because it did not produce any emotional suffering for Harris or injure her psychological well-being, nor was there any substantial effect on her job performance. The Sixth Circuit Court of Appeals affirmed this judgment. The Supreme Court reversed.

Justice Sandra Day O'Connor, writing for a unanimous court, ruled that establishing a hostile working environment does not require some showing of psychological or emotional injury. However, she hastened to add, the mere utterance of a sexual remark that offends someone does not constitute harassment. Rather, the ruling steers a "middle path" between acute sensitivities on the one hand and nervous breakdowns on the other. This is done by applying both the **reasonable person standard** "as well as the victim's subjective perception" in identifying abusive work situations. In other words, O'Connor offers a compromise position in which a hostile work environment is one that *both* the objective and impartial person *and* the immediately involved and quite partial woman (or "reasonable person in the victim's shoes") would find to be hostile or abusive. Thus the Supreme Court stopped short of exclusively endorsing the reasonable woman standard found in *Ellison*.

Whistleblowing and Loyalty

Throughout this chapter, we have talked about the duties of companies and the rights of employees. In this last section, we will focus on the duties of employees and the rights of companies. Specifically, we will examine the duty of employees to blow the whistle, and its conflict with another duty employees have to be loyal to their employers. Employees *blow the whistle* when they reveal company information to prevent or to explain actions that can be harmful to people or the environment.

Instances of whistleblowing are regularly in the news (Miceli, Near, and Schwenk 1991). *The Wall Street Journal* reported that Timothy Kerr, an employee of Boeing, launched a $10 billion lawsuit against his company for producing defective aircraft (Faye 1997). In another case, William Watt filed a suit against the Fluor Corporation under the 1986 False Claims Reform Act (see Selected Cases, below). He eventually received $1.1 million for his efforts, including $3 million for problems created by Fluor when he quit (Smith 1997).

We will presume that employees have a duty to respect their employers' property, whether it is in the form of funds, equipment, or information. This duty is just an instance of everyone's duty to respect the property of others. As we will see in the discussion of ethics, below, there are different ethical explanations of this duty. All of these explanations agree, however, that private property rights are not absolute, and that they can be overridden by a variety of concerns, such as the need to prevent a felony or to prevent great harm to the public or the environment.

Justified whistleblowing must meet three criteria (Duska 1997). First, the whistleblower should be able to prove to a reasonable person that the company is planning to do something or has done something harmful or illegal. Simply believing the company is too big or does not care enough about its customers is not enough. Second, the harm must be great enough to justify revealing proprietary information. The fact that the company does not pay its parking tickets is not a grave enough harm to disclose to the press. Third, the employee must have tried to resolve this matter with management; whistleblowing is a last resort, not a first step. This last criterion can be ignored if the harm is great and imminent.

In our discussion of the ethics of whistleblowing, we will rely on the following example.

Three employees are asked by their company, which is under contract from the federal government, to dump dangerous chemicals in an unpopulated desert area. This dumping will save the company approximately $700,000, which the company is falsely claiming to have spent to get rid of the waste properly. The source of the damage will be hard to determine.

The chemical will leach into the ground water. The employees who are told to dump the chemicals know that it is illegal, but they believe that there is some chance the ground water will dilute the chemicals safely. If people come into contact with the water and the chemical is not sufficiently diluted, they will burn their skin and increase their risk of cancer. Should these employees blow the whistle?

Ethics

Promoting Self-interest: Egoism   Employees who adopt self-interest as their sole ethical principle believe that their only duty is to themselves; they would not acknowledge any duty to the company.

If these employees were aggressively self-interested they might seek opportunities to increase their wealth or to get a better position in the company. They could increase their wealth in at least two ways. First, they could sue the company for defrauding the government under the 1986 False Claim Reform Act (see Selected Cases, below). This act allows the court to impose treble damages, which in the chemical dumping case described above would be $2.1 million. The informer can be awarded up to 30 percent of the money recovered, or $630,000, or, alternatively, the employees could go to their manager and threaten to sue unless they received cash payments, promotions, or other benefits.

If these employees were contemplatively self-interested, they would look for a way to avoid conflict and worry. They would be very hesitant to blow the whistle as that would cause them prolonged conflict. Blowing the whistle is a long, drawn out process that is emotionally draining on the whistleblower (Botsko 1994). Although the False Claims Reform Act protects whistleblowers against reprisals, whistleblowers are often isolated and reviled by fellow workers. Contemplatively self-interested employees would much prefer to move to a different part of the company where they would not be responsible for this problem. If the chemical dumping problem was just one of many stressful problems these employees faced, contemplatively self-interested employees would look for another, less stressful, job.

Promoting Personal Relationships: Care Employees using the care perspective would evaluate whistleblowing in terms of how it affected their personal relationships.

Passive carers would try to please those with whom they are most closely related. If their families were in favor of honesty, they would blow the whistle. The monetary reward would be important if they could use it to help friends and family pursue their projects, not for what it could buy for the whistleblower. For example, the money might be used to help a needy cousin go to college. Passive carers would have a difficult time making a decision if those for whom they cared disagreed about what the best course of action is.

Active carers try to promote the well-being of their relationships, too, but they do not automatically accept others' views of what a healthy relationship is. For example, if the family of a whistle blower cared mainly about money, the whistleblower would consider what the money would be used for. If it was going to be used for gambling and drugs, the active carer would not want to give the family money. If the money was to be used for more productive purposes, such as education or a retirement fund, the active carer could agree to these goals.

Active carers would also consider the relationships of those whom the contaminated ground water could harm. Paying attention to these victims would probably move the active carer to do something about the dumping and the cheating. However, blowing the whistle would be the active carer's last choice, because whistleblowing almost always destroys work relationships. Instead, these employees would try to work within the company to correct these problems. If this did not work, and there were no other ways to correct the problems, active carers would blow the whistle.

Promoting Group Good: Utilitarianism Utilitarian employees would consider the impact of the dumping and cheating on the society as whole. If they believed that blowing the whistle would benefit the society more than not blowing the whistle, they would inform the proper officials of the company's plans. If they thought that revealing the plans would do more harm than good, they would keep quiet. How they calculated these harms and benefits would depend, in part, on whether they took a strict or a flexible view of social rules.

Using strict rule utilitarianism, employees should blow the whistle if doing so follows the rules of their society. There are plenty of social rules, both formal and informal, that permit and even, at times, require the employees to blow the whistle. *Informal* social rules require us to protect the innocent.

There are two types of innocent victims here: the people who might come into contact with the ground water and the taxpayers who are cheated out of $700,000. Further, the company's reports to the government will be false, violating the social rule that requires us to tell the truth. There are also many *formal* rules that permit and urge employees to blow the whistle in a case like this. We have already mentioned one, the 1986 False Claim Reform Act. There are many other laws that support and supplement this act (see Selected Cases, below). Given the strength and number of social rules that support blowing the whistle, strict utilitarian employees would have plenty of reasons to reveal the company's plans.

Employees using flexible rule utilitarianism would blow the whistle only if it were likely to promote more happiness than any other act. Since future happiness is often difficult to calculate, we should generally obey the rules of society, because these tend to promote group happiness. The only exception to following standard rules is when doing so would *certainly* cause *great* harm.

There are also rules that require employees to be loyal and not to reveal proprietary information. Flexible rule utilitarians would have to weigh these rules against the rules that support blowing the whistle. Suppose the employees go to their manager and tell them their concerns. The manager responds sympathetically, saying that she, too, is concerned, but then she goes to her boss and makes the following deal. If no one blows the whistle about this plan, which is too late to stop, the company will take care of toxic waste properly in the future. Further, they will implement a company policy regarding toxic waste that is more strict than the government rules require, thus creating more good than harm. However, if the employees blow the whistle, the company will fight it, causing a great deal of time and money to be spent on court costs by the company and the government.

Flexible rule utilitarian employees could agree to this as long as they had good reason to trust the company to follow through on its promises. Given that the company is already untrustworthy, the employees would have to demand access to company information that would show whether or not the company was keeping its word.

Respecting Dignity and Rights: Intrinsic Value Employees relying on human dignity and fairness would acknowledge the rights of companies to private information. But that would only be the beginning of their analysis. They would also look at how dumping the chemical affects others. Dumping these chemicals puts human beings at risk for the sole purpose of saving money. This treats people as mere means to an end, and not as valuable in themselves. These employees could also note that the laws that govern dumping were adopted in a relatively fair process, a process that allowed input from a variety of different parties and interests. The enactment of environmental laws makes it clear that the body politic wants to stop the unsafe dumping of toxic chemicals. Dumping the chemicals violates the free choices of millions of citizens.

Employees relying on property rights would recognize their duty not to give away company property. However, they would also acknowledge the need to obey the law and the need to prevent great harm to innocent people. According to the rights-based social contract theory, the state was created by its citizens to protect themselves. On these grounds, an employee would be justified in blowing the whistle.

International Issues

The definition, use, costs, and benefits of whistleblowing are the same at the domestic and international levels. What is different are the conditions, laws, and cultures in which whistleblowing occurs.

Great Britain, for example, does not have laws like the United States that protect and reward whistleblowing. Parliament considered its first real whistleblower protection in the 1990s. There was concern in Great Britain that a great deal of money was being lost because of fraud and shoddy work, but that there was no good way to find out these problems. Protecting whistleblowers encourages workers to come forward. Sponsors of the bill also hoped that the legislation would encourage companies to make it easier for employees to voice concerns to management, hopefully stopping problems before they occur (Borrie 1996).

Not all countries are so anxious as Great Britain to encourage whistleblowing. For example, Cambodian nationals blew the whistle on their own country at the International Conference on the Reconstruction and Rehabilitation of Cambodia in 1995. The subject of the conference was whether Cambodia should receive more foreign aid. Various speakers, including the former finance minister, Sam Rainsy, argued that graft (payoffs to government officials for contracts and other favors) and human rights abuses were reasons to stop foreign aid.

There are some cases of whistleblowing in the United States that have international aspects. For example, the Foreign Corrupt Practices Act (FCPA), passed in 1977 and amended in 1988, makes it a crime for U.S. companies to bribe foreign officials. Whistleblowing in these cases would necessarily concern information outside our borders (Dienhart 1999).

Economics

Society The social point of view evaluates the *practice* of whistleblowing, not individual acts of whistleblowing. The social issue is whether society should encourage whistleblowing, discourage it, or remain neutral.

Good economic reasons exist to encourage whistleblowing. Whistleblowing gets information to consumers, producers, and to government officials that they need to make informed decisions. In the chemical dumping case, consumers need to be aware of the dangerous water. By avoiding the water they avoid costly medical bills and lost wages, which drain national wealth. The government can take appropriate action to stop the dumping before it occurs if the whistleblowing precedes the dumping, or the government can force the company to pay for cleaning up the area if they find out after the fact. Both actions will help deter other producers from illegal dumping.

Social reasons to be wary of encouraging whistleblowing by giving rewards to whistleblowers are also important. Rewards provide incentive for employees to avoid discouraging their companies from committing illegal acts, so that the employees can get a reward for blowing the whistle. Or, if the reward is based on the dollar amount of damage or fraud caused by a company, employees have an incentive to wait to blow the whistle until the wrongdoing is extensive enough to yield a substantial reward.

Although these are real problems with encouraging whistleblowing, they concern the way whistleblowing is rewarded and investigations conducted. They do not speak to the key point that whistleblowing provides the market with important information. Some of these facts will be misleading, but that is true for all information channels: word of mouth, newspapers, radio, television, and the Internet. The market has developed mechanisms for evaluating data from these sources; there is no reason why they could not use these same mechanisms to evaluate information arising from acts of whistleblowing.

The third social option is to remain neutral, that is, not to encourage or discourage whistleblowing. When we examine this option more closely, however, we see that this is not a real option. Once someone blows the whistle, there will be a chain of consequences for the whistleblower and the company. If the whistleblower is treated as a hero, this will encourage whistleblowing, but if he or she is fired and the company suffers no harm as a result, this will discourage disclosures. Since whistleblowing can be evaluated by the news media, the courts, or legislative bodies, society has some choice in identifying those institutions that determine what the social point of view is, but in any case it is inevitable that some social view(s) will develop.

Consumers Timely whistleblowing benefits consumers because they get more information about the products they buy and use. In the chemical dumping case, they are protected from skin burns and cancer. Although this may be a small group, because the dumping area is in a remote, sparsely populated region, the harm is potentially great to those who are affected; this is a risk consumers do not want to take. Consumers also save money if employees blow the whistle, because the company doing the dumping, and not taxpayers, will be forced to pay for the cleanup and any damages.

Producers Although society and consumers have good reasons to support whistleblowing, producers would seem to have good reasons to be against it. Not only does whistleblowing release private information, it brings investigators into the company, using company resources in nonproductive ways. Whistleblowing can also undermine employee morale, cause good managers and employees to look for jobs elsewhere, and ruin a company's reputation.

However, managers who look at whistleblowing more deeply realize that it is almost always the last step following a series of management errors. First, there must be some corporate decision that will or has harmed people or the environment in significant ways. This decision is the first management error. Second, there is no way for those who disagree with such a decision to voice their concerns within the company. This is the second management error. Good managers, recognizing the possibility of whistleblowing, will design management systems that make illicit decisions less likely, and that provide ways for employees to voice their concerns about decisions they think are ethically or legally questionable.

Law

In this chapter we focus on various moral and legal aspects of the relationship between employees and their employers. In the other sections of this chapter, our concern has been with the obligations employers owe to their employees: do not discriminate, respect employee privacy, provide a safe working environment, pay a fair wage, among others. We now address a different perspective on the issue. What are the legal obligations employees owe to their employers? And when may those obligations be overridden by a weightier legal obligation to report wrongdoing by employers?

About half of America's workers are either members of a union or employed by government. Their duties to their employers are spelled out in a union contract or specified by applicable civil service laws. That still leaves approximately 70 million people who do not belong to a union, and who are not government workers. In order to find their legal obligations, these **at-will** employees (see Terms and Conditions of Employment, also in this chapter) must look to the common law, and a legal area contained therein known as agency law. In this area, the employee is referred to as the *agent*, that is, one who acts on behalf of an employer, who is called the *principal*.

Since rules governing the agent's duties to the principal have rarely been the subject of federal or state legislative efforts, it remains for the common law and *Restatements of the Law* to specify the nature of this relationship. According to the *Second Restatement of Agency Law*, the agent is a fiduciary, from the Latin *fidere*, meaning "to trust." This signifies that the principal trusts the agent to perform certain duties on behalf of the principal. The foundational obligation of the agent to the principal is the duty of loyalty.

Employee Loyalty This duty demands faithful and trustworthy service to the principal. It requires that the agent follow instructions carefully and with diligence, keep exact records, and provide accurate and thorough information. Perhaps most centrally, the *Second Restatement* avers that loyalty requires the agent "to act solely for the benefit of the principal in matters entrusted to him, . . . to take no unfair advantage of his position in the use of information or things acquired by him or because of his position, . . . [and] not to act or speak disloyally in matters which are connected with his employment." This duty also prohibits an employee from disparaging the principal's products, competing with the principal's business interests, or participating in work slowdowns or sabotage.

One facet of the duty of loyalty described in the *Second Restatement* is a duty to avoid *conflicts of interest*; this prohibits employees from acting as agents for persons whose interests are incompatible with their employers' business interests. An agent who acts for the benefit of business competitors of the principal is obviously involved in a conflict of interest, and is plainly a disloyal employee. Not so obvious conflicts are also included here, such as supplying information detrimental to the employer to political organizations that operate with the express intention of putting the principal out of business. These potential sources of employee disloyalty are primarily conflicts between the principal's interests and those of the principal's competitors or opponents, with the agent as the mechanism, so to speak, of the conflict. The interests of the disloyal agent may or may not come into play here. So another potential source of unfaithfulness arises when the agent's personal interests are incompatible with the principal's business interests. Acting to realize these personal interests is also outlawed by a general duty of loyalty; the agent must refrain from acting in ways that promote his or her interests at the cost of those of the principal.

A second manifestation of loyalty is found when the *Second Restatement* describes a duty of *confidentiality*. An employee must avoid "using or communicating information confidentially given to him by the principal" in ways that damage the employer, unless that information is a matter of public knowledge. Assurances of confidentiality enhance the flow of information necessary for the effective and efficient operation of a business, and such assurances are clearly prompted by a trustworthy agent demonstrating loyalty to the principal. Disclosure of information harmful to the principal is disloyal.

One of the best examples of such potentially damaging information is a **trade secret**. The *Second Restatement of Torts* defines a trade secret as "any formula, pattern, device or compilation of information which is used in one's business, and which gives [a business person] an opportunity to obtain an advantage over competitors who do not know or use it." This would include such items as the ingredients or chemical composition of some product or specifics of how it was made, the design of a machine, results of marketing surveys, customer lists, or methods of quality control.

Trade secrets are distinguished from other sorts of confidential material according to whether the information is used in manufacturing a product or in providing a service. In contrast, employee salaries are typically confidential but they are not a feature of a product or service provided to consumers. According to the *Second Restatement*, what makes something a secret in business is a function of several factors, such as: how widely the information is known in the company and in the industry as a whole; what efforts have been made to develop and to conceal the information; and its value to the company and its competitors.

The legal problems surrounding the duty of loyalty, and its derivative obligations of confidentiality and avoiding conflicts of interest, tend to crystallize on trade secrets. Because a trade secret is information an employer intends to conceal, confidentiality is obviously required to effect this state of affairs. So maintaining confidentiality requires that an employee privy to the information be a loyal agent of the principal. Yet individuals often change jobs within a particular industry and, when they do so, the confidential information goes with them; the information may benefit the new employer, as well as the employee, and produce a competitive advantage over the old employer. Disloyalty clearly arises when such conflicts of interest occur between an employee and a current employer concerning a trade secret. But is there any duty of loyalty to a *former* employer? Who owns the trade secret?

The *Second Restatement* goes on to qualify the obligation to be loyal toward one's employer with two provisos: (1) Agents' loyalty to the principal does not require them to carry out orders that are illegal or unethical (though "unethical" is not defined); and (2) agents are permitted, though not required, to disclose illegal activities or intentions by the principal to the proper authorities (disclosure of unethical conduct is not mentioned here). This second qualification of the duty of loyalty brings us to the issue of whistleblowing.

Whistleblowing   For most of the history of our country, the law provided no assurance to individuals reporting improper conduct by their employers that they would not be harassed, intimidated, demoted, transferred, or simply fired. This gap in the law was a by-product of the buyer's market for labor that arose out of the Industrial Revolution during the last half of the nineteenth century, a time when wealthy capitalists exercised nearly total control over the allocation of millions of jobs, and therefore enjoyed unrestrained discretion over the terms and conditions of employment.

Potential whistleblowers also faced the formidable doctrine of **employment at-will**. The idea here is just that, in the absence of an express contract, employee and employer alike were entitled to terminate the working relationship at any time for any reason. This might seem fair until one recognizes that an employer would likely have a far easier time hiring another worker than the employee would have finding another job. The dominion of the capitalists and the disadvantageous state of affairs that prevailed for workers led to the rise of labor unions (for more detail on the historical developments of the labor environment, see Terms and Conditions of Employment, in this chapter).

Although the False Claims Act of 1963 did allow workers to sue their employers who engaged in illegal activity, no safeguards against retaliation aimed at the whistleblowers were provided until amendments passed in 1986 (see Selected Cases, below). The Railway Labor Act of 1926 (RLA), 45 U.S.C. §152, was the first attempt by Congress to prevent the discharge of workers who participated in activities contrary to their employer's interest. The provisions of the RLA were confined to the railroads and other common carriers, but they did prohibit employers from retaliating against employees for their union activities. Similar protections were extended a decade later to members of all labor unions in the National Labor Relations Act of 1935   (NLRA), 29 U.S.C. §§142 *et seq.* Section 8 of the NLRA declares it an unfair labor practice to fire union members for filing charges or giving testimony against their employers, or in some other way to discriminate based on union membership (the RLA and NLRA are also discussed in more detail in Terms and Conditions of Employment, Selected Cases, this chapter).

For 30 years following the enactment of the NLRA, the beneficiaries of such federal laws were exclusively union members, and the protected activities involved conduct related to unions. Thus, until fairly recently, the two key features of whistleblower protection—*who* is protected and *what* actions are protected—were rather narrowly confined to a minority of the American labor force and a small range of activities.

It was only with the enactment of Title VII of the Civil Rights Act of 1964 (see below; also Discrimination and Affirmative Action, Law, in this chapter) that workers in all areas of employment were afforded some measure of security when reporting the wrongdoing of their employers. Unfortunately, the protection only concerned reports of illegal discrimination, and not other sorts of unlawful actions. In 1970, the Occupational Safety and Health Act (OSHA), (see also Health And Safety, Selected Cases, this chapter), supplied employees with assurances when they called attention to dangerous working conditions. OSHA regulations, including whistleblower protection, apply to many different industries, so they are drafted in broad language and cover a variety of circumstances. Employers are prohibited from retaliating against employees who exercise their rights, under OSHA, to request inspections, accompany inspectors, and refuse to work in life-threatening situations. As the 1970s wore on to the 1980s, more statutory protections for whistleblowers, cutting across various industries, were enacted, increasing the number and types of violations that an employee could feel safe in disclosing. Many of these newer statutes are found in environmental law. The Department of Labor is the agency responsible for administering these laws, arising out of a variety of congressional actions. All of these forbid reprisals against an employee for commencing proceedings, for testifying against his or her employer, or in some other way participating in the prosecution of violations of environmental law. Reinstatement, back pay, and attorneys' fees may be awarded to vindicated whistleblowers. The relevant statutes include (see Chapter 5: The Environment, for more on these and other such laws): the Hazardous Substances Release Act (42 U.S.C. §9610), the Clean Air Act (42 U.S.C. §7622), and the Comprehensive Environmental Response, Compensation and Liability Act of 1980 (42 U.S.C. §9610).

Together with these industrywide regulations, today there are many more that are specific to particular industries and focus on matters of special concern to that industry. For example, the Mine Safety and Health Act, 30 U.S.C. §815, allows miners to demand immediate inspections of safety hazards and gives them the right to walk off the job if their concerns are not adequately addressed. The Federal Mine Safety and Health Administration is required to promptly investigate complaints of retaliation in response to miners' protests, and to order reinstatement of miners within 15 days after they have blown the whistle.

Today, about two-thirds of the states have their own whistleblower protection laws in addition to the federal regulations discussed or mentioned above. State regulations vary widely. Some cover all public employees, and workers in the private sector too—California is an example. Others, such as Alaska, include only state or local government employees and have no protections at all for other public employees, like those working at state universities, or for those in the private sector.

Selected Cases, Statutes, and Regulations

False Claims Act of 1863, 31 U.S.C. §§3729–3733 During the Civil War, unscrupulous individuals took advantage of shortages of food, clothing, tools, and labor, among other things, by charging the federal government outrageous prices to supply these items, or by issuing bills for goods that were never received. In an effort to curb the rampant profiteering, Congress passed the False Claims Act, authorizing private citizens to sue, in the name of the federal government, any company engaged in this sort of fraudulent activity. To encourage citizens to file lawsuits, the act allowed them to recover up to one-half of the amount fraudulently obtained from the federal government, and the cost of the suit. A person filing such a suit is called a *qui tam* plaintiff, meaning the individual is suing on his or her own behalf "as well as" on behalf of the government.

Unfortunately, as originally written in 1863, the act did not allow the government itself to intervene in the suit and, although the employees of profiteering contractors were permitted to blow the whistle on their own employers and sue them, retaliation against these employees was not expressly prohibited. Very few *qui tam* plaintiffs sued their employers. Both of these gaps were filled by subsequent amendments, though it took many years to do so.

Amendments to the act passed in 1943 addressed a problem also generated by war, but now the trouble was not the profiteers, but rather the private citizens bent on stopping the profiteering. Individuals were filing lawsuits against fraudulent defense contractors based on public reports of criminal indictments brought by the federal government. Under the original act, a *qui tam* plaintiff was entitled to pursue the litigation, even if the government wanted to settle with the defendant. The new law required that *qui tam* suits be dismissed if they were based solely on information possessed by the government, and it also gave government the option to take over prosecution of such suits. If this option was selected, the *qui tam* plaintiff was eligible to receive only 10 percent, at most, of the amount recovered. If the government did not take over the case, the plaintiff's recovery was limited to 25 percent or less.

The 1943 amendments had the effect of discouraging citizens from blowing the whistle on fraudulent contractors; after all, they lowered the recovery percentage and provided for the forfeiture of the suit to the government, both without providing any protection for the whistleblower. The 1986 amendments, also called the False Claims Reform Act, rectified this situation by raising the financial incentives for private citizens to sue on behalf of the government, and by supplying safeguards for employees who fear reprisals if they report abuses.

Along with the imposition of treble damages (recovery at three times the amount fraudulently acquired), the Reform Act allowed *qui tam* plaintiffs to receive at least 15 percent and as much as 25 percent of the proceeds when the government takes over the legal action, and a minimum of 25 percent and a maximum of 30 percent when it does not. Perhaps more importantly, the statute prohibits any reprisals against employees who disclose information regarding false claims to any government or law enforcement agency, or against employees who participate in prosecutions or investigations of false claims. Workers who successfully demonstrate in a federal district court that they were prey to retaliation from their employers may be awarded reinstatement (if fired), restoration of seniority (if demoted), double the amount of pay lost with interest, compensation for special damages, and attorneys' fees.

Title VII of the Civil Rights Act of 1964, 42 U.S.C. §§2000e *et seq*. After the passage of the National Labor Relations Act of 1935 (see Law: Whistleblowing above), years went by without further congressional action providing security for whistleblowers. Finally, in 1964 a law was written explicitly authorizing employees to testify against their employers, while also prohibiting retaliation for that testimony. The focus of Title VII of the Civil Rights Act is to criminalize discrimination in employment on the basis of race, color, religion, sex, or national origin (for details, see Discrimination and Affirmative Action, in this chapter). But it also includes wholesale whistleblower protections considerably broader than those found in later federal statues that apply generally to many different forms of businesses (also see Whistleblowing above).

Section 704(a) of Title VII states that it is illegal to discriminate against an employee or applicant because he has "*opposed* any practice made an unlawful employment practice...or because he has made a charge, testified, assisted, or *participated* in any manner in an investigation, proceeding, or hearing." (Emphasis added.) What is unusual here is the protection provided for two distinct kinds of whistleblowing. The **opposition clause** affords protection to individuals who simply voice their objections to what they perceive to be discriminatory practices, without becoming involved in the prosecution of such practices. This means that coworkers who express their support of individuals filing complaints with the Equal Employment Opportunity Commission need not fear reprisals. The opposition clause has been interpreted very broadly by the judiciary. For example, one court has held that it protected an employee who said that a collective bargaining agreement adversely effected women, but who did not say that the agreement violated Title VII (*Gifford v. Atchison, Topeka & Santa Fe Railway*, 685 F.2d 1149 [9th Cir. 1982]). In another case, the clause was used to reinstate a manager who had been fired for hiring a black man, even though he had made no statements whatever about his employer (*EEOC v. St. Anne's Hospital*, 664 F.2d 128 [7th Cir. 1981]).

The **participation clause** is more typical of whistleblower protection laws generally because it covers employees who are actively engaged in the process of bringing charges of discrimination against their employers. This clause has also been read by the courts as reaching a wide range of individuals involved in employers' improper conduct. Not only are those filing complaints against current employers included, so are those complaining about the practices of former employers (*Barela v. United Nuclear Corporation*, 462 F.2d 149 (10th Cir. [1972]). Even workers who *might* be called as witnesses in Title VII discrimination cases (*EEOC v. Plumber's Local 189*, 311 F. Supp. 464 [1970]) as well as the spouses of those filing complaints (*Kornbluth v. Stearns & Foster Company*, 73 F.R.D. 307 [1976]) are covered.

In 1986 the Supreme Court validated a thesis that some lower courts had been circulating for several years: Sexual harassment is a form of sex discrimination in violation of Title VII of the Civil Rights Act (*Meritor Savings v. Vinson*, 477 U.S. 57 [1986]. *Williams v. Saxbe*, 413 F. Supp 654 [1976], appears to be the first such finding. See Sexual Harassment, in this chapter, for details). Since that time, individuals blowing the whistle on sexual harassment have been one of the most frequent targets of retaliation. Both the opposition and participation clauses provide safeguards for employees filing a complaint of this nature.

***Pickering v. Board of Education*, 391 U.S. 563 (1968)** Marvin Pickering was a high school teacher in Township School District 205, Will County, Illinois. In September 1964 Pickering wrote a letter that was published in the local newspaper, severely criticizing the school board for its allocation of funds garnered from bond sales in 1961. He charged that the board had misled the community by utilizing a sizable portion of this money to finance the construction of athletic facilities and the operation of various athletic programs. He also claimed that the superintendent of schools had attempted to prevent teachers from opposing a second bond issue that had been defeated just before Pickering wrote his letter.

The board of education responded by firing Pickering. During the hearing subsequent to his dismissal (as required by Illinois law), the board made several allegations. Among other charges, it claimed that the statements contained in Pickering's letter were uniformly false, that these false statements would not only disrupt faculty discipline, they would also breed conflict and dissension throughout the community, and that Pickering had unfairly impugned the integrity and competence, and damaged the reputations of the board members and school administrators. Pickering's defense was that the dismissal was a violation of his First Amendment right to freedom of speech. However, the Illinois Supreme Court ruled that accepting a position in the public schools imposes a duty on an individual to refrain from making such statements about the administration of schools.

The Supreme Court reversed that decision. Justice Thurgood Marshall's majority opinion agreed that since Pickering's letter was directed at issues of legitimate public concern, his First Amendment rights had been violated by the dismissal. Furthermore, Marshall was unable to find any evidence that faculty discipline or harmony was undermined, or that there was any reason to believe that the community or the school system had been adversely affected in any substantial way. However, he was careful to point out that the free speech rights of public employees are not absolute: A citizen's interest in offering a public opinion must be balanced against the state's interest in the efficient operation of a public service.

Pickering has served as a precedent-setting case for the role of First Amendment freedom of expression as a safeguard against retaliation prompted by whistleblowing specifically, and against job dismissals generally. It was especially important at the time, as whistleblower protections were then confined to members of labor unions (as provided by the National Labor Relations Act; see above, Whistleblowing) and to those complaining of violations of Title VII of the Civil Rights Act (see above). *Pickering* added whistleblower protection for government workers, and seven years later, the Supreme Court extended that precedent to private sector contractors dealing with the federal government (*Holodnak v. Avco Corporation*, 423 U.S. 892 [1975]).

With the passage of a variety of federal and state statutes in the late 1970s and 1980s containing clauses protecting whistleblowers in both the public and private sectors, the influence of *Pickering* has diminished somewhat. Nonetheless, there are still thousands of workers and numerous complaints that are not covered by those statutes. For them, and in these cases, *Pickering* provides security (as does *Palmateer v. International Harvester Company*; see below). However, the implication of Justice Marshall's opinion is clear: The First Amendment shields those who complain about matters of public concern in a way that does not seriously disturb the functioning of the employment situation. And that is a crucial qualification.

Civil Service Reform Act of 1978, 5 U.S.C. various sections Until the enactment of the Civil Service Reform Act (CSRA), millions of people employed by the federal government had no protection against reprisals if they felt compelled to complain about government waste or about fraud committed by businesses providing goods and services to their federal employers. The False Claims Act did permit individuals to sue businesses that submitted false claims for payment to the government, and allowed plaintiffs to recover some portion of the damages; but until the 1986 amendments, the False Claims Reform Act, a federal employee pursuing such a claim had no protection against harassment, demotion, or even dismissal (see above).

Although the primary purpose of CSRA was to restructure the agencies responsible for administering the federal system of employment, as well as to provide procedures to ensure that federal employees were evaluated on their personal merit and not according to their political connections, it also instituted protections for employees disclosing illegal or improper government conduct. The act replaced the former Civil Service Commission with two new organizations. The administration of federal employees became the responsibility of the Office of Personnel Management. The Merit Systems Protection Board (MSPB or the Board) is charged with ensuring that the new merit system is followed by government agencies, and with providing security for whistleblowers.

The special counsel of the MSPB (an attorney and staff) investigates allegations of retaliation against whistleblowers, and petitions the Board to order a halt to the reprisals. The CSRA expressly forbids retaliation against employees who complain to supervisors, the special counsel, or to the inspector general of their particular agency about improper conduct. Any violation of law or regulation, any instance of mismanagement, waste of funds, abuse of authority, or serious threat to public health and safety are fair game for protest without fear of retribution. The special counsel also has the authority to initiate disciplinary proceedings against individuals who improperly discipline whistleblowers.

Employees are also entitled to take their cases directly to the MSPB. Any decision rendered by the Board, whether following an investigation by the special counsel or from an employee's petition, may be appealed through the U.S. Circuit Courts of Appeals. Legal remedies for wronged whistleblowers include reinstatement and the awarding of attorneys' fees (if the special counsel is not involved). Wrongdoers may be reprimanded or suffer dismissal and disbarment from federal civil service for up to five years.

***Wexler v. Greenburg*, 160 A.2d 430 (Pa. 1960)**   This decision by the Pennsylvania Supreme Court is one of the most significant trade secret cases because it specified criteria for determining both who owns a trade secret and when an employer is legally entitled to relief for the disclosure of that confidential information. The main figure in this dispute is a chemist named Alvin Greenburg. For eight years, Greenburg worked for Buckingham Wax Company, a floor care products manufacturer, eventually rising to the head of their product development and testing division. In this capacity, he analyzed the products of Buckingham's competitors—polishes, cleaners, sealants, preservatives—while developing new formulas and modifying old ones. Greenburg then left Buckingham and took a job as chief chemist for Brite Products, a floor care products retailer that had been supplied exclusively by Buckingham. Now that Greenburg was on board, Brite utilized his knowledge, acquired while he was at Buckingham, to manufacture its own products, and it soon closed its account with its old supplier. Buckingham filed suit to put a halt to the use of the formulas Greenburg had developed there, claiming that they were trade secrets that had been illegally obtained, and Brite had no right to use them.

The lower court decision held that Greenburg had violated a duty of confidentiality by disclosing the formulas to Brite Products. However, the state supreme court pointed out that Greenburg had not become aware of the formulas because his former employer had disclosed them to him; rather, Greenburg had created the formulas himself. This fact provides the crux of the decision. In order for there to be an obligation of confidentiality, two conditions must be satisfied: (1) an employee must be informed *by his or her employer* of a preexisting trade secret, and (2) the employee must acknowledge and use the trade secret, implying a promise to maintain confidentiality. This means that an employer is protected against the use of such information by others only when disclosure violates an obligation of confidentiality (or when it was obtained illegally, such as by theft, bribery, or industrial espionage, but this is not at issue here). Because condition (1) did not obtain, and because

Greenburg's merely apprising Buckingham of the new formulas he had developed could not be construed as implying a pledge of secrecy on his part, there was no duty of confidentiality to be violated. The trade secrets were Greenburg's property to do with as he wished.

***Carpenter v. United States*, 484 U.S. 19 (1987)** This is the definitive word to date from the high Court on a loyal employee's duty to keep certain information confidential and avoid conflicts of interest. It began in 1982 when R. Foster Winans started writing a column for the *Wall Street Journal* called *Heard on the Street*. Winans's column investigated various stocks and offered advice to readers on whether or not the securities discussed were a good investment. In a short time, the perceived quality and integrity of the column began to have some effect on market activity: Stocks that Winans said were a good investment seemed to rise in value, while those he cautioned against declined.

The *Journal* had an explicit policy that any information presented in *Heard on the Street* was the property of the newspaper and must be kept confidential prior to publication. Despite this rule, in October 1983 Winans and his roommate, David Carpenter, along with two stock brokers, Peter Brant and Kenneth Felis, devised a scheme to take advantage of the market information Winans had acquired in advance of its publication in the column. This allowed them to buy and sell securities based on the likely impact of the information subsequently published in the *Journal*. Over a four-month period, the conspirators realized $690,000 in profits on these transactions. Unfortunately for them, correlations were noticed between the trading on their accounts and the contents of various *Heard on the Street* articles, and the Securities and Exchange Commission (SEC) launched an investigation. In March 1984 the conspirators had a falling out, and Winans and Carpenter confessed to the SEC.

Although Winans was prosecuted by the SEC for insider trading (see Chapter 2: The Consumer—Finance, Selected Cases; Securities Exchange Act of 1934), the Court's decision provides a clear statement for employees of the judicial view of confidentiality and conflict of interest. The Supreme Court split four to four on this case, which has the effect of affirming the circuit court's judgment, and in any case, Justice Byron White's opinion in favor of the affirmation substantially agreed with the lower courts.

The district court and the Second Circuit Court of Appeals both held that Winans had violated a duty of confidentiality to his employer, the *Journal*, by misappropriating the market information and, in so doing, committed fraud against the newspaper as well. Using this confidential information for his personal gain put Winans in a conflict of interest with the *Journal* for two reasons. First, confidential information acquired in the course of conducting business is the property of the employer, who has an exclusive right to it; Winans appropriation of confidential information defeated this entitlement. Second, the *Journal*'s interest in Winans discharging his fiduciary duty by maintaining that confidentiality was thwarted when he failed to do so. The message is clear: Employees who use confidential information for their own benefit are engaged in a conflict of interest with their employers, and these employees are quite likely to be found legally liable for their conduct.

Whistleblower Protection Act of 1989, 5 U.S.C. §7701 According to the Civil Service Reform Act of 1978 (CSRA), the special counsel of the Merit Systems Protection Board (MSPB) has substantial investigative and prosecutorial powers to be exercised on behalf of whistleblowers employed by the federal government (see the entry for CSRA above). However, during the 1980s, the special counsel was often criticized for failing to investigate allegations of retaliation against whistleblowers, and for revealing the identities of several individuals who had attacked their employers, allowing these agencies to strike back at them. The Whistleblower Protection Act is intended to remedy these problems.

It does so, first, by imposing deadlines on the special counsel for the prosecution of whistleblower complaints, and requiring that the complaining employees be informed of the progress of the investigation. The special counsel must also submit an annual report to Congress detailing the number of complaints filed and how they were resolved. Moreover, there is a strict prohibition against revealing the identity of any whistleblower whose case is still pending; the only exceptions to this rule are when the revelation would prevent criminal activity or when failing to disclose would produce an imminent threat to public safety. The act further requires agencies that have been directed by the MSPB to pay damages to wronged employees to distribute that relief promptly, even though the case may still be working its way through the appeals process. Finally, whistleblowers who request transfers to other agencies in order to avoid reprisals are accommodated by the act.

References: Andrews, Edmund L. 1997. "European Court Backs Hiring Women to Correct Past Discrimination," *New York Times* Cybertimes (Nov. 12).

Baldwin, Tom. 1997. "Substance Abuse Checks Put to the Test in Maine," *Journal of Commerce and Commercial* (Mar. 14): 1B(2).

Ballam, Deborah A. 1995. "The Traditional View on the Origins of the Employment-At-Will Doctrine: Myth or Reality?" *American Business Law Journal* 33 (1): 1–50.

Barlow, Wayne E., Diane Hatch and Betty Southard Murphy. 1997. "Recent Legal Decisions Affect You." *Workforce* 76 (3) (March): 110.

"Big Companies May Boost the Risk of Employee Drug Use at Small Businesses," *Wall Street Journal* (May 13, 1997): pA1(W) pA1(E), col 5.

Birkner, Lawrence R. and Ruth K. Birkner. 1997. "Committment, Vision and Compliance In Occupational Health and Safety." *Occupational Hazards* 59 (2): 20–21.

Boatright, John. 1997a. *Ethics and the Conduct of Business.* 2d ed. Upper Saddle River, NJ: Prentice Hall.

———. 1997b. "Comparable Worth." In *The Encyclopedic Dictionary of Business Ethics* Malden, MA: Blackwell Publishers Inc.

Boler, Jean. 1998. (Boler is an attorney in private practice who specializes in class action employment law). Interview with author (Dienhart).

Borrie, Gordon. 1996. "Blowing the Whistle: Business Ethics and Accountability," *Political Quarterly* 67 (2): 141–150.

Botsko, Carleen A. and Robert C. Wells. 1994. "Government Whistleblowers: Crime's Hidden Victims." *The FBI Law Enforcement Bulletin* 63 (7): 17–21.

Bowers, Faye. 1997. "$10 Billion Suit Claims Boeing Produced 'Defective' Aircraft." *The Christian Science Monitor* 89 (234): 1.

Boxhill, Bernard R. 1978. "The Morality of Preferential Hiring." *Philosophy and Public Affairs* 7: 246–268.

Bravo, Ellen and Ellen Cassedy. 1992. *The 9–5 Guide to Combating Sexual Harassment.* New York: John Wiley & Sons, Inc.

Bucholz, Rogene. 1997. "Privacy." In *The Encyclopedic Dictionary of Business Ethics*. Malden, MA: Blackwell Publishers Inc.

Chlopecki, Mary and Ellen Duffy McKay. 1997. "The Dollar Impact of the 1991 Civil Rights Act." *HR Focus* 74 (9): 15.

Cohen, Warren. 1997. "The Long Road to a Model Workplace." *U.S. News and World Report* 122 (7) (Feb. 24): 57

Conference Board, The. 1998. http://www.ron-brown-award.org/ronbrown/ winners.html

Davidson, Dan. 1988. "Employee Testing: An Ethical Perspective." *Journal of Business Ethics* 7: 211–217.

DesJardins, Joseph R. 1985. "Fairness and Employment-at-Will." *Journal of Social Philosophy* 16: 31–38.

DesJardins, Joseph R. and John J. McCall. 1985. "A Defense of Employee Rights." *Journal of Business Ethics* 4: 367–376

Devine, Phillip. 1987. "Comparable Worth." *International Journal of Applied Ethics*. 3: 11–19.

Dienhart, John W. 1999. (forthcoming). *Institutions, Business, and Ethics*, New York: Oxford University Press.

Dillon, Sam. 1997. "U.S. Labor Forges Ties Across Mexican Border." *New York Times* CyberTimes (Dec. 20).

Duska, Ronald. 1997. "Whistle-blowing." In *The Encyclopedic Dictionary of Business Ethics*, Malden, MA: Blackwell Publishers Inc.

Dyer, Clare. 1996. "Changes Pose Threat to 10 Million." *The Guardian* (Mar. 8): 6.

Eckholm, Erik. 1998. "New China Leader Promises Reforms for Every Sector." *New York Times* (Mar. 20): A1.

Ezorsky, Gertude. 1991. *Racism and Justice: The Case for Affirmative Action*. Ithaca: Cornell University Press.

Feary, Vaughana Macy. 1997. "Sexual Harassment: Why the Corporate World Still Doesn't 'Get it'." In *Ethical Theory and Business*, Tom L. Beauchamp and Norman E. Bowie, eds., 5th ed. Upper Saddle River, NJ: Prentice Hall.

Flynn, Gillian. 1996. "Why at-Will Employment is Dying." *Personnel Journal* 75 (5): 123–126.

———. 1997. "A Pioneer Program Nurtures a Harassment Free Workplace." *Workforce* 76 (10): 38(6).

"Free at Last?" 1997. *The Economist* 40 (Mar. 8): 342 (8007).

Hasnas John. 1997. "Sexual Harassment." In *The Encycopedic Dictionary of Business Ethics*. Malden, MA: Blackwell Publishers Inc.

Hill, Judith M. 1987. "Pay Equity." *International Journal of Applied Philosophy* 3: 1–9.

Hume, David. 1748. *An Enquiry Concerning the Principals of Morals*. In *Hume's Moral and Political Philosophy*, Henry D. Aiken, ed. 1970. Darien, CN: Hafner Publishing Co.

Grcic, Joseph. 1997. "Worker Safety." In *The Encycopedic Dictionary of Business Ethics*. Malden, MA: Blackwell Publishers Inc.

Greenberg, Eric Rolfe. 1996. "Drug-testing now standard practice." *HR Focus* 73 (9): 24.

Groarke, Leo. 1990. "Affirmative Action as a Form of Restitution." *Journal of Business Ethics* 9: 207–213.

Hayek, F. A. 1994. *The Road to Serfdom*. Chicago: University of Chicago Press.

Henley, Jon, Alex Duval Smith, Sarah Boseley and David Hencke. 1997. "Drug Traces Suggest Drink Problem." *The Guardian* (Sept. 11): 2.

Johnson, Mark. 1993. *Moral Imagination: Implications of Cognitive Science for Ethics*. Chicago: University of Chicago Press.

Laabs, Jennifer J. 1997. "Cashing in on Safety," *Workforce* 76 (8) (Aug.): 53–57.

LaBar, Gregg 1997. "Contingent Worker Safety: A Full-Time Job in a Part-Time World." *Occupational Hazards* 59 (10): 92(6).

Lawrence, Anne T. 1993. "Johnson Controls and Protective Exclusion from the Workplace." In *Cases in Ethics and the Conduct of Business*, John Boatright, ed. 1995. Upper Saddle River, NJ: Prentice Hall.

Lee, Barbara A. 1989. "Something Akin to a Property Right: Protections for Job Security." *Business and Professional Ethics Journal* 8: 63–81.

Lindgren, J. Ralph. 1981. "The Irrelevance of Philosophical Treatments of Affirmative Action." *Social Theory and Practice* 7: 1–19.

Lipman, Ira A. 1995. "Drug Testing Is Vital In The Workplace." *USA Today* 123 (2596): 81–82.

Looney, Deane H. 1996. "Response to Fine, Reeves and Harney's Article on Employee Drug Testing." *Public Administration Review* 56 (3): 314–314.

Maitland, Ian. 1989. "Rights in the Workplace: A Nozickian Argument." *Journal of Business Ethics* 8 (12): 951–954.

"Mattel Sets Conduct Code for Suppliers." 1997. *New York Times*. CyberTimes (Nov. 20).

Miceli, M. P., Near, J. P., and Schwenk, C. R. 1991. "Who Blows the Whistle and Why?" *Industrial & Labor Relations Review* 45: 113–130.

Mill, John Stuart. 1859. *On Liberty*. In *The English Philosphers from Bacon to Mill*, Edwin A. Burtt, ed. New York: The Modern Library, 1939.

Moorman, Jane. 1995. "The Two Year Rule Is Shown the Door." *The Guardian* (Aug 12): 2.2.

National Bureau of Economic Research. 1997. "The Economic Analysis of Substance Abuse," *NBER Reporter* (summer): 22(2).

Nickel, James W. 1978–1979. "Is There a Human Right to Employment?" *Philosophical Forum* 10: 149–170.

Nozick, Robert. 1974. *The State, Anarchy, and Utopia*. New York: Basic Books.

Paine, Lynn Sharp. 1994a. "Managing for Organizational Integrity." *Harvard Business Review* (March–April).

Paine, Lynn Sharp and J. Katz. 1994b. "Levi Strauss & Co.: Global Outsourcing." Harvard Case Study #395127.

Paul, Ellen Frankel. 1989. *Equity And Gender: The Comparable Worth Debate*. New Brunswick: Transaction Books.

Phillips, Michael. 1991. "Preferential Hiring and the Question of Competence." *Journal of Business Ethics* (Feb.): 161–163.

Pojman, Louis P. 1992. "The Moral Status of Affirmative Action." *Public Affairs Quarterly* 6: 181–206.

Polter, Julie. 1997. "M-I-C-K-E-Y, Kathie Lee and Me," *Sojourners* 26 (2): 12(2).

Purdy, Laura M. 1984. "In Defense of Hiring Apparently Less Qualified Women." *Journal of Social Philosophy* 15: 26–33.

Quintanilla, Carl. 1997. "Chances Are If You Are White Collar, You Aren't Being Drug-Tested." *The Wall Street Journal* 165 (Aug. 19): A1(W) A1(E).

Radin, Tara J. and Patricia H. Werhane. 1996. "The Public/Private Distinction and the Political Status of Employment." *American Business Law Journal* (Special Issue on Business Ethics) 34 (2): 245–260.

Rafalko, Robert J. 1994. "Remaking the Corporation." *Journal of Business Ethics* 13: 625–636.

Richardson, Margaret R. 1997. "Comprehensive Evaluations: Safety's Annual Checkup." *Occupational Hazards* 59 (3): 51–53.

Robson Ann P. and John M. Robson Mill, eds. 1994. *Sexual Equality: Writings by John Stuart Mill, Harriet Taylor Mill, and Helen Taylor*. Toronto: University of Toronto Press.

Rodriguez, Americo Pla. 1995. "The Protection of Workers' Privacy: the Situation in the Americas." *International Labour Review* 134 (3): 297–313.

Sassen, Robert F. 1976. "Affirmative Action and the Principle of Equality." *Studies in the Philosophy of Education* 9: 275–295.

"Schoolgirls as Sex Toys." *New York Times* 146 (4)(April 6, 1997): E2(N), E2(L), 1.

Sethi, Prakash S. 1984. *The False Promise of the Japanese Miracle*. Boston: Pitman.

Shrage, Laurie. 1987. "Some Implications Of Comparable Worth." *Social Theory and Practice* 13: 77–102.

Simon, Herbert. 1995. "Organizations and Markets." *Journal of Public Administration Research and Theory* 5 (3): 273–93.

Smith, Elliot Blair. 1997. "Fluor Settles Whistle-Blower Suit for $8.4 Million," *The Orange County Register* 623 (June 23): B1091.

Sowell, Thomas. 1990. *Preferential Policies: An International Perspective*. New York: William and Morrow & Company, Inc.

Sueyoshi, Akiko. 1997. "Breaking the Stereotypes." *UNESCO Courier* 6 (4)(July–August): 6–10.

Thayer, Nate. 1995. "Blowing the Whistle: Dissenters Slam Rights Record Ahead Of Aid Forum." *Far Eastern Economic Review* 158 (11) (March 16): 28.

Wall Street Journal. 1997b. On-line publication, Nov. 8.

Waluchow, Wil. 1988. "Pay Equity: Equal Value To Whom?" *Journal of Business Ethics* 7: 185–189.

Werhane, Patricia H. 1983. "Accountability and Employee Rights," *International Journal of Applied Ethics* 1: 15–26.

———. 1994. "Moral Imagination and the Search for Ethical Decision Making in Management," Presented at the University of Virginia's Ruffin Lectures, 1994.

Williams, Patricia. 1997. "Anita Hill's Second Act," *Harper's Bazaar* 3431 (4): 220(4).

Wood, Donna 1994. *Business and Society.* 2d ed. New York: Harper Collins.

CONTEMPORARY ETHICAL ISSUES

Chapter 5:
The Environment

E very product offered in commerce—every article of clothing, every automobile and house,
every ear of corn and slab of steak, every piece of
paper and computer disc, every glass of beer and
gallon of gas—was taken from the earth. The items
that are the stock and trade of business are ham-
mered and crafted out of the raw materials available on this planet for human consumption. This
very often requires the suffering and death of many
living things. Moreover, in the process of fashion-
ing these materials into consumer goods, and in
the process of using them and using them up, they
are in various ways returned to the environment
from whence they came. And in those processes,
environmental problems are created.

Introduction

Pollution and Waste

Air Pollution and Toxic Waste   The world runs
on fossil fuels: coal, natural gas, petroleum products. Billions of tons of these substances are
extracted from the earth every year, processed by

large corporations and by governments, and sold to consumers for many billions of dollars. These substances are then burned to produce energy. The burning of fossil fuels lights, heats, and cools our homes, offices, and factories, energizes our cars, trains, trucks, ships, and planes, and powers all manner of machines, from the metal press stamping out car fenders to the circular saw cutting the boards to frame a home. But the burning also produces enormous quantities of two dangerous gases: sulfur dioxide (SO_2) and nitrogen oxides (NO_x). During 1993, the United States generated about 45,000 tons of SO_2 and NO_x (Environmental Protection Agency 1995). That works out to one quarter of a million pounds every single day in this country alone. Sulfur dioxide and nitrogen oxides are highly corrosive gases that bond readily to particles of dust and smoke, allowing them to be transported long distances in the atmosphere. The gases can cause serious lung and respiratory tract damage to humans and animals, and are the major contributors to acid rain, which kills trees, vegetation, and aquatic life.

The processes required to manufacture consumer goods employ a wide variety of toxic chemicals, and produce a great deal of waste that must be disposed of; much of this waste is also toxic. About 70,000 different chemicals are in everyday use around the world, with up to 1,000 new ones added every year. The harmful effects of these chemicals, to humans, animals, and the environment, are often not immediately known. For example, pesticides and herbicides are used extensively in agriculture and in food processing, yet many of these poisons were used for years before their carcinogenic effects were well enough understood to ban their manufacture entirely—DDT is probably the most notable instance.

The chemical compound known as dioxin causes immune system damage, infertility, cancer, and death. Dioxin is a by-product of chlorine, and it is produced whenever some industry uses or burns chlorine or chlorine-derived products. One of the largest users of chlorine is the paper and pulp industry; vast quantities of chlorine are utilized in the bleaching process. Incinerating paper thus generates dioxin. The most common chlorine-based product is the plastic-like material called PVC (polyvinyl chlorine); the manufacturing process of PVC releases dioxin, as does any burning of the material. Ordinary plastic is perhaps the most common material used in the manufacture of consumer goods. Yet three of the key ingredients in plastic production are clearly dangerous to human health and well-being. Acrylonitrile is a carcinogen that releases the toxic chemical hydrogen cyanide when plastic is burned; benzene causes anemia and leukemia; and vinyl chloride causes cancer, liver damage, and birth defects.

Solid Waste and Water Pollution Combined, more than 22,000 generators in the various manufacturing industries, and in agriculture and mining, produce about 235 million tons of solid waste every year in the process of running their businesses and providing consumers with merchandise (Environmental Protection Agency 1994). Where does all this waste go? There are some 220,000 industrial waste dumps in this country, and most of them are unlined surface impounds. In addition, there are thousands of *wildcat* *dumps*—unregulated, often abandoned sites—most of which have been created by firms in the chemical and petroleum industries.

After we are through using these consumer goods supplied by business and industry, we throw them away. Where is "away"? Of course these items don't just vanish into thin air; most persist in more or less their original form, but now they are stored in the garbage. But what then is "the garbage"? Typically, the final resting place of our waste is a landfill or a body of water: We bury our garbage in the earth or at sea. We produce enormous amounts of waste material. Over 200 million tons of solid waste are generated every year by people living in America's cities; that's about five pounds per person every single day (Environmental Protection Agency 1994). About half of this total is paper products, glass, and plastic. The municipal dumps that are the ultimate fate for many of these items are significant sources of pollution. For instance, old car batteries and TV picture tubes exude lead, and old refrigerators, stoves, and other appliances release polychlorinated biphenyls (PCBs), extremely toxic organic compounds.

Dumping waste and sewage into bodies of water is an age-old method of ridding ourselves of garbage, and so it is one of our oldest pollution problems. Indeed, the first federal law regulating waste disposal concerned discharge into the navigable waters of the nation (the Rivers and Harbors Act of 1899, see below, Environmental Law: Introduction). Untreated human waste and sewage are a significant contributor to water pollution, but the majority of the problem can be traced to business and industry. Food processing, the lumber industry, and animal feedlots generate very large amounts of organic wastes. When discharged into water, these wastes use up all the available oxygen and render the water uninhabitable for aquatic life. Coal mining operations contaminate local waters with sulfuric acid and iron particles. Metal processing plants use acid to scrub metals, and use water to wash off the acid, which is then flushed into streams and rivers. Many industrial manufacturing processes, such as paper production, and the electric power industry use enormous amounts of water as a coolant; the heated water is then pumped back into its source. All these discharges also kill the fish and most of the other complex organisms inhabiting the waters, and prevent life from regenerating there.

Agricultural and industrial water pollution also presents a more immediate threat to human health. Zinc refineries and certain fertilizers used in agriculture produce cadmium, a heavy metal that even at low concentrations can pose serious medical problems when it contaminates a water source: a degenerative bone disease, heart disease, or vomiting and diarrhea at a minimum. Another extremely toxic heavy metal, mercury, has been used as a fungicide, a pesticide, and is a by-product of the combustion of fossil fuels. It has found its way into water supplies and aquatic life through runoff and leaching into ground water. Mercury's effects on humans are disastrous: brain damage, paralysis, and death. PCBs were widely used in this country for many years as a coolant in electrical transformers, as lubricants, and as flame retardants. Their manufacture and use were banned in the United States in 1979, but they don't just go away and other countries continue to produce them. PCBs are accumulating in the world's oceans, especially in coastal areas, and are moving through the food chain; minute amounts are lethal to humans.

Animals in Business

Animals as Food Products   After enduring varying degrees of confinement and coercion, a vast number of animals are killed and their bodies are crafted or carved into consumer products. Every pork chop and hamburger, steak and sausage, surf and turf, as well as every breast, thigh, or drumstick bought and sold in commerce, and all fur, leather, and suede came from an animal that was killed in order to supply consumers with that product. Many animals are killed. In 1995 about 165 million cattle, calves, sheep, lambs, and hogs went to a slaughterhouse in the United States, along with 7.2 billion chickens and 280 million turkeys (American Meat Institute 1996). This works out to about 240 animals every second of every day. Global figures are unknown. A brief outline of some of the business practices involving these animals should make the moral problems clearer.

Most cows used for meat are born on a ranch or beef farm, and spend one or two years with the herd, primarily fending for themselves on pasture or rangeland. At some point during this period, the cattle are branded in order to identify them as the property of the ranch, dehorned so that they won't spear each other or the cowboys, and all males are castrated in order to prevent unwanted pregnancies; the use of painkillers during these procedures is absent or rare. When the rancher believes the time is right, the animals are rounded up and shipped without food or water in large, tightly packed tractor-trailers to a feedlot for "finishing."

The average feedlot may hold as many as 25,000 cows in a series of corrals edged by a concrete feed trough. Here, they are fed a high calorie diet consisting mainly of corn and soy meal, usually laced with a growth promotant to accelerate the process of bringing them to the market weight of about 1000 pounds. Some beef producers buy "feeder calves" of four to six months old and ship them immediately to feedlots for fattening. When the market weight is attained, the cows are loaded on the trucks once again and transported to the slaughterhouse. Upon arrival, the animals are driven single file down a corridor into a restraint device; once immobilized, they are stunned by a mechanical blow to the head. Death is then accomplished by decapitation or evisceration (Mason and Singer 1990).

The methods and structure of pig farming vary widely, according to whether the operation is a small, family-owned farm of less than 100 animals, or a huge, corporate farm that processes hundreds of thousands of pigs each year. Like all animal agriculture, there has been a clear trend in the last 20 years or so toward concentrating the business into a number of large corporations. Due to this trend, most pigs spend their entire lives—about six months—in large, warehouse-like buildings that are designed to feed, water, and remove the manure of thousands of animals automatically. In order to control their growth and development, and to facilitate this automation, some degree of confinement is required, ranging from complete detainment for each individual in a narrow stall, to holding areas confining several pigs at a time.

Pregnant sows spend the 16-week gestation period in stalls or larger pens; the last week of the pregnancy and the first two or three weeks after the birth of the piglets, the sow is restricted to the tight quarters of a farrowing stall, where she cannot walk or turn around. Newborn pigs are injected with antibiotics, their "needle" teeth are clipped, their tails removed, and their ears notched for identification. After weaning at about two weeks, males are castrated, and all pigs are taken to the automated growing building. They remain here for about 20 weeks, and are then shipped off to the slaughterhouse. Here, the pigs are typically rendered unconscious by an electric current, and then killed by bleeding or evisceration (Mason and Singer 1990).

Chickens begin their brief lives in a hatchery; once they break out of their eggs, their fate is a function of the facility in which they find themselves. If it is for egg production, males must first be separated from females. The males are usually killed: they may be decapitated, asphyxiated with carbon dioxide, piled into heavy-duty plastic bags and suffocated, or simply ground up alive as meal for other animals. The beaks of the females are immediately cut off so they will not peck and injure one another in the crowded conditions of a fully automated "layer house" holding as many as 80,000 birds. There, the laying hens are confined to 12-inch by 18-inch cages, stacked in tiers, typically three to five birds per cage. Because light increases egg production, they are exposed to very long periods without darkness. After a year to 18 months, their productivity decreases substantially and the hens are killed.

"Broiler" chickens, mostly males, are raised in large warehouses with populations of about 25,000; they too are debeaked and their toes are removed, both measures to reduce injuries to one another. At little more than six weeks old, they reach their market weight of about four pounds. The chickens are then packed alive into crates and shipped to the slaughterhouse. Here, they are hung by their feet from shackles on a conveyor line; after a dip in an electrically charged water tank, intended to stun them to unconsciousness, their necks are passed over a rotating circular blade and they bleed to death (Mason and Singer 1990).

Animals in Consumer Products Testing Business uses animals as a resource to serve human needs and interests in another way. Every year, numerous corporations subject millions of animals to a variety of laboratory procedures in order to test the safety, effectiveness, and toxicity of many different drugs, consumer goods, and medical equipment and procedures. Many animals are also used to gather biological and psychological data, and to serve as teaching tools in medical and veterinary schools. The exact numbers exploited in these ways vary widely, depending on the source consulted; Estimates can go as high as 70 million and as low as 20 million. The disparity is primarily explained by the fact that the Animal Welfare Act (see below, Environmental Law, Selected Cases) does not require facilities to report the number of mice and rats used, so their numbers are estimates and guesses. The most accurate figure is probably somewhere in between, at around 30 million (Orlans 1993).

It is well accepted, however, that biomedical research and education account for about 80 percent of all animals used for testing and experimentation in this country. Our focus here is on the remaining 20 percent, almost all of which are enlisted for the testing of consumer products. Other than being marketed as consumer products themselves in the form of food for human consumption, this is the primary purpose for animals in business. At the lowest estimate, corporate America uses at least 4 million animals per year for this purpose, or 14 million according to the high figure; virtually all of these are killed shortly after the end of the experimentation.

Of these animals, perhaps 80 percent are mice and rats, and about 15 percent are rabbits, hamsters, and guinea pigs. Birds, dogs, and cats comprise most of the remainder; occasionally cows and pigs are put to use. Primates account for only about 1 percent of test subjects because they are the most expensive animal to use for this end. These animal subjects are exposed to many different household goods, including a wide variety of cosmetics, such as eye shadow, mascara, blush, nail polish, suntan lotion, deodorant, cologne, shaving cream, hairspray, and mouthwash; and numerous cleaners, such as dish, laundry, and hand soap, glass and oven cleaners, toothpaste, shampoo, air freshener, and floor and furniture polish. The intention behind the exposure is to produce results that will help prevent or treat human illness or injury. Typically, the testing proceeds by introducing these substances into or onto the bodies of the subject animals in order to determine either the toxicity or the lethality (acute toxicity) of the substance. A toxicity test is usually designed to measure the tissue damage caused by a particular substance, while a lethality test determines the dosage level required to induce death in the animal.

Two of the most common toxicity tests were developed by John Draize, a scientist working for the Food and Drug Administration in the 1940s. In the Draize Eye Irritancy test, a liquid, flake, granule, or powdered substance is placed in a rabbit's eye, and the effects of the substance are observed and recorded at regular intervals, typically 24, 48, and 72 hours, and at four and seven days. The other eye serves as the control. The rabbits are usually restrained in stocks or boxes from which only their heads protrude, thus preventing them from scratching at their eyes and compromising the test; their eyelids are held open with clips. Rabbits are especially appropriate subjects for the Draize test because they have no tear ducts from which tears would flow and dilute the substance, which would also compromise the test.

Draize also developed a skin irritancy test, commonly administered to rabbits as well. In this procedure, the hair on the backs of the animals is shaved and the skin is slightly abraded. The substance to be tested is then put on a piece of gauze and taped in place on the abrasion; the entire trunk of the rabbit is then wrapped in some impermeable material, such as rubberized cloth. After a period of 24 hours, the wrapping is removed and the lab technicians observe and record the effects of the substance on the rabbits' skin. The wrapping is then replaced and further observations made after two more days; another round of testing will typically follow on previously unexposed areas of skin (Zurlo 1994).

The most widely applied acute toxicity test is the so-called LD-50, or lethal dose for 50 percent. The development of this procedure has been traced to J. W. Trevan, a British pharmacologist. In 1927 Trevan was attempting to standardize the potency of some highly toxic drugs, notably digitalis, insulin, and diphtheria toxin. He came up with the idea of injecting groups of rats and mice with various doses of the drugs to see exactly how much would kill half of a test group; that lethal dose could be then precisely measured and designated as the level of acute toxicity. Over the years, as chemicals came to dominate so many aspects and products of our industrialized society, the LD-50 test was adopted as the standard measure of acute toxicity.

The standard procedure for this test has as many as 100 or more animals exposed to the test substance by oral ingestion or inhalation. Oral ingestion is the most common method and rats are the most common test subject. Scientists make initial estimates of the toxicity range of the substance, and then varying doses are administered to groups of animals until 50 percent of one group dies. These dead animals are then autopsied to determine the cause of death. After two weeks, the surviving animals are killed and examined for further data on the effects of the test substance (Zurlo 1994).

The use of animals in business thus appears to cause a great deal of pain, suffering, and death. Is that a moral problem? Do human interests rule the day here? Whose interests count, and why? How much do they count?

Business and Its Responsibilities

This litany of the harmful effects of business and industry on humans and other living things raises a number of interesting questions. The most immediate one is whether corporations have moral or legal obligations to avoid causing these harmful consequences, or at least to produce *less* harmful ones. As we will see below in Environmental Law, all branches of the federal government have answered the legal dimension of this question with an emphatic "yes," though somewhat qualified in the case of animals. Lawmakers and judges have created a plethora of legal responsibilities that business must fulfill. Right now, our concern is with the *moral* responsibilities of business regarding the environment.

Some have denied that business has any such moral duties. Norman Bowie, for one, has argued that the environmental responsibilities of business are confined to those the law imposes, though he adds that corporations are morally required not to obstruct environmental legislation (Bowie 1990). Others have been quick to repudiate this notion. W. Michael Hoffman has pointed out that, due to the profound impact corporations have on the environment, and the vast intellectual and material resources they can muster to address these problems, business does indeed have moral responsibilities in this area (Hoffman 1991). Today, it is safe to say that there is a great deal of agreement among business persons, scholars, and citizens alike that corporations do have moral obligations to practice business in a manner that at least minimizes harm to the environment and to animals. This view presupposes that a business can have moral and social responsibilities that go beyond, or are independent of, what the law requires. As we saw in Chapter 3: The Corporation, there are good reasons to hold that this is the case.

There is much debate about how corporations are to minimize environmental harms, and what is the proper role of government regulation and public opinion in these determinations. For example, hazardous waste cannot be totally eliminated in a modern, industrialized society, and it will not simply disappear, so where do we put it? The standard answer is some version of the NIMBY reply ("not in my backyard"). The next question then concerns the equitable distribution of the burdens associated with a hazardous waste site. But the more fundamental philosophical question asks: burdens to *whom*? Whose interests are at stake and do they really *matter*, from the moral point of view?

Or consider the notion of *sustainable development*. This is one of the most popular ideas in discussions of business and the environment today. Roger Burritt and Patricia McCreight define sustainable development as "attempting to get industry to perceive the environment as an asset—one to be nurtured, one to maintain, one to invest in, one to protect for present and future generations." (Burritt and McCreight 1998: 48). The definition suggests that nature is simply a resource or tool, an *asset* to be wisely exploited for the benefit of people living today and in the future. Is this all the nonhuman world is worth? Similarly, the International Chamber of Commerce has written a Business Charter for Sustainable Development. This document lists a number of principles that are intended to promote this goal. The first states that "Corporate priority [is]…to establish policies, programs, and practices for conducting operations in an environmentally sound manner." Other principles include "To develop and provide products or services that have no undue environmental impact" and "To educate, train, and motivate employees to conduct their activities in an environmentally responsible manner" (Willums and Goluke 1992).

Who exactly are the intended beneficiaries of acting responsibly in this way? Why should the effects of business on the environment be sensible and appropriate? Setting aside the issue of just what an "undue" impact is and what environmental soundness signifies, the obvious answer to these questions is, again, these policies promote human well-being. And again, the deeper question of moral philosophy concerns whether or not humans are the *only* beings to be considered here. If so, why? What is required in order to be worthy of respect, a holder of moral rights, to be more than just a thing to be used? After all, air and water pollution, hazardous waste, and toxic chemicals also adversely affect wild animals, plants, and entire ecosystems. Do corporations have responsibilities to *them* as well? And if so, what about the legions of domestic animals who are confined and killed, or forced to undergo painful experiments? Should business strive to avoid harming nonhuman beings for their own sake, or simply as a means to benefit people?

For moral philosophers like us, these are penetrating and fascinating issues. Yet business is about commerce, profit, money. Though, as we have suggested, there is widespread agreement that business is not simply about money, our study of business ethics can no more ignore economic issues here, than we can in discussing any other area of corporate practice. So certain economic matters must be addressed in this chapter also, such as these: Because less harmful processing and manufacturing can be accomplished with various pollution abatement devices, should business be required to pay for these devices in order to discharge their moral and legal obligations? Should consumers pay for them? Or should business simply pay for the right to pollute? Essentially, the question here is just this: Can pollution problems be solved by the operation of free markets? Moreover, the use of animals is a prominent and quite lucrative aspect of commerce. Improving the lives of these animals costs money, and ending such uses would cost jobs and possibly jeopardize human safety. Could such radical changes really be worth it?

Environmental Ethics

When business activity produces pollution or depletes resources, resulting in harm to people, there is little doubt that something needs to be done about it, and very soon. As the scope of business and industrial pollution mushroomed, and the extent of its adverse effects became widely known in the 1960s, this sense of moral urgency spurred Congress into writing a vast amount of environmental legislation, imposing standards on corporations and providing penalties for violating them (see below, Environmental Law). The justification of this regulation of corporations is found primarily in a moral and political demand to stop or at least reduce these harmful effects on people, not only for the good of the community now and in the future, but also because citizens are entitled to air and water that does not deteriorate their health and well-being. The presupposition, the unquestioned assumption, of these principles is that human persons, collectively and individually, have a very important standing or status before the law. The main questions to be puzzled over are basically practical ones, such as how this good is to be effectively and fairly realized, or economic ones concerning how much clean air and water are worth, and how the abatement devices are to be paid for (see also below, Environmental Economics). It is simply given that people have **legal standing**.

Introduction

The great significance of this status is that it gives people an entitlement to positive action on their behalf, a claim to action that promotes their interests. Public policy is then constructed and political institutions are arranged in order to consider those interests, sometimes as of paramount importance, and to require some positive action. To consider people in this way is to attribute **legal standing** to them: this is to say that people have legally protected interests that can be injured by the actions or failures to act on the part of others. A *legal remedy* attempts to heal the injury by awarding money or other property, and by punishing the wrongdoer. To have legal standing is synonymous with having legal rights.

To illustrate the role of legal standing and to prepare ourselves for the moral point ahead, consider for a moment the famous environmental case of *Sierra Club v. Morton*, decided by the Supreme Court in 1972 (for more details, see Environmental Law, Selected Cases, below). Members of the Sierra Club attempted to stop the construction by Walt Disney Enterprises of a ski resort in the Sierra Nevada mountains of California. A majority of the Court ruled against the Club members because they *lacked* standing to sue: They had not shown how the development would injure any of their membership by defeating a legally protected interest. Had they shown this, the interests of a small group of individuals may well have prevailed over a large corporation.

Although the Sierra Club did not win its case, Justice William O. Douglas's dissent from the majority addressed the core philosophical and legal issue: the nature of legal standing. He contended that if the Sierra Club had no standing to sue, then wilderness *itself* could have legal standing with a legally protected interest not to be injured, polluted, or otherwise despoiled. The legal remedy would be to clean up the pollution, return the effected area to its natural state, or prevent development in the first place. Yet how could inanimate, nonconscious things have *interests*?

Douglas was strongly influenced in his dissent by a long, rather hastily prepared essay by University of Southern California Professor of Legal Philosophy Christopher Stone. In *Should Trees Have Standing?* Stone observed that to have legal standing is to "*count* jurally—to have a legally recognized worth and dignity in [one's] own right, and not merely as a means to benefit [others]" (Stone 1974: 11). He went on to argue that natural objects like trees, rivers, and ecosystems should count in this way because they have wants and needs that can be thwarted by human activity; this damage constitutes an injury to *them*. People could represent the interests of natural objects just as they represent children and the mentally disabled who are not competent to represent themselves, though they undoubtedly have legally protected interests (Stone 1974).

Both Douglas's opinion and Stone's essay garnered a fair amount of notoriety among those concerned with environmental affairs, but the idea that natural objects have legal standing has never been taken seriously by the law. Nonetheless, about the same time that Douglas and Stone were writing, philosophers began in earnest to consider the very similar notion of **moral standing**.

Moral Standing   To trace the analogy with legal standing, we can say that to have moral standing is to *morally* count. English philosopher G. J. Warnock, among the first to investigate the issue, defines those with moral standing as those "hav[ing] a claim to be considered by rational agents to whom moral principles apply" (Warnock 1971: 148). By *rational agent*,

Warnock means a **moral agent**: These are persons who know the difference between right and wrong, and can act accordingly. In most basic terms, the moral principles that apply to agents require treating those who have moral standing with an attitude of respect. This attitude acknowledges that those with moral standing are more than mere things to use. Minimally, this would require telling the truth, keeping promises made, and refraining from causing harm through coercion, deception, or producing pain (Warnock 1971).

A metaphor might be useful here. Moral standing is rather like an umbrella. An umbrella is a protective device constructed of some impermeable substance, shielding those underneath it from inclement weather; these inclemencies are deflected by the barrier. Think of moral standing as a kind of *moral* umbrella, one constructed of various moral principles, such as "tell the truth," or "do not harm." These principles provide protection from "inclement" human action; they deter invasions of the interests of someone ensconced underneath the moral barrier by requiring moral agents to be honest and avoid hurting that individual, among other things. To have moral standing is to stand under this umbrella and enjoy the benefits of a shield against other people who might rain on your parade.

So who is standing under the moral umbrella? The question is not only profoundly interesting philosophically, it is of great practical significance as well. First, it is crucial for moral agents to know to whom they owe various duties of respect and honesty, of nonviolence and beneficence. In order to act as a moral being—as one concerned to do the right thing, to do right by others—a moral agent needs to know who are the beneficiaries of these obligations. As a corporate moral agent, a business cannot take effective measures to avoid harming others without a full understanding of precisely what others it would be morally wrong to harm.

Also, the answer to the question is obviously crucial for those beneficiaries. When you stand under the moral umbrella you are owed concern and consideration as an individual worthy of respect. To put it another way, you have a *right* to this respect. This is a very good position to occupy. Those without moral standing can be kicked around, used and abused, and moral agents need not fear impropriety, guilt, blame, or punishment. On the other hand, your moral standing allows you to enjoy the benefits of moral principles that constrain agents and, at least to some extent, guide them toward serving your personal interests.

The problem of identifying those who have moral standing is a relatively new one for philosophical contemplation. Prior to the 1970s moral philosophy at the normative level had been almost entirely devoted to sorting out various decision-making procedures for arriving at morally correct action: How should we conduct ourselves in our relations with others? It was simply assumed that the "others" here are other humans. But what exactly is it about humans, or any other sorts of beings, that identifies them as having moral standing? Philosophers have devoted a great deal of attention to this question over the last 30 years, and it resides at the core of environmental ethics.

The traditional, though usually implicit, answer to the question was that possessing the capacity of *rationality* is the essential requirement for having moral standing. This capacity is at once both a necessary and sufficient condition to identify a being worthy of respect and consideration, one who has moral rights. This special ability to reason not only served to distinguish the morally worthy from the morally worthless, but it also specified the identity of those with moral standing, and those without it, in a very rigid manner. It seemed clear to all who reflected on the matter that only humans are rational.

Historically then, philosophy began to reflect on this core issue from the perspective of respect for individual rights. As time went on, through the call and response of debate and discussion, the moral vision of philosophers began to expand from here, and other morally salient features were championed. Tracing the course of this dialogue will provide an illuminating survey of a problem situated at the foundations of ethics. As we will see, three of our ethical points of view for moral decision making presuppose distinctive conceptions of *whose* rights and interests must be respected and considered, conceptions that have also been expanded.

Respecting Dignity and Rights: Intrinsic Value

The first explicit statement of the view that rationality is both necessary and sufficient for moral standing is from the eighteenth-century German philosopher, Immanuel Kant. In his *Fundamental Principles of the Metaphysics of Morals*, he wrote

> Now, I say, man and, in general, any rational being exists as an end in himself and not merely as a means to be arbitrarily used by this or that will. In all his actions, whether they are directed to himself or to other rational beings, he must always be regarded at the same time as an end…. Beings who…are not rational beings, have only a relative worth as means and are therefore called "things"; on the other hand, rational beings, are designated "persons," because their nature indicates that they are ends in themselves, that is, as something that must not be used merely as a means. Such a being is thus an object of respect…(Kant 1785: II, §48).

In this passage, Kant distinguishes persons from things according to their rational capacities; Rational beings have "absolute worth" as "ends in themselves." To count in this way is to have a value that is not reducible to one's usefulness, a special worth and dignity that must be recognized by others. This special worth is called **intrinsic value**, a value one has for one's own sake, as an end. Intrinsic value contrasts with **extrinsic value**, or the value something has as a tool or a resource. Nonrational beings have only extrinsic value, according to how useful they are for serving our ends. The intrinsically valuable have a worth that goes well beyond any usefulness. The appropriate attitude toward a being with intrinsic value is respect. To have intrinsic value is thus to have moral standing, and for many philosophers, both concepts are synonymous with having moral rights.

In his *Lectures on Ethics*, Kant in effect states that animals have no moral standing; since they are not rational, we have no duties directly *to them*; our duties are owed only to those with intrinsic value. We may be required not to hurt animals, but that can only be because we have duties to their human owners not to damage their property (Kant 1782). Although Kant says that "any rational being" has intrinsic value, his vision of moral standing is usually described as **anthropocentric**: It is centered on or confined exclusively to humans. The implications of Kant's theory for the conduct of corporations might be described as business as usual. Business practices regarding normal, adult consumers are the focus of moral appraisal, and our concern for animals or the environment is merely instrumental to our concern for human well-being.

What is rationality? The concept, like many, has been voluminously analyzed by philosophers, but in simplest terms we can say that rationality includes such high-order cognitive capacities as the ability to reason from particular cases to universal rules, to apply rules to new and novel situations, and to solve abstract problems through the manipulation of symbols; further, these abilities require a well-developed language. To take an elementary example, only a rational being could understand a general moral principle, say, "lying is wrong," recognize a particular case of lying, and draw the conclusion that it would be wrong to tell a lie here.

Although rationality has been regarded by many as definitive of moral standing and required for moral rights holding, it has an obvious problem: It leaves nonrational *humans* morally unaccounted for. Infants and children, at least until they reach some more advanced age, are not rational in this morally loaded sense. Neither are severely mentally disabled humans of any age, those afflicted with serious mental dysfunctions such as Alzheimer's disease or schizophrenia, and certainly not those who are comatose. What about them? Do they have no protections afforded by the moral umbrella? Is it morally permissible to use them as tools for our ends?

Most people would quickly answer "no." Then what gives children and the mentally impaired moral standing? Perhaps these nonrational humans have moral rights simply because they are human: Being a member of the species *Homo sapiens* entitles one to moral consideration. However, this answer also raises a serious problem. Peter Singer, Professor of Philosophy at Monash University in Australia, has argued that selecting species membership as the qualification for moral standing is no different from appealing to race or sex for the same purpose. After all, the racist and the sexist claim that a morally arbitrary feature of humans is indicative of moral importance: Being of a certain race or sex is supposed to bring special value, privileges, and priorities with it. But why? Especially if one considers that the matter of one's race or sex is something over which one has no control, placing such weight upon them seems to be quite unfair and of no moral significance. For Singer, and others, this moral irrelevance applies to species as well, and he identifies **speciesism** as another form of bigotry (Singer 1990).

Interests Many philosophers abandon rationality as the key to moral standing and select some other feature or features. In an early discussion of the moral standing of animals, University of Arizona Professor of Philosophy Joel Feinberg argued that we have duties to animals simply because they have *interests* that can be promoted or harmed by our actions. By interests, he meant that animals have certain mental states, such as "conscious wishes, desires, hopes; or urges or impulses, or unconscious drives, aims or goals; or latent tendencies, direction of growth, and natural fulfillments" (Feinberg 1974: 49). For Feinberg, rationality is *not* necessary for having moral rights; having interests is both necessary and sufficient. He concludes that the "higher" animal forms do indeed have moral rights. This gives us a **nonanthropocentric ethic**, one that extends moral standing beyond the human. Notice, however, that by fastening onto various mental states, Feinberg's extension of moral standing only goes so far, excluding nonconscious entities like plants and "lower" animal forms from the protections of the moral umbrella: They have neither rights nor intrinsic value.

Another philosopher, influenced by Kant and Feinberg, who also develops a rights-based view of moral standing is Tom Regan of North Carolina State University. Regan too emphasizes respect for the unique dignity and worth of each individual, what he calls *inherent value*. Regan's understanding of inherent value is very close to Kant's notion of *absolute worth* or intrinsic value. All three concepts refer to the kind of value one has for one's own sake, independently of any use that can be made of one. Those who are inherently/intrinsically valuable are ends in themselves, and it is morally wrong to treat them as means or tools for the ends of others (Regan 1985).

Despite their agreement on the nature of this special value, Regan and Kant part company on what is needed to have it. Kant said rationality was required, but for Regan a being need only qualify as a *subject-of-a-life*. This condition is not as difficult to satisfy as Kant's, but it still involves some fairly sophisticated mental equipment:

> To be a subject-of-a-life is to...have beliefs and desires; perception, memory, and a sense of the future, including their own future; an emotional life together with feelings of pleasure and pain; preference and welfare interests; the ability to initiate action in pursuit of their desires and goals; a psychophysical identity over time; and an individual welfare in the sense that their experiential life fares well or ill for them independently of their utility for others (Regan 1983: 243).

Regan determines that mammals of at least one year old are subjects-of-a-life. This includes the overwhelming majority of the animals that serve as commodities or resources in business activity. Their inherent value means that they have a right to respectful treatment, among other rights, and this imposes a duty on us to act accordingly: We must avoid treating them as resources that we may exploit for our purposes. Such service is, for Regan, an obvious violation of the right all these animals have to respectful treatment. It follows from this view that a lot of business enterprises are engaged in seriously immoral conduct. If Regan is correct, justice demands enormous changes in the way corporations do business with animals, and indeed he calls for the total abolition of such practices (Regan 1983, 1985).

It also follows from this view that future generations of *humans* have no rights either. According to Feinberg and Regan, rights-holding requires the possession of an array of mental states, but because future generations do not exist, they do not possess anything, let alone mental states. Although this implication of the rights view has seemed problematic to some, others have embraced the conclusion. Richard DeGeorge points out that not only is it the case that future people do not now exist, they may never exist; they are simply products of the imagination that cannot be hurt, punished, mistreated, or acted upon in any way (DeGeorge 1980). Thomas Schwartz has called this the *disappearing beneficiaries problem* and suggests that it not only denies any rights to future generations, it also makes it senseless to say we have any obligations to them.

Gregory Kavka has a solution to the problem that offers a way to move past the focus on rights, and anticipates subsequent developments in moral philosophy. Granted that future people do not now have any interests, so there are no specific individuals who have a claim against us to act on their behalf; nonetheless, it is extremely likely that there will be such people, and they could be harmed by the environmental policies we pursue today. For Kavka, these facts provide powerful reasons to say that we do have obligations to future generations, even though, strictly speaking, they have no rights (Kavka 1978). This suggests that mental states might be dispensable for moral standing.

The rights-based view has been quite influential, despite its troubles with future generations, and notwithstanding a variety of other objections. Prominent among these is concern about the attribution of interests to animals that forms the basis of their status as rights holders, an objection that strikes at both Regan and Feinberg. R. G. Frey contends that in order for animals to have interests they must have desires and beliefs, a claim with which Regan and Feinberg would apparently agree. If an animal has an interest in something—say food or water—it must want that thing, but wanting something means that the animal must believe it does not have that thing. The problem, according to Frey, is that believing something requires the command of a fairly sophisticated language, something animals do not have. This sets off a chain reaction: if no language, then no beliefs; and if no beliefs, then no desires; and if no desires, then no interests; and if no interests, then no rights (Frey 1980).

Biocentric Ethics   Others have criticized Feinberg and Regan for being too narrowly concerned with the mental states of individuals, while neglecting the morally important features of living, nonconscious beings. Their rights view, while nonanthropocentric, is nonetheless **cerebrocentric**: It is centered on the mind or the brain. In contrast, a **biocentric ethic** moves beyond the mind and centers on life itself as the basis of moral consideration. The first explicit statement of a biocentric view in western philosophy came from Albert Schweitzer, a German philosopher, theologian, and medical doctor who provided health care for Africans during much of the first half of this century. In 1915 it occurred to him that a truly moral being is one who holds what he called a *reverence for life*. For him, every living thing is deserving of the same esteem with which a person regards his or her own life (Schweitzer 1990).

Many years later, Kenneth Goodpaster offered essentially the same opinion when he asserted that from the moral point of view, what matters about a being is not that it has some *mental* life, but that it has life itself:

> Neither rationality nor the capacity to experience pleasure and pain seem to me necessary (even though they may be sufficient) conditions on moral considerability. And only our hedonistic and concentric forms of moral reflection keep us from acknowledging this fact. Nothing short of the condition of *being alive* seems to me to be a plausible and nonarbitrary condition (Goodpaster 1978: 310).

Shortly thereafter, in a book titled *Respect for Nature*, Brooklyn College Professor of Philosophy Paul Taylor developed a biocentric ethic in great detail; he makes the point this way:

> To have the attitude of respect for nature is to regard the wild animals and plants of Earth's natural ecosystems as possessing inherent worth. That such creatures have inherent worth may be considered the fundamental value presupposition of the attitude of respect.... If it is true that a living thing has inherent worth, then it possesses such worth regardless of any instrumental value it may have...(Taylor 1986: 71, 75).

The respect due to rational beings on the basis of what Kant called their *absolute worth*, and the dignity accorded animals when recognizing what Regan calls their *inherent value* is transferred by Taylor to all living beings— animals *and* plants. His notion of *inherent worth* is thus another variant on the concept of intrinsic value: The inherent worth of a living thing is not a function of its usefulness as a tool or instrument for the purposes of others.

Why do all living things have inherent worth? Taylor's answer moves through several stages. First, he observes that all living things are *teleological centers-of-life*, a phrase reminiscent of Regan's *subject-of-a-life* criterion. However, Taylor often avoids talk of rights, and his classification is more inclusive because it is not wholly a function of complex mental states. For him, a teleological center-of-life is any being whose "internal functioning as well as external activities are all goal-oriented, having the constant tendency to maintain the organism's existence through time and to enable it successfully to perform those biological operations whereby it reproduces its kind and continually adapts to changing environmental events and conditions" (Taylor 1986: 121). Each living thing has a good of its own because it has a direction or end toward which it is heading: In the Greek, this is a *telos*.

The fact that each living thing has a good of its own, even if the organism is unaware of this fact, is not enough to attribute inherent worth to it. That is accomplished by adopting what Taylor calls the *biocentric outlook*: This is a basic understanding of the natural world and our place in it. We hold this view when we recognize that humans are not inherently superior to any other species, that all living things, including humans, are pursuing their own good as interdependent components in a vast ecological system. Once we adopt the biocentric outlook, we recognize the inherent worth and dignity of all living things, and thus acknowledge their moral standing and the duties we owe to them (Taylor 1986).

What might biocentric ethics mean for business practices? Extraordinary changes are in order in the use of animals in agriculture and products testing, much like those advocated by Regan. Taylor does argue in favor of vegetarianism, and his position seems clearly to reject animal testing. But more than that, biocentric ethics must also take account of *all* living individuals in determining the morally correct course of action. Insofar as business practices impact any living things, their welfare or good must be considered. In building a shopping mall, for example, a business enterprise would need to morally consider not merely the impact on people's lives, but also the displacement of animals caused by the development, any animal deaths that might result, and the likely event that a large number of plants would be destroyed in the process. Obviously, this is far more than any corporation has ever been morally required to confront, and this would be standard procedure, not a rare exception. Although one might be inclined to wonder whether Taylor's biocentric ethics would ever allow *any* business development, he does offer several *priority principles* that are designed to deal with situations in which human interests conflict with the interests or good of living things (Taylor 1986). But would human interests ever prevail?

Taylor's ethical theory does not confine moral standing to beings with a well-developed mental life, as does the cerebrocentric ethics of Feinberg and Regan, but it still shares an important feature with a mind-centered view: Biocentric ethics is highly individualistic. Each particular organism, as a teleological center-of-life, has a good of its own that is ripe for recognition by enlightened moral agents who have adopted the biocentric outlook. Joseph DesJardins, a philosopher at the College of St. Benedict in Minnesota, succinctly describes a serious dilemma Taylor faces here. Imagine that you want to dig up part of your yard and put in a brick patio. This will result in the destruction of many, though small, living things, each of whom, according to Taylor, have moral standing. Would this be wrong? If it is, then his biocentric ethics is far too demanding and simply unworkable. If it is morally permissible to build the patio, why should your fairly trivial desire to have a patio be important enough to utterly destroy living things that are merely seeking their own good? One duty Taylor favors calls for making restitution to organisms we harm, but how can you do that for the living things you killed to put in your patio? Plant more vegetation elsewhere? DesJardins observes that this answer seems to point to a duty to the *species* involved, not the individuals (DesJardins 1993).

DesJardins's criticism here begins a movement away from a concentration on the rights and intrinsic value of individuals, and toward a broader moral vision that takes in the good of the group. We now turn to this alternative point of view.

Promoting the Good of the Group: Utilitarianism

Although Kant's focus on rationality held sway in Western moral philosophy for many years, a force to erode it was set in motion even before Kant took pen to paper. It was in large measure the arguments of an eighteenth-century Scottish philosopher, David Hume, that initiated the movement away from rationality and toward other, less restrictive capacities. Hume argued against the view that moral action was a function of reason and intellect. He observed that what motivates us to act is the prospect of pain or pleasure resulting from the action. In contrast, rationality is essentially concerned with logic and empirical knowledge, these being, according to Hume, incapable of motivating us to do anything. Since reason alone doesn't move us, but moral issues do move us to act, morality is strictly speaking not a product of reason, but of the "passions" (Hume 1739). Hume thus severely demoted the role of rationality and intimately bonded morality to our "sentiments," our feelings and emotions.

Although Hume was mainly concerned with clarifying the nature of moral judgments as made by rational agents, his position paved another way for including nonrational humans among those with moral standing. It also has the added advantage of being consistent with ordinary moral thinking about them. Recall that Kant's view had some trouble accounting for the moral standing of nonrational human beings. We considered whether membership in the human species might solve the problem, but, as Peter Singer has charged, that is simply a prejudice; the best answer seems to be to drop rationality and move on to less restrictive capacities. After all, our care for and consideration of children, as well as the mentally disabled and dysfunctional, is produced, not by the accident of their biological classification, but by the fact that they have various *sensations*, particularly their feelings of pleasure and pain. Rational or not, certainly all human beings are **sentient**: They experience sensations that they are apt to seek out and avoid. Sentience can then replace rationality as that special part of a human's nature that signals moral standing, both for the rational and nonrational.

Sentience This move opens the floodgates. There is little doubt that humans are not the only sentient beings on this planet. Jeremy Bentham, an

English philosopher influenced by his contemporary David Hume, emphasized the capacity to experience pleasure and pain as the determinant of moral consideration, and quickly realized that many animals are capable of these experiences. In an often quoted passage, Bentham suggests the arbitrariness of requiring rationality for moral consideration and the consequence of its rejection when he speculates that

> The day *may* come when the rest of the animal creation may acquire those rights that never could have been withholden from them but by the hand of tyranny...the blackness of the skin is no reason why a human being should be abandoned without redress to the caprice of a tormentor. It may one day come to be recognized that the number of legs, the villosity of the skin, or the termination of the *os sacrum*, are reasons equally insufficient for abandoning a sensitive being to the same fate. What else is it that should trace the insuperable line? Is it the faculty of reason, or perhaps the faculty of discourse? But a full-grown horse or dog is beyond comparison a more rational, as well as a more conversable animal, than an infant of a day or a week, or even a month, old. But suppose they were otherwise, what would it avail? The question is not, Can they reason? nor Can they talk? but, *Can they suffer*? (Bentham 1789: 283)

Bentham draws his "insuperable line" around the capacity for experiencing certain mental states, the capacity for sentience. Why here? In a book provocatively titled *Animal Liberation*, Peter Singer explains that this capacity is just what we are considering in deciding how we should conduct ourselves toward others:

> [T]he only legitimate boundary to our concern for the interests of other beings is the point at which it is no longer accurate to say that the other being has interests. To have interests, in a strict, nonmetaphorical sense, a being must be capable of suffering or experiencing pleasure. If a being suffers, there can be no moral justification for disregarding that suffering, or for refusing to count it equally with the like suffering of any other being. But the converse of this is also true. If a being is not capable of suffering, or of enjoyment, there is nothing to take into account. (Singer 1990: 171)

Notice that Singer's understanding of interests is narrower and, because of that, more inclusive that what Feinberg and Regan mean by interests. For Singer, having interests requires only the capacity to feel pleasure and pain. Rather more sophisticated mental states like having desires and beliefs, a sense of time, memory, hopes, or a psychophysical identity are all jettisoned in favor of the simpler and more primitive ability to experience suffering and enjoyment. So while Feinberg and Regan might be reticent to include fish, for example, under the moral umbrella, Singer does not hesitate to do so. There is, however, one point of contact between these philosophers: All exclude *nonsentient* animals (perhaps insects), all plant life, and other natural objects like rocks and dirt. Bentham and Singer's ethics are also mind-centered or cerebrocentric.

These two philosophers are **utilitarians**. As we know, a utilitarian is required to perform that action that produces the greatest amount of—that *maximizes* the—good for everyone concerned. What is best for the group is most important, morally speaking, not necessarily what is best for some individual member of the group. The good here is defined in various ways by various utilitarians, but all fasten on some positive mental state, such as happiness, pleasure, or the satisfaction of desires and preferences. Right actions are those that produce more happiness or pleasure for everyone affected by the action than any alternative, and wrong actions are those that produce pain, or at least less pleasure than would be produced by some alternative conduct. As utilitarians, Singer and Bentham are simply tracing out the logical implications of their theory: if in moral decision making one is concerned about maximizing pleasure and minimizing pain, and if one holds that certain nonhuman animals experience pleasure and pain, then one is led inexorably to include them under the moral umbrella.

After detailing the vast amounts of suffering endured by animals "down on the factory farm" and as "tools for research," Singer concludes that vegetarianism is morally required, and that animals should be liberated from their bondage as subjects in experimentation and research (Singer 1990). Adopting his position on animal ethics would certainly lead to profound changes in the use of animals in business. Corporate concern for nonsentient nature need only be mindful of what would best promote the welfare of humankind and those animals whose rather advanced mental capacities qualify them for moral standing. The good of insects and plants, and the health of ecosystems, become no more than a means to the well-being of these advanced creatures. This is unlike biocentric ethics and, as we shall see in a moment, it is contrary to ecocentric ethics as well. This does not mean that, for Singer, only the animals humans have domesticated have interests or, for Regan, rights to be respected; wild species also count morally, and so they are deserving of protection. Their numbers are currently being decimated by business activities that destroy habitat, such as mining and agriculture, and the cerebrocentric ethics of Singer (and Regan) do take a moral accounting of this.

Singer's utilitarian approach to moral standing and its implications for our treatment of animals has been criticized in many different ways. For example, some have wondered if the rejection of animal eating and experimentation can really be sustained from the utilitarian point of view. After all, research using animals as subjects has resulted in enormous benefits for many humans, and for animals themselves, and presumably will continue to do so; numerous advances in medicine and product safety have come about following these researches, and much human pain and suffering has been avoided (Cohen 1986). Moreover, the welfare of those who work in animal agriculture and those who eat animals would be significantly affected by a turn to universal vegetarianism (Frey 1983). Would we really produce the most good for everyone concerned by ending these practices?

A related criticism focuses on the egalitarian nature of Singer's defense of animals. For utilitarians, everyone's interests are equal: As Singer said, equal suffering is to be counted equally, whether experienced by a human or non-human; and as Bentham said, all count for one and none count for more nor less than one. Bonnie Steinbock has worried that this means that someone who fed starving dogs instead of starving children may be doing nothing wrong, or at least, so long as the total good is the same, it doesn't matter who gets fed. This cannot be correct, she says; animal interests matter, morally speaking, but human interests count for more. Why? According to Steinbock, humans are more valuable, from the moral point of view, because they are responsible moral agents who have a "desire for self-respect." Furthermore, people can see that the interests of others give them reasons to act on their behalf. Animals can do none of this (Steinbock 1978).

Others have criticized Singer for his preoccupation with the mental states of individuals, while ignoring the morally important features of collections of individuals, such as species, and even entire ecosystems. These objections do not fault Singer for his insistence on calculating group welfare, it's just that his understanding of the morally relevant group is far too narrow. This next step in expanding the boundaries of moral standing is perhaps the most revolutionary. Until now, we have been in familiar territory, working with individual, living beings who feel pain and pleasure, or also have desires and interests, or who pursue a basic good that can be helped or harmed. In contrast, **ethical holism** holds that collectives of individual entities have a moral status that is in some way independent of the moral standing of the parts of the group. In environmental ethics, the collective of primary moral concern here is the *ecosystem*. So now we move on to **ecocentric ethics**: Entire forests, deserts, oceans, lakes, wetlands, and grasslands, along with the myriad species that populate them, all have moral standing.

Ecocentric Ethics

As the name suggests, ecocentric ethics is based upon the relatively new science of ecology. It began in the 1860s when the German biologist Ernst Haeckel combined two Greek words—*oikos*, meaning "home," and *logos*, meaning "study of"—to form *ecology*, the study of the environment or where and how things make their home. Wilderness enthusiast John Muir grasped the core idea of ecology as early as 1869: "When we try to pick out anything by itself, we find it hitched to everything else in the universe" (Muir 1911: 211). Ecology teaches that the separate elements that constitute an ecosystem are all connected with one another as parts of a unified whole, and none can be understood in isolation. The health of an ecosystem is a function of the sum total of the interrelationships among the various elements, not the fate of this or that individual element, whether human or nonhuman, living or nonliving.

The importation of ecology into ethics began with pioneering forester and wildlife manager Aldo Leopold and his "land ethic." Leopold explains the insights of ecology with his metaphor of the Land Pyramid. The Pyramid represents an ecosystem, powered by the sun's energy and resting on a foundation of the soil. The structure is arranged according to food chains: Moving from the base toward the apex, the creatures in each succeeding layer are less numerous than and feed mainly on those in levels below it. This means that the layers of the Pyramid are closely interrelated. Each species is seen as a link in these chains, and since a given species may eat many others, it may be a link in many chains. The ecosystem is stable and properly integrated when these complex interdependencies are organized so that its smooth functioning as an energy unit is maintained. This state of affairs constitutes, for Leopold, *land health*. When these interdependencies are disrupted, the energy flow is altered or obstructed and the functioning of the unit breaks down (Leopold 1949).

Ecocentric ethics emerges when, endowed with this ecological understanding, we come to regard the ecosystem as coextensive with the *moral* community: "The land ethic simply enlarges the boundaries of the [moral] community to include soils, waters, plants, animals, or collectively: the land" (Leopold 1949: 204). This produces a moral point of view that is holistic, focusing moral concern on the condition of the ecosystem as a whole instead of on the welfare of the particular individuals found within it. In this way, the good of the moral community becomes inseparable from the "health" of the land. Leopold's fundamental moral principle of the land ethic is this:

> [Q]uit thinking about decent land use as solely an economic problem. Examine each question in terms of what is ethically and aesthetically right, as well as what is economically expedient. A thing is right when it tends to preserve the integrity, stability, and beauty of the biotic community. It is wrong when it tends otherwise (Leopold 1949: 224–225).

University of Wisconsin philosopher J. Baird Callicott is the foremost expositor and elaborator of Leopold's land ethic. Callicott supplies a good summation of the ecological motivation behind ecocentric ethics generally, and explains the relevance of ecology to the land ethic in particular when he writes:

> Since ecology focuses upon the relationships between and among things, it inclines its students toward a more holistic vision of the world. Before the emergence of ecology as a science the landscape appeared to be, one might say, a collection of objects, some of them alive, some conscious, but all the same, an aggregate, a plurality of separate individuals. With this atomistic representation of things it is no wonder that moral issues might be understood as competing and mutually contradictory clashes of "rights" of separate individuals, each separately pursuing its "interests." Ecology

has made it possible to apprehend the same landscape as an artic-
ulate unity…. The land ethic calls our attention to the recently
discovered integrity—in other words the unity—of the biot[ic
community] and posits duties binding upon moral agents in relation to that whole (Callicott 1989: 22–23).

Other ecology-based moral systems have been developed over the last 30
years or so, and all pay homage to Leopold's land ethic. Along with Callicott's
extensive development of the theory (Callicott 1989), these views have gone a
long way toward situating morality in an ecologically informed context. One
such view is from Colorado State University philosopher Holmes Rolston.
He argues that if we accord moral standing to animals and plants because they
have interests, or merely because they are alive, we need to realize that their
interactions with the physical environment made them what they are in the
first place. Because the ecosystem is causally responsible for those very aspects
of a creature showing it to be worthy of moral consideration, we ought to
value the ecosystem just as much and in the same way that we value the individual (Rolston 1989).

More influential for environmental activists has been the ecocentric ethic
known as *deep ecology*. As originally sketched by Norwegian philosopher Arne
Naess, deep ecology takes a holistic and nonanthropocentric approach to
environmental problems: We need to explore the underlying causes of pollution and resource depletion, rather than narrowly—or shallowly—focusing
on how these problems effect humans in affluent countries (Naess 1973). Bill
Devall and George Sessions are two prominent deep ecologists or *ecophiloso-
phers* who have articulated eight basic principles of the theory. Among them
are the affirmations that the nonhuman world has intrinsic value, and that
bountiful and diverse ecosystems are valuable in themselves (Devall and
Sessions 1985). Naess offers a similar set of principles, which he calls the deep
ecology *platform* (Naess 1989).

Ecocentric ethics does not require of business the expansive moral deliberations called for by biocentric ethics, nor the radical transformations advocated by Singer and Regan in the way business proceeds. Ecocentric ethics is
not concerned with the fate of this or that individual in an ecosystem, rather
it is the health and stability of the system as a whole that morally matters.
Many ecocentric philosophers have pointed out that the animals used in business are not really part of this system in the first place, being more accurately
described as living artifacts created by humans; from the ecocentric perspective they are of little moral relevance.

Eric Katz has taken this tack while trying to reassure business interests
about their use of domesticated animals. He argues against both Singer's animal liberation and Regan's animal rights on ecocentric grounds. Katz claims
that Singer's preoccupation with animal pain is misguided because of the practical difficulties in determining which animals are sentient, and because the
concern with pain is ecologically naive. As for Regan, Katz points out that
since many "marginal" humans—those who are not rational—are in fact not

given equal rights, Regan has no grounds for complaining that nonrational animals are arbitrarily excluded from moral consideration while these marginal humans are included. Katz concludes:

> An ethic of ecological holism would require major revisions in [business] activities regarding wildlife and the natural environment. Industry would be compelled to adopt alternative technologies with low impact on natural evolutionary processes, such as solar power and organic pesticides. These reforms would affect the animal kingdom in positive ways, for reducing air and water pollution benefits all organic life. However the reforms required…are minuscule compared to the reforms demanded by the animal liberation [and rights] movement[s] (Katz 1990: 231).

Ecocentric ethics has been subjected to a number of criticisms. Probably the most serious charge is that the land ethic and deep ecology elevate the stability and integrity of the ecosystem to a position of moral priority over the rights of the individual. After all, if it is permissible to kill deer in order to preserve land health (as both Leopold and Callicott assert), and if people have no privileged place in the ecosystem (an idea seconded by Naess, Devall, and Sessions), are we not also permitted to reduce the number of humans whose overpopulation is so environmentally destructive? That cannot be correct. This problem has led some philosophers to brand ecocentric ethics as "totalitarian" (Kheel 1985) and "fascist" (Regan 1983).

Nurturing Personal Relationships: Care

The newest voice in environmental ethics has emerged from the social and philosophical movement known as feminism. Although the use of the singular term suggests that there is a unified theory with definitive features here, there are in fact several different feminisms. Alison Jaggar has explained a useful classification of feminism into four basic types.

Liberal feminism affirms that there are no morally relevant differences between men and women, that all persons are rational, autonomous beings deserving of equal consideration and respect. Liberal feminists are thus very concerned to secure equal rights and equal opportunity for women. *Marxist feminism* focuses on the economic exploitation of women confined to domestic labor; housework and child care are devalued by men, but are required in order for them to succeed in the public world of production and wage earning. The solution is for "women's work" to become appropriately valued and for women to participate in other forms of labor. *Socialist feminism* sees the Marxist focus on economic oppression and an economic solution as too narrow; a full accounting of the problem must also recognize the impact of traditional gender roles and the way sexual identity is culturally defined. Finally, *radical feminism* concentrates on how these gender roles have been foisted upon women; the feminine has been defined by men as emotional and passive, essentially sexual in nature and centered on child care. Many radical feminists call for separation from men entirely, while others advocate emphasizing and extolling the different ways in which women experience and value the world, especially emphasizing personal relationships of caring and nurturing (Jaggar 1983).

Ecofeminism   Out of this medley has come **ecofeminism**. The various feminisms transfer into the arena of environmental issues in various ways, but the core idea concerns what Karen Warren has called the *logic of domination*. Here, men and women are distinguished according to certain features, the male set of features is regarded as superior, and the superiority justifies the dominance and authority of men. The standard pattern identified by Warren is that men are seen as rational, a characteristic that is superior to women's emotional nature; the subordination of women is then regarded as appropriate (Warren 1987). Ecofeminism is the exploration of how this logic manifests itself in the human relationship with nature. Warren writes that "there are important connections—historical, experiential, symbolic, theoretical— between the domination of women and the domination of nature, an understanding of which is crucial to both feminism and environmental ethics" (Warren 1990: 126).

The main connection arises from the logic of domination. Women are identified with nature and nature is identified as a woman; Both are seen as essentially wild and irrational resources to be harnessed by rational, intellectual men. The masculine is associated with the superior traits of reason, the mind, objectivity, culture, and civilization, while the feminine is equated with inferior emotions, subjectivity, and nature. Evelyn Fox Keller cites a clear instance of this logic from Francis Bacon, widely regarded as the founding father of modern science. Bacon writes that because the goal of science is to "establish a chaste and lawful marriage between Mind and Nature," he will be "leading to you Nature with all her children to bind her to your service and make her your slave" (Keller 1985: 36). Warren and Keller find such metaphors very revealing, and they conclude that our environmental predicament will not be improved until we overthrow the oppressive patterns of masculinist thinking that produced them.

Carol Adams has identified similar connections in the practice of eating animals for food. She too writes of a logic of domination, which she calls the *texts of meat*. Adams refers here to the symbolic meanings that meat consumption has in our political-cultural context. Citing many examples drawn from mythology, scripture, folklore, anthropology, sociology, linguistic and etymological analysis, and cultural observations, Adams argues that the message of meat eating is that it is the special province and sometimes the privilege of men, representing virility, authority, and superiority. Animals and women are viewed by men as objects to be dominated and used. For Adams, this shows that the oppression of women and the eating of animals are interlocked (Adams 1990).

For many ecofeminists, especially for those influenced by the more radical variety of feminism, the solution to our environmental problems can be found in the *ethics of care*. Inspired by the work of such original theorists as Carol Gilligan (1982) and Nel Noddings (1984), these ecofeminists reject what they see as masculine notions of rights, obligations, and justice characterizing traditional ethical theory, where morality is a field of competition and conflict between self-interested egos. Instead, values and dispositions formerly regarded as peculiarly female and distinctly inferior, are celebrated and elevated to a position of moral superiority. Abstract discussions about moral standing that are preoccupied with the rights of nature and our duties to nonhuman beings are then diluted or jettisoned entirely in favor of moral thinking centered on caring and nurturing, cooperation and accommodation, friendship and relationship. So instead of pondering whether or not the mental states of animals give them rights, or the connection between the good of living things and their inherent value, the care ethic tells us to consider our relationships with animals and the environment generally. Do our interactions with the nonhuman world manifest care and concern? Do we act as friends of nature, engaging in a nurturing and loving relationship with our natural surroundings?

Warren offers an instructive example of how the care ethic is activated in this context; notice, she says

> the difference in attitudes and behaviors toward a rock when one is "making it to the top" and when one thinks of oneself as "friends with" or "caring about" the rock one climbs. These different attitudes and behaviors suggest an ethically germane contrast between two different types of relationship humans or climbers may have toward a rock: an imposed conqueror-type relationship, and an emergent caring-type relationship.... Ecofeminism makes a central place for values of caring, love, friendship, trust, and appropriate reciprocity.... It thereby gives voice to the sensitivity that in climbing a mountain, one is doing something in relationship with an "other," an "other" whom one can come to care about and treat respectfully (Warren 1990: 135–136).

Criticism of ecofeminism as a distinct plank in a feminist platform has been rather slow to develop so far, perhaps due to its recent arrival on the scene. Those voicing reservations have questioned the close bond that ecofeminists try to forge between the oppression of women and the degradation of the environment, both explained as manifestations of patriarchal domination. These critics have difficulty seeing how rejecting cultural and political practices that oppress women necessarily leads us to greater respect for nature.

Margarita Garcia Levin, a philosopher at Yeshiva University, argues that it does not follow from the fact that a single pattern of thought justifies both the domination of women and the domination of nature, that to discard one is to discard the other. A logic of domination may lead men to treat women and nature alike and badly, but this "does not imply that a change in the treatment of women requires a change in the treatment of nature. What is needed is the additional premise that the oppression of women and nature is equally wrong…. Absent that premise…it might be wrong for men to dominate women, but perfectly all right for men, and women, to dominate nature" (Levin 1994: 137). In other words, one can agree that the exploitation of women is immoral, but deny that the exploitation of nature is immoral. Women are different from animals, plants, and ecosystems in a host of morally important ways, indicating that women have a moral standing not found in nonhuman nature.

An ecofeminist approach might require the greatest revisions for business practices of all these ethical theories. Or it might not. As far as we know, no one has looked at issues concerning business and the environment with an ecofeminist gaze, so our conclusions here are speculative. But this perspective would appear to recommend that business practices turn away from the legalistic obsession with conflicting interests, rights, and justice that characterize Singer, Regan, and Taylor, and instead ponder the sort of relationship corporations have with nature. This seems to suggest a very open-ended approach, depending on the scope of the association with nature adopted by the moral agents running the corporation.

If business persons could establish a caring, nurturing, empathetic, and friendly relationship with every aspect of the human and nonhuman world, corporate decisions would need to be made in a context in which not only people, but animals, plants, and all living things, as well as nonliving things, and the ecosystem itself must be considered. Karen Warren's position suggests such a maximally broad range of moral concern (recall her example of rock climbing; Warren 1990). Mark Starik has incorporated some elements of the ecofeminist view in adapting the stakeholder model of management (see Chapter 3: The Corporation) to include the whole of nature, human and nonhuman, individuals and collectives. Although he appeals to a number of other ingredients, such as various economic, political, social, and legal factors, he does arrive at this most expansive vision that ecofeminism makes available (Starik 1995).

On the other hand, it is by no means necessary for the moral reach of ecofeminism to be quite so wide. Nel Noddings, for one, confines the extent of caring and nurturing to all and only living things, suggesting a significant overlap with biocentric ethics, though hers is more holistically oriented than the standard life-centered view (Noddings 1984). It also seems open to ecofeminism to further limit the scope of moral concern along cerebrocentric lines, depending on persons' psychological ability to affectively connect with other beings. Whether this is a defensible basis for moral decision making in business, regarding the environment or any other object of moral concern, is a project that ecofeminism still needs to work out.

Environmental Economics

The moral questions that arise when we look closely at business's use of the environment in general and animals in particular cannot be thoroughly addressed in isolation from the economic issues involved. A lot of money is at stake: These uses produce a great deal of wealth, and modifying our behavior according to certain moral requirements would be quite costly, not only in monetary terms but also in terms of human well-being. Many people make their living in animal agriculture and in meat packing and processing, industries that moreover inject billions of dollars into the nation's economy. Our confidence that the products we buy are safe and effective arises in large part from their having been proven so through animal testing. The price of morality is especially worrisome when environmental problems are tackled. Consider air and water pollution. Pollution abatement devices and measures are typically very expensive. Are they really worth the expense? If so, then who pays for them? Can we really afford not aggressively pursuing abatement? Many have argued that these questions are best answered when we recognize that pollution, like other environmental concerns, is essentially an economic problem that can be solved by economic means. Let's investigate this issue first.

Society: The Price of Pollution

Electricity is probably society's most vital commodity. So imagine a company—call it Municipal Electric Power Company (MEP)—that is in the business of producing and selling electricity to the residents of a medium-sized city. Much of the electric power generated in this country results from burning coal, so let's say that MEP must buy this fossil fuel. Of course MEP must also pay individuals to operate and maintain the machinery required to generate the power, and the company has to buy the machines themselves. The cost of fuel, labor, and equipment is the price MEP pays to produce electricity. However, these costs do not represent the true, total costs of producing electricity. As we saw above in Business and the Environment, the burning of fossil fuels produces large amounts of sulfur dioxide and nitrogen oxides; both have been implicated in lung and respiratory tract illness, and as the major factor causing acid rain. Furthermore, the smoke and soot from the burning create particulates that settle on cars, windows, porches, walkways, plants, just about everything.

It costs money to fix the health problems caused by MEP's burning of coal. Cleaning up the mess from the smokestacks also must be paid for. From the economic point of view, the problem here is that MEP is not paying these costs. MEP is only paying for the *internal* or *private* costs of fuel, labor, and machinery, while the **external** or **public** costs of medical care and cleanup are borne by the residents of the municipality. What it really costs to generate electricity is the *sum total* of both internal and external costs—this is the **social cost** of producing electricity—yet MEP is paying much less than this total. Why is this a problem? Many would be inclined to say that this is a problem because it is *unfair*, that the people affected by the smoke do not *deserve* to be harmed in these ways, and that MEP has a *duty* to assume these external costs.

But from the economic perspective, all this moralizing is beside the point. The real problem here, the economists say, is that the market for electricity is not **efficient**.

Efficient Markets   The standard definition of efficiency employed by modern economists was devised early in this century by Vilfredo Pareto. An inefficient market is one in which some transaction would make at least one party to an exchange better off without making anyone else worse off. An **efficient market** is one in which no transaction could make anyone better off without making someone else worse off. *Better off* refers to the satisfaction of people's desires and preferences, *worse off* to their frustration: You are better off in state of affairs A then you would be in state of affairs B if more of your desires are satisfied in A than in B; in B you are worse off than in A. An efficient market occurs when we have the highest possible sum total of satisfied desires, as measured by the aggregation of everyone's satisfactions and frustrations. This maximum indicates a **pareto optimal** distribution of satisfactions and frustrations. Efficiency is thus defined by the utilitarian standard. It is one in which *utility is maximized*: Everyone has as much of what they want without making anyone else worse off in the process. This is regarded as the apotheosis of market exchanges, and for economists, it should be the goal of public policy.

In the electricity market described above, there is indeed a transaction that would make at least one party to the exchange better off without making anyone else worse off. To see this, we first must recognize that since MEP is not paying the true cost of supplying electricity, this commodity is *underpriced*; if MEP had to pay the external costs as well the internal ones, the company would certainly charge more per kilowatt hour. But in that case, demand would decline and, with it, supply would too. This means, without taking on the external cost, MEP's electricity is not only underpriced, it is also *overproduced*: More electricity is being generated then consumers would demand if they had an accurate measure of the true costs to society of its production. Human and other resources are being wasted to produce excessive amounts of electricity, and the excess electricity is itself wasted.

A more efficient market could be created if MEP took on the total social cost of generating electricity: MEP needs to internalize those external costs. This would occasion an increase in rates, of course, and a decline in demand, but supply would be adjusted accordingly and MEP could realize a net increase in profit, or at least no loss. For their part, consumers would see higher prices for electricity. However, the cost of medical care and cleanup would be covered, perhaps by taxes MEP pays to fund public health services and municipal maintenance, or the pollution that caused these problems in the first place would be reduced as MEP buys abatement devices. Either state of affairs would be viewed by people as an improvement, that is, they would be more satisfied than when electricity prices were lower but pollution and health problems were greater. Additionally, resources would no longer be wasted. According to this economic analysis, the key for solving the pollution problem here is to get MEP to internalize the external costs, and so produce an efficient market where utility is maximized. Society as a whole is then better off.

Consumers: The Market Solution

One of the first statements of the economic solution to pollution problems was famously (or infamously) presented by William Baxter in a book provocatively titled *People or Penguins: The Case for Optimal Pollution*. He formulates the thesis this way:

> To assert that there is a pollution problem or an environmental problem is to assert, at least implicitly, that one or more resources is not being used so as to maximize human satisfactions. In this respect at least environmental problems are economics problems, and better insight can be gained by the application of economic analysis (Baxter 1974: 17).

In light of this thesis, the "optimal" level of pollution is simply that amount found in an efficient market: It is "[j]ust those amounts that attend a sensible organized society thoughtfully and knowledgeably pursuing the greatest possible satisfaction for its human members" (Baxter 1974: 8).

Baxter's formulation clearly exhibits the two primary features of the economic approach to environmental issues. First is the view that we can achieve the highest sum total of human satisfaction (maximize utility) through the unencumbered workings of the market. For economists, satisfaction or happiness is a function of the cost of goods offered on the market. The cost of something is determined by how much consumers are willing to pay for it: The more they are willing to pay, the greater the satisfaction in obtaining the item.

Now the cost of some item is not merely handing over some amount of money. Baxter points out that it is also what consumers are willing to do without in exchange for some commodity. For example, you may have to choose between spending $20 on eating out or $20 on a new shirt; if you choose the shirt, its real cost includes the lost opportunity to go out to eat. In buying the shirt, you are willing to forgo—another sense of *to pay*—a restaurant meal, but in making this choice you believe you will be happier with the shirt and without the dinner then you would be with the dinner and without the shirt. For Baxter, then, the costs associated with pollution include more than just the monetary value of abatement devices or health care, it also includes other goods consumers must give up. This is the familiar notion of making tradeoffs. In reducing pollution, we continue making tradeoffs until the next tradeoff would produce a decrease in total utility.

To return to our electricity example, Baxter's market solution says that we can determine how much pollution is optimal according to how much consumers are willing to pay to reduce it, or, to put it another way, according to how much people are willing to pay for clean air. As MEP raises the price of electricity in order to fund tax levies or buy abatement devices, people's willingness to pay the rate hikes brings tradeoffs: They get cleaner air or low-cost health care but they also have to turn down the air conditioner or buy fewer shirts or go out to eat less often. Yet the sacrifice is worth it to them—up to a point anyway. That point is where the costs of pollution reduction begin to outweigh the benefits, and utility is no longer maximized. The economic solution says that public policy should be structured to bring us right up to, but not past that point. This is *optimal pollution*.

The second prominent feature of the economic approach is its distinctively anthropocentric alignment. The only satisfaction or happiness of any relevance here is human; the desires and preferences of nonhuman species simply do not count when calculating total utility. Baxter makes this feature very clear (as well as the significance of his book's title) when he notes that some people are worried (in the early 1970s) that penguins might be harmed by exposure to DDT:

> My criteria are oriented toward people, not penguins. Damage to penguins, or sugar pines, or geological marvels is, without more, simply irrelevant. One must go further, by my criteria, and say: Penguins are important because people enjoy seeing them walk about rocks.... I have no interest in preserving penguins for their own sake (Baxter 1974: 5).

Standard economics is concerned with what consumers value, this being understood as a function of what they want, what makes them happy. Human happiness is an end in itself, and all else is valuable only when it serves that end. This is the familiar notion that only people (or their mental states) have **intrinsic value**, while animals, plants, and indeed all of the nature world are merely instrumentally valuable as resources or tools to promote our satisfaction.

Classical economics is driven by the utilitarian conception of social welfare, but as we saw above with Bentham and Singer, it is difficult to confine the utilitarian standard to humans only. In that case, the market solution to environmental problems would seem to have to take account of the wants and preferences of *all* sentient beings. But of course, nonhuman animals are not and cannot be participants in market exchanges; they demonstrate no "willingness to pay" indicating how much they value clean air or water or anything for that matter, so there is nothing that can be quantified in order to calculate total utility. For many, this indicates a major flaw in the economic analysis: It claims to promote social welfare, but excludes a significant class of beings who experience satisfaction and frustration because their manifestations of utility cannot be measured. Yet air and water pollution affect all those who breathe and drink. Perhaps the fundamental problem is an approach that requires economic measurements of what individuals value.

Criticism of the Market Solution   This leads us to the principal objection that has been directed at the market solution to environmental problems. The basic charge is that this approach is too narrow and short-sighted. A leading figure in the attack has been University of Maryland Professor of Philosophy

Mark Sagoff. According to Sagoff, the market solution fails to recognize two crucial and interdependent features of human beings, features that cannot be quantified and measured as market behavior. First, economic analysis does not recognize that people are *citizens* in addition to being individuals out to get what they want. Economics regards human beings in one-dimensional terms: we are *consumers* and nothing else. What's the difference? Sagoff writes that

> We act as consumers to get what we want *for ourselves*. We act as citizens to achieve what we think is right or best *for the community*. The question arises, then, whether what we want for ourselves individually as consumers is consistent with the goals we would set for ourselves collectively as citizens (Sagoff 1981: 1285).

Consumers have desires for things, to obtain or consume them, and these desires are satisfied by paying the costs necessary to do so; this is all a consumer is interested in. Economists then think that all that needs to been done is to figure out how to ensure that as many consumer desires as possible are satisfied without making anyone else worse off: the **efficient market**. *Worse off*, recall, is understood here in terms of frustrated desires. Sagoff points out that the economic vision is myopic. As a consumer—as someone trying to get what I want—I may loathe riding the bus (crowded, inconvenient) and I wouldn't dream of buying returnable containers (too much bother), but as a citizen, I vote for propositions that tax gasoline to fund public transportation and that outlaw nonreturnables (Sagoff 1981).

This brings out the second human feature missed by the economic analysis, and the point of Sagoff's consumer versus citizen distinction: People are motivated not merely by their wants and preferences, but also by their beliefs, values, and convictions. The problem is that the market solution can only take account of *market* values as a function of what we, as consumers, individually desire. These are measured according to how much we are willing to pay for something, and the more we will pay, the more we want that thing. Market conditions in which these desires are maximized are then seen as the goal of public policy. Where do our beliefs and convictions about beauty, dignity, integrity, spirituality, and propriety fit into this picture? How can *moral* and *aesthetic* values, spiritual significance, and symbolic meanings be quantified and measured? How much are you willing to pay to preserve the integrity of the rainforest? Sagoff claims that these are nonmarket values and beliefs that, as such, do not fit into the economic picture, and cannot be accounted for there (Sagoff 1990).

Why should beliefs and convictions that cannot be assigned a market value be reckoned with at the level of public policy? Sagoff argues that because we don't need to give reasons for our wants and preferences, or defend them in any way, they are purely subjective: "I want to drive my car everywhere. Why, you ask? I like the ease and convenience. Why, again? Well, I just do—stop bothering me." This has long been a problem for utilitarianism generally: The focus on maximizing wants and preferences seems to ignore the fact that some desires are foolish, perverse, immoral, or just plain criminal. Yet, economists have often seen the subjectivity of this kind of valuing as a laudable aspect of the ethical neutrality of economics. Sagoff disagrees. He observes that, in contrast to wants and preferences, our beliefs and convictions about what is morally and aesthetically worthy of an enlightened citizenry can be defended with reasons, that they are in this sense objective matters of fact and knowledge that can be correct or mistaken. What is more, they express our identity as members of a community pursuing a vision of the common good. Surely, such items must have a prominent, if not preeminent, place in the formation of social policy (Sagoff 1981).

Sagoff concludes:

> Our environmental goals—cleaner air and water, the preservation of wilderness and wildlife, and the like—are not to be construed, then, simply as personal wants or preferences; they are not interests to be "priced" by markets or cost-benefit analysis, but are views or beliefs that may find their way, as public values, into legislation. These goals stem from our character as people, which is not something we choose, as we might choose a necktie or a cigarette, but something we recognize, something we are. These goals presuppose the reality of public or shared values that we recognize together, values that are discussed and criticized on their merits and are not to be confused with preferences that are appropriately priced in markets (Sagoff 1990: 28–29).

Environmental economists have not been persuaded by Sagoff's objections. In response, they have charged him, and those who take a similar line, with a kind of myopia of their own. Just as Sagoff claims that the economic analysis fails to distinguish people as citizens from people as consumers, economists claim that Sagoff fails to distinguish *economic* values from *market* values. Perhaps economists look at human beings and see only consumers, but Sagoff looks at economics and sees only prices established by markets. However, the determination of economic value is not constrained by the actual operation of real markets.

Social scientist Steven Edwards has pressed this reply to Sagoff's critique. He claims that Sagoff, among others, has overlooked the **contingent valuation method** of determining economic value. This procedure consists of surveys asking people how much they would be willing to pay for environmental public goods, such as clean air or wilderness areas or the preservation of species. On the basis of their responses, *shadow prices* are assigned to these goods; this is how much, say, wilderness areas would cost if there really were a market for buying and selling them. Thus, our environmental goals *can* be construed as preferences that can be priced in *hypothetical* markets: This is "the monetization of nonmarket values associated with the natural environment" (Edwards 1987).

In other words, Edwards insists that people *are* simply consumers after all, that moral, aesthetic, and spiritual values can be quantified as personal preferences, and that environmental policy should be arranged so as to maximize the satisfaction of these preferences, along with others, according to the *existence value* of the natural object in question. Efficient markets (real and hypothetical) can take account of the happiness and satisfaction we derive from environmental goods.

Producers: Economics and Animals in Business

Although every aspect of environmental economics involves producers, consumers, and society generally, the ethical issues surrounding the use of animals in business supply an especially good example of the moral and economic pressures that can be exerted on corporations in particular. Consider the ethics of using animals for food. Those who advocate vegetarianism are advocating the end of an industry responsible for injecting billions of dollars into the nation's economy.

Animal Agriculture   In 1995 nearly one-half of all cash receipts from agriculture in this country were garnered from the marketing of more than 7.5 billion cows, sheep, hogs, and poultry; that is a total of $118.5 billion. The popular vision of agriculture is that these animals are raised on numerous small, family-owned farms and ranches, where the business is passed on from father to son as a time-honored family tradition. On this view, the end of animal eating means more than just lost revenue, it is the demise of core family values and a highly regarded way of life. The reality of animal agriculture is quite different. More than half of the sales receipts—$62 billion—in this business are accounted for by just 20 national and international corporations, and one-third of all sales ($39 billion) are enjoyed by the "Big Four" meat processors and packers: Con Agra, Inc. of Omaha, Nebraska; IBP, Inc. of Dakota City, Nebraska; Cargill Meat Sector of Minneapolis, Minnesota; and Tyson Foods, Inc. of Springdale, Arkansas (American Meat Institute 1996).

Although animal agriculture is controlled by big business interests and not small family operations, there are still many people whose livelihood depends upon the killing and eating of animals. In 1995 the meat and poultry packing and processing industry employed about 500,000 workers, earning an average of nearly $11 per hour (American Meat Institute 1996). The employees of this industry are responsible for approximately $11.4 billion of the national economy. This economic resource would be eliminated by a national movement to vegetarianism, and the ripple effects to other areas of business would be significant. What are these people supposed to do for a living? How could such a disaster for social welfare be justified? Bowling Green University philosopher R. G. Frey, among others, has claimed that the demise of the meat industry and its satellites that would attend a wholesale conversion to vegetarianism would be catastrophic to social welfare. Frey lists 14 different ways in which widespread vegetarianism would adversely affect human well-being, primarily in the form of economic losses for those employed in the industry and other dependent businesses (Frey 1983).

Although this seems not to be Frey's intent, we see here the germ of a market defense of animal agriculture. Overall human satisfaction would appear to be dealt a severe blow if the meat market were eliminated, rendering the market for food into a highly inefficient form. Of course *animal* satisfaction could be substantially increased, but as we saw above, this particular manifestation of utility does not and indeed cannot count as a factor for determining pareto optimality. Yet such a market defense is not obviously sustainable—it must also consider significant sources of human unhappiness attending meat eating. One such source is the fact that jobs in the meat industry are among the most dangerous in America. In 1994, 24 out of every 100 workers in meat packing suffered an injury on the job; the rate was 15 of 100 for meat processing. Compare this to a national average for all other jobs of less than 6 in 100. Moreover, there are approximately 5 million vegetarians in this country, the vast majority of whom, presumably, are not pleased with the existence of the meat market.

At any rate, Frey's point is that even counting animal happiness as a variable in a utilitarian calculation, we could not maximize utility by becoming vegetarians. Frey is directing this objection against Singer's utilitarian-based defense of vegetarianism, but we do not have to be utilitarians to feel its force. The fact is that the end of animal eating would likely have seriously adverse effects on the economic, or just plain well-being of many people.

Two major responses to these economic problems are available to vegetarians. First, Tom Regan (1983) and others have observed that the end of animal eating would not come overnight. Those who appeal to these economic factors in opposing vegetarianism seem to think that the switch would occur quickly, and we would suddenly be faced with the disastrous collapse of a major industry along with the immediate unemployment of hundreds of thousands of workers. Fortunately, the vegetarian could say, this is very unlikely to occur. What is much more plausible is that a change (if there ever is to be one) would take place over an extended period of time, perhaps several or even many generations. As more and more people make the switch to vegetarianism, and parents raise their children on a meatless diet, the demand would slowly diminish; this lowers prices and occasions reductions in the supply. Wages are frozen or cut. Current employees thus actively and (it is assumed) successfully seek other employment opportunities. Fewer workers are required in the industry, a fact that becomes common knowledge, so fewer people pursue employment there; vacancies and retirements are not replaced. Gradually, the business fades away or persists at a fraction of its former scale.

It is also plausible to assume that new food processing options and opportunities that do not involve animal flesh would open up as demand for meatless alternatives increases. One can even suppose that individuals would jump from meat processing and packing jobs to vegetable processing and packing jobs. Satellite industries formerly wholly or partly dependent on meat could hook on to new markets in soy burgers, textured vegetable protein (tvp) products, and a variety of foods in which meat ingredients are replaced with more vegetables (for example, casseroles, lasagna, and many types of pasta dishes). It is thus possible to imagine a scenario, though perhaps not an entirely smooth and seamless one, in which the market for food is not significantly altered as a gradual, national movement to vegetarianism proceeds.

Those who reject animal eating have another reply to the appeal to the economic realities of the industry as a justification for maintaining the practice. Bluntly and simply stated, this reply is just "So what?" So hundreds of thousands of people loose their jobs and an enormous economic resource is shut down. What does this matter if the basis of this economy is patently immoral? The slave-based economy of the antebellum South produced prodigious amounts of money for the southern economy, wealth that would have to be transferred to the laborers if they were actually paid a decent wage, and wealth that would be significantly diminished by a substantial improvement in the terms and conditions of their employment. That transfer and those improvements, had they occurred overnight, would have dealt a staggering blow to the southern economy, but "So what." A slave-based economy is immoral and needs to be abolished, no matter the cost. Why should it be any different for animals?

Tom Regan has made this point in the context of a rights-based theory founded on his notion of inherent value:

> Farm animals raised for human consumption are today treated as renewable resources.... [This] is to fail to treat them with the respect they are due as possessors of inherent value. It is, then, to treat them unjustly, and this finding makes all the moral difference in the world when the farmer claims that he is "within his rights" in raising these animals for human consumption. He *would* be "within his rights"*only if* those who were harmed by what he does (namely, the animals he raises) *were treated with respect*. But they are not treated with respect, and cannot be, so long as they are treated as if they are renewable resources. This is why, on the rights view, farmers who raise animals for human consumption are engaged in an unjust practice....Morally, this practice ought to cease, and consumers ought to cease to support it (Regan 1983: 345–346).

Regan adds that an appeal to economic harm does not give anyone the right to protection from that harm if the rights of others are violated by an unjust institution.

Animals as Test Subjects   Economic concerns are frequently cited to combat those who are concerned with environmental protection, or with the deaths of animals at the hands of those in the meat packing and processing industries. Although, as we noted above, it is not completely obvious that the economic analysis favors the perpetuation of the meat market, nonetheless such an appeal is very plausible. In an interesting turnabout, economic considerations seem clearly to weigh against the use of animals as subjects for consumer products testing. Alternative methods of testing that utilize computer models or *in vitro* (literally, "in glass") techniques are almost invariably far cheaper than using animals, take much less time, and appear to be just as effective. After all, test animals must be purchased, facilities to house them maintained, people paid to make sure that the animals are fed and watered, and their cages cleaned, and a number of handlers and experimenters must also be paid. This all adds up.

Consider one of the most utilized alternatives to the Draize Eye Irritancy Test (see above, Introduction, Animals in Business: Animals in Consumer Products Testing). The *Eytex* method, developed by InVitro International of Irvine, California, assesses irritancy with a vegetable protein derived from the jack bean plant. Researchers at InVitro constructed a synthetic matrix of protein that mimics the reaction of a cornea when exposed to some foreign substance. When test compounds cause the protein matrix to become opaque, the degree of opacity corresponds to a degree of irritancy: The more opaque, the greater the irritant. Eyetex can be used to determine the toxicity of more than 5,000 different chemicals. The economic advantages of Eytex are obvious: One testing kit suitable for testing three different concentrations of some chemical costs about $100, while a Draize test of comparable range would cost more than $1000 to pay for the animals, the equipment, the facility, and the personnel. A significant part of these savings results from the time required; while a standard Draize test may take one to three weeks, Eyetex results typically can be obtained in one day or less (Welsh 1990).

A second instance of economically advantageous alternatives to animal testing is a variety of cell culture procedures. The basic idea here is to measure the effect of different dilutions of a test substance on a specific number of cultured cells; cell death or any substantial changes are observed and recorded after the test substance is added to the culture. For example, the *agarose diffusion method* was originally designed in the early 1960s to determine the toxicity of plastics and other synthetic materials used in medical devices, such as heart valves, intravenous lines, and artificial joints. It has only recently been put to use by manufacturers of consumer products, such as the Noxell Corporation. In this method, human cells and a small amount of the material to be tested for toxicity are placed in a flask. The two substances are separated by a thin layer of agarose, a derivative of the seaweed called agar. If the test material is toxic, an area of dead cells will appear surrounding the substance; degree of toxicity can be determined by the extent of cell damage. Once more, agarose diffusion is extremely cost effective, with a price tag one-tenth that of toxicity testing using animals, and results are available much more quickly (Welsh 1990).

The 10 to 1 ratio seems to hold across the board for alternatives to animal testing. The General Accounting Office has reported that the average *in vitro* test costs about $50,000 per product, while animal tests of a similar scope cost an average of $500,000 per product.

Of course, the animal rights advocate, or simply one who is concerned with animal pain and suffering, could argue that the economic benefits of alternatives to animal testing are morally irrelevant. Even if these alternatives were not so much cheaper, the fact remains, they would insist, that animals are treated as instruments for serving human purposes, or their misery is regarded as having little or no moral significance. In either instance, the animal advocate would demand some justification for a view that denies animals moral standing, or only accords one so meager that we may treat them as "tools for research."

Environmental Law

Introduction

Environmental law is the newest legal arena in which business must maneuver. Prior to 1970 there really was no cohesive body of law concerning the environment; no law school or MBA program had a course in environmental law, and the United States had no national policy addressing environmental problems with federal regulation. Part of the problem was a lack of scientific knowledge, but also there was too much reliance on the states to formulate standards and enforce them. Both tasks, if addressed at all, were accomplished unevenly and inconsistently. Occasionally, private citizens would sue industrial polluters for nuisance, trespass, or negligence; such isolated litigation did not produce any widespread or lasting impact. And prior to 1960 the use of animals in business was completely unregulated: There were no federal laws whatever providing standards for slaughtering food animals, and it was not until 1970 that procedures for handling animals in testing and research became subject to statutory requirements.

Pollution The initial foray into federal regulation of air quality occurred in 1955 with the Air Pollution Control Act; however, this statute did little more than allocate money to study air quality control. It was substantially altered with the first national air quality legislation, the Clean Air Act of 1963, (42 U.S.C. §§7401–7642). Administered by the Department of Health, Education, and Welfare (HEW), the law imposed no requirement to reduce pollution; rather the focus was on investigating sources of pollution and making recommendations to states interested in tackling the problem. States were free to ignore the recommendations if they chose. Nonetheless, the act did provide for both the development of air quality criteria and for a federally mandated abatement of action if air pollution presented a danger to the health and welfare of citizens.

The Air Quality Act of 1967 consisted of further amendments to the Clean Air Act. Most notable among them was the imposition on the states of required air quality standards. The applicable standards were tailored according to the regional weather and landscape. Unfortunately, the Air Quality Act was not very successful. It was ineffective primarily because the states were given too much flexibility in setting standards and establishing time limits for compliance, and the act failed to specify just what level of air quality indicates pollution. Moreover, states were allowed to consider the practicability and feasibility of pollution control, a permission that was typically used as a loophole to escape abatement measures. Amendments in 1970 fixed these problems (see Selected Cases: Clean Air Act of 1970, below). The brand new Environmental Protection Agency (see Selected Cases, below) generated national standards within a year and the states were given nine months to describe how they intended to meet those standards. The practicability/feasibility loophole was eliminated and pollution defined.

Federal regulation of water pollution began much earlier than legislation aimed at improving air quality, but since water rights had traditionally been left to the states, there was not much real effect here either. The Rivers and Harbors Act of 1899 (30 Stat. 1121) restricted discharges into navigable waters; the Public Health Service Act of 1912 (42 U.S.C. §§201 *et seq.*), allowed the federal government to investigate public health problems caused by water pollution; and the Oil Pollution Act of 1924 (33 U.S.C. §§431–437), prohibited discharge of oil into coastal waters (it was eventually repealed). Enforcement was lax, and judicial interpretation of the acts was rare and quite general. Little change occurred.

The Federal Water Pollution Control Act of 1948 did little more than provide some financial assistance and research support for states concerned with water quality. The Water Quality Act of 1965 (33 U.S.C. §§1251 *et seq.*) increased federal involvement with state efforts primarily by requiring states to either set their own water quality standards or have federal standards imposed upon them. Though a step in the right direction, industry ably resisted such standards as bad for business and the states opposed a greater federal presence in an area traditionally left to them. Finally, two major events in the summer of 1969 generated enough public concern to effectively stimulate Congress. The Cuyahoga River, near Cleveland, Ohio, caught fire; and about one-quarter billion gallons of oil leaked into the Pacific Ocean from an offshore drilling platform on the California coast. Both incidents received a great deal of media attention. It was time for some big changes.

As we saw in Environmental Ethics, above, the ultimate justification for this sort of legislation is that people are harmed by the effects of pollution, and they are entitled to air and water that does not deteriorate their health and well-being. This justification presupposes that people have **legal standing**. The doctrine of legal standing holds that in order to enjoy the protections afforded by law, an individual must suffer an injury, generically understood as an invasion of one's interests, and it must be possible to remedy this injury in some manner provided by law. To have legal standing is to have legal rights (for more details, see below *Sierra Club v. Morton*). Clearly, you have legal standing and, just as clearly, your chair does not. If sulfur dioxide emissions from the local power plant damage your lungs, your interest in a healthy respiratory tract has been defeated. In simpler terms, you have been injured. Your injury can be compensated with monetary payments (though perhaps not adequately). On the other hand, the chair you're sitting in can be "remedied" if it is damaged—it can be repaired—but it has no interests in any legally relevant sense: it has no desires that can be satisfied or frustrated, and it cannot suffer, or experience pain or happiness. Where do animals fit in?

Animals   The legal standing of animals used in business and those wild animals affected by business activity is not entirely clear. Several federal cases, including one reaching as high as the Supreme Court, involve lawsuits filed by individuals concerned for the well-being of animals. However, these cases were decided according to human interests in the animals, not according to the interests the animals have in their own well-being. For example, a case involving the killing of seals ultimately turned on what sort of injury members of a wildlife advocacy group might suffer, not on any injury to the seals. The Marine Mammal Protection Act bans killing or importing marine mammals in the United States, but it also allows the director of the National Marine Fisheries Service the discretion to waive the ban. When Director Kreps decided to issue permits to the South African government for the taking of a certain number of Cape fur seals, the Animal Welfare Institute (AWI) sued, hoping to maintain the proscription. The District of Columbia Court of Appeals ruled in favor of the AWI on the grounds that allowing the hunt would invade their members' interest in observing, photographing, and delighting in the seals in their natural habitat. The interest the seals might have in not being killed was not considered, indicating that they had no legal standing in this case (*Animal Welfare Institute v. Kreps*, 561 F.2d 1002 [D.C. Cir. 1977]).

Another wildlife advocacy organization pushed its lawsuit all the way to the Supreme Court, arguing that its membership would be adversely affected by actions harmful to animals. The International Convention for the Regulation of Whaling had declared a moratorium on the killing of whales, yet Japanese business interests had continued to pursue and take whales despite the prohibition. The American Cetacean Society tried to induce the secretary of commerce to notify the president that Japan was in violation of the international regulation, which would require the president to impose economic sanctions against that country. Although the Court decided that the secretary was not required to inform the president of the violation, it did agree that the Cetacean Society had legal standing to sue. This was because their members' interest in whale watching and study would be thwarted by continued hunting. Here too, there was no suggestion that the whales themselves could have any cause of legal action against the Japanese hunters (*Japan Whaling Association v. American Cetacean Society*, 478 U.S. 221 [1986]).

Although these cases, and others like them, suggest that animals do not have any legal standing in their own right and can only receive legal protection when humans take an interest in them, every state does have some version of an anticruelty to animals statute. Most of these laws apply to any animal, and in general they prohibit cruel mistreatment—such as torturing, mutilating, wounding, or overworking an animal, or failing to provide food, water, or shelter for it. *Cruelty* is typically defined as inflicting unnecessary or unjustified pain and suffering. Such statutes suggest that animals do have legal standing and some legal rights: the right not to be tortured, for example, and the right to be supplied with adequate sustenance. Yet, as we have seen (above, Introduction to this chapter), business enterprises involved in agriculture and products testing subject enormous numbers of animals to varying degrees of coercion and confinement, cause them pain and suffering, and then kill them. How can this be legal?

There are two answers here. First, it is plausible to hold that anticruelty statutes do not actually accord animals legal standing and rights after all. The American Law Institute, an association of legal scholars, canvassed state anti-cruelty legislation, and drafted a paradigm statute for inclusion in the Model Penal Code. The drafters determined that the prevailing justification for these statutes was to prevent affronts to human sensibilities—to protect those who would be displeased with demonstrations of cruelty to animals—and maintain the moral fiber of the community. If the Institute is correct about this, then we have no *direct* legal duties to animals, only indirect duties that are really to people of tender sensibilities and to the public at large (see also Kant's view of our duties to animals, above in Environmental Ethics, Respecting Dignity and Rights). And because the use of animals by business is nearly always concealed from public view, these problems do not arise.

The other answer is that these business practices involving animals are not really cruel after all, and so they are specifically exempted by the relevant statutes. All state anticruelty statutes explicitly announce that the provisions of the law do not apply when raising animals for food or when using them in research and experimentation. The states have uniformly adopted the view that so long as the federal anticruelty laws are followed—the Humane Methods of Slaughter Act and the Animal Welfare Act (see both in Selected Cases, below)—animal agriculture and testing do not raise any legal issues. In that event, these practices are not cruel because any pain and suffering endured is necessary or justified.

So what is the legal standing of animals? Apparently, it all depends. Wild animals would appear to have none, as indicated by the two cases discussed above (see also Selected Cases: *Lujan v. Defenders of Wildlife*), and by the fact that sport hunting and commercial trapping are legal in every state. The Model Penal Code suggests that domesticated animals have no legal standing either, because our duties with regard to them are really owed to other people. If, however, this is just a part of the justification for anticruelty legislation, and such laws are directed toward the welfare of the animals themselves, then they do have legal standing and the legal right not to be treated cruelly. Obviously though, animals have no legal right to life, and what is or is not cruel seems to be a function of what humans regard as necessary or justifiable.

Selected Cases, Statutes, and Regulations

Environmental Protection Agency, Presidential Reorganization Order (1970) President Richard Nixon created the Environmental Protection Agency (EPA) by consolidating the various functions of the Federal Water

Quality Administration, the National Air Pollution Control Administration, the Atomic Energy Commission, and others. The mission of the EPA is to control and decrease air and water pollution, especially that produced by solid waste, pesticides, radiation, and toxic substances. Cooperation and coordination with state and local officials are seen as essential.

The EPA is intended to exercise regulatory authority over every aspect of pollution abatement: research, creating standards and the policies that express them, monitoring for pollution, and enforcing the regulations. These diverse functions are allocated to six different administrative departments in the EPA. The checkered history of the agency includes the frequent criticism that this structural intention is usually just a management ideal, that there is far too little coordination and communication among the departments to effectively accomplish their presidentially appointed mandate. During its nearly three decades of existence, the EPA has been regularly plagued with administrative turmoil, the subject of frequent assaults from all fronts: business, environmental groups, the Congress, and the executive branch that created it. Some stability seems to have arrived at the EPA since the appointment in 1993 of Carol Browner as chief administrator.

National Environmental Policy Act of 1970, 42 U.S.C. §§4321 *et seq*. The National Environmental Policy Act (NEPA) mandates that any proposed legislation, regulation, or other federal government action take account of the effects on the natural environment before proceeding. This mandate is accomplished through two main devices:

The first device is the **Council on Environmental Quality** (CEQ), the federal watchdog on environmental policy. Three people sit on the council, one of whom is designated as the chair. The main function of the CEQ is to advise the president on the current state of the nation's environment. Data is gathered and analyzed by the counselors and their staff, legislation recommended, urgent issues requiring attention identified, and every year a publication detailing their findings is released: the *President's Annual Report on Environmental Quality*.

During the 1970s the chair of the CEQ was very much involved in federal policy issues concerning the environment, attending meetings of the President's Domestic Policy Council, representing the president at international conferences, and coordinating federal agency activities involved with the World Commission on Environmental Development. All that changed with the Reagan administration in the 1980s. The CEQ budget was reduced by more than 80 percent, and staff was cut by a similar percentage. President Clinton attempted to abolish the CEQ in 1993 and replace it with the new Office of Environmental Policy, but House opposition led him to revitalize the CEQ and merge it with the new office.

The second device is the required filing of an **Environmental Impact Statement** (EIS) for every major federal government activity that has a significant impact on the environment. "Federal activities" are construed broadly to include any project requiring federal licensing or involving government money. No precise dollar amount is specified as indicating a "major" activity, just those that require a substantial investment of human and financial resources.

The meaning of "significant impact on the environment" has been the subject of much debate both inside and outside of courtrooms. In 1979 the CEQ tried to clarify the issue with the pronouncement that the significance of an environmental impact was a function of the *context* and the *intensity* of the activity. The context was determined by assessing the long- and short-term effects on the local area, the region, and society generally. The intensity of the impact involved a number of factors, including the degree to which public health and safety may be affected, the likelihood of controversy generated by the activity, its effects on places with historical, cultural, or scientific value, and whether any environmental protection law may be violated.

The filing of an EIS has been contentious from the beginning, and not just because some of the terms are vague. The procedural requirements are time-consuming and costly. A team of specialists (engineers, geologists, accountants, and the like) is required to prepare a draft report, one that is typically circulated within the agency contemplating the project, to be reviewed by others. The reviewers' comments may lead to significant revisions. Once the draft is complete, it is read and criticized by the CEQ, and published in the *Federal Register* for public comment. Further revisions may then follow, or even a rewriting of the entire EIS, before a final draft is issued. The process usually takes six to nine months, and considerably longer if legal challenges arise.

Every EIS must address five items:

1. The adverse and beneficial effects of the proposed activity on the environment
2. Any unavoidable negative environmental impact
3. Alternatives to the proposal
4. The short-term uses of the environment and their relationship to long-term productivity
5. The resources that are irretrievably committed

The typical EIS is a few hundred pages in length.

Clean Air Act of 1970, 42 U.S.C. §§7401 *et seq.* By 1970 it had become apparent in Congress that both the Clean Air Act of 1963 and its 1967 amendment (see Introduction, above) were making very little progress, and abatement efforts by state governments were not doing any better: The nation's skies were getting dirtier, not cleaner. This act represents a new covenant between state and local governments. Primary responsibility for monitoring, controlling, and preventing pollution is allocated to the states, while the EPA (a federal office) is charged with setting air quality standards, conducting research, and supplying the states with technical and financial assistance. The EPA may also help the states in the implementation and enforcement of regulations. The act was amended in 1976 and 1990.

At the core of the act are the **national ambient air quality standards** (NAAQSs). These standards are maximum allowable limits for those pollutants that were determined by the EPA to be harmful to human health and well-being: carbon monoxide, sulfur dioxide, nitrogen dioxide, ozone, lead, and suspended particulates. The states are responsible for reducing the level of the pollutants to the national standards, or below them. A state implementation plan (SIP) must be submitted, explaining how the standards will be achieved within the three-year time period allowed by the act. The states are given the discretion to distribute the burdens of reducing pollution among the various industries.

Because reducing air pollution costs money and usually requires special devices, businesses are often tempted to avoid the standards by pleading that they cannot afford the equipment needed to meet them, or that the necessary equipment is not currently available. However, the Supreme Court has ruled that economic or technological feasibility is not to be considered in the formulation of SIPs. In *Union Electric Company v. EPA* (427 U.S. 246 [1976]), the Missouri power company, Union Electric, objected to the NAAQS imposed upon it for sulfur dioxide emissions in the St. Louis metropolitan area. Union Electric argued that the standards were economically and technologically impractical. The court rejected the argument because the statute does not allow such factors to mitigate the NAAQSs promulgated by the EPA. After this decision, SIPs have been seen as focused on promoting public health in ways that are "technology forcing." This interest in clean air is so important that if the technology does not exist, it must be invented.

New source performance standards (NSPSs) apply to new sources of pollution, namely, recently constructed plants and older plants that have been modified. These standards are usually more stringent than those for older operations, and are a function of the best system of emissions reduction that has been "adequately demonstrated." Soon after the act was passed, controversy arose over what the *adequate demonstration* of an emissions reduction system was. Corporations claimed that the phrase meant that the standards were achievable by any business presently in operation. The District of Columbia Circuit Court disagreed. In a decision very much like that in *Union Electric Company*, the court held that NSPSs are forward looking and technology forcing, not focused on the current state of affairs of pollution control (*Portland Cement Association v. Ruckelshaus*, 486 F.2d 385 [D.C. Cir. 1973]).

The 1990 amendments to the Clean Air Act added two new pollution control programs. The *Air Toxins Program* was prompted by the realization that by 1989 only eight of the nearly 200 toxic pollutants identified by the EPA during the early 1970s had received federal regulations. This program is intended to compel industrial plants to drastically reduce their emissions of these pollutants. The *Acid Rain Control Program* calls for a 50-percent reduction in sulfur dioxide emissions by 2000. Because burning coal produces sulfur dioxide (see below, Surface Mining Control and Reclamation Act), this reduction objective sits uneasily with congressional action aimed at increasing the use of coal for our energy needs. The 1990 amendments also prohibit the use of chlorofluorocarbons and carbon tetrachloride by 2000.

Clean Water Act of 1977, 33 U.S.C. §§1251–1387   This congressional action began as the Federal Water Pollution Control Act of 1972 (FWPCA) and stated that "The objective of this Act is to restore and maintain the chemical, physical, and biological integrity of the Nation's waters." The legislative intent of the FWPCA was to protect all the waters of the United States and make them safe for aquatic life, fishing, and swimming. In 1977 various amendments to the FWPCA produced a comprehensive and complex system of water pollution control.

The EPA devised the **National Pollutant Discharge Elimination System**. The core of the system is a series of effluent discharge standards, initially set by the EPA for each of 27 categories of industry, such as rubber, plastics, and forest products; 13 more categories of industry were subsequently added. Every business within each group is required to use the same pollution control technology. The EPA issues permits to companies, specifying regulations on the discharge of pollutants at *point sources*, discrete locations where effluent is released. Any discharge without a permit is illegal. The permits specify the control technology required, the dates of compliance, and the maximum allowable discharge. They also contain provisions for modifying the discharge standards in case it is determined that stricter control is necessary to achieve the goals of the act.

Discharge regulations vary depending on whether the effluent is from a new or existing source, and on the category of pollutant. New sources have stricter pollution regulations because it is easier and less expensive to design plants with effective discharge control than it is to retrofit already existing plants. Pollutants are classified as conventional, nonconventional, or toxic. Conventional pollutants (suspended solids and fecal matter, for example) are the most leniently regulated, requiring only that **best conventional pollution control technology** (BCT) standards are achieved. Toxic and nonconventional pollutants are subject to the more rigorous requirements of the **best available technology economically achievable** (BAT). The main difference between the two is that BCT standards result from balancing the costs of the technology with the benefits of reducing the pollution, while BAT standards take only the benefits into account.

The Clean Water Act also proscribes the discharge of thermal pollution, or heated water. Electric power plants and many types of manufacturing plants produce enormous amounts of very hot water or other heated materials. Because such emissions cause ecological instability by decreasing the oxygen content of water and by harming fish, birds, and mammals that use the waterways, they are subject to federal regulation. Generally, industrial plants are required to reduce the temperature of liquid discharges to a maximum of 104°F.

Over the last 20 years, the Clean Water Act has significantly reduced water pollution emanating from industrial point sources, but a major fount of ongoing pollution is *nonpoint sources*. These discharges occur, for example, when storm water carries pesticides and fertilizers as runoff from fields, or from the accumulated effect of oil dripping from motor vehicles. The Water Quality Act of 1987 attempts to address this problem in two phases. In the first phase, permits to discharge are issued to municipalities; in the second phase, just begun in 1995, specific regulations are issued for specific polluters identified as nonpoint sources.

Violations of this law can bring fairly severe penalties. A corporation that knowingly endangers the public safety by polluting waters faces a fine of $1 million or $25,000 per day for negligent violations. An individual who by polluting water places another person in imminent danger may be fined $250,000 and imprisoned for up to 15 years. The EPA can also seek court injunctions and fines. Citizens may sue corporations or other persons whose pollution adversely effects them.

***Sierra Club v. Morton*, 405 U.S. 727 (1972)** This famous Supreme Court case concerns the deep legal and philosophical question of **standing** (see also above, Environmental Ethics: Introduction). To have *standing* is to be legally entitled to initiate a lawsuit. To do that, a person must be sufficiently affected by the matter at hand, and the problem must be resolvable by legal action. As traditionally defined, the impact and resolution require three elements: (1) an actual or imminent injury, which is understood as an invasion of a legally protected interest, (2) a causal relationship between the injury and the challenged conduct, and (3) a likelihood that the injury will be remedied by a favorable decision. In environmental law, the first element is especially important because environmental protection requires the identification of a party who would be injured by environmental use, and to qualify as an injured party one must have a legally protected interest. Now, of course, people have such interests, but does a wilderness area?

The wilderness in question is the Mineral King Valley on the west side of the Sierra Nevada Mountains, Tulare County, California. The area was designated as part of the Sequoia National Forest in 1926 and in the late 1940s the Forest Service began to consider Mineral King as a potential site for recreational development. In 1965 the Forest Service invited bids from developers for the construction and operation of a combination ski resort and summer recreation area. Walt Disney Enterprises submitted the winning bid: a $35 million complex of motels, restaurants, parking lots, ski trails and lifts, and other structures designed to accommodate an estimated 14,000 visitors daily. A 20-mile-long road, to be constructed by the state of California, was needed to provide access to the facility, and a high-voltage electricity line would supply power.

In 1969 the Sierra Club filed suit against Rogers Morton, secretary of the Department of the Interior and chief administrator of the Forest Service. In its complaint filed in federal district court, the Club claimed that the proposed development violated various federal rules governing the preservation of national forests, and it sought permanent injunctions against the approval of the project. The district court granted a preliminary injunction, but the Ninth

Circuit Court of Appeals vacated it on the grounds that the Sierra Club had failed to establish its standing as a party that would be injured by the development.

Justice Potter Stewart's majority opinion affirmed the judgment of the appellate court. The Sierra Club had no standing in this suit because it had failed to demonstrate or even to assert that any of its members would be affected in any substantial way by the Disney project. Although the Club did claim that the interests of future generations in the aesthetic enjoyments of the valley would be thwarted, Stewart pointed out that a legally relevant injury did not consist in the invasion of *any* recognizable interest, it must be an *actual* injury sustained by the person seeking judicial review of the matter. Since the Sierra Club was not suing on behalf of future generations, much less on behalf of the valley itself, it needed to show that at least some of its membership would be harmed, and this was not shown.

This case produced a dissenting opinion nearly as well known as that of the majority. Justice William O. Douglas, a long-time devotee of wilderness preservation and conservation, argued that because the interests of natural objects can be injured in a legally cognizable way, they can be seen as having legal standing in themselves. Human persons can speak for these natural objects just as they do for individuals who are not legal persons, such as corporations and children. Although this appeal has never been taken seriously in law, it has fueled years of debate in the literature of environmental philosophy. In the courts, as this case shows, injured parties remain those with legally protected interests, and they are the ones (or their proxies) who have the right to sue for redress. Despite the fact that the Sierra Club had failed to meet this requirement here, its suit did have two results favorable to those concerned with environmental protection. First, it indicated that an organization whose members would be adversely effected by environmental regulation would have standing. Second, the Mineral King project was never carried out. The Valley remains undeveloped to this day.

Lujan v. Defenders of Wildlife, 504 U.S. 555 (1992) This is the most recent major case on the issue of legal standing and concern for the environment, and it also has far-reaching implications for international business. The precedent set in *Sierra Club v. Morton* (see above) and in another key Supreme Court case decided shortly thereafter, *United States v. Students Challenging Regulatory Agency Procedures (SCRAP)* (412 U.S. 669 [1973]), seemed to bode well for environmental protection groups. In the *SCRAP* case, the student group sought an injunction prohibiting the Interstate Commerce Commission (ICC) from allowing the railroads to collect a 2.5 percent surcharge on transported goods before completing an environmental impact statement (for more on environmental impact statements, see above, National Environmental Policy Act). SCRAP argued that each of its members suffered specific harms as a result of the surcharge, including price increases on products shipped by rail, and adverse effects on their recreational and aesthetic opportunities in the natural areas surrounding the Washington, D.C., area where they lived. The ICC claimed that SCRAP, like the Sierra Club in

Morton, lacked standing to sue, but this time Justice Stewart's majority opinion went against business interests. He was sufficiently persuaded that
SCRAP would be injured by the surcharge.

With these two cases in the judicial background, things looked good for
the Defenders of Wildlife when they filed suit in a district court against
Manuel Lujan, secretary of the interior. The Defenders pointed out that the
Endangered Species Act of 1973 (16 U.S.C. § §1531 *et seq.)* requires each federal agency to consult with either the Department of the Interior or the
Department of Commerce to determine whether the agency's proposed business enterprise would imperil the habitat or the existence of any endangered
or threatened species. However, U.S. funds had been slated for an irrigation
project in Sri Lanka, threatening an endangered elephant species, and for
rebuilding the Aswan Dam on the Nile River in Egypt, menacing a rare
species of crocodile, and no such consultation was required. The Defenders
argued that this determination mandated by the Endangered Species Act
applies to activities funded by U.S. money in foreign countries as well, not just
in the United States. They anticipated that the funding would be withdrawn
once the statute was brought to bear on the status of the two animal species.

Lujan countered that the Defenders lacked standing to sue because the
group had not shown that their members were in fact injured by the failure to
apply the statute to the foreign projects. The Defenders responded that since
they represent members of an organization who had personally visited the
sites to study the endangered species, the matter of their standing had been
established. They cited *Morton* as the relevant precedent. Although initially
the district court accepted Lujan's argument and dismissed the suit, after the
Eighth Circuit Court of Appeals reversed and remanded the judgment, the
district court ordered Lujan to publish a new regulation, extending the
required consultation to actions taken in foreign nations. The appellate court
then affirmed this judgment.

Despite the two favorable decisions in *Morton* and *SCRAP* that anticipate
this case, the Supreme Court dismissed the Defenders' suit for lack of standing. Justice Antonin Scalia's majority opinion employed a narrow definition of
legal standing; in order to have standing, he argued, parties must show that
they have been "injured in fact," and this requires showing "a concrete and
particularized, actual or imminent invasion of a legally protected interest."
The Defenders did not show this: They did not prove that one or more of
their members would be directly affected in this way by the foreign projects,
and affidavits claiming an intention to visit the sites at some unspecified future
time do not establish an "imminent" injury. Finally, to the Defenders' notion
that injury would be caused to anyone anywhere in the world with an interest
in studying or observing these endangered species, Scalia opined that it was
just too speculative and nonconcrete to be taken seriously.

***Lucas v. South Carolina Coastal Council,* 505 U.S. 1003 (1992)**   The
Fifth Amendment to the Constitution is probably best known as the one that
protects an accused person from self-incrimination (pleading the Fifth), and
from being tried twice for the same crime (double jeopardy). Less well known

is the role of this amendment in environmental law. The **takings clause** of the Fifth Amendment reads: "nor shall private property be taken for public use, without just compensation." This means that the government must pay a fair price to the owner of property appropriated for public purposes. The clause has at least two important implications for business and the environment. First, unlike the protection against self-incrimination, the takings clause applies to corporations as well as individuals. But more significantly, it also has quite an influence on government regulation of natural resources held as private property. If the preservation of a wetland, for example, activates the Takings Clause, then government—the American people—will have to *pay* for the wetland, rather than simply seize it. Paying for something, instead of getting it for free, often provides a powerful incentive not to acquire the thing at all.

In 1986 David Lucas paid $975,000 for two residential lots on the Isle of Palms in Charleston County, South Carolina. He intended to have single-family dwellings constructed on these lots. Before he could begin construction however, South Carolina passed the Beachfront Management Act in 1988, which prohibited the erection of any permanent structure on beaches that had been subject to erosion over the previous 40 years. This area included Lucas's property, thus scuttling his plans to build condominiums. Lucas sued the state, charging that the Beachfront Management Act rendered his property virtually valueless, and thus amounted to a taking without just compensation in violation of the Fifth Amendment. The South Carolina Court of Common Pleas agreed with Lucas and ordered the state to pay him just over $1.2 million, but the South Carolina Supreme Court reversed that decision. In the reversal, the court argued that construction on the beach presented a serious threat to a public resource and, in that situation, no compensation was required.

The U.S. Supreme Court reversed the reversal. The six to three majority opinion, written by Antonin Scalia, presented the following principle: When a state regulation eviscerates a citizen's property of all economic worth, it is inappropriate to embark on a case-specific investigation in search of a compelling public interest that would justify not compensating the owner for his or her loss. The South Carolina Supreme Court was mistaken in pursuing this investigation. Unless state laws of property and nuisance foreclose compensation, a citizen's understanding of state power over private property must hold sway. That understanding, according to Justice Scalia, does not abide with the notion that title to property is at the mercy of a state's discretion to eliminate all that property's monetary value. Instead, people believe that the state will pay for the property taken. Lucas was entitled to his $1.2 million.

The significance of this decision is clear: State legislatures desiring to protect natural areas held by private citizens may well need to pay millions of dollars in "just compensation" for them. And that cost can be a substantial deterrent to environmental protection. Property owners, especially business persons like David Lucas, may be encouraged by these results, which suggest that a serious obstacle to business development—namely, state regulation—has been significantly diminished.

These lessons of *Lucas* were reinforced by a similar and more recent Supreme Court case. In *Dolan v. City of Tigard* (114 S. Ct. 2309 (1994)), Florence Dolan sought a permit to expand her plumbing and electric supply store in Tigard, Oregon. The city agreed to grant the permit on two conditions: Dolan must relinquish one portion of her property for use as a public greenway to minimize flooding likely to result from the expansion, and she must set aside another for a pedestrian and bicycle pathway to alleviate congestion in the area. Dolan sued, arguing that the two conditions were not reasonably related to her expansion plans; therefore, the city's requirements constituted a taking for which, under the Fifth Amendment, she was entitled to just compensation. Although the Oregon Supreme Court sided with the city of Tigard, the U.S. Supreme Court ruled for Dolan. Chief Justice William Rehnquist's five-to-four majority opinion declared that the construction required by Dolan's expansion plans did not have a close enough connection with the city's conditions to justify imposing an uncompensated burden.

Resource Conservation and Recovery Act of 1976, 42 U.S.C. §§6901–6991   The Solid Waste Disposal Act of 1965 (42 U.S.C. § §3251 *et seq.*), was the first attempt by Congress to regulate pollution caused by hazardous waste. However, major responsibility for setting standards was left to the states until the Act was amended by the Resource Conservation and Recovery Act (RCRA) in 1976 and the EPA took over. Today, state and local governments must actively manage solid waste according to nationwide regulations, aided by technical and financial support from the federal government. The RCRA defines hazardous wastes as solid wastes (these include liquids and gases) that cause increased mortality rates or severe illness if dispersed or improperly handled. Hazardous wastes are identified according to their level of ignitability, corrosivity, reactivity, and toxicity. (Hazardous waste and toxic waste are not necessarily the same thing; see Toxic Substances Control Act below.)

The RCRA authorizes the EPA to control hazardous substances in two different ways. First, facilities that treat, store, or dispose of hazardous wastes (TSDFs) must obtain permits in order to operate. Permits are issued once the EPA is satisfied that its standards for treatment, storage, disposal, documentation, and inspection are met. These standards vary in large part depending on the methods employed by the particular TSDF: tanks, surface impoundments, landfills, or incinerators, to name a few. Second, waste material is tracked through a series of manifests from its point of origin to the TSDF where it ends up. This is known as *cradle-to-grave* tracking. The industry generating the waste initiates the documentation that is then passed on to one or more transporters. The receiving TSDF also signs off and returns a copy to the generator; manifests that are not returned to the generator within 45 days must be reported to the EPA. Since the journey of the material from the generating facility through various transporters to the treatment plant is thoroughly documented, the assignment of responsibility for mishandling or accidents is made easier.

Toxic Substances Control Act of 1976, 15 U.S.C. §§2601–2671 The Toxic Substances Control Act (TSCA) gives the EPA authority to regulate toxic chemicals. These are substances that cause harmful effects in living organisms. By 1979 the EPA had compiled a list of all the chemicals moved across state lines as commercial traffic, an inventory numbering nearly 50,000. The agency can control chemicals by issuing rules for the production, distribution, use, and testing of a chemical. If a chemical is shown to present an unreasonable risk to human health, the EPA can order a halt to all production and distribution of it. The EPA's Interagency Testing Committee is authorized to direct manufacturers to either test their chemicals or give reasons why no testing is necessary. As of this writing, only about one-quarter of the listed chemicals have been tested for toxicity.

The EPA also investigates the development of new chemicals. A manufacturer wishing to use an unlisted substance must provide the agency with a pre-manufacturing notice (PMN) at least 90 days before the substance is scheduled to be made or imported. The PMN must contain quite a bit of information about the chemical, including its molecular structure, its purpose, its possible health hazards, any by-products of its manufacture, how much of it and where it would be produced. Most importantly, all test data related to the effect of the new chemical on human health must be included in the PMN and submitted to the EPA. The agency may promulgate rules requiring various warnings or it may ban the chemical altogether.

Surface Mining Control and Reclamation Act of 1977, 30 U.S.C. §§1201 *et seq.* Coal is formed when trees, shrubs, and other vegetable matter dies and then decomposes while buried under mud or rock. Over millions of years, the pressure and lack of oxygen forms the decaying plant material into a solid substance that will burn when ignited, thus producing energy. America has enormous amounts of coal, located primarily in the Appalachian region and on the western and midwestern plains, constituting 90 percent of our hydrocarbon reserves. Today, coal-fired generating plants supply about half of the nation's electricity, and about 25 percent of all our energy needs. Because coal is plentiful, relatively cheap to extract, and reduces our dependence on foreign oil, there has been over the last 25 years a push to increase our reliance on it. Indeed, the Powerplant and Industrial Fuel Act of 1978 (42 U.S.C. § §8301–8433), required many electricity generating installations to switch from oil or gas to coal in order to produce power.

Unfortunately, burning coal to generate power causes some serious environmental problems, not the least of which is the emission of sulfur dioxide, a major factor in acid rain (see above, the Clean Air Act and the Acid Rain Program). Just as troubling are the effects of the procedure for removing coal from the earth. Commonly referred to as *strip mining*, the process varies somewhat depending on the topography of the land but the basic idea is the same: the coal is accessed by removing and discarding the material (the *overburden*) under which it is buried. The results of this process include sterile land rendered useless for agricultural purposes, excessive soil erosion, water pollution from mining runoff, destruction of ecosystems, and loss of habitat for many species.

The Surface Mining Control and Reclamation Act (SMCRA) was passed by Congress to address these environmental problems caused by strip mining for coal, and by subsurface mining that affects the surface. Especially targeted is pollution resulting from exposure to heavy metals and from silt runoff during mining operations. The SMCR authorized the creation of a federal agency to enforce the Act, the Office of Surface Mining Reclamation and Enforcement (OSM), housed in the Department of the Interior. The statute stipulates that the OSM must not employ any individuals associated with any authority or program promoting the use or development of coal.

The OSM is charged with correcting past abuses in the mining industry and ensuring that future abuses do not occur. Mining companies are required to restore the land to approximately its original condition before the operation began its work; this restoration might include reproducing the original contours of the earth, and making sure the land can be used for the same purpose for which it was utilized before the mining occurred. In any case, reclamation efforts typically include replacing rock and topsoil, and replanting the surface. Companies are responsible for the successful revegetation of the mined area for the next five years, or, where average annual rainfall is less than 26 inches, the term of responsibility runs for ten years. Mining companies must apply for permits before they can begin operations, and no permit will be issued without a reclamation plan. These plans are approved by either the OSM or some authorized state agency.

The SMCRA survived a constitutional challenge in *Hodel v. Virginia Surface Mining & Reclamation Association, Inc.* (452 U.S. 264 (1981)), a case that also had wider implications for environmental regulation of business by the federal government. The mining association argued that the SMCRA requirement to restore stripped land to its approximate original condition amounted to an unconstitutional regulation of private property rather than a legitimate exercise of federal authority to manage business. The **commerce clause** of the Constitution (Article I, Section 8) empowers the legislature to regulate commerce *between* or "among" the various states, but the miners were hard-pressed to see how the restoration rule applied to a mining operation in Virginia (or some other state) had anything to do with that.

The Supreme Court ruled unanimously against the mining association. Congress has the authority to regulate a business activity, even though it is confined within the borders of a particular state, if it is reasonable to believe that the activity does influence commerce with other states. The court held that, because strip mining is well known to adversely impact the land in a wide variety of ways, it does indeed have this interstate effect. In that case, the only remaining question was whether the SMCRA is an effective means for accomplishing the goal set by Congress, namely, to reclaim land despoiled by mining. The SMCRA was held to be an effective means for this end.

Comprehensive Environmental Response, Compensation, & Liability Act of 1980, 42 U.S.C. §§9601–9675 The purpose of this Act

(CERCLA, or the Superfund) is to solve the problem of accidentally spilled hazardous waste and its storage in dump sites. The problem was originally addressed through a $1.6 billion trust fund. In 1986 the Superfund Amendment and Reauthorization Act (SARA), an amendment to CERCLA, increased the money available for cleanups to $9 billion. About three-quarters of this money comes from the petroleum and chemical industries, and corporate income taxes. In 1992 $1.75 billion in federal revenues was added to the Superfund, mostly through taxes on products containing hazardous substances, such as gasoline.

CERCLA requires the owners of hazardous waste dumps to notify the EPA of just what sort of waste is buried in their dumps. For its part, the EPA is required to identify sites where hazardous wastes have been disposed, stored, or abandoned, and rank these sites according to the severity of the health risk they pose. Those with the highest ranking are placed on a National Priority List, and receive first consideration for cleanup. Before any site is cleaned, engineering and scientific studies determine the best method of proceeding. To date, the EPA has located over 25,000 such sites.

CERCLA imposes liability for the cleanup and for any damages on those companies that generate and dispose of hazardous waste. The liability imposed here is **strict**: subject companies are responsible for cleanup and damages whether or not they were negligent or in any other way at fault in their actions (for more on strict liability, see Chapter 2: The Consumer— Product Safety, Law; Introduction). Companies are required to carry liability insurance to cover any damages resulting from the release of hazardous substances. Liability may be escaped if it can be shown that the release was caused by an "act of God" (a natural phenomenon, such as an earthquake), an act of war, or the acts or omissions of a third party. Generally, parent companies are not liable for cleanup costs incurred by their wholly owned subsidiaries, unless the parent exercises substantial control over the offending subsidiary. Mergers typically result in the surviving or acquiring company assuming responsibility for the pollution caused by the acquired company, even if the dumping occurred prior to the formation of any statutes making it illegal. The EPA is authorized to use Superfund money to clean up problem areas when the responsible party cannot be found.

Humane Methods of Slaughter Act of 1960, 7 U.S.C. §§1901–1906
Legislation designed to regulate the killing of animals for human consumption began in 1955 with a bill sponsored by Senator Hubert Humphrey and Representative Martha Griffiths. This initial attempt was vigorously opposed by the U.S. Department of Agriculture (USDA) and the meat packing industry, so little was accomplished for several years. Resistance in Congress was worn down over time and, culminating in an all day filibuster by Senator Humphrey, both Houses finally passed the bill. The Humane Slaughter Act was signed into law by President Eisenhower in 1960. As originally written, the statute applied only to packers supplying meat to the federal government, but that still accounted for 80 percent of American plants. Amendments in 1978 extended coverage to all meat packers in this country, and further required that

meat imported into the United States must also be slaughtered according to the provisions of the Act. Moreover, these amendments gave federal inspectors the authority to stop processing lines until violations are corrected.

All meat sold in this country must originate from animals killed at a federal or state facility approved by the USDA. The Act provides the rules for the proper handling and killing of the approximately 100 million cows, pigs, sheep, goats, and horses slaughtered each year. Poultry are specifically excluded from the provisions of the Act, as are animals ritually slaughtered according to religious traditions. While awaiting slaughter, animals must be driven into and out of the holding corrals in a "humane" manner, basically meaning that good faith efforts must be made to minimize their excitement and discomfort. Metal pipes and sharp objects are not permitted for this purposes; electric prods and canvas slappers are permitted but should be used as little as possible. All animals must have access to water and, if they are held more than 24 hours before being slaughtered, food must be provided. Animals confined overnight must have sufficient room to lie down. Animals that have fallen down for any reason should not be dragged; immediate slaughter may be necessary for such animals. Corrals, ramps, and driveways are to be maintained in good condition with sharp objects, splinters, broken boards, and the like, removed or repaired. Floors should be made slip resistant to provide secure footing.

The Act requires that animals be stunned into unconsciousness before they are killed. Exclusions for religious reasons allow killing fully conscious animals, as required, for example, by Jewish dietary laws specifying kosher slaughter. After the initial stunning, the death of the animal may result from evisceration, bleeding, or beheading; the Act does not specify a method here. The stunning may be accomplished with either an electrical device or a stungun. The typical electric stunner consists of a pair of large tongs with round disks at the ends; when placed on either side of the head, the disks pass an electrical charge into the brain, rendering the animal unconscious. Electric stunners are very commonly used for smaller animals like sheep and pigs in bigger slaughtering operations.

Cattle are almost always knocked out with stun-guns. These devices come in various sorts. Least often employed is the free fire cartridge, which is basically a bullet fired into the head; this is rare because it is the most expensive, and is confined to animals whose head meat is condemned as unfit for consumption. The bolt stunner and the concussion stunner are the most common instruments: with the bolt method, either an exploding cartridge or a blast of air drives a piston and an attached rod forward, penetrating the skull and brain of the animal, the bolt then retracting. The concussion works in the same way but does not penetrate the brain.

Animal Welfare Act of 1970, 7 U.S.C. §§2131–2157 This is the first, and remains the only, major federal legislation governing the use of animals in research and testing. It began as the Laboratory Animal Welfare Act of 1966, a statute inspired, not by concern for the treatment of animals in research facilities, but by a rash of thefts of family pets for use in experimentation. Congressman Resnick introduced the original bill in 1965 after becoming involved in an attempt to help a family recover a dog that had been stolen and taken by a dealer to a laboratory. Indeed, the preamble explicitly states that the primary purpose of the Act was to protect the owners of dogs and cats from the theft of their pets. In addition to these, the other animals covered are primates, guinea pigs, hamsters, and rabbits, but record keeping is only required for the dogs and cats.

Rats and mice are not covered by the Act (neither are birds), and subsequent Amendments have not included them, even though about 80 percent of animal subjects come from these two rodent species (see above, Environmental Ethics, Introduction; Animals in Consumer Products Testing). This exclusion was successfully challenged in federal district court by the Animal Legal Defense Fund and the Humane Society. They argued that their primary function as animal welfare organizations was the dissemination of information to their members and the public regarding the human use of animals, a function thwarted by the exclusion. However, this decision was vacated on appeal by the District of Columbia Circuit Court of Appeals (*Animal Legal Defense Fund v. Espy*, 23 F.3rd 496 (1994), and the issue has not been revived.

The Act is enforced by the U.S. Department of Agriculture (USDA) through the Animal and Plant Health and Inspection Service (APHIS), an administrative agency of the USDA. The secretary of the USDA is directed to set standards for the care and treatment of animals by dealers and research facilities. These standards include minimum requirements for feeding, watering, sanitation, shelter, and "adequate veterinary care," but initially did not include any guidelines whatever for the treatment of animals during the actual research. Dealers must be licensed, and, as originally written, the statute requires that they must identify or mark all and only the dogs and cats transported. All and only research facilities using dogs and cats must be registered with the federal government, and researchers must obtain dogs and cats from a licensed dealer only. Penalties for violation include revocation of a dealer's license and imprisonment for up to one year and a fine of up to $1000. Research facilities can be fined $500 per day.

In 1970 a number of major changes to the Act began with its name, and this is what we now know today as the Animal Welfare Act (AWA). The definition of *animal* was extended to include any "warm-blooded animal [that] the Secretary may determine is being used, or is intended for use, for research, testing, experimentation, or exhibition purposes, or as a pet," and record keeping was now required for all of these, and not just dogs and cats. Farm animals are excluded as are, again, rats, mice, and birds. The definition of "research facility" was also expanded to cover any individual, organization, or institution, including those of higher education, using or intending to use animals for these purposes. Additionally, "exhibitors" were brought under the regulation of AWA, defined as any persons exhibiting animals for compensation, such as in auctions, circuses, zoos, and carnivals (but rodeos are not included). These activities became subject to APHIS inspection. Dealers now include those supplying animals for education, exhibition, or as pets (though pet shops themselves are not covered by AWA). The concept of "adequate veterinary care" was fine-tuned to make explicit reference to the use of anesthetic and tranquilizing drugs, although the decision of precisely when these drugs are appropriate was left to the researchers. Finally, the 1970 Amendments created penalties for those who interfered with inspectors.

Major changes to the AWA occurred again with the 1985 Amendments. Perhaps foremost among them is that every research facility is required to establish an Institutional Animal Care and Use Committee (IACUC). The chief executive officer of each facility appoints the committee members; there must be at least three members, and both a veterinarian and a person concerned about animal welfare who is not affiliated in any way with the facility must be among them. The IACUC is required to conduct semiannual inspections of the facility and then file a complete report of their findings with APHIS.

Also included was the first regulation of the way in which experimentation is conducted; one amendment directs researchers to minimize pain and distress, as well as consider alternatives to procedures that cause pain. The withholding of anesthetics is permitted only when scientifically necessary; the researchers are left to determine when that necessity obtains. Further amendments require that dogs must be exercised and "a physical environment adequate to promote the well-being of primates" must be provided. Also, animal handlers are given mandatory training in humane methods of animal maintenance and experimentation. Finally, APHIS is required to inspect each research facility at least once a year.

An amendment in 1990 brought AWA back to concern for people's dogs and cats. Also known as the Pet Protection Act, regulations are now imposed on random source animals used in research. These are dogs and cats obtained at pounds or animal shelters, and the amendment requires these facilities to hold the animals for at least five days before selling them to a licensed dealer. The point is to give the human owners some opportunity to recover their pets, or provide some time for adoption. Some states prohibit shelters from supplying animals for research, and some shelters euthanize animals before the five-day period or have policies against supplying dealers; in these cases, this AWA amendment is superseded. Before a dealer can sell a random-source dog or cat, he or she must provide the buyer with documentation containing information about the dealer, the animal, the pound or shelter from which the animal was obtained, a statement from that facility that the animal was held for at least five days, and the date of acquisition.

Although the AWA applies to all animals used in consumer products testing, it should be noted that the Food and Drug Administration (FDA; see Chapter 2: The Consumer—Product Safety, Law) does not require cosmetics manufacturers to test their products for safety, either by using animals or any other method. However, if the safety of a cosmetic product has not been substantiated in some way, the manufacturer is required by the FDA to label the item in this manner: "Warning—the safety of this product has not been determined." Since this labeling would undoubtedly discourage sales, and since the failure to label accordingly would provoke costly lawsuits and federal regulatory action, the FDA policy has the practical effect of ensuring exhaustive product testing in the cosmetic industry. Recognizing this, the FDA has explicitly disavowed the LD-50 test, while also proclaiming that the Draize eye and skin irritancy tests are preferable to methods that do not utilize animals; this is because the FDA believes that nonanimal tests do not conclusively demonstrate safety.

References: Adams, Carol. 1990. *The Sexual Politics of Meat: A Feminist-Vegetarian Critical Theory*. New York: Continuum Books.

American Meat Institute. 1996. *Meat and Poultry Facts*. Washington D.C.

Baxter, William. 1974. *People or Penguins: The Case for Optimal Pollution*. New York: Columbia University Press.

Bentham, Jeremy. 1789. *Introduction to the Principles of Morals and Legislation*. London: Athlone Press, 1970.

Bowie, Norman. 1990. Morality, Money, and Motor Cars. In *Business, Ethics, and the Environment: The Public Policy Debate*, W. Michael Hoffman, Robert Frederick, and Edward Petry, eds. New York: Quorum Books.

Burritt, Roger and Patricia McCreight. 1998. Environmental Compliance By Industry. Vol. 2 of *Encyclopedia of Applied Ethics*, San Diego, CA: Academic Press.

Callicott, J. Baird. 1989. *In Defense of the Land Ethic*, Albany: State University of New York Press.

Cohen, Carl. 1986. "The Case for the Use of Animals in Biomedical Research," *New England Journal of Medicine* 315: 865–870.

DeGeorge, Richard. 1980. The Environment, Rights, and Future Generations. In *Responsibilities to Future Generations*, Ernest Partridge, ed. Buffalo, NY: Prometheus Books.

DesJardins, Joseph R. 1993. *Environmental Ethics*. Belmont, CA: Wadworth Publishing.

Devall, Bill and George Sessions. 1985. *Deep Ecology: Living as if Nature Mattered*. Salt Lake City: Peregrine Smith Books.

Edwards, Steven. 1987. "In Defense of Environmental Economics," *Environmental Ethics* 9: 73–85.

Environmental Protection Agency. 1994. *Characterization of Municipal Solid Waste in the United States*. Washington D.C.: US Government Printing Office.

———. 1995. *National Air Pollution Emission Trends 1900–1993*, Washington D.C.: US Government Printing Office.

Feinberg, Joel. 1974. The Rights of Animals and Unborn Generations. In *Philosophy and Environmental Crisis*, William T. Blackstone, ed. Athens, GA: University of Georgia Press.

Frey, R. G. 1980. *Interests and Rights*. New York: Oxford University Press.

———. 1983. *Rights, Killing, and Suffering*. Oxford: Blackwell.

Gilligan, Carol. 1982. *In A Different Voice*. Cambridge, MA: Harvard University Press.

Goodpaster, Kenneth. 1978. "On Being Morally Considerable." *The Journal of Philosophy* 75: 308–325.

Hoffman, W. Michael. 1991. "Business and Environmental Ethics." *Business Ethics Quarterly* 1: 169–184.

Hume, David. *A Treatise of Human Nature*. 1739.

Jaggar, Alison. 1983. *Feminist Politics and Human Nature*. Totowa, NJ: Rowman & Allanheld.

Kant, Immanuel. 1782. Duties to Animals and Spirits. In *Lectures on Ethics*, Louis Infield, trans. 1963. New York: Harper & Row.

———. 1785. *Fundamental Principles of the Metaphysics of Morals*.

Katz. Eric. 1990. Defending the Use of Animals in Business: Animal Liberation and Environmental Ethics. In *Business, Ethics, and the Environment: The Public Policy Debate*, W. Michael Hoffman, Robert Frederick, and Edward Petry, eds. New York: Quorum Books.

Kavka, Gregory. 1978. The Futurity Problem. In *Obligations to Future Generations*, R. I. Sikora and Brian Barry, eds., Philadelphia: Temple University Press.

Keller, Evelyn Fox. 1985. *Reflections on Gender and Science*. New Haven, CN: Yale University Press.

Kheel, Marti. 1985. "The Liberation of Nature: A Circular Affair." *Environmental Ethics* 7: 135–149.

Leopold, Aldo. 1949. *A Sand County Almanac*. New York: Oxford University Press.

Levin, Margarita Garcia. 1994. A Critique of Ecofeminism. In *Environmental Ethics*, Louis Pojman, ed. Sudbury, MA: Jones and Bartlett Publishers.

Mason, Jim and Peter Singer. 1990. *Animal Factories*. New York: Harmony Books.

Muir, John. 1911. *My First Summer in the Sierra*. Boston: Houghton Miflin Books.

Naess, Arne. 1973. "The Shallow and the Deep, Long-Range Ecology Movement." *Inquiry* 16: 95–100.

———. 1989. *Ecology, Community, and Lifestyle*, David Rothenberg, trans. Cambridge: Cambridge University Press.

Noddings, Nel. 1984. *Caring: A Feminine Approach to Ethics and Moral Education*. Berkeley, CA: University of California Press.

Orlans, Barbara. 1993. *In the Name of Science: Issues in Responsible Animal Experimentation*. New York: Oxford University Press.

Regan, Tom. 1983. *The Case for Animal Rights*. Berkeley, CA: University of California Press.

———. 1985. The Case for Animal Rights. In *In Defense of Animals*, Peter Singer, ed. Oxford: Blackwell.

Rolston, Holmes. 1989. *Environmental Ethics*. Philadelphia: Temple University Press.

Sagoff, Mark. 1981. "At the Shrine of Our Lady of Fatima, or Why Political Questions Are Not All Economic." *Arizona Law Review* 23: 1283–1298.

———. 1990. *The Economy of the Earth: Philosophy, Law, and the Environment*. New York: Cambridge University Press.

Schwartz, Thomas. 1978. "Obligations to Posterity." In *Obligations to Future Generations*, R. I. Sikora and Brian Barry, eds., Philadelphia: Temple University Press.

Schweitzer, Albert. 1990. *Out of My Life and Thought*, A. B. Lemke, trans. New York: Holt Publishers.

Singer, Peter. 1990. *Animal Liberation*. New Revised Edition. New York: Avon Books.

Steinbock, Bonnie. 1978. "Speciesism and The Idea of Equality," *Philosophy* 53: 247–256.

Starik, Mark. 1995. "Should Trees Have Managerial Standing? Toward Stakeholder Status for Non-Human Nature," *Journal of Business Ethics* 14: 207–217.

Stone, Christopher. 1974. *Should Trees Have Standing?* Los Altos, CA: William Kaufman Publishers.

Taylor, Paul. 1986. *Respect for Nature*. Princeton, NJ: Princeton University Press.

Warnock, G. J. 1971. *The Object of Morality*. New York: Methuen Books.

Warren, Karren. 1987. "Feminism and Ecology: Making Connections," *Environmental Ethics* 9: 3–20.

———. 1990. "The Power and the Promise of Ecological Feminism," *Environmental Ethics* 12: 125–146.

Welsh, Heidi. 1990. *Animal Testing and Consumer Products*. Washington D.C.: Investor Responsibility Research Center.

Willums, J. O. and U. Goluke. 1992. *Business and Sustainable Development*. Oslo: International Environmental Bureau of the International Chamber of Commerce.

Zurlo, Joanne, Deborah Rudacille and Alan Goldberg. *Animals and Alternatives in Testing*. New York: Mary Ann Leibert Publishers, 1994.

CONTEMPORARY ETHICAL ISSUES

Chapter 6: Codes of Ethical Conduct

Over the last 20 years or so, a growing number of corporations, organizations, associations, and other institutions have devised codes of ethical conduct. Ethical codes are becoming more common for two reasons: First, there has been a great deal of external criticism of business from government, consumers, and the media, and the threat of such reproach is ever-present. Second, there is the perhaps more disturbing problem of internal unrest arising from dissatisfied employees who perceive some social or institutional injustice (see also Chapter 4: The Employee—Whistleblowing and Loyalty). These two sources have generated an increased awareness of unethical business activity, and have caused a significant level of doubt and suspicion to grow in the minds of the public.

Although the need to monitor and regulate business is clear, the appropriate source of regulation is not. Business people do not look favorably on the idea of government or some other outside agency taking up the task: They fear that such external regulation would greatly disrupt the efficiency, cohesiveness, and profit margin of the corporation, as well as violate basic freedoms and property rights.

The alternative seems to be the self-regulation provided by an ethical code, and almost every company of any size has one.

The website of DePaul University's Institute of Business and Professional Ethics features a page with many different ethical codes from a variety of professions and organizations. Its address is http://www.depaul.edu/ethics/codes1.html. Many more can be accessed on the World Wide Web simply by utilizing any of the available search engines and asking for "ethical codes." Most companies are typically happy to provide their codes to interested persons upon written request.

Even a casual perusal of ethical codes will impress the reader with the great diversity found in ethical codes. Some come in slim pamphlets of just a couple of pages, others are substantial documents containing 50 pages or more, and nearly everything in between occurs, too. Some codes are highly detailed, discussing specific situations and alternative courses of action, while others are very broad, offering only rather vague recommendations to promote human well-being or to be a responsible citizen. These two categories of detailed and general ethical codes will be treated in more depth below.

Codes of conduct not only vary widely in their length and specificity, but in their moral emphasis as well. A particular code may offer directives about the workings of the institution as a collective of individual members, and stress conduct that seems aimed more at producing a successful business than morally appropriate behavior. The line between what constitutes potentially lucrative business practices and what constitutes virtuous conduct is often a fine one. Indeed, some argue that morally upright behavior just *is* good business. Despite the ambiguity and the variations mentioned above, some common themes of ethical codes can be identified.

Conflicts of interest are often mentioned or discussed in detail. Such conflicts may arise on an individual level when an employee is trusted to fulfill a certain professional responsibility, but chooses to act in his or her own interest instead. They also can occur as conflicts between the interest of the public and the interest of the business serving the public. The public trusts business, with the expectation that business will fulfill its responsibilities to the public; this conflict is especially acute when the self-regulating business defines both what the public interest is and its corresponding responsibility to it. In either case, there is a potential for a breach of trust between two parties.

Human well-being is an important category in many ethical codes, but it is not often clearly defined. Frequently, there is an umbrella statement to the effect that employees and managers should enhance human well-being, but the code does not specify the scope of that claim or define precisely what well-being is. Other codes are somewhat more enlightening. For example, the code of the Australian Institute of Engineers states that engineers should promote the common good by acting from common values, such as equal opportunity among individuals, social and environmental justice, unity of purpose (among people and engineers), and the support and growth of community health, safety, and welfare.

Issues of privacy and confidentiality, especially in the last decade, have been increasingly emphasized by corporations when creating and revising their ethical codes. The sort of issues under consideration range from the privacy of company accounts to employees' personal privacy. Many codes among members of accounting and banking associations discuss the responsibility to keep clients' accounts private. Information technology groups, such as the Association of Computer Machinery, are increasingly concerned with the need for care and confidentiality.

A prominent feature of nearly every ethical code is honesty. In one way, honesty is presupposed by ethical codes, because, although there may be penalties for failing to fulfill certain corporate objectives, codes can only be effective if those governed by them make an honest effort to comply. Many critics question the effectiveness of ethical codes because of this inherent weakness: A set of rules that relies primarily on the integrity of those who are meant to be regulated by the code raises perhaps the most fundamental conflict of interest issue.

The matter of gifts appears in ethical codes far less frequently than conflicts of interest or privacy. This issue may seem fairly insignificant, but in certain situations it is problematic. Gift giving can result in dishonest relationships and conflicts of interest. Often inherent in receiving gifts is the threat that honesty will be sacrificed for personal gain. Within the category of gift giving and receiving is political contributions. There is here a similar potential for dishonesty and promoting self-interest over corporate interest, and corporate interest over public interest by swaying or influencing public policy toward corporate ends. This aspect of business also needs monitoring, given the possibility of dishonest transactions.

Finally, most ethical codes include a set of guidelines prescribing how a corporation ought to relate to its competitors. Once again, this issue addresses such concerns as honesty, fairness, and straightforwardness.

Whatever its length or specific content, an ethical code's fundamental purpose is to guide and unify the members of various institutions when they encounter ethical questions in their daily operations or in unusual, isolated circumstances. Further, codes identify corporate goals and objectives and steer employees toward them. What is definitive of the various types of codes is a set of normative statements expressing how members of the group ought to fulfill the institution's mission and objectives.

General Ethical Codes

General ethical codes try to provide an ethical framework that can guide an individual's actions and decisions. Although the code typically recommends morally good, fair, and just behavior, a clear definition of these concepts is often absent. Also usually missing is a description of appropriate penalties or consequences for violations.

The basic features of general ethical codes are well represented by Johnson & Johnson (J&J), the world's largest health care products company. This company has a long tradition of formulating and modifying its ethical code. J&J calls its ethical position a *credo*. A credo is an institutional philosophy, usually no more than several paragraphs in length, intended to create a sense of corporate cohesion among the individuals of the institution. Due to its generality, a credo is often not especially useful for answering specific ethical questions.

J&J was one of the first of a rather small number of institutions that recognized the importance of a unifying company philosophy and ethical statement. As far back as 1935, J&J began defining its responsibilities and obligations to **stakeholders** such as customers, employees, stockholders, and the communities in which they worked and lived. J&J has made numerous revisions of its credo over the past two decades, though the core intent and motivation remain the same. The most significant and dynamic changes occurred when the company added phrases pertaining directly to issues of family life, and the protection of and respect for the natural environment. The credo as it stands presently is this:

Our Credo

We believe our first responsibility is to the doctors, nurses and patients, to mothers and fathers and all others who use our products and services. In meeting their needs everything we do must be of high quality. We must constantly strive to reduce our costs in order to maintain reasonable prices. Customers' orders must be serviced promptly and accurately. Our suppliers and distributors must have an opportunity to make a fair profit.

We are responsible to our employees, the men and women who work with us throughout the world. Everyone must be considered as an individual. We must respect their dignity and recognize their merit. They must have a sense of security in their jobs. Compensation must be fair and adequate, and working conditions clean, orderly and safe. We must be mindful of ways to help our employees fulfill their family responsibilities. Employees must feel free to make suggestions and complaints. There must be equal opportunity for employment, development and advancement for those qualified. We must provide competent management, and their actions must be just and ethical.

We are responsible to the communities in which we live and work and to the world community as well. We must be good citizens— support good works and charities and bear our fair share of taxes. We must encourage civic improvements and better health and education. We must maintain in good order the property we are privileged to use, protecting the environment and natural resources.

Our final responsibility is to our stockholders. Business must make a sound profit. We must experiment with new ideas. Research must be carried on, innovative programs developed and mistakes paid for. New equipment must be purchased, new facilities provided and new products launched. Reserves must be created to provide for adverse times. When we operate according to these principles, the stockholders should realize a fair return.

The core of the J&J credo speaks to the idea of both personal and company responsibility. This is a standard feature of general and detailed ethical codes alike. The responsibility not only calls for action on the part of the company as a whole, but also on the part of the individual. The code is classified as general because, although there are a number of normative statements as to what one ought to do as a member of the company, there is very little specificity. For instance, the credo at one point speaks of the need for management to act in a just and ethical way, but there is little instruction for how to be just and ethical, nor are there any penalties stated for unjust or unethical behavior.

These sorts of blanket ethical statements are present in many general codes and arise in a wide range of ethical claims; they are by no means unique to J&J's credo. To take just one other of many instances of this tendency, the ethical code of the National Association of the Remodeling Industry opens by directing all members to observe the highest levels of honesty, integrity, and responsibility in the conducting of business. This broad statement does not describe precisely what things ought to be done and what things ought to be avoided.

J&J's credo begins, as many general codes do, with imperatives concerning what an employee of the company ought to do to fulfill his or her corporate responsibilities. In dealing with customers, employees are directed to perform high quality work, strive to reduce costs, maintain reasonable prices, and respond to customer orders promptly and accurately. These sorts of responsibilities might seem less questions of ethics and more questions of good business, but are nevertheless present in general ethical codes. The final paragraph asserting the responsibility to stockholders is plainly aimed at the financial bottom line. However, the financial aspects of a company have ethical aspects too. The owners have invested their money and employees have invested their time. The company needs to be financially healthy to meet its obligations to these stakeholders.

The second paragraph of J&J's ethical code describes the company's responsibilities to its employees, another common feature of general codes. As with J&J, one often finds ethical claims involving such things as respect for the merit and dignity of the individual employee, equal opportunity for and development and advancement of employment, and, beyond that, consideration for the individual's family.

The third responsibility of the company and its members stated in J&J's credo is to the many communities in which they do business: One ought to be a good citizen by supporting good works, charities, better health education, and civic improvements. Again, lacking any specific instructions for ethical action or sanctions for unethical action, these sorts of statements serve merely to give a moral tone to the company. After all, the statement "support good works" is filled with ambiguity; it makes no mention of what works are good and how one ought to support those works. Nonspecific claims about such things as goodness and responsibilities to do good are very common in general codes. In contrast, detailed codes typically explain what these goods are. For example, the code of the American Society of Civil Engineers asserts that an engineer's knowledge ought to be used to benefit the community's welfare; this is then more clearly described as the need for a member of the society to consider the health, safety, and welfare of the public at all times in making professional decisions, and includes guidelines for how to do that.

Although J&J's credo does not provide a comprehensive or specific inventory of company policy, it does provide a general sense of corporate unity. Depending upon the strength and scope of individuals' response to a firm's ethical statement, it may or may not be capable of holding a company together when morally problematic situations arise. There are numerous variables to consider when judging a code's effectiveness, and thus it is difficult to locate weakness and strengths in ethical codes. In the case of J&J, despite its brevity and sketchiness, its code has lasted for over 60 years (with revisions), and was a source of great company strength in unifying and guiding it through such events as the Tylenol crisis of 1982 through 1986.

During these four years, the pain reliever Tylenol was tainted with the lethal drug cyanide, and J&J was threatened with ruin. Although the ethical statement did not contain any specific instructions on how the company and its employees ought to respond to such a terrible event, it did help to guide them in making particular and crucial ethical decisions in the course of the ordeal. The general code has remained effective for J&J in maintaining their reputation as an honest institution and for drawing their employees together.

Detailed Ethical Codes

In contrast to general codes, a detailed code may have multiple functions, including defining general business policies, stating professional obligations, presenting penalties for breaking international, national, and institutional laws, while creating rules and making claims about personal character. A detailed code is highly structured and often strictly categorized, with elaborations on each important category. Frequently, a detailed code is comprehensive enough to take the place of positive law, not only by prohibiting certain activities, but also by providing enforcement measures and penalties for violations. The addition of sanctions is a key feature distinguishing general from detailed ethical codes.

The main feature that sets the two types of codes apart is the degree to which detailed codes elaborate upon business policies and professional obligations. For example, the National Societies of Professional Engineers (NSPE) has a code of ethics containing a large amount of description and elaboration on these issues, explaining both what one ought to do and how one ought to accomplish specific things. A major concern of the engineering profession is the health, safety, and welfare of the public. A general ethical code would simply state that this is a major concern and not go much further, but in a detailed code like that of the NSPE, there is a great deal of description of how one ought to go about ensuring that this concern is properly realized.

Very often, the first category of a detailed code discusses moral concerns and obligations of the company or association connected to it, expressing fairly sweeping moral responsibilities. In the categories that follow, these general objectives are placed within the context of specific professional circumstances, and explicated in terms of specific situations. The ethical code of the NSPE follows this format. The NSPE code is presented in three main categories titled Fundamental Canons, Rules of Practice, and Professional Obligations. The first category offers wide-ranging responsibilities, with few instructions, in only six sentences. However, the code then moves on to greater detail in the categories that follow. The second one, Rules of Practice, speaks to issues of duty and more definite responsibilities. This category has within it more elaboration, with five sections and nearly 20 subsections. The final category, Professional Obligations, discusses further responsibilities one has as a member of the NSPE and as an engineer. It is filled with numerous positive and negative commands, is quite lengthy, and contains a great amount of specificity as well.

Examination of a particular detailed ethical code will further promote our understanding of the defining qualities of these codes, and will also create a contrast, allowing us to see the general ethical codes more clearly. We will examine the code of the Association of Computer Machinery (ACM). The ACM, founded in 1947 in response to the unveiling of the first electronic digital computer (ENIAC) the year before, is the largest and longest running international scientific and educational computer society in the world. The ACM was formed to exchange information and ideas that would nurture the development and advancement of computing technology. Membership includes such professionals as engineers, practitioners, researchers, mathematicians, educators, developers, and managers, all of whom are involved to support the creation and application of information technologies.

The ACM mission statement provides a rationale for the rest of the code. It includes a declaration of an institution's purpose, motivation, and objectives, along with suggestions for how to pursue these. The mission statement of ACM is:

> ACM is an international scientific and educational organization dedicated to advancing the art, science, engineering, and application of information technology, serving both professional and public interests by fostering the open exchange of information and by promoting the highest professional and ethical standards.

Most corporations and associations carry a mission statement, though they vary in the way they are used. A general ethical code would say little more than the ethical assertions presented in the ACM's statement, while a detailed ethical code takes those assertions, describes them clearly, and then applies them. A detailed code will elaborate upon each key point in the mission statement, explaining its importance both as a discrete moral pronouncement and as a part of the whole ethical statement. A step usually ignored in general codes is an explanation of the importance of an ethical item and how it ought to be actualized. Various excerpts from the detailed ethical code of the ACM will show how this step can be taken.

The ACM's code is organized into four main titles, consecutively: General Moral Imperatives, More Specific Professional Responsibilities, Organizational Leadership Imperatives, and Compliance With the Code. Each of these is further divided into several subsections. The ACM's categories are not common to all detailed codes, but the ideas presented in each category typically are. Consider the first one:

General Moral Imperatives

1.1 Contribute to society and human well-being.

This principle concerning the quality of life of all people affirms an obligation to protect fundamental human rights and to respect the diversity of all cultures. An essential aim of computing professionals is to minimize negative consequences of computing systems, including threats to health and safety. When designing or implementing systems, computing professionals must attempt to ensure that the products of their efforts will be used in socially responsible ways, will meet social needs, and will avoid harmful effects to health and welfare.

In addition to a safe social environment, human well-being includes a safe natural environment. Therefore, computing professionals who design and develop systems must be alert to, and make others aware of, any potential damage to the local or global environment.

The first sentence asserts the importance of human rights across all cultures. This is a normative claim expressing how one should act, and that one needs to concern one's self with the well-being of others. This sort of obligation to those outside the corporation is a common characteristic among detailed ethical codes.

The next paragraph in Section 1.1 expresses a second moral obligation connected to that mentioned above: the duty to safeguard the natural environment. In order to feel more secure in our social environments and to protect human well-being in the complete sense, there is a need for the protection of the natural environment. There is a suggested union between social justice and environmental justice, and the presentation of a moral obligation to promote that justice. Fulfilling this obligation would seem to serve the association's business interest by building a sound reputation, but in the code it comes without the attachment of a profit motive.

Here is another excerpt from this first title of the ACM's code:

1.4 Be fair and take action not to discriminate.

The values of equality, tolerance, respect for others, and the principles of equal justice govern this imperative. Discrimination on the basis of race, sex, religion, age, disability, national origin, or other such factors is an explicit violation of ACM policy and will not be tolerated.

Inequities between different groups of people may result from the misuse of information and technology. In a fair society all individuals would have equal opportunity to participate in, or benefit from, the use of computer resources regardless of race, sex, religion, age, disability, national origin or other such similar factors. However, these ideals do not justify unauthorized use of computer resources nor do they provide an adequate basis for violation of any other ethical imperatives of this code.

Section 1.4 is stated partially in response to state and federal law and partially as an affirmation of the association's own ethical principles. The first paragraph expresses the role of tolerance, equality, respect for others, and the pursuit of equal justice, and then adds the strict requirement to avoid discrimination on the basis of race, sex, religion, age, disability, and national origin.

Discrimination in employment is prohibited by law, and thus it makes sense that it would be prohibited by the ACM. The devotion to tolerance, equality, and respect creates a sort of ethical shelter that can also be used to house numerous moral problems falling outside the scope of the law. Although the action-guiding nature of a commitment to equality, etc., appears fairly general here, the sections that follow make it clear that nondiscriminatory practices are intended to realize these values. In contrast, the general ethical code of the Institution of Electrical and Electronics Engineers (IEEE), consisting of ten brief statements, mentions the same need for the fair treatment of all persons regardless of race, religion, gender, disability, age, and national origin, but gives no indication of just what this means or how it's supposed to be realized.

The ACM continues to enumerate the ethical imperatives for its membership in another title:

More Specific Professional Responsibilities

2.3 Know and respect existing laws pertaining to professional work.

ACM members must obey existing local, state, province, national, and international laws unless there is a compelling ethical basis not to do so. Policies and procedures of the organization in which one participates must also be obeyed. But compliance must be balanced with the recognition that sometimes existing laws and rules may be immoral or inappropriate and, therefore, must be challenged.

Violation of a law or regulation may be ethical when that law or rule has an inadequate moral basis or when it conflicts with another law judged to be more important. If one decides to violate a law or rule because it is viewed as unethical, or for any other reason, one must fully accept responsibility for one's actions and for the consequences.

2.7 Improve public understanding of computing and its consequences.

Computing professionals have a responsibility to share technical knowledge with the public by encouraging understanding of computing, including the impacts of computer systems and their limitations. This imperative implies an obligation to counter any false views related to computing.

In Section 2.3 we have both a call to follow the laws of numerous jurisdictions, and to challenge those laws. This statement is somewhat broad but also contains detail. Since it does not describe particular instances or circumstances in which ethical judgment may override the law, there is a lack of detail. However, the very idea that one as a member of the association might have to ethically judge a given situation as inconsistent with the prevailing rule is entirely absent in general codes. Other detailed codes are highly specific in this area. For example, the National Society of Professional Engineers' code of ethics, although recognizing possible conflict between law and conscience, states clearly that its members should never consider or participate in collective coercive action such as strikes and picket lines.

Obligations to uphold the integrity of the profession by enlightening consumers about its advantages and flaws, and by correcting any mistaken opinions regarding it, such as in Section 2.7, are rather common in detailed codes. Here again we tread a fine line between moral action and good business practice.

This narrow margin is embraced in Title 4 of ACM's code, Compliance with the Code:

As an ACM member I will...

4.1 Uphold and promote the principles of this Code.

The future of the computing profession depends on both technical and ethical excellence. Not only is it important for

ACM computing professionals to adhere to the principles expressed in this Code, each member should encourage and support adherence by other members.

This category goes on to mention a key feature that distinguishes detailed from general codes: penalties for violations of the code:

As an ACM member I will...

4.2   Treat violations of this code as inconsistent with membership in the ACM.

Adherence of professionals to a code of ethics is largely a voluntary matter. However, if a member does not follow this code by engaging in gross misconduct, his or her membership in the ACM may be terminated.

The presence of sanctions is not a necessary condition for defining a code as detailed, but if they are found in a code, it is almost always a detailed one. Penalties vary in specificity, both in the way they respond to a specific unfulfilled task and the way they are described in writing. The severity and strength of a sanction depends on a few key items: whether or not the corporation has a higher or lower degree of self-regulation, the type of service or business the corporation is involved with, and the degree of importance the violation holds to the corporation and other involved parties. Probably the most common penalty found in corporations' and associations' codes is termination, but many also have less severe punishments.

To close this chapter, we should mention that in 1995 the U.S. Department of Commerce released a statement of Model Business Principles in an effort to encourage business and industry to voluntarily formulate codes of ethical conduct. The principles listed in this document are similar to the ones we have mentioned: a safe and healthy workplace, avoiding discrimination of protected classes, responsible environmental protection, recognition of the right to organize and bargain collectively, and encouraging "good corporate citizenship" and a "positive contribution to the communities in which the company operates."

CONTEMPORARY ETHICAL ISSUES

Chapter 7:
Biographical Sketches

John D. Aram

Professor of Management Policy at the Weatherhead School of Management at Case Western Reserve University. Professor Aram is also director of the Executive Doctorate in Management Program, a three-year, interdisciplinary program of doctoral studies for advanced practitioners that utilizes intensive residencies with electronic communication. Much of his past work, including his most recent book, *Presumed Superior: Individualism and American Business* (Prentice-Hall, 1993), examines individuals, collectivities, and their interactions in the context of business and society. Currently his writing addresses interactions between capitalism, society, and political institutions in the challenge of combining liberal and community values.

Tom L. Beauchamp

Professor of Philosophy and Senior Research Scholar, Georgetown University, Washington, D.C. Professor Beauchamp was born in Austin, Texas. He took graduate degrees from Yale University and the Johns Hopkins University, where he received his Ph.D. in 1970. He then joined the faculty of the Philosophy Department at Georgetown University, and in the mid-1970s he accepted a joint appointment at the Kennedy Institute of Ethics. He has written *Case Studies in Business, Society, and Ethics* (Prentice-Hall, 4th ed. 1997); edited *Ethical Theory and Business* (Prentice-Hall, 5th ed. 1997), with coeditor Norman Bowie; and authored *The Virtuous Journalist* (Oxford, 1988), a study of media ethics and the publishing industry. Professor Beauchamp has written numerous articles in business ethics and medical ethics, and has lectured at over 100 American and European universities on problems of philosophical and practical ethics.

John R. Boatright

Raymond C. Baumhart, S.J., Professor of Business Ethics and Professor of Management in the School of Business Administration at Loyola University, Chicago. Dr. Boatright is the author of the textbook *Ethics and the Conduct of Business* (Prentice Hall, 2d ed. 1998), and the editor of a casebook, *Cases in Ethics and the Conduct of Business*, both published by Prentice Hall. He recently completed a book, *Ethics in Finance*, and his current research and writing focus on the roles of shareholders and other constituencies in corporate governance. Dr. Boatright is president of the Society for Business Ethics for 1997–1998, and he serves on the executive committee of the Society for Business Ethics, and on the editorial boards of the *Journal of Business Ethics* and *Business Ethics Quarterly*. An honors graduate of the College of Wooster, he received his M.A. and Ph.D. in philosophy from the University of Chicago.

Norman E. Bowie

Elmer L. Andersen Chair in Corporate Responsibility in the Departments of Philosophy and Strategic Management and Organization at the University of Minnesota. Professor Bowie is the author, editor, coauthor, or coeditor of 12 books and 50 articles on business ethics and political philosophy. He is past president of the Society for Value Inquiry, the Society for Business Ethics, and the former Executive Secretary of the American Philosophical Association. He served a term as chair of the Department of Strategic Management and Organization. In 1996–1997 he was a fellow in the Program in Ethics and the Professions at Harvard University.

F. Neil Brady

Professor of Public Management and Associate Director of the Center for the Study of Values in Organizations in the Marriott School of Management at Brigham Young University. There, Professor Brady teaches management ethics. Previously, he taught for 11 years at San Diego State University, where he also served as the chair of the Department of Management. He has a Ph.D. in philosophy from the University of Texas at Austin. He has published about 30 articles in a variety of journals on ethics, and he is the author of two books: *Ethical Managing* (Prentice Hall, 1989) and *Ethical Universals in International Business* (Springer-Verlag, 1997). Professor Brady's works have won regional and national awards, and his present interests focus on relationships among ethics, economics, and ecology.

George Brenkert

Visiting Professor of Management at Georgetown University, currently on leave from the University of Tennessee, Knoxville. He received his B.A. from Colgate University, and an M.A. and Ph.D. from the University of Michigan. He specializes in the areas of business ethics, social and political philosophy, and ethics. He serves on the Editorial Review Board of *Business Ethics Quarterly* and is a member of the executive committee of the Society for Business Ethics. Dr. Brenkert has published extensively in business ethics and is currently writing a book on the ethics of marketing.

Rogene A. Buchholz

Legendre-Soule Professor of Business Ethics at Loyola University of New Orleans. Professor Buchholz received his Ph.D. from the Graduate School of Business at the University of Pittsburgh, and previously taught at the University of Minnesota, Washington University at St. Louis, and the University of Texas at Dallas. His articles have appeared in *Human Relations, Journal of Management Studies, Industrial and Labor Relations Review, Harvard Business Review, Journal of Business Ethics, Business and Society*, and *Business Ethics Quarterly*. He is the author or coauthor of ten books in the areas of business and public policy, business ethics, and the environment, including a recently published textbook in business ethics. Professor Buchholz is currently coauthoring a book for the Ruffin series on business ethics, and has served on the editorial board of several journals and as chair of the Social Issues in Management Division of the Academy of Management.

Gerald F. Cavanagh, S.J.

Charles T. Fisher, III, Chair of Business Ethics and Professor of Management at the University of Detroit Mercy. Professor Cavanagh is the author of five books, the latest, *American Business Values with International Perspectives* (Prentice Hall,1998), and numerous articles. He has lectured worldwide on business ethics, held the Dirksen Chair of Business Ethics at Santa Clara University and the Gasson Chair at Boston College, and was academic vice-president and provost at the University of Detroit Mercy. He was chair of the Social Issues Division of the Academy of Management and the All-Academy Task Force on Ethics. Professor Cavanagh is currently researching global codes of ethics and the virtue of courage within the firm.

Philip L. Cochran

Associate Professor of Business Administration and director of the Business Ethics Program at the Smeal College of Business Administration at Penn State University. Professor Cochran holds a B.S. in aerospace engineering and a B.S. in management from the Massachusetts Institute of Technology. He also holds an M.B.A. in finance, an M.A. in economics, and a Ph.D. in business, government, and society from the University of Washington. He has spoken at numerous conferences, including being a keynote speaker at the Second Russian Business Ethics Conference in Moscow. He is the recipient of a 1994 Howard Chase Award, and an M.B.A. Excellence in Teaching Award, and an AT&T Innovations in Distance Education Grant. Professor Cochran was the first president of the International Association for Business and Society and is a past chair of the Social Issues in Management Division of the Academy of Management; he also serves on the editorial boards of several journals.

Thomas Carson

Professor of Philosophy at Loyola University Chicago. Professor Carson publishes in ethical theory and business ethics. His major publications include *The Status of Morality* (Kluwer, 1984) and an anthology, *Morality, Value, and the Good Life* (Oxford, 1997). His papers on business ethics address such topics as bribery, conflicts of interest, deception in negotiations, deception in advertising, the ethics of sales, and corporate social responsibility. Several of his papers have been widely reprinted; several were coauthored with Richard Wokutch (Professor of Business at Virginia Tech). Professor Carson is now writing a book titled *Lying and Deception: Theory and Practice*, which will combine his work on ethical theory and business ethics.

John R. Danley

Professor of Philosophy at Southern Illinois University at Edwardsville, where his areas of interest include political theory, ethics, and applied ethics. Professor Danley has a B.A. from Kalamazoo College, an M.Div. from the Union Theological Seminary (NY), and an M.A. and Ph.D. from the University of Rochester. He is the author of *The Role of the Modern Corporation in a Free Society* (Notre Dame University Press, 1994), and his articles have appeared in *Philosophy & Public Affairs*, *Philosophical Studies*, the *Journal of*

Business Ethics, and elsewhere. He is involved in an interdisciplinary team-taught course in business and society. Professor Danley is a member of the American Philosophical Association, the Academy of Management, the International Association of Business and Society, and the International Society for Business, Economics, and Ethics.

Michael Davis

Senior Research Associate at the Center for the Study of Ethics in the Professions, Illinois Institute of Technology, Professor Davis received his Ph.D. from the University of Michigan in 1972. He has published more than 100 articles (and chapters), authored two books, and coedited two others. His research interests include conflict of interest, codes of ethics, professions, and the teaching of ethics.

Richard T. De George

University Distinguished Professor of Philosophy and Business Adminis-tration, and Director of the International Center for Ethics in Business at the University of Kansas. Professor De George received his Ph.D. from Yale University. He has been a research fellow at Yale University, Columbia University, Stanford University, and the Hoover Institution. He is the author of over 150 articles and the author or editor of 18 books, including *Ethics, Free Enterprise, and Public Policy* (Oxford 1978); *Business Ethics* (Prentice Hall, 4th ed. 1995); and *Competing With Integrity in International Business* (Oxford, 1993). He is on the editorial boards of several business ethics journals, and has served as a consultant on business ethics for a number of firms. Professor De George has served as president for the American Philosophical Association, the Society for Business Ethics, and the International Society of Business, Economics, and Ethics.

Joseph R. DesJardins

Professor of Philosophy and chair of the department formed jointly by the College of St. Benedict and St. John's University in Collegeville, Minnesota. Professor DesJardins received his Ph.D. from the University of Notre Dame and taught at Villanova University before moving to Minnesota. His research interests are business ethics and environmental ethics, and par-ticularly the environmental responsibilities of business. He is the coeditor, with John McCall, of *Contemporary Issues in Business Ethics* (Wadsworth, 3d ed. 1996), and the author of *Environmental Ethics* (Wadsworth, 2d ed. 1997). Professor DesJardins has also published numerous articles on such topics as employee rights, employee privacy, and business and the environment. He serves as the editor for the *Newsletter for the Society of Business Ethics*.

Thomas Donaldson

Mark O. Winkelman Professor at the Wharton School of the University of Pennsylvania, where he teaches business ethics. Professor Donaldson has authored or edited numerous books, including: *Ethics in International Business* (Oxford University Press, 1989); *Ethical Issues in Business* (Prentice-Hall, Inc., 5th ed., 1996), coedited with Patricia Werhane; *Case Studies in Business Ethics* (Prentice-Hall, Inc., 4th ed., 1996), coedited with Al Gini; and *Corporations and Morality* (Prentice-Hall, Inc., 1981). His writings have appeared in publications such as *The Academy of Management Review*, the *Harvard Business Review*, *Ethics*, and *Economics and Philosophy*. He is a founding member and past president of the Society for Business Ethics, and is a member of the editorial boards of a number of journals, including the *Academy of Management Review* and *Business Ethics Quarterly*. Professor Donaldson has lectured and consulted to many corporations, including AT&T, Walt Disney, IBM, Motorola, Johnson & Johnson, the IMF, Bankers Trust, and the World Bank. He has appeared on national television and served as the host for a one-hour, nationally televised PBS special, *Business Ethics*.

Thomas W. Dunfee

Kolodny Professor of Social Responsibility and Director of the Carol and Lawrence Zicklin Center for Business Ethics Research at The Wharton School of the University of Pennsylvania. Professor Dunfee's current research interests focus on social contract theory and business ethics, the concept of a marketplace of morality, and developing ethical standards for business transactions. He is particularly interested in global applications of these ideas. Professor Dunfee has been a visiting professor at four universities, has published in a wide variety of journals, has consulted to law firms and corporate and government clients, has served as an expert witness in several cases, and has been a judge for a variety of ethics awards.

Ronald F. Duska

Professor of Ethics and holder of the Charles Lamont Post Chair of Ethics and the Professions at The American College. Professor Duska received his Ph.D. in philosophy from Northwestern University. He is a specialist in the area of ethical theory and business ethics, and the author, coauthor, or editor of numerous books including: *Business Ethics, Organizational Behavior in Insurance* (1992); and *Ethics and Corporate Responsibility: Theory Cases and Dilemmas*. He has also written many articles on philosophy and business ethics, and is currently working on a book of readings by American College authors entitled *Compliance, Ethics and Consumer Expectations*. He has lectured and published extensively, both in the United States and internationally, and has served as an editor and reviewer for numerous business and professional ethics publications. Professor Duska is currently executive director of the Society for Business Ethics and editor of the Society's newsletter, and Senior Fellow at The Olson Center For Applied Ethics at the Darden School, University of Virginia.

Robert E. Frederick

Associate Professor of Philosophy and Chair of the Philosophy Department at Bentley College in Waltham, Massachusetts, Dr. Frederick is also Research Scholar at the Center for Business Ethics at Bentley and editor of *Business and Society Review*. He received a B.A. degree in economics from Rice University and an M.A. and Ph.D. in philosophy from Brown University. Dr. Frederick has published a number of articles in philosophy, business ethics, and environmental ethics, and he has edited or coedited nine books on various topics in applied ethics and philosophy, including *Business, Ethics, and the Environment* (Greenwood, 1990); *Emerging Global Business Ethics* (Greenwood, 1993); and *Business Ethics: Readings and Cases in Corporate Morality*. He has served as a consultant on business ethics for corporations and academic institutions and has delivered addresses on business and environmental ethics to a variety of professional organizations. Prior to joining Bentley and the Center, Dr. Frederick worked for nine years for a large financial institution in Atlanta, Georgia, where he was vice president for administrative services.

William C. Frederick

William C. Frederick is a research scholar, lecturer, and reviewer in the field of business ethics and corporate responsibility, with a Ph.D. in economics and cultural anthropology from the University of Texas. He has specialized in the study of managers' values as they are influenced by corporate culture and nature. He helped write several editions of the textbook *Business and Society*, a book on *Social Auditing*, and is author of *Values, Nature, and Culture in the American Corporation*. Professor Frederick is a past president of The Society for Business Ethics and served on the faculty of the University of Pittsburgh from 1963–1991.

R. Edward Freeman

Elis and Signe Olsson Professor of Business Administration and Director of the Olsson Center for Applied Ethics at the Darden Graduate School of Business Administration, University of Virginia at Charlottesville. Freeman has a Ph.D. in philosophy from Washington University, and a B.A. in mathematics and philosophy from Duke University. His most recent books are *Ethics and Agency Theory* (with Norman Bowie, Oxford, 1992), *Business Ethics: The State of the Art* (Oxford, 1992), and *Corporate Strategy and the Search for Ethics* (with D. Gilbert, Jr., Prentice Hall, 1988). He is currently writing, with Patricia Werhane, *The Dictionary of Business Ethics*, a volume in Blackwell's *Encyclopedia of Management*, and with J. Pearce and R. Dodd, *Shades of Green: Business Ethics and the Environment*, an attempt to show how environmental values can be used to craft sustainable competitive advantage. Freeman has received the Sixth Annual Outstanding Teaching Award from the Wharton Advisory Board, a Top Ten Teachers Award from the Wharton MBA program, and in 1986 was named Teacher of the Year at the Carlson School of Management, University of Minnesota. In 1992 he was chosen for the Outstanding Faculty Award by the Darden student body.

Peter A. French

Marie E. and Leslie Cole Chair in Ethics and Professor of Philosophy at the University of South Florida. Dr. French is the director of The Ethics Center and chair of the Department of Philosophy of the University of South Florida. He has a B.A. from Gettysburg College, an M.A. from the University of Southern California, and a Ph.D. from the University of Miami. He is the author of 16 books, including *Corporate Ethics* (1994), *Responsibility Matters* (1992), *Corporations in the Moral Community (1992)*, *Collective and Corporate Responsibility* (1984), and *Corrigible Corporations and Unruly Laws*. Dr. French's work on corporate responsibility and business ethics is the subject of a book, *Shame, Responsibility, and the Corporation*, that features essays written by some of the world's leading philosophers. Senior editor of *Midwest Studies in Philosophy* and editor of the *Journal of Social Philosophy*, Dr. French has published dozens of articles in the major philosophical and legal journals and reviews.

Al Gini

Associate Professor of Philosophy and Adjunct Professor in the Institute of Industrial Relations at Loyola University, Chicago. Professor Gini received his Ph.D. from Loyola University, Chicago. He is the managing editor and cofounder of *Business Ethics Quarterly*. and had a regular column in *The Small Business Journal*. Besides lecturing to community and professional organizations, he also does consulting on corporate ethics and employee relations and can be heard regularly on National Public Radio's Chicago affiliate, WBEZ-FM. His published work includes *Philosophical Issues in Human Rights* (with Patricia Werhane and David Ozar; Random House, 1986), *It Comes With the Territory: An Inquiry Into the Nature of Work* (with T.J. Sullivan; Random House, 1989), *Case Studies in Business Ethics* (with Thomas Donaldson; Prentice-Hall, 1993) and *Heigh-Ho!—Funny, Insightful, Encouraging and Sometimes Painful Quotes About Work* (with T.J. Sullivan; ACTA Publication, 1994).

Kenneth Goodpaster

David and Barbara Koch Chair in Business Ethics at the University of St. Thomas, St. Paul, Minnesota. Professor Goodpaster earned his A.B. in mathematics from the University of Notre Dame and his A.M. and Ph.D. in philosophy from the University of Michigan. While at the Harvard Business School, he authored *Managerial Decision Making and Ethical Values* (1989) and *Ethics in Management* (1984). His *Policies and Persons: A Casebook in Business Ethics* is due out in a third edition in 1998. Work in progress includes a monograph on management and moral philosophy entitled *The Moral Agenda of Management*. He has published articles in a wide variety of professional journals, including the *Journal of Philosophy*, *Ethics*, *Environmental Ethics*, the *Journal of Business Ethics*, and the *Harvard Business Review*. Professor Goodpaster is on the editorial boards of the principal journals and has authored three encyclopedia articles on business ethics.

Laura Pincus Hartman

Wicklander Chair in Professional Ethics at DePaul University and Associate Professor of Management at DePaul's Kellstadt Graduate School of Business. Professor Hartman is also the director of DePaul's Institute for Business & Professional Ethics. She graduated from the University of Chicago Law School and *magna cum laude* from Tufts University, and is a member of the Illinois bar. She is cofounder and past chair of the Employment and Labor Law Section of the Academy of Legal Studies in Business, and past editor of the Section's newsletter. Professor Hartman has done extensive research and consulting with *Fortune 500* companies, American academic institutions, and educational institutions in Latin America on the ethics of the employment relationship. Her work has culminated in the publication of several textbooks, including *Employment Law for Managers* and *The Legal Environment of Business: Ethical and Public Policy Contexts* (Irwin, 1996) and *Perspectives in Business Ethics* (McGraw Hill, 1997). Professor Hartman's articles have been published in or accepted for publication by *Hofstra Law Review*, *Columbia Business Law Journal*, *Harvard Journal of Law & Technology*, *Journal of Business Ethics*, *Labor Law Journal*, *Journal of Individual Employment Rights*, and *Journal of Legal Studies Education*.

W. Michael Hoffman

Executive Director of the Center for Business Ethics at Bentley College in Waltham, Massachusetts, a 21-year-old research and consulting institute. Dr. Hoffman received his Ph.D. in philosophy at the University of Massachusetts and has been a professor for 29 years in higher education. He has authored or edited 15 books, including *Business Ethics* (McGraw-Hill, 3rd edition 1995) and *The Ethical Edge* (1997), and has published more than 50 articles. Dr. Hoffman consults on business ethics for universities, government agencies, and corporations, and serves as an expert witness on ethical issues that arise in litigation. He was a founding member and president of the Society for Business Ethics, served as an advisor to the U.S. Sentencing Commission, and was the first executive director of the Ethics Officer Association.

Daryl Koehn

Cullen Chair of Business Ethics at University of St. Thomas in Houston, Texas. Koehn earned a Ph.D. in philosophy at the University of Chicago, an M.B.A. in finance at Northwestern University, and an M.A. in politics, philosophy, and economics at Oxford University. She is the author of *The Ground of Professional Ethics* (Routledge, 1994) and *Rethinking Feminist Ethics: Care, Trust and Empathy* (Routledge, 1998), and is the editor of a forthcoming volume, *Trust: Barriers and Bridges*. She currently is at work on a book on the relevance of Japanese and Chinese ethics to business practice. In addition to writing and teaching, she is in great demand as a public speaker and regularly consults with businesses and government agencies to help them develop ethics education programs.

Richard L. Lippke

Professor of Philosophy at James Madison University, Professor Lippke earned his doctorate in philosophy from the University of Wisconsin-Madison in 1982. He is the author of *Radical Business Ethics* (Rowman & Littlefield, 1995), and several articles that have been reprinted in leading business ethics texts. His writings analyze issues in business ethics within the contexts provided by theories of social and economic justice. His examination of issues such as advertising, employee privacy, insider trading, and employee freedom of speech utilizes a perspective that is critical of many of the institutions and practices of advanced capitalist societies. Professor Lippke's broader interests include ethical theory and the normative analysis of social and public policy issues.

Tibor R. Machan

Tibor R. Machan has been a contributor to the literature of business ethics on such issues as corporate social responsibility, insider trading, cigarette advertising, truth in advertising, government regulation, and other subjects. He edited *Commerce & Morality* (Rowman & Littlefield, 1988), and coedited *Rights and Regulation* (Ballinger, 1983). Several of his books address business ethics: *Capitalism and Individualism* (St. Martin's Press, 1990), *The Virtue of*

Liberty (Foundation of Economic Education, 1994) and *Private Rights and Public Illusions* (Transaction Books, 1995). Professor Machan believes business is an honorable profession. It needs the study of ethics qua standards of professional conduct. The discipline is best approached from an neo-Aristotelian teleological, not a deontological, framework.

John J. McCall

John J. McCall holds a B.A. from LaSalle University and an M.A. and Ph.D. from the University of Notre Dame. He is on the faculty of Saint Joseph's University in Philadelphia, where he has taught business ethics at the undergraduate, graduate, and executive levels for the past 15 years. He is also an affiliated faculty of the Ethics Program at the Wharton School of the University of Pennsylvania. He has written on welfare reform, products liability, employee rights, corporate dismissal policies in the U.S. and Europe, downsizing, and employee participation in corporate decision making. Professor McCall is coauthor/coeditor, with Joseph R. DesJardins, of *Contemporary Issues in Business Ethics* (Wadsworth, 1996).

Dennis J. Moberg

Professor of Management and Scholar at the Markkula Center of Applied Ethics at Santa Clara University. Possessing a D.B.A. from the University of Southern California, Professor Moberg is a social scientist who attempts to integrate his discipline with business ethics. His recent work is in virtue ethics, but he has also worked on issues of utilitarianism and justice. All of his work focuses on intraorganizational concerns. He has analyzed organizational politics, hierarchic relations, and the roles of character, wisdom, and vice in shaping how employees should behave.

Laura L. Nash

Director for the Program on Business Values and Leadership at the Harvard Divinity School's Center for the Study of Values in Public Life. Professor Nash received her M.A. and Ph.D. from Harvard University, and began work on business ethics in 1980 while on the faculty of the Harvard Business School. Her research and consulting has concentrated on topics where there has formerly been little discussion of ethics: early corporate ethics programs, business ethics and academia, mission statements, racial integration and the corporation, the changing employment contract, religious values and business, and corporate culture. Among Professor Nash's publications are *Good Intentions Aside: A Manager's Guide to Resolving Ethical Problems* (1991) and *Believers in Business: Resolving the Tensions between Christian Faith, Business Ethics, Competition, and Our Definitions of Success* (1994).

Lisa H. Newton

Professor of Philosophy and Director of the Program in Applied Ethics at Fairfield University in Fairfield, Connecticut. Professor Newton has authored or coauthored several textbooks in the field of ethics, including *Wake Up Calls: Classic Cases in Business Ethics* (1996), *Watersheds: Cases in Environmental Ethics* (2d ed. 1997), and *Taking Sides: Controversial Issues in Business Ethics and Society* (4th ed. 1996). She has also authored over 70 articles on ethics in politics, law, medicine, and business, and was the writer and ethics consultant for Media and Society's 1990 series, *Ethics in America*, still occasionally aired on public television. Professor Newton also serves as a consultant in business ethics for companies and professional associations.

Lynn Sharp Paine

Professor at the Harvard Business School, Paine heads up the school's initiative on Leadership, Values, and Corporate Responsibility. She holds a doctorate in moral philosophy from Oxford University and a law degree from the Harvard Law School. A member of the Massachusetts bar, she practiced law with the Boston firm of Hill & Barlow after graduating from law school. She has also served as a consultant for executive and management education for the Ethics Resource Center in Washington, D.C., and has been involved in consulting and organizational development activities for numerous companies and industry groups. Paine's current research focuses on management and organizational value systems, with special emphasis on ethical aspects of globalization. Author of numerous articles and dozens of case studies, she has written most recently on organizational ethics strategies. Her publications have appeared in a variety of books and journals including the *Harvard Business Review, California Management Review, Journal of Business Ethics, Philosophy and Public Affairs*, and the *Wisconsin Law Review*. Paine is the author of *Leadership, Ethics, and Organizational Integrity* (Richard D. Irwin, Inc., 1997), a text and casebook.

S. Prakash Sethi

Academic Director of Executive Programs, Baruch College, The City University of New York. Professor Sethi holds an M.A. in economics from Delhi University, India, and an M.B.A. and Ph.D. from Columbia University. He is one of the pioneers in research dealing with issues of corporate social responsibility, business ethics, and international business and public policy. He has authored, coauthored, or edited 24 books and over 150 articles in academic, professional, and practitioner journals. Over the last few years, he has been engaged in research on codes of conduct for multinational corporations, and the impact of market-competitive conditions on business ethics practices on the part of corporations. Among his publications pertaining to these topics are: *Up Against the Corporate Wall: Modern Corporations and*

Social Issues of the Nineties (Prentice Hall, 1990); *Multinational Corporations and the Impact of Public Advocacy on Corporate Strategy* (Kluwer, 1994); "Working with International Codes of Conduct: Experience of U.S. Companies Operating in South Africa," and "Ethical Behavior as a Strategic Choice by Large Corporations: The Potential Impact of Industry Structure and Market Place Competition."

Bill Shaw

Woodson Centennial Professor of Legal and Ethical Studies in Business at the University of Texas at Austin. Professor Shaw is the author or coauthor of three texts and numerous journal publications on the legal environment of business. He has served as the president of the Academy of Legal Studies in Business and editor-in-chief of the *American Business Law Journal*. He is a licensed attorney, arbitrator, business consultant, and is currently a member of the editorial board of the *Journal of Business Ethics*. Professor Shaw has taught graduate and undergraduate business law and business ethics courses for more than 30 years.

William H. Shaw

Professor of Philosophy and Chair of the Philosophy Department at San Jose State University, where he has taught for 11 years. Dr. Shaw holds a B.A. from Stanford University and a Ph.D. from the London School of Economics at the University of London. He is the author of *Business Ethics* (Wadsworth, 2d ed. 1995), and coauthor of *Moral Issues in Business* (Wadsworth, 7th ed. 1998). He writes primarily on issues in social and political philosophy and in theoretical and applied ethics. Other publications of his include *Marx's Theory of History* (Stanford 1978) and *Moore on Right and Wrong: The Normative Ethics of G. E. Moore* (Kluwer 1995). He has also edited or coedited several anthologies, including *Justice and Economic Distribution* (Prentice-Hall, 2d ed. 1991), *Philosophy of Law* (Prentice-Hall, 2d ed. 1993), and *Social and Personal Ethics* (Wadsworth, 2d ed. 1996).

Robert (Bob) Solomon

Quincy Lee Centennial Professor and a member of the Academy of Distinguished Teachers at the University of Texas at Austin. Professor Solomon has spent the past 15 years thinking, writing, and talking about professional and business ethics. He is the author or editor of nearly 30 books, among them *Above the Bottom Line* (Harcourt Brace Jovanovich, 2d edition, 1993), *It's Good Business* (Atheneum, 1985, and Rowman and Littlefield, 1998), and *Ethics and Excellence* (Oxford University Press, 1992). Professor Solomon has provided ethics programs for Chase Manhattan Bank in New York, AT&T, IBM, Conoco Oil, Southwestern Bell, and other *Fortune 500* companies. He has taught at Princeton, UCLA, and Harvard, and has been visiting professor at several universities overseas.

Linda Klebe Treviño

Professor of Organizational Behavior at The Pennsylvania State University, where she has been on the faculty since receiving her Ph.D. in management in 1987. Her research on the management of ethical conduct in organizations is widely published in academic journals. Professor Treviño has also coauthored a textbook with Katherine Nelson entitled *Managing Business Ethics: Straight Talk About How to Do it Right* (John Wiley & Sons, 1995). Her current research focuses on the management of ethical conduct in organizations, including: (1) determinants of moral awareness, (2) understanding what works and what doesn't in ethics management, and (3) an organizational justice approach to understanding reactions to discipline, diversity, and downsizing.

James Weber

Associate Professor and Director of the Beard Center for Leadership in Ethics, Dusquesne University. Dr. Weber received his Ph.D. in business administration from the University of Pittsburgh. As Director of the Beard Center, Dr. Weber provides ethics training seminars for business and community organizations and organizes discussion forums on critical ethical issues in business. His research interests include the assessment of values, moral reasoning, and ethical behavior. He has been published in *Business & Society*, *Journal of Business Ethics*, *Business Ethics Quarterly*, *Research in Corporate Social Performance and Policy*, and *International Journal of Value-based Management*, and is the coauthor of the ninth edition of *Business and Society: Corporate Strategy, Public Policy, Ethics* (Irwin/McGraw-Hill, 1998). Dr. Weber has served as the program chair for the Social Issues in Management division of the Academy of Management and the International Association for Business and Society.

Patricia H. Werhane

Ruffin Chair of Business Ethics in the Darden Graduate School of Business Administration at the University of Virginia. Professor Werhane teaches business ethics, strategic human resource management, and business ethics and literature. She received her B.A. from Wellesley College, and M.A. and Ph.D. from Northwestern University. She is a founding member and past president of the Society of Business Ethics, and is editor-in-chief for *Business Ethics Quarterly*, the journal for the society. From 1989 to 1992 she was chairperson of the Ethics Advisory Council for Arthur Andersen and Company, which engaged in a five-year Teaching Business Ethics project on the integration of business ethics into traditional business school disciplines. Professor Werhane is the author or editor of eight books, including *Ethical Issues in Business* (Prentice Hall, 1996), edited with Tom Donaldson, now in its fifth edition; *Persons, Rights, and Corporations* (Prentice Hall, 1985); *Profit and Responsibility*; and *Philosophical Issues in Human Rights* (edited with David Ozar and A. R. Gini, Random House, 1986). She has also written a number of articles and papers on such topics as employee and employer rights, whistleblowing, mergers and acquisitions, responsibilities of multinational corporations, and insider trading. She is currently working on a book that will outline frameworks of moral reasoning for management decision making.

Donna J. Wood

Professor of Business Administration at the Katz Graduate School of Business, University of Pittsburgh. Professor Wood received her Ph.D. in sociology from Vanderbilt University. She is a founder and officer of the International Association for Business and Society, and has been chair of the Social Issues in Management Division of the Academy of Management. Her interests, reflected in many journal articles and books, include corporate social performance and stakeholder theory, international business and society, collaborative social problem solving, public-private enterprise, business ethics, and business-government relations.

CONTEMPORARY ETHICAL ISSUES

Chapter 8: Business Organizations and Associations

There are literally thousands of business associations and organizations in existence today. Whether they function on a community, state, provincial, national, or international level depends much upon the specific objective pursued by the association or organization, and the concerns of its membership. Associations and organizations formed to promote and support ethics in business come in a variety of types or categories, including: nongovernmental organizations (NGOs), professional associations, not-for-profit organizations, and privately formed monitoring and surveillance associations. As a subset of such business groups in general, the number of associations and organizations for the promotion of business ethics, specifically, is not large, but their membership is growing. Support for ethics in business and the prevention of corruption has become an increasingly prevalent concern in the last decade for the general public, suggesting that a future increase of associations and organizations can be expected. A selection of associations and organizations most directly concerned with issues in business ethics follows.

Academy of International Business (AIB)
University of Hawaii at Manoa—SBA
2404 Maile Way
Honolulu, HI 96822
(808) 956-3665
Fax (808) 956-3261
e-mail: aib@gusadm.cba.hawaii.edu
James R. Wills, executive secretary

Founded in 1959, the association contains a multinational assortment of university professors, researchers, writers, managers, executives, and attorneys working in the field of international business education. AIB encourages the advancement of knowledge of international business operations by promoting and using teaching materials, and initiating an information exchange between academia, business, and government.

Publications: Academy of International Business Membership Directory, biennial; *Academy of International Business Newsletter*, quarterly; *International Business Curricula: A Global Survey*; *Journal of International Business Studies*, quarterly.

Other Available Information: Membership details (2,500 members), inventory of collegiate courses in international business, survey of research projects and educational materials, an annual award of recognition (Dissertation Award), newsletter, numerous publications, conventions, and meetings.

American Assembly of Collegiate Schools of Business (AACSB)
600 Emerson Road, Suite 300
St. Louis, MO 63141-6762
(314) 872-8481
Fax (314) 872-8495
Website: http://www.aacsb.edu
William K. Laidlaw Jr., executive vice-president

Founded in 1916, membership includes accredited and nonaccredited schools offering courses in accounting and business administration, business firms, governmental and professional organizations, and educational institutions and organizations. The association serves as a professional association for management education, collecting statistics, conducting research, and providing professional development programs.

Available Information: Committees, special programs, task forces, numerous publications, newsletter, meetings, and conferences.

American Society of Civil Engineers (ASCE)
World Headquarters:
1801 Alexander Bell Drive
Reston, VA 20191-4400
(703) 295-6000
Fax (703) 295-6222

Washington, D.C., Office:
1015 15th St. NW, Ste 600
Washington, DC 20005
(202) 789-2200
Fax (202) 289-6797

New York Office:
345 East 47th St.
New York, NY 10017
(212) 705-7010
Fax (212) 705-7712

Founded in 1852, the ASCE represents over 120,000 civil engineers world-wide, and is America's oldest national engineering society. The ASCE is committed to advancing the practice of civil engineering and furthering professional knowledge.

Publications: ASCE *newsletter;* more than 25 *ASCE Journals;* Civil Engineers, magazine; *Lessons from the Oklahoma City Bombing: Defensive Design Techniques,* 1997.

Other available information: Membership details (120,000 members), civil engineers database, job information, conferences and conventions, continuing education, and public/government relations.

Automotive Service Association (ASA)
P.O. Box 929
Bedford, TX 76095-0929
(817) 283-6205 voice
(800) 272-7467
Fax (817) 685-0225
e-mail: asainfo@asashop.org
G.W. "Bud" Merwin III, president

Founded in 1951, the ASA has been the leading organization for owners and managers of automotive service businesses that strive to deliver excellence in service and repairs to consumers. The ASA advances the "professionalism and excellence in the automotive repair industry through education, representation and member services."

Other Available Information: Membership details (12,000 members), ethical code of association, association history.

Business Enterprise Trust, The
204 Junipero Serra Boulevard
Stanford, CA 94305
(415) 321-5100
Fax (415) 321-5774
e-mail: bet@betrust.org.

Founded in 1989, an organization promoting social leadership in business.

Other Available Information: Membership details, educational materials (videos and films, etc.), business enterprise awards, nomination information.

Business for Social Responsibility
1683 Folsom Street
San Francisco, CA 94103-3722
(415) 865-2500
e-mail: dhuson@bsr.org
Robert H. Dunn, president

This organization, founded in 1992, serves members involved with small, medium-sized, and large businesses. They work to promote good and responsible business, offering resources for businesses facing ethical decisions.

Other Available Information: Membership details (800 members), conventions, meetings, and an annual conference.

Council for Ethics in Economics (CEE), The
125 East Broad Street
Columbus, OH 43215-3605
(614) 221-8661
Fax (614) 221-8707
e-mail: cee@businessethics.org
David C. Smith, president

Founded in the late 1970s, CEE is an association of leaders in business, education, religion, and other professions working together to strengthen the ethical fabric of business and economic life. The council identifies and responds to emerging issues important for ethical economic practices and assists in the resolution of these issues locally, nationally, and internationally.

Publications: Ethics in Economics, quarterly; *The Ethics of Business in a Global Economy,* 1993; *Ethics in Business: Faith at Work,* 1995; *A Global Ethic: The Leadership Challenge,* 1996.

Other Available Information: Membership details, conferences, meetings, educational materials, audio tapes, videos, CD-ROM on business ethics, and international and national council programs.

Computer Dealers and Lessors Association (CDLA)
1200 19th Street, NW, Ste 300
Washington, DC 20036
(202) 429-5150
Fax (202) 223-4579
e-mail: cdla@cdla.org

Founded in 1974, the CDLA promotes ethics in the industry of computer leasing and remarketing. Members of CDLA are associated with companies that buy, sell, and lease new and used high-technology equipment. CDLA members also include: maintenance companies, refurbishment/reconfiguration firms, transportation companies, financial institutions, OEM finance companies, software distributors, and industry consultants.

Publications: Membership Directory, annual; *CDLA Survey of the Computer Leasing & Remarketing Industry News Digest*, monthly; *CDLA Code of Ethics & Procedural Manual*; *CDLA Information Resource Guide*; *DataLine Magazine*; *Alert Notices*.

Other Available Information: Membership details (300 member companies), industry statistics, meetings, conventions, seminars, workshops, code of ethics, and numerous other services.

Computer Users For Social Responsibility (CUSR)
1726 Lenox Road
Schenectady, NY 12308
(518) 374-1088
Fax (518) 374-1088
Don Ritter, executive officer

The members of the association exchange their knowledge, understanding, information, and resources of personal computers for community service, and to people involved in other community-driven projects (i.e., teaching a disabled person to use a PC).

Other Available Information: Membership details.

Corporations For Cultural and Social Development (CODECAL)
Carrera 15, Numero 37-58
Apartado Aereo 20439
Bogota, Colombia
57 1 2878540
Fax 57 1 2878701
Jaime Diaz, director

Founded in 1972, the association promotes education on social issues, and its areas of concern include: human rights, international relations, environment, community action, and counseling.

Publications: Codecal Bulletin, semiannual (Spanish); *Booklets*; *A Guide To Adult Programs*.

Other Available Information: Membership details, materials in English, French, and Spanish, educational programs for adults and children, computer database, mailing lists, statistics, and educational textbooks.

European Business Ethics Network (EBEN)
Small Business Research Centre
Kingston University
Kingston Hill, Kingston-upon-Thames
Surrey, KT2 7LB, United Kingdom
0181 547 724
e-mail: 1.spence@kingston.ac.uk
Contact: Laura Spence

Founded in 1987, EBEN is a not-for-profit association. Network members include business people, public sector managers, and academics. The role they play is to stimulate and facilitate meetings of minds, discussion, and debate on common ethical problems and dilemmas.

Publications: EBEN Newsletter; Market Morality and Company Size, 1991; Business Ethics in a New Europe, 1992; Ethics and Consultancy: European Perspectives, 1995; Facing Public Interest: The Ethical Challenge to Business Policy and Corporate Communications, 1995.

Other Available Information: Membership details, mission statement, listing of events, meetings, and conferences, press releases.

Hastings Center
255 Elm Road
Briar Cliff Manor, NY 10510
(914) 762-8500
Fax (914) 762-2124
Daniel Callahan, president

Founded in 1969, the Hastings Center is a multinational organization concerned with medical and professional ethics. Professionals that are of interest to the center include physicians, nurses, lawyers, administrators, public policy makers, and academic and health care professionals. Conducts research and is concerned with issues relevant to ethics. The Hastings Center was formerly the Institute of Society, Ethics and the Life Sciences.

Publications: Hastings Center Report, bimonthly; *IRB: A Review of Human Subjects Research,* bimonthly; various monographs and reports.

Other Available Information: Membership details (11,500 members), consulting services, in-house and international educational opportunities, international fellowships, library, and awards of recognition.

Institute for Business & Professional Ethics, The
DePaul University
One East Jackson Boulevard
Chicago, IL 60604
(312) 362-6569
e-mail: LPincus@wppost.depaul.edu
Laura B. Pincus, director

Founded in 1985 by a joint effort of the Colleges of Liberal Arts and Sciences and Commerce at DePaul University, the Institute is one of the first ethics-related resources to pioneer a hypertext-linked ethics network throughout the Internet. The mission of the Institute is to foster ethical behavior. The main focus is on teaching and training individuals to think before they act. The aim is not to design or impose rules, regulations, and controls, but instead to concentrate on stirring an individual's conscience by stimulating moral imagination, by encouraging ongoing ethical debate, and by insisting upon individual responsibility.

Other Available Information: Membership details, book reviews, journals, current events listing for ethics, meetings, conferences (calendar of events), directory, other professional resources.

Interfaith Center On Corporate Responsibility (ICCR)
475 Riverside Drive, Room 566
New York, NY 10115
(212) 870-2293
Fax (212) 870-2023
Timothy H. Smith, executive director

Founded in 1974, the Interfaith Center assists members in incorporating social and ethical responsibility into their investing, by promoting an exchange of information, views, and effective strategies for enabling such activities. The center supports and is involved with research on specific corporations and industries, working to discover materials and the existence of corporate responsibility.

Publications: Corporate Examiner, 10 annually; *Newsletter*; church-sponsored books, proxy resolutions, research papers, briefs.

Other Available Information: Membership details (members: 25 Protestant denominations and 250 Catholic orders), numerous working and researching groups, and information about collaborations with government representatives, sponsors from industries and corporations, foundations, and universities.

International Association for Business and Society (IABS), The
General Information: e-mail to dnigh@darla.badm.scarolina.edu
Professor Doug Nigh
Membership Information: e-mail to lewelln@univscum.csd.scarolina.edu
Professor Patsy Lewellyn

Founded in 1990, IABS is a society devoted to research and teaching on the relationships between business and society. It comprises more than 300 professors worldwide, from 100 universities in 20 countries. It includes, among others, research on corporate social responsibility and performance, emerging social issues for business, business ethics, environmental affairs, and business and government relations.

Publications: Business & Society, quarterly; *IABS Newsletter*, three times a year.

Other Available Information: Membership details, annual international conference, course information, e-mail network discussion.

National Association of Business Consultants (NABC)
175 Fifth Avenue, Suite 2158
New York, NY 10010
(800) 571-NABC
Bruce Miles, executive director

Founded in 1984, the association's members include financial planners, accountants, bankers, lawyers, sales and marketing staff, educators, engineers, and social workers. The association seeks to maintain the highest level of ethics in the business of consulting.

Publication: The Communicator, quarterly.

Other Available Information: Membership details (10,300 members), a membership directory, conventions, and meetings.

National Catholic Coalition For Responsible Investment (NCCRI)
1000 Sixth Street
Charleston, WV 25302
(304) 342-2716
Fax (304) 344-1678
Richard Zelik, chairperson

Founded in 1973, NCCRI was established to encourage Catholic institutions that own stock in corporations to realize the ethical and religious role the investor ought to play in making decisions. The coalition is affiliated with the Interfaith Center on Corporate Responsibility.

Publications: Directory, periodical.

Other Available Information: Membership details (200 members), quarterly meetings, and workshops.

Privacy International (PI)
666 Pennsylvania Avenue S.E.
Suite 303
Washington, DC 20003
(202) 544-9240
Fax (202) 547-5481
e-mail: pi@washofc.cpsr.org.
Contact: Simon Davies, Marc Rotenberg, David Banisar

An independent nongovernmental organization (NGO) established in 1990 to protect personal privacy and to monitor surveillance by government, financial institutions, international agencies, media, political groups, police, and other organizations.

Publication: The International Privacy Bulletin, quarterly.

Other Available Information: Membership details, mission statement, listings of international covenants and laws, listings of various national constitutions, lists of printed social, political, and cultural policies.

Society For Business Ethics (SBE)

The American College
270 S. Bryn Mawr Avenue
Bryn Mawr, PA 19010
(610) 526-1387, (610) 687-6819
Fax (610) 526-1359
e-mail: DUSKA@aol.com
Ronald Duska, executive director

Founded in 1979, the association has within its membership a multinational assortment of philosophy and theology professors, business school professors, and business executives. The association promotes and facilitates information exchange in business ethics.

Publications: Journal of Business Ethics, quarterly; *Society for Business Ethics Newsletter*, quarterly.

Other Available Information: Membership details (800 members), meetings, and conventions.

Transparency International (TI)

Association Headquarters:
Heylstrasse 33
D-10825 Berlin, Germany
(49) 30-787 59 08
Fax (49) 30-787 57 07
Peter Eigen, chairman (Germany); Jeremy Pope, managing director (New Zealand)

USA National Chapter:
1615 L Street, NW, Suite 700
Washington, DC 20036
e-mail: TIUSA@aol.com
(202) 682-7048
Fax (202) 857-0939
Mr. Fritz Heimann, chairman; Mrs. Nancy Zucker Boswell, managing director

A coalition against corruption in international business transactions. TI is a not-for-profit, nongovernmental organization, established to fight corruption in international business transactions. International and national coalitions encourage governments to establish and implement effective laws, policies, and anticorruption programs.

Publications: Sharpening the Responses Against Global Corruption, TI Annual Report 1996; *Building a Global Coalition Against Corruption*, TI Annual Report 1995; *Accountability & Transparency in International Economic Development*, 1994; "Combating Corruption Around the World." *Journal of Democracy* 7 (1) 1996; *National Integrity Systems: The TI Source Book*, 1996.

Other Available Information: Mission statements, association objectives and strategies, pamphlets, numerous multilingual publications.

CONTEMPORARY ETHICAL ISSUES

Chapter 9:
Reference Material

There is an enormous amount of reference material in the field of business ethics. This material can be divided into two broad categories: print and nonprint. Print materials include a wide variety of books and journals. Nonprint materials include films and videotapes. In this chapter, we present a selective inventory of what we regard as the most important items for those who wish to pursue business ethics in a variety of media.

Selected Print Materials

The decade of the 1990s has seen an explosion of books and other print materials in business ethics and in business law. Our listing below is therefore far from comprehensive, but it does, we think, provide a good representation of many of the best works that the student of business ethics will find especially useful and instructive. In a field that changes almost daily, we have emphasized the newest, and most up-to-date items in an attempt to stay on the cutting edge. We have grouped these materials under five headings.

First, in **General Business Ethics**, we subdivide the area into **Anthologies, Case Studies**, and **Monographs.** The anthologies typically include some text written by the editor or editors outlining the basics of ethical theory, along with introductions of varying length to the various topics in business ethics; a variety of readings from several different authors offers diverse perspectives on the topics discussed. Most of these anthologies also include specific cases illustrating the issues. Case studies are entire books that focus exclusively on particular situations, almost always drawn from actual circumstances that occurred in the business context. The monographs consist of material wholly written by a single author, presenting his or her view of the relevant issues, though different authors tend to emphasize different issues. Usually the authors compare their views with those of other scholars. What all these types of books in this first category have in common is their treatment of most or all of the core concerns of business ethics, concerns that we also have addressed here: product safety, advertising, discrimination, whistleblowing, the environment, and so on.

Our second category is **Issues In Business Ethics.** Here we list a number of works written entirely by the authors (very few are edited anthologies) that focus on particular topics, and we group them under our chapter headings: The Consumer, The Corporation, The Employee, and The Environment. We have also added a section listing some works on international business ethics; this area has really taken off in the last few years, with several book-length studies devoted entirely to it. These books typically deal with most of the standard issues as applied to an international context. Not every issue we discuss has an entire book devoted to its subject matter. For example, so far as we know, a comprehensive, book-length treatment of the uses of animals in business and the moral issues generated there has yet to be written.

The extent to which these general and issue-oriented materials in business ethics address business law varies widely; in some, there is very little discussion of the law; in others, there is quite a lot. For those who are seriously interested in the law, we recommend study of the books in our third and fourth categories.

These last two categories mirror the first and second ones, but in the area of business law. **General Business Law** texts are typically not anthologies; instead they are running narratives written exclusively or predominantly by the authors, organized according to the major areas of business law. These areas often correspond to our key issues in business ethics; however, sometimes a prominent area in business ethics is little discussed in business law texts, and sometimes a topic of prime importance in business law is just briefly treated in most general business ethics anthologies. For example, every business ethics anthology has significant material—often an entire chapter—on employee privacy, while business law texts tend to skim over the issue. On the other side, consumer finance is a major feature of business law, especially securities regulation, yet few business ethics texts go beyond a couple of papers on insider trading. For those with deeper interests in specific topics, whether from a moral or legal perspective, we recommend focusing on issues-oriented texts.

Issues In Business Law, our fourth category, concentrates on particular legal problems pertinent to the study of business ethics. Once again, these books are not anthologies and not every issue in business ethics has a book-length treatment of the impact of law in that area. For these topics, texts in general business law are the best source of information and analysis, though depth of detail is absent. The reader will notice a preponderance of books concerning corporate law and employment law, and it does seem to us that most recent work in the field has focused on this area.

We do not include a section on reference works devoted to business ethics because at this time there is just one such item. We predict that this is the next wave in the study of business ethics. It has just begun with a new publication edited by R. Edward Freeman and Patricia Werhane, *The Blackwell Encyclopedic Dictionary of Business Ethics* (Malden, UK: Blackwell, 1997. 416p. ISBN 1-55-786942-1). A useful secondary source of reference is contained in the *Encyclopedia of Applied Ethics* (San Diego, CA: Academic Press, 4 volumes, 1998). The set contains a number of entries that address issues in business ethics: corporate responsibility, affirmative action, strikes, consumer rights, and others.

Finally, our fifth category is **Journals**. Here, we first list the four major journals that are currently devoted entirely to the study of business ethics. We also provide an inventory of a number of philosophy, business, and law journals that often contain insightful papers on business ethics and business law. For these materials, we note the title, place of publication, publisher, year of inception, and frequency of publication.

General Business Ethics

Anthologies

Beauchamp, Tom L. and Norman E. Bowie, eds. *Ethical Theory and Business*. Upper Saddle River, NJ: Prentice Hall, 5th ed. 1997. 661p. ISBN 0-13-398520-2.

Davies, Peter W., ed. *Current Issues in Business Ethics*. New York: Routledge, 1997. 224p. ISBN 0-41-512450-6.

DesJardins, Joseph R. and John McCall, eds. *Contemporary Issues in Business Ethics*. Belmont, CA: Wadsworth, 3d ed. 1996. 560p. ISBN 0-53-425542-6.

Donaldson, Thomas and Patricia H. Werhane, eds. *Ethical Issues in Business: A Philosophical Approach*. Upper Saddle River, NJ: Prentice-Hall, 5th ed. 1996. 516p. ISBN 0-13-50440-5.

Freeman, R. Edward, ed. *Business Ethics: The State of the Art.* New York: Oxford University Press, 1992. 225p. ISBN 0-19-508198-6.

Harwood, Sterling, ed. *Business As Ethical & Business As Usual: Text, Readings, and Cases.* Sudbury: Jones & Bartlett Publishers, 1995. 672p. ISBN 0-86-720971-2.

Hoffman, W. Michael and Jennifer Mills Moore, eds. *Business Ethics: Readings and Cases in Corporate Morality.* New York: McGraw-Hill, 3d ed. 1995. 640p. ISBN 0-07-029349-X.

Newton, Lisa H. and Maureen M. Ford, eds. *Taking Sides: Clashing Views on Controversial Issues in Business Ethics and Society.* New York: McGraw-Hill, 5th ed. 1998. 384p. ISBN 0-69-739108-6.

Sethi, S. Prakash, Paul Steidemeier, and Cecilia M. Falbe, eds. *Scaling the Corporate Wall: Readings in Business and Society.* Paramus, NJ: Prentice Hall, 1997. 515 p. ISBN 0-13-490145-2.

Shaw, William H. and Vincent Barry, eds. *Moral Issues in Business.* Belmont, CA: Wadsworth Publishing, 7th ed. 1997. 608p. ISBN 0-53-452452-4.

White, Thomas I., ed. *Business Ethics: A Philosophical Reader.* Upper Saddle River, NJ: Prentice Hall, 1993. 867p. ISBN 0-02-427221-3.

Case Studies

Beauchamp, Tom L. *Case Studies in Business, Society, and Ethics.* Upper Saddle River, NJ: Prentice Hall, 4th ed. 1998. 304p. ISBN 0-13-398512-1.

Collins, Denis and Thomas O'Rourke. *Ethical Dilemmas in Business.* Cincinnati: South-Western Publishing, 1994. 64p. ISBN 0-53-883512-5.

Donaldson, Thomas and Al Gini, eds. *Case Studies in Business Ethics.* Upper Saddle River, NJ: Prentice-Hall, 4th ed. 1996. 352p. ISBN 0-13-3842433-0.

Goodpaster, Kenneth, John B. Matthews, and Laura Nash. *Policies and Persons: A Casebook in Business Ethics.* New York: McGraw-Hill, 3d ed. 1997. 576p. ISBN 0-07-024509-6.

Jennings, Marianne M. *Case Studies in Business Ethics.* Saint Paul, MN: West Publishing, 1993. 350p. ISBN 0-31-401261-3.

Newton, Lisa H. and David Schmidt. *Wake Up Calls: Classic Cases in Business Ethics.* Belmont CA: Wadsworth Publishing, 1996. 256p. ISBN 0-53-425338-5.

Paine, Lynn Sharp. *Cases In Leadership, Ethics and Organizational Integrity: A Strategic Perspective.* Burr Ridge, IL: Richard D. Irwin, 1996. 320p. ISBN 0-25-619790-3.

Sethi, S. Prakash. *Up Against the Corporate Wall: Cases in Business & Society.* Paramus, NJ: Prentice Hall, 6th ed. 1996. 496p. ISBN 0-13-488371-3.

Monographs

Barton, Laurence. *Ethics: The Enemy in the Workplace.* Cincinnati: South-Western Publishing, 1995. 384p. ISBN 0-53-883873-6.

Boatright, John R. *Ethics and the Conduct of Business.* Upper Saddle River, NJ: Prentice Hall, 2d ed. 1997. 416p. ISBN 0-13-551798-2.

Bowie, Norman E. and Ronald Duska. *Business Ethics.* Englewood Cliffs, NJ: Prentice Hall, 2d ed. 1990. 160p. ISBN 0-13-095910-3.

Buchholz, Rogene A. and Sandra B. Rosenthal. *Business Ethics: The Pragmatic Path Beyond Principles to Process.* Paramus, NJ: Prentice Hall, 1998. 544p. ISBN 0-13-350786-6.

DeGeorge, Richard T. *Business Ethics.* Upper Saddle River, NJ: Prentice-Hall, 4th ed. 1995. 612p. ISBN 0-02-328020-4.

French, Warren A. and John Granrose. *Practical Business Ethics.* Englewood Cliffs, NJ: Prentice Hall, 1995. 235p. ISBN 0-02-338863-3.

Jackson, Jennifer. *An Introduction to Business Ethics.* Malden, UK: Blackwell Publishers, 1996. 272p. ISBN 0-63-119533-5.

Larson, Andrea and R. Edward Freeman. *Women's Studies and Business Ethics: Toward a New Conversation.* New York: Oxford University Press, 1997. 208p. ISBN 0-19-510758-6.

Lippke, Richard L. *Radical Business Ethics.* Lanham, MD: Rowman & Littlefield, 1995. 240p. ISBN 0-84-768069-X.

Machan, Tibor R. *Commerce and Morality: Alternative Essays in Business Ethics.* Lanham, MD: Rowman & Littlefield, 1988. 264p. ISBN 0-84-767586-6.

Michalos, Alex C. *A Pragmatic Approach to Business Ethics.* Thousand Oaks, CA: Sage Publications, 1995. 248p. ISBN 0-80-397085-4.

Pincus, Laura B. *Perspectives in Business Ethics.* Burr Ridge, IL: Irwin Professional Publishing, 1997. 840p. ISBN 0-25-623317-9.

Solomon, Robert C. *Above the Bottom Line: An Introduction to Business Ethics*. Orlando, FL: Harcourt Brace & Company, 2d ed. 1994. 528p. ISBN 0-15-501051-4.

Stewart, David. *Business Ethics*. New York: McGraw-Hill, 1995. 313p. ISBN 0-07-061544-6.

Velasquez, Manuel. *Business Ethics: Concepts and Cases*. Prentice-Hall, 4th ed. 1997. ISBN 0-13-350851-X.

Weiss, Joseph. *Business Ethics: A Managerial Stakeholder Approach*. Cincinnati: South-Western Publishing, 2d ed. 1997. 304p. ISBN 0-534-92512-X.

Wood, Donna J. *Business and Society*. Reading, PA: Addison-Wesley Educational Publishers, 2d ed. 1994. ISBN 0-67-352263-6.

Issues In Business Ethics

The Consumer

Chonko, Lawrence B. *Ethical Decision Making in Marketing*. Thousand Oaks CA: Sage Publications, Sage Series on Business Ethics, vol. 1, 1995. 328p. ISBN 0-80-395545-6.

Dadd-Redalia, Debra. *Sustaining the Earth: Choosing Consumer Products That are Safe for You, Your Family, and the Earth*. New York: Hearst Books, 1994. 352p. ISBN 0-68-812335-X.

Dobson, John. *Finance Ethics: The Rationality of Virtue*. Lanham, MD: Rowman & Littlefield, 1997. 272p. ISBN 0-84-768402-4.

Maldonado-Bear, Rita. *Free Markets, Finance, Ethics, and Law*. Paramus, NJ: Prentice Hall, 1993. 434p. ISBN 0-13-457896-1.

Owen, David G. *Product Liability and Safety*. Eagan, MN: Foundation Press, 3d ed. 1997. 204p. ISBN 1-56-6625807.

Phillips, Michael J. *Ethics and Manipulation in Advertising: Answering a Flawed Indictment*. Westport, CN: Greenwood Publishing Group, 1997. 224p. ISBN 1-56-720063-X.

Williams, Oliver F. *Ethics and the Investment Industry*. Lanham, MD: Rowman & Littlefield, 1989. 260p. ISBN 0-84-767613-7.

The Corporation

Aram, John D. *Presumed Superior: Individualism and American Business.* Englewood Cliffs, NJ: Prentice Hall, 1992. 224p. ISBN 0-13-720699-2.

Cannon, Tom. *Corporate Responsibility: Issues in Business Ethics, Governance and Responsibilities.* Philadelphia: Trans-Atlantic Publications, 1994. 384p. ISBN 0-27-360270-5.

Cowan, Robin and Mario J. Rizzo, eds. *Profits and Morality.* Chicago: University of Chicago Press, 1995. 192p. ISBN 0-22-611632-8.

Danley, John R. *The Role of the Modern Corporation in a Free Society.* South Bend, IN: Notre Dame University Press, 1994. 376p. ISBN 0-26-801647-X.

Frederick, William C. *Values, Nature, and Culture in the American Corporation.* New York: Oxford University Press, 1995. 320p. ISBN 0-19-509674-6.

French, Peter A. *Corporations in the Moral Community.* Orlando, FL: Harcourt Brace Publishers, 1992. 176p. ISBN 0-03-030782-1.

———. *Corporate Ethics.* Orlando, FL: Harcourt Brace Publishers, 1995. 380p. ISBN 0-15-501124-3.

Gilbert, Daniel R. *Ethics Through Corporate Strategy.* New York: Oxford University Press, 1996. 192p. ISBN 0-19-510855-8.

Green, Ronald M. *The Ethical Manager: A New Method for Business Ethics.* Paramus, NJ: Prentice Hall, 1993. 448p. ISBN 0-02-346431-3.

Hartman, Edwin M. *Organizational Ethics and the Good Life.* New York: Oxford University Press, 1996. 232p. ISBN 0-19-510077-8.

Hoffman, W. Michael and Dawn-Marie Driscoll. *The Ethical Edge: Tales of Organizations That Have Faced Moral Crises.* Portland, OR: MasterMedia Publishing, 1997. 256p. ISBN 1-57-101051-3.

Kaufman, Allen, Lawrence Zacharias, and Marvin Karson. *Managers vs. Owners: The Struggle for Corporate Control in American Democracy.* New York: Oxford University Press, 1995. 304p. ISBN 0-19-509860-9.

Punch, Maurice. *Dirty Business: Exploring Corporate Misconduct.* Thousand Oaks, CA: Sage Publications, 1996. 304p. ISBN 0-80-397604-6.

Treviño, Linda K. and Katherine A. Nelson. *Managing Business Ethics: Straight Talk about How to Do It Right.* New York: John Wiley & Sons, 1995. 352p. ISBN 0-47-159848-8.

The Employee

Cahn, Steven M., ed. *The Affirmative Action Debate.* New York: Routledge, 1995. 224p. ISBN 0-41-591493-0.

Cohen, Carl. *Naked Racial Preference: The Case Against Affirmative Action.* Lanham, MD: Madison Books, 1995. 240p. ISBN 1-56-833053-7.

Cox, William N. *A Guide to Effective Employee Relations for the 90's.* Holland, MI: CR & Associates, 1991. 245p. ISBN 1-88-042900-4.

Decker, Kurt H. *Privacy in the Workplace: Rights, Procedures & Policies.* Horsham: LRP Publications, 1994. 540p. ISBN 0-31-872686-6.

Edwards, John R. *When Race Counts: The Morality of Racial Preference in Britain and America.* New York: Routledge, 1995. 272p. ISBN 0-41-507293-X.

Ezorsky, Gertrude. *Racism and Justice: The Case for Affirmative Action.* Ithaca: Cornell University Press, 1991. 136p. ISBN 0-80-149922-4.

Ezorsky, Gertrude, ed. *Moral Rights in the Workplace.* Albany, NY: State University of New York Press, 1987. 312p. ISBN 0-88-706362-4.

Gini, Al R. *It Comes with the Territory: An Inquiry Concerning Work and the Person.* New York: Random House, 1989. 448p. ISBN 0-39-438298-6.

Larmer, Robert A. *Ethics in the Workplace: Selected Readings in Business Ethics.* Saint Paul, MN: West Publishing, 1996. 600p. ISBN 0-31-406802-3.

LeMoncheck, Linda. *Sexual Harassment: A Debate.* Lanham, MD: Rowman & Littlefield, 1997. 192p. ISBN 0-84-768425-3.

Messing, Karen. *One-Eyed Science: Occupational Health and Women Workers.* Philadelphia: Temple University Press, 1998. 264p. ISBN 1-56-639598-4.

Rosenfeld, Michel. *Affirmative Action and Justice: A Philosophical and Constitutional Inquiry.* New Haven, CN: Yale University Press, 1993. 384p. ISBN 0-30-004781-9.

Stockdale, Margaret S. *Sexual Harassment in the Workplace: Perspectives, Frontiers, and Response Strategies.* Thousand Oaks, CA: Sage Publications, 1996. 303p. ISBN 0-80-395793-9.

Taylor, Bron R. *Affirmative Action at Work: Law, Politics, and Ethics.* Pittsburgh: University of Pittsburgh Press, 1991. 288p. ISBN 0-82-295453-2.

Vallance, Elizabeth. *Business Ethics at Work.* New York: Cambridge University Press, 1995. 200p. ISBN 0-52-140568-8.

The Environment

Buchholz, Rogene A. *Principles of Environmental Management: The Greening of Business.* Paramus, NJ: Prentice Hall, 2d ed. 1998. 433p. ISBN 0-13-684895-8.

Business Ethics Quarterly 5, no. 4 (1995). Chicago: The Society for Business Ethics. Special Issue on "Corporations and the Environment."

Grayson, Lesley. *Business and Environmental Accountability.* Mahwah, NJ: Lawrence Erlbaum Associates, 1993. 100p. ISBN 0-94-665582-0.

Hoffman, W. Michael, Robert Frederick, and Edward S. Petry, eds. *Business, Ethics, and the Environment: The Public Policy Debate.* Westport, CN: Greenwood Publishing Group, 1990. 352p. ISBN 0-89-930603-9.

Westra, Laura and Patricia Werhane. *The Business of Consumption: Environmental Ethics and the Global Economy.* Lanham, MD: Rowman & Littlefield, 1998. 360p. ISBN 0-87-768669-8.

International

Cavanagh, Gerald F. *American Business Values with International Perspectives.* Upper Saddle River, NJ: Prentice Hall, 4th ed. 1998. 314p. ISBN 0-13-518234-4.

De George, Richard T. *Competing with Integrity in International Business.* New York: Oxford University Press, 1993. 233p. ISBN 0-19-508226-5.

Donaldson, Thomas. *The Ethics of International Business.* New York: Oxford University Press, 1989. 196p. ISBN 0-19-507471-8.

Elfstrom, Gerard. *Moral Issues and Multinational Corporations.* New York: Saint Martin's Press, 1991. 176p. ISBN 0-31-205314-2.

Wood, Donna J. and Steven L. Wartick. *International Business and Society.* Malden, UK: Blackwell Publishers, 1997. 256p. ISBN 1-55-786944-8.

General Business Law

Bohlman, Herbert M. *The Legal, Ethical and International Environment of Business.* Saint Paul, MN: West Publishing, 3d ed. 1996. 620p. ISBN 0-31-406456-7.

Cheeseman, Henry R. *The Legal and Regulatory Environment: Contemporary Perspectives in Business.* Paramus, NJ: Prentice Hall, 1997. 750p. ISBN 0-13-237280-0.

Phillips, Michael J. *The Legal, Ethical, and Regulatory Environment of Business.* St. Paul, MN: West Publishing, 5th ed. 1995. 972p. ISBN 0-31-403920-1.

Pincus, Laura B. and Tony McAdams. *The Legal Environment of Business: Ethical and Public Policy Contexts.* Burr Ridge, IL: Irwin Professional Publishing, 1996. 704p. ISBN 0-25-617051-7.

Shaw, Bill M., Art Wolfe, and Steven Salbu. *The Structure of the Legal Environment of Business.* Cincinnati: South-Western Publishing, 3d ed. 1996. 772p.ISBN 0-53-884428-0.

Stone, Christopher D. *Where the Law Ends: The Social Control of Corporate Behavior.* Prospect Heights: Waveland Press, 1991. 273p. ISBN 0-88-133632-7.

Issues In Business Law

The Consumer

Abbott, Howard. *Safer By Design: A Guide to the Management and Law of Designing for Product Safety.* Brookfield: Ashgate Publishing, 2d ed. 1997. 200p. ISBN 0-56-607707-8.

Fueroghne, Dean K. *Law and Advertising.* Chicago: Copy Workshop, 1995. 600p. ISBN 0-96-214158-5.

Huber, Peter W. *The Liability Maze: The Impact of Liability Law on Safety and Innovation.* Washington, D.C.: Brookings Institution, 1991. 514p. ISBN 0-81-573760-2.

Oditah, Fidelis. *The Future for the Global Securities Market: Legal and Regulatory Aspects.* New York: Oxford University Press, 1996. 312p. ISBN 0-19-826219-1.

Page, A. C. *Investor Protection.* Evanston, IL: Northwestern University Press, 1994. 384p. ISBN 0-29-782131-8.

The Corporation

Adams, Edward S. *Corporations and Other Business Associations: Statutes, Rules and Forms.* Saint Paul: West Publishing, 1997. 1146p. ISBN 0-31-422738-5.

Bowman, Scott R. *The Modern Corporation and American Political Thought.* University Park: Pennsylvania State University Press, 1996. 424p. ISBN 0-27-101472-5.

Easterbrook, Frank H. *The Economic Structure of Corporate Law.* Cambridge: Harvard University Press, 1996. 384p. ISBN 0-67-423539-8.

Fisse, Brent. *Corporations, Crime, and Accountability.* New York: Cambridge University Press, 1994. 288p. ISBN 0-52-144130-7.

Gilson, Ronald J. *The Law and Finance of Corporate Acquisitions.* Westbury, CN: Foundation Press, 1995. 1603p. ISBN 1-56-662067-8.

Jamieson, Katherine M. *The Organization of Corporate Crime: An Inquiry into the Dynamics of Antitrust Violation.* Thousand Oaks, CA: Sage Publications, 1994. 114p. ISBN 0-80-395200-7.

Kovaleff, Theodore P., ed. *The Antitrust Impulse: An Economic, Historical, and Legal Analysis.* New York: M.E. Sharpe, 2 vol., 1994. 1298p. ISBN 1-56-324085-8.

McCahery, Joseph. *Corporate Control and Accountability: Changing Structures and the Dynamics of Regulation.* New York: Oxford University Press, 1994. 472p. ISBN 0-19-825827-5.

Mitchell, Lawrence E. *Corporate Finance and Governance: Cases, Materials, and Problems.* Durham, NC: Carolina Academic Press, 2d ed. 1996. 1113p. ISBN 0-89-089864-2.

Mussati, Ciuliano. *Mergers, Markets and Public Policy.* Norwell: Kluwer Academic Publishers, 1995. 232p. ISBN 0-79-233643-7.

Schneeman, Angela. *The Law of Corporations, Partnerships and Sole Proprietorships.* Albany, NY: Delmar Publishers, 2d ed., 1997. 656p. ISBN 0-82-737569-7.

Wells, Celia. *Corporations and Criminal Responsibility.* New York: Oxford University Press, 1995. 192p. ISBN 0-19-825947-6.

The Employee

Bible, Jon D. and Darien A. McWhirter. *Privacy in the Workplace.* New York: Quorum Books, 1990. 306p. ISBN 0-89-930473-7.

Blosser, Fred. *Primer on Occupational Safety and Health.* Washington, DC: BNA Books, 1992. 374p. ISBN 0-87-179741-0.

Caplan, Lincoln. *Up Against the Law: Affirmative Action and the Supreme Court.* New York: Twentieth Century Press, 1997. 90p. ISBN 0-87-078409-9.

Conte, Alba. *Sexual Harassment in the Work Place: Law and Practice.* New York: John Wiley & Sons, 2d ed. 2 vol. 1995. 1000p. ISBN 0-471-01446-X.

Fiscus, Ronald J. *The Constitutional Logic of Affirmative Action.* Durham, NC: Duke University Press, 1996. 176p. ISBN 0-82-231770-2.

Forbath, William. *Law and the Shaping of the American Labor Movement.* Cambridge: Harvard University Press, 1991. 211p. ISBN 0-67-451782-2.

Gilliom, John. *Surveillance, Privacy, and the Law: Employee Drug Testing & the Politics of Social Control.* Ann Arbor: University of Michigan Press, 1994. 200p. ISBN 0-47-210493-4.

Gutman, Arthur. *EEO Law and Personnel Practices.* Thousand Oaks, CA: Sage Publications, 1993. 320p. ISBN 0-80-395222-8.

Lindemann, Barbara and David D. Kadue. *Sexual Harassment in Employment Law.* Washington, D.C.: BNA Books, 1992, supplement, 1997. 882p. ISBN 0-87179-704-6.

Moran, John J. *Employment Law: New Challenges in the Business Environment.* Paramus, NJ: Prentice Hall, 1996. 608p. ISBN 0-13-448250-6.

Moran, Mark M. *The OSHA Answer Book: The Employer's Manual That Answers Every OSHA Question.* Orange Park: Moran Associates, 3d ed. 1996. 316p. ISBN 0-96-322967-2.

Petrocelli, William. *Sexual Harassment on the Job.* Berkeley, CA: Nolo Press, 3d ed. 1997. 320p. ISBN 0-87-337403-7.

Twomey, David P. *Labor and Employment Law: Text and Cases.* Cincinnati: South-Western Publishing, 10th ed. 1998. 784p. ISBN 0-53-885439-1.

Vincoli, Jeffrey. *Making Sense of OSHA Compliance.* Rockville, IL: Government Institutes, 1997. 294p. ISBN 0-86-587535-9.

Westman, Daniel P. *Whistleblowing: The Law of Retaliatory Discharge.* Washington, D.C.: BNA Books, 1991. 250p. ISBN 0-87-179661-9.

The Environment

Francione, Gary L. *Animals, Property, and the Law.* Philadelphia: Temple University Press, 1995. 349p. ISBN 1-56-639284-5.

Kubasek, Nancy K. and Gary Silverman. *Environmental Law.* Paramus, NJ: Prentice Hall, 2d ed. 1996. 292p. ISBN 0-13-541202-1.

Percival, Robert V. and Dorothy C. Alevizatos. *Law and the Environment: An Interdisciplinary Reader.* Philadelphia: Temple University Press, 1997. 464p. ISBN 1-56-639524-0.

Patton-Hulce, Vicki R. *Environment and the Law: A Dictionary.* Santa Barbara, CA: ABC-CLIO, 1995. ISBN 0-87-436749-2.

Rosenberg, Ronald H. *Environment, Property and the Law: Federal and State Case Decisions.* New York: Garland Publishing, 1998. 350p. ISBN 0-81-532696-3.

Valente, William D. *Introduction to Environmental Law and Policy: Protecting the Environment Through Law.* Saint Paul, MN: West Publishing, 1995. 464p. ISBN 0-31-404356X.

Weinberg, Philip. *Environmental Law: Cases and Materials.* Bethesda, MD: Austin & Winfield, 2d ed. 1998. 424p. ISBN 1-57-292080-7.

Journals

Business Ethics Journals

Business and Professional Ethics Journal. Troy, NY: Human Dimensions Center, Rensselaer Polytechnic Institute, 1981–present, quarterly.

Business Ethics Quarterly. Chicago: The Society for Business Ethics, 1991–present, quarterly.

Journal Of Business Ethics. Dordrecht, the Netherlands; Boston: D. Reidel Publishing, 1982–present, quarterly.

Teaching Business Ethics. Dordrecht, the Netherlands: Kluwer Academic Publishers, 1st volume in 1997, quarterly.

Other Journals that Address Business Ethics

Business and Society. Chicago: Walter E. Heller College of Business Administration, Roosevelt University, 1960–present, three times a year.

Business Horizons. Bloomington, IN: Indiana University Graduate School of Business, 1958–present, bimonthly.

Business Quarterly, The. London, Ontario: School of Business Administration, The University of Western Ontario, 1950–present, quarterly.

California Management Review. Berkeley, CA: Graduate Schools of Business Administration, University of California, 1958–present, quarterly.

Columbia Law Review. New York: Columbia University, 1901–present, 8 issues yearly.

Executive Excellence. Provo, UT: Learning Associates International, 1984–present, monthly.

Harvard Law Review. Cambridge, MA: Harvard Law Review Association, 1887–present, monthly.

Harvard Business Review. Boston, MA: Harvard University, 1922–present, bimonthly.

Hastings Center Report, The. Hastings-on-Hudson, NY: Institute of Society, Ethics and the Life Sciences, 1971–present.

Journal of Applied Philosophy. Abingdon, Oxfordshire, UK: Society for Applied Philosophy, 1984–present, biannually.

Journal of Social Philosophy, The. St. Petersburg, FL: University of South Florida, 1975–present, quarterly.

Public Affairs Quarterly. Bowling Green, OH: Philosophy Documentation Center, Bowling Green State University, 1987–present, quarterly.

Selected Nonprint Resources

Educational Videos and Films

Thousands of educational videos and films have been produced in the last 25 years or so describing every aspect of business practice. Among these are many dozens of titles attempting to provide a better and more complete understanding of ethics in business. In compiling this educational resource, we have selected a representative sampling of videos that address most of the areas of business ethics that have occupied our study. Some areas of ethical concern in business are little treated; for example, our research has yielded only one video on privacy in the workplace. Other topics are covered in great depth; one obvious trend in nonprint, educational materials treating business ethics is a concentration on sexual harassment: There are at least 40 such videos currently available.

The entries below are ordered alphabetically by the **Title** of the movie, followed by its running time, stated in minutes, and the year of its release, if available. The producer and distributor are then credited along with the distributor's address and telephone number. A short description of the subject matter follows. All these productions are in color and available in the VHS format.

Advertising
Length: 20 minutes
Date: 1985
Producer: TV Ontario/USA
Distributor: TV Ontario/USA
1140 Kildaire Farm Road, Suite 308
Cary, NC 27511
(800) 331-9566

Although geared toward younger audiences, this production addresses some moral problems with advertising directed at children. The purpose of advertising is explained, as well as how it can influence and mislead. The pervasiveness of advertising is also noted.

Advertising Alcohol—Calling the Shots
Length: 30 minutes
Date: 1992
Producer: Cambridge Documentary Films
Distributor: Cambridge Documentary Films
P.O. Box 385
Cambridge, MA 02139
(617) 354-3677

This is a visual and conceptual examination of the techniques used by advertisers to sell alcohol. The film argues that alcohol advertising exploits the fears and desires of young people in order to create a new generation of alcohol consumers. Such ads ignore or misrepresent the warning signs of alcohol abuse and claim that alcohol consumption promotes happiness, success, sexual vitality, prestige, athletic ability, and creativity—qualities that are in fact destroyed by such abuse.

Affirmative Action Versus Reverse Discrimination
Length: 60 minutes
Date: 1984
Producer: WNET-TV (New York)
Distributor: Annenburg/Corporation for Public Broadcasting
P.O. Box 2345
South Burlington, VT 05407
(800) 532-7637

Now somewhat dated, this debate still represents the best educational material available covering both sides of a very controversial issue. The panel discussion features Ellen Goodman, former EEOC chair Eleanor Holmes Norton, Washington Post columnist William Raspberry, and United Federation of Teachers President Albert Shanker. The primarily question considered is whether quotas based on race and gender are constitutional. Part of a series on the Constitution created by Fred Friendly.

Anatomy of a Corporate Takeover

Length:	60 minutes
Date:	1989
Producer:	Columbia University
Distributor:	Annenburg/Corporation for Public Broadcasting
	P.O. Box 2345
	South Burlington, VT 05407
	(800) 532-7637

This is part five of PBS's *Ethics in America* series, produced by Fred Friendly. It features a roundtable discussion, against the backdrop of specific instances of corporate mergers, by several prominent authorities on the ethics of corporate mergers. Includes T. Boone Pickens, economist Lester Thurow, Senator Tim Wirth, and chief executives from Borg-Warner, Goodyear, and Berkshire Hathaway.

B, E & K Campaign—The Workers Fight Back and Worker's Enemy

Length:	20 minutes
Date:	1989
Producer:	United Brotherhood of Carpenters and Joiners
Distributor:	AFL-CIO
	Education Department
	815 16th St. NW
	Washington, DC 20006

Two 10 minute short films about a large, nonunionized construction firm called B, E & K. The company builds new production facilities, primarily in the paper industry, but it also provides corporate clients with various services designed to break labor strikes. The first film describes the efforts of the Carpenters and the United Paperworkers unions to enlighten workers and their communities about B, E & K's tactics, while the second short details what those tactics are. Although not an objective look at the issue, these films provide a good overview of workers' values and attitudes, and what is at stake for them.

Beyond Borders—Ethics in International Business

Length:	30 minutes
Date:	1992
Producer:	Ethics Resource Center
Distributor:	Ethics Resource Center
	1120 G St. NW, Suite 200
	Washington, DC 20005
	(800) 777-1285

Five dramatizations examine the conflicts that may arise in international trade. The video directs and promotes the discussion of such issues as: cultural differences, the Foreign Corrupt Practices Act, and company standards that conflict with business and social practices in different countries.

The Burial Ground
Length: 30 minutes
Date: unavailable
Producer: Commonwealth Films
Distributor: Commonwealth Films
223 Commonwealth Ave.
Boston, MA
(617) 262-5634

A dramatization of a company improperly disposing of hazardous wastes and the tragic consequences that follow. The emphasis here is on the company's moral and legal responsibility for proper disposal, and the penalties imposed by law and by public opinion for noncompliance.

Business Ethics
Length: 19 minutes
Date: unavailable
Producer: CareerTrack Publications
Distributor: Cambridge Educational Films
P.O. Box 2153
Department CC13
Charleston, WV 25328
(800) 468-4227

The presentation of a number of ethically perplexing scenarios arising in the corporate context, asking viewers how they would respond to the questions raised. This video helps to give teachers a way of discussing morally troubling situations that arise in doing business, and allows students to begin to form their own opinions about what they understand to be ethical and unethical, without undue influence from their instructors.

Business Ethics
Length: 58 minutes
Date: 1994
Producer: Kantola Productions
Distributor: Video Learning Systems Inc.
345 W. Lancaster Ave.
Haverford, PA 19041
(800) 622-3610

Professors Thomas Dunfee and Diane Robertson of the University of Pennsylvania Wharton School of Business focus on developing basic ethical practices in a business setting. They show how to make high ethical standards a continuing feature of decision making in the corporation. Dunfee and Robertson also explain ways to recognize potential moral problems before they arise, and offer methods for making people feel confident and comfortable about voicing their moral concerns.

Buying Trouble: Ethics Issues in Purchasing
Length: 30 minutes
Date: 1989
Producer: Ethics Resource Center
Distributor: Barr Media Group
12801 Schabarum Ave.
P.O. 7878
Irwindale, CA 91706
(800) 234-7878

An investigation of how pressure can be placed on purchasing decisions by those who are outside of the decision, such as coworkers and suppliers. The presentation promotes discussion of various issues, including: favoritism, collusion, gifts and bribes, and reciprocal favors. It further focuses on the causes of these pressures, and what can be done about them when they occur.

Chico Mendes—Voice of the Amazon
Length: 57 minutes
Date: 1989
Producer: Better World Society
Distributor: Cinema Guild
1697 Broadway, Suite 506
New York, NY 10019
(800) 723-5522

Examines the life and work of Chico Mendes, an environmentalist and rubber tapper who fought for both the preservation of Brazil's rainforest and the welfare of the peasants against business and government interests. His assassination in December 1988 unleashed a global outcry to check the political and economic forces that produce environmental degradation and human oppression.

The Dirty Dozen—OSHA's 12 Most Common Violations
Length: 16 minutes
Date: unavailable
Producer: Commonwealth Films
Distributor: Commonwealth Films
223 Commonwealth Ave.
Boston, MA
(617) 262-5634

A description of the 12 most common, yet serious, safety violations found in business and industry. These infractions of Federal Standards for General Industry are detailed in a way that assists supervisors in examining their own workplaces and making adjustments, if necessary. Examples drawn from case studies are used to show how workers can be protected.

Employment and Discrimination Law Under the New Supreme Court Majority—The Court Turns Right
Length: 210 minutes
Date: 1989
Producer: American Law Institute/American Bar Association
Distributor: American Law Institute/American Bar Association
      4025 Chestnut St.
      Philadelphia, PA 19104
      (215) 243-1661

An in-depth examination and analysis of the startling and substantial changes in employment law following in the wake of several Supreme Court decisions during the 1988–1989 term. The effects of these changes continue to resound today. Special attention is given to the landmark cases *Richmond v. J.A. Croson* and *Wygant v. Jackson Board of Education.*

Employment-at-Will on Trial
Length: 280 minutes
Date: 1987
Producer: American Bar Association
Distributor: American Bar Association
      541 Fairbank Court
      Chicago, IL 60611
      (800) 964-4253

Extensive instruction for lawyers, human resource managers, and personnel executives on the legal and ethical aspects of at-will employment. A wealth of useful information is provided, including how to identify problematic situations in hiring and firing, how to design policies that reduce the likelihood of lawsuits, and how judges and juries assess the trial process and evaluate witnesses.

Ethics and Work with Joanne Ciulla
Length: 30 minutes
Date: 1995
Producer: PBS
Distributor: PBS
      1320 Braddock Place
      Alexandria, VA 22314
      (800) 344-3337

Joanne Ciulla of the University of Pennsylvania Wharton School of Business discusses ethics in business, and the meaning of work in the American culture. She argues that people are often consumed by their work to such an extent that they sacrifice almost everything for the sake of their careers, even families and children.

Ethics at Work

Length: 30 minutes
Date: 1992
Producer: Ethics Resource Center
Distributor: Ethics Resource Center
    1120 G St. NW, Suite 200
    Washington, DC 20005
    (800) 777-1285

The video presents ethical issues that can arise in multinational business operations. Includes such issues as: marketing to different cultures, environmental responsibility, technology transfer, Foreign Corrupt Practices Act, and foreign partnerships and acquisitions.

Ethics in Advertising

Length: 30 minutes
Date: unavailable
Producer: Nebraska Educational TV Council for Higher Education
Distributor: Nebraska Educational TV Council for Higher Education
    P.O. Box 8311
    Lincoln, NE 68501

A discussion of taste and truthfulness in advertising. The focus is on an explanation not only of the relevant federal regulation for all advertising media, but also effective means of self-regulation in the industry.

Ethics in American Business

Length: 180 minutes
Date: 1988
Producer: WTVS-TV (Detroit)
Distributor: Coronet/MIT Film & Video International
    4350 Equity Drive
    Columbus, OH 43228
    (800) 321-3106

A prolonged and detailed discussion of how business executives can promote ethical conduct in the business activities of their employees. A number of executives from several large American companies are featured, explaining the process of developing ethical codes of conduct.

For the Life of the Product

Length: 20 minutes
Date: 1992
Producer: Commonwealth Films
Distributor: Commonwealth Films
    223 Commonwealth Avenue
    Boston, MA
    (617) 262-5634

An exploration of product liability law and its application to a manufactured consumer good. The development of a product is traced from its inception, through its manufacture, and on to its distribution. Paralleling this, the life of a consumer from birth to adulthood is depicted, culminating in her purchasing the product. An injury results and a suit for damages follows. Describes key issues for manufacturers, including safety standards, hazards analysis, postsale product monitoring, recalls, and replacing defective merchandise.

Gateway to Opportunity—Interviewing Job Applicants with Disabilities

Length:	18 minutes
Date:	unavailable
Producer:	Commonwealth Films
Distributor:	Commonwealth Films
	223 Commonwealth Ave.
	Boston, MA
	(617) 262-5634

Instructions for managers and supervisors on how to prepare for and interview a disabled person. Areas of possible discrimination and violation of the Americans with Disabilities Act are stressed.

Hamburger—Jungleburger

Length:	58 minutes
Date:	1986
Producer:	Icarus Films
Distributor:	Icarus Films
	200 Park Ave. S, Suite 1319
	New York, NY 10003
	(212) 674-3375

This is an examination of the impact of the fast food industry on third-world countries. Costa Rica is highlighted, where two-thirds of the beef raised is exported, despite the fact that meat consumption in the country is declining. Graphically displays the staggering effects of the fast food industry on the Costa Rican rainforest, and the use of herbicides on the health of the people.

Handling Employee Terminations

Length:	22 minutes
Date:	unavailable
Producer:	Commonwealth Films
Distributor:	Commonwealth Films
	223 Commonwealth Ave.
	Boston, MA
	(617) 262-5634

A video geared toward supervisors who have decided to fire an employee. Instructions are provided on how to correctly process performance and disciplinary terminations in order to avoid legal problems. Dramatizations of actual cases present a five-step procedure to facilitate the process.

In Defense of Animals

Length:	28 minutes
Date:	1989
Producer:	Julie Akeret
Distributor:	Bullfrog Films, Inc.
	P.O. Box 149
	Oley, PA 19547
	(800) 543-3764

Philosopher and animal rights activist Peter Singer explains the moral and practical arguments against eating animals and using them for research and experimentation.

Inside the Poison Trade

Length:	52 minutes
Date:	1990
Producer:	Coronet/MIT Film and Video International
Distributor:	Coronet/MIT Film and Video International
	4350 Equity Drive
	Columbus, OH 43228
	(800) 321-3106

In the late 1980s more than 20 ships loaded with industry-produced toxic waste left European ports, bound for various third-world countries. The growing problem of toxic waste dumping is the centerpiece of this production, especially Italy's role in exporting its refuse. Numerous interviews with waste brokers, public officials, environmental workers, and concerned citizens are featured.

Marketplace Ethics

Length:	29 minutes
Date:	1990
Producer:	Ethics Resource Center
Distributor:	Barr Media Group
	12801 Schabarum Ave.
	P.O. Box 7878
	Irwindale, CA 91706
	(800) 234-7878

The ethical problems that arise in the sale and marketing of products are detailed here. This production argues for establishing company standards concerning product representation, rejecting gifts, and dealing with whistleblowing, competitor relationships, and consumers.

A Matter of Judgment—Conflicts of Interest in the Workplace
Length: 30 minutes
Date: 1986
Producer: Ethics Resource Center
Distributor: Barr Media Group
               12801 Schabarum Ave.
               P.O. Box 7878
               Irwindale, CA 91706
               (800) 234-7878

An investigation of various areas of business that may lead to conflicts of interest, including vendor relationships, hiring practices, abuses of the consultant-client relationship, and involvement with the family. Short skits are presented to illustrate legally suspect activities and to provoke critical moral thinking.

The Mine Field: A Comprehensive Primer on Legal Compliances and Ethical Conduct
Length: 22 minutes
Date: 1991
Producer: Commonwealth Films
Distributor: Commonwealth Films
               223 Commonwealth Ave.
               Boston, MA
               (617) 262-5634

A summary of several of the legal compliance issues affecting business: environment, sexual harassment, employee health and safety, equity and employment, competition, and information regulations. Actual situations are effectively utilized to emphasize the importance of compliance, and the penalties for failing to do so.

A Need to Know
Length: 25 minutes
Date: 1990
Producer: Commonwealth Films
Distributor: Commonwealth Films
               223 Commonwealth Ave.
               Boston, MA
               (617) 262-5634

A how-to guide for complying with securities laws, especially those regarding insider trading. These points are made through dramatization and discussion. This video is approved by the Securities and Exchange Commission for compliance education, which is required for officers, directors, managers, and financial personnel of banks and other financial institutions.

Pollution Liability—Managing the Challenges of Coverage and Defense

Length: 210 minutes
Date: 1991
Producer: American Law Institute/American Bar Asssociation
Distributor: American Law Institute/American Bar Asssociation
4025 Chestnut St.
Philadelphia, PA 19104
(215) 243-1661

Although somewhat dated in a legal field of constant modification, this is a thorough overview of most of the major federal environmental laws, such as CERCLA, SARA, RCRA, and various Clean Air Act amendments. The video also reports on outcomes for business in pollution liability during 1990, and details the approaches that seem to be working in the rapidly evolving field of dispute resolution, pollution management, and insurance litigation.

Privacy in the Workplace—Unreasonable Intrusion or Legitimate Interest?

Length: 50 minutes
Date: 1992
Producer: American Law Institute/American Bar Asssociation
Distributor: American Law Institute/American Bar Asssociation
4025 Chestnut St.
Philadelphia, PA 19104
(215) 243-1661

A close examination of a number of privacy issues in the workplace, arising in both the public and private sectors. Drug testing and polygraphs are high-lighted. The balancing test used by judges is described, showing how employers should proceed with caution when assessing the reasonableness and lawfulness of searches, testing, and surveillance on the job.

Sexual Harassment—How to Protect Yourself and Your Organization

Length: 126 minutes
Date: 1993
Producer: CareerTrack Publications
Distributor: Cambridge Educational Films
P.O. Box 2153
Department CC13
Charleston, WV 25328
(800) 468-4227

The video presents three concise and comprehensive sections on sexual harassment, defining what is and what is not considered harassment. Further, procedures for handling sexual harassment are presented, both for the victim and for managers who must deal with complaints. Describes skillful and legal methods for resolving instances of sexual harassment, as well as how to initiate new policies or modify existing ones to better handle such cases if they arise.

Sexual Harassment Video—Serious Business
Length: 25 minutes
Date: 1994
Producer: Council on Education in Management
Distributor: Council on Education in Management
                325 Lennon Lane
                Walnut Creek, CA 94598
                (800) 942-4494

This production makes the case that preventing or eliminating sexual harassment will benefit all employees as well as the entire organization. It examines the impact of hostile working environment situations, the consequences of third-party harassment, proper reporting of complaints, confronting the harasser, the problem of false accusations, and other issues.

Someone is Watching—Versions A and B
Length: 25 and 28 minutes
Date: unavailable
Producer: Commonwealth Films
Distributor: Commonwealth Films
                223 Commonwealth Ave.
                Boston, MA
                (617) 262-5634

These two films are introductions to the basic principles of correct business practices. They outline antitrust legislation, including the Sherman Act, the Clayton Act, and the Federal Trade Commission Act. Federal sentencing guidelines for white-collar crimes are also explained. Industry-specific dramatizations of certain business situations subject to legal review are presented. Version A is for manufacturing industries, and Version B is for service industries.

When Products Harm
Length: 33 minutes
Date: 1991
Producer: Commonwealth Films
Distributor: Commonwealth Films
                223 Commonwealth Ave.
                Boston, MA
                (617) 262-5634

This video promotes product liability awareness for manufacturers by presenting dramatizations of lawsuits directed toward manufacturers. The video goes on to discuss specific precautions and steps manufacturers can take to avoid such legal suits. The overall emphasis is company responsibility.

Whistleblowers

Length:	24 minutes
Date:	1989
Producer:	Films for the Humanities and Sciences
Distributor:	Films for the Humanities and Sciences
	P.O. Box 2053
	Princeton, NJ 08543
	(800) 257-5126

The story of four whistleblowers who learned that personal integrity can only be maintained at a very high cost. Suggestions for protecting whistleblowers are presented, and criteria are offered for distinguishing honesty and disloyalty on the job.

Who's Killing Calvert City?

Length:	60 minutes
Date:	1990
Producer:	PBS
Distributor:	Documentary Consortium
	Address unavailable

Calvert City, Kentucky, enjoyed the economic benefits of its three chemical plants for many years, but then the toxic waste began to cause serious environmental and health problems. The conflict between environmentalists and chemical manufacturers is presented through interviews with experts and local citizens. One of PBS's *Frontline* episodes.

Entertainment Videos and Films

Thousands of feature films have been produced over the last 70 years or so, but very few have focused on ethical conduct in the practice of business, or raised important moral questions in a corporate context. The films we have selected and synopsized below represent a fairly comprehensive list of this meager collection. Their story lines are often some version of the standard Hollywood formula in which the lines between good and evil are crisply drawn, and good invariably triumphs. In the business setting, the formula is this: An individual or a few individuals of upstanding and righteous character are pitted against big, bad, big business, represented impersonally by an ill-defined "company" or group of "bosses" or represented personally by a particularly corrupt owner or executive who serves as a touchstone of evil. Moral ambiguity or an even-handed treatment of opposing sides tends to be absent. Almost always, the morally righteous individuals prevail in the conflict. This recipe is especially evident when the central conflict concerns labor-management issues (*American Dream* is a notable exception, see below), but is typical of most any film on the ethics of business.

The entries below are ordered alphabetically by the **Title** of the movie, along with the Motion Picture Association of America (MPAA) rating (PG, PG-13, R), or (no rating) if the date of release precedes the institution of the MPAA rating system, or if the movie was made for television; next is the video's running time, stated in minutes, and the year of its release; the director, writer (if available), and principle actors are also credited. A short description of the plot follows, emphasizing its relevance to business ethics.

Acceptable Risks (no rating)

Length: 97 minutes
Date: 1986
Director: Rick Wallace
Actors: Brian Dennehy, Cicely Tyson, Kenneth McMillan, Christine Ebersole

Citichem plant manager, played by Brian Dennehy, is ordered to cut costs at the price of employee safety and public health. Battling against corrupt politicians and morally bankrupt corporate executives, Dennehy fights to reinstate safety standards. Cicely Tyson portrays the city manager, allied with Dennehy, who tries to warn the town of the threat of chemical disaster. Made-for-television melodrama.

The Agency (R)

Length: 94 minutes
Date: 1981
Director: George Kaczender
Actors: Robert Mitchum, Lee Majors, Valerie Perrine, Saul Rubinek

Subliminal advertising is employed by an unscrupulous ad agency in an attempt to manipulate public behavior and opinion. Based on a Paul Gottlieb novel.

American Dream (PG-13)

Length: 100 minutes
Date: 1989
Director: Barbara Kopple

A documentary from Barbara Kopple about a meat packers' union in Austin, Minnesota, struggling to negotiate pay raises with the Hormel Corporation. Local P-9 bypasses their international chapter and hires a labor consultant to market their cause while polishing the public's tarnished view of unions. Meanwhile, a significant contingent of P-9 members begins to question the union's methods and goals. Unlike Kopple's earlier union documentary, *Harlan County U.S.A.* (see below), this one features the perspectives of all sides in the conflict. The voices of the strikers, the dissident union members, Hormel executives, and representatives of the international chapter of the union are all heard, leaving the viewer to decide who is right.

389

Barbarians at the Gate (R)

Length:	107 minutes
Date:	1993
Director:	Glenn Jordan
Writer:	Larry Gelbart
Actors:	James Garner, Jonathan Pryce, Peter Riegert, Joanna Cassidy

Set in the "greed is good" financial atmosphere of the 1980s, this film presents the $25 billion battle over RJR Nabisco, which was working on the development of "smokeless cigarettes." James Garner portrays the CEO of RJR Nabisco, F. Ross Johnson, who is confident that the smokeless cigarettes will cause a substantial increase in the price of Nabisco stock. When test-marketing indicates dim prospects for the new cigarettes, Johnson attempts a leveraged buyout of the company in order to avert the product's failure. Unfortunately, he runs into stiff competition when he meets Kravis (Pryce), a "master dealer." Based on the book by Bryan Burrough and John Helyar. Made for cable television.

Black Fury (no rating)

Length:	95 minutes
Date:	1935
Director:	Michael Curtiz
Actors:	Paul Muni, Barton MacLane, Henry O'Neill, Karen Morely

One of the first plight-of-the worker movies. Paul Muni portrays coal miner Joe Radek, an eastern European immigrant, who protests the terrible working conditions in the mines. Company thugs beat him up and kill his friend. Although basically apolitical, Radek then barricades himself in a mine and draws national attention to the miners' predicament. Authentic and realistic for the time, but with a standard happy ending.

The Burning Season

Length:	123 minutes
Date:	1994
Director:	John Frankenheimer
Writers:	Michael Tolkin, William Mastrosimone, Ron Hutchinson
Actors:	Raul Julia, Edward James Olmos, Sonia Braga, Luis Guzman, Nigel Havers

One of Raul Julia's last roles, here he portrays Chico Mendez, a Brazilian socialist engaged in the struggle to save the homes and land of people living in the Western Amazon rainforest. He assists them in forming a union and holding off the coming of a railroad that will allow land speculators and cattlemen easy access to the jungle. Mendes and his followers are violently opposed by corrupt politicians who are bankrolled by corporate interests. Mendes's efforts ended in 1988 when he was murdered. Filmed on location in Mexico. Based on the book by Andrew Revkin.

Business As Usual (PG)

Length:	89 minutes
Date:	1988
Director:	Lezli-Ann Barrett
Writer:	Lezli-Ann Barrett
Actors:	Glenda Jackson, Cathy Tyson, John Thaw, Craig Charles

When one of her employees is sexually harassed, a timid boutique manager (Glenda Jackson) comes to the victim's defense. She gets fired for her trouble, but fights back and creates a national furor over the issue and women's rights in general. Set in Liverpool, England, the film is an angry prolabor, anti-Margaret Thatcher period piece.

The Devil and Miss Jones (no rating)

Length:	90 minutes
Date:	1941
Director:	Sam Wood
Writer:	Norman Krsna
Actors:	Robert Cummings, Jean Arthur, Charles Coburn, William Demarest

A millionaire executive from a huge corporation (Charles Coburn) poses as an ordinary salesclerk in order to expose union organizers. Instead, he finds that management supervisors are the bad guys, and another lowly clerk (Jean Arthur) is a captivating love-interest.

Disclosure (R)

Length:	129 minutes
Date:	1994
Director:	Barry Levinson
Writer:	Paul Attanasio
Actors:	Michael Douglas, Demi Moore, Donald Sutherland, Caroline Goodall

Michael Douglas is a likeable and responsible "family man" working as a corporate executive. His boss, who also happens to be his ex-lover (Demi Moore), attempts to seduce him, but when he rejects her come-ons, she accuses him of sexual harassment. The film addresses many issues in corporate politics, especially the *quid pro quo* form of sexual harassment. Based on the novel by Michael Crichton.

Executive Suite (no rating)

Length:	104 minutes
Date:	1954
Director:	Robert Wise
Writer:	Ernest Lehman
Actors:	William Holden, June Allyson, Barbara Stanwyck, Fredric March, Walter Pigeon, Shelley Winters, Dean Jaggar

One of the first dog-eat-dog dramas about high finance and big business, this movie is based on the novel by Cameron Hawley. It is a multifaceted drama that examines the intense power struggles in big business, following the death of the owner of a gigantic furniture company. Became a short-lived TV series.

The Firm (R)

Length:	154 minutes
Date:	1993
Director:	Sydney Pollack
Writer:	Robert Towne, David Rayfiel
Actors:	Tom Cruise, Jeanne Triplehorn, Gene Hackman, Wilfred Brimley, Ed Harris, Holly Hunter, Hal Holbrook, Gary Busey

Tom Cruise portrays a recent Ivy League law school graduate who accepts a fantastic position at a wealthy law firm in Memphis, Tennessee. To the ambitious and idealistic graduate, everything seems perfect, but as he soon finds out, nothing is completely free and easy. The plot is filled with turns and twists, with several moral dilemmas. Though somewhat predictable, it does provides some surprises as well. Based on the novel by John Grisham.

Glengary Glen Ross (R)

Length:	100 minutes
Date:	1992
Director:	James Foley
Writer:	David Mamet, based on his Pulitzer Prize-winning stage play
Actors:	Al Pacino, Jack Lemmon, Ed Harris, Alec Baldwin, Kevin Spacey

A film presenting the lives of a collection of real estate salesmen working relentlessly to keep their jobs by selling more than their coworkers, who are also competitors. The film presents 48 hours of their lives, with all of the trials and tortures of ruthless business. The characters find themselves in many ethical binds, and the way out is a rough road.

Gung Ho (PG-13)

Length:	111 minutes
Date:	1985
Director:	Ron Howard
Writers:	Babaloo Mandel, Lowell Ganz
Actors:	Michael Keaton, Gedde Watanbe, George Wendt, Mimi Rogers, John Turturro, So Yamamura

A failing automobile factory in a small town is bought by a Japanese corporation that then takes over management of the plant. Cultural and business practices come into conflict in the process, and Michael Keaton is selected as the one to keep the peace. Although primarily a comedy, the film offers an interesting treatment of the Japanese focus on corporate cohesion in opposition to the American rugged individual looking out for number one.

Harlan County U.S.A. (PG)

Length:	103 minutes
Date:	1977
Director:	Barbara Kopple

Barbara Kopple's documentary covers a strike by Kentucky coal miners. Like nearly every union film, the story told is entirely from the point of view of the workers and their families, and thus lacks the moral ambiguity of her later documentary *American Dream* (see above). One cannot help but sympathize with their plight in this fascinating and gripping look at the emotional turmoil that attends a union shut down. 1976 Academy Award for Best Feature Documentary.

How To Succeed In Business Without Really Trying (no rating)

Length:	121 minutes
Date:	1967
Director:	David Swift
Writers:	David Swift, Abe Burrows
Actors:	Robert Morse, Michele Lee, Rudy Vallee, Anthony Teague, Maureen Arthur

A classic musical comedy about a window washer who works his way to the top of a company by using his charm. Robert Morse reprises the role that won him a Tony Award on Broadway. The script is loosely based on a nonfiction work of the same title by Shepherd Mead, whose book Morse buys on his first day of work at the Worldwide Wicket Company. The lyrics of the music present numerous ideas and situations concerning corporate conduct.

The Hucksters (no rating)

Length:	115 minutes
Date:	1947
Director:	Jack Conway
Actors:	Clark Cable, Deborah Kerr, Sydney Greenstreet, Ava Gardner, Keenan Wynn, Edward Arnold

A scathing critique of the advertising and radio industries. Clark Cable battles for honesty and integrity against a swarm of lackeys and yes-men. Sidney Greenstreet portrays a despotic and predatory president of a soap company, out to swindle consumers in the name of the almighty dollar. Deborah Kerr's first American movie.

Matewan (PG-13)

Length:	130 minutes
Date:	1987
Director:	John Sayles
Writer:	John Sayles
Actors:	Chris Cooper, James Earl Jones, David Strathairn, Mary McDonnell, William Oldham, Kevin Tighe, Nancy Mette, Jo Henderson, Josh Mostel

Based on a factual account of the infamous coal miners' strike and accompanying bloodshed in Matewan, West Virginia, in 1920. Chris Cooper portrays a soft-spoken but intense union organizer, trying to avoid violence, while James Earl Jones is a miner, initially and unknowingly brought in as a replacement worker, who then sides with the union. The local sheriff (David Strathairn) is caught between the combatants, trying to keep the peace while enforcing the law. Though it's clear that the company is evil and the miners represent the forces of good, the film exhibits the complexity of organizing men of disparate backgrounds to fight for a common cause. John Sayles has a stunning cameo as a pro-management preacher.

Jerry Mcguire (R)

Length:	135 minutes
Date:	1996
Director:	Cameron Crowe
Writer:	Cameron Crowe
Actors:	Tom Cruise, Cuba Gooding, Jr., Renee Zellweger, Kellie Preston, Bonnie Hunt, Jerry O'Connell, Glen Frey

Tom Cruise is the title character, a professional sports agent who decides to restore a sense of morality and "goodness" in the profession. After his honorable conduct gets him fired from a mega-agency, Mcguire starts his own company and allies himself with his most obnoxious and least important client (Cuba Gooding, Jr.). He struggles to maintain his new commitment to ethical business practices, while at the same time keeping his head above water. His secretary, and love interest, stands by him throughout, which causes Mcguire to consider what he truly values most.

9 to 5 (PG)

Length:	111 minutes
Date:	1980
Director:	Colin Higgins
Writer:	Patricia Resnick
Actors:	Jane Fonda, Lily Tomlin, Dolly Parton, Dabney Coleman, Sterling Hayden

The presentation of a comic caricature of corporate life, focusing on three women (Jane Fonda, Lily Tomlin, and Dollie Parton in her acting debut) working under the direction of a male chauvinist boss. The three are consistently treated unfairly by their sexist, tyrannical boss, and are continuously ground under his thumb. Three mishaps occur, one to each of the female employees, that threaten to cost them their jobs. The three decide to fight back by kidnaping their boss and, while he is "out of the office," try their hands at running the corporation. He returns after many comedic episodes to find things much changed.

Norma Rae (PG)

Length:	114 minutes
Date:	1979
Director:	Martin Ritt
Writers:	Harriet Frank, Jr., Irving Ravetch
Actors:	Sally Field, Ron Liebman, Beau Bridges, Pat Hingle

Sally Field is Norma Rae, a poor and uneducated textile mill worker. With the help of a New York labor organizer (Liebman), she manages to unionize the mill in an attempt to improve the dreadful working conditions and low wages. Naturally, she is opposed by management at every turn. Based on a true story.

On the Waterfront (no rating)

Length:	108 minutes
Date:	1954
Director:	Elia Kazan
Writer:	Budd Schulberg
Actors:	Marlon Brando, Rod Steiger, Lee J. Cobb, Karl Malden, Eva Marie Saint

Tough, realistic portrayal of New York dock workers embroiled in union violence. Marlon Brando portrays Terry Malloy, a former boxer who "could have been a contender," but now is just another union lackey. His older brother (Rod Steiger), the corrupt lawyer for the longshoreman's local, leads Terry into criminal activity. He now must choose between his loyalty to his brother and the union boss (Lee J. Cobb) and remaining true to personal principles already damaged by participation in the union's strongarm tactics.

Other People's Money (R)

Length:	101 minutes
Date:	1991
Director:	Norman Jewison
Writer:	Alan Sargent
Actors:	Danny DeVito, Penelope Ann Miller, Dean Jones, Gregory Peck, Piper Laurie

This is the story of a "corporate raider" with a heart of stone. "Larry the Liquidator," played by Danny DeVito, has a passion for taking over other corporations, and has now set his gaze on the family-owned New England Wire and Cable Company. In the process of this quest, he meets Kate Sullivan (Penelope Ann Miller), the daughter of the owner (Gregory Peck) and also the company's legal advisor and advocate. Larry falls in love with Kate, but realizes his pursuit of her father's company will cost him her affections. Their relationship mirrors the central conflict at the core of takeovers: concern for the welfare of employees whose jobs will be eliminated versus the pursuit of profits that is the goal of stockholders and corporate raiders alike. The film effectively states this conflict but does not resolve it.

Patterns (no rating)

Length: 83 minutes
Date: 1956
Director: Fielder Cook
Writer: Rod Serling
Actors: Van Heflin, Everett Sloane, Ed Begley, Beatrice Straight

Trenchant Rod Serling drama, based on his 1956 *Kraft TV Theater* play. Van Heflin begins work at a huge New York office that is ruthlessly controlled by Everett Sloane. A penetrating psychological exploration of power struggles in a large corporation, depicting the manipulations and Machiavellian attitudes of executives clawing their way to the top of the corporate ladder.

The Player (R)

Length: 123 minutes
Date: 1992
Director: Robert Altman
Writer: Michael Tolkin, based on his novel
Actors: Tim Robbins, Greta Scacchi, Fred Ward, Whoopi Goldberg, Peter Gallagher, Dean Stockwell, Cynthia Stevenson

A film about the movie industry and the greed and ruthlessness that drive it. The focus is on Griffin Mill, portrayed by Tim Robbins, a young studio executive who finds himself in a precarious position after being suspected of the murder of a disgruntled screenwriter. In the "tradition" of Hollywood, Griffin takes whatever steps necessary to save himself, pushing the right buttons, stabbing the right backs, and effectively personifying "Hollywood ethics." Chock full of moral questions—such as, why do the wicked prosper in business while the good suffer? The film has an all-star cast, including a few dozen celebrity cameos.

Quiz Show (PG-13)

Length: 133 minutes
Date: 1994
Director: Robert Redford
Writer: Paul Attanasio
Actors: John Turturro, Rob Morrow, Ralph Fiennes, Paul Scofield

A morally complex film about a series of TV game show scandals that occurred in the 1950s. The quiz show of the title is called *Twenty-One*, and features Herbert Stempel (John Turturro), a long-standing contestant and perpetual winner. Stempel is ousted by the program's sponsor after the show's ratings begin to suffer. Stempel's new competitor, the charming intellectual Charles Van Doren (Ralph Fiennes), takes over the winning streak, and ratings and revenues soar. A federal agent, who is also an avid fan of *Twenty-One*, becomes suspicious of the winning streak and investigates. Believing that Van Doren's reign is a sham, he sets out to expose him as a fraud. The story contains many elements of rich ethical dilemmas, such as corporate greed, class rivalry, and the power of the TV industry. Based on Richard Goodwin's book *Remembering America: a Voice From the Sixties.*

Roger and Me (R)

Length: 90 minutes
Date: 1989
Director: Michael Moore
Writer: Michael Moore

An often funny but ultimately depressing documentary follows Michael Moore as he attempts to track down General Motors Chairman Roger Smith. Moore wants to talk to Smith about the GM plant closings in Flint, Michigan. The shutdowns put 30,000 people out of work, resulting in poverty and despair for many of the city's inhabitants. Along the way he meets, among others, a family evicted just before Christmas, a woman who makes her living raising and selling rabbits for human consumption, and a soon-to-be Miss America with some rather vapid thoughts about the socio-economic impact of Smith's decision. Appearances by Bob Eubanks, Pat Boone, and Anita Bryant.

Silkwood (R)

Length: 131 minutes
Date: 1983
Director: Mike Nichols
Writers: Nora Ephron, Alice Arlen
Actors: Meryl Streep, Kurt Russell, Cher, Diana Scarwid, Fred Ward, Bruce McGill

This is the story of Karen Silkwood, a woman who died in a car accident in 1974 under suspicious circumstances. Silkwood (Meryl Streep) works in an Oklahoma nuclear plant, and while on the job a number of incidents occur that produce harmful and unhealthy consequences. These health risks and the reasons why they occurred are left unexplained by her employers, thus provoking Karen to speak out and act against the injustice and irresponsibility. There is much good acting here and weighty moral questions concerning the responsibilities an employer has to his or her employees for their health and safety.

Skyscraper Souls (no rating)

Length: 98 minutes
Date: 1932
Director: Edgar Selwyn
Actors: Warren William, Maureen O'Sullivan, Gregory Ratoff, Anita Page

Warren William stars as David Dwight, a ruthless businessman and megalomaniac. His goal is to have complete control of a 100-story office building, and he'll do anything to get it, including manipulate stock prices, trample lives, and double-cross lovers. Everything and everyone is cannon fodder for his march to conquest. Based on the book *Skyscraper* by Faith Baldwin.

The Triangle Factory Fire Scandal (no rating)
Length:	100 minutes
Date:	1979
Director:	Mel Stuart
Actors:	Tom Bosley, David Dukes, Stephanie Zimbalist, Charlotte Rae, Stacey Nelkin

Based on an actual event, a huge fire at the Triangle Factory that killed 145 garment workers. The tragedy led to major changes in industrial fire and safety codes. Made for television.

Tucker: The Man and His Dream (PG)
Length:	111 minutes
Date:	1988
Director:	Francis Ford Coppola
Writers:	Arnold Schulman, David Seidler
Actors:	Jeff Bridges, Martin Landau, Joan Allen, Dean Stockwell, Frederic Forrest, Christian Slater, Lloyd Bridges

The more-or-less true story of Preston Tucker and his quest to realize the "American Dream." Tucker (Jeff Bridges) is an amazing idealist and 1940s entrepreneur, working to build the car of the future and a successful company in the process. Due to the greed and power of his opponents, the "Big Three" car manufacturers, Tucker is effectively driven out of the business. His passion to do what is good for consumers and his family while pursuing the "American Dream" is destroyed by the ruthlessness of corrupt business.

Wall Street (R)
Length:	126 minutes
Date:	1987
Director:	Oliver Stone
Writers:	Oliver Stone, Stanley Weiser
Actors:	Michael Douglas, Charlie Sheen, Martin Sheen, Daryl Hannah, Sean Young, James Spader, Hal Holbrook

Michael Douglas, as Gordon Gekko, is the perfect personification of greed. An entreprenuer after the inside information on Wall Street, he is deceptive and slick in his securities trading and seeks the upper hand or no hand at all. A young associate, Bud Fox (Charlie Sheen), much to the disappointment of his father (Martin Sheen), gets roped into illegal insider trading by Douglas's shining "sales-pitch." The film thrives on and has much to say about the ideas underlying 1980s materialism, and the "bigger and more is better" mentality that comes with it. It is fast paced, and filled with thought-provoking dialogue that leads to questions of how we ought to be and what we ought to do, both in business and in our personal lives.

The Wheeler Dealers (no rating)

Length: 100 minutes
Date: 1963
Director: Arthur Hiller
Actors: James Garner, Lee Remick, Jim Backus, Phil Harris, Shelly Berman

A Texas millionaire (James Garner) disguises himself as a poor drifter, and takes his act on the road to New York City, specifically, Wall Street. Upon arriving there, Garner stops to talk with a stock analyst (Lee Remick). From his appearance, the analyst's boss judges him to be a bit "slow," and orders her to sell the cowboy worthless stock. The stock turns out to be worth a fortune, thus giving Garner the upper hand. The film dallies with ideas and issues surrounding the ethics of investing on Wall Street, and does so in a comedic way.

Working Girl 1988 (R)

Length: 115 minutes
Date: 1988
Director: Mike Nichols
Writer: Kevin Wade
Actors: Melanie Griffith, Harrison Ford, Sigourney Weaver, Joan Cusack, Alec Baldwin, Riki Lake, Olympia Dukakis

A good-hearted secretary (Melanie Griffith), continually under the thumb of her devious employer, struggles for her chance to shine in the brokerage business. Her ever-scheming boss is a manipulative character (Signourney Weaver) who uses her power to stifle any ideas that her employees might have about upward mobility or changes for the better. Griffith finally gets her chance when her boss breaks her leg, and takes a leave of absence from the office. As the Working Girl begins to call the shots, she runs into a handsome businessman (Harrison Ford), and romance soon follows.

CONTEMPORARY ETHICAL ISSUES

Glossary

act utilitarianism   A form of utilitarianism. Utilitarianism is the doctrine that we should promote the good of all. Act utilitarianism holds that we should try to promote the good of all in every action. This is opposed ' to **rule utilitarianism**, which holds that we should act according to rules that promote the good of the group. (*See* Chapter 1: Introduction—Tools of Business Ethics, Ethics.)

administrative law judge (ALJ)   A judge who specializes in hearing cases concerning the legality of regulations issued by federal agencies; corporations that believe an agency has overstepped its rule-making authority may appeal to an ALJ for relief.

affirmative action   Federal law requiring businesses that contract or subcontract with the government to take positive steps to ensure that employees and prospective employees are treated fairly, without regard to their race, color, religion, nationality, sex, age, or disability; these features are to be ignored in recruitment, hiring, and promotions. (*See* Chapter 4: The Employee—Discrimination and Affirmative Action, Selected Cases: Executive Order 11246)

agency problem   An agent is a person who acts on the behalf of another person, called the principal. Doctors, accountants, and managers are all agents because they are hired by principals to perform specific tasks: cure diseases, prepare tax returns, manage businesses. By convention and by law, agents are supposed to act to promote the interests of the principal. The agency problem concerns means of insuring that agents do this, especially in cases when agents can promote their own interests at the expense of the principal. (*See* Chapter 3: The Corporation—Corporate Social Responsibility)

agency shop   Labor union rule requiring nonunion employees to pay an "agency fee" that is equivalent to union dues. (*See* Chapter 4: The Employee—Terms and Conditions, Selected Cases: Taft-Hartley Act)

anthropocentric ethic   A human-centered ethical theory holding that only *Homo sapiens* have **moral standing** (*See* Chapter 5: The Environment—Environmental Ethics, Respecting Dignity and Rights)

asymmetric information   A condition in which one person or group has more information than another person or group. In transactions, purchases, and trades, those with more information can take advantage of those with less. (*See* Chapter 2: The Consumer—Introduction, Protecting Consumers: Imperfect Market)

autonomy   Descriptively, this term refers to the capacity of human beings to make their own free choices. This fact of human nature is connected with the ethical view that humans have a right to make their own free decisions. (*See* Chapter 4: The Employee—Terms and Conditions of Employment)

best available technology economically achievable (BAT)   Federal standards for the discharge of toxic and nonconventional pollutants into the nation's waters are subject to BAT standards. These standards take the costs of regulation into account but they are not to be balanced against the benefits achieved. (*See* Chapter 5: The Environment—Environmental Law, Selected Cases:; Clean Water Act)

best conventional pollution control technology (BCT)   Federal standards for the discharge of conventional pollutants (suspended solids and fecal matter, for example) into the nation's waters are subject to BCT, which balances the costs of the technology with the benefits of reducing the pollution. (*See* Chapter 5: The Environment—Environmental Law, Selected Cases: Clean Water Act)

biocentric ethic   A life-centered ethical theory holding that all and only living things have **moral standing**. (*See* Chapter 5: The Environment—Environmental Ethics, Respecting Dignity and Rights)

black codes   Discriminatory and segregationist measures found mainly in the southern states, designed to maintain white domination of blacks following the Civil War. Such measures included literacy tests, poll taxes, and other Jim Crow laws. (*See* Chapter 4: The Employee—Discrimination and Affirmative Action, Law: Introduction)

bona fide benefit plan   Discrimination against an individual 40 years old or more is legally permissible if it is based on a legitimate system of employment benefits that are a function of age, such as retirement requirements. Sufficient defense against allegations of violating the Age Discrimination and Affirmative Action in Employment Act. (*See* Chapter 4: The Employee— Discrimination and Affirmative Action, Law)

bona fide occupational qualification (BFOQ)   Discrimination against protected classes is legally permissible if it is based on a genuine qualification necessary for adequately performing the functions of the job. Sufficient defense against allegations of violating Title VII of the Civil Rights Act or the Age Discrimination and Affirmative Action in Employment Act. (*See* Chapter 4: The Employee—Discrimination and Affirmative Action, Selected Cases: *International Union, et al. v. Johnson Controls, Inc.*, and *Western Air Lines v. Criswell*)

bona fide seniority system (BFSS)   Discrimination against protected classes is legally permissible if it is based on a legitimate system of rewarding individuals for their service to the company. Sufficient defense against allegations of violating Title VII of the Civil Rights Act or the Age Discrimination and Affirmative Action in Employment Act. (*See* Chapter 4: The Employee— Discrimination and Affirmative Action, Selected Cases: *Firefighter's Local Union No. 1784 v. Stotts*)

bounded rationality   To say that we have bounded rationality means that we have limited information, limited time, and limited reasoning power. Because of bounded rationality, we almost always act in conditions of uncertainty. (*See* Chapter 1: Introduction—Tools of Business Ethics, Ethics)

business cycles Economies alternate between good and bad economic times. In good economic times people have jobs and stock prices increase. In bad economic times, people lose jobs and stocks decrease. Most economists believe that economies go in cycles, though there is no way to predict when a particular cycle will begin or end. (*See* Chapter 2: The Consumer—Finance, Economics)

business necessity Discrimination against protected classes is legally permissible if it is required in order to achieve a legitimate business purpose in a safe and efficient manner. Sufficient defense against allegations of violating Title VII of the Civil Rights Act. (*See* Chapter 4: The Employee—Discrimination and Affirmative Action, Selected Cases: *International Union v. Johnson Controls, Inc.*)

capital Goods that are produced, such as money and machinery, that are then used to produce more goods. Capital is distinguished from land and labor, which are also used to produce goods. (*See* Chapter 1: Introduction—What Is Business Ethics?, The Roots of Business Ethics)

capital structure This term refers to the way in which a company is financed. The crucial difference between capital structures, in most cases, is how much of a company is financed by debt (such as bonds) and how much by equity (such as common **stock**). (*See* Chapter 3: The Corporation—The Nature and Structure of the Corporation, Economics)

cared-for This term is used by those who espouse the care ethic. It is an easy way to refer to someone's close friends and family members. (*See* Chapter 2: The Consumer—Advertising, Ethics)

cerebrocentric ethic A mind-centered ethical theory holding that only beings with certain mental states have **moral standing**; precisely what mental states are required for moral standing depends on the theory advocated. (*See* Chapter 5: The Environment—Environmental Ethics, Respecting Dignity and Rights)

civil law Legal rules providing the least severe punishments for violation, that is, fines and **injunctions**, not incarceration. Conviction for violating a civil law requires only a finding that the "preponderance of the evidence" indicates wrongdoing, not a unanimous jury verdict finding guilt "beyond a reasonable doubt."

Commerce Clause Article I, Section 8 of the Constitution empowers Congress to regulate commerce between or "among" the various states; this gives the federal government authority to regulate business activity in order to develop a national market and to encourage free trade among the states.

common law Legal rules based on judges' understanding of prevailing social customs or practices, or what seems appropriate or reasonable in the particular circumstances of the case at hand. This "judge-made" law arises when courts must make decisions in the absence of guiding statutes or regulations.

common stock company A company that is financed by the sale of common **stock** is a common stock company. A share of common stock entitles its owner to vote for members of the board of directors. The board of directors determines the general policy of the company and the distribution of profits to owners. (*See* Chapter 1: Introduction—What Is Business Ethics?, The Roots of Business Ethics)

comparable worth The values of two different jobs can be compared in order to determine whether the wages offered for them are fair and equitable. Numerical values are assigned to various aspects of each job (e.g., how much education is required, how much supervision the employee receives, and what risks characterize the working conditions); the numbers are summed and the totals and wages compared. (*See* Chapter 4: The Employee—Discrimination and Affirmative Action, Law; Comparable Worth: *County of Washington v. Gunther*)

comparative advantage First introduced by Adam Smith, comparative advantage refers to a country's being able to produce a product more efficiently than other countries. Each country should focus on what it does best and trade for products that it does not produce well. (*See* Chapter 1: Introduction—Tools of Business Ethics, Economics)

compensation Compensation used to be called "pay." Since pay is usually associated with cash, it no longer describes the many ways in which employers compensate employees for their labor. In addition to money, employees can now receive medical benefits, child care benefits, retirement contributions, and stock options. (*See* Chapter 4: The Employee—Discrimination and Affirmative Action)

consent order Directive issued by a federal agency to a corporation or other business to halt what the agency believes to be an illegal business practice or to act affirmatively in some legally required way; the business agrees to comply with the order without admitting guilt.

consumer acknowledgment of danger   Sellers cannot be found **strictly liable** for failing to warn of widely recognized dangers, nor will liability be imposed if it can be proved that the consumer knew and appreciated the risks associated with the product, and voluntarily accepted those risks. (*See* Chapter 2: The Consumer—Product Safety, Law: Defending Against Liability)

consumer misuse   Manufacturers and sellers can defeat consumer allegations that they are liable for damages by demonstrating that the consumer's conduct with regard to the product was in some way inappropriate, and that therefore the personal injury resulted from the consumer's own negligence, hypersensitivity, or misuse. (*See* Chapter 2: The Consumer—Product Safety, Law: Defending Against Liability)

contingent valuation method   A procedure for determining the economic value of goods that are not subject to market transactions. In environmental affairs, surveys ask people how much they would be willing to pay for certain public goods, such as clean air or wilderness areas or the preservation of species. On the basis of their responses, "shadow prices" are assigned to these goods; this is how much they would cost if there really were a market for buying and selling them. (*See* Chapter 5: The Environment—Environmental Economics, Consumers)

contract theory   A theory that determines when producers are responsible for harm caused by their products. According to the contract theory, companies can be held responsible only if they have a contract with the person who is harmed. This contract can be explicit or implied. Contrast with **due care** and **social cost** theories. (*See* Chapter 2: The Consumer—Product Safety, Theories of Responsibility for Harm)

cost-benefit analysis   A decision-making procedure in which the price of a certain policy is compared with its advantages; the policy is implemented only if the costs do not exceed the benefits. *See also* **feasibility analysis**. (*See* Chapter 4: The Employee—Health and Safety, Selected Cases: *American Textile Manufacturers Institute Inc. v. Donovan*)

criminal law   Legal rules providing the most severe punishments for violation, including imprisonment, probation, fines, and capital punishment. Due to the severity of the sanctions, conviction under the criminal law requires a unanimous decision by members of a jury who are convinced "beyond a reasonable doubt."

deceptive sales practice (1) A representation or omission of fact that is (2) likely to mislead consumers acting reasonably under the circumstances, and (3) the representation or omission is material. (*See* Chapter 2: The Consumer—Advertising, Selected Cases: *In re Cliffdale Associates, Inc.*)

defendant The party responding to a lawsuit, accused of some legal wrongdoing; can be a person or an organization, such as a corporation.

discriminatory pricing Business practice of charging different consumers different prices for the same commodity; declared illegal by the Clayton Act. (*See* Chapter 3: The Corporation—Antitrust Issues, Law: Clayton Act)

disparagement A false statement made by a business concerning a competitor's product that tends to diminish respect for or confidence in the product by impugning its quality; this is an illegal marketing technique. (*See* Chapter 2: The Consumer— Advertising, Law: Lanham Act)

disparate (adverse) impact Outcome of a company policy that has different consequences for different individuals according to their race or gender, even though there is no intent to discriminate; this is illegal discrimination in violation of Title VII of the Civil Rights Act of 1964. (*See* Chapter 4: The Employee— Discrimination and Affirmative Action, Selected Cases: *Griggs v. Duke Power Company*)

disparate treatment Results when a company policy is formulated with the intent to discriminate on the basis of race or gender; this is illegal discrimination in violation of Title VII of the Civil Rights Act of 1964. (*See* Chapter 4: The Employee—Discrimination and Affirmative Action, Selected Cases: *Griggs v. Duke Power Company*)

dividing markets Agreements between corporations to split a market into geographical regions or to allocate territories to different businesses, with the competitors agreeing not to interfere in one another's region; declared illegal by the Sherman Antitrust Act. (*See* Chapter 3: The Corporation—Antitrust Issues, Law: Sherman Antitrust Act)

due care An agent acting for a principal (*see* **agency problems**) should inform the consumer of the risks. This includes more than what the agent happens to know at a given time. Due care requires that the agent should do enough research to know common facts and risks. (*See* Chapter 2: The Consumer—Finance: Ethics)

due care theory According to the due care theory of product liability, a company is required to do all that it reasonably can to ensure that its products are safe for their intended uses. As long as it does this, the company cannot be held responsible for harm caused by its products. The **social cost theory** and **contract theory** are different theories of product liability. (*See* Chapter 2: The Consumer—Product Safety: Theories of Responsibility for Harm)

Due Process Clause Statement in the Fifth and Fourteenth Amendments to the Constitution prohibiting government from "depriv[ing] any person of life, liberty or property without due process of law." (*See* Chapter 4: The Employee—Discrimination and Affirmative Action, Selected Cases: Public Works in Employment Act; Terms and Conditions, Law: **Employment At Will**; Chapter 3: The Corporation—Economics, Law: The Rights of Corporations)

ecocentric ethics An ethical theory holding that entire ecosystems have **moral standing**. (*See* Chapter 5: The Environment—Environmental Ethics, Promoting the Good of the Group)

ecofeminism A philosophical and social movement that identifies similarities between the oppression of women and the degradation of the environment; the solution to both problems is to overcome the patriarchal domination that causes them. (*See* Chapter 5: The Environment—Environmental Ethics, Promoting Personal Relationships)

economies of scale Mass production allows products to be made inexpensively because the cost of production is spread over many units. These economies of (large) scale are most noticeable in products such as cars and refrigerators. It would be very expensive to build just a few cars or refrigerators. Setting up factories to make thousands of these items allows each unit to be very inexpensive compared to the cost of making just a few. (*See* Chapter 3: The Corporation—Mergers and Acquisitions, International Issues, Economics).

efficient market An allocation of goods and services in which no transaction could make anyone better off without making someone else worse off. "Better off" refers to the satisfaction of people's desires and preferences, "worse off" to their frustration. See also **pareto optimal**. (*See* Chapter 5: The Environment— Environmental Economics, Society)

employment at will Employment principle holding that both the employer and the employee are entitled to make any sort of contract that they find mutually acceptable, without interference by external forces; unless they specifically agree otherwise, each may end the relationship at any time. (*See* Chapter 4: The Employee—Terms and Conditions of Employment)

entrepreneurial Entrepreneurial individuals aggressively pursue business opportunities, usually by starting their own businesses. The term has become used more widely to refer to individuals who have a good sense of market opportunities, even when these are pursued within organizations. (*See* Chapter 4: The Employee—Sexual Harassment, Ethics)

environmental impact statement (EIS) A document that must be filed for every major federal government activity that has a significant impact on the environment. An EIS must address: (1) the adverse and beneficial effects of the proposed activity on the environment; (2) any unavoidable negative environmental impact; (3) alternatives to the proposal; (4) the short-term uses of the environment and their relationship to long-term productivity; and (5) the resources that are irretrievably committed. (*See* Chapter 5: The Environment—Environmental Law, Selected Cases: National Environmental Policy Act)

Equal Protection Clause Statement in the Fourteenth Amendment to the Constitution guaranteeing every person equal protection of the law (*See* Chapter 3: The Corporation—Economics, Law: The Rights of Corporations; Chapter 4: The Employee—Discrimination and Affirmative Action, Law: Introduction; Selected Cases: *City of Richmond v. J.A. Croson Company*)

ethical holism A moral theory holding that collectives or wholes of individual entities, such as an ecosystem, have a moral status that is independent of the **moral standing** of the parts of the group. (*See* Chapter 5: The Environment—Environmental Ethics, Promoting the Good of the Group)

ethical personality: Our ethical personality consists of how we interpret and rank the principles of self-interest, care, utilitarianism, and **intrinsic value**. (*See* Chapter 2: The Consumer—Finance, Economics)

European Commission This commission is the central administrative body for the **European Union**. It proposes legislation and monitors member nations to make sure that the treaty creating the EU is enforced. (*See* Chapter 3: The Corporation—Mergers and Acquisitions, International Issues)

European Union (EU) Fifteen European countries that have banded together in order to reduce, and eventually eliminate, restrictions on trade between member states. The EU is planning to introduce a common currency, called the *Euro*, in 1999. As of March 1998, 11 member countries are planning to adopt the new currency. (*See* Chapter 3: The Corporation—Mergers and Acquisitions, International Issues)

express warranty An affirmation of fact, explicitly stated verbally or in writing, or created by a description or sample of the product, that the item meets certain standards of quality, performance, or condition. The terms *warranty* or *guarantee* need not be used to create an express warranty, nor are sellers required to offer such warranties. (*See* Chapter 2: The Consumer—Product Safety, Law: Modern Legal Remedies)

external cost A cost generated by economic activity that is not included in the transaction, so one party to the exchange assumes a burden not accounted for in the pricing of the good; for example, generating electricity produces pollution, but the costs of the health problems caused by the pollution are not borne by the power company and hence not included in the price of electricity. See also **social cost**. (*See* Chapter 5: The Environment—Environmental Economics, Society)

externalities When a business transaction affects those outside the transaction, these effects are called externalities. Externalities can be negative or positive. An example of a negative externality is the harm cause by air pollution to those who have no relationship with the polluting company. An example of positive externality is a golf course driving up prices of local real estate for those who have no relationship to the golf course. (*See* Chapter 1: Introduction—Tools of Business Ethics, Economics)

extrinsic value The value something has as a tool or instrument for the purposes of others; valuable as a means to an end and not for its own sake. Contrasted with **intrinsic value**. (*See* Chapter 5: The Environment—Environmental Ethics, Respecting Dignity and Rights)

fair market prices Fair market prices are what goods and services would cost in an open, competitive market. The phrase is found in discussions of utility pricing when there is no competition. Regulatory agencies establish formulas suggesting what price these services would have in a competitive environment. The result of this calculation is the fair market price. (*See* Chapter 1: Introduction—Tools of Business Ethics, Economics)

feasibility analysis An alternative to **cost-benefit analysis**, in which standards of employee health and safety are set according to what can be accomplished. OSHA is not required to take the cost of compliance to employers into account but only the technological feasibility of eliminating the hazards. (*See* Chapter 4: The Employee—Health and Safety, Selected Cases: *American Textile Manufacturers Institute Inc. v. Donovan*)

fiduciary relationship A relationship in which one person holds or controls something of value for another is a fiduciary relationship. Managers have fiduciary relationship with owners and banks have fiduciary relationships with depositors. (*See* Chapter 2: The Consumer—Finance, Ethics)

financial instruments A document that indicates that one party has debt to another. Financial instruments can range from informal IOUs to municipal bonds used to finance government projects. (*See* Chapter 2: The Consumer—Finance)

foreclosure sale The holder of a **mortgage** to **real property** is entitled to sell the property if the money is not repaid by the borrower who used the land to secure the loan. (*See* Chapter 2: The Consumer—Finance, Law: Credit)

***forum non conveniens*, doctrine of** The jurisdiction of a particular court (the forum) should be rejected on the grounds that litigating the case there would involve difficulties (*non conveniens* or "inconveniences") that do not obtain in some other court. If the appeal is successful, the case is dismissed in one jurisdiction and moved to another. (*See* Chapter 2: The Consumer—Product Safety, Selected Cases: *Dow Chemical Company v. Alfaro*)

free market approach A market is free when it has as little government intrusion as possible. Adherents of this approach argue that free markets are desirable because they fulfill demand more efficiently than other systems. Government does need to supply a basic economic infrastructure, such as a court system and a monetary system, as well as internal security (police) and external security (the army), but nothing more. Contrast with the imperfect market approach. (*See* Chapter 2: The Consumer—Introduction, Protecting Consumers)

free riding   People and organizations ride free when they get the benefits of a program or good without paying for it. For example, those who evade taxes are riding free on goods and services, such as roads and schools, that are paid for by those who do pay their taxes. (*See* Chapter 2: The Consumer—Finance, Economics)

garnishment   A creditor's right to a debtor's property that is in the possession of some third party, commonly the debtor's wages held by his or her employer; debtors' funds in the possession of banks may also be garnished. (*See* Chapter 2: The Consumer—Finance, Law: Credit)

general duty clause   Requires employers to provide their employees with a job and a work environment free from recognized hazards that cause or are likely to cause illness, injury, or death. (*See* Chapter 4: The Employee—Health and Safety, Selected Cases: Occupational Safety and Health Act)

group boycotts   A group of corporations stipulates certain conditions of business to firms outside the group or refuses to deal with them altogether; declared illegal by the Sherman Antitrust Act. (*See* Chapter 3: The Corporation—Antitrust Issues, Law: Sherman Antitrust Act)

homestead exemption   A debtor who defaults on a loan may retain some portion of the value of a personal residence; usually also exempts furniture, clothing, pets, vehicles, and tools of one's trade from seizure. (*See* Chapter 2: The Consumer—Finance, Laws: Credit)

honest claims doctrine   Claims made by management during labor negotiations that the company is unable to pay a certain wage increase must be substantiated with credible evidence. (*See* Chapter 4: The Employee—Terms and Conditions, Selected Cases: *NLRB v. Truitt Manufacturing Company*)

host nation   When a company has offices or operations in another country, that country is called the host nation. (*See* Chapter 3: The Corporation—The Nature and Structure of the Corporation, International Issues)

hostile working environment   A form of sexual harassment in which conduct in the workplace has the purpose or effect of unreasonably interfering with an individual's job performance or creating an intimidating, hostile, or offensive employment environment. (*See* Chapter 4: The Employee—Sexual Harassment, Law: Introduction; Selected Cases: and *Henson v. City of Dundee* and *Harris v. Forklift Systems, Inc.*)

hot-cargo contract An unfair labor practice in which an employer agrees with a union to refrain from dealing with nonunion employers. (*See* Chapter 4: The Employee—Terms and Conditions, Selected Cases: Landrum-Griffin Act)

humanism The doctrine that human beings are the center of ethical value. Although humanism is compatible with most religions, it often puts God in the background. Deism is a form of humanism that holds that God does not interfere with humanity. God created the world, and then stepped back to let things turn out according to the laws of nature and human free will. (*See* Chapter 1: Introduction—What Is Business Ethics?, The Roots of Business Ethics)

impartial principle A principle is impartial when it evaluates all cases and/or people in the same way. Justice, fairness, and utilitarianism are impartial principles. This is contrasted with partial principles that do not evaluate all cases in the same way. Care and egoism are partial ethical principles. (*See* Chapter 4: The Employee—Terms and Conditions of Employment, Ethics)

imperfect market approach This approach is based on the view that the **free market approach** does not recognize that markets often fail to meet consumer demand efficiently. Pollution, worker safety, and product liability are just a few of the areas in which government can intervene to make markets more responsive to demand. (*See* Chapter 2: The Consumer—Introduction, Protecting Consumers)

implied warranty of fitness for a particular purpose When a seller knows the specific purpose for which a product has been purchased, makes a statement that the product will serve this purpose, and the buyer depends on the seller to select the necessary item for that purpose, a guarantee is thereby implied that the item will function properly. (*See* Chapter 2: The Consumer—Product Safety, Law: Modern Legal Remedies)

implied warranty of merchantability The act of selling a labeled and packaged product to someone implies that a merchant is guaranteeing that the item is fit to be used for the purposes for which it was produced. (*See* Chapter 2: The Consumer—Product Safety, Law: Modern Legal Remedies)

individual with a disability A person with (1) a physical or mental impairment that substantially limits one or more of his or her life activities; or (2) who has a record of such impairment; or (3) who is regarded as having such an impairment. (*See* Chapter 4: The Employee—Discrimination and Affirmative Action, Selected Cases: Americans with Disabilities Act)

infomercials Infomercials are programs of a half-hour or more that are designed to sell specialty or niche products such as exercise equipment or food processors. They have developed because it is often less expensive to buy a half-hour of TV time at off hours than to buy a 30-second commercial. (*See* Chapter 2: The Consumer—Introduction, Protecting Consumers)

infrastructure Infrastructures provide a framework that makes commerce possible. They are both physical and social. Physical infrastructures consist of such things as roads, bridges, and gas pipelines. Social infrastructures consist of rules and **institutions**, such as promises and court systems. (*See* Chapter 1: Introduction—The Tools of Business Ethics, Economics)

injunction An order issued by a court to an individual or an organization to act or to refrain from acting in some specified way.

insider trading An investment practice in which an individual working inside a corporation makes money by purchasing **securities** in the corporation before favorable information is released to the general public, or avoids a loss by selling securities of the corporation prior to the disclosure of unfavorable information. Outlawed by the Securities Exchange Act of 1934. (*See* Chapter 2: The Consumer—Finance, Selected Cases: Securities Exchange Act)

International Monetary Fund (IMF) The IMF is a bank created after World War II to help countries with problems concerning international finance. Member countries deposit funds in the bank, which are then loaned to countries who have trouble repaying international loans. The IMF usually requires countries to reform their economic practices before lending them money. (*See* Chapter 2: The Consumer—Finance, International Issues)

intervening event If merchandise is materially altered or modified in a way that causes an injury, the original seller of the item is not at fault for the harm. (*See* Chapter 2: The Consumer—Product Safety, Law: Defending Against Liability)

intrinsic value The value someone has for his or her own sake, as an end, and independently of any use to which the individual can be put.

Often regarded as synonymous with having **moral standing** and contrasted with **extrinsic value**. (*See* Chapter 5: The Environment—Environmental Ethics, Respecting Dignity and Rights)

legal standing A special status before the law, required for an individual to initiate a lawsuit. Its three main elements are (1) an actual or imminent injury (an invasion of a legally protected interest); (2) a causal relationship between the injury and the challenged conduct; and (3) a likelihood that the injury will be remedied by a favorable decision. Synonymous with having legal rights. See also **moral standing**. (*See* Chapter 5: The Environment—Environmental Ethics; Environmental Law, Selected Cases: *Sierra Club v. Morton* and *Lujan v. Defenders of Wildlife*)

lie detector Any device used for the purpose of rendering a diagnostic opinion regarding the honesty or dishonesty of an individual. (*See* Chapter 4: The Employee—Privacy, Selected Cases: Employee Polygraph Protection Act)

lobbyists Corporations and other special interest groups hire lobbyists to persuade legislators and regulators to approve policies favorable to the interest group. General Motors, for example, spends millions of dollars in Washington, DC, in the hope of making laws and regulations that are favorable to car manufacturing. (*See* Chapter 3: The Corporation—Antitrust Issues, Economics)

macroeconomics The study of economic relationships in large social systems, such as a nation. For instance, a macroeconomic study might explore the relationship between productivity and personal income in order to understand national wealth. Contrast with **microeconomics.** (*See* Chapter 1: Introduction—Tools of Business Ethics, Economics)

management buyout (MBO) When managers of publicly traded company buy the company they manage, this is called a management buyout. (*See* Chapter 3: The Corporation—Mergers and Acquisitions)

marginal cost The cost of making one more unit of production. This concept can help us understand **economies of scale**. If refrigerators are built one at a time, by hand, the marginal cost of the tenth refrigerator will be the same as the first one. However, if we build a factory to produce refrigerators, the marginal cost of the first refrigerator is enormous, since it includes the cost of making the factory. However, when the millionth refrigerator rolls out, its marginal cost will be much less than the first one. (*See* Chapter 2: The Consumer—Advertising, Economics: Society)

market penetration This is jargon for how much of the market a particular company or product has. (*See* Chapter 3: The Corporation—The Nature and Structure of the Corporation, International Issues)

microeconomics The study of relatively self-contained markets that exist within larger markets. For example, examining car prices and production rates is a microeconomic study of the automobile industry. (*See* Chapter 1: Introduction—Tools of Business Ethics, Economics)

minority business enterprise (MBE) A company whose ownership is at least 50 percent black, Hispanic, Asian, or American Indian. (*See* Chapter 4: The Employee—Discrimination and Affirmative Action, Selected Cases: Public Works in Employment Act of 1977)

mixed economy A mixed economy is one in which the factors of production are regulated both by the market and by government. Consider the market for food. What food is produced is determined by market factors such as the tastes and preferences of consumers. Yet, the government has many regulations intended to promote safe food products. Almost every nation in the world has a mixed economy. Only North Korea and Cuba still have government-controlled economies. China and Vietnam are moving from government-controlled economies to mixed economies. (*See* Chapter 2: The Consumer—Introduction, Protecting Consumers)

monopolistic behavior Market behavior that can occur without having a true monopoly. When there are only a few producers of a product, the companies can behave in monopolist ways by agreeing to fix prices or by dividing the market so that each company will have monopoly in that area. (*See* Chapter 3: The Corporation—Mergers and Acquisitions, Economics)

monopolistic competition Exists when we have items featuring certain qualities that others cannot copy, but these qualities are not essential to the usefulness of the product. This is especially true for brand names. (*See* Chapter 1: Introduction—Tools of Business Ethics, Economics)

monopoly A market condition in which there is only one seller for a particular good or service; most forms of monopoly are outlawed by antitrust laws. See also **trust**. (*See* Chapter 1: Introduction—Tools of Business Ethics; Chapter 3: The Corporation—Antitrust Issues, Law, Antitrust Law, Economics). Legal monopolies are either "natural," as when demand for a product may be limited to what one company can produce, or when a small town cannot support more than one business of a certain type; or due to "superior business acumen," in which a monopoly is acquired by superior skill, foresight, or industry. (*See* Chapter 3: The Corporation—Law; Sherman Antitrust Act)

moral agent   A person or rational being who knows the difference between moral right and wrong, and can act accordingly; one who has moral responsibilities and duties. (*See* Chapter 5: The Environment—Environmental Ethics)

moral standing   A special status before the enlightened conscience, it is having a claim to be considered by moral agents, or to be the beneficiary of the moral duties and responsibilities binding upon moral agents. Sometimes regarded as synonymous with having moral rights. See also **legal standing** and **intrinsic value**. (*See* Chapter 5: The Environment—Environmental Ethics, *passim*)

mortgage   A security interest held in **real property**, that is, land, including any buildings, trees, crops or plants generally, soil, and minerals found there. (*See* Chapter 2: The Consumer—Finance, Law: Credit).

national ambient air quality standards (NAAQSs)   The maximum allowable limits for pollutants determined by the Environmental Protection Agency to be harmful to human health and well-being. These pollutants are carbon monoxide, sulphur dioxide, nitrogen dioxide, ozone, lead, and suspended particulates. (*See* Chapter 5: The Environment—Environmental Law, Selected Cases: Clean Air Act)

national pollutant discharge elimination system   A series of effluent discharge standards, set by the Environmental Protection Agency, for each of forty categories of industry. Every business within each group is required to use the same pollution control technology. (*See* Chapter 5: The Environment—Environmental Law, Selected Cases: Clean Water Act)

natural monopolies   Monopolies are natural when adding another producer would increase the price of products. (*See* Chapter 1: Introduction—Tools of Business Ethics, Economics)

negligence A quality of an action or failure to act that creates an unreasonable risk of harm with a resulting injury; for injuries caused by consumer products, this high risk of injury may be due to negligence in the design, manufacture, or inspection of the product, or by a failure to warn of the danger. (*See* Chapter 2: The Consumer—Product Safety, Law: Modern Legal Remedies)

niche market A specialty market within a larger, more homogeneous market. For example, espresso is a niche market within the larger coffee market. (*See* Chapter 4: The Employee—Discrimination and Affirmative Action and Affirmative Action; Economics)

nonanthropocentric ethic An ethical theory rejecting the idea that only humans have **moral standing**; precisely what entities besides humans have moral standing depends on the theory advocated. (*See* Chapter 5: The Environment—Environmental Ethics, Respecting Dignity and Rights)

oligopolistic competition Competition is oligopolistic when there are only a few companies that produce a product, such as automobiles and airplanes. The number of companies is limited because of the high cost of manufacturing. (*See* Chapter 1: Introduction—Tools of Business Ethics, Economics)

opportunity cost When we do one thing rather than another, the value of the best opportunity that we do not pursue is our opportunity cost. In general, you want opportunity costs to be less than the value you received from the course of action you did pursue. For example, when you take a job, there are other jobs that you are not taking. The value of the best job you do not take is your opportunity cost. (*See* Chapter 1: Introduction—What Is Business Ethics?, The Roots of Business Ethics, Chapter 5: The Environment—Environmental Economics, Consumers)

opposition clause Statement in Title VII of the Civil Rights Act that makes it illegal to discriminate against employees who voice their objections to what they perceive to be discriminatory employment practices, without themselves becoming involved in the prosecution of such practices. (*See* Chapter 4: The Employee—Whistleblowing and Loyalty, Selected Cases: Title VII of the Civil Rights Act)

pareto optimal A distribution of goods and services resulting from market exchanges in which everyone has as much as they want without making anyone else worse off. See also **efficient market**. (*See*

Chapter 5: The Environment—Environmental Economics, Society)

participation clause Statement in Title VII of the Civil Rights Act that makes it illegal to discriminate against employees who are actively engaged in the process of bringing charges of discrimination against their employers. (*See* Chapter 4: The Employee—Whistleblowing and Loyalty, Selected Cases: Title VII of the Civil Rights Act)

perfect competition A state of competition in which products are very similar and there are many producers. The virtue of perfect markets is that they are completely driven by demand. It is impossible for any one producer to affect prices. Although there are no truly perfect markets, commodity markets in grain and other agricultural products come close. (*See* Chapter 1: Introduction—Tools of Business Ethics, Economics)

plaintiff The party filing a complaint in a lawsuit, charging some legal wrongdoing; can be either an individual or an organization, such as a corporation.

pluralism An ethical view that asserts that there are several equally valuable ethical principles. Most other ethical theories argue for one supreme principle of morality, such as justice or the good of the group. (*See* Chapter 1: Introduction—Tools of Business Ethics, Ethics)

populism A political movement that began in the late 19th century. Populists were against the U.S. transition from an agricultural-based economy to an industrial-based economy. Although the Populist party no longer exists, the term is still used to indicate the values championed by populists. (*See* Chapter 3: The Corporation—Antitrust Issues, Economics)

price fixing An agreement by competitors in the same market to set or "fix" prices at a certain amount; declared illegal by the Sherman Antitrust Act . (*See* Chapter 3: The Corporation—Antitrust Issues, Selected Cases: Sherman Antitrust Act)

primary consumers People who buy products and services that they will use themselves. Contrast with **secondary consumers**. (*See* Chapter 2: The Consumer—Introduction, Protecting Consumers)

principal *See* **agency problems**. (*See* Chapter 3: The Corporation—Corporate Social Responsibility)

probable cause The Fourth Amendment to the Constitution states that "[t]he right of the people to be secure in their persons, houses, papers, and effects, against unreasonable searches and seizures, shall not be violated, and no Warrants shall issue, but upon probable cause, supported by Oath or affirmation." The courts have interpreted this clause to mean that before a search or seizure can be legally carried out, law enforcement officials must present their reasons for wanting to do so to a judge, swearing that the facts they allege are true; the judge then decides if the search is justified and, if so, issues a warrant. (*See* Chapter 4: The Employee—Privacy, Law: Right to Privacy; Selected Cases: *Marshall v. Barlow's Inc.*)

protected classes Groups of people who are identified for antidiscrimination protection in employment by Title VII of the Civil Rights Act of 1964. These classes are defined by race, color, sex, nationality, and religion. (*See* Chapter 4: The Employee— Discrimination and Affirmative Action, Law: Introduction)

puffery When advertisers use vague claims to make their products look good, such as "you'll feel great after washing your hair with X" or "our customers say our ribs are the best in the midwest," they use puffery. (*See* Chapter 2: The Consumer—Advertising: Economics)

***qui tam* plaintiff** An individual who sues a corporation on his or her own behalf "as well as" (translated from the Latin) on behalf of the government. (*See* Chapter 4: The Employee—Whistleblowing and Loyalty, Law: Introduction)

quid pro quo Latin phrase meaning "this for that," referring to a form of sexual harassment in which a position, promotion, or other employee benefit is offered in return for sexual favors. (*See* Chapter 4: The Employee—Sexual Harassment, Law: Introduction; Selected Cases: *Barnes v. Costle* and *Williams v. Saxbe*)

real property Land (real estate), and buildings, trees, crops, plants, soil, and minerals that are part of a tract of land. (*See* Chapter 2: The Consumer—Finance, Law: Credit)

reasonable person (man) standard First formulated in the 1837 English case *Vaughan v. Menlowe*, this standard refers to the ordinary person of average prudence and common sense, who exercises commonplace levels of care and skill. (*See* Chapter 2: The Consumer—Advertising, Selected Cases: *In re Cliffdale Associates, Inc.*)

reasonable woman standard Modification of the **reasonable man standard**, tailored to sexual harassment cases; requires that the alleged harassment be judged from the perspective of the female recipient of ordinary sensitivity. (*See* Chapter 4: The Employee— Sexual Harassment, Selected Cases: *Ellison v. Brady*)

registration statement A document filed with the Securities and Exchange Commission, as required by Section 5 of the Securities Exchange Act of 1934, that registers the selling of **securities** with the federal government. The statement contains descriptions of the securities to be sold, how the proceeds from the sale will be used, the nature of the business, the structure of management in the business, any pending litigation it faces, the degree of competition in the industry, and any other special risk factors. (*See* Chapter 2: The Consumer—Finance, Law: Investments)

reinforcement view of law Law reinforces important ethical and legal relationships. For example, the difference between a promise and a contract is that the latter is enforced by law. Societies spend money and time to enforce contracts because they are essential for the production and distribution of products. (*See* Chapter 1: Introduction—Tools of Business Ethics, Law)

requirement of privity In order for a consumer to recover damages for harm caused by a product, a contract providing for damages in specific circumstances is required. (*See* Chapter 2: The Consumer—Product Safety, Law: Privity and Liability)

resale price maintenance A form of **price fixing** that occurs when a producer tries to impose either maximum or minimum prices on a wholesaler or retailer that the producer supplies. (*See* Chapter 3: The Corporation—Antitrust Issues, Selected Cases: Sherman Antitrust Act)

respondeat superior Latin meaning "the boss has to answer for what his workers do," and implying that an employer is responsible for the illegal behavior of his or her employees if he or she knew or should have known about it. (*See* Chapter 4: The Employee— Sexual Harassment, Selected Cases: *Barnes v. Costle*)

reverse discrimination Charge of unfair discriminatory practices directed against an individual who is not identified as a member of a legally protected class, that is, white males. (*See* Chapter 4: The Employee—Discrimination and Affirmative Action, Selected Cases: *United Steelworkers of America & Kaiser Aluminum v. Weber* and *Wygant v. Jackson Board of Education*)

right to privacy Protects a person's interest in having possession of certain information about himself or herself; often characterized as a right to be left alone. Unstated in the Constitution, the right to privacy has been judicially recognized, most notably in *Griswold v. Connecticut*, as implied by various amendments to the Constitution. (Chapter 4: The Employee—Privacy, Law)

right to publicity Protects a public person's commercial interest in the use of his or her identity, and entitles either a celebrity or an ordinary citizen to authorize the publication of a picture of that identity; such publication without consent violates this right. (*See* Chapter 2: The Consumer—Advertising, Selected Cases: *Onassis v. Christian Dior, New York, Inc.*)

right to refuse work When an employee (1) acting on good faith, reasonably believes that the working conditions pose an imminent risk of death or serious injury, and (2) has reason to believe that the risk cannot be avoided by any less disruptive course of action, then he or she may refuse to perform job-related tasks without fear of discharge or other negative employment consequence. (*See* Chapter 4: The Employee—Health and Safety, Selected Cases: *Whirlpool Corporation v. Marshall*)

right-to-work laws State laws prohibiting **union shops** or **agency shops**. Outlawing these shops has the practical effect of banning unions, since a state thereby removes all incentives to form a union in that state. (*See* Chapter 4: The Employee—Terms and Conditions, Selected Cases: Taft-Hartley Act)

rule 10b–5 The Securities Exchange Act of 1934 makes it illegal "to employ any device, scheme, or artifice to defraud" or "to engage in any act, practice, or course of business which operates or would operate as a fraud or deceit upon any person in connection with the purchase or sale of a security." The phrase is not used in the Act, but Rule 10b–5 has been interpreted to prohibit **insider trading**. (*See* Chapter 2: The Consumer—Finance, Selected Cases: Securities Exchange Act)

rule of reason Legal rule that only unreasonable restraints of trade violate section 1 of the Sherman Antitrust Act; developed after judicial recognition that any agreement between corporations, and any government regulation, restrains trade to some extent. (*See* Chapter 3: The Corporation—Antitrust Issues, Selected Cases: Sherman Antitrust Act)

rule utilitarianism A form of utilitarianism. According to rule utilitarianism, we should act from rules that promote the well-being of the group. Rule utilitarians maintain that we must have reasonably good information about the future in order to conduct business efficiently. We can construct the future in many ways, for example, by using contracts. But contracts only work if people generally follow the rules governing contracts. See **act utilitarianism** for a different view. (*See* Chapter 1: Introduction—Tools of Business Ethics, Ethics)

script   A script is a sequence of behaviors that we do almost automatically in specific situations. For example, you see a red light, and you begin slowing down your car and get ready to stop. Scripts are necessary because of **bounded rationality**. Since we have limited rational powers, we cannot actively think about everything we do. Most of our lives, in fact, are scripted. This allows us to think about things that we cannot script and that are of special importance to us, such as our relationships with family and friends, our careers, and perhaps religious issues. (*See* Chapter 1: Introduction—Tools of Business Ethics, Ethics)

secondary agreements   An unfair labor practice in which an employer with whom a union does not have a dispute agrees not to make purchases from another employer with whom the union does have a dispute. (*See* Chapter 4: The Employee—Terms and Conditions, Selected Cases: Landrum-Griffin Act)

secondary consumers   Persons who use products and services that are bought by others. For example, almost all of us are secondary consumers of public roads, the police and national defense. In a family, those who do not select the food they eat are secondary consumers. (*See* Chapter 2: The Consumer—Introduction, Protecting Consumers.

securities   Methods of investing money in some business enterprise: **stocks**, bonds, debentures, notes, investment contracts, certificates of interest, and profit-sharing agreements. Investors expect that buying these securities will produce profits for themselves, as a result of the efforts of others. (*See* Chapter 2: The Consumer—Finance, Law: Investments)

sentience   The capacity to experience sensations, especially pleasure and pain. (*See* Chapter 5: The Environment—Environmental Ethics, Promoting the Good of the Group)

social cost   The total cost to society of the production and consumption of some consumer good; for example, the cost of generating electricity includes the labor, equipment, and fuel necessary to produce power, as well as the various health and sanitation problems resulting from industrial pollution. See also **external cost**. (*See* Chapter 5: The Environment—Environmental Economics, Society)

social cost theory Focuses on the entire cost of something, not just on what the producers have to pay to make it. For example, if making steel causes pollution that harms property and health, the social cost would include the property loss and medical costs. (*See* Chapter 2: The Consumer—Product Safety, Theories of Responsibility for Harm)

social institutions Social institutions provide a structure for social interactions. They exist to ensure that important values and relationships are preserved. For example, marriage is institutionalized because it is so important to raising children. The corporate structure is also an institution. The way that it organizes capital, management, and labor to produce goods efficiently is a central part of contemporary society. (*See* Chapter 1: Introduction—Tools of Business Ethics, Ethics)

speciesism Regarded by some philosophers as a form of bigotry holding that the moral value of a being is determined by that individual's species; often compared to racism and sexism. (*See* Chapter 5: The Environment—Environmental Ethics, Respecting Dignity and Rights)

stakeholder view The view that management needs to consider all **stakeholders** when making a decision. (*See* Chapter 3: The Corporation—Corporate Social Responsibility)

stakeholders This term refers to those who are affected by and can affect business transactions. These include stockholders, but also employees, suppliers, bondholders, and communities, to name a few. The term arose as business ethicists began to argue that managers should consider the effects of their decisions on a wide range of people, not just the owners. (*See* Chapter 1: Introduction—What Is Business Ethics?, The Roots of Business Ethics)

state-of-the-art defense A manufacturer can avoid liability for harm caused by a consumer product by claiming that the designing and marketing of the product employed the most advanced knowledge and technology available, and any injuries were unavoidable or unforeseeable given the most current information and procedures. (*See* Chapter 2: The Consumer—Product Safety, Law: Defending Against Liability)

stock An ownership right to some portion or "share" of a company's profits. Classified as "preferred" or "common": preferred stockholders receive their interest payments or dividends before common stockholders. (*See* Chapter 2: The Consumer—Finance, Law: Investments)

strict liability The attribution of legal responsibility for injury regardless of the intentions or reasonableness of the liable party. In consumer product safety, strict liability may apply whenever damages result from a product with a defect that presents an unreasonable danger to a consumer, whether or not the defect was known about or should have been known about. (*See* Chapter 2: The Consumer—Product Safety, Selected Cases: *Greenman v. Yuba Power Products.*) In cases of sexual harassment, strict liability is enforced when the harasser is shown to be a supervisor or agent of the company; the employer is legally responsible for the wrongdoing whether or not the employer knew of the activity or should have known. (*See* Chapter 4: The Employee—Sexual Harassment, Law: Introduction.) Strict liability is also connected to **social cost theory**. It usually applies only in cases in which great harm is possible, such as in food production or in discrimination. (*See* Chapter 2: The Consumer—Advertising: Ethics)

strict scrutiny An especially close judicial examination activated when a fundamental right, such as the right of every person to equal protection under the law, is threatened by a statute. (*See* Chapter 4: The Employee—Discrimination and Affirmative Action, Selected Cases: *City of Richmond v. J.A. Croson Company* and *Adarand Constructors v. Pena*)

supremacy clause Article VI, Section 2 of the Constitution declares that federal laws are the supreme laws of America, and state or local laws conflicting with them are unconstitutional.

takings clause Statement in the Fifth Amendment to the Constitution that reads: "nor shall private property be taken for public use, without just compensation." This means that the government must pay a fair price to the owner of property appropriated for public purposes. (*See* Chapter 5: The Environment—Environmental Law, Selected Cases: *Lucas v. South Carolina Coastal Council*)

tort An action that injures someone in some way, but it is not criminal behavior and does not involve breach of contract; injuries caused by consumer products are considered torts. (*See* Chapter 2: The Consumer—Product Safety, Law: Modern Legal Remedies)

trade secret Information, formula, program device, pattern, method, technique, or process that (1) derives economic value from not being generally known, and (2) is the subject of reasonable efforts to maintain its secrecy. (*See* Chapter 3: The Corporation—Economics, Law: Corporate Crime, and Selected Cases)

transaction costs All the costs of acquiring a product minus the purchase price. If you buy a used car for $10,000, and spend $500 evaluating the car, the transaction cost is $500. Transaction costs can be significant in many cases. For example, many theorists argue that government needs to protect property and enforce contracts. In these roles, government is a transaction cost. (*See* Chapter 4: The Employee—Terms and Conditions, Ethics)

trust A group of several corporations, initially competitors in the same industry, that have banded together; with the unification, competition shifts to those who are not allied with the trust. See also **monopoly**. (*See* Chapter 3: The Corporation—Antitrust Issues, Law)

Tree Fruits principle Striking workers may peacefully picket a secondary employer (one who receives goods from the struck employer) so long as the object of the protest is a particular product and not the business as a whole. (*See* Chapter 4: The Employee—Terms and Conditions, Selected Cases: *NLRB v. Fruit and Vegetable Packers*)

tying agreements A company makes the sale of one product, A, conditional on the purchase of a second product, B; the buyer wants A, but cannot get it unless B is purchased. Declared illegal by the *Clayton Act*. (*See* Chapter 3: The Corporation—Antitrust Issues, Selected Cases: Clayton Act)

Uniform Commercial Code (UCC) Rules written by legal scholars of the American Law Institute and the National Conference of Commissioners on Uniform State Laws. These rules apply to most transactions necessary for exchanging consumer goods, including issuing and using credit, but do not have the force of law until state legislatures adopt them. (*See* Chapter 2: The Consumer—Product Safety, Law: Modern Legal Remedies; Finance, Law: Credit)

union shop A labor union rule requiring an employee to join a union (typically within one month of being hired), and requiring an employer to discharge an employee who does not join. (*See*

Chapter 4: The Employee—Terms and Conditions, Selected Cases: Taft-Hartley Act)

usury laws These set the upper limits on interest rates, and vary from state to state; they are intended to protect unsophisticated or desperate borrowers from falling prey to unscrupulous individuals who would otherwise charge exorbitant rates of interest. (*See* Chapter 2: The Consumer—Finance, Law; Credit) In medieval times usury was a mortal sin and illegal; it referred to the practice of charging interest. (*See* Chapter 1: Introduction—What Is Business Ethics?, The Roots of Business Ethics)

workers' compensation State laws (all 50 states have them) requiring businesses who meet certain criteria to provide their employees with compensation for work-related injuries. (*See* Chapter 4: The Employee—Health and Safety, Selected Cases: Occupational Safety and Health Act)

World Bank This organization was formed at the same time as the **International Monetary Fund**. The World Bank offers low-cost loans to underdeveloped countries when private lending cannot be found. These loans are usually given to help countries build the physical infrastructure, such as roads, bridges, and dams, that is necessary for economic development. (*See* Chapter 2: The Consumer—Finance: International Issues)

yellow-dog contract An unfair labor practice in which a clause in an employment contract stipulates that employment is conditional on the refusal to join a union. (*See* Chapter 4: The Employee—Terms and Conditions, Law: Labor Unions)

CONTEMPORARY ETHICAL ISSUES

Court Cases, Federal Statutes, and Agencies

Cases

Citations in **bold** are described in detail at the page(s) indicated. Citations not in bold are mentioned at the page(s) indicated.

Federal Statutes and Administrative Agencies

Statutes in **bold** are described in detail at the page(s) indicated; those not in bold are mentioned at the page(s) indicated. Alternative designations for certain statutes are listed in parentheses. Agencies are not bolded; the enabling legislation for each and acronyms are listed in parentheses.

Index

Terms in **bold** are also found in the Glossary. Court cases, administrative agencies, and federal statutes are indexed in a separate section. Individuals and companies named as litigants in these cases are not indexed here.

John W. Dienhart is Professor of Philosophy at St. Cloud State University, St. Cloud Minnesota.

Jordan Curnutt is Assistant Professor of Philosophy at St. Cloud State University.